RUSSIA'S RULERS
UNDER THE OLD REGIME

Dominic Lieven

Russia's Rulers
under the Old Regime

Yale University Press
New Haven and London

Set in Linotron Bembo by Best-set Typesetter Ltd, Hong Kong.
Printed and bound at the Bath Press, Avon, Great Britain.

Library of Congress Cataloging-in-Publication Data

Lieven, D. C. B.
    Russia's rulers under the old regime/by Dominic Lieven.
        p.   cm.
    Bibliography: p.
    Includes indexes.
    ISBN 0–300–04371–6 (cased)
    ISBN 0–300–04937–4 (pbk.)
    1. Soviet Union — Kings and rulers — Biography.   2. Nicholas II,
Emperor of Russia, 1868–1918 — Friends and associates.   3. Soviet
Union — Nobility — History — 19th century.   4. Soviet Union — Politics
and government — 1894–1917.   5. Elite (Social sciences) — Soviet
Union.   I. Title.
DK253. L54   1989
947.08'092'2 — dc19

For Mikiko and Alekachan

CONTENTS

PREFACE

In his work on the seventeenth-century Russian ruling élite Robert Crummey chose to concentrate on the members of the Boyar Duma.[1] He did so although, as he himself states, the Boyar Duma was probably not the most powerful governmental institution in this era. The key political figures in the realm were not so much the members of the Duma as a whole as a close inner group of boyars who surrounded the Tsar, together with a handful of senior officials (*d'yaki*) who dominated the executive departments (*prikazy*). The Boyar Duma included these men but also others of lesser political significance. Moreover the pattern of recruitment was not uniform throughout the years 1613 to 1689, both the administrative experience and political weight of new recruits on the one hand and the balance between aristocrats and 'new men' on the other differing from one period to another.

Crummey states that he is interested not in the Boyar Duma as an institution but rather in its members. 'The present work', he writes, 'approaches the members of the Duma, not as a body but as a group of important individuals.... This study, then, proceeds on the assumption that, to use somewhat dated language, the Duma's ranks included the "power élite" of Muscovy.' Though the power of individual members of the Duma was indeed different, nevertheless 'we find there almost all of the leading bureaucrats and generals of the realm'. A 'collective biography' of the members of the Boyar Duma is, in Crummey's opinion, the best method available for isolating and studying the rulers of seventeenth-century Russia.

Much of what Crummey writes about his work applies to the present book, which is essentially a study of the late nineteenth and early twentieth-century Russian imperial ruling élite. It is true that my work is more than just a profile of Russia's rulers in the reign of Nicholas II. Chapter 1, for instance, studies the development of this élite since its inception, as well as the crucial relationship between monarchy, aristocracy, gentry and bureaucracy in Russia as it changed over the centuries. The last chapter looks at the causes of the élite's demise in 1917. Both these chapters are interpretative essays, as is inevitable when dealing with such huge subjects. Other chapters contain information not just on the ruling élite but also on the civil service as a whole; but my book's core is a study of the rulers of late

[1] R.O. Crummey, *Aristocrats and Servitors: The Boyar Elite in Russia, 1613–1689* (Princeton, N.J., 1983).

imperial Russia, based on the 215 men appointed to the State Council by Nicholas II between 1894 and 1914.

The Council itself, founded in 1810, was a body designed to advise the Emperor on civil legislation and the budget.[2] The monarch was, however, not obliged to consult the State Council on such matters, still less to follow the advice of its majority. Up to 1906 all members of the Council were appointed by the Emperor, but in that year both the Council's membership and its functions were transformed. Under the new bicameral constitutional system the Council became the upper house, with a veto over legislation and much of the budget. Its size more than doubled, half its members now being elected by the 'great corporations' of the Empire, such as, for instance, the nobility, the Orthodox Church, the zemstvos, universities and stock-exchange committees. With one relatively minor exception, the composition of the Council's appointed membership remained the same after 1906 as before.

For the purposes of this book, however, the role of the State Council or its power as an institution is irrelevant. It would matter very little to me had the Council been as insubstantial and indeed almost non-existent a body as the contemporary British Privy Council. What does matter to me, as it did to Crummey for the Boyar Duma, is that the appointed members of the State Council can with justice be described as the ruling élite of late imperial Russia. Here we have almost all the ministers and top central government officials of Nicholas II's reign, together with the most prominent judges, military men, provincial governors and conservative academics. We find too among the 215 members of the Council a handful of key figures among the aristocracy and landowning gentry.

It is true that this group of 215 men does not take in all those who played a major role in Nicholas II's ruling élite. Many leading figures in the reign of the last Romanov emperor had been appointed to the Council under Alexander III, and a few others only reached the Council during the First World War. Moreover, certain government ministries were somewhat over-represented in the State Council, while others saw surprisingly few of their top officials nominated to the Empire's highest legislative body. This im-balance was partly a reflection of the Council's functions: a legislative body required jurists and veterans of the State Chancellery, expert in drafting laws. The monarch's own views also influenced the Council's make-up, since all appointments, at least formally, came from the Winter Palace. This helps to explain why provincial governors were so heavily represented in the State Council, for Nicholas II desired to place at the heart of the central government men with experience of local conditions.

There were other factors: the number of Council members who had formerly been high officials of the powerful Ministry of Finance would, for instance, undoubtedly have been greater had not some leading figures in this department found lucrative private employment on retirement, thus

---

[2] On the institution and its role see, e.g., V.G. Shcheglov, *Gosudarstvennyy Sovet v Rossii* (Yaroslavl, 1903); M. Szeftel, *The Russian Constitution of April 23 1906: Political Institutions of the Duma Monarchy* (Brussels, 1976); and P. Chasles, *Le Parlement russe. Son organisation. Ses rapports avec l'empéreur* (Paris, 1909).

debarring themselves from membership. Moreover, there was one difference between those members appointed between 1894 and 1906 and those nominated to the Council in the 'constitutional era'. In the former period many generals and admirals were appointed to the Council as a dignified sinecure on their retirement from active service. After 1906, however, when the Council came to play a major role in parliamentary politics and its debates were open to the press and the public, the government could less easily afford to have elderly 'non-political' and silent military veterans slumbering in stately retirement in the Council's comfortable armchairs. In 1894 to 1906 almost 40 per cent of those appointed to the Council were admirals and generals, although many of the latter had actually spent part or even most of their careers in civilian posts. Between 1906 and 1914, however, the proportion of military men appointed to the Council dropped by almost one-half.

With these qualifications, however, if one wishes to study Nicholas II's ruling élite the membership of the State Council is the best place to start. This becomes clear when one tries to think of alternative groups one might choose to study. If for instance it was felt that a group of 215 men was too small a sampling, one might look alternatively at the 5,417 officials in the top four ranks of the civil service in 1914. Given the chaos into which the system of ranking had descended by the Empire's last years, however, this large group of men would be not only unwieldy but totally heterogeneous, containing every level of official from minister to desk officer. And if, more realistically, one sought to study the members of some body other than the State Council, such as for instance the Senate, the problem would be, *inter alia*, that because of the Senate's role as, in part, Russia's supreme court, that institution inevitably contained a greatly disproportionate number of jurists.

One objection to using the appointed membership of the State Council as a guide to the imperial ruling élite might be that the power wielded by members of the Council was very unequal. Among the 215 men one finds both the Empire's most important political leaders and senior expert officials little known outside their own departments. To meet such an objection one might try to locate a narrower but truer 'power élite' among, for instance, the ministers appointed by Nicholas II. But this would be to waste the valuable material, often in the form of unpublished memoirs, diaries and letters, on which one can draw when studying the whole group of 215. Moreover, even if one's study were confined to Nicholas II's ministers, one would still be concerned with a group of men whose power varied radically. Is the weight of a State Controller or Minister of Communications really to be compared with that of the head of the Ministry of Internal Affairs? Nor did a department's power necessarily remain constant, as a comparison of the Ministry of Agriculture's role before and after 1906 illustrates. Finally, the personality of a minister inevitably had a huge influence on the actual power he wielded, as did the extent to which a statesman or leading official enjoyed the trust and support of the monarch.

The aim of this book is to understand what kind of men governed Russia in the Empire's last years. The work is in part a study of politics and bureaucracy, of education and culture. Above all, however, it is a collective biography. The book's fundamental aim is to explore the values, opinions and mentalities of the ruling élite and to explain how these were shaped. Its basic structure is that of a biography. Chapters 1 and 2 trace the history of the Russian ruling élite from its early medieval origins and provide as full information as possible on the backgrounds, wealth and career patterns of those who governed the Empire under Nicholas II. Next I study the up-bringing and education of these men, seeking to understand both the intellectual training they acquired and the values they absorbed in the course of their childhood and adolescence. From there the book moves on to the careers of the members of the State Council; it hopes to illustrate how men rose to the top of the imperial government and whether their experience in the civil service contributed to the development of a general 'bureaucratic élite' mentality and a set of political conceptions. I then go on to study the different groupings, social, ethnic and departmental, within the ruling élite, since I believe that it is in many ways more accurate to view distinct group characteristics and mentalities as existing rather than some general 'bureaucratic élite' stereotype. Chapters 6, 7 and 8 are biographies of P.N. Durnovo, A.N. Kulomzin and the brothers Alexander and Aleksei Obolensky respectively. In these chapters but above all in chapter 9 I also attempt to provide an overall survey of the political problems facing the élite and how it understood and responded to them.

Throughout the book I try never to allow the reader to forget that the members of the State Council were individuals, each one of them the complex product of a separate personal development. Not merely are three whole chapters devoted to the biographies of individual men, but short biographical sketches are frequently to be found in the text. My aim in adopting this approach is twofold: I am anxious to balance a quantitative, 'scientific' and generalizing approach to understanding the ruling élite with attention to the individuals who were its basic component and reality. Moreover, in my view an impressionistic, detailed use of biography is uniquely able to give the reader an imaginative feel for the subject, without which no amount of scientific method can hope to convey a true sense of the past's reality.

It is now twelve years since I began this study, though in the course of these years I have also at times worked on other subjects. Over this long period I have covered a vast amount of material, not all of which could, for reasons of space, be listed in a bibliography unless considerable cuts were made in the text itself. I have therefore cited in full in the end notes those secondary sources on which I have drawn directly, and have limited my bibliography to primary sources, both published and unpublished, and to works of reference. I am unhappily aware that this may inconvenience some readers and depress others who find no reference to their own books and articles in the present work. All I can say in defence is that to list some relevant secondary literature but not all of it would be to make invidious choices, particularly since in many cases it is works seemingly somewhat removed from this book's subject which have inspired me to my most constructive thoughts. Of course my debt to historians, past and present, of imperial Russia is immense. Often this debt is made clear in the end notes, or in the

Index of Authors Cited. I am, however, very conscious of the fact that much valuable work relevant to Russian politics, government and society under the Old Regime goes unmentioned.

In the course of twelve years the debts one amasses to both individuals and institutions are considerable. First and foremost I should mention my supervisor, Professor Hugh Seton-Watson. It was Hugh who encouraged me to take up the present theme, not to fight shy of biography, and to toughen myself against the attacks (often of course fully justified and generally useful) by academic colleagues on my scholarship, subject matter, methodology, opinions or social origins. With growing age and self-confidence I began to appreciate not only Hugh's intelligence but also his kindness and his wisdom. It is a real sadness to me that he is no longer alive to see this book published. Second only to Hugh Seton-Watson comes my debt to the late Leonard Schapiro, my 'grandfather' at LSE, a man whose intellectual qualities and deep culture went along with a personality whose warmth, kindness and generosity I shall always remember with the greatest affection. I am truly grateful to have studied under two such men as Seton-Watson and Schapiro, and to have come to count both of them as my friends.

No other debt is quite so great, but many are nevertheless not small. Peter Reddaway, whose departure to America ended many years of close and trusting collaboration at LSE, heads the list of those who have helped me with my work. My thanks are also due to Professor Richard Pipes, Professor Olga Crisp, Mr Harry Willetts, Prince Dimitri Shakhovskoy, Professor Geoffrey Hosking, Professor E.D. Chermensky, and to Professor Norman Stone, who, together with Simon Schama, taught me at Cambridge. I am also very grateful for the help I have received from Professor Walter Pintner, that most modest and kindly of American professors. I owe a big debt to my colleagues in the Government Department at the LSE, a civilized community whose brains I have picked over the years, and perhaps most of all to the department's conveners in the last nine years, William Letwin, Maurice Cranston, George Jones and Kenneth Minogue. In their very different ways these four have contributed greatly to making the department a pleasant place in which to think, research and write despite the hugely increased teaching and administrative load which has descended on all of us in recent years and which has at times driven scholarship into the early hours of the morning. Mrs Marian Osborne, my secretary, has uncomplainingly become a leading expert on the State Council as a result of typing frequent articles and now a book on the subject. She deserves all my thanks. So too do Mrs Paula da Gama Pinto and Ms Susan Kirkbride who helped with typing the text.

As regards institutions, pride of place belongs to the Central State Historical Archive (TsGIA) in Leningrad, whose staff made a tremendous contribution to this book. So too, with a trifle less good will and efficiency, did the staffs of the Central State Archive of the October Revolution (TsGAOR) and of the Manuscript Section of the Lenin Library (RO) in Moscow. Useful help was also given to me by the staffs of the main Lenin Library in Moscow and the Library of the Academy of Sciences in Leningrad. I am also much in debt to the staff of the Bakhmetev Archive of

Columbia University (CUBA) and of the British Library of Political and Economic Studies at LSE (particularly Brian Hunter), the British Library, Harvard University's Law and Widener libraries, the Bayerische Staats-bibliothek and the Bodleian. A special word of thanks is owed to Dr John Screen and his excellent staff at the library of the School of Slavonic Studies in London. Nor should the helpfulness of library staff in Helsinki, in rapidly sending me photocopies ordered from afar, be forgotten. Although both at the Kennan Institute for Advanced Russian Studies in Washington, and during my tenure of a Humboldt fellowship in Germany under the guid-ance of Professors Rudolph Vierhaus and Gerhard Ritter, I was researching for my next book, on the European aristocracy in the nineteenth century, some of the ideas absorbed in that year helped me in re-drafting portions of some chapters of this book. Both the institutions and individuals in question also therefore deserve my thanks. So too do the *Jahrbücher für Geschichte Osteuropas, Slavonic and East European Review, Cahiers du monde russe et soviétique* and *Historical Journal* for allowing me to use material previously published in part by them. I also owe a big debt to Mrs Humphrey Brooke, Prince George Vasilchikov, Professor Prince Dimitri Obolensky, Prince N.N. Obolensky, Prince A. Obolensky and Baron A.P. Bilderling, who kindly allowed me to use the private papers and photographs of their ancestors.

In preparing this book for publication I have had the noble support of Robert Baldock of Yale University Press and of Catharine Carver, to both of whom I owe great thanks. A more civilized publisher and a more pains-taking and efficient copy editor are, I am sure, not to be found on this planet.

Last but definitely not least come the various members of my family: my parents, who supported and encouraged me through difficult years as a graduate student; my uncle Leonid, a constant source of interest and enthusiasm; my brother Anatol, whose broad knowledge and intelligence made him an ideal sounding board for my ideas; my wife, Mikiko, not one of nature's historians, whose love and sympathy triumphed over her amazement at having married 216 people, all but one of them long since dead.

D.C.B.L.

London, March 1988

Chronology

IMPERIAL RUSSIA 1825–1917

1825	19 Nov	Death of Alexander I; accession of Nicholas I
	14 Dec	Decembrist rising
1826	3 July	Formation of Third Section (i.e. security police department)
1830	11 Dec	Polish revolution begins.
1833	1 Jan	Completion of the Code of Laws
1848	12 Feb	Overthrow of Louis-Philippe of France; beginning of European revolution
	2 Apr	Formation of Buturlin committee on censorship: beginning of last and most oppressive phase of Nicholas I's reign
1854	16 Mar	France and Britain declare war on Russia: beginning of Crimean War.
1855	18 Feb	Death of Nicholas I; accession of Alexander II
1856	18 Mar	Treaty of Paris ends Crimean War.
1861	19 Feb	Emancipation of the serfs
1863	10 Jan	Polish revolution begins.
1864	1 Jan	Introducion of zemstvo statute
	November	Introduction of judicial reform
1866	4 Apr	Karakozov attempts to assassinate Alexander II.
1871	28 Apr	Treaty of Frankfurt ends Franco-Prussian War.
1873–4		Narodnik (Populist) movement begins.
1874	1 Jan	Introduction of universal military service in Russia
1877	12 Apr	Beginning of Russo-Turkish War
1878	24 Jan	Vera Zasulich shoots General F.F. Trepov.
	1 July	Treaty of Berlin
1881	1 Mar	Assassination of Alexander II; accession of Alexander III
1882	30 May	Count D.A. Tolstoy becomes Minister of Internal Affairs.
1889	12 July	Introduction of *Zemstvie nachal'niki* (land commandants)
1890	12 June	Zemstvo counter-reform

1892	18 Aug	S. Yu. Witte becomes Minister of Finance.
1893	23 Dec	Russo-French military alliance ratified.
1894	20 Oct	Death of Alexander III; accession of Nicholas II
1897	3 Jan	Currency reform: Russia adopts the gold standard for the rouble.
1898	1 Mar	First congress of Social Democratic party
	15 Mar	Russia leases Port Arthur from China: beginning of confrontation with Japan.
1902	January	First appearance of the newspaper *Osvobozhdenie*, organ of the liberal opposition movement
	March	Agrarian disturbances in Poltava and Kharkov
	2 Apr	Assassination of Minister of Internal Affairs, D.S. Sipyagin; replaced by V.K. Plehve.
1903	August	Trans-Siberian railway opened for through traffic.
1904	26 Jan	Japanese attack Port Arthur.
	15 July	Assassination of V.K. Plehve; replaced by Prince P.D. Svyatopolk–Mirsky: onset of a thaw
	20 Dec	Fall of Port Arthur
1905	9 Jan	Bloody Sunday: troops fire on demonstrators in St. Petersburg.
	14 May	Battle of Tsushima
	23 Aug	Treaty of Portsmouth ends Russo-Japanese War.
	17 Oct	Imperial manifesto promises a constitution. Witte appointed chairman of the Council of Ministers.
	23 Oct	P.N. Durnovo appointed (acting) Minister of Internal Affairs.
	3 Dec	Petersburg Soviet arrested.
	8–9 Dec	Collapse of attempted general strike
	18 Dec	Moscow rising defeated.
1906	23 Apr	Replacement of S. Yu. Witte and P.N. Durnovo by I.L. Goremykin and P.A. Stolypin
	26 Apr	Publication of Fundamental Laws
	27 Apr	Convocation of First Duma
	9 July	Dissolution of First Duma
	10 July	Appointment of P.A. Stolypin as chairman of the Council of Ministers
	9 Nov	Decree eases withdrawal from village communes. Beginning of the Stolypin land reforms
1907	3 June	Second Duma dissolved. Electoral law changed.
	19 Aug	Russo-British convention signed. Beginning of 'Triple Entente'
	24 Sept	Austria annexes Bosnia-Hercegovina.
	1 Nov	Third Duma opens.
1909	25 Apr	Nicholas II vetoes Naval General Staff bill. Stolypin's government begins to move further to the right.
1911	4 Mar	State Council rejects Western Zemstvo bill.
	5 Sept	Death of P.A. Stolypin

	11 Sept	V.N. Kokovtsov appointed chairman of the Council of Ministers.
1912	4 Apr	Troops fire on workers in Lena goldfields. Strikes begin.
	September	Elections to the Fourth Duma
	18 Oct	Outbreak of first Balkan War
1913	21 Feb	Tricentenary of Romanov dynasty
1914	31 Jan	I.L. Goremykin replaces V.N. Kokovtsov as chairman of the Council of Ministers.
	19 July	Germany declares war on Russia.
1915	6 June	Dismissal of N.A. Maklakov, the Minister of Internal Affairs, as a concession to the Duma
	23 Aug	Nicholas II assumes command at military headquarters.
	25 Aug	'Progressive Bloc' formed in the Duma.
	3 Sept–9 Feb 1916	Duma in recess
1917	2 Mar	Abdication of Nicholas II

GLOSSARY

boyar	the top rank in pre-Petrine Russia's court aristocracy
chin	rank
desyatina	measure of land = 1.09 hectares
d'yak	a senior official in the pre-Petrine civil service
druzhina	military household
Gosudarstvennyy Sekretar'	usually translated as 'Imperial Secretary': the head of the State Chancellery
gradonachal'nik	city governor
gymnasium	high school
Herrenhaus	the Prussian upper house
intelligent	member of the intelligentsia: the word had radical or at least liberal political connotations in imperial Russia
ispravnik	the police chief in a district (*uezd*)
meshchanstvo	the urban lower middle class
Oberhofmarschall	effectively the no. 2 at the Russian imperial court, second only to the Minister of the Court
obrok	money rent paid by serfs
obshchina	peasant village commune
Okhrana	'special sections' (*okhrannye otdeleniya*), i.e. security police
okol'nichii	the second rank in pre-Petrine Russia's court
pomest'e	an estate held conditionally on service tenure; the distinction between such estates and *votchiny* (see below) was in practice already slight by the seventeenth century
pravoved	student at the imperial School of Law
prikaz	a government department in pre-Petrine Russia
raznochinets	a term coming into use in the second half of the nineteenth century to denote educated people, usually in universities or professions, who were divorced from one of the estates (*sosloviya*) into which Russian society was divided
Realschule	high school putting more stress on mathematics, science and modern languages than the classical gymnasium
soslovie	estate: Russian citizens belonged to one of a number of estates (nobility; honorary citizens; merchants; clergy; *meshchane*; peasants)

starosta	peasant village headman
starshina	peasant *volost'* (see below) headman
stolovaya	dining hall
Svod Zakonov	Code of Laws
szlachta	the Polish petty nobility
Trudoviki	the 'labour' (radical-socialist) group in the first two Dumas
tseremoniemeister	chamberlain at the imperial court
uezd	district; a province (*guberniya*) consisted of a number of *uezdy*
uryadnik	junior police officer
voevoda	district governor in pre-Petrine Russia
votchina	hereditary estate in pre-Petrine Russia
volost'	one of a number of units (*volosti*) into which a district (*uezd*) was divided; sometimes translated as 'county', 'canton' or 'parish'. The *volost'* administration and court had authority only over peasants.

Author's Note

All dates in the text are in the Julian calendar, used in imperial Russia. Russia was twelve days behind the rest of Europe in the nineteenth century and thirteen days behind in the twentieth century.

As regards transliteration, I have followed a modified version of the American system. Where surnames of Western origin are concerned, I have always tried to render them in their original form, since to my mind the direct transliteration of these names from the Russian looks ugly and even at times absurd.

D.C.B.L.

Previous page: The re-formed State Council (1906–17) in session.

CHAPTER 1

FROM THE TARTARS TO
THE TWENTIETH CENTURY:
THE STATE AND ITS RULERS

The élite which governed Nicholas II's Russia had a long history. Many of the families represented in the State Council between 1894 and 1914 were older than the Romanov monarchy; some were more ancient even than the Muscovite state itself. Certainly in terms of genealogical antiquity the Russian ruling élite in the late Victorian and Edwardian eras was in no way inferior to its English or German counterparts. The opposite may indeed have been the case.[1]

Of the families represented in the State Council, the most ancient were those descended from Russia's original royal house, one branch of which had provided Moscow's own grand princes until 1598. Of the 215 appointed members of Nicholas II's State Council, 10 were princes who traced their descent from Rurik, the founder of the Russian 'state' and dynasty in the ninth century.[2] Among the 10 men were 3 Obolenskys, 2 Dolgorukys, 2 Volkonskys, 1 Vyazemsky, 1 Lobanov-Rostovsky and 1 Khilkov. All these men traced their ancestry back to the rulers of the grand principality of Kiev, which had held sway over the whole Rurikid inheritance in the dynasty's early years. the Obolenskys, Dolgorukys and Volkonskys were, however, descended from the branch of the Rurikid clan which had come to rule the principality of Chernigov in the Middle Ages, while the Vyazemskys, Lobanov-Rostovskys and Khilkovs traced their ancestry to Vladimir Monomakh (1053–1125), the grand prince of Vladimir. Of Monomakh's great-grandsons, the sons of Grand Prince Vsevolod Yurevich of Vladimir, the eldest, Konstantin (1185–1219), founded the ruling house of Rostov to which the Lobanov-Rostovskys belonged. A younger son, Ioann (1197–1239), was the ancestor of the rulers of Starodub, who included the princes Khilkov. Between the two brothers came Yaroslav Vsevolodovich (1190–1246), the ancestor of the ruling houses not only of Moscow but also of Tver, Suzdal and Galich.[3]

In the medieval era the many branches of the Rurikid clan all played a part in the constant struggles between principalities and the frequent conflicts over the succession within individual Rurikid families.[4] All suffered the loss of full sovereignty after the Tartar invasions of the thirteenth century. Whereas, however, in the thirteenth to fifteenth centuries the princes of north-eastern Russia remained autonomous under the ultimate authority of the Tartar Horde, most of the domains of the southern and western princes were swallowed up by the growing Lithuanian empire. This fundamental split affected the manner and timing of the princes' eventual absorption into the Muscovite state. The principalities of north-eastern Russia were taken first, the Starodub Rurikids losing their independence in the mid-fifteenth century and the Rostov, Tver and Yaroslavl branches in 1485. Between that date and the destruction of Ryazan, the last independent principality of the north-east, in 1517, Moscow also secured the allegiance of many princes of the eastern border region of Lithuania through a mixture of conquest, inducements and displays of its might. In 1494, for instance, Vyazma, the apanage of the Vyazemsky princes, was overrun by Muscovite forces.[5]

The picture is further complicated by the fact that well before Moscow moved into the Lithuanian borderlands some princes had abandoned their possessions in the grand duchy of Lithuania and taken service under Moscow. Members of the Obolensky family, for instance, were already prominent at the Muscovite court in the mid-fifteenth century. Nor were such princely immigrants always Rurikids. For much of the fifteenth century the single most powerful family at the Muscovite court were the Patrikeevs, descendants of Gedymin (d. 1328), the ruler of Lithuania. Prince Yuri Patrikeev, the great-grandson of Gedymin, married the daughter of Grand Prince Vasili I of Moscow in 1418. In 1499 the Patrikeevs lost their stranglehold on power, largely because their increasing monopoly of top positions had become insupportable to other aristocratic clans. Nevertheless, two sons of Boyar Ivan Vasilevich ('Bulgak') Patrikeev survived the family's disgrace and founded dynasties which were to play a major role in Russian history both in the sixteenth century and subsequently. One of these dynasties was the Golitsyns and the other the Kurakins. Both families had a representative among the appointed members of Nicholas II's State Council.[6]

In the late fifteenth and early sixteenth centuries the various princely families were unequal not only in power and wealth but even in their formal status in the Muscovite kingdom. Formally speaking, the princes of the former sovereign north-eastern territories and princes who had abandoned their lands in Lithuania and been granted Muscovite *votchiny* (hereditary estates) ranked somewhat below the so-called 'service princes'. The latter, whose apanages were on the Lithuanian–Muscovite border, retained their lands and a considerable autonomy in their first years under Moscow's rule. This situation was not, however, to last for long in the face of the centralizing tendencies of the Muscovite state. The Vyazemskys, for example, lords of a strategic frontier area, were quickly deprived of their apanage and granted lands elsewhere. Other more powerful 'service princes' saw their families absorbed into the central Muscovite élite, destroyed or encouraged to die out. Though even at the end of the sixteenth century some families, the Trubetskoys, Cherkasskys and Odoevskys for instance, were still described as 'service princes', the title no longer had any meaning. Semi-autonomous princes with deep historical roots in a particular region were a thing of the past.[7]

From the perspective of a Western historian studying Russia's failure to produce an independent territorial aristocracy capable of checking royal power this fact may well be a source of regret. It is, however, clear that it was not only the coercive power and centralizing tendencies of the Muscovite state but also in the long run the aristocracy's own interests that contributed to the consolidation of the absolute monarchy. The relative poverty of the north Russian economy, not to mention the custom of dividing lands among all the male heirs, meant that princely families which attempted to maintain themselves as territorially-based landowning aristocrats were soon in trouble. In contrast, fighting for a place within the Muscovite state's ruling élite offered risks but also great rewards. Over the centuries this state proved to be one of the most effective machines for the exploitation of national resources and for territorial expansion ever known to the human race. A large portion of the huge spoils of exploitation and conquest was annexed by the clique of aristocratic families that dominated Russian politics from the foundation of the Muscovite state down to the end of the eighteenth century. These families, in a sense the largest shareholders in the Russian state, had every reason to associate its fortunes with their own and to see themselves in the long run as major beneficiaries of the power and unity generated by monarchical absolutism.

Inevitably, within the ruling élite, the competition among leading families for the spoils of office was intense. In the two centuries after their absorption into Muscovy, some of the princely families subsequently represented in Nicholas II's State Council did better than others. By the end of the seventeenth century, for instance, both the Vyazemsky and the Volkonsky families were quite large, 36 of the former and 30 of the latter owning inhabited estates in 1699. Whereas some of the Volkonskys were beginning to secure appointments as boyars and *okol'nichie* (boyar, 2nd rank) in the seventeenth century, the Vyazemskys had yet to make a major impact within the Russian ruling élite. For both families, however, the eighteenth century was to be more rewarding than the seventeenth. In contrast, the Obolenskys, of whom only eight owned inhabited estates in 1699, had occupied key political posts since the mid-fifteenth century and were still to be found in prominent places 200 years later, while the power of the Dolgorukov clan, initially a branch of the Obolenskys, became ever greater as the seventeenth century progressed. The Khilkov and Lobanov-Rostovsky families, both small by the standards of the Vyazemskys and Volkonskys, contained a number of boyars and *okol'nichie* in both the sixteenth and seventeenth centuries. Even more impressive was the record of the Golitsyns and Kurakins, who seem to have come closest in both centuries to holding positions as boyars as an hereditary right.[8]

For the State Council's ancient princely families to survive and flourish over so many generations required both luck and skill. Right down to the eighteenth century and even to some extent beyond, European aristocratic families faced a dilemma. On the one hand, high and unpredictable mortality rates, especially among children, made it essential to produce many male heirs if a family's survival was to be ensured. Indeed, even in the eighteenth century there were spectacular examples of seemingly large families suddenly becoming extinct.[9] On the other hand, supporting its male heirs could strain a family's fortunes to breaking point, driving it out of the upper reaches of noble society. Varying customs as regards inheritance affected the way in which aristocracies in the European states met this challenge. In Russia, as to a somewhat lesser extent in Prussia, the division of lands among a nobleman's sons could threaten a family's ability to maintain its wealth and status over many generations. One effect of this in both countries was to increase the dependence of the nobility on the absolutist state, whose army and bureaucracy provided a source of wealth and status alternative to landownership. On the other hand, in many of the Catholic regions of Germany, while strict systems of primogeniture and the discouragement of younger sons from marrying kept wealth within a family, the shortage of heirs could prove a danger.[10]

The fortunate aristocratic family produced just enough heirs to survive, thereby avoiding an excessive strain on its finances. Only luck could secure such a result, however, since birth control, even if practicable, exposed a family to great risks in view of the high mortality rates among children and adolescents. On this score the luckiest of the State Council's eight ancient princely families were the Kurakins who, over the centuries, produced a small number of male children, many of whom either remained unmarried or died without heirs. As a result Kurakin princes were rare, prominent and rich, the State Council's A. A. Kurakin inheriting 30,000 *desyatiny* (1 *ds.* = 1.09 ha).[11] In contrast, one reason why Prince D.P. Golitsyn was landless, despite the wealth and prominence of his eighteenth-century ancestors, was that the Golitsyn family had been forced to divide its inheritance among too many sons.[12] Within an aristocratic clan the number of male heirs could be of decisive importance in determining the relative wealth of the family's many branches. Prince L.D. Vyazemsky, for instance, who inherited 16,200 *desyatiny*, was far richer than most Vyazemskys largely because he was the sole male heir of one whole branch of the family. To the extent that it is possible to judge from his genealogy, his wealth does not seem to have derived from any spectacular careers or marriages of his ancestors, none of whom were particularly remarkable.[13]

Though a family might preserve its fortune and eminence by limiting the number of its heirs, it could not initially acquire either wealth or status in this manner. In Russia, as indeed in most European aristocracies, service to the crown was a key factor in a family's initial acquisition of great estates and a leading position within the social élite. But the maintenance of this wealth and status entailed, in Russia, a greater dependence of the aristocracy on the state than was true in many other European societies.

Some of the reasons for this have already been noted. The poor soil and relatively primitive economy of the Muscovite heartland, together with the custom of partible inheritance, would have made it difficult for a rich, independent Russian territorial or commercial aristocracy to develop before the seventeenth century, even if the Muscovite élite had not concentrated its attention on the court and on service. Nor was aristocratic property secure against confiscation, even to the extent that was true elsewhere in Europe. On the other hand, the seventeenth- and eighteenth-century Russian state was a bountiful provider of land to its leading statesmen and countiers—not in the poor soil of northern Russia but in the much more fertile territories of the Central Black Earth zone, the Volga provinces, the Ukraine and the Southern Steppe. It is not surprising that Russian aristocratic families who were rich in the nineteenth and twentieth centuries often owed much of their wealth to generous land grants made by the state in the previous 250 years.[14]

Of the State Council's 'ancient princes', the richest were A.S. and N.S. Dolgoruky, A.A. Kurakin, M.S. Volkonsky, Alexander Obolensky, V.S. Obolensky-Neledinsky-Meletsky, L.D. Vyazemsky and N.V. Repnin(-Volkonsky). All were very wealthy men and all, with the exception of Vyazemsky, were direct descendants of men at the summit of the Russian government or armed forces in the eighteenth century. In some cases it is possible to show that estates still in the possession of these men were originally imperial land grants, but even where this cannot be done it is legitimate to assume that their wealth owed something to the position of their ancestors. Con-

An ancient élite. Prince Alexander Obolensky, a member of Nicholas II's State Council, in the court dress of his ancestors.

versely, among the Council's poorer princes were A.B. Lobanov-Rostovsky and, in particular, M.I. Khilkov; although both men inherited considerable social status, it is probably to the point that neither was descended directly from noblemen who played a key role in Russian eighteenth-century politics and government.[15]

Service was not, however, the only or even necessarily the most usual means by which a Russian aristocratic family acquired wealth. Even in the eighteenth century, those who reached the pinnacle of the civil and military service by no means necessarily received generous land grants. On the contrary, the awarding of such grants, not to mention their size, was subject to imperial whim.[16] More important, a family could acquire great wealth in the last three centuries of the Old Regime by means that were purely private and had nothing to do with the state. The failure to stress this point can lead to exaggerated estimates of aristocratic dependence on the monarchy, and to misapprehensions about the relationship of state and society in imperial Russia. Moreover, even when an individual was enriched through service in the seventeenth and eighteenth centuries, his good fortune was seldom the product either of purely arbitrary imperial favour or of sheer professional merit. On the contrary, a man's birth and aristocratic connections were usually of great relevance to his ability either to make a successful career in that era or to come within range of imperial favour. Social status was a cause as well as a result of most successful careers. Study of the history of Russia's élites suggests that it is unrealistic to speak of the domination of society by the state or vice versa, state and society being linked in ways more complex and equivocal than such simplistic theories suggest.[17]

Of the purely private means of acquiring wealth employed by the aristocracy, marriage was one of the most important. An aristocrat was well placed to marry not only one of his peers but the heiress of a leading statesman or favourite, or of a wealthy industrialist or financier. Such marriages helped to consolidate the social élite, to integrate new elements into it, and to bring great wealth to old families.[18] Members of the eight princely families mentioned so far tended strongly to marry within their own circle. Very often their wives brought with them considerable dowries.[19] Frequently rich men married rich women. Sometimes, however, as in the case of the Obolensky family, a fortune inherited through women and derived from industry and finance rescued an ancient 'dynasty' somewhat impoverished by the division of its estates among numerous heirs.[20] Of the Council's 12 'ancient' princes, the biggest landowners were A.S. Dolgoruky and M.S. Volkonsky. Both men came from rich families, though, interestingly, in both cases the family had suffered and recovered from the confiscation of its estates. Both Dolgoruky and Volkonsky acquired enormous extra landholdings through their wives. In the case of the former, Olga Petrovna Dolgoruky (née Shuvalov) brought to her husband some 39,000 desyatiny of land in Tambov province derived originally from an eighteenth-century imperial grant to the Naryshkin family.[21]

Though important, marriage was by no means the only way in which a family might increase or preserve its fortune without recourse to state grants. An individual could squander his patrimony or even abandon it, as D.P. Golitsyn's grandfather did by quitting Russia, marrying a Pole and becoming a Catholic.[22] He could, on the other hand, live within his means and, at least from the eighteenth century onwards, seek to gear his crops to market conditions and to engage in any number of industrial or commercial activities.[23] Certainly some of the Council's 12 'ancient princes' supervised their estates with great care and attention.[24] In addition, merely to transfer one's landownership from the Muscovite heartland to the richer lands to the south, whether through purchase, inheritance or land grant, was virtually to ensure oneself a much greater income. This process was occurring throughout the last three and a half centuries of the Old Regime as regards the nobility as a whole, the great landowners (whom I shall call 'magnates') in particular, and the State Council's 'ancient princely' families specifically.[25] Of the 12 men in question, only M.I. Khilkov still had most of his land within the boundaries of pre-1550 Muscovy, and his small estate was in any case retained for sentimental reasons or as a summer retreat rather than as a commercial proposition.[26] Indeed, the pattern of the Russian princes' landowning over the centuries is reminiscent not of any other European aristocracy but of American planters on the move from ravaged Tidewater estates to the richer lands of Mississippi and Alabama. The comparison is relevant to many old gentry families as well. That Russia was in part a frontier society, with a sometimes migrant gentry, provides one possible explanation of why local traditions and roots may sometimes have been weak among the Russian nobility. It may also explain why, despite multiple inheritance and for all the frequent unprofitability of Russian agriculture, so many old Russian families succeeded in surviving for so long. Not only did the state provide them with jobs and incomes, but also they could draw on a fund of land which, at least until the nineteenth century, seemed inexhaustible.

In the initial period of Muscovite history, during the fourteenth century, princely families descended from Rurik and Gedymin played no role at Moscow's court. Themselves cadets of royal houses, they saw no reason to take service with their cousin of Moscow who, grand prince or not, they regarded as by no means superior to themselves. A very few princely families, notably the Patrikeevs and Obolenskys, were in Muscovite service by the mid-fifteenth century, as we have seen, but the great majority of princely houses did not begin to serve Moscow until the last years of that century. There followed a period in which princes served in Moscow's armies to win their spurs and prove their loyalty to their new overlord. Many years of such military service was in any case the norm, even for members of long-established and trusted Muscovite noble families, before being appointed as boyars. It was only from the 1520s and 1530s onwards that members of princely families came to equal, and even temporarily to outnumber, non-titled Muscovite aristocrats in the so-called Boyar Duma – in other words the grand prince's body of top advisers. By this time, however, the Muscovite grand principality was already two centuries old, its institutions, ruling élite and political culture well rooted, the pattern of relations between the grand prince and his leading subjects set.[27]

The hard core of Moscow's boyar aristocracy was formed in the

1330s and 1340s. In this period immediately after the Golden Horde recognized Ivan Kalita as grand prince, a number of families entered Moscow's service who were to dominate the principality's political life over the next two centuries. Initially not more than 20 in number, and never more than 35, this tight clique of aristocratic families provided two-thirds of the non-princely boyars and *okol'nichie* throughout the late fifteenth and even the sixteenth centuries. The families established at the Muscovite court by the mid-fourteenth century included some who were to play a prominent role in the history not only of Muscovite but also of imperial Russia. Among them were the ancestors of the Romanovs, Sheremetevs, Saltykovs, Vorontsovs, Pushkins, Kutuzovs, Buturlins, Khvostovs and Saburovs – some of whom were to be represented among the appointed members of Nicholas II's State Council.[28]

Muscovite politics were those of the *druzhina*, the royal military household of comrades-in-arms from which the leading lieutenants of the warrior grand prince came. Relations between the prince and his boyars were those, ideally, of a band of warrior brothers, defined by custom and mutual personal loyalties rather than institutionalized or enshrined in law. Royal leadership was undisputed, partly because unity of command was a military necessity amidst the constant warfare of the Russian north-east, but also because the prince was the essential arbiter in the competition for status and power among the boyar clans. If the monarchy disappeared, as it did to all intents and purposes in the dynastic wars of the mid-fifteenth century, in Ivan IV's minority and during the Time of Troubles, there was always a risk that the political system, deprived of its central focus, would disintegrate. Nevertheless, even with a competent adult monarch on the throne, aristocratic power remained very great. The leading aristocratic families supplied the ruler's top counsellors, the boyars, virtually by hereditary right. Until the sixteenth century their retinues also made up the bulk of his army. Muscovite aristocrats were not, however, territorial magnates seeking to protect their corporate rights or local autonomy from the encroachments of the central power. Their estates were scattered across the whole of Muscovy, their vision an imperial one encompassing the whole of the former territories of Monomakh. These were not men who opposed the central power or sought to constrain its growth, for they were, together with the royal family to which many aristocratic houses were linked by marriage, themselves part of that central power, from whose expansion and conquests they were the major beneficiaries.[29]

In the sixteenth century, however, both the traditions of Muscovite politics and government and the position of its élite families came under great strain. The tremendous expansion of Moscow under Ivan III, Vasili III and Ivan IV necessitated the development of an effective administration. The *prikaz* system (departments of the court and government were called *prikazy* in pre-Petrine Russia) established in the 1550s was to survive until the reforms of Peter I.[30] Meanwhile, the need for larger armies, the requirement to organize effective cavalry units from the great numbers of servitors now dispersed over a huge territory, led to the development of the so-called middle-service gentry. This group, which barely supported itself on small properties granted by the crown under conditional tenure, was increasingly desperate to control the movement of the handful of peasant families on whose work the cavalryman's welfare depended. Though they formed the core of the state's armed forces until the second half of the seventeenth century, the middle-service gentry were in political terms very weak, and in no sense challenged the aristocratic élite for control over the state.[31]

Within the élite itself, however, the competition for power and status among aristocratic families became fiercer in the sixteenth century. This partly reflected the growing size of the families traditionally constituting the Muscovite élite. Fortunately for itself, the Moscow aristocracy effectively barred the boyar families of Tver, Ryazan, Novgorod and other newly annexed territories from high political or military office, though it was unable to do the same as regards the numerous princely families, and had indeed to make way for a number of converted Tartar princelings as well. In addition, in the second half of the sixteenth century the élite was subjected to the increasingly demented rule of Ivan IV, who launched Moscow on a long-drawn-out war with Poland and Sweden which his kingdom was not yet capable of sustaining. On the domestic front Ivan caused chaos by dividing his state into two territorial units, the so-called *zemshchina* and *oprichnina*, and mounting a vicious assault on the aristocracy and on other sections of the population as well. To compound this folly he almost destroyed the royal house itself, leaving his state to face a dangerous future without the legitimate monarchical authority on which political stability depended. Discussing the tsar's policy towards the political and social élite, Robert Crummey concludes that 'in the end, his government had done virtually nothing to change the structure of political power in which the monarch ruled with and through an intricate network of aristocratic clans. Instead, he had lashed out indiscriminately, destroying individuals and households, and demoralizing the rest of the ruling élite'.[32]

As the leading contemporary Western expert on the seventeenth-century Russian ruling élite, Crummey is well placed to discuss the long-term impact of Ivan IV on the composition of the Russian aristocracy. He shows how the early Romanov regime successfully reconstituted the old boyar aristocracy, favouring members of the traditionally leading families in order to consolidate and stabilize the ruling élite, build up support for itself and recreate political stability. The dominant feature of the seventeenth-century élite, stressed both by Crummey and Ya. E. Vodarsky, seems indeed to be continuity with the past, both as regards the circle of ruling families and the nature of politics.[33]

This continuity was admittedly by no means total. In the last years of his reign Aleksei Mikhailovich recruited far more 'new men' into the Boyar Duma than had been the case under his father. Individuals from the lower reaches of the court nobility who were expert in military or diplomatic affairs found it easier to rise into the boyar élite than had previously been the case. A.L. Ordin-Nashchokin, V.N. Panin and I.I. Chaadaev belonged, among others, to this group. Moreover, the Romanovs' decision not to court political trouble by marrying into the boyar élite, but rather to choose their brides from somewhat lower down in the Moscow nobility, catapulted certain previously obscure families such as the Naryshkins, Apraksins, Streshnevs and Miloslavskys into the top rank of the aristocracy.[34]

Nevertheless, on the whole the seventeenth century was a good one for the Russian traditional élite. As Crummey notes, few once-great families declined in this period and the dramatic executions and confiscations of property that had marked Ivan IV's reign were not repeated.[35] Within the boyar élite there existed an inner core of aristocratic families, almost all of them long established at the summit of Moscow society, whose adult male members joined the Boyar Duma as of quasi-hereditary right. The Golitsyns, Kurakins, Sheremetevs and Lobanov-Rostovskys were at this group's centre. Vodarsky shows that this inner core of old families, together with the new royal in-laws, were far wealthier than other seventeenth-century boyars. He also illustrates how much richer these families became in the course of the seventeenth century. Moreover, in this period the old aristocracy succeeded in taking control of the *prikazy* away from the professional bureaucracy, whose expansion and growing expertise in the sixteenth century might conceivably have posed a threat to aristocratic power.[36]

On the whole the Romanov regime had good reason to be satisfied with its achievements in the first three-quarter century of its rule. Inheriting chaos from the Time of Troubles, the regime had quickly restored domestic stability and the state's military power. One of the prices paid for this, namely the final enserfment and deprivation of rights of the peasantry, was of little concern to the élite, though the occasionally violent response to repression on the part of the masses did cause worry. In the course of the seventeenth century Russia's territory and resources had been expanded enormously, greatly increasing the wealth of the élite and providing the state with a more nearly adequate base from which to challenge Swedish and Polish power than had existed under Ivan IV. The administrative system which had developed was formidably effective as regards the taxation, conscription and control of the population. A 'new model army' had been created, even if its control by foreigners, at a time when the Russian service gentry's traditional military role had become redundant, was not a situation the state was likely to tolerate for long. Moreover, although the *prikaz* system appeared to be irrational and inefficient, in some ways the top level of government functioned rather more effectively under Aleksei Mikhailovich than was the case under the last Romanov monarch, Nicholas II. Seventeenth-century Russia was if anything closer to having a succession of 'premiers', who co-ordinated governmental affairs; moreover monarchical absolutism was buttressed by an effective private royal secretariat and had its embodiment, in Aleksei Mikhailovich, in an autocrat capable of imposing his will and personality on his chief advisers.[37]

Even a nodding acquaintance with the reign of Tsar Aleksei inspires doubt as to whether a fundamental shift occurred in the reign of Peter I and whether the Petrine era can truly be described as ushering in the modern period of Russian history. Historians, however, require some system of periodization, and the split between pre-Petrine and Petrine Russia is by now well established. Moreover, in categorizing the members of Nicholas II's State Council according to their social origins I have labelled all those men whose families were already noble in pre-Petrine Russia as belonging to the traditional Russian ruling élite. Let us therefore look briefly at these well-established gentry families in order to gain a sense of their origins and history over the centuries.

Of these gentry families, those which were oldest and most prominent in the pre-Petrine era were listed in the so-called 'Velvet Book', drawn up in the 1680s, and based almost entirely on the *Rodoslovets Gosudarev* of 1555; the families recorded in the book were all over 400 years old by 1900. By that time, of the 334 families listed in the Velvet Book, 100 still existed, of which 67 came from the old untitled nobility. Of the 67 families, 6 were represented by, in all, 9 appointed members of Nicholas II's State Council. All six families were descended from leading aristocratic houses in fourteenth-century Muscovy.[38]

The Sheremetevs were the best-known of the six families. One branch, created counts in 1706, was extremely rich for a litany of reasons which will be familiar from my discussion of the Council's princely families. Ancestors prominent in the eighteenth and seventeenth centuries (not to mention earlier) received huge grants of land,

Monarchy and aristocracy: the Winter Palace and (*left*) the Sheremetev palace in Petersburg.

virtually all of which was eventually inherited by Count S.D. Shere-metev and his brother Alexander, the only male counts Sheremetev in their generation. To them too fell the vast eighteenth-century Cherkassky inheritance in Nizhniy Novgorod and Voronezh, as well as the many properties purchased by the family in Kostroma, Penza, Saratov, Kursk, Smolensk, Oryol and Simbirsk. The Sheremetevs were also represented in the State Council by Count Serge Dmitrie-vich's distant cousin and brother-in-law, General Serge Alekseevich. The latter, not particularly wealthy but a courageous and excep-tionally well-connected soldier, had an aristocratic military career in which front-line service in the Caucasus during the Shamyl era was followed by a series of posts at court.[39]

The Council's two Sheremetevs were 'types' familiar in the his-toriography of the Russian nobility: one a great landowning mag-nate, the other a scion of the junior branch of a prominent family who found a comfortable haven in the bosom of a monarchical and aristocratic state. The history of the Khvostovs is rather more un-usual and more interesting, given the preconceptions frequently held about the nature and history of the Russian nobility. The Khvostovs, a leading boyar family in the mid-fourteenth century, descended into the service of an apanage prince and thence into the ranks of the provincial gentry after losing a power struggle with the Velyaminov family in 1356. The Khvostovs then lived for five centuries in the upper but not the upmost reaches of the Tver gentry, producing no leading servitors and receiving no land from the state. The number of males in the family was not abnormally small. Nevertheless, on the eve of Emancipation the father of the Council's two Khvostovs still owned 529 'souls' and over 5,000 *desyatiny* in Tver. After his marriage to a Zhemshchuzhnikov who owned an estate roughly similar in size to his own, in agriculturally much richer Oryol, A.N. Khvostov transferred there and it was in Oryol that all his sons inherited their properties. After five centuries in the political wilder-ness the Khvostovs suddenly made a major impact on Russian politics in the era of Nicholas II. Of four Khvostov brothers, one became a minister, another a member of the State Council, the third a senator; the fourth, a zemstvo provincial chairman, was killed in Stolypin's house in 1906 when revolutionaries attempted to blow up the premier. Moreover, one of the four brothers' sons became Minister of Internal Affairs during the First World War.[40]

One lesson to be drawn from the history of the Khvostovs might well be that concerted brotherly support was a useful aid in one's career. More fundamentally, however, the Khvostovs' fate shows that it was possible for old families to survive and even flourish in Russia's provinces without recourse to state aid. The experience of the Saburovs was rather similar to that of the Khvostovs, though the family survived near the top in Russian politics rather longer and even provided a tsarina in the early sixteenth century. Nevertheless, the Saburovs were not recipients of land grants during the Russian state's territorial expansion, but remained relatively prosperous through their own efforts. In part the family may have achieved this by moving from the Muscovite heartland to the Black Earth province of Tambov. In addition, at least one Saburov enriched herself in early nineteenth-century Tambov by founding a prosperous wool factory. Of the Council's two Saburov brothers, one owned, in the late nineteenth century, 1,300 *desyatiny* and the other 5,800. Like the Khvostovs, the Saburovs' story was that of brothers returning to prominence after their family had spent many centuries in the political wilderness. As with the Khvostovs, however, the political wilderness did not entail a slide into impoverishment.[41]

I.D. Tatishchev's family had played a more prominent role in post-Petrine Russia than either the Khvostovs or the Saburovs. The Tatishchevs had also been courtiers and comfortable landowners in the seventeenth century. I.D. Tatishchev's grandfather, a full general and a Knight of Saint Andrew, was created a count in 1801 and granted 1,200 serfs, in addition to land already owned in Petersburg and Pskov provinces. Nevertheless, I.D. Tatishchev may well have been telling the truth when he wrote in his service record that he owned no land. A career soldier, like others of his kind he may have been happy to leave the cares of estate management to his brothers. It is, however, most unlikely that lack of land meant Tatischev enjoyed no sort of private income. For a young officer in the Preobrazhensky Guards this would have been almost inconceivable. And for Tatishchev, whose mother, S.I. Kusova, was the daughter of a millionaire businessman, it was altogether improbable. Not only were the Tatishchevs a wholly military family; every generation had served in the Preobrazhensky regiment from the unit's creation in the 1690s down to the eve of the First World War, when I.D. Tatishchev's eldest son retired as the regiment's colonel. One of Tatishchev's uncles had been killed at Austerlitz, another, a Semyonovsky, died at Borodino. The effect of such traditions and memories on the mentality of the ruling élite can scarcely be overestimated.[42]

The Ignat'evs, descended from the Pleshcheev family of boyars, had never played a prominent role in military or political affairs before the nineteenth century. In the pre-Petrine era the family had been on the Moscow noble rolls and had owned estates in the Rzhev distirct of Tver. P.N. Ignat'ev, offspring of this prominent but by no means aristocratic provincial family, was the only son of a Tver nobleman who was marshal of his province in the late eighteenth century. The career of this relatively well-off young officer in the Preobrazhensky regiment in the 1820s blossomed after his troops were among the first loyal units to move on to the Palace Square under Nicholas I's eyes during the Decembrist rebellion. Ignat'ev married into the wealthy Maltsov business family and owned 1,226 serfs in 1860. He ended his career in the 1870s as a count. a full general and the chairman of the Committee of Ministers. Both his sons played major political roles as strong authoritarians and Russian nationalists in the last decades of the Old Regime. It says something for the exclusiveness of the aristocratic élite of Petersburg society in the late nineteenth century that the Ignat'evs, for all their prominence and their respectable ancestry, were never much welcomed or accepted as equals by the Dolgorukys, Shuvalovs and their ilk. Instead, A.P. Ignat'ev's home became the centre for 'Monday evening receptions. . .specially dedicated to church matters', to which bishops and laymen interested in the Orthodox Church flocked. Among the frequent guests was the ultra-conservative V.P. Meshchersky, the editor of *Grazhdanin* and a kinsman of Ignat'ev's wife. The countess, a provincial gentry nationalist of the purest breed, was described in old age as representing 'that type of old-fashioned dowager whom one so rarely meets nowadays in society. Tall and rather awe-inspiring in appearance, she disdains new fashions and attends balls and evening parties in a high-necked, dark silk gown with a black lace handkerchief pinned over her hair'.[43]

The Samarins, descended from the old Kvashnin family of boyars, yielded nothing in their conservativism and Russian nationalism either to the Ignat'evs or to Count S.D. Sheremetev. Some direct ancestors of A.D. Samarin had occupied prominent government posts in the seventeenth and eighteenth centuries, though one, Nicholas Mikhailovich (d. 1762), had also amassed a large fortune privately, through business activity in Archangel province. Even in the twentieth century some Samarins were extremely wealthy and owned large estates. A.D. Samarin himself seems to have possessed only a small property, but he was certainly not poor. His wife, Vera Mamontov, was the daughter of one of the richest members of the Moscow business community. Marshal of Moscow province and a Muscovite through and through, A.D. Samarin was a very different type both from the Petersburg officials who dominated the State Council and the often highly cosmopolitan aristocrats of Petersburg's drawing-rooms. The nephew of Yuri Samarin, the famous slavophil, and the younger brother of Fyodor Samarin, the philosopher, Alexander Samarin was also closely linked by marriage to the princes E.N. and S.N. Trubetskoy, key figures in the Moscow intellectual community in the early twentieth century. The network of nationalist, intellectual, business and aristocratic connections at whose centre A.D. Samarin stood was a purely Muscovite phenomenon which had no real counterpart in late imperial Petersburg.[44]

The Sheremetevs, Khvostovs, Saburovs, Ignat'evs, Tatishchevs and Samarins were not wholly typical of the group of families represented in the State Council which had belonged to the pre-Petrine nobility. In comparison with the group as a whole, the six families were all older and usually rather grander as well. Since families belonging to that pre-Petrine nobility accounted, however, for at least one-third of the 215 members of Nicholas II's ruling élite, it is impossible to go into detail about each of them. Instead, I shall seek to discover patterns in the histories of these families.

Some members of the State Council from old gentry families either owned no land and had become pure service dynasties, or held very small estates which can have been little more than summer retreats. In the great majority of cases men in this position came from the gentry of the Central Industrial and northern provinces of the Muscovite heartland, where agriculture was seldom very profitable and Emancipation had removed the main source of gentry wealth, namely the dues (*obroki*) of their serfs.

One not untypical old gentry family from the north were the Tyrtovs. After Ivan III destroyed the independence of Novgorod in the 1480s, he granted estates to a number of Muscovite families, among them the Tyrtovs. The ancestor of the State Council's Admiral P.P. Tyrtov, Vasili Matveevich Tyrtov, had participated in the siege of Moscow during the Time of Troubles and as a reward was granted further land in the Torzhok district. By 1900 the estate of Mironezhe held by P.P. Tyrtov and his brothers and sisters had been in the family's possession for over 300 years. Maybe for that very reason the eleven brothers and sisters had not divided the estate, but rather held it in common, one unmarried sister living there permanently. Mironezhe cannot have brought the Tyrtovs much profit, and their other lands had been sold after Emancipation. Fortunately for them, however, the Tyrtovs were not only a landowning but also a service family, with a long military and in particular a naval tradition. P.P. Tyrtov's father had lived the not untypical life of the pre-Emancipation nobleman. After serving for twenty years and rising to the rank of lieutenant-colonel, he retired to his estates, held various elected positions in local government and brought up his family of eleven children. Of his sons, one, P.P. Tyrtov, became naval minister, another was a full admiral and the commander of the Black Sea fleet, a third was a naval captain, a fourth a lieutenant-general, a fifth a major-general, and a sixth the procurator of the Kazan district court. The Tyrtovs' history underlines the vital significance of state jobs for the families of the declining northern landowning class, while emphasizing too the strength of the military and patriotic tradition in this milieu. Among the Tyrtovs' close relations by marriage were, for instance, the Seslavins and Rimsky-

Korsakovs, names which had a special meaning for any Russian patriot conscious of his country's history.[45]

Among the members of the State Council who came from old northern gentry families but had inherited little or no land were N.M. Anichkov,[46] A.S. Taneev,[47] Count M.N. Murav'yov,[48] A.A. Polivanov,[49] I.P. and N.N. Shipov,[50] V.N. Kokovtsov,[51] V.V. Verkhovsky[52] and Prince A.A. Shirinsky-Shikhmatov.[53] In a number of cases the fact that an individual owned no estate did not mean that his family had dropped out of the landowning gentry. Generals A.A. Polivanov and N.N. Shipov both had brothers who were land-owners and noble marshals, while both the father and the son of V.V. Verkhovsky owned large, though possibly not very valuable, estates in Kostroma province. Unless, however, one counts A.D. Zinov'ev's estates in Petersburg and Vitebsk provinces,[54] A.N. Ku-lomzin[55] and Count A.P. Ignat'ev were the only members of the State Council from old gentry families who themselves owned size-able estates in a region ruled by Moscow before 1550 but who did not at the same time possess much larger and more profitable estates elsewhere.

More common were men from old gentry families who, like A.S. Bryanchaninov and D.S. Sipyagin, combined ownership of estates in the Muscovite heartland with the possession of more profitable lands in more recently colonized regions. Though, for instance, Bryan-chaninov, a former officer in the Chevaliers Gardes, cannot have been poor as a young man, his inherited estate of 1,160 *desyatiny* in Vologda in the far north was much less valuable than the 5,074 *desyatiny* owned by his wife in Samara.[56] In a number of cases families initially from the northern gentry had transferred their landholdings entirely to other regions. The Tyutchevs, originally from Yaroslavl but by the nineteenth century big landowners in Oryol, were a pro-minent family who made such a move.[57] So too were the Stolypins, initially from the Tver and Moscow gentry, who by the nineteenth century owned big estates in the Volga provinces and other lands in Penza and Kovno.[58] In addition, of course, among the 215 members of the State Council were some representatives of old families of the Black Earth provinces. According to P.P. Semyonov, for instance, his family were Ryazan boyars in medieval times. Whether or not this was the case, he certainly came from an old Ryazan family and still owned estates in the province, though his wife's property in Samara was more valuable.[59] N.A. Myasoedov, whose family held junior court rank in the pre-Petrine era and already held estates in Tula in the 1580s, still owned land in the province in the early twentieth century, though his property in Saratov was much larger.[60] Another old Tula family represented in the State Council were the Arsen'evs, at least one of whose estates had been in the family for over 250 years by the time of the revolution.[61] Equally, the estate of Lipovka in Oryol, which had been in the Bekhteev family for 400 years, was still owned by S.S. Bekhteev in 1910.[62] On the whole these members of the Black Earth gentry were much more likely to be able to live off the proceeds of land-owning than their northern peers; but agricultural depression and division of estates among the heirs took a toll in their ranks too, especially in an era when the old escape route of taking up virgin land in newly colonized areas no longer existed.[63]

Most of the old gentry families represented in the State Council remained in the upper reaches of provincial society down to the lifetime of the Council's members. In a few cases, however, families which were not particularly prominent in the pre-Petrine era rose into the aristocracy in the 150 years after 1700. A vital prerequisite for this ascent was the rise of an ancestor to the top of the military or civil service, or occasionally just his ability to attract imperial favour. The general rule was that a brilliant career, which might in itself have brought rich financial rewards in the form of imperial land grants in the eighteenth century, was far less likely to do so as the nineteenth century wore on. Thus the Taneevs, who provided three long-serving chiefs of the Emperor's Own Personal Chancellery in the nineteenth and early twentieth centuries, remained by no means well off and also in this period lost the small estates they had once possessed in Vladimir and Tver.[64] At the other extreme the Shuvalovs, favourites and chief advisers to the Empress Elizabeth in the mid-eighteenth century, were showered with such wealth that Count Paul Shuvalov was still a very rich man at the end of the nineteenth century despite the existence of nine other counts and thirteen countesses Shuvalov in his generation. Admittedly, a 'sensible' policy of marriage only to their peers had helped to maintain the family's wealth.[65]

Even Paul Shuvalov's fortune was, however, dwarfed by that of P.P. Durnovo, who together with his wife owned 123,000 *desyatiny*, and of N.P. Balashov, who shared 522,000 *desyatiny* with his brother, Ivan. The means by which Durnovo and Balashov acquired these huge estates were rather similar and distinctly interesting. Though the Durnovos had the longer pedigree, neither family was particularly distinguished in the pre-Petrine era. Neither man's ancestors had held court rank in the seventeenth century or before, the highest post attained being that of *voevoda* (provincial chief administrator). The ascent of both families began in the eighteenth century. Dmitri Ivanovich Balashov entered the civil service in 1734, worked subsequently in both Petersburg and the provinces, and after 52 years' service became a senator in 1786. His son Alexander, born when his father was already a senior civil servant, started service in aristocratic style in the Corps des Pages and Preobrazhensky Guards, 'but having only a modest fortune he found the regiment too expensive for him and transferred, with the rank of lieutenant-colonel, into the Astrakhan Grenadier Regiment'. Subsequently A.D. Balashov's career flourished. He became an aide-de-camp general, a member of the State Council and, from 1810 to 1816, Minister of Justice. N.D. Durnovo was 17 years younger than D.I. Balashov and made a military career, starting service in the Semyonovsky Guards, becoming an aide-de-camp general and a senator and in 1816, the year of his death, aged eighty-three, receiving a grant of 1,828 serfs in Minsk.

So far the stories of the Balashovs and Durnovos are typical of those of a number of men from provincial noble families who rose through the Table of Ranks to top positions in the state's service. What singled out both families were the marriages they made in the late eighteenth and early nineteenth centuries. N.D. Durnovo's son Dmitri married into the Demidov family with its colossal, initially merchant, fortune, while A.D. Balashov acquired much of the huge Myasnikov business inheritance – also, like that of the Demidovs, built initially around Urals industry. Subsequently, P.P. Durnovo's fortune was much increased by the fact that, firstly, all his Durnovo uncles died without heirs; secondly, he was an only son; and thirdly, his wife, born a Princess Kochubei, brought with her an immense dowry. The Balashovs' wealth grew over the generations in even more spectacular fashion. Through their mother, the daughter of Field Marshal Prince I.F. Paskevich-Erivansky, the two Balashov brothers inherited big estates in Mogilyov. This inheritance paled into insignificance beside the 170,000 *desyatiny* brought to N.P. Balashov from his marriage to Countess Catherine Shuvalov, who received this immense concentration of wealth from her uncle, the last of the princes Vorontsov.[66]

The theme of this chapter so far has been continuity and the dominant position of the aristocracy within the ruling élite of Muscovite Russia. The same trend is visible in the reign of Peter I. Though a number both of foreigners and of Russians of modest origin held high rank under Peter I, the bulk of the Petrine élite was drawn from the pre-Petrine aristocracy, and the dominance of old aristocrats was more marked the closer one got to the key posts. Generous land grants went largely to families springing from the traditional élite, and it was their sons, rather than those of newcomers or foreigners, who were most likely subsequently to hold high office. Peter in other words forced the old élite to serve in the manner which he considered appropriate. He forced them to re-educate themselves so that they could serve effectively. Had he wished to replace the old élites or weaken their position he could have turned to the sons of his professional civil servants, the *d'yaki*. Instead he chose to bend the old aristocracy and service gentry to his will and goals.[67]

To what extent this picture of continuity and a dominant aristocracy applies to the ruling élite in the reigns of Elizabeth, Catherine II and Paul is not clear. No one has studied the later eighteenth or indeed nineteenth-century élites with the care Brenda Meehan-Waters has devoted to the rulers of Petrine Russia. In the eighteenth century the Russian nobility as a whole was diluted, becoming far less homogeneous than it had been even in the pre-Petrine era. Even leaving aside the increasing horde of personal nobles, the influx into the hereditary nobility of Polish *szlachta* (lesser gentry), the Cossack *starshina* (officers), the various elements that made up the nobility of recently colonized New Russia, and ennobled officers and officials promoted through the Table of Ranks ensured this result. Whether the same was true of the aristocracy or ruling élite is, however, a quite different matter.[68]

The great expansion of Russia in the eighteenth century allowed the monarch to make generous grants of land and serfs even without exercising his prerogative of handing state or formerly Church peasants to private owners. Some imperial favourites benefited in spectacular fashion from this fact and joined the ranks of the landowning magnates. In the reigns of Elizabeth, Catherine II and Paul, for instance, the Razumovskys, the Shuvalovs, A.P. Bestuzhev, N.I. Panin, A.A. Bezborodko, Dashkova, the Orlovs, A.S. Vasil'chikov, A.B. Kurakin and I.P. Kutaysov, among others, were recipients of lavish imperial favours.[69] Though a few favourites such as Menshikov and Kutaisov[70] were complete outsiders, most came from families which were at least sufficiently part of the élite to have placed their sons as officers in the regiments of the Imperial Guard. Some were aristocrats by birth.[71] Even where this was not the case, a favourite had every incentive to marry into the aristocracy, partly for social reasons and partly, as in Potyomkin's case, because to be politically effective any favourite needed allies in the established aristocratic class.[72] In the seventeenth century, as we have seen, the Russian aristocracy flourished while absorbing a handful of suddenly rich and influential royal in-laws from previously relatively minor noble families. What the Naryshkins and Streshnevs were in the seventeenth century, the Orlovs and Shuvalovs were in the eighteenth. Moreover, if there were rather more favourites than there had been in-laws, there was also a great deal more in the way of spoils of territorial expansion to be shared out among the whole élite, old and new. There is little reason to doubt that the old aristocracy absorbed the newcomers without difficulty.

As to the balance of power between 'autocracy', aristocracy and gentry in eighteenth-century Russia, the so-called 'class nature' of the absolutist state, even the terms in which the question is posed are a cause of misunderstanding and imprecision.[73] The Russian hereditary nobility, extremely heterogeneous in this era, had no common aspirations, values and interests save a dislike of serf rebellion and, in most cases, a pride in Russia's military power. The court aristocracy was more homogeneous, partly because it was more deeply and wholly westernized, but it was also divided into hostile competing families and other cliques. 'Autocracy' is a confusing concept, in part because for some it signifies the monarch personally, for others both the sovereign and his chief advisers. Even the word 'state' can be misleading when applied to the Russian eighteenth century, for in that era Russia was certainly not governed by a large and semi-autonomous bureaucracy, professionally trained, with its own ethos, purposes and leaders, serving some collective vision of the common good embodied in the concept of the state. Political power was contested by court factions, each one anxious to use the governmental machine to further the interests of its own clique and to provide patronage for its clients.[74] The extent to which 'the state' could remain independent of these cliques and impose 'its' own aims still depended greatly on the abilities, age, temperament and desires of the ruling monarch.

Nevertheless, certain commonsensical points can be made. The Russian hereditary nobility was not a class, let alone a ruling class. Even had it possessed common aspirations, it had no means to articulate them or force them on the state's rulers. On the other hand, it is undoubtedly true that, as Catherine II found to her cost in the Pugachov rebellion, the monarchy could not even have guaranteed order in the provinces, let alone governed there in any constructive manner, without the active collaboration of provincial landowners.[75] As regards the sovereign's relationship with the court aristocracy, the single most important point to note is that Russia was an absolute monarchy at the beginning of the eighteenth century and an absolute monarchy at the end of it. No institutions had been created through which the social élite could exercise control over monarchical power in a legitimate, consistent and regular manner. Undoubtedly one important reason for this was that aristocratic factionalism allowed the monarch to play divide and rule. Moreover, if some elements of the Russian aristocracy had come to absorb Western notions of a semi-constitutional nature, others remained happy with the existing political system from which they derived so many benefits. The monarch's ability to promote and reward personal favourites, non-aristocratic officials or non-Russians helped to consolidate his personal power.[76]

Nevertheless governing without, let alone against, the leading court factions was both difficult and dangerous. The coups by which monarchs were overthrown were the work of cliques rather than classes, but they did sometimes reflect broader interests and aspirations than those of a mere court faction.[77] In particular, the conspirators who overthrew Paul I in 1801 were motivated not only, as in 1762, by dislike of the monarch's foreign policy, but also by the fact that, in James Kenney's words, 'it was indeed Paul's intent to destroy what he viewed as the harmful and counter-productive pretensions of the aristocracy'. Commenting that 'the conspirators formed a homogeneous group drawn from the highest layer of Russian society', Kenney sees behind the assassination 'the hatred of the aristocracy as a whole for the Emperor Paul'. Paul once made the comment, often cited, that there were no *grands seigneurs* in Russia save men who were speaking to the monarch and even then only so long as the conversation lasted. This did not represent late eighteenth-century Russian realities, and the Emperor paid for his miscalculation with his life.[78]

John Keep notes that Paul I's reign represented 'a shift in the locus of executive power away from the aristocratic élite to professional administrators', as well as a change in the ethos of public service best described as militarization. He sees Paul's reign as a forerunner to that of Nicholas I, when the rigid military-bureaucratic state truly came into its own. In many ways not only the conspiracy of 1801 but also elements of the uprising of 1825 can be seen as aristocratic responses to the development of Romanov bureaucratic absolutism, though the Decembrists were much less selfishly concerned with purely aristocratic interests than had been the case in 1801. If in 1825 the young conspirators' ambitious and idealistic programme led to a good deal of uncertainty, by comparison with the simple goal and ruthless execution of the coup of 1801, they at least had a clear sense of the need to consolidate the gains of successful rebellion immediately in institutional controls over monarchical power. Inevitably, however, the Decembrist revolt merely deepened the suspicion of the Russian aristocracy that always lurked in the hearts of Paul I and his sons. In the thirty years after 1825 Russia was ruled by a monarch of immense conscientiousness with a Petrine vision of universal service and whose sympathies lay in the minute regulation of society by the state. Moreover, in Nicholas's lifetime the great expansion of the bureaucracy, its organization into hierarchical ministerial apparatuses and its liberation from the control of aristocratic cliques allowed the monarch to believe that such salutary regulation was in fact occurring in accordance with his wishes.[79]

In recent years Nicholas's bureaucracy has been the subject of considerable study in the West. For H.J. Torke the major characteristics of the Russian civil service were its lack of professional auto-

Monarchy and bureaucracy towards the end of the Old Regime. Nicholas II visiting Riga is greeted by civil servants in summer uniforms.

nomy, expertise or ethos. Unlike its Prussian counterpart it had neither the corporate rights guaranteed by the *Allgemeine Landrecht*, nor yet a clear sense of service to the communal welfare enshrined in an abstract ideal of the state.[80] Without challenging Torke's view that the Russian civil service as a whole was corrupt, inefficient, arbitrary and concerned with its own welfare rather than the communal interest, some American scholars have recently cast a somewhat redeeming light on certain aspects of Nicholas's bureaucracy. What emerges clearly from the work of these scholars is that by the 1850s Russia possessed an élite officialdom fully committed to the service of a state whose only legitimate function in their eyes was the welfare of the community. These men were expert career officials, firmly rooted in the ministerial apparatus, and possessed of an ethos distinct in most cases from that of the landed aristocracy or gentry. They expected the state to play the leading role in bringing reform and modernization to Russian society and, if permitted by the monarch and his entourage, were willing and able to take the burden of leadership on their own shoulders. Moreover, although convinced that in the short term ultimate authority must be retained by the civil service, many of these men had a vision of civil society's development which encompassed the increasing devolution of power into non-bureaucratic hands.[81]

Whereas the pre-reform bureaucracy has attracted much excellent scholarship in recent years, there is no work devoted exclusively either to the institutions or to the personnel of the civil service as a whole in the reigns of the last three Romanov monarchs. Nor is there a study of the ruling élite at any point between 1855 and 1914, though very useful work has been done by both Soviet and Western scholars on the nobility and on government–gentry relations.[82] Apart from more general surveys which include the period 1855–1917,[83] and what can be gleaned from books both on politics and specific fields of policy, the scholar interested in the late imperial ruling élite or the civil service is left with a handful of specialist studies, among them a work on the Ministry of Internal Affairs which concludes with 1881;[84] a forthcoming book on the provincial governors;[85] a study of the relations between Alexander III and the State Council;[86] a number of articles on officials of the Ministry of Internal Affairs;[87] and some rather misleading statistics on the members of the State Council under Nicholas II.[88]

From these and other sources[89] much can of course be gleaned about the Russian bureaucracy and ruling élite in the last decades of the Empire. The civil service grew greatly, it is clear, in size, professional expertise and efficiency. If the bureaucracy's lower ranks in the provinces were not overimpressive, taken as a whole the civil service had left the era of Gogol far behind, particularly of course as regards the central ministries and the administrative élite. The many well-educated and often public-spirited officials who filled the bureaucracy's ranks held attitudes generally rather far removed from old-fashioned concepts of dynastic service and were devoted instead to a vision of the common weal. By 1900 the civil service taken as a whole was certainly distinct from the landowning class, having its own ethos, interests and purposes, even if certain groups of officials such as governors or members of the bureaucratic élite were more likely than others to share the values and loyalties of the aristocracy and gentry.

In politics much had changed since the days of medieval or Catherinian Russia when, in J.P. LeDonne's view, the family was still the dominant institution, the main source of 'identity, a refuge, and a source of rewards'.[90] It is true that ties of blood and marriage, comradeship at school and in the service, still counted for much. Nevertheless an official's life now turned round his department or ministry, which imposed its own interests and viewpoints on those who served within it. Unquestionably politics now was much more the struggle of ministries than a conflict among cliques of families. Moreover, at the top of the bureaucracy there were cleavages between men known to hold differing principles and to take different views as to the best way to survive the political crisis increasingly threatening the Old

Regime's stability. Even a very superficial knowledge of Russian politics would indicate that some high officials favoured liberalization, greater autonomy for society and increased participation of that society in politics, while others remained committed to authoritarian, bureaucratic and centralized rule. It is no secret that the monarch's general commitment to the second group and its ideas was of great significance in determining Russia's political course in the last decades of the Empire.

The relation between bureaucracy and monarch was one of mutual dependence. The monarch could not govern Russia alone. To run an increasingly complex society intelligently required that he listen to advisers and experts, often bowing to their conclusions. Yet even top officials had scant ground on which to unite and impose their views on a recalcitrant monarch, for ultimately all authority and all legitimacy flowed from him. On major political questions he remained the ultimate arbiter and decision-maker. However, the balance of power among monarch, bureaucracy, aristocracy and gentry was not static. Between 1861 and 1905 the civil service gained in power and autonomy at the expense of the traditional social élites, even if many of its chiefs shared the values and loyalties of those élites. On the other hand, the years 1906–17 witnessed a dramatic resurgence of strength on the part of the gentry and the aristocracy, as these groups were at last provided with institutions through which they could express their views and wield an influence on governmental policy.

CHAPTER 2

PROFILE OF AN ELITE

I

In an essay on the nineteenth-century Russian aristocracy Jerome
Blum wrote in 1977 that 'the majority of the closest advisers and
leading generals of the last tsar...were commoners by birth'.[1] If
'commoners' means non-nobles, then Blum's statement could scarcely be less accurate. As Table A shows, 90 per cent of the members of
the State Council were born into the hereditary nobility, an estate
which in 1914 made up roughly 1 per cent of the Empire's population. Of the remaining 10 per cent, the great majority were the sons
of professional men or of junior state officials. Only two men, A.A.
Makarov and N.S. Tagantsev, were born into the merchant estate,
two more, D.I. Pikhno and N.I. Zverev, coming from the *meshchanstvo* (i.e. urban small tradesmen, artisans and other 'lower middle-
class' elements). One man, A.P. Nikol'sky, was a priest's son, and

MEN APPOINTED TO THE STATE COUNCIL 1894–1914

Table A: *Social Origins*

No.	Council members							
	Civilians 146		Generals 58		Admirals 11		Total 215	
	No.	%	No.	%	No.	%	No.	%
Noble	128	87.7	55	94.8	11	100	194	90.2
Professional	11	7.5					11	5.1
Commercial	2	1.4					2	0.9
Clergy	1	0.7					1	0.5
Meshchane	2	1.4					2	0.9
Other	1	0.7					1	0.5
Unknown	1	0.7	3	5.2			4	1.9

none were the sons of peasants, nomads or cossacks – categories which, taken together, accounted for roughly 8 out of every 9 imperial subjects. Clearly, the imperial ruling élite was recruited from a social group that was, relative to the Empire's total population, very narrow.

This situation was obviously dangerous. Parts of Russian society were changing very rapidly in Nicholas II's reign. Portions not only of the working class but even of the peasantry were beginning to organize and to make political demands on the state. Mentalities were shifting. The members of a ruling élite drawn from such a relatively narrow circle, very distinct from the bulk of the population, might find it very hard to appreciate, let alone accommodate, changes within the peasantry and working class. For the latter it might be even harder to feel empathy for a state run by people with values so very different from their own. Nor was it only the masses from whom the ruling élite was far removed. The new groups spawned by the massive expansion of the economy and educational system under Nicholas II were also faced with this élite drawn almost exclusively from the traditional noble and official ruling circles. Even the leaders of the powerful Moscow industrial and financial bourgeoisie lived, in K.A. Krivoshein's words, on a different planet from the Petersburg official élite, at least until the twentieth century.[2]

The continued domination of top governmental posts by the traditional élites was in part the result of a deliberate policy of the imperial regime. It is true that the basic principles of Peter I's civil service legislation were never rescinded: merit, education and experience were the key formal criteria for advancement, and even the highest posts always in principle remained open to anyone possessing these qualifications, whatever their origins. On the other hand, in both the eighteenth and nineteenth centuries legislation gave advantages to the hereditary nobility in service and sought to limit the movement of non-nobles into the bureaucracy's higher ranks.[3]

As we shall see, however, educational levels rather than social origins had by the mid-nineteenth century become the key formal barriers to entry into the administration's top flight, and the government's policy on education was a more effective obstacle to non-nobles reaching top office than any remaining bias in the civil service regulations themselves. Though the Russian gymnasium and university were scarcely by contemporary European standards socially exclusive, the imperial government looked askance at the effects of social mobility through the educational system and, particularly in the early 1850s and 1880s, did its best to stem it. Probably more important in the long run, the government refrained from creating a simple educational ladder whereby a student might progress easily from the district school to the all-important gymnasium. Certainly even in the 1860s the key educational institutions from which Russia's future rulers were drawn were still largely noble preserves. Even in the universities, the most 'democratic' educational path into the higher civil service, 73 per cent of all students in 1862 were still the sons of nobles and officials.[4] Nor was there any dramatic shift in this figure later in the 1860s and early 1870s, least of all in the law faculty of Petersburg University, which was the main source of recruits to the higher civil service from Russian universities.[5] The Alexander Lycée and the School of Law, key training establishments for the official élite, remained noble monopolies. Moreover, as regards the army, although Dimitri Milyutin's reforms opened the officer corps to non-nobles, the Military Schools, the essential training ground for the future military élite, remained dominated by nobles in the 1860s. Thus even in the Aleksinsky Military School in Moscow, an anything but aristocratic institution, between 1864 and 1869 81 per cent of the cadets were noble.[6]

Yet though the contrast between a traditional élite and an increasingly educated and industrialized society was real and vital, its basic causes should not be sought in governmental policy or regulations. One has to remember that Nicholas II's ruling élite was the product of the Russia of the 1840s to 1870s, not of the 1890s and 1900s.[7] The Russian Empire was governed by a largely bureaucratic élite, made up of men who, if they were to acquire political power, had to enter the state's service in their early twenties and commit themselves to spending at least 25 years climbing the official ladder to top governmental posts. It scarcely needs to be emphasized that the Russia of the 1860s, when most future members of the State Council either had entered or were entering the state's service, was a very different country indeed from twentieth-century Russia.

When noting the domination of the late imperial ruling élite by hereditary nobles, it is important to remember the size and nature of the groups with which noblemen were in competition for official jobs in the 1860s and 1870s. It is pointless to mention here that the hereditary nobility made up only 1 per cent of the population. Peasants are not serious competitors for top official posts in any traditional agrarian society untouched by revolution, even in the immediate pre-industrial period. For the traditional élite, members of professional, clerical and commercial families are likely to provide much more dangerous competition. In Russia, however, even in 1897, the hereditary nobility, 1.2 million strong, numbered two-thirds as many as the non-noble professional, clerical and merchant estates combined. Russian noblemen in the 1860s and 1870s also still enjoyed great advantages of wealth, culture and connections over the three non-noble groups, in competing for official posts. Moreover, in the immediate post-Emancipation period the merchant estate was still in general a highly conservative and parochial group, devoted to its own affairs. The sons of the clergy, in Protestant countries a vital source of recruits for the civil service, were by European standards exceptionally poor, ill-educated and of low social standing. In addition, in the 1860s, because of the low level of capitalist development in Russia and the swollen condition of the state's apparatus, much of the professional class, including most of its élite, belonged to the hereditary nobility.[8]

To understand the significance of statistics about Russian officials' 'estate' origins, one needs to put the Russian hereditary nobility in a European perspective. Comparisons with the English nobility are of course impossible, though if one included in the term 'nobility' not merely the peerage but also the landed gentry and 'gentlemen' of England, as M.L. Bush does, they would become more viable.[9] German comparisons are more to the point. In nineteenth-century Prussia, for instance, as in Russia, there were considerable numbers of nobles living little better than peasants and competing hungrily for lowly jobs in the state's service. Both countries also had a large and impoverished Polish *szlachta*. The Prussian gentry, like its Russian counterpart, was infused with a strong ethic of service, and had learned to assimilate large numbers of ennobled state officials and even army officers.[10] In Bavaria and Württemburg a personal nobility existed, similar in principle to that existing in Russia.[11] In Austria, undoubtedly the state most nearly akin to Russia in this context, hereditary nobility was attainable automatically through the award of certain decorations or simply through long and blameless service.[12]

Yet the very fact that the Russian hereditary nobility tended to share all the 'open' features of its British and German counterparts helped to make it a distinctly 'democratic' variation on the European noble theme. When a comparative European perspective is adopted, the dominant position of the Russian hereditary nobility in Nicholas II's ruling élite seems not too remarkable. John Armstrong stresses the overwhelming predominance of the well-educated and well-off in leading positions in nineteenth and twentieth-century European civil services.[13] In England, for instance, the upper classes wholly dominated rural local government through unpaid JPs until the late 1880s, while control of the key positions in the central Home Office was largely in the hands of the professional upper middle class well beyond that date.[14] The Foreign Office by contrast remained to a considerable extent the preserve of Old Etonians down to 1914, while of the army's 19 full generals in 1912, 6 came from the aristocracy, 5 from the landed gentry, and all the rest from the middle class.[15]

In Prussia too, nobles, like the British aristocracy and gentry a narrower group than the Russian hereditary nobility, still held a great many key posts in 1914. In the provincial administration of the Ministry of Internal Affairs the three most influential positions were those of *Oberpräsident*, *Regierungspräsident* and *Landrat*. Nobles by birth made up 83 per cent of the first group, 51.4 per cent of the second, and 56.2 per cent of the third.[16] As regards Prussia's full generals, in 1909 considerably more than half came not merely from noble families, but from lines which had been noble well back into the mid-eighteenth century. As much as 63 per cent of General Staff officers were born into the nobility.[17] Meanwhile a historian of the German diplomatic corps writes that 'the Foreign Office prized no quality so much as noble lineage', a comment amply borne out by the statistics on the social origins of German diplomats.[18]

Comparisons between Russia on the one hand and Britain and Germany on the other are useful in showing that not only in Russia but also in Europe's two leading industrialized states a traditional élite continued to play a major role in government right down to 1914. They also remind one that, by the standards of the Prussian nobility or of the families included in Burke's genealogies of the British aristocracy and landed gentry, the Russian hereditary noble estate was a relatively large and heterogeneous group, which, particularly in the first two-thirds of the nineteenth century, included a very large proportion of Russian educated society.

Two further points, however, should be made. One is that, whatever the comparisons with other European countries, it remains true that in a period of intense social conflict within Russia the domination of the imperial state by members of the traditional noble estate was bound both to weaken the regime's legitimacy in the eyes of other groups and to reduce its ability to mediate effectively between conflicting forces in society. A second point is that, unlike Russia, neither Britain nor any of the German states was governed by a monarch, officials and generals alone. All these countries had parliaments, none of them as gentry-dominated, by the twentieth century, as were the Russian Third and Fourth Dumas.[19] Although the traditional ruling class may have been as dominant in British and German administrative, diplomatic and military élites prior to 1914, or conceivably even more, than was the case in Russia, those élites no longer bore the entire burden of directing society or of mediating between conflicting groups, ideologies and interests.

Men whose families were already part of the pre-Petrine ruling élite can safely be regarded as having been fully Russian centuries before the reign of Nicholas II. The same cannot necessarily be said about individuals whose families became Russian subjects during or after the Petrine era. Of this latter group almost all came from lands to the west or, in the case of Finland, north-west of the Russian Empire. Sixty-one men, 28 per cent of the total, had 'Western' surnames, of whom two were of French descent, two were Greek and one was Portuguese.[20] Six men came from Finland, though judging by their surnames, all were in ethnic terms Swedes.[21]

Much the largest section among the Council's 61 'non-Russians' was, however, made up of men of German origin, of whom there were 48 in all. About half of these men came from families indigenous to the Baltic provinces of Estland, Livland and Courland; the ancestors of the others had immigrated directly to Russia from Germany.[22] Within the latter group there were a few men whose families had been nobles in their homelands before emigrating to Russia.[23] In most cases, however, the original immigrants had been men of relatively modest backgrounds for whom emigration to Russia brought much greater possibilities of advancement than they would have enjoyed at home, since Russian society was hungry for the technical skills they possessed. Technological, medical and educational skills were particularly valued,[24] and it is interesting that, where immigrant families tended towards military occupations, they very often served in the technical branches of the army. Nor was this tradition by any means extinct among the members of the Council themselves. Of the Council's four engineer generals, for instance, N.K. Schaffhausen, P.F. Unterberger and P.F. Röhrberg were the descendants either of the Baltic German bourgeoisie or of German immigrants. The family of Peter Röhrberg, whose father was a General of Engineers, whose brother was a civil engineer and Privy Counsellor, and whose grandfather had been the director of a state-owned sail-making factory, represented the quintessence of the German professional middle-class tradition within the Empire's high civil and military officialdom.[25]

Within the group of 'German', originally bourgeois service families, the distinction between men whose ancestors had immigrated from abroad, and others who sprang from the Baltic provinces was of no great significance. This was especially true when, as often happened, members of originally Balt middle-class families severed their links with the provinces and merged into the Russian service nobility. The same could be the case even with cadets of the Baltic gentry families, some of whom, as we shall see, had by the late nineteenth century nothing either 'Balt' or 'landed' about them save their names. In general, however, it is important to make a clear distinction between members of the Baltic landed gentry and other men of German origin in the service of the Russian crown. This remains the case even when these 'other Germans' came from aristocratic families and owned estates in non-Baltic areas of the Empire. The Baltic gentry, or rather those members of it who were still rooted in their homeland, had traditions, ways and prejudices which set them quite sharply apart from all other elements in the imperial landed and service nobility.[26]

Within the State Council there were in all 16 men who belonged to Baltic gentry families. Of those families, some, such as the Medems, Lievens and Uxkulls, had been in the Baltic provinces since the early years of the German settlement.[27] Others, such as the Lambsdorffs, Budbergs and Korffs, though already noble in the medieval era, had come to the Baltic region in the fifteenth and sixteenth centuries.[28] From the medieval period down to the eighteenth century all these families were part of a single Germanic North European military and landed society, Protestant since the sixteenth century, which stretched from Mecklenburg in the west to Estland in the east.[29] Two other Baltic gentry families, the Staals and Rennenkampfs, can be traced back to the sixteenth century in the Baltic provinces, but were only ennobled in 1684 and 1728 respectively.[30]

The youngest of the Baltic gentry families represented in the Council were the Wahls. Their ancestor, Johann Heinrich, had made money in the second half of the eighteenth century partly through minor office but also by leasing land from the gentry. His wealth opened the way to his being ennobled by the Holy Roman Emperor in 1795. In the agricultural crisis of the 1820s, when many estates went on the market at low prices, Johann Heinrich's son Karl Gustav, already the lessor of a large property, was able to buy a considerable amount of land and rise into the Baltic gentry. The manner in which the Wahls rose from bourgeoisie to nobility was typical for late eighteenth-and early nineteenth-century Prussia, where large numbers of bourgeois tenant farmers achieved wealth and ennoblement through efficient exploitation of the soil and cunning use of shifting land prices. It was not at all typical, however, of Russia, whose serf-owning gentry in the early nineteenth century were less exposed than the Prussian nobles to the disciplines of capitalist competition, and whose laws still in any case forbade the purchase by commoners of inhabited land. The Baltic gentry therefore stood somewhere between their Russian and Prussian peers: like the Prussians they were participants, far earlier than the Russian landowners, in the international grain market; on the other hand, Baltic law, like Russian, forbade the acquisition of noble estates by commoners until the 1860s.[31]

The best shorthand method of judging whether an individual from an originally non-Russian family was by the second half of the nineteenth century assimilated into the Russian ethnic and cultural community, is to see whether the man's family had converted to Russian Orthodoxy. Entrance into the Orthodox Church brought a family to the core of Russian ethics, history and, to some extent, culture. Even more importantly, it nearly always meant that members of a non-Russian family had acquired Russian wives. Once the initial religious and cultural taboo of marrying an Orthodox, and thereby almost always accepting that one's children would be brought up in the Russian state religion, was broken, there was every chance of further

MEN APPOINTED TO THE STATE COUNCIL 1894–1914

Table B: *Religion*

No.	Council members							
	Civilians 146		Generals 58		Admirals 11		Total 215	
	No.	%	No.	%	No.	%	No.	%
Orthodox	128	87.7	44	75.9	8	72.7	180	83.7
Protestant	13	8.9	9	13.1	3	27.3	25	11.6
Catholic	2	1.4	1	1.7			3	1.4
Unknown	3	2.1	4	6.9			7	3.3

intermarriage in later generations and thus complete assimilation into the Russian community.

It is therefore very significant to discover from Table B that only 28 men, 13 per cent of the total number, were non-Orthodox, almost all of them being Protestants; whereas of the group of 2 'Frenchmen' and 1 'Portuguese', two-thirds were Orthodox, all 6 Finns were Protestants. Frenchmen or Portuguese emigrating to Russia and becoming Russian subjects had made a conscious choice to break the links with their homelands. In addition, had they sought to choose wives from the French or Portuguese women living in Russia their range of choice would not have been wide. It is therefore no surprise that the only non-Orthodox of the group, V.I. Guerrier (Ger'e), married a Russian and had three Orthodox children.[32] The Finns on the other hand were born into a settled national community which was entirely Protestant. Even so, service to the Russian state took these six men, spiritually perhaps as well as physically, outside their own national community and three of them married Russians.[33]

As regards the Council's 'Germans', the members of the Baltic gentry families were distinctly less Russian than the others. The latter, who for want of a better term I will call 'German bourgeoisie', included 32 people, of whom 10 were Protestant (31.25 per cent) and 1 a Roman Catholic. Of these 11 men, 6 had Orthodox wives. Among the Baltic gentry, on the other hand, 9 of the 16 men (56.25 per cent) were Lutheran. Of these 9 men, two-thirds had Protestant wives, while Count O.L. Medem contrived to marry a Naryshkin and yet still produce Protestant children.[34]

In attempting to gauge the extent to which these high officials from the Baltic gentry had retained the peculiar stamp of their class, I compared them to the marshals and *Landrats* of the three Baltic provinces in 1914.[35] The latter represent the Baltic landowning class in its purest form. The marshals and *Landrats* were, it is safe to assume, all landowners in the three provinces and almost all of them had received their higher education either at Dorpat or at German institutions abroad. In contrast, only 2 of the group of 16 owned estates in the Baltic provinces and all had attended Russian institutions of higher education. Thus the Baltic noblemen in the Council, if still distinctly less assimilated as a group than the 'German bourgeois' officials, were much less uniformly un-Russian than the leaders of the landowning gentry in the three Baltic provinces. This fact, together with the relatively small size of the group of Baltic gentry within the Council, leads me to conclude that one should not exaggerate the weight of the 'Baltic barons' in high governmental circles in the last years of the Old Regime.

It is as important to discover which ethnic groups were not represented in the Russian ruling élite as to study the representatives of those that were. In 1897 roughly 2.7 per cent of the imperial population were Tartars from the Volga and Crimea, another 4.2 per cent other Moslems, largely from Central Asia and Azerbaijan. None of these Moslem communities had any representatives in the State Council. Nor did the 2.9 per cent of the population who were Latvians, Lithuanians or Estonians, or the 2 per cent who were Armenians and Georgians. The Council did contain two Roman Catholic Poles, but this was a serious under-representation of a nation which made up 6.3 per cent of the overall imperial population.[36] Like the Poles, but to an even greater and more bitter extent, Jews were regarded as enemies by the state's rulers, and not only did the Council contain no members of the Jewish faith, it had no representatives of families of Jewish origin; moreover, to the extent that it is possible to guess people's origins from their names, none of the members had married Jewesses or were the sons of Jewish mothers. This policy of wholesale exclusion deprived the ruling élite of recruits from what was probably the ablest and most energetic of the Empire's minorities, helping in the process to make that minority a breeding ground for future revolutionary leaders.

Of all the Russian Empire's minorities the Ukrainians were, however, both the biggest and the one whose weight within the ruling élite it is most difficult to assess statistically. Orthodox and Slav, they cannot be differentiated from their Russian peers either by religion or, easily, through their surnames. Common sense suggests, however, that for someone wishing to rise to the State Council it would have been risky to display any sign of Ukrainian consciousness more marked than a rather superficial interest in 'Little Russian' folklore. Certainly there is no evidence that any member of the State Council either regarded himself as a Ukrainian, or was seen by others as having any particularly Ukrainian characteristics or loyalties. On the contrary, the evidence that does exist points consistently in the opposite direction. Thus A.P. Rogovich, the only member of the Council to belong to a family listed in Modzalevsky's genealogy of the old Ukrainian nobility, not only owned land in Moscow province but was also the son-in-law of the Russian nationalist thinker, M.N. Katkov.[37] Another Ukrainian closely tied to Russian nationalist circles was Professor D.I. Pikhno.[38] Of the two other landowners of undoubtedly Ukrainian origin in the Council, N.I. Shebeko belonged to the cosmopolitian aristocratic circles of Petersburg, while P.A. Poltoratsky owned an estate in Tver.[39] All in all it is safe to conclude that the 18 per cent of the population who could on the basis of their mother tongue be considered Ukrainians had no representatives in the State Council.

The only source of income common to all members of the State Council was their salary. In 1909 the appointed members of the upper house received between 10,000 and 20,000 roubles a year. At the bottom end of the scale were junior or newly appointed individuals; in addition, men enjoying large private incomes tended to draw the minimum salary. Seniority, coupled with imperial good will, secured one a higher salary, but the top end of the scale was filled largely by former ministers.[40] Precisely how many members of the State Council had no source of income but their salary it is impossible to say, for reasons which will become clear. Evidence exists that many of the 215 men, including some from aristocratic backgrounds, were entirely dependent on their salaries; but the proportion cannot have been greater than 40 per cent and was probably lower.

As regards types of income other than salaries, there is often little evidence. This is particularly true where ownership of stocks and bonds is concerned. We know that a few of the Council's richest landowners derived extra income, often considerable, from this source, but these men were in every way untypical of the bulk of the members of the Council, and how many of the latter drew an income from stocks and bonds can only be guessed. Of the 137,825 nobles living in Petersburg in 1910, 49 per cent are said to have lived on income from securities, and it would be remarkable if this figure did not include many of the non-aristocratic members of the State Council, especially since some of those who owned no real property came from seemingly wealthy families.[41]

Only a few senior officials owned urban property from which they could draw rents, though the number who did so was somewhat less minuscule than the service records suggest.[42] Very few members of the State Council were, it seems, owners or directors of industrial or commercial companies, save where these were situated on their rural estates or connected with those estates' exploitation.[43] A handful of men wrote books or newspaper articles, though there is no reason to believe that this was a particularly lucrative source of income, even for them.[44] We can be confident that for the overwhelming majority of senior officials, ownership of rural estates was much the most important source of income apart from their salary. Moreover, most of the small number of wealthy directors of companies or owners of large holdings of bonds or shares were also aristocrats and large landowners.

In some circumstances a man could derive an income from the land without himself owning an estate. Landless members of the Council whose parents possessed properties were of course generally supported by their fathers during their training, and possibly in the early stages of their careers as well. In a few cases subsidies derived from family-owned property may have continued for much longer. V.V. Wahl, for instance, was the eldest son of a landowner whose property was subsequently inherited by a younger brother. It is of course possible that, as an adult, Wahl received nothing from his family's estate, but that seems unlikely. Nor is it probable that V.V. Verkhovsky, the son and later the father of large landowners, derived no income from his family's property.[45]

The statistics on landownership in Tables C, D and E do not of course reflect such details. Nor, it should be stressed, can they be absolutely precise about the extent of landownership within the Russian ruling élite. Large quantities of noble land were bought and sold throughout Nicholas II's reign, and the statistics on high officials' landowning inevitably differ from year to year.[46] Nor would the arbitrary selection in these tables of a single base year, even if the sources made this possible, have solved all the problems, for the 'cyclical mobility' which T. Shanin sees as the key determinant in changing peasant landownership[47] applied to some extent to noblemen as well. A nobleman in his twenties or thirties, who had still to inherit most or all of his parents' land, would be shown in his service record as landless; forty years on, however, part of his property might already have been dispersed to his heirs. Interesting examples of such 'cyclical mobility' exist among the members of the State Council.[48] As a result, the overall figures for landowning depend, as does the landowning group to which one assigns an individual, on the year from which one draws one's statistics.

My 'solution' to this problem was, for the civilian members of the Council, to use 1908 as my base year. If a member of the Council was already dead by that year, I looked at the *spiski* for 1904 or, if necessary, 1895. On the one occasion when *spiski*'s evidence was at odds with that in a service record prepared at roughly the same date, I gave preference to the latter.[49] Service records were my basic source

MEN APPOINTED TO THE STATE COUNCIL 1894–1914

Table C: *Landowning*

Council members	Total 215	
	No.	%
No land	91	42.3
1–499 *ds.*	20	9.3
500–999 *ds.*	15	7
1,000–4,999 *ds.*	45	21.4
5,000–9,999 *ds.*	12	5.6
10,000 *ds.*	21	9.8
Unknown	10	4.7

ds. = desyatiny (= 1.09 hectares)

Area of land whose ownership can be distinguished between husbands and wives:

1,090,228 *ds.*	= 100%
of which 872,515 *ds.* owned by husbands	= 80.03%
217,713 *ds.* owned by wives	= 19.97%

Area of land owned by husbands whose origin can be distinguished:

561,589 *ds.* = 100%
of which 451,422 *ds.* = 80.4% inherited
100,588 *ds.* = 17.9% bought
9,609 *ds.* = 1.7% received by imperial grant

of information on the Council's generals and admirals. Where, however, the section of a service record on landowning was left blank while other sources stated that the man in question owned estates, I have credited those sources and altered my statistics accordingly.

Table C shows that 57.7 per cent of the members of the State Council owned land. Of these 124 men, 10 possessed estates of unknown size; as Table D makes clear, however, the remaining 114 men owned almost 1,350,000 *desyatiny*. The main conclusion to be drawn from these statistics is that even under Nicholas II the Russian ruling élite had an immense, direct material interest in landownership. Discussion of governmental policy, particularly during the agrarian crisis of 1905–6, can scarcely afford to neglect this fact.

The other major conclusion to be drawn from Table D is that within the landowning group there was extreme inequality. If for

MEN APPOINTED TO THE STATE COUNCIL 1894–1914

Table D: *Distribution of Land*

Size of estate (*ds.*)	No. of owners	% of total group	Av. size of landholding (*ds.*)	Total area landholding (*ds.*)	% of total
1–499	20	17.5	236	4,724	0.35
500–999	15	13.2	713	10,699	0.82
1,000–4,999	46	40.4	2,551	117,335	8.7
5,000–9,999	12	10.5	6,399	76,790	5.7
10,000–30,000	8	7.0	17,568	140,547	10.42
30,000–100,000	10	8.8	44,542	445,419	33.0
100,000 +	3	2.6	184,351	553,053	41.0
Total	114	100		1,348,577	100

instance one takes those owning 500 to 5,000 *desyatiny* as 'middle-sized landowners' one finds that this section comprises 61 men, or 53.6 per cent of the total group, while only owning 9.5 per cent of the land. By contrast 13 men, 11.4 per cent of the total, owned just under three-quarters of all the land known to have been possessed by the members of the ruling élite. Even if one registers the fact that none of the estates of unknown size was in the 30,000-plus category,[50] the immense weight of a few huge landowners within the ruling élite remains evident.

Knowing an estate's size may, however, be a very inadequate guide to its value. In 1905 the average price of land per *desyatina* was, to take but a few representative examples, 13.02 roubles in Vologda, 29.95 roubles in Kostroma, 55.97 roubles in Pskov, 87.46 roubles in Saratov, 125.6 roubles in Oryol, 156.14 roubles in Kiev and 197.85 roubles in Kherson.[51] Divergences such as these could play havoc with an attempt to differentiate among members of the ruling élite merely on the basis of the extent of their landowning. Table E, which illustrates the value of the land owned by the members of the Council, is an attempt to overcome this problem. The attempt is by no means perfect. We do not possess figures for all the provinces, and senior officials did not always state clearly where their estates were, so that only 88 per cent of the land covered by Table D is included in Table E. Moreover, the average land price for an area as large as a province obviously cannot tell one the value of an individual estate. Nevertheless, the statistics in Table E constitute a useful check on the conclusions drawn from Tables C and D.

MEN APPOINTED TO THE STATE COUNCIL 1894–1914

Table E: *Distribution of Land – Value*

Size of estate (*ds.*)	Total area landholding (*ds.*)	% of total	Av. price per *d.* (rs.)	Value in roubles	% of total
1–499	4,724	0.4	84.19	397,702	0.4
500–999	10,109	0.85	111.5	1,127,408	1.16
1,000–4,999	107,881	9.09	92.4	9,969,122	10.28
5,000–9,999	76,790	6.5	79.2	6,079,403	6.27
10,000–29,999	110,214	9.3	162.3	17,889,600	18.45
30,000–99,999	378,103	31.9	66.5	25,152,625	25.93
100,000 +	498,638	42	72.9	36,372,391	37.5
Total	1,186,638	100	81.73	96,988,251	100

d. = *desyatina*   rs. = roubles

Table E shows that the ruling élite did indeed have a large vested interest in landownership, while at the same time extreme inequality reigned within the propertied group. Although the main conclusions drawn from Tables C and D are confirmed, they are also somewhat modified. The estates of the 13 largest landowners were of less than average worth: constituting 73.9 per cent of the total area of landholding, they made up only 63.4 per cent of its value. By contrast, the estates of between 10,000 and 30,000 *desyatiny*, though comprising only 9.3 per cent of the total known land, were of exceptional value to their owners.[52] Table E seems indeed to show that if one is seeking to distinguish exceptionally wealthy magnates from the bulk of the landowning group, then 10,000 *desyatiny* is the best boundary. At the other end of the scale the value of estates of between 500 and 1,000 *desyatiny* confirms that their owners had a considerable stake in landownership.[53] Finally, it is interesting, even comforting, to note that the average value per *desyatina* of the land owned by the ruling élite (81.73 roubles) is almost precisely the same as that cited by Proskuryakova for the land owned by the nobility as a whole (80.97 roubles).

The service record shows not only how much land was owned by a particular member of the State Council, but also whether an estate was the property of the man or of his wife, and whether it was inherited or purchased. Caution is required in using these records, for given the extent to which noble estates were bought and sold between

MEN APPOINTED TO THE STATE COUNCIL 1894–1914

Table F: *Distribution of Land – Regions*

	No. of landowners	Av. size of estate (ds.)
North	1	1,160
Ural	2	3,400
Northwestern	21	4,640
Baltic	4	1,767
Lithuania	5	3,582
Central Industrial	30	3,355
Byelorussia	9	13,794
Central Black Earth	38	4,381
Mid-Volga	29	6,656
Left Bank Ukraine	11	1,973
South West	15	6,272
South Steppe	9	4,172
South East	13	12,025

1861 and 1914, it cannot be assumed that a member of the Council who described his land as purchased was a new recruit to the land-owning class. In fact, roughly four-fifths of the land belonging personally to the members of the Council (i.e. not to their wives) was inherited, which emphasizes the extent to which one is dealing with an hereditary élite. Of the total land owned by both husbands and wives, 19.97 per cent belonged to the latter. Interestingly, even a woman with brothers sometimes possessed a great deal of land, most of which subsequently of course remained with her husband's family.[54]

The service records also inform one of where the estates owned by members of the Council were located, and it is on the basis of this information that Tables F and G were compiled. The tables too need to be treated with some caution, particularly where the number of landowners in a province or region is fewer than 10, and the overall average is easily distorted by one or two huge estates. Nevertheless Table F correctly informs us that most of the land owned by members of the Council was in the Central Black Earth, Central Industrial, mid-Volga and Northwestern regions. The most fully modernized and most prosperous regions of Russian noble agriculture, namely the Baltic, Southwest and Southern Steppe, seem to have been under-represented.[55] The large average size of estates in the mid-Volga region is confirmed (Table G) by the figure for Saratov, a centre both of high officials' landowning and peasant radicalism. By contrast Moscow was the homeland of the small estate. In general indeed the same is true both of Novgorod province and of the Central Industrial region as a whole. Here one finds many small estates of little eco-

MEN APPOINTED TO THE STATE COUNCIL 1894–1914

Table G: *Distribution of Land – Provinces*

	No. of landowners	Av. size of estate (*ds.*)
Saratov	15	9,283
Orël	12	4,062
Novgorod	11	6,656
Tambov	11	5,972
Tula	10	2,231
Moscow	10	991

nomic value which were either held on to for sentimental value, some of them being old family possessions,[56] or acquired less for agricultural purposes than as a country retreat. At the same time both the Northwestern (including Novgorod) and Central Industrial regions also contain a small number of huge estates, often given over to forestry, which somewhat distorts the overall picture.

Finally, what should be said here on the huge subject of the means by which the members of the State Council exploited their property? Even a cursory glance at the list of estates provided by *Vsya Rossiya* yields some useful insights into the economic activities of members of the imperial ruling élite. In the first place, little energy seems to have been devoted, at least in 1900, to growing grain. Landowners mention meat and dairy farming much more often than the production of cereals. Equally frequent are mentions of fruit farming, fisheries, horse studs and, not surprisingly, forestry. A great deal of effort seems to have gone into the exploitation of estates for industrial and commercial purposes. Sometimes this merely meant leasing land or buildings, but more often landowners or their stewards were directly involved in production. The frequency with which flour mills, distilleries, cheese factories and sugar refineries are mentioned is not perhaps surprising; but one also hears of quarries and mines, of glass, timber, starch, glue and brick factories, not to mention fulling mills.[57]

The list is quite impressive. The members of the Council, or their stewards, seem to have shown imagination and initiative in responding both to the possibilities inherent in landowning and to the cereal crisis of the late nineteenth century. At first glance their attitude seems to have been anything but a *Cherry Orchard* style of fatalism. However, the sheer diversity of their activities would have made it difficult to unite in defence of any common economic interest, save the preservation of private, large-scale landowning, though the uses to which these men put their estates sometimes provided them with natural links to the leaders of Russia's industrial economy. Thus Count Aleksei Bobrinsky was the chairman of the All-Russian Society of Sugar Manufacturers, and his brother-in-law, Prince Alexander Obolensky, was the chairman both of the Congress of Glass Manufacturers and of its standing committee; the latter was also a member of the Council of Representatives of Trade and Industry.[58]

My aim in investigating the antiquity of the families represented in the State Council was to discover to what extent the imperial ruling élite was still under Nicholas II dominated by old gentry families, or whether, on the contrary, top positions in the imperial service were by now largely filled by men from newly ennobled families. I took as my starting point Dolgorukov's lists of noble famiIes which could trace their origins back to before 1600,[59] then sought to establish that each individual on the Council bearing the name of one of these old families was actually a member of that family. As Table H shows, in this task I was by no means wholly successful. Nevertheless I found sufficient evidence on which to come to clear conclusions about the

MEN APPOINTED TO THE STATE COUNCIL 1894–1914

Table H: *Antiquity of Families*

	No.	% of total
Council members	215	100
	(Certain/Possible)	
Descendants of Rurik and Gedymin established in Russia prior to 1600	13	6
Those belonging to noble families cited by Dolgorukov as existing in Russia before 1600	38/8	17.7/3.7
Total of those belonging to noble families existing in Russia before 1600	51/59	23.7/27.4
Noble families established in Courland, Livonia and Estland before 1600	12	5.6
Noble families existing elsewhere in Europe before 1600	5/6	2.3/2.8
Total of all those belonging to noble families before 1600	68/77	31.6/35.8

strength of the old gentry element in Nicholas II's ruling élite.

Of those members of the State Council whose families can be traced back to the Russia of pre-1600, 13 men were descendants of Rurik or of Gedymin, the medieval ruler of Lithuania,[60] 8 more came from families mentioned in the Velvet Book, the seventeenth-century genealogy of the most distinguished old gentry families,[61] and 30 men belonged to other noble families which Dolgorukov traces back to before 1600.[62] Another 8 men may or may not have belonged to the old Russian noble families whose names they bore.

To discover the overall weight of the old gentry element in the Council one must add to the Russian group those men whose families were already noble outside the borders of Russia in 1600. In all 17 men, the overwhelming majority of them from the Baltic gentry, belong definitely to this group.[63] Apart from the Balts there are 3 men from the Polish nobility, a group which includes the 2 Svyato-polk-Mirskys since, regardless of their ultimate descent from Rurik, they were indubitably members of the Polish gentry in the sixteenth and seventeenth centuries.[64] Of the families that emigrated to Russia in the eighteenth and nineteenth centuries only the Heidens and Kaufmanns, as well as perhaps the Schaffhausen-Schönberg-och-Schaufuss line, could trace their origins as nobles to before 1600.[65]

The conclusion to be drawn from Table H is therefore that, according to Dolgorukov, at the very least 31.6 per cent of the members of the Council belonged to families already noble before 1600. A minimum of 51 men, 23.7 per cent of the total, were members of families already part of the Russian nobility before that date. In his very influential work on the Russian nobility Romanovich-Slavatinsky wrote that, 'if one is to trust Prince Dolgorukov's genealogical books then amidst the purely Russian nobility there are not many thoroughbred families.... What significance do 882 families, of which many have died out, possess in the general mass of the hereditary nobility, which consisted of 603,973 people of both sexes in 1858?'[66] If Table H is correct, then Russia's 'thoroughbred' families clearly retained a much greater significance than Romanovich-Slavatinsky imagined. Certainly the table supports E. Amburger's stress on continuity within the ruling élite and Meehan-Waters's argument that Peter I by no means destroyed or displaced from power the traditional Russian ruling class.[67]

How accurate are Dolgorukov's lists? To the professional genealogist they undoubtedly present some problems. For instance, Bobrinsky states that the Sukhotins, Tyrtovs, Bulygins and Sazonovs, all traced back to the sixteenth century by Dolgorukov, were only ennobled in the seventeenth century. Conversely, Bobrinsky, backed by Ikonnikov, confirms that the Stolypins, not mentioned by Dolgorukov, belonged to the sixteenth-century Russian nobility.[68]

For our purposes, however, it matters very little whether a family was ennobled in 1575, 1615 or even 1650. Indeed one could make a strong case for saying that 1600 is too early a date, and that 'old Russian nobility' would be more sensibly taken to mean the pre-Petrine élite. Even if one took 1700, or perhaps 1690, as the dividing line, one would still be ensuring that members of the State Council described as 'old Russian nobles' had at least six generations of Russian noble ancestors in their families. This is surely a more than adequate definition of old nobility.

When we try to discover whether a man belonged to a Russian family ennobled in the seventeenth century whose surname he shared, we find in 9 cases that we cannot be certain; although the evidence is on one or two occasions quite convincing,[69] I have left all 9 of these men in the 'uncertain' category. In 17 other cases we can, however, be sure of an individual's belonging to a Russian gentry family ennobled in the seventeenth century.[70] Thus a total of 68 members of Nicholas II's ruling élite, 31.6 per cent of the whole number, definitely belonged to old Russian noble families, while another 17 men (7.9 per cent of the 215) may have done so. We will not therefore be far wrong if we say that not less than a third of the members of the State Council were from families belonging to Russia's pre-Petrine social élite.

Quite clearly, then, members of the traditional Russian ruling class, in the strictest definition of the words 'traditional' and 'Russian', retained a considerable hold on political power until the end of the Old Regime. One is not talking here about an amorphous and heterogeneous group such as the hereditary noble estate, but rather of the traditional core of the Russian landowning élite. One may ask, nevertheless, whether this old noble group retained any sense of cohesion. Did it still own land or have independent wealth, or had it merged entirely into a wider and often landless service class, for whose members family genealogies, estates and traditions were little more than a curiosity?

Let us see whether the 'old Russian noblemen' were indeed richer and more landed than other members of the late imperial ruling élite. Of the 51 men from families which Dolgorukov traces to before 1600 (Group A in Table I), 6 (11.8 per cent) were landless and 5 (9.8 per cent) owned estates of unknown size. The remaining 40 men owned 700,669 *desyatiny* at an average value of 86.5 roubles a *desyatina*. Thus, 51 men, 23.7 per cent of the total number of members of the State Council, owned 52 per cent of the land owned by those members; and half the total number of men who owned estates of unknown size also belonged to this group. Moreover the estates owned by these 51 men were of more than average value. To the 17 men who belonged to families ennobled in seventeenth-century

MEN APPOINTED TO THE STATE COUNCIL 1894–1914

Table I: *Old Russian Nobility – Landowning*

No./% of total	Group A 51/23.7		Group B 19/8.8		Total Groups A & B 70/32.6		Total members 215/100	
Size of estate (*ds.*)	No. of owners	%	No. of owners	%	No. of owners	%	No. of owners	%
No land	6	6.6	3	3.3	9	9.9	91	100
1–499	6	30	2	10	8	40	20	100
500–999	3	20	1	6.7	4	26.7	15	100
1,000–4,999	13	28.3	6	13.0	19	41.3	46	100
5,000–9,999	5	41.7	2	16.7	7	58.3	12	100
10,000 +	13	61.9	5	23.8	18	85.7	21	100
Unknown	5	50	0		5	50	10	100
Total known landholding	Area (*ds.*) 700,669	% 51.97	Area (*ds.*) 427,171	% 31.56	Area (*ds.*) 1,127,840	% 83.53	Area (*ds.*) 1,348,577	% 100
Av. value per *d.* (rs.)	Group A 86.5		Group B 77.1		Groups A & B 82.9		Total members 81.73	

Russia, we should add the two counts Bobrinsky, descendants of the liaison between Catherine II and Prince Grigori Orlov, who in everything but the most pedantic genealogical sense belonged unequivocally to the old Russian nobility,[71] thus making a second group (B) of 19 men. Of these 3 were landless and 1 man owned an estate of unknown size. The rest owned among them 427,171 *desyatiny*, or 31.56 per cent of the ruling élite's total landownership, at an average value of 77.1 roubles per *desyatina*.

What emerges from Table I is that the men who can be described as 'definitely members of the old Russian nobility', 70 in all, or 32.6 per cent of the total membership of the State Council, owned 83.53 per cent of the land owned by its members, at an average value of 82.9 roubles per *desyatina*. Of the 70 men only 9 (12.9 per cent) owned no land (the equivalent figure for the whole group of 215 being 42.3 per cent). Table I, far from suggesting that the old Russian noble group within the State Council had dissolved without trace into an amorphous hereditary noble service class, emphasizes rather the continuing distinctness of this group, its firm links to landowning society, and its considerable wealth. In general Table I stresses still further the force of continuity within the ruling élite.

An interesting comparison can be drawn between the 'old Russian' and 'old Balt' groups in the State Council. Of the 13 'old Balts' – the

12 men whose families were noble before 1600 being joined by G.G. Staal, whose ancestors were ennobled in 1684[72] – 5 were landowners (38.5 per cent), a figure low even by the standards of the whole group of 215. Of the 5, Budberg owned an estate of unknown size, Nolde's property was tiny, while Lieven, Medem and Toll owned 12,411 *desyatiny* among them. By comparison with the 'Old Russian nobles', the Council's 'old Balts', almost always divorced from their traditional landowning roots in the Baltic provinces, were generally neither rich nor landed. On the other hand, adding the 13 'old Balts' to the 70 'old Russian nobles' emphasizes still further the weight of tradition and continuity within Nicholas II's ruling élite. Certainly it is a remarkable fact that together the 85 men whom one can definitely describe as 'old nobles' owned 85.2 per cent of all the land in the possession of the 215 members of the State Council.[73]

Forty-one members of the State Council had inherited titles. Of these, 12 were barons,[74] 12 were counts, 16 were princes, and 1 was a prince with the title of 'Serene Highness' (i.e. *svetleyshiy knyaz'* rather than simply *knyaz'*). What significance did these titles have?

Contrary to belief in the West, the number of titled families in Russia was not large in proportion to the whole hereditary noble estate, let alone the overall population. At the beginning of the twentieth century there were 830 titled families in Russia, a figure which may be compared with the 570 British families headed by peers in 1914.[75] Titles in Russia were significant, being an almost certain indication either, in the case of many of the princes, that the family was genuinely ancient, or that it had at some point stood high in the favour of the Romanov monarchs. The very fact that 41 of the 215 members of the State Council had inherited titles shows that the titled nobility still enjoyed considerable political power. Moreover, of the 147 largest landowners in early twentieth-century Russia, half were titled.[76]

Nevertheless, it is quite true that no title, even the grandest one, was in itself a certain sign of a man's wealth, connections or social status. So long as titles and lands were shared among a man's sons this was bound to be the case. Moreover, the older the family the more likely it was that some of its cadets would be penniless and without social standing. The examples of two titled members of the State Council are illuminating in this respect.

A.A. Lieven was the Council's only Serene Highness, a title he inherited from his great-grandmother, who had been unique in her time in her closeness to the Romanov family, and had been showered with wealth and lands. Not much of these, however, had descended to this particular great-grandson. A.A. Lieven's grandfather, Karl, had fathered too many sons, who, moreover, had shared out his pro-

MEN APPOINTED TO THE STATE COUNCIL 1894–1914

Table J: *Titled Members of the Council*

	Barons	Counts	Princes	Total
No.	12	12	17	41
Russian (R)/ non-Russian (NR)	R 0/NR 12	R 7/NR 5	R 14/NR 3	R 21/NR 20
Ancient	R 0/NR 8	R 5/NR 4	R 14/NR 3	34 [R 19/NR 15]
Landed	R 0/NR 5	R 5/NR 4	R 13/NR 3	30 [R 18/NR 12]
Landholdings: Unknown size	R 0/NR 2	R 0/NR 0	R 1/NR 0	3 [R 1/NR 2]
500 + *ds.*	R 0/NR 2	R 5/NR 3	R 10/NR 3	23 [R 15/NR 8]
5,000 + *ds.*	R 0/NR 0	R 4/NR 2	R 9/NR 2	17 [R 13/NR 4]
10,000 + *ds.*	R 0/NR 0	R 4/NR 0	R 8/NR 1	13 [R 12/NR 1]

perty in a most unequal manner. Nor were the estates of the Orthodox and 'Russian' branch of A.A. Lieven's family as valuable as those of his Baltic cousins. Lieven still possessed powerful connections at court and, partly through his wife, a Golitsyn, was a by no means inconsiderable landowner. But his grand and pompous title did not mean that he was one of the richest members of the Council, nor give him a social status superior to that of untitled landowning magnates such as N.P. Balashov or P.P. Durnovo.[77]

As interesting is the case of Prince D.P. Golitsyn, another member of an old family and one which had made a great impact on Russian history over the centuries. By the mid-nineteenth century, however, the Golitsyn princely clan was immense even by Russian standards. In Dimitri Petrovich's generation there were 168 princes and princesses Golitsyn, some of them inevitably far richer and better connected than others. Thus, while one finds mention of some Golitsyns in the works of Minarik and Anfimov on Russia's greatest landowners, D.P. Golitsyn was landless. Not surprisingly, a character in one of Golitsyn's novels bemoans the need to maintain the dignity of an ancient name and title on the bare salary of a state official.[78]

Table J shows that of the Council's 41 titled nobles, 21 (51.2 per cent) belonged to families which were already Russian by 1600. Thirty-four of the 41 belonged to families already noble by 1600 (82.9 per cent), a figure which rises to 36 (87.8 per cent) if one includes the two Bobrinskys. Thirty men, 73 per cent of the total, owned land: 3 of them possessed estates of unknown size, while 23 men (56.1 per cent) owned estates of at least medium (500 + *ds.*) size, 17 (41.5 per cent) owned big estates, and 13 (31.7 per cent) owned latifundia of over 10,000 *desyatiny*. The latter figure enables us to see that 13 of the 21 members (61.9 per cent) of the Council who owned latifundia belonged to the titled nobility.

There were major differences both between and within the Council's three ranks of titled noblemen. All the barons were, for instance, non-Russians. None owned big estates, though A.A. Budberg, one of the 'unknowns', probably did. The 12 barons divide neatly into two groups. Eight of them, all the barons who were from old families, came from the Baltic gentry. Of these 8, however, apart from E. Yu. Nol'de, who had a tiny estate, only Budberg owned land. Nor, again apart from Budberg, were their fathers either wealthy or prominent, much the highest rank achieved by any of the 7 fathers being lieutenant-general.[79] Of the 4 non-Balt barons, none came from old families, but 3 owned respectable estates and all 4 had very well-placed fathers, 3 of whom were full generals, including 2 aides-de-camp generals and 1 commandant of Tsarskoe Selo, and 1 of whom was an ambassador.[80]

Among the counts and princes only one man, Count P.I. Kutaysov, did not come from an old family.[81] Russians, as we have seen earlier, tended to be much more landed than non-Russians. Of the Russian counts only M.N. Murav'yov and I.D. Tatishchev were landless. Of the princes only D.P. Golitsyn owned no land, though M.I. Khilkov's estate was only 225 *desyatiny*. With the exception of P.I. Kutaisov and Prince A.A. Shirinsky-Shikhmatov,[82] all the counts and princes on the Council could claim that their families belonged to that real, albeit almost indefinable, élite which can be described as the Russian aristocracy. Among the Russian princes, A.A. Kurakin, the Dolgoruky brothers, D.P. Golitsyn, A.B. Lobanov-Rostovsky, M.S. Volkonsky, N.V. Repnin, M.I. Khilkov, the Obolensky brothers, and V.S. Obolensky-Neledinsky-Meletsky were direct descendants either of one of the 179 officials holding the top four military or civil ranks in 1730 (i.e. the *Generalitet*), or of seventeenth-century members of what Crummey describes as the Boyar Duma. The Dolgoruky brothers, Golitsyn and Kurakin had ancestors in both these élite bodies, as did the counts S.D. Sheremetev and P.A. Shuvalov, the Sheremetevs being particularly prominent, along with the Dolgorukys, Kurakins and Golitsyns, throughout the period between 1613 and 1730.[83]

MEN APPOINTED TO THE STATE COUNCIL 1894–1914

Table K: *Sons of Top Officers
and Officials*

Total	28	
	No.	%
Old Russian nobles	12	42.9
Old Baltic nobles	2	7.1
Old nobles (total)	17	60.7
Titled	14	50
Landowners	24	85.7
Landholdings:		
Unknown size	3	10.7
500 + *ds.*	21	75
5,000 + *ds.*	12	42.9
10,000 + *ds.*	8	28.6

Although, taken together, a man's wealth, the antiquity of his family, and his inheritance of titles are accurate guides to his social standing, they can usefully be supplemented by other information. One such piece of information is the role played by a man's family in the state's service. It would be of great value to know the jobs held by the fathers and grandfathers of all the members of the State Council, but although I have considerable information on this score, to seek complete knowledge on this point is to ask for the moon. It is possible to know which of the 215 men were the sons of members of the State Council, full generals and admirals, or senior Privy Counsellors, posts which were among the roughly 150 top positions in the Russian Empire, constituting the summit of the service élite. Table K investigates the 28 men, 13 per cent of the total membership of the State Council, who make up this group.

The table allows one, up to a point, to see whether by the end of the nineteenth century an hereditary service élite, distinct from the traditional landowning aristocracy, was developing. The answer, to the extent that a sample of 28 can provide one, seems to be negative. The greater number of the 28 men came from well-established families, but the few who did not seem to have merged without difficulty into the traditional ruling élite. Twelve of the 28 men (42.9 per cent) came from the old Russian nobility and 17 (60.7 per cent) from the old nobility as a whole. Moreover, if one includes the two counts Bobrinsky, the figures become 50 per cent and 67.9 per cent respectively. Given what has been said earlier, it comes as no surprise that all but 2 of the owners of more than 5,000 *desyatiny*, and all but 1 of the latifundia owners, belonged to the old nobility.

Of the 9 men (32.1 per cent) remaining, 4 were barons – V.B. Frederycksz, A.N. Meller-Zakomel'sky, A.P. Mohrenheim and I.O. Velho. None of them was in any sense a 'new man', since all four families had received their titles in the eighteenth century. Since then all these families had become formidable service dynasties, in each case producing a surprising number of top generals and officials.[84]

Of the 5 others, untitled, 2 were members of the quartet of Trepov brothers, a foursome who played a major role in Russian politics during Nicholas II's reign. The Trepovs' father, Aide-de-Camp General Fyodor Fyodorovich, ennobled in 1867, was in a sense a 'new man'. As the illegitimate son of the commandant of the palace at Gatchina, Trepov was, however, born on the steps of the throne, with advantages most 'new men' did not possess. Of his many children, all his sons had spectacularly successful careers, while his daughters seem to have had no difficulty in marrying into well-established gentry and official families.[85]

The 3 others, also sons of top servicemen, were N.A. Bezak, P.A. Kharitonov and A.P. Salomon. The fathers of all 3 men were born into not particularly well-known or prominent hereditary noble families, but all 3 were educated at the Tsarskoe Selo/Alexander Lycée, which means that their own fathers must already have occupied relatively senior service positions. The education and connections gained at the Lycée no doubt aided the careers of A.P. Bezak, A.A. Kharitonov and P.I. Salomon. The elder Salomon's service brought him into close contact with the Oldenburg family and this powerful connection was inherited by his son, who worked under Prince Alexander of Oldenburg and also served for four years as secretary to Princess Eugénie. Two generations at the top of the imperial civil service, however, brought the Salomons social status but little wealth.[86]

This last was not true of either the Kharitonovs or, particularly, the Bezaks. The latter, one of the originally German bourgeois families discussed above, were differentiated from most of their peers not by their rise through the state's service, from relative obscurity to high official position, but rather by their having been able to amass a considerable fortune through successful state service in the nineteenth century. As was often the case with German bourgeois families, the first Bezak was a pastor, whose son Christian entered Russian service as a professor in 1760. Scholarship prevailed for one more generation, but Alexander Bezak (1795–1868) became a General of Artillery and aide-de-camp general. Clearly Alexander Bezak was *persona gratissima* with Alexander II, since he was made a Knight of Saint Andrew, the rarest and most treasured honour any serviceman could receive. Bezak's son, Nicholas, educated at the Corps des Pages, commissioned into the Preobrazhensky Guards, and serving, as a young man, as a junior ADC (*fligel'-adyutant*) to Alexander II, started his career with all the advantages of a fully fledged aristocrat. To the large estates Bezak inherited from his father, the Romanovs added a further 6,000 *desyatiny* granted to N.A. Bezak personally – much the largest land grant made to any of the 215 members of the State Council. Nicholas Bezak's sons served in the ultra-exclusive Chevaliers Gardes, married into the old Russian nobility, and, in one case, provided an ADC to the Grand Duke Nicholas Mikhailovich.[87]

Of the four families which rose to prominence in the nineteenth century, the Kharitonovs had the fewest links to the Romanovs. For our present purposes, however, the most interesting point about P.A. Kharitonov is his marriage to the daughter of Aide-de-Camp General Konstantin Kaufmann, the conqueror of Khiva and Bokhara, and the owner of large estates granted to him by the crown. Through this marriage Kharitonov became the first cousin of P.M. Kaufmann, a member of the State Council from 1906, whose own father had been appointed to the Council in 1882.[88] This alliance between two families, both of which rose during the nineteenth century from the ranks of the everyday service nobility into Petersburg high society, is an example of the links which often bound together members of Nicholas II's ruling élite in tight but interlocking 'family-style' groups, created by blood, marriage, education or service.

Two such family-style groups, one created by education, the other by service, are a useful guide to the social status of members of the Council. Four schools in imperial Russia were geared to educating boys from the social élite, while four regiments of the Imperial Guard were, for their officers, not just military units but also exclusive clubs. The four schools were the Corps des Pages and the School of Guards Sub-Ensigns and Cavalry Junkers, both military institutions, together with the Alexander Lycée and School of Law, which were civilian boarding schools. The military units were the two senior regiments of the First (Heavy) Guards Cavalry Division, namely the Chevaliers Gardes and the Horse Guards, the Emperor's Own Life Guard Hussar Regiment of the Second (Light) Guards Cavalry Division, and the Preobrazhensky regiment, which was the senior unit within the Guards Infantry.

Entry into any of these institutions required a certain inherited social status. In the four educational institutions this was to some extent required by law. To enter these schools one had not only to be a nobleman but also, for most of the nineteenth century, to belong to

MEN APPOINTED TO THE STATE COUNCIL 1894–1914

Table L: *Graduates of Privileged Schools*

	Corps des Pages		School of Guards Sub-Ensigns & Cavalry Junkers		Alexander Lycée		School of Law		Total	
No.	15		16		21		27		79	
	No.	%	No.	%	No.	%	No.	%	No.	%
Old Russian nobles	7	46.7	6	37.5	12	57.1	9	33.3	34	43.0
Old Baltic nobles	1	6.7	0	0	0	0	6	22.2	7	8.9
Old nobles (total)	10	66.7	6	37.5	13	61.9	16	59.3	45	57.0
Titled	7	46.7	4	25.0	4	19.0	5	18.5	20	25.3
Landowners	12	80.0	9	56.25	14	66.7	13	48.1	48	60.8
Landholdings:										
Unknown size	2	13.3	1	6.25	2	9.5	0	0	5	6.3
500 + *ds.*	9	60.0	7	43.8	8	38.1	11	40.7	35	44.3
5,000 + *ds.*	6	40.0	2	12.5	1	4.8	3	11.1	12	15.2
10,000 + *ds.*	5	33.3	0	0	1	4.8	2	7.4	8	10.1
Sons of service élite	7	46.7	1	6.25	5	23.8	4	14.8	17	21.5
None of these categories	1	6.7	4	25.0	3	14.3	8	29.6	16	20.3

a specific section of the nobility. The Corps des Pages, which educated only those boys whose grandfathers or fathers had reached the top three ranks (i.e. lieutenant-general, vice-admiral or Privy Counsellor or above) in the state's service, was the most demanding, the other three schools contenting themselves with the requirement that fathers should have attained the sixth (i.e. lieutenant-colonel or equivalent) or sometimes the fifth rank, or that the noble family in question should be titled or able to trace its origins back to the seventeenth century. In addition, most boys at these schools, with the exception of cadets at the Corps des Pages and the, admittedly numerous, state scholars at the Lycée and School of Law, had to pay quite high fees.[89] Although in the four exclusive Guards regiments there were, in legal terms, no social requirements as regards entry, a cadet would not have been accepted unless he came from a prominent noble family, nor could he have survived as an officer without a considerable private income.[90]

That one needed to be of relatively high social status to enter these exclusive educational and military institutions is, however, only half the point. By studying at these schools or serving in these regiments one also greatly increased one's social standing, not to mention one's career prospects. Not for nothing did the *Almanach de Saint Petersbourg* always take care to note whether a man had been a page, a Lycéen, or a graduate of the School of Law, for the prestige and influence of these institutions was very great. Indeed, for a young man starting his career, the 'right' school or regiment was in many cases at least as important an advantage as landowning or family background.

It is therefore of interest that 79 men, 36.7 per cent of the total membership of the State Council, were educated at one of these four prestigious schools. From Table L it is clear, however, that the former pupils of these schools were by no means all from old, aristocratic or wealthy families, and that entry into these educational institutions was therefore to some extent a means of rising socially within the nobility. Forty-eight men at these schools (60.8 per cent) came from old noble or titled families, but two-fifths of the group of 79 did not. Whereas there was a very close correlation between landowning, a family's antiquity, titles, and a father's membership of the service élite, the same is less true as regards the origins and places of education of the Council members. A disproportionate percentage of the State Council's 85 'old nobles' (52.9 per cent) and an even larger percentage of the sons of the 28 top state servants (60.7 per cent) were educated at the four privileged schools, but the same was not true of the Council's landowners. Of the 94 members of the Council who definitely owned over 500 *desyatiny*, only 35 (37.2 per cent) were educated at one of the four schools, the equivalent figure as regards owners of over 10,000 *desyatiny* being 38.1 per cent. Moreover, if one defines aristocracy in the tightest possible way by counting only those men who were titled, owned over 10,000 *desyatiny* and belonged to families noble before 1600, then only 5 of this group of 13 (38.5 per cent) were educated at privileged schools, three going to the Corps des Pages and one apiece to the Lycée and School of Law. Of the remaining 8 men, 4 went to university and 3 were educated at home. No doubt at this exalted level one had no need of the connections or the prestige that education at a privileged school entailed. Certainly there was a contrast between the education of the 28 sons of top officials, generals and admirals on the one hand, and the schooling of the 13 aristocratic landowning magnates on the other.

It is clear from Table L that the only one of the four privileged schools which could truly claim to be aristocratic was the Corps des Pages. A much higher proportion of its cadets came from titled or wealthy families than in the other three schools. It also had much more than its share of the sons of top officials, generals and admirals. Second to the Corps des Pages as regards the social status of its pupils came the Alexander Lycée, with the School of Law not far behind.

MEN APPOINTED TO THE STATE COUNCIL 1894-1914

Table M: *Men Commissioned into the Four Most
Exclusive Guards Regiments*

Total	23	
	No.	%
Old Russian nobles	13	56.5
Old Baltic nobles	1	4.3
Old nobles (total)	15	65.2
Titled	12	52.1
Landowners	18	78.3
Landholdings:		
Unknown size	3	13
500 + *ds.*	14	60.9
5,000 + *ds.*	11	47.8
10,000 + *ds.*	8	34.8
Sons of service élite	10	43.5
Corps des Pages	6	26.1
School of Guards Sub-Ensigns	7	30.4
None	0	0

A peculiarity of the School of Law was its relatively large share of Baltic noblemen, 6 out of the total group of 13 (46.2 per cent). Moreover two more Baltic noblemen of more recent origin, K.K. Rennenkampf and Alexander Knirim, were also educated at the School.

Another striking aspect of the statistics for the School of Law is that 8 (30 per cent) of its pupils were not from old or titled noble families, nor landowners, nor the children of top officials. This probably reflects the fact that, even by comparison with the Lycée, the School's intake of boys from everyday service–noble families was relatively large. It is important to remember, though, how exclusive is Table L's category of 'sons of service élite', i.e. of top state officials, generals and admirals. Since 'top' in this context means only the two senior ranks, even the sons of lieutenant-generals and Privy Counsellors do not figure in these statistics. In fact 6 of the 8 former pupils at the School were from modest noble families, but the fathers of both K.K. Rennenkampf and P. Khr. Schwanebach had reached the third rank in the state service. Finally, there is the rather puzzling evidence from the School of Guards Sub-Ensigns, whose cadets seem to come from families rather less old and landed than the memoir material might suggest. It is perhaps relevant, however, that 3 cadets at this school came from families which may well have belonged to the old Russian nobility but whose ancestry I cannot establish.[91]

To conclude this section we have in Table M information on the 23 men who commenced their service by taking up commissions in one of the army's four most exclusive regiments. Given the extent to which these regiments were the preserve of old, rich and well-connected noble families, the overall picture presented by this table is not surprising; nor is the fact that at least[92] 73.9 per cent of the 23 men came from old or titled noble families. Some details are of interest: Of the 13 men educated at military schools, all attended the Corps des Pages or School of Guards Sub-Ensigns. Of the 10 other members of this exclusive group, 4 were educated at home, 3 at the law faculty of Petersburg University, and 3 at the Alexander Lycée.

II

Having attempted with due statistical solemnity to pin-point the social status of all the members of the State Council, it is a relief to recognize that some individuals escaped from their assigned places and came to possess a social standing to which neither their birth nor wealth, education or any other statistically discoverable factor entitled them. These are the Phineas Finns of this world, who by dint of intelligence, charm, good looks or luck find an entrée into circles to which the sociologist feels they should not belong. Perhaps they arrive in such circles by charming a daughter of some powerful person. More prosaically, but just as possibly, they may be the kindly and assiduous partner of some dowager at bridge.

One such Phineas Finn in the State Council was Alexander Vlangali, the son of a naval officer of modest rank, and of Greek origin. A.A. Polovtsov, who knew Alexander Vlangali well, writes that he was 'small in stature, kindly, but by no means brilliant'. Vlangali graduated from the Mining Institute, an educational institution which was the farthest extreme from aristocratic. By dint of some merit, some protection and more luck, Vlangali transferred in mid-career into the diplomatic service and rose within it. An amiable, courteous, amusing and attentive bachelor, he was expert at making himself known and liked in society. Polovtsov reports that Vlangali, as Assistant Minister of Foreign Affairs, 'was not slow in becoming a favourite of all Saint Petersburg and especially of female society. Every place where two candles were burning he was invited, beginning with the grand duchesses'.[93]

Vlangali's career is a useful reminder that we should not attempt to judge even the upper reaches of Russian society in too inflexible a manner. Petersburg was not Vienna, and Russia's 'First Society' was not yet as far removed from the world of politics and officialdom as were most of the great aristocratic families of the Austrian half of the Habsburg Monarchy.[94] Nor were the Russians as obsessed by a ponderous form of ancestor worship. In Petersburg as in London, character, wit and manners, especially of course when allied to wealth and high official position, could effect an entry into aristocratic circles. Nevertheless, birth, wealth and titles were the stuff of high society. Not for nothing were two of Russia's leading late nineteenth-century genealogists, themselves aristocrats, appointed members of the State Council.[95]

To understand how high society operated, a by no means irrelevant task if one wishes to understand Russian politics, requires a grasp of personalities and personal relationships some of which, like those of Vlangali, are invisible to the statistical or genealogical eye.[96] A certain knowledge of genealogy and of the links formed through blood and marriage is, however, also required. Indeed, if one is attempting to 'layer' the members of the ruling élite according to their wealth and status, knowledge about their connections can be vital. By the measurements used so far in this chapter, for instance, General S.A. Sheremetev, not even a Guardsman, would seem a relatively poor and run-of-the-mill member of the non-aristocratic branch of a distinguished old noble family. The picture is rather different when one discovers that he was, through his mother, a first cousin of the extremely wealthy and influential Count Serge Dimitrievich Sheremetev, that one of his sisters had married a Count Bobrinsky, and one of his brothers had wed a first cousin of Alexander III.[97]

To construct a table which would illustrate all the relationships and connections running through Petersburg's social and political élite is impossible. One can, however, gain some sense of the central core of that élite by looking at the members of the small and exclusive Imperial Yacht Club. One knowledgeable observer described the Club as 'a power in Petersburg society, I would almost go as far as to say a tyranny'.[98] Between 1909 and 1913, unfortunately the only years for which I have information, 14 members of the State Council were also members of the Club. Of these P.A. Stolypin, the Premier, was an honorary member, while A.P. Izvol'sky and S.D. Sazonov, both Foreign Ministers, were virtually *ex officio* members of this Club in which the diplomatic corps congregated, as was Baron V.B. Frederycksz, the Minister of the Imperial Court. The only slight 'surprise' among the Club's members is Roman Rosen, who although a baron and a cadet of one of the Council's oldest families, would probably not have belonged to this exclusive set had he not also been an ambassador.[99]

The other 9 members of the club were N.P. Balashov, Count Aleksei Bobrinsky, Princes Alexander and Nicholas Dolgoruky, P.P. Durnovo, Princes Alexander and Aleksei Obolensky, Count S.D. Sheremetev and Prince B.A. Vasil'chikov. All of these men were from old Russian noble families. Between them they owned 679,409 *desyatiny*, or 50.4 per cent of the total known landholdings of the 215 members of the State Council. We need look no further for the aristocratic core of the ruling élite, or for its institutional head-quarters.

The 9 men just mentioned clearly had the lineage and wealth that are key determinants of aristocracy. Did they also have an aristocratic sense of themselves, as being a separate and exclusive group at the summit of the Russian nobility? One can measure this by seeing whom they married and whether they made up a tight family circle. The Russian social élite, like the British aristocracy, did not erect elaborate codes like those of the German great nobles (*Standesherren*), which often forbade marriage to anyone not of the same rank and lineage (though usually permitting it, unless forbidden on other grounds, to members of families ennobled before 1582).[100] In Russia, despite the genuinely ancient, and indeed royal, origins of the oldest families, such a code, which would have forbidden a Dolgoruky to marry a Balashov or even perhaps a Shuvalov, would have been con-sidered absurd. Where new nobles combined wealth, social status acquired through a brilliant career in the state service, and acceptable manners and opinions, marriage into the traditional aristocratic élite was by no means excluded in principle. Nevertheless Table N shows that at the summit of the Russian nobility there existed a tiny cluster of families whose inter-relationships and marriage customs were not so different from those of Appalachian mountaineers or New Guinean tribesmen isolated from the rest of mankind. In the face of this strik-ing evidence of the concentration of wealth, lineage and high political office in a restricted group, it would be a brave person indeed who denied the existence of a Russian aristocracy.

Table N represents genealogy at its simplest: were one to include all the cousins, even the first cousins, of these individuals, more members of the State Council could be fitted into the chart, but the result would be bewildering.[101] Even in its simplified form, Table N includes 7 of the 9 members of the Yacht Club in 1913, and 9 of the 13 members of the State Council who were titled, owned over 10,000 *desyatiny*, and could trace their noble ancestry to before 1600. Of the whole group of 215 men appointed to the State Council between 1894 and 1914, 16 appear on this chart, as do another 6 men appointed to the Council before this period. At the centre of Table N stand Count Aleksei Bobrinsky and Prince Alexander Obolensky, who were brothers-in-law. Their father-in-law was A.A. Polovtsov, the

Table N: *Aristocratic Connections*

Those with names in italics were members of the State Council.

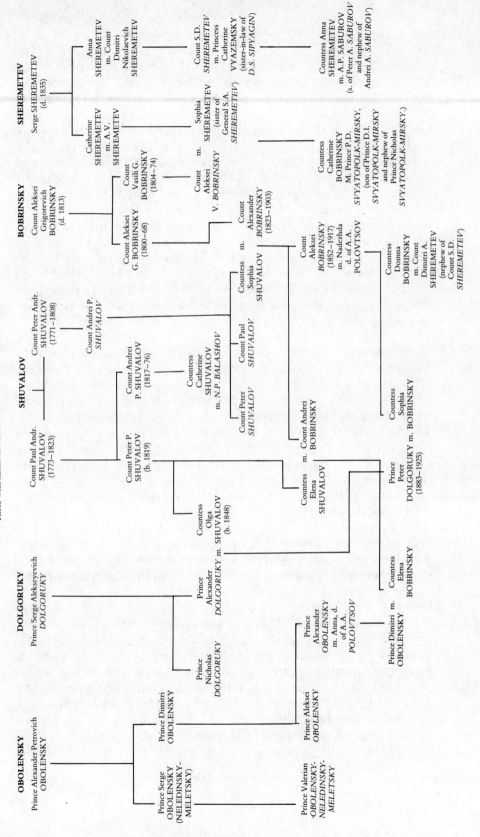

Imperial Secretary (*Gosudarstvennyy Sekretar'*) and a member of the State Council under Alexander III, who had married the heiress to a banking fortune. Obolensky and Bobrinsky each had a father and brother on the Council, as were Obolensky's first cousin, Valerian Obolensky-Neledinsky-Meletsky, and Bobrinsky's two Shuvalov uncles.[102]

Let us now bring together evidence of wealth, connections and lineage to define the group I shall henceforth label as 'aristocratic magnates'. If we begin by assigning to this group all 13 men who were titled, owned over 10,000 *desyatiny* and belonged to families noble before 1600;[103] then add N.P. Balashov and P.P. Durnovo, both of whose families by the nineteenth century stood at the very centre of the Petersburg aristocracy;[104] and if we concede that, though owning slightly less than 10,000 *desyatiny*, Prince N.V. Repnin and Prince P.D. Svyatopolk-Mirsky belonged unequivocally among the aristocratic magnates on the strength of their wealth, connections and lineage,[105] we have in all 17 members of this group.

To create some coherent sense of the social groups from which the whole ruling élite was drawn, we need now to organize the members of the State Council into distinct categories on the basis of their backgrounds, taking social and ethnic origins together. There would seem to be three such categories, each with its own sub-sections: (1) The 61 'non-Russians', i.e. Europeans whose families emigrated to Russia or came from areas absorbed into the Russian Empire in the Petrine era or after; as we have seen, this group can be divided into three major sub-sections, namely the Finns, the 'Baltic barons', and the Germans of non-noble origin. (2) Russians belonging to well-established noble families; this group too has its sub-sections, the most exclusive of which, the 'aristocratic magnates', has just been defined. (3) Men of Russian or occasionally perhaps Ukrainian origin who were non-nobles or, if they were born into the hereditary nobility, came from families of very modest and recent noble origin.

Group (1) requires no further comment at this point. Defining the limits of group (2) is, however, a problem. The 70 'old Russian nobles' whose families were ennobled in the pre-Petrine era of course belong to this group, as do at least some of the 17 men whose surnames were the same as those of old noble families but whose origins I have been unable to trace. In addition, however, men born in the mid-nineteenth century whose fathers and grandfathers were already by around 1800 relatively wealthy noble landowners or prominent officers should certainly be seen as belonging to the established gentry: to argue otherwise is to confuse genealogical snobbery with social reality. This group includes M.G. Akimov, N.S. Ganetsky,

S.S. Goncharov, A.D. and I.L. Goremykin, P.K. Gudim-Levkovich, N.A. Makhotin, P.A. Poltoratsky, N.I. Shebeko, L.P. Sofiano, V.A. Sukhomlinov and S.I. Timashev.[106] If full information existed the list would undoubtedly be considerably longer. In all it is most unlikely that fewer than 100 of the 215 members of the Council came from well-established Russian noble families; this group is therefore very much the largest of the three. Nor should it be forgotten that by 1800 a few of the families of German bourgeois origin, such as the Härbels (Gerbel),[107] were also established and Russianized nobles.

Group (3), made up of Russians of modest origin, consists of not many more than 50 men. Of the 15 of these men not born into the hereditary noble estate, the 5 sons, all of them Russian, of the merchant class, *meshchanstvo* and clergy have already been named. The other 10 men were for the most part the sons of state officials. Among these, M.D. Dmitriev, K.S. Nemeshaev and S.V. Rukhlov seem to have come from particularly lowly origins,[108] but the rest of the group, to the extent that it is possible to judge, may have been the sons of middle-ranking officials.[109] P.M. Romanov was the son of a private tutor,[110] S.F. Platonov described himself, not very revealingly, as an 'honorary citizen',[111] and A.F. Koni was the son of a journalist and teacher, who became something of a figure in Russian literary circles.[112]

Koni is in fact the only one of these 15 men to have inherited a considerable degree of social standing. Had his father, F.A. Koni, who was himself the son of a Moscow merchant, continued to teach in cadet corps rather than moving into the field of private literary activity, there is every chance that he would have acquired hereditary nobility. In this case the career of the elder Koni would have looked more like that of some of the ennobled fathers of members of the State Council. As it was, A.F. Koni was, together with A.P. Nikol'sky, N.S. Tagantsev, N.I. Zverev and D.I. Pikhno,[113] the purest *razno-chinets* and *intelligent* to be appointed to the State Council between 1894 and 1914. His distinctly atypical opinions may well have owed something to the fact that he was unique among the members of the Council in coming from a non-noble, non-official and yet quite prominent Petersburg intelligentsia family.

Approximately 35 men belonged to what might be described as the Russian new nobility: in other words their fathers or perhaps grandfathers had been ennobled. Unfortunately, information about these men's families is extremely scarce. Their service records merely state baldly that they are hereditary nobles, the genealogists shun such modest families, and one is often forced to accumulate scraps of what is almost anecdotal material.

In imperial Russia, in the overwhelming majority of cases, ennoblement resulted from service in the armed forces or the bureau-cracy. A few men were ennobled for personal service to the monarch, but very few indeed acquired nobility as a result of the wealth or status they had gained in industry or commerce, let alone agricul-ture. The only family represented in the State Council to follow this path to ennoblement were the Goncharovs, wealthy industrialists who were raised to the nobility in 1744. The Goncharov family was, however, well established in the Russian gentry by the time of S.S. Goncharov's birth. His father's generation indeed moved in court circles, one of his aunts marrying A.S. Pushkin.[114] Within the ranks of the State Council there were no representatives of recently en-nobled families of the industrial or commercial bourgeoisie.

Some of the new noble families represented on the Council had achieved social mobility through the army or financial administra-tion,[115] some through medicine, and others through education. The father of A.V. Krivoshein, for instance, was a peasant's son who rose from the ranks to become a lieutenant-colonel in the artillery. As a result A.V. Krivoshein was able to acquire a complete secondary and higher education, which, by the second half of the nineteenth century, was almost a *sine qua non* for anyone ambitious for a career in the civil service, and an absolute necessity for a man without powerful connections.[116]

The father of N.I. Bobrikov was of clerical origin but trained as a doctor, thus following a pattern more frequently found among the German bourgeois families represented in the Council than among the Russians.[117] Ivan Vasilevich Bobrikov served in the field of mili-tary medicine and ended as a permanent member of the Military-Medical Educational Committee.[118] His son Nicholas was educated at the First Cadet Corps and entered service in a Grenadier regiment. The key to his successful career, as became ever more generally the case in the late nineteenth-century army, was his entry into and gra-duation from the General Staff Academy. With this certificate under one's belt, especially after 1878, social barriers to advancement be-came relatively unimportant. Despite his modest origins Bobrikov was for 14 years chief of staff of the Guards Corps, in which position he was able to acquire some very powerful patrons. In a way that was by no means untypical among Russian service families, Bobri-kov's successful career was mirrored by that of his two brothers, one of whom became a full general and the other a Privy Counsellor.[119]

The most spectacular examples of family advancement among the members of the State Council were, however, the brothers Ivan and Nicholas Zinov'ev. Their grandfather was a peasant from Yaroslavl, but their father was well enough educated eventually to become a professor at both the Demidov Lycée and the Lazarev Institute of Eastern Languages. Aleksei Zinov'ev was clearly a formidable

MEN APPOINTED TO THE STATE COUNCIL 1894–1914

Table O: *Social Status*

Council members	Total 215	
	No.	%
Bourgeois (0 pts.)	66	30.7
Minor gentry (1 pt.)	28	13.0
Gentry (2–5 pts.)	77	35.8
Aristocrats (6–9 pts.)	27	12.6
Magnates (10 pts.)	17	7.9

Points awarded:

1 pt. = ownership of 500 + *ds.* land
     family well-established nobility, inherited title of baron
     son of officer or official of top 3 ranks, noble marshal, man holding court rank
     grandson of officer or official of top 2 ranks
     attendance at Alexander Lycée, School of Law, School of Guards Sub-Ensigns
     started service with commission in Imperial Guard

2 pts. = ownership of 4,000 + *ds.* land
     inherited title of count or prince
     son of senator or of officer or official of top 2 ranks
     grandson of member of State Council or ADC general
     attendance at Corps des Pages
     started service in one of 4 most exclusive Guards regiments

3 pts. = ownership of 10,000 + *ds.* land
     son of member of State Council or ADC general

4 pts. = ownership of 30,000 + *ds.* land

linguist and a man of immense drive and ambition. He pushed his own son Nicholas so hard that the latter finished a full gymnasium course by the age of eleven, subsequently graduating from both the Lazarev Institute and the Konstantin Surveyors' Institute. Meanwhile Ivan Zinov'ev was trained in Middle Eastern affairs and languages, thus acquiring the arcane field of expertise almost essential for a man with ambitions to rise in the highly aristocratic foreign service. Aleksei Zinov'ev's efforts paid off brilliantly. Nicholas Zinov'ev became Assistant Minister of Internal Affairs, while Ivan rose to be an ambassador, a Knight of Saint Andrew, and official Russia's best-known expert on the Middle East.[120]

Individual examples of social mobility, however interesting and illuminating, do not, however, bring one much closer to the clear overall sense needed of where each member of the State Council stood in the social and official pecking order. Table O is an attempt to convey the information gathered thus far through a system based on points.

This table is designed to illustrate both differences in social status and the extent to which a man's background, school and regimental links and his family's service pedigree were likely to have influenced his career. In it one is indeed seeking to measure how a young man entering service stood in both the social and official hierarchies, which in mid-nineteenth-century Russia were very closely linked but not identical. The 66 men (30.7 per cent) who earned no points I will henceforth call 'bourgeois'. The 28 (13.0 per cent) with 1 point will be called 'minor gentry'. In all 77 men (35.8 per cent) had between 2 and 5 points, and all of these I will describe as 'gentry'. Those who scored between 6 and 9 points,[121] 27 in all (12.6 per cent), I call 'aristocrats'. When dealing with the ultimate élite of 'aristocratic magnates' I break my own rules, however, at this level what counted above all was wealth and, particularly, belonging to one of a very small group of closely related families. In this case I have simply retained my already defined group of 17 (7.9 per cent) 'magnates'.

As regards their careers, the members of the State Council can be divided into a number of distinct, though overlapping, groups. Amidst a ruling élite which was more than two-thirds civilian the Council's 58 generals seem – but, as we shall see, only to a certain extent were – a clearly different and separate military minority. As one can see from Tables P and Q, in terms of their social status the generals were close to the average among the members of the State Council, though they were distinctly less likely to own estates than was the case with their civilian counterparts.[122] Eight of the 58 men had entered the army without any formal military education. On the other hand 86 per cent had attended one or another of Russia's cadet corps and almost two-thirds of them had a military higher education as well (Table S).[123]

Study of the careers of senior military officers reveals that the early twentieth-century Russian army was dominated by two élites. On the one hand there was a social élite made up of Guards officers, on the other an intellectual élite heavily weighted with officers of the artillery, engineers and sappers.[124] In 1908, of the army's 1,424 generals 35.7 per cent had started their service in the Guards, and 35 per cent in the artillery, engineers and sappers of the line. Among the 58 generals in the Council, 33 (57 per cent) entered service in the Guards and only 10 (17.2 per cent) in the three technical branches of the army of the line. Thus the Council's generals represented the army's social rather than its intellectual élite. It was on the whole generals from the social élite who, while retaining their military rank, served in the civil administration: in 1908, of the 144 generals in civilian posts, 47.2 per cent had entered service in the Guards, the percentage of 'civilian' generals becoming greater in proportion to the social exclusiveness of specific Guards regiments.[125]

Similar tendencies can be seen in the careers of the 58 generals who became members of the State Council. Of these, 23 served only in purely military jobs, and 26 held civil service positions at some stage in their careers. In addition, 9 men who had otherwise purely professional military careers also served as governor-general in one or other of the Empire's outlying regions – a position which entailed both military and civil responsibilities but which could not by itself move a man into the category of 'civilian' general. The Council's 58 generals can therefore be divided into a 'military' group of 32 and a 'civilian' one of 26. The contrast between the social origins of these two groups is striking. In terms of the points system on which Table P is based, the 32 'military' generals average 1.8, and their 26 'civilian' counterparts 4.1 – the latter figure surpassed only by the marshals, diplomats and provincial governors. It is hardly surprising to discover that of the 15 generals who started their careers in one of the army's four most exclusive regiments, 12 belonged to the 'civilian' group.[126]

It seems clear therefore that in many cases 'civilian' generals were using their powerful connections to make careers outside the army. Since on the whole a 'civilian' general was considerably less likely to have attended the General Staff, Artillery or Engineering academies than his military counterpart, one reason for his transferring to the civil service may have been that promotion to top positions in the army was likely to be increasingly difficult for him.[127] In addition, a civilian official was almost always better paid than his military peers.[128]

The point in his career at which a 'civilian' general transferred out of the army differed greatly. Nor was such a transfer always permanent, some men returning to senior military commands after periods in civilian posts. At one extreme among the 'civilian' generals is A.I. Kosych, who commanded a regiment, brigade, division and corps,

MEN APPOINTED TO THE STATE COUNCIL 1894–1914

Table P: *Social Status by Groups*

	Aristocratic magnates (10 pts.)		Aristocrats (6–9 pts.)		Gentry (2–5 pts.)		Minor gentry (1 pt.)		Bourgeois (0 pts.)		Total		Av. pts.
	No.	Pts.	No.	Pts.	No.	Pts.	No.	Pts.	No.	Pts.	No.	Pts.	
All generals	6	60	8	58	17	43	7	7	20	0	58	168	2.9
Civilian generals													4.1
Military generals													1.8
Jurists	1	10	3	20	22	62	10	10	10	0	46	102	2.2
Procurators													2.08
State Chancellery/CCMS	1	10	4	25	14	40	6	6	5	0	30	81	2.7
HIMC/EMI	0	0	3	21	6	21	1	1	1	0	11	43	3.9
Marshals													
District	6	60	3	21	8	27	0	0	1	0	18	108	6
Provincial	7	70	2	12	7	22	0	0	0	0	16	104	6.5
Governors	5	50	12	77	15	49	2	2	7	0	41	178	4.3
MIA/Central govt. officials	3	30	7	45	16	51	4	4	10	0	40	130	3.25
Financial officials					6	13	3	3	8	0	17	16	0.94
Professors					1	2			9	0	10	2	0.2
MFA	3	30	3	20	7	23			2	0	15	73	4.9
Ministers	3	30	9	61	26	71	6	6	19	0	63	168	2.67
All members of State Council	17	170	27	186	77	220	28	28	66	0	215	604	2.81

ABBREVIATIONS:

CCMS = Chancellery of the Committee of Ministers
EMI = Empress Marie's Institutions
HIMC = His Imperial Majesty's Own Personal Chancellery
MFA = Ministry of Foreign Affairs
MIA = Ministry of Internal Affairs

and who spent only four years out of the army, as governor of Sara-tov.[129] At the other extreme are such 'generals' as F.F. Trepov or the princes P.D. Svyatopolk-Mirsky and L.D. Vyazemsky, whose truly military careers were confined to a few years' service as subalterns in the most exclusive regiments of the Guards cavalry.[130]

With the exception of two railway engineers, 'civilian' generals transferred, as one would expect, into generalist rather than specialist branches of the civil service. Much the most popular department was the Ministry of Internal Affairs, in which 13 generals served as gover-nors and 5 as officers of the Gendarmerie, or political police. Never-theless, at various times in Nicholas II's reign generals were to be found at the head of the department of education, of the State Con-trol and of the Imperial School of Law. Even the military generals did not have wholly stereotyped careers, nor did they necessarily hold command positions in fighting units. The Russian army was a vast and heterogeneous body, in which it was possible to pursue a number of distinct careers.[131] Thus, to take but one example, P.L. Lobko had never held a civilian post prior to his appointment as State Controller in 1899, but he had also never commanded any unit larger than a platoon. Instead he had decades of experience as a professor and practitioner of military administration.[132]

Of the 215 members of the State Council, 27 had served as district and/or provincial marshals of the nobility. As one might expect, they were by far the most aristocratic and most landed group (Tables P and Q) within the ruling élite.[133] They were also (Table S) well-educated. Most of the district marshals and more than two-thirds of the provincial marshals had attended Moscow or, more often, Petersburg University, a point which emphasizes yet again that the products of the privileged schools were not necessarily more aristocratic than former university students.

Even the district marshals had in general considerable official experience prior to their election. All 18 men had previously been in the state's service, half as officers in the armed forces and half as civil servants. In addition, 9 of these men had also been zemstvo deputies or honorary justices of the peace. Elected district marshal at an aver-age age of thirty-two, their average term in office was 7.3 years. After retiring as marshal most of these men maintained their involvement in local government. Seven became marshals of their province, 4 be-came vice-governors and 3 were appointed directly to governorships. Older, richer, more aristocratic and usually more experienced than the district marshals, the provincial marshals were nevertheless simi-lar to their juniors in most ways.[134] On retiring from their positions, 6 provincial marshals were appointed directly to the State Council, 4 became governors, and 1 served briefly as a vice-governor.

The split in the subsequent careers of the provincial marshals, between those appointed directly to the State Council and those assigned
to top governmental posts in the provinces, reflects a basic division
within the Council's group of 27 marshals, and indeed within the
whole function which a marshal was called upon to fulfil. On the
one hand a marshal was the elected representative of the nobility,
responsible to his peers for managing the business of the noble estate
and for bringing its needs to the attention of the government. Yet in
practice, even indeed to some extent in law, he was also an unpaid
state official, who played a key role in local government.[135] The ambitions and aims of the Council's marshals reflected this dual function.
Some saw their job as marshal as one step in a successful career in the
imperial service. Others had no such ambitions, and saw themselves
above all as spokesmen for the landed nobility. Different sections of
the landowning class found their representatives in the second group:
P.A. Krivsky, S.S. Bekhteev and A.A. Arsen'ev were spokesmen
above all for the wealthier strata of the traditional provincial gentry;
O.R. Ekesparre was the veteran defender of the Protestant Baltic
landowning class; Count Alexis Bobrinsky and A.P. Strukov were
magnates. In each case, however, the mentality of the marshal in
question was much more that of a noble than an official, his eyes
being fixed more on his peers' opinion than on his own prospects for
a civil service career.[136]

More of the appointed members of the State Council had served in
the Ministry of Internal Affairs than in any other government department.[137] The careers of these 65 men help to illustrate two significant ways in which officials of this ministry differed from those
serving in most other departments. Firstly, men tended to serve in
this department for a shorter period than in the more specialist ministries. The 65 members of the State Council, for instance, averaged
13.4 years' service in the Ministry of Internal Affairs, only 5 (7.7 per
cent) of them staying in the department for more than 25 years and
another 22 (33.8 per cent) for 15 to 24 years. Secondly, the relationship between service in Petersburg and in the provinces differed in
this department from the normal civil service pattern. In the nineteenth century a clear distinction existed between the 80 per cent of
officials who worked in the provinces and the 20 per cent who worked
in Petersburg. The pay, conditions of service and career prospects of
the latter group were far better, which explains why bureaucratic
'high flyers' usually sought to remain in the capital.[138] We shall see
the effects of this tendency on officials in other ministries; the point
to note here is that the careers of the 65 officials of the Ministry of
Internal Affairs seem to conflict with normal 'high-flying' practice.
Of the 51 men who served for more than six years in this ministry,

MEN APPOINTED TO THE STATE COUNCIL 1894–1914

Table Q: *Landowning by Groups*

	Total	Unknown		No land		1–499 ds.		500–999 ds.		1,000–4,999 ds.		5,000–9,999 ds.		10,000 + ds.	
		No.	%	No.	%	No.	%	No.	%	No.	%	No.	%	No.	%
MFA	15	1	6.7	7	46.7	1	6.7	1	6.7	2	13.3			3	20
Financial officials	17	0		8	47.1	5	29.4	2	11.8	2	11.8				
State Chancellery/CCMS	30	1	3.3	9	30	6	20	1	3.3	8	26.7	2	6.7	3	10
HIMC/EMI	11	2	18.2	4	36.4	1	9.1			4	36.4				
Jurists	46	0		20	43.5	4	8.7	1	2.2	16	34.8	3	6.5	2	4.3
Governors	41	4	9.8	8	19.5	1	2.4	5	12.2	11	26.8	5	12.2	7	17.1
MIA/Central govt. officials	40	3	7.5	10	25	3	7.5	5	12.5	12	30	2	5	5	12.5
Marshals															
District	18	2	11.1	0		2	11.1	0		5	27.8	5	27.8	4	22.2
Provincial	16	1	6.25	0		1	6.25	0		4	25	3	18.75	7	43.75
Generals	58	2	3.4	34	58.6	2	3.4	3	5.2	9	15.5	1	1.7	7	12.1
Professors	10	1	10	7	70	2	20								
Ministers	63	3	4.8	25	39.7	7	11.1	6	10.3	14	24.1	6	10.3	2	3.4

For abbreviations see Table P (p. 66)

only 7 (13.7 per cent) had never held a provincial job, whereas 17 (33.3 per cent) had never worked in the department's central offices in Petersburg.

It was, however, by no means the case that these 65 men all had worked their way up through junior or middle-ranking positions in the provincial offices of the Ministry of Internal Affairs. On the contrary, only N.A. Zinov'ev and A.P. Rogovich could claim to having taken that road to high office.[139] The great majority of the former provincial officials of the Ministry of Internal Affairs had served only as vice-governor of a province. For almost all the 16 vice-governors, service in that post had been a relatively brief (average three years) training for their subsequent appointment to a governorship.[140] Of the 41 governors, 14 were promoted from vice-governorships, 7 had been serving as marshals, and 8 had come straight from the army.[141] In contrast, only 6 men were officials of the Ministry of Internal Affairs (other than vice-governors). Study of their past careers thus suggests that the 41 governors were not in the majority of cases recruited from long-serving officials of the Ministry of Internal Affairs.[142]

As Table P illustrates, among the 215 members of the State Council only the marshals and diplomats were of higher social status than the governors. As regards landowning (Table Q), only the marshals scored more points than the governors. When one considers the functions a governor fulfilled, this is not surprising. The governor was a generalist, his major responsibility being for order and good government in the province he headed. The overall welfare and prosperity of the population were also his concern. Not only in Russia but also in late nineteenth-century England and Prussia, men from upper-class and landowning backgrounds tended to dominate in such key 'generalist' posts in provincial and rural local government.[143] As regards education (Table S), the main difference between the governors and other top civilian officials was that 35.7 per cent of the former (i.e. 15 men) had been educated at military schools. Since, as we have seen, 13 of the 41 governors were generals, this is scarcely remarkable. Moreover, apart from these 15 men all the other governors had a civilian higher education.

Table R shows that there was a correlation, at least as regards magnates and bourgeois, between a man's social status and the age at which he was appointed to a governorship. This suggests that favouritism and powerful connections may have been a factor in these appointments. Length of service as governor differed enormously and in a seemingly random manner. Thirteen men served for less than 5 years, 13 for 11 years or more, N.I. Petrov and Prince A.B. Lobanov-Rostovsky for only 1 year, and P.A. Poltoratsky for more than 30. The great majority of the 41 men passed from governorships

MEN APPOINTED TO THE STATE COUNCIL 1894–1914

Table R: *Age on Appointment to Governorships*

Governors	No.	Av. age on appointment (years)
Aristocratic magnates	5	36.6
Aristocrats	12	40.1
Gentry	15	40.9
Minor gentry	2	39.5
Bourgeois	7	54.8

to top positions in Petersburg, usually in the State Council, the Senate, or as heads of department or chief administrations in the Ministry of Internal Affairs.[144] Though P.A. Stolypin was unique among the 41 men in jumping straight from a governorship to ministerial office, Nicholas II clearly approved of this experiment and repeated it with N.A. Maklakov.[145]

The 40 men who served in the central offices of the Ministry of Internal Affairs came on the whole from more modest backgrounds than the governors and were less likely to own land. Nevertheless, as regards both status and land they surpassed most other groups of central government officials (Tables P and Q). The fact that 11 of the 40 men attended military schools distinguishes this group from the jurists, financial officials or men who had served in the State Chancellery or Chancellery of the Committee of Ministers. Once again, however, it needs to be stressed that all the other 29 men had a higher civilian education.

The movement of officials into and away from the central offices of the Ministry of Internal Affairs is interesting. The relationship between the army and these departments was one-way, 4 military men entering the Ministry's central administration. Movement between the State Chancellery (and Chancellery of the Committee/ Council of Ministers) and the central administration of the Ministry of Internal Affairs was both greater in volume and two-way. There were 5 transfers into the ministry from the chancelleries and 7 in the opposite direction. The two main sources from which senior central officials of the Ministry of Internal Affairs were recruited were, however, governors and judicial officials. Thirteen former governors, most of whom had previously served as marshals and/or officers, were promoted to top positions in the ministry. Moreover, all the

Ministers of Internal Affairs among the 215 members of the Council came either from the gubernatorial group or from former judicial officials. The latter group, which included V.K. Plehve, P.N. Durnovo, I.L. Goremykin, A.A. Makarov, A.I. Lykoshin, A.V. Krivoshein and V.N. Kokovtsov, played an exceptionally important political role in the reign of Nicholas II.[146] Moreover, the former judicial officials among the 215 members of the State Council who switched into the Ministry of Internal Affairs were only the tip of the iceberg. Thus, to take but one example, all the chiefs of the Police Department, which N.A. Maklakov described as 'the main part of this [i.e. Internal Affairs] ministry', were procurators.[147]

Of the 215 members of the State Council, 55 had served in the judicial department. Their careers generally followed a very different pattern from those of the former officials of the Ministry of Internal Affairs. On average these 55 men served 23.6 years in the judicial department, 27 men (49 per cent) having worked there for more than a quarter of a century, and a further 10 men (18.5 per cent) for 15 to 24 years. Moreover, of the group of 46 men who had served in the department for 6 or more years (henceforth described as 'jurists'), 22 (47.8 per cent) never worked outside Petersburg in the whole course of their careers.

In terms of social status, the 'jurists' were from rather more modest backgrounds than the average member of the State Council. The group of 46 men also had slightly, but only slightly, more than its share of officials who owned either no land or very small estates. In this respect Russia followed the Prussian model, whereby judicial officials were generally of lower social origins than men involved in general administration. Nevertheless in Russia, not as in Prussia, the group of top jurists could not be labelled as bourgeois. This is not only because (see Table P) the jurists' average number of points puts them in the gentry bracket, or because 47.8 per cent of them owned medium-sized or large estates; in addition, although the group included very few magnates or aristocrats, the jurists did include a considerable number of men from well-established, often distinguished, gentry families.

As one might expect, the jurists were a very well-educated group. Only one man, P.N. Durnovo, had not been through a higher civilian education, and he compensated for this by graduating from the Military Judicial Academy. Probably the most interesting fact about the jurists' education is, however, that almost half the group was educated at a single, relatively small institution, namely the School of Law. A correlation of information about education and careers can produce interesting results. We have already seen both that 'high flyers' preferred to serve in Petersburg and that almost half the 'jurists'

MEN APPOINTED TO THE STATE COUNCIL 1894–1914

Table S: Places of Education by Groups

	Generals	Marshals District	Marshals Provincial	Governors	MIA/Central govt officials	Jurists	State Chancellery/CCMS	HIMC/EMI	Financial officials	Professors	MFA	All members of State Council
Gen. Staff Academy (+ other higher mil. acad.)	30 (+7)			1	1	1	1					
Naval Cadet Corps	1					1	1					10
Other cadet corps	19			1	3	2						22
Artillery & Engineering schools	8				2	1						7
First Cadet Corps	5											10
Nicholas Cavalry S./S. of Guards Sub-Ens. & Cavalry junkers	10	2	2	4	3				1			16
Corps des Pages	8	2	6	4							3	15
Middle	1						2	1			1	5
Other civilian schools: Higher	1					2	1		1	1	2	12
School of Law		3	1	5	5	22	7	4			1	26
Alexander Lycée	2		1	5	6	3	6	2	5		4	21
Other univ.				1	2	2	1			1	1	7
Moscow Univ.		4	3	5	4	10	5	1	1	6	3	28
SPB Univ.	1	5	8	9	11	8	9	3	6	3		38
Home	3	1	1									6
Total	58	18	16	41	40	46	30	11	17	10	15	215

For abbreviations see Table P (p. 66)

succeeded in spending their entire careers in the capital. Where one served depended enormously on where one had been to school. Thus, whereas the 25 'jurist' graduates of the School of Law and Lycée worked outside Petersburg, on average, for 2.7 years, the remaining 21 'jurists' served in the provinces for 11.2 years. Nor does the disparity between the two groups lessen when one looks at the proportion, rather than the number of years, of these men's judicial service spent outside Petersburg.

What one is seeing here are the results of the capture of the judicial department's appointments system by old boys of the Imperial School of Law. Contemporaries often comment on the liking of graduates of the School for service in the capital; nor was Kireev mistaken in believing that 'this horrible School of Law *Kahal* support each other *per fas et nefas*'.[148] Clearly in the judicial or procuratorial service, so long as one had attended the School one's possibly modest personal background was of little importance. The Ministry of Justice had indeed to an extent created its own departmental family-school, its own pecking order as regards a man's origins. Given the requirements for entry to the School, it would be absurd to pretend that this departmental status system was unconnected with that of Russian society as a whole. Nevertheless, the School of Law accepted many boys from relatively modest noble families and graduated them with major potential advantages as regards future service – a clear illustration that an individual's position in the social hierarchy was not the only guide to his prospects as a young entrant in the civil service. In a manner unsurprising, given Russia's history, the state, acting to some extent independently of the social hierarchy, could intervene decisively to alter a boy's prospects and social status even before he entered its service.

Those who served in the judicial department nearly always began their careers there, the only exceptions being young officials who had served initially in other departments but transferred into the rapidly expanding Ministry of Justice soon after the 1864 reforms. The reason is obvious: a judicial official required a legal education and experience which made it virtually impossible for an outsider to transfer into the department in mid-career. Of the 46 'jurists', 34 (74 per cent) had served as procurators, 27 (58.7 per cent) as officials in the Senate's chancelleries, and only 20 (43.4 per cent) as judges in the district courts and judicial chambers. Moreover, 'jurists' tended on average to serve as judges for much shorter periods than as procurators. A study of careers within the judicial department may therefore tell one something about the best way to the summit of this particular branch of the civil service. In this department the route to success had little connection with social origins; the procurators were drawn from families no more upper-class than those of judicial officials as a whole. As regards their careers, however, one should note the ease with which procurators transferred to and from other branches of the judicial department, even indeed other parts of the civil service. Such transfers cannot have increased the procuracy's ability to maintain its independence as an 'organ of surveillance' over the rest of the government.[149]

For most 'jurists', appointment to the Senate was the final stage – save of course membership of the State Council itself – of their careers. Thus 33 (71.1 per cent) of the 46 men were senators. On the other hand, among the 215 members of the State Council there were 34 other senators who came from the ranks of the 'non-jurists'. Whereas some men actually served in the Senate, others merely bore the honorary title of senator; of the 33 'jurist' senators, 85 per cent actually served in the Senate, whereas among the 'non-jurists' only half did so. Moreover, within the Senate there was a distinction between the civil and criminal appeals departments, all of whose members were 'jurists', and the First, Second and Heraldry departments, which were often staffed by 'non-jurists'.

Transfers out of the judicial department into other ministries were numerous and important. Almost three-quarters of such transfers were either to the Ministry of Internal Affairs or to the State Chancellery and Chancellery of the Committee of Ministers. The hold of former 'jurists' on top positions both in the Ministry of Internal Affairs and in the two great central chancelleries can be measured statistically: of the 10 Ministers of Internal Affairs within the group of 215, 7 had served previously as judicial officials; of the 6 chiefs of the State Chancellery and Chancellery of the Committee of Ministers, all but 1 had transferred into the chancelleries from the judicial department.

For the basic cause of this preponderance of judicial officials in key positions within Nicholas II's government we must look back to the 1860s. In the wake of the radical judicial reform of 1864, able young men had poured into the Ministry of Justice, anxious to combine a career with the realization of their ideals about legality, and thankful to achieve responsibility at an early age instead of suffering the tedium and servility that went with most junior positions in other departments.[150] Thus Gurko recalls that 'a veritable constellation of talented contemporaries... assisted in creating our new court system',[151] and Kulomzin states that 'the flower of the younger generation of that day' chose the judiciary for their careers.[152] These men acted as a leaven for large sections of Russian central officialdom. Chiefs of other departments looking for able young men to fill vacant posts tended to cast their eyes towards the Ministry of Justice.[153] Moreover, since the influx of such young men into the Ministry in the 1860s was bound at a later period to create sharp competition for top judicial posts, ambitious 'jurists' had an incentive to seek better career prospects by transferring to other ministries.[154]

Thirty members of the group of 215 had previously served in the State Chancellery or Chancellery of the Committee/Council of Ministers, institutions which acted as secretariats respectively to the State Council and to the Committee/Council of Ministers.[155] Among the members of the State Council the former officials of these chancelleries were of about average social status (Table P). Roughly half of the 30 owned medium-sized or large estates (Table Q) and all but 2 had a higher civilian education (Table S). Seven of these 30 men had also served in the Emperor's Own Personal Chancellery or the Petitions Chancellery, as had 4 other men who had never worked in either of the two central governmental chancelleries.

As a group the 11 officials of the 'monarchical chancelleries' were of higher social status than the 30 men who had served in the governmental chancelleries, but the institutions in which they worked were of far less significance than the State Chancellery or Chancellery of the Committee/Council of Ministers. Indeed the great preponderance of governmental over 'monarchical' officials in this group of 34 accurately reflects the shift in the administration's centre of gravity since the days when Nicholas I's Personal Chancellery had been the headquarters of the Russian government.[156] Both N.M. Korkunov and G. Yaney confirm that by the last quarter of the nineteenth century the latter role had devolved on to the two great governmental chancelleries.[157]

The 34 former chancellery officials served shorter terms within these institutions and were much more likely to transfer to or from other departments than was the case with the 'jurists'. Thus the 34 served on average 13.9 years in the chancelleries, 8 (23.5 per cent) men working there for over 25 years and 5 (14.7 per cent) for 15 to 24 years. In contrast to the 'jurists', less than one-quarter of the 34 began their careers in the central chancelleries, most officials having to display their excellence in other departments before being admitted to the élite co-ordinating institutions of the Petersburg bureaucracy.

Of the 34 transfers into the chancelleries, 90 per cent were from the departments of Justice, Internal Affairs and Finance. The largest element here were the 14 transfers from the judicial department; of the 12 men involved, two-thirds had been educated at privileged schools and only 1 had ever served outside Petersburg. The chancelleries were therefore in the main recruiting a particular, and privileged, strain of judicial officials. A British diplomat once wrote, partly in jest, that there existed before 1939 an inner circle of key posts through which bright young men progressed during their assured rise to the top of the Foreign Office.[158] A similar inner circle linked education at the School of Law with jobs in the central departments of the Ministry of Justice or the Senate's chancellery, followed by a move into one of the two great governmental chancelleries. After a more or less prolonged sojourn in one or the other of the latter, a man jumped straight on to the State Council or into the Senate. The careers of P.A. Kharitonov, Baron Ju. A. Uxkull, Baron E. Yu. Nolde, K.K. Rennenkampf and N.A. Voevodsky (among others) typify this 'inner circle', though it is worth stressing that none of these men ever held ministerial office and that this group therefore never exercised direct responsibility for the implementation of government policy.[159]

In contrast to the 'jurists', only 3 of the chancelleries' 10 former officials from the Ministry of Internal Affairs had never served in the provinces, though immediately prior to their transfer 7 of the 10 men had been working in the ministry's central offices. The former Ministry of Internal Affairs officials were, however, the exception to the general rule that officials of the central chancelleries had little experience of provincial service. Thus almost two-thirds of the 34 had never worked outside Petersburg, a proportion matched only by the Council's financial officials. If transfers into the chancelleries were monopolized by the ministries of Internal Affairs, Justice and Finance, precisely the same was true (though to a somewhat lesser extent) of movement in the opposite direction.[160] Thus at the very centre of the Petersburg governmental machine one finds a small inner group of élite officials circulating among these four departments.

Nineteen members of the State Council served in the Ministry of Finance, 3 of them dividing their careers between this department and the State Control, the ministry's junior ally in the struggle to maintain budgetary limits in the face of the attacks of the spending departments.[161] In addition, one man, V.P. Cherevansky,[162] devoted his entire civil service career to the State Control.

The small size of this group of 20 men, whom I shall call financial officials, is surprising, given the great importance of the Ministry of Finance in late nineteenth and early twentieth-century Russian government. One explanation is that in the last years of the imperial regime an increasing number of financial officials tended on reaching senior rank to take up lucrative jobs in private finance and business, rather than moving to much less well-paid positions in the State Council. Leading examples of this tendency were V.I. Timiryazev, A.I. Putilov, A.I. Vyshnegradsky, V.I. Kovalevsky, P.L. Bark and M.M. Fyodorov.[163]

Although none of these 20 members of the State Council had ever served outside the civil service, the movement between private and governmental positions was not entirely one way. As Minister of Finance both Witte and Kokovtsov fought hard to increase the recruitment into their department of experienced men from the private sector.[164] Moreover, for more than half of the last 35 years of the Old Regime the Ministry of Finance was headed by N.Kh. Bunge, I.A. Vyshnegradsky, S.Yu. Witte and P.L. Bark, all of whom had worked for many years outside the civil service. This ability and willingness to draw into the state's service leading figures from the rapidly expanding world of Russian industry and finance suggests a certain degree of governmental adaptability to the demands of a changing economy and society.

The careers of the 20 financial officials in the State Council were in some ways similar to those of the 'jurists', in other ways more akin to those of the men who had served in the central governmental chancelleries. Like the 'jurists' the financial officials were for the most part specialists, who devoted much or all of their careers to one branch of the governmental apparatus. On average the 20 men had served for 23.7 years in the financial departments, half having worked there for more than a quarter of a century, and 30 per cent more for 15 to 24 years. On the other hand, like the former officials of the central chancelleries, the 17 long-serving financial officials (i.e. those who had served in this branch for 6 years or more) had limited experience outside Petersburg. Eleven of the 17 men had never served outside the capital and a considerably larger number had never served in provincial branches of the Ministry of Finance.

Although many of the 20 financial officials devoted much of their lives to the financial departments, a few had complicated careers entailing many shifts between ministries. Apart from the very close links between the Ministry of Finance and the State Control, most transfers occurred between the financial departments and the State Chancellery or Chancellery of the Committee/Council of Ministers. V.N. Kokovtsov, N.N. Pokrovsky, V.V. Verkhovsky, S.A. Mordvinov and I.P. Shipov moved between these two branches,[165] some of them on a number of occasions, and the significance of this group is reflected by the fact that it contains no less than three ministers.

Tables P, Q and S show that the long-serving financial officials were well educated, but came from distinctly modest backgrounds when measured against their peers in other ministries. Less than a quarter of the 17 men owned medium-sized or large estates. Nevertheless, it would be a mistake to imagine that, on starting their careers, all these men were outsiders to the Petersburg official 'establishment'. Between them old school links, ties of blood and marriage, together with old friendships forged in service or in Petersburg society, set up in this group a tight, interlocking set of relationships which created its own family atmosphere, with the concomitant elements of mutual support, claustrophobia and jealousy.

When, on his appointment as Minister of Finance in 1904, V.N. Kokovtsov spoke of the 'family' which he was rejoining, his words were more literally true than he perhaps intended. The new Minister was succeeding his ailing first cousin and old Lycée friend E.D. Pleske. Pleske's uncle and Kokovtsov's father-in-law was F.A. Oom, secretary to the Empress Marie Fyodorovna and an old, originally university, friend of F.G. Terner, the Assistant Minister of Finance under I.A. Vyshnegradsky. Kokovtsov's son-in-law, N.N. Fliege, another Lycéen, was the great-nephew of N.Kh. Bunge, Vyshnegradsky's predecessor as Minister of Finance.[166] The web of relationships joining these men was slightly less dense than that linking the Council's aristocratic magnates and is of course more difficult to illustrate through a genealogical chart. But that did not mean that the links were any less strong, effective or important.

Of those ministries not so far mentioned in this chapter, a number were very sparsely represented among the members of the State Council. The Cinderella status of the Ministry of State Properties, which in 1894 was transformed into the Ministry of Agriculture, is emphsized by the fact that not one long-serving official of this department sat in the State Council.[167] The 7 Ministers of Agriculture or State Properties within the group of 215 were all either former officials of the ministries of Internal Affairs or Finance, or landowning magnates. Equally, the subordinate position of the Church and of the Holy Synod in Russian politics is emphasized by the fact that only 2 men from this department, V.K. Sabler and Prince A.A. Shirinsky-Shikhmatov, sat in the Council. Nor were civilian engineers much better represented: 5 men, of whom all but Prince M.I. Khilkov had formal engineering training, were members, but civilian engineers never played a role in the civilian government that approached the importance their military equivalents had in the army.[168]

Ten members of the State Council were professors at Russian universities. Of these all but 1 were 'bourgeois' and none is known to have owned a large or medium-sized estate. Nine men had been educated at university and 1 at a medical college. Of the 10 professors, 3 never served in the administration and were appointed directly to the Council from their professorial chairs as a result of their personal stature and political views. Two men combined holding a chair with part-time service in the State Chancellery or Senate. Three of the professors served as Minister of Education, bringing with them as deputies the two other men, who were in each case colleagues at their university. Before becoming Minister, both N.P. Bogolepov and A.N. Schwartz had served as curator of an educational district, as had 4 other members of the State Council. Of this foursome, K.P. Yanovsky and N.M. Anichkov were former teachers and career officials at the Ministry of Education, while P.P. Izvol'sky and A.A. Saburov were drawn from outside the educational department.[169]

Finally we come to the Ministry of Foreign Affairs. Thirteen members of the Council served as ambassadors and two others became top officials in the ministry in Petersburg. Though almost half these men owned no land, the 15 diplomats, in line with general European practice, were from much grander social backgrounds than any of the domestic civil servants. The greater number of them were former students at the Lycée, which supplied all but two of Russia's Foreign Ministers in the half-century before 1914.[170] As regards careers, Prince N.S. Dolgoruky and Count P.A. Shuvalov were generals with very powerful connections who had no experience in the foreign service prior to their appointment as heads of mission.[171] Of the remaining 13 men, all had served in this department for over a quarter of a century, but whereas 11 men had spent almost their entire careers abroad, Prince V.S. Obolensky-Neledinsky-Meletsky and Count V.N. Lambsdorff had never left Petersburg.[172]

The last group of officials deserving separate mention are the 63 members of the State Council who also served as ministers.[173] While it is by no means true that all 63 of these men exercised more power or influence, as ministers, than colleagues in the Council who had never held ministerial office, it is the case that the 'average' minister was politically more significant than the 'average' ordinary member of the State Council. In political terms therefore we can with some justice describe the 63 ministers as an élite within an élite.

It is of importance that the average age of the 63 men on their appointment as minister was 53.7 years, their average term in office being just less than 4 years. Moreover the figure for average length of ministerial service is distorted by the long terms served by a handful of men,[174] some of whom worked in relatively apolitical posts such as Minister of the Imperial Court or secretary to the Committee of Ministers. The median figure for term in office, two years, indicates the relatively rapid turnover which existed in key political posts before the ministerial leap-frog of the First World War.

As regards their social backgrounds and the extent of their landholding, the 63 ministers were roughly typical of the whole group of 215. If on the one hand their social status (Table P) was marginally lower than average, the proportion of ministers who owned medium-sized or large estates was marginally higher. Among the 'aristocratic magnates', it is true, only B.A. Vasil'chikov, P.D. Svyatopolk-Mirsky and Aleksei Bobrinsky served as ministers, but the group of 63 contained many quite large landowners from established, and indeed sometimes ancient, families. Of the men in this group who played key political roles in Nicholas II's reign, P.A. Stolypin, D.S. Sipyagin, Prince Aleksei Obolensky, I.G. Shcheglovitov, I.L. Goremykin, A.N. Kulomzin, S.D. Sazonov and the various members of the Saburov, Khvostov and Izvol'sky families are the best known.

We have already noted the important role played by former jurists at the head both of the State Chancellery and the Ministry of Internal Affairs. Outside the civilian departments concerned with domestic affairs, ministers were always long-serving experts in the particular field covered by their ministry. Thus diplomats ran the Foreign Ministry, admirals ran the navy,[175] while all the Council's Ministers of War were not only generals but moreover 'military' rather than 'civilian' generals. Domestic civil servants virtually never transferred into what, to use modern jargon, one might describe as the agencies of national security. By keeping internal and external policy in strictly separate hands the government increased the risk that none of its top officials would have sufficient knowledge and experience to achieve a balanced and rounded view of the state's overall policy.

Finally, it should be noted that far fewer generals became heads of civilian ministries than had been the case in the mid-nineteenth century.[176] Apart from the largely apolitical Minister of the Court, V.B. Frederycksz, the only general who served for any length of time as a civilian minister was P.L. Lobko, the State Controller from 1899 to 1905. In addition, however, one general briefly headed the Ministry of Education, another the Communications Ministry, and a third the Ministry of Internal Affairs.

In conclusion let us summarize the key points made in this chapter. Out of all the detail 14 main points emerge.

(i) The Russian ruling élite under Nicholas II was largely drawn from the traditional source, namely the landowning and official classes. Roughly one-third of the members of the State Council came from families already part of the Russian nobility before 1700. About 60 per cent of the 215 men belonged to families already well established as part of the landowning gentry in the lifetimes of the members of the State Council's grandfathers.

(ii) Of the remaining 40 per cent, most were the sons or grandsons of men who had been ennobled, though in some cases they were from families that had belonged to the minor nobility for longer, while in others the member of the State Council himself came into the nobility. In the overwhelming majority of cases, military or civil service was the route to ennoblement and social mobility. Among the 40 per cent of 'new nobles' there were many families of modest German origin.

(iii) The ruling élite was overwhelmingly Russian or russianized. The only other considerable group among the 215 men were the Germans, though even most of these were Russian in all but name. Cadets of Baltic gentry families were, by comparison with other Germans, rather more, but by no means entirely, proof against russianization.

(iv) The ruling élite had an immense stake in landowning. Well over half owned land, most of them possessing medium-sized or large estates. Within the landowning group wealth was, however, very unevenly divided. A small group of 8 magnates owned more than half of all the land possessed by the members of the State Council.

(v) There was a very marked correlation between a family's antiquity and its ownership of land. The 70 men who definitely belonged to families part of the Russian nobility before 1700 made up 32.5 per cent of the total membership of the ruling élite and owned 83.5 per cent of its land. This underlines the extent to which one is dealing with a wealthy and hereditary ruling class.

(vi) At the centre of the group of old Russian families was a small and closely-knit core of immensely wealthy magnates who were aristocrats by any conceivable definition of the word. These men had far more in common with the Hungarian or Bohemian aristocracy than with the Prussian service gentry. The age when magnates dominated politics in Russia was over, however. Ministers were seldom magnates, though the latter still exerted a major influence through ministerial connections, the court, and, after 1905, the legislature and newly formed landowners' pressure groups as well.

(vii) Education at one of the privileged schools was an important factor in influencing career prospects. By no means all the boys at the Lycée or School of Law, however, came from aristocratic or prominent gentry families; the two schools in fact to some extent acted as a force for social mobility within the nobility.

(viii) Rural local government (elected service as marshals and appointed service as governors), together with diplomacy, were much the most popular areas of activity for the Council's aristocrats and members of prominent gentry families. Careers in education and finance were followed by men from the most modest backgrounds. Judicial officials were on the whole from less elevated social backgrounds than men involved in general administration, but the 'jurists' were nevertheless usually of gentry rather than bourgeois origin.

(ix) The ruling élite was largely civilian. Generals, many of whom were in any case not true military specialists, played a major role only in the Ministry of Internal Affairs.

(x) Conversely, officials from the domestic civil service virtually never transferred into the military, naval or diplomatic departments and had almost no experience as regards problems of national security.

(xi) A number of civilian ministries (e.g. State Properties, Education, State Control, Synod, Communications) were of secondary importance and played little part in forming the official élite. The domestic governmental élite was dominated by officials from the ministries of Internal Affairs, Justice and Finance, together with men who had served in the State Chancellery or the Chancellery of the Committee of Ministers.

(xii) In this official élite one sub-group was the upper-class, landed and often ex-Guards element predominant in the top provincial posts of the Ministry of Internal Affairs, sometimes holding the highest positions in the ministry's central administration, but seldom pushing its way into other key departments. P.A. Stolypin, Prince P.D. Svyatopolk-Mirsky and D.S. Sipyagin, to take but three major examples, belong in this category.

(xiii) A second sub-group, to be found particularly in the judicial and financial departments, was made up of specialists who had spent all or most of their careers in a single ministry. I.G. Shcheglovitov was one such specialist who played a key role in Nicholas II's government. In general, however, even financial and judicial ministers from this group (e.g. E.D. Pleske and S.S. Manukhin) were of relatively limited importance.

(xiv) Finally, one has a sub-group of officials who passed from one key department mentioned to another, sometimes serving in three of them but seldom in four. These men came closest to forming imperial Russia's true mandarinate. Usually possessing a legal education and very often qualifying as 'jurists', these men's careers also frequently revolved around the State Chancellery and Chancellery of the Committee/Council of Ministers. This sub-group played a political role of unique importance in Nicholas II's Russia. Here, for instance, one finds V.N. Kokovtsov, A.V. Krivoshein, V.K. Plehve, P.N. Durnovo, A.S. Stishinsky, S.E. Kryzhanovsky and A.N. Kulomzin, each one of whom was both a highly professional civil servant and a hard-bitten expert at bureaucratic politics.

CHAPTER 3

Educating Rulers

The oldest member of the State Council, Count L.L. Heiden, was educated at home in the reign of Alexander I. The youngest, A.D. Samarin, left Moscow University in the last years of Alexander III's reign. The upbringing and education of the Council's members thus span eight decades of the nineteenth century, though the greater number of the group were children and adolescents in the years between 1835 and 1880. Even in this latter period, however, Russian society changed greatly, and with it the Russian family and Russia's schools and universities.

The members of Nicholas II's ruling élite fall into three distinct categories as regards their education. Eighty-one men attended military schools, 71 at army and 10 at naval cadet corps. Seventy-three members of the Council studied at university, 28 at Moscow, 38 at Petersburg, and 7 at one or another of the other imperial universities. Among the 73 students at university, the overwhelming majority had previously graduated from a gymnasium. Finally, 47 men studied at one or the other of the Empire's prestigious civilian boarding schools for nobles only, the Alexander Lycée and the School of Law.[1] There were great differences in the quality and type of education offered to these three groups of men, and even within a particular group, there might be all the difference in the world between a boy's training in a run-of-the-mill cadet corps of the 1840s and the ultra-exclusive Corps des Pages fifteen years latter.

Moreover, if it is difficult to generalize about the formal education received from a range of institutions, it is even harder to gauge the effect of their domestic environment as children and adolescents on the future members of the ruling élite. The difficulty is partly lack of information. But the very fact that these members of the State Council reached the summit of the Russian governmental system shows that they were in one way or another exceptional, so that even if, for instance, one could make confident judgements about the impact of a particular educational institution on the greater number of its students, it would be unwise to assume that it had a similar influence on these 215 men.

Between leaving school and achieving a senior governmental post each member of the State Council of course shed some influences and absorbed others. In addition, as a civil servant he worked under the constraints of bureaucratic hierarchy and discipline, acting not in a void but in the context of his particular job and of wider political realities. To take a concrete example: Russian legal education in the 1840s and 1850s may have been inadequate; and in the late nineteenth century senior officials in the Ministry of Internal Affairs trained as jurists may have overriden legality in pursuit of political objectives. The two points may be connected;[2] on the other hand, it may be that the functions the Ministry of Internal Affairs existed to fulfil, combined with the very nature of Russian society and politics in the last decades of the Old Regime, made it very difficult for these men unreservedly to uphold the rule of law.

In Russian noble families at the beginning of the nineteenth century, patriarchy ruled supreme.[3] The father, tsar within the family, not only held unchallengeable authority but also felt the need to exercise it in an aloof, arbitrary and commanding manner. Emotion was not the key to family relationships, whether between husbands and wives or between parents and children. Even had the father, trained in most cases in a military school, been capable of exhibiting emotion, he would have feared to do so, for emotion was unstable, unreliable, and could undermine the discipline and self-control which parents sought to implant in their children, especially in their sons.

The family existed to train young men to fill a foreordained place in a fixed and ordered society. Allowing a child's personality to develop unhampered was by no means the aim, for human nature was not trusted, and in any case the boy must be moulded to meet the demands of his future, almost certainly military and serf-owning, life. The individual was trained in obedience but equipped with the self-discipline and toughness which would fit him one day to command. Excessive sensitivity was discouraged. Subordination both to one's superiors in age and status, and to the collective of family and state was required.

Nevertheless, the strength of that requirement should be measured not by the standards of the contemporary North American or West European bourgeois family but rather by those of other sections of the European nobility at the time. Judged in this way, the Russian noble family of 1800 to 1850 would often have seemed a generation or so behind the times, but neither the brutality by which obedience to authority was enforced[4] nor the extent to which the individual was subordinated to the collective would have seemed excessive. The younger sons of the Russian nobility were not, for instance, as in some other parts of Europe, expected to live landless and celibate lives so that all property could pass by primogeniture and a family's status be ensured forever.[5]

Four stages of an aristocratic upbringing. The photographs are of Prince Anatol Pavlovich Lieven as infant, child, student (at right) in the law faculty of Petersburg University, and officer of the Chevaliers Gardes. His wife, a Saltykov, was the sister-in-law of Aleksei Dimitrievich Obolensky.

In the course of the nineteenth century the traditional relationships and values of the Russian noble family were undermined by ideas of individualism derived from the West. Stress on the rights and personality of the individual led to an interest in psychology and in the early pre-rational years of childhood when much of this personality was formed. Experts on child-rearing urged parents to be closer to their children, to encourage their confidences and not to shrink from or suppress all emotion.[6] The development of these tendencies should be seen as part and parcel of the gradual westernization of the Russian nobility, but more specific factors were also involved. The collapse of traditional values in Russia was longer delayed than in much of the rest of Europe because between 1770 and 1815 the Russian nobility was removed geographically from the turmoil of secularization, revolution, emancipation of serfs and occupation by the French which engulfed much of the continental nobility.[7]

For Russian nobles the period of upheaval was delayed until the 1850s and 1860s. Defeat in the Crimea called into question the viability of the values and institutions on which the 'Nicholas system' was based. Among them were the patriarchal, authoritarian family and the subordination of the individual to the collective. Emancipa-

tion of the serfs had many causes, of which the Crimean defeat and the gradual westernization of the élite were probably the most vital. Since serfdom was seen as the cornerstone of an unfree society, Emancipation symbolized the liberation of more than just serfs. Nor should the practical impact of 1861 on the noble family be under-estimated. The patriarchal father no longer had to play the part of little king among his serf subjects. Moreover, if the cultivation of natural relationships was made more possible, it also became more necessary. In some cases at least, inability to afford the traditional household of tutors, governesses and servants brought parents closer to their children of necessity. In any event, as Russian society began to change there were advantages to a more flexible training of the personality which would allow a young man to cope with the de-mands of a more complicated and less predictable world.

The young Russian nobleman of the 1860s and 1870s was probably freer and of a more complex nature than his father, but also quite probably less secure, less self-confident in his values and in his treat-ment of others, and more tortured. Writing in 1910, the columnist 'Vol'nyy' argued that the older generation, tempered in the tough school of Nicholas I's Russia where rules were clear-cut and con-fidently imposed, were a distinctly stronger breed than their sons, an altogether more nervous and complicated group, wracked by far greater doubts and insecurities than their parents.[8]

The memoirs of members of the State Council add detail and provide a necessary corrective to such broad generalizations. The Russian nobility, as we have seen, was anything but homogeneous. Fyodor Terner, for instance, was an hereditary nobleman, Orthodox from birth, but his background was wholly unlike that of the reasonably well-off provincial Russian landowner taken as a model in recent discussions of the domestic upbringing of noblemen. In all but strictly legal terms Terner was a member of the German-Russian professional middle class, and his upbringing reflected this fact. The Terners' cosy bourgeois home, its relationships sanctified by a considerable dose of sentimentality, was very much a closed refuge from the world's storms. Fyodor Terner records that all his basic moral values he owed to his parents, other influences having made little impact on him. Nevertheless, he writes, to discuss his family life in a book would be 'a type of profanity', for it would mean revealing this fundamentally private and separate sphere of life to outsiders.[9]

Alexander Mosolov, born in 1844, was on the face of it much more typical of the Russian provincial nobility than was Terner. Inevitably, however, once one concentrates on the life of an individual many generalizations about upbringing come to seem at best half-truths. Mosolov came from an old gentry family, a fact in which he took considerable pride, and one that was financially at the top end of the provincial gentry. The Mosolovs' wealth derived from ironworks employing serf labour and quickly disappeared after Emancipation. A.N. Mosolov's father, Nicholas, was a captain in the Guards cavalry who retired after inheriting rich estates and married a non-noble doctor's daughter. Nicholas Mosolov spoke perfect French, excellent English, loved music and possessed a fine library. His wife, also an excellent linguist, was close to her children and herself taught her son Alexander to read; later the children had a series of foreign tutors and governesses. A.N. Mosolov recalls with great nostalgia the happy, secure and cultured family life he had as a child.

At the age of ten this idyll ended when he was dispatched by his father to the Naval Cadet Corps in Petersburg. Nicholas Mosolov chose this school partly from a family tradition, but also out of patriotic indignation at Russia's defeats in the Crimean war, without taking into account his son's personality or inclinations. A.N. Mosolov wanted, he says, to be a diplomat or a writer, indeed anything but a sailor. He longed for the more civilized atmosphere of the Lycée or School of Guards Sub-Ensigns among boys of his own class, rather than the provincial noble 'semi-savages' who packed the Naval Cadet Corps. Yet for all his loathing of the corps, Mosolov records that he cried bitterly on hearing of the death of Nicholas I, so great was his adoration for this monarch whom he had never seen.

The years of Mosolov's adolescence brought major problems and insecurities. By the age of seventeen, transferred at last to the School of Guards Sub-Ensigns, be had begun to write poetry and had become deeply interested in Russian, French, English, Italian and classical literature. He was also, he records, in some respects 'abnormal' and 'sickly', a violent hypochondriac and extremely nervous. Political events contributed to Mosolov's insecurity. When the news broke of Alexander II's intention to liberate the serfs, his brothers and he were greatly alarmed and felt the ground to be shifting under their feet. The new, usually radical and even republican ideas that began to be discussed among his schoolmates tormented him.

For a time Mosolov shared the liberal, westernizing views current among his peers, but by the early 1860s he had swung back to the beliefs traditional in his family. His father, whom A.N. Mosolov deeply admired for his patriotism as well as his personal qualities, died in 1861, partly it seems from an inability to reconcile himself to Emancipation, not to mention the drastic financial losses it entailed for his family. In M.N. Murav'yov, his first chief in the civil service, Alexander Mosolov found something of an alternative father-figure; Murav'yov's conservative and Russian-nationalist views confirmed the instinctive loyalties Mosolov had derived from his childhood. A.N. Mosolov clung to these loyalties and convictions for the rest of his life, holding to them quite possibly with all the more determination because they were linked to his lost childhood world of security and material comfort.[10]

Even Alexander Mosolov's rather full, intelligent and sensitive memoirs leave one guessing as to some aspects of his upbringing and the influence that upbringing may have exerted on him, particularly of course on his private and sexual life. Most other memoirs by members of the Council are less frank, and of course only a small minority of the members left a record of their childhood and adolescence. It is significant, however, that among those who did leave autobiographies, very few reached adulthood before the death of one at least of their parents.[11] Some indeed were orphans from relatively early childhood, and the effects of such a loss could be great not only in psychological terms but also in determining future careers.

The early lives of two members of the Council, P.P. Semyonov and V.N. Kokovtsov, illustrate this point. Semyonov was born in 1827 into an old Ryazan family of boyars, a fact in which he took great pride. His grandfather's ancestral estate had, he writes, been in the family's possession for centuries. The Semyonovs' service and sacrifice in the ranks of the Russian army over the generations are stressed in his memoirs, as are the high cost in eighteenth- and early nineteenth-century Russia of educating young men, and especially of supporting them while in service in the Guards. P.P. Semyonov's

V.N. Kokovtsov

mother's family, of Huguenot origin, were blood relations of the Semyonovs, and his childhood and adolescence were spent amidst a dense network of cousins from prominent provincial families of the Central Black Earth region. The main meeting-place of the families remained Moscow rather than the imperial capital. At home in their comfortable country house – built of stone, a rarity among the Ryazan gentry – family prayers were said every morning. Semyonov's mother spoke to her children only in French, and on certain days the children were allowed to speak only French or German. Both the Semyonov parents were highly cultured and took a great interest in contemporary Russian literature and theatre.

This seemingly secure household was devastated by the death of Semyonov's father in 1832, followed within two years by the onset of his mother's madness. Semyonov's experiences in the following years would have broken a less resistant and independent person, but they appear to have strengthened him and allowed him to develop interests he could only have come to at a later age had his upbringing been more closely supervised. Aided intermittently by one tutor or another, Semyonov was deeply immersed in Russian, German, French and English literature by the age of thirteen. Having free run of a decent library and an extensive garden and estate, the boy largely educated himself in what was to be his lifelong passion, namely botany. Meanwhile his character was tempered by having, when still almost a child, had to manage an insane mother, mediate between her and the servants, and play a considerable role in running both household and estate. After such experiences, the School of Guards

Sub-Ensigns came almost as a relief, and his subsequent expeditions in the remote Tyan-Shan area amidst warlike pagan tribes were as nothing compared to the strains of Semyonov's childhood and early adolescence.[12]

The family of V.N. Kokovtsov was a little less distinguished and considerably poorer than either the Semyonovs or the Mosolovs. Kokovtsov's uncle was, however, the Novgorod provincial marshal, and parts of his father's estate had been granted to the Kokovtsovs by Tsar Aleksei Mikhailovich in the mid-seventeenth century. As V.N. Kokovtsov underlines, however, it was difficult to squeeze a decent living from an estate in northern Russia. He describes a very simple and unspoiled childhood in which apples were a treat and there could be no thought of foreign travel. Kokovtsov lived a rather untrammelled life in the countryside until the age of ten, his father being too busy running the estate to pay close attention to his son.

Kokovtsov's parents worried constantly about the difficulty of educating their children at home. Their estate was isolated, roughly 100 kilometres from the nearest town, almost 150 from the railway, and with no other large or even middle-sized gentry properties in the neighbourhood. Tutors and governesses came readily enough for the summer, but the winter was cold and long, there were few books to read and little to do, and teachers therefore changed frequently. Vladimir Kokovtsov had no schoolbooks and received no systematic education until the age of ten, though the local priest taught him religion, and German and French tutors instructed him in the rudiments of their languages.

Kokovtsov writes that he loved his parents and their estate, but that it was clear that a decent education was only to be had in Petersburg. Thence he was dispatched in 1863, his family remaining in the country. Loneliness was soon compounded by tragedy, when his mother died suddenly, aged only thirty-seven. Kokovtsov recalls that her death turned him into a far more serious child than before; thenceforth his behaviour improved dramatically, he worked very hard and was regularly top of his class. At the Alexander Lycée his lack of any family in Petersburg meant that he went out much less than his schoolmates, was far lonelier, and had more time and a psychological need to read and work. The seeds of the future exceptionally hard-working and self-disciplined statesman are clearly evident. So no doubt too is the depth of Kokovtsov's love for the Lycée, for in the school's civilized atmosphere and the close solidarity of his class he could find a substitute for the comradeship and security of family life.[13]

The 81 members of the State Council who had passed through military schools were undoubtedly, as a group, the worst educated section of the ruling élite. Because the government was less willing, after 1906, to appoint generals to the State Council than had previously been the case, the military members of the group of 215 were somewhat older on average than their civilian counterparts. This helps to explain why 37 of the group of 81 had been educated wholly or almost wholly in cadet corps in the reign of Nicholas I.

For all the inadequacies of Nicholas's cadet corps, it is important to remember the benefits they brought to Russia and its army. As General Lalaev correctly pointed out, among officers newly commissioned between 1856 and 1861 only 26 per cent had studied at a cadet corps. The general intellectual level of the remaining 74 per cent, for the most part educated at home and trained through brief service in the ranks, was 'incomparably lower' than that of the cadet corps graduates.[14]

It is certainly fairer to judge Nicholas's cadet corps in terms of what had preceded them rather than to set them against some ideal vision of a modern education. Under Alexander I there had been no system of military education as such, but rather a number of wholly uncoordinated institutions each pursuing its own objectives. The 1830 Statute of Military Educational Institutions helped to bring this chaos to a halt by imposing qualifications of age and literacy on would-be entrants, setting out programmes of education, intellectual and otherwise, and regularizing the procedures by which cadets passed through the corps and were commissioned into the army. Subsequently the Chief Administration of Military Educational Institutions, under the Grand Duke Mikhail Pavlovich, established examinations to test would-be teachers and regularized a system of inspectors to ensure that standards were maintained and rules enforced. The edicts of the Chief Administration and of its Teaching Committee show that their hearts were sometimes in the right place. Exhortations went out, for instance, to take into account the younger cadets' age in enforcing discipline; to encourage thought rather than rote learning; to take cadets off on tours of museums and factories; and to uphold authority by example and moral suasion rather than terror. In 1835, regretting that the state lacked funds to provide a musical education for cadets, the Grand Duke Mikhail nevertheless ordered that encouragement should be given to private lessons in free time, since 'music, like all the arts, elevates a man's spirit, gives him new means to be pleasing in society and sometimes serves as a comfort in difficult moments in life'.[15]

To an even greater extent than is normally the case, however, the ideals and rhetoric of educational institutions failed to coincide with reality. As regards the intellectual training of cadets, this was by no means wholly the fault of the authorities, who frequently bewailed the fact that, owing to the low level of culture and education in

Russian society, boys entering the cadet corps between the ages of ten and twelve were often scarcely more, and sometimes less, than literate.[16] 'This kind of boy, entering the corps, has to be taught virtually everything, often beginning with the alphabet', complained one report in 1852.

The situation was compounded by the fact that, for the great majority of cadets, the nine years at a cadet corps were the only formal education they would receive. Yet these boys, the élite of the army's officer corps, must be provided with the educational qualifications for later admission to the General Staff Academy. Moreover, many cadets would later hold top civil service and government posts, which meant that they must also be given a general education and the cultural grounding that, had they not gone to boarding school, their family milieu might in theory have provided. To meet all these requirements courses became impossibly broad and superficial. In 1852 a senior cadet studied a bewildering mixture of technical military subjects, law, mathematics and natural science, history, statistics, two foreign languages, Russian and religion.[17]

Given such a curriculum, no teacher on earth could have been fully effective, but those who actually taught in cadet corps were often sadly inadequate. Provincial corps were the most likely to suffer from very bad teachers, but even in the capitals much depended on the interest or lack of it shown by the corps authorities in attracting skilful instructors to their schools. Moreover, even a conscientious teacher in this era was inclined to see his job as being to train the memory of his pupils, impart information and enforce the habit of hard, systematic and painstaking work; encouraging independent thought was seldom the ideal. Even these goals were, however, by no means always attained, largely because of the hopelessness of the military tutors who were supposed to supervise the cadets' private study and drill them in their courses. General M.I. Lelyukhin, a cadet at the Second Cadet Corps between 1837 and 1845, recalls that 'the intellectual development of the cadets was exceptionally limited: they studied a lot but fully absorbed very little, mostly because of the lack of tutors who could have helped the cadets prepare their lessons'.[18]

Incapable of exercising much moral, let alone intellectual, influence on the cadets, the military tutors concentrated instead on enforcing rigid and unquestioning obedience to authority, impeccable drill, and a smart external appearance. Corps authorities often shared this sense of priorities and higher authorities rarely probed behind this surface of order and efficiency even if indeed they wished to do so. Especially after 1848, a button undone was too often seen as incipient anarchism, a smart bearing as a guarantee of political reliability and good character. At all times in Nicholas's reign the latter qualities were viewed as of much greater significance for a cadet than were intellectual achievements. Thus the cadet corps 'programme' of 1845 stressed that the ideal pupil was 'a Christian; loyal; Russian; a good son; a reliable comrade; a modest and educated young man; a painstaking, patient and efficient officer'.[19] Education of the intellect came low on the list and even there was only acceptable if clothed in modesty.

Of course one must remember that the cadet corps were military institutions whose fundamental task was the education of future officers. Given the nature of warfare, especially in the early nineteenth century, there was good reason to stress the qualities of self-sacrifice, physical courage and toughness, the ability to function under conditions of great physical and mental stress, strong collective loyalties, and a wholehearted and simple love of sovereign and country. Not surprisingly, studies of Prussian or Austrian cadet corps in this era, even indeed of Sandhurst in a later period, show very many similarities to the cadet corps of Nicholas I.[20]

Nevertheless the evils of the Nicholas cadet corps are obvious and were not even, in the event, justified by the officer corps's performance in time of war. Unthinking discipline was imposed by sometimes vicious means. P.N. Ignat'ev, for instance, director of the Corps des Pages, ordered one boy to be flogged, a great dishonour in the aristocratic circles from which that Corps was largely drawn. When the cadet nearly succeeded in committing suicide to avoid this disgrace, Ignat'ev still insisted that the sentence be carried out on the boy's recovery from his serious wounds. Rigid discipline allied to regulation of almost every moment of a cadet's day inevitably crushed sparks of individuality. Nor could the individual survive the extreme pressure on cadets to conform to the mores of their peers, or the savage persecution of junior classes by senior. This last probably reached its high point in the sadistic tortures perpetrated in the Artillery School, but the rule of the fist was general in all the cadet corps.[21]

This genuinely totalitarian form of education seems to have suited many boys, who adapted cheerfully to life in the corps. General Lelyukhin, for instance, could not remember any comrades in his year who hated the school's authorities or the training they imposed.[22] No doubt this was partly because the corps's values were in harmony with those of the provincial gentry families from which most of the cadets were drawn. Bred in a relatively tough, wild and unsophisticated environment, these boys needed little encouragement to accept the rule of the fist, let alone the right of those senior in age and status to exact deference from their juniors.

A product of the School of Guards Sub-Ensigns, which as we shall see was in most ways a more sophisticated and intelligent institution than the average cadet corps, recalls that his peers took great pride in their excellent drill and observance of military minutiae. Most cadets retained a strong and naïve set of religious beliefs, anti-Orthodox jokes being greatly disapproved of. Far from hating the cadet corps or the 'Nicholas system' as a whole, the boys had no sympathy whatever for liberal ideas. All believed that Russia was the greatest and most powerful country on earth and that her army was invincible. The cadets took immense pride in their country's might, its embodiment, the majestic and awe-inspiring Nicholas I, being seen as almost divine. With the acceptance of such values by cadets on the one hand and the determined and self-confident imposition of rigid rules and beliefs by the corps authorities on the other, it is not surprising that military training under Nicholas I was in many ways an exceptionally effective process of character-formation.[23]

Nevertheless, the system inevitably claimed its victims, as some at least of the corps histories concede.[24] Even in his sixties A.N. Mosolov was still expressing his loathing and resentment of the Naval Cadet Corps,[25] and one can only guess at the impact it made on him. Nor, to take but one example, can one gauge the influence of an adolescence spent in the Corps des Pages in the 1850s on V.N. Lambsdorff, the exceptionally sensitive and nervous homosexual who subsequently became Foreign Minister. More important, however, than the psychological traumas of individual cadets are the ways in which the corps shaped the minds and personalities of the ruling élite as a whole.

D.M. Lyovshin, the historian of the Corps des Pages, writes that the Nicholas cadet corps developed the will of a majority of the boys, the minds of a minority and the sensitivities of very few.[26] M. Maksimovsky, the author of a history of the School of Engineers, comments that because boys entered the cadet corps around the age of ten their characters were often shaped by the corps atmosphere, which was anything but conducive to sensitivity or tenderness, and bred, in addition, little respect for the intellect. Mixing together boys aged from nine to twenty in a closed educational institution and allowing the older cadets great leeway to tyrannize was a standing invitation to homosexuality. Nevertheless, in Maksimovsky's view the cadet corps created a marked sense of comradeship among the boys and produced 'firm, strong, courageous' characters. Writing in the late 1860s, he commented that cadets of that day were more humane, cultured and adult, but lacked some of the naïve and direct sincerity of their predecessors of the Nicholas era.[27]

D.V. Denisov was a great deal more critical of the training of the minds and personalities of the future ruling élite in Nicholas's cadet corps. Denouncing the corps's failure even to attempt to develop independent minds, allowing them on the contrary to be destroyed at first flowering by the weight of collective opinion and anti-intellectualism, Denisov bewailed the ruinous consequences of creating future rulers unable to reason, 'a mob of incapable men, stubborn in their own ignorance'.[28] A.A. Polovtsov would have agreed with Denisov's comment. Convinced that, for all its failings, his own education at the School of Law had been far superior to anything available at a cadet corps, he was often scathing about colleagues whose training had been purely military. Count Peter Shuvalov, for instance, was in Polovtsov's view a naturally highly gifted man, but his education had not trained him to think with depth or clarity. Equally, if Prince Gregory Golitsyn, the governor-general of the Caucasus, was much better equipped to command and obey than to discuss or reason, that had far more to do with his (lack of) education than with failings in his basic personality or intelligence. There can indeed be little doubt that an education confined to Nicholas's cadet corps was a hopelessly inadequate, and indeed in some ways positively dangerous, training for a Russian statesman of the turn of the twentieth century.[29]

Between 1857 and 1862, when many of the future members of the State Council were at cadet corps, the corps went through a period of transition and crisis. The values and institutions of the Nicholas era were exposed to criticism and increasing condemnation in Russian society. In the sphere of education the very influential articles of N.I. Pirogov struck at the roots of the Nicholas system.[30] Since so much of the prestige and legitimacy of Nicholas's regime had been based on patriotic faith in Russian power and prestige, the defeat in the Crimea caused major soul-searching. Corps authorities were less confident about imposing the old values, and cadets less willing to accept them. Authority wavered and was uncertain, its zigzag course inevitably causing trouble through its mixture of insecurity, concession and repression. Some of the changes which occurred in the cadet corps in this period were very fruitful. Both the authorities and the boys in many cases took intellectual training far more seriously than in the past. Respect for independent thinking was often combined with a much more civilized atmosphere in the corps, brought about on occasion by the revolt of a junior class or by intervention on the part of the authorities to end the traditional tyranny of senior cadets.[31]

Where a corps's authorities were less flexible, however, or had a particularly low standing in the eyes of the cadets, there could be serious trouble. Lack of faith in the existing political and military system, the sunken prestige of the latter, could combine with contempt for military tutors, still often crude and uneducated, to produce an atmosphere of revolt. At the intellectually outstanding Engineering Academy in 1860 the whole of the top class, V.V. Wahl and his peers, left after a clash with the authorities over the expulsion of one cadet.[32] From 1858 until the early 1860s a major fall in discipline was evident at, to take but two examples, the First Cadet Corps in Petersburg and the First Moscow Cadet Corps. Massive infraction of rules concerning private literature, frequenting of inns and theatres, and clothing was combined with student insolence towards the authorities and the large-scale vandalism of state property, At the First Moscow Cadet Corps examination results also plunged.[33] Not surprisingly, regimental commanders began to complain that cadets joining their units lacked discipline and showed no great energy or enthusiasm for military service.[34]

To their credit, the military authorities responded effectively to the growing problems of the cadet corps. The special commission on military education established on 12 October 1862 decided that the key failing of the cadet corps was that they had not kept step with changes that had occurred in Russian society and the Russian mentality since 1856. Accepting Pirogov's view that the basis for any specialist training must be a complete general education, the commission condemned the cadet corps's excessively wide-ranging curricula and their mixing of general and technical-military subjects. Henceforth general education was to take place in military gymnasia from whose programmes technical training and drill would be excluded. Their curricula followed very closely those of the civilian *Realschule*, with mathematics and modern languages heavily stressed. Meanwhile military education was confined to newly-established two-year military schools, designed to teach well-educated young men the skills needed by an officer up to the rank of colonel. In 1863 General N.V. Isakov was appointed head of the military education administration, a post he held for the rest of Alexander II's reign.[35]

On the whole, Isakov's policy was a triumphant success. The amount of time spent on general education, the breadth and coherence of the curriculum, the quality of both teachers and tutors, and the whole intellectual and moral atmosphere of the military gymnasia were a vast improvement on the old cadet corps. The reason lay in part simply in the development of Russian society; there now existed a pool of university-educated teachers and cultured tutors, as well as adequate textbooks, to a degree that had never been true in Nicholas's Russia. The efforts of Isakov and his subordinates were also, however, very important. The military authorities put great effort into selecting and training teachers and tutors, founding their own pedagogical journal. Although in form Russian general education in military institutions was similar to the Prussian, both countries adopting *Realschule* courses for their basic middle-school curricula, the atmosphere of the Prussian cadet corps remained much more militarized, the prestige of intellectual training much lower, and the glorification of traditional military values such as 'character' and toughness more all-pervasive.

Moreover, in many respects the Russian military gymnasia under the benign supervision of the civilized D.A. Milyutin and N.V. Isakov compared favourably with the regular classical gymnasia run by the Ministry of Education. The general dislike in Russian educated society for D.A. Tolstoy's classical gymnasia was indeed one reason why military middle schools flourished in Alexander II's reign. Russian boys in general saw much more sense in the *Realschule* curriculum than in the classics, and the best teachers were often attracted to military gymnasia by the courses taught there, by the relative liberalism of the military authorities, and by the relations between teacher and taught, which were warmer than in the classical gymnasia. In themselves of course the military gymnasia were not a sufficient training ground for statesmen, but as a grounding for subsequent higher education they would have been more than adequate.[36]

Inevitably, any brief general survey of Russian military education is bound to gloss over distinctions between the various corps and schools. These distinctions could, however, be very great. Sometimes a single personality, usually but not always that of the director, could stamp itself on an institution, significantly changing its nature. Though A.N. Mosolov thoroughly disliked the Naval Cadet Corps from the start, he found its director, B.A. Glazenapp, a decent and humane man. The same could not be said for his replacement in 1856, Vice-Admiral Davydov, 'an antediluvian savage', whose ferocity poisoned the lives of the cadets and finally persuaded even Mosolov's conservative father to remove his son from the corps.[37]

More lasting than the influence of personalities were fundamental differences in the character of the institutions. The artillery and engineering schools, for instance, as training grounds for technically sophisticated branches of the service, maintained entrance requirements and intellectual standards which were at all times well above those of the average cadet corps. Thus Maksimovsky writes that 'the type of so-called "old cadet", who not only did no theoretical work but openly ignored everything taught him in class and only took any notice of practical soldiering, never existed and never could have existed in the engineering school'.[38]

Equally distinct from the run-of-the-mill cadet corps were the two aristocratic institutions that existed in Petersburg, namely the Corps des Pages and the School of Guards Sub-Ensigns and Cavalry Junkers. Although in 1854 only 2 per cent of Russian army cadets attended the Corps and 2.9 per cent the School, of the 71 members of the State Council educated at military institutions 21 per cent were former pages and 22.5 per cent products of the School of Guards

The products of an aristocratic military education. The Chevaliers Gardes on parade.

Sub-Ensigns. No other institutions even approached these two in the number of future members of the Council whom they educated.[39]

The aristocratic nature of the Corps des Pages fundamentally affected the training of its cadets. In the Nicholas era the senior class of pages was even more convinced of its prerogatives, even less inclined to submit to the influence of mere tutor-officers of much lower social origins, than was the case in other corps. On the other hand, the tutors in the School of Guards Sub-Ensigns and the First Cadet Corps, as well as in the Corps des Pages, tended to treat their well-connected young charges with a good deal more politeness than was the norm in most corps. Boys with the highest grades in class acted as pages at court in their senior years, and the desire to be included in this group was one of the few incentives to academic study in the Nicholas era. Memoirs of the period frequently express the pages' awe at the mystique and splendour of the court, which could leave a lasting impression and form the basis of later loyalties, as well as of extremely powerful connections.[40]

The history of the Corps des Pages from the 1840s to the 1870s combined some elements common to military educational institutions with others that were unique. In the pre-Crimean era, typically, intellectual education was given relatively low priority by the Corps authorities and had little prestige among the pages. The strongest single influence in the school in those years was Girardot, the Company Commander, who was in charge of all non-academic aspects of the pages' lives. One of the last in a line of French émigrés who strove to bring the manners and sympathies of the French Old Regime to the Russian high nobility, Girardot added an aristocratic touch to the externals commonly stressed in cadet corps by putting a heavy emphasis on mastery of perfect French, impeccable service at court as pages, and refined elegance, tact and manners in society.[41]

In the second half of the 1850s, the whole atmosphere of the Corps des Pages changed dramatically. The attention paid to intellectual education both by the authorities and the boys greatly increased. In part this reflected the replacement of one, indifferent, Inspector of Classes, I.F. Ortenburg, by another, excellent, one, P.P. Vinckler. The latter ensured that, in contrast to the Nicholas era, the Corps got the best and liveliest teachers available in Petersburg. If better teaching and tutoring were one cause of greater enthusiasm for learning among the pages, another was simply the mood dominant in Russian society at the time. According to Prince Peter Kropotkin, the pages in the late 1850s began to discuss social and political questions for the first time. Knowledge suddenly took on prestige while in many cases pages resented the tedium and waste of time involved in service at court. Teachers genuinely attempted to widen horizons and encourage critical thought, those who instructed the cadets in the natural sciences arousing such enthusiasm that the pages set up their own independent laboratory.

Amidst this revolution in the established ways of Nicholas's Corps des Pages, Girardot was increasingly isolated and soon retired. Meanwhile in 1857 the rule of the fist exercised by the senior class was overthrown by a revolt of their juniors who, having shaken off the constraints of deference, discovered that force could actually be opposed to force. In time the enthusiastic liberalism of the late 1850s and early 1860s faded in the Corps des Pages, as in upper-class society as a whole, but intellectual standards were never again lowered. Thus M.M. Osorgin, who attended the Corps in the late 1870s, records that the teaching 'was simply brilliant. The majority of the professors were outstanding'.[42]

Even by the standards of the Corps des Pages, the cadets at the School of Guards Sub-Ensigns and Cavalry Junkers were considered wild, the young cavalrymen being particularly notorious. The persecution of juniors was developed into a fine art in the School, as in the Corps des Pages, though a major turn for the better came in very similar fashion after 1857.[43] Cadets at the School had a slightly different profile from pages, according to P.P. Semyonov. The pages had close relatives in high places in the service. Most boys at the School, however, came from old and wealthy landowning families in which, in general, the tradition was to serve in the army for a few years before retiring to one's estates. Half the boys in Semyonov's time brought a servant with them to the School. In the last decade of Nicholas I's reign, when many future members of the State Council attended the institution, there was every justification for the School's historian to comment that its character 'was in many ways distinct from that of the cadet corps of those days'.[44]

Above all, the School of Guards Sub-Ensigns stood out for its academic excellence. If the courses taught were about as varied as a normal cadet corps curriculum, the standards required of the boys both on entry and subsequently were far higher than in the other military educational institutions. The quality of teaching was also much superior. In part this simply reflected the School's wealth, based on high fees, and the upper-class origins of its cadets. The boys came from much better educated and more highly cultured families than the run-of-the-mill cadet-corps product, which in 1838 had made it possible, for instance, to demand high standards of French and German grammar, composition and conversation from would-be entrants.[45]

As the history of the Corps des Pages showed, however, wealth alone was not a guarantee that a school's authorities would pay serious attention to academic study. At the School of Guards Sub-Ensigns it was once again a question of personalities. The School's director in the 1830s was Baron Schlippenbach, a harsh martinet determined that drill and discipline should be excellent but little interested in the academic side of school life. In 1843, however, Schlippenbach was succeeded by A.N. Suthof, who held the directorship for the rest of Nicholas's reign. Suthof was by no means inattentive to drill, external smartness and good discipline, indeed no director of any military school who ignored these matters would have survived for long under Nicholas I. But he also put great stress on education, attracting excellent teachers to the School, including many of the livelier university professors, and doing everything possible to encourage the boys' interest in their studies.

P.P. Semyonov, who was at the School under Suthof, writes that the teaching was excellent, the curriculum more stimulating than that of the average cadet corps, and the teachers almost all greatly respected by the boys. Subjects were taught, especially in the natural sciences, that were outside the normal gymnasium curriculum. The School encouraged independent thinking, Semyonov says, and considerably broadened his view of life. Coming from such a man these are compliments indeed, and in fact the School's academic quality was widely recognized. In 1861 V.V. Wahl, surrounded by graduates of the cadet corps during his first posting in Warsaw, wrote with relief that 'among my new comrades were some young officers from the School of Guards Sub-Ensigns and Cavalry Junkers in Petersburg, coming from good families and well educated, who were interested in more serious questions and with whom it was pleasant to spend one's time'.[46]

Discussing the impact on the ruling élite of education in Russian gymnasia is distinctly less satisfactory than studying the cadet corps. In the first place, there were 74 gymnasia in 1855, 146 in 1871, and almost double that number by the late 1880s. Inevitably standards varied and it is risky to generalize; yet one cannot, as with the cadet corps, pick out one or two institutions where a large percentage of the members of the élite studied. Moreover, unlike the cadet corps, the gymnasium was generally a day school, its purpose being less to mould the whole personality than to train the intellect.[47]

Throughout the nineteenth century the Russian gymnasium aimed to hone the mind. As elsewhere in Europe, in the first half of the century great stress was laid on rote-learning in an effort to train the memory. Under both Nicholas I and Alexander II the educational authorities tried to inculcate the habit of regular, systematic work, close attention to detail, and a rigorous, logical approach to thinking. Refinement of sentiment had no place in the educational system: Russian gymnasium boys under Nicholas I learned a great deal about contemporary Romantic literature, but they did so from each other not from their teachers. The latter employed themselves teaching declensions in Latin grammar and the propositions of mathematical logic. Nor, did the Russian school have any truck with English ideas of games-playing as a source of character formation.[48]

The education provided at the gymnasium was linked to no indigenous tradition. No effort was made to devise courses which might be of particular interest to Russian children, or which Russian educated society might deem necessary and significant. Nor were the schools much used to indoctrinate patriotic or monarchist values, partly because teachers were not trusted to do this but also because this was not considered a proper function of the school. Courses followed closely the French and German models. Careful attention was paid to the way in which Russian history was taught, but it was by no means the gymnasium's main subject. Under Nicholas I pride of place went to Latin, mathematics and modern languages. Subsequently, under Count D.A. Tolstoy, classics became even more prominent, to the loudly expressed dismay of Russian society. In part the classics were unpopular because ancient Greece and Rome were considered alien to Russian traditions and their study seemed irrelevant to contemporary social needs. Moreover, although even under Tolstoy classics took up less of a Russian pupil's time than was the case in Prussia or Saxony, there were fewer competent teachers of Latin and Greek in Russia than in those countries. This contributed to the boredom of classics lessons, and in the (somewhat naïve) view of A.N. Schwartz 'did more to harm classical education as regards Russian society than any other factor'.[49]

Tolstoy and his followers well understood that their educational programmes were unpopular, but regarded this as a failing on the part of Russian society rather than of themselves. I.D. Delyanov, for instance, bemoaning the lack of self-discipline, order and consistency in Russian life, believed that these were failings the educational system must counter and eradicate.[50] Inevitably this effort, often incompetently carried out, to thrust down pupils' throats 'dull, taxing and definitely not politically relevant' courses aroused anger against the gymnasium, which in Allan Sinel's words often became 'an object of derision and hate'.[51] Of course such schools could play little part in shaping a boy's values, save in a distinctly negative manner.[52]

Were one discussing the alienation of society from the state, or the formation of a radical youth culture in Russia, the evil effects of Tolstoy's gymnasia might well need to be underlined. Yet they are barely relevant here, since by definition the men we are discussing were neither radicalized nor alienated from the government and its service. Thomas Darlington, the contemporary English expert on Russian schools, was largely unaffected by Russia's political battles over education and capable of making useful comparisons with the rest of Europe; discussing the education in gymnasia under Nicholas I, Darlington commented in 1909 that pupils 'were as a rule well taught up to the standard of that time'. Of the late nineteenth century he wrote that, 'the Russian boy who has completed a course in the gymnasium or the *realschule* is undoubtedly better developed intellectually than an English public-school boy of the same age'.[53]

Armed with his 'certificate of maturity' from a gymnasium the Russian boy had the right to enter any of the Empire's universities. Virtually all the future members of the State Council studied at either Petersburg or Moscow; but by the standards of a cadet corps or a privileged boarding school for nobles, a university was a large and amorphous institution. In 1865, for instance, Petersburg had an enrolment of 785 and Moscow 1,741. Although most of the future members of the State Council studied law at university, a sizeable minority did not, since civil service entrance requirements specified only the need for a degree, not its nature. Different faculties, however, placed very different burdens on their students. At Petersburg, no sensible student entered the faculties of mathematics or natural science unless he meant to work hard, but the law faculty, the natural target for the many intending civil servants who flocked to university, was noted for the laziness and, sometimes, high life of its students – a pattern familiar in many German universities as well.[54] V.D. Zherebtsov, who studied in the faculty of law in the early 1880s, commented that in his department, 'together with able, business-like and serious workers, there was a mass of superficially thinking young men who had gone to university not to study but only to gain diplomas'. Given the laxness and inconsistency of the examination system, it was not difficult for such students to gain diplomas with a minimal amount of work in the first three-quarters of their course.[55]

Nor is the difference between faculties the only consideration in assessing the impact of university life on students. The universities were extremely vulnerable to political currents, which affected both what was taught and the atmosphere within the student body. The fact that Moscow and Petersburg were great cities, not university towns, made it difficult to live untroubled by political currents and the day-to-day excitements of city life. Scattered across these cities, students tended to form very distinct groups. 'Aristocrats' and 'seminarists' were in their different ways distinct subdivisions within the student body, easily spotted by their life-style, clothes and solidarity. The same was true of non-Russians. Moreover students from families living in Petersburg or Moscow often remained quite separate from 'immigrants', keeping themselves aloof and spending much of their time with friends from their old gymnasium. Because both the education and socialization of students occurred at least as much through their comrades as their teachers, it is worth recognizing just how varied life at university could be.[56]

Since the law faculty of Petersburg University trained many more future members of the State Council than any other university department, we may look initially at the education it provided for its students. An anonymous memoirist of the 1840s devoted most of his time and energy, as did many of his German contemporaries both at Dorpat and in Germany itself, to the student corporation, Ruthenia. Like German students then and later, the memoirist and his fellows were very solemn and serious about their corporation's rules and about suspected insults to its members. He recalls that students of his day were much more childlike than subsequent generations, and worried less about the world's problems. He and his circle seldom attended lectures, swotted like madmen prior to examinations, and had little interest in politics. For most students, he adds, what counted was whether the professor was lively, not whether he was a good scholar. Most of the teaching was dry and dull, except in the mathematics department, and students taught each other more than they learned from their professors.[57]

As one might have suspected, the life of this cheerful student had little in common with that of the diligent and serious-minded F.G.

Terner, who graduated with distinction from the cameralist section of the Petersburg law department in this period. He notes in his memoirs that in the 1840s, corporations still existed at Petersburg but only aristocrats and some Russian-Germans belonged to them. Terner had nothing to do with this side of university life. Nor on the whole did he attend lectures in the law department; since the notes were published, he says, this was unnecessary. Political economy, which in later life became his speciality, had no interest for him at university. Instead he broadened his mind by attending lectures on natural history, natural science and minerology. The university examination system was, he adds, extremely inefficient and arbitrary. Nevertheless, on the whole Terner was satisfied by his education. Unlike later, he wrote, professors did not play to the student gallery by making liberal gestures, and relations between staff and students were informal and easy.[58]

In the last years of Nicholas I's reign the atmosphere in the Petersburg law department was harsher than in Terner's day. F.N. Ustryalov writes that students admired Herzen and accepted his ideas on trust, but were careful to discuss them only in very small groups of intimate friends. A few professors, such as I. Ya. Gorlov, were potentially interesting but constrained hopelessly by political currents of the time. Much more serious was the dry and boring way in which most professors delivered their lectures. Moreover they seldom provided information on practical aspects of jurisprudence, or an interesting survey of legal theory. Instead they tended to expound existing Russian laws. Though, like Terner, Ustryalov admired some of the law professors, particularly I.E. Andreevsky, V.A. Milyutin and D.I. Meyer, he learned as much from lecturers in other faculties as from the lawyers. In addition, he notes, the cameralist course was unsystematic and rather superficial in the range of subjects it sought to study.[59]

The contrast between Ustryalov's memoirs and those of V.V. Sorokin, who studied in the law faculty in the late 1850s, is striking. On the one hand there is the crude repressiveness of the curator, obligatory drill, teaching circumscribed by political constraints and students keeping a low profile. On the other, students are the social lions of the hour, cockily abandoning their lectures to preach radical doctrines to attentive members of the older generation. Sorokin's reminiscences certainly bear out the view that students of this era were more disposed to enthusiasm, idealistic visions and café conversation than to systematic study of their subjects. Professors were admired if they were eloquent and, above all, if they appeared to share the students' moral and political commitments. A comparison of Petersburg University with Dorpat in the late 1850s and early 1860s shows that the Dorpat students had a better grasp of their subjects, faced stiffer examinations and in academic terms simply studied more professionally than their Russian peers.[60]

The evidence cited so far supports Torke's thesis that Russian legal education in the 1840s and 1850s tended to be unsystematic, made little effort to study problems of jurisprudence, and spent too much time explaining Russian laws and too little on comparative and theoretical legal studies.[61] In addition, although there were many advantages to future statesmen in tackling history, political economy and statistics as well as purely legal subjects, the range of the curriculum was probably too wide.[62] What also clearly emerges is that, despite having some fine professors, in the period prior to the very late 1850s the Petersburg law faculty was much inferior to its rival in Moscow.

Indeed when one talks about the golden age of the Russian university with respect to the 1840s, it is always Moscow University that one has in mind. Commenting that in this period 'Moscow University became the centre of all intellectual development in Russia', Chicherin writes that he entered its halls as if going to church. Among a galaxy of famous names, Redkin, Kavelin, Granovsky, Solov'yov, Mulhausen and Shevyryov stand out. Thomas Darlington, not on the whole given to hyperbole, comments that 'seldom in the history of any country has so much intellectual power been concentrated within the walls of a single teaching institution as was to be found in the University of Moscow in the Forties'. Other scholars stress the inspirational quality of Moscow's professors in this decade, as well as the fact that their commitment to Hegelian philosophy gave them a great sense of the law's role in the general progress of mankind. The university suffered severely in Nicholas's last years, Chicherin writing that by 1855 'it was impossible for the soul not to grieve that an institution so recently standing so high should have fallen so low'. Nevertheless, as the memoirs of A.N. Kulomzin show, for all the constraints that existed in the early 1850s, students still derived considerable inspiration from their years at Moscow University, where the liberal spirit in political and legal matters had been tempered rather than extinguished by mere external repression. Kulomzin concludes that what the university provided was not so much factual knowledge, on which in any event most of the law professors were weak, but rather 'a large store of general intellectual development and especially of idealism'.[63]

With the death of Nicholas I and the thaw that occurred under his son, Moscow University breathed more freely again. In 1863 the universities gained a considerable degree of autonomy. Already in the 1850s the quotas which Nicholas had imposed on the number of students and the restrictions on the content of courses had been lifted. Thus in 1859 Moscow University regained the right to teach comparative European constitutional law (i.e. 'State Law of the European Powers'), which was important both as a symbol of the thaw and as a step towards a more analytical approach to legal studies. In the first years of Alexander II's reign the universities resumed their place in the forefront of the movement for the liberalization and westernization of Russian society. For many of the law professors in particular, the creation in 1864 of an incorruptible, efficient and egalitarian system of justice embodied the ideals for which they had striven in the Nicholas era. They had good reason to believe that without their own efforts and those of the students whom they had inspired with a commitment to justice and legality the new judicial statutes would have been inconceivable.[64]

In the new era, however, Petersburg University's law department stood on the same level or even higher than that of Moscow.[65] The curriculum followed by law students was narrowed and better integrated, the rather chaotic cameralist course being scrapped. Above all, however, Petersburg acquired outstanding professors both in the legal field and in other faculties. Even before the University's temporary closure in December 1861, the law faculty had acquired C.D. Kavelin and P.G. Redkin. In the 1860s and 1870s these were joined by A.D. Gradovsky, N.S. Tagantsev, V.I. Sergeevich, F.F. Martens and N.M. Korkunov, to name but a few. These were men of very high intellectual calibre and reputation, who could hold their own with the professors of any university in Europe. In many fields of the law their immense and careful scholarship is still required reading.[66]

V.O. Zherebtsov entered Petersburg's law faculty in the early 1880s, but most of the professors whose courses he describes had been teaching in the 1870s and sometimes even in the 1860s. Zherebtsov makes clear the exceptionally high intellectual standard of the teaching, but he also stresses, in contrast to memoirists of the 1840s and 1850s, that courses were in general well-organized and lectures delivered with clarity and rhetorical skill. In Zherebtsov's view very few professors were not up to their jobs. Lecture courses were, with only two or three exceptions, analytical and intellectually demanding, the old rote-learning of legal catechisms being a thing of the distant past.[67]

It is clear from Zherebtsov's comments, and indeed from reading the works of the Petersburg professors themselves, that the student who wished to think and learn about government, law and administration, Russian and European, had every opportunity to do so in the post-1863 era. How much a student did actually learn was, however, to a considerable extent a question of choice. The examination system, as we have seen, did not force the student to work equally and consistently hard at all his subjects. A few students, alienated from authority by social trends in the 1860s and 1870s, educated each other in groups of like-minded friends and largely ignored official teaching. A much larger contingent, interested only in a final degree, exploited the attractions of Petersburg life and the weaknesses of the examination system. Nevertheless, only an extremely dogmatic and opinionated radical, or a student of exceptional laziness and intellectual drowsiness could have passed through the Petersburg law faculty under Alexander II without any broadening of his mind or sharpening of his wits.

The Alexander Lycée and the School of Law were founded in 1811 and 1835 respectively with the aim of attracting young noblemen into the civil service.[68] Lycéens were intended for the service as a whole, *pravovedy* (i.e., graduates of the School of Law) for the judicial department. Both schools attracted the patronage and close attention of members of the imperial family and to be a graduate of either gave a man a great advantage in rank (*chin*) on entering the service – a factor of real significance in the first half of the nineteenth century when rank was still of key importance in promotions and appointments.[69] Against the sombre background of the early nineteenth-century civil and judicial service, the honesty, idealism and good educations of the Lycéens and *pravovedy* caused them to stand out brightly.

In the second half of the century, however, the universities began to turn out honest, often idealistic and more thoroughly educated young men on a scale that neither of the privileged schools could match. The *raison d'être* of the two schools became somewhat unclear. If they survived, it was in part because parents welcomed the chance to send their sons to a prestigious school whose old boys were a powerful clique in Russian government. The Lycée, where Greek had never been taught, also benefited from the unpopularity of Tolstoy's classical gymnasia, just as both schools gained from parents' concern at what they felt to be the disorder and radicalism of the universities. From the state's point of view the privileged schools were a reliable source of loyal cadres at a time when university education seemed to breed radicalism and was at times subject to disruption. Above all, the two schools survived because they had put down such deep roots in Russian upper-class society in general and the bureaucratic élite in particular. To question the utility of institutions whose, often very loyal, old boys literally swarmed in the State Council, the Senate and in ministerial office would have been hopeless and foolhardy.[70]

As regards academic education the two institutions faced the same basic difficulty, which was indeed insoluble because of their nature and functions. Graduates of the Lycée and School of Law were supposed to be ready to take up posts in the civil service and not, moreover, as clerks but in responsible positions. On the other hand, both schools were closed educational institutions whose inmates, even in the top class towards the end of the nineteenth century, were kept under constraints and discipline much more suitable for school-boys than mature students. It was impossible to keep young men in boarding schools much beyond the age of twenty, indeed many Lycéens and *pravovedy* graduated in their late teens. Quite rightly, Professor Ya.K. Grot reminded the Lycée's graduating class in 1856 that 'you are still at an age when many are only just beginning a university education'. Nevertheless, on graduation the products of both schools were expected to have completed not only a full inter-mediate education but also a good part of a higher, largely legal, education as well.[71]

Inevitably the education received was somewhat rushed, superficial and difficult to absorb. Even in 1885, after certain improvements had been made, Professor N.M. Korkunov complained that the Lycée's students had to finish in three years a bundle of courses on which gymnasium boys often spent twice as long. The same complaint was made by former pupils at both schools in the 1860s and 1870s. Moreover, if entrance requirements for the two schools were rela-tively exacting, they did not guarantee that most of the boys admit-ted would have the brains to learn compressed courses at the required speed. Rushed through their intermediate education, students reached the senior, 'university', courses too young and too ill prepared intel-lectually to grasp much of what they were being taught. Thus the professors from Petersburg University who taught most of these senior courses were forced to scale down both the breadth and the analytical content of their lectures in the realization that unless they did so all but the very clever students would be left floundering.[72]

To make the situation worse, the sixteen-year-old Lycéen or *pravoved* entering the senior classes had to absorb in three years most of the elements of a four-year university law degree. Lecture hours tended to be increased in an effort to provide boys with the knowl-edge they required, but one effect of this was to deprive students of the time for independent study in which the concepts thrown at them could have been absorbed and pondered. This problem was re-cognized by the authorities and efforts were made in the 1860s and 1870s to weed out unnecessary subjects, free more time for pre-paration and, especially at the Lycée, to encourage students to dis-play original thought in their written work. So long, however, as boarding schools were expected to provide the fundamentals of both an intermediate and higher education no fully satisfactory solution was possible. L.S. Birkin, for instance, who graduated from the Lycée in 1871, wrote that his education gave him 'a small stock of ready formulas relating to the law but I can't say that it roused in me a sufficiently conscious attitude even towards these formulas; it taught me to think in a very imperfect way and perhaps not at all'. Seeking an explanation for the Lycée's failure to educate him properly, Birkin blamed not the teachers, who 'inspired and inspire only a very real respect and sincere gratitude', but rather the whole organization and teaching plan of the Lycée, together with the fact that he was 'too young', being barely nineteen on graduation.[73]

Other failings in the academic education offered by the two schools were in general less basic, and more the products of their era. After some students were overheard in 'seditious' conversation in 1849, a military regime was imposed on the School of Law, with all the brutality, stress on externals, and lack of attention to intellectual training this implied. In both schools in the 1840s and 1850s teaching was often boring and ill designed to train thinking minds. Tutors were even more of a problem than professors, and remained so for rather longer. Syuzor's comment on the School of Law's teachers is, however, not only correct but fully applicable to the Lycée as well. 'Disposing always', he wrote, 'of ample material means and giving suitable rights in the service, the School always attracted good scholars and teachers as its professors and teaching personnel. One can with absolute confidence say that for each of its subjects the School had the best teachers of its time.' Thus the eminent professors of the Petersburg law faculty who sent the inmates of the privileged schools to sleep in the 1840s and 1850s made, as we have already seen, a similar impact on university students. And the much more complimentary comments about teachers in the 1860s onwards from memoirs of those at the privileged schools reflect a similar advance in university standards of teaching.[74]

One should not, however, discuss the failings of an education at one or other of the privileged schools in isolation. How did the formal education there compare, for instance, with what was on offer at cadet corps, gymnasia or universities? By comparison with most cadet corps, particularly before 1863, the academic standards were incomparably superior, entrance and graduation examination requirements far higher, the student community much more cultured. Since boys, particularly in the 1840s and 1850s, were more likely to educate each other than to be taught effectively in class, the last point was all-important. Neither at the School of Law nor, even less, at the Lycée was there ever anything approaching the rule of the fist or the conscious anti-intellectualism that dominated most of Nicholas I's cadet corps. On the contrary, there was often considerable respect for scholarship, and for literature and music. By comparison with a gymnasium, the courses at the privileged schools were fuller and taught by teachers with higher reputations. Moreover, teaching was not bedevilled by the animosities that reigned in the classical gymnasia.

As regards the universities, and it is generally with these that the privileged schools are compared, it is unquestionable that a diligent university student interested in doing more than merely pass examinations was intellectually far ahead of a graduate of the privileged schools. The student doing the minimum necessary to secure a diploma in law was a rather different case, and would indeed have been forced to work more diligently at a privileged school. On the other hand, as Serge Witte rightly pointed out, young men at the Lycée or at the School of Law, however clever, were still effectively pupils, acquiring knowledge rather than developing their intellects independently in the much wider, freer and more combative student community of a university.[75]

Although inevitably there were strong similarities between the academic courses followed at the privileged schools and at universities, in general the two types of educational institution and their student bodies were very different. Especially from the 1860s on, the university student was often scruffy and poor, unsure of being able to support himself through his courses and frequently full of anger both against the educational system and the imperial government.[76] The student in the senior classes of a privileged school on the other hand was materially secure, with few doubts as to his ability to complete the course or fears as to his subsequent career prospects. Encouraged to take pride in his elegant behaviour and, especially at the Lycée, to become fluent in French, he wore an old-fashioned uniform with a tricorn hat and a sword. The uniform set him apart from other students, the sword symbolized the aristocratic pretensions of the Lycée and the School of Law and the ethic of *noblesse oblige* which they sought to inculcate in their pupils. Few boys at either school would have doubted N. de Basily's comment that 'the students were united by a solid *esprit de corps*', N.N. Fliege adding that 'a feeling of comradeship, of the honour of our uniform, of corporate spirit, was very strongly developed among all of us'. In a word, the Lycéen or *pravoved* knew he was a member of an élite and was proud of the fact.[77]

This sense of élitism was owed to many factors. Their noble origins to some extent set the Lycéens or *pravovedy* apart from other students in the second half of the nineteenth century, given the democratization of the gymnasia and universities. On the other hand – though, judging from class lists, the proportion of boys from aristocratic or prominent gentry families increased in the nineteenth century – a considerable number always came from relatively poor and undistinguished noble families.[78] The schools indeed owed their aristocratic aura less to the social origins of their pupils than to the self-image and history of the Lycée and School of Law as institutions. Both schools had been founded by the Romanovs,[79] and the imperial family never ceased to show them attention and favour, one aspect of this being the advantages in rank which civil service entrants from the Lycée and School of Law enjoyed by comparison with university graduates.

As important, by the second half of the nineteenth century, was the prominence attained by so many former students of the two schools, particularly of course in the civil service. When, as was very often the case, one of these old boys stressed his loyalty to his school, greeted the young Lycéen or *pravoved* as a member of his own extended school family,[80] and participated enthusiastically in school festivities and committees,[81] the proud sense of belonging to a worthy and distinguished élite was reinforced. In some families numerous members had been educated at the Lycée or School, and loyalty to one or other of the institutions was particularly deep-rooted,[82] which further contributed to the basic solidarity in values, loyalties and aspirations between the schools' authorities and their charges.

This solidarity enabled the authorities of the two schools, in total distinction from those who ran the universities and gymnasia, to hold their charges' loyalty and emotional sympathies, and to steer the boys in what were seen as desirable directions. These last included a cult of loyalty to the dynasty and service to the state, both of which were closely associated in rhetoric and ceremony with the traditions and values of the Lycée and School themselves. So too was the insistence that each student should live and act nobly, behaving with honesty and truthfulness, and serving his country with patriotic unselfishness if he was to be worthy of his predecessors at the two schools and the traditions they had bequeathed. Professor Grot's call to the Lycée's graduating class of 1856 to 'have only one thing in view, everywhere and in all circumstances, regardless of any outward advantages, to act nobly and in good conscience', was very much in tune with the two schools' ethical ideals. Moreover, to do them justice, the authorities at both schools, who were on the whole humane, honourable and intelligent men, went some way to embodying these principles at most periods of the schools' histories.[83]

Baron F.F. Wrangel, a key figure at the Lycée in the 1870s and 1880s, stressed to tutors that they must get to know each of their charges. Truthfulness and honesty were basic attributes of a noble character and 'every effort should be devoted to the eradication of lies and deceit'. Boys must be trained to have an 'always polite and respectful attitude to their elders'. It was vital to inculcate a strong sense of honour in the students. Such concepts had deep roots in the Lycée and it was important to use the senior class to win allegiance to them from their juniors, since the older boys often had greater moral influence than the tutors. 'The public opinion of one's comrades and, so to speak, the corporate feeling about morality are among the most important educative factors in a closed educational establishment.' The collective wisdom and solidarity of the class and the whole student body should be respected, and boys encouraged to fend for themselves with minimal interference in most cases from the authorities.[84]

Although in both schools the potential in using the senior boys to uphold traditions and supervise behaviour was understood, fears of brutality and, still more, homosexuality, put limits on the creation of a prefectoral system. After 1846 the senior and junior courses were kept separate at the School of Law, the boys sharing only the church and the hospital. Similar restrictions existed for decades at the Lycée, though by the last years of the nineteenth century they were 're-duced', since the authorities by then had greater trust in the senior course. An English-style system of prefects was never instituted in the School of Law, however, and prevailed in the Lycée to only a very limited extent in its last years. Efforts at the School of Law to appoint a prefect in each class ran up against the very strong feeling of solidarity and equality that united boys in the same year of study.[85]

A teacher at the Lycée in the 1870s wrote that 'the pupils are strongly united amongst themselves and are ready to defend the interests of the class and, individually, of each of their comrades. In their mutual relations there exists the principle of mutual trust, comradeship, straightness and honesty, to a certain extent even of chivalry'.[86] The comment may seem somewhat sentimental and idealized, but it is echoed in many old boys' memoirs.[87] Of course collective solidarity could mean collective tyranny. An informal 'Court of Honour' of old *pravovedy* persuaded Peter Ilyich Tchaikovsky that he would do better to commit suicide than allow his homosexuality to be publicly revealed to his own and the School's dishonour.[88]

This 'court' had its counterpart in similar bodies which sat in the School and, it seems, the Lycée, to recommend the punishment or expulsion of boys who had offended the institution's honour and its moral code.[89] In the view of V.N. Kokovtsov, this code was fundamentally sound and valuable. Great comradeship and mutual accommodation prevailed in his class, and there was little competition, no considerations of differing wealth and status, and no thoughts about future careers to divide the boys. In his class at the Lycée, he says, there existed a sense of equality, of very decent treatment of one's classmates and of tolerance for varying opinions and habits. Among them the class, the Lycée's traditions and the attitude of the authorities created 'a general, definite set of conceptions, obligatory for all, and an unwritten code absorbed by all of what was and was not "done", what one should strive to do and what one should avoid'. These fundamentally humane values influenced a Lycéen for the rest of his days.[90]

So far the Lycée and the School of Law have been discussed together, almost as if they were the same institution. While it is true that they had many characteristics in common, especially when compared with the cadet corps or universities, considerable differences did exist between them as regards both the academic training and the atmosphere. The School of Law's formal education was geared to a single clearly defined goal, namely the production of judicial officials. Although in the 1850s a number of non-legal subjects were still taught in the School's three upper, 'university' classes, this almost entirely ceased in 1863.[91] Meanwhile the lower three 'intermediate' classes came more and more closely to resemble a gymnasium, with even Greek playing a prominent role between 1876 and 1896, in foolish emulation of Tolstoy's schools. From the start, however, the School of Law, designed to turn out officials rather than legal scholars, put a praiseworthy emphasis on jurisprudence in its senior classes, which set it apart from the universities. As early as the 1840s *pravovedy* were analysing actual cases from the archives of the Ministry of Justice and the Senate, and although one rather bilious former student denied that this training, any more than the lectures on senatorial procedures, was of much value, it no doubt spared young *pravovedy* the confusion felt by Lycéens who, 'on entering service, had never before seen a single administrative file or held in their hands a single volume of the code of laws'.[92]

The degree to which *pravovedy* were educated outside the classroom varied from era to era and from one year's intake of boys to another. The mere fact, however, that a family sent its sons to the School rather than to a cadet corps, at least before the 1860s, suggests that it was slightly more cultured than the bulk of the provincial nobility. The atmosphere in the School in the 1840s gained somewhat from the close and civilizing presence of Prince Peter of Oldenburg, and music and drama were officially encouraged in a way that was not to occur again before the 1880s. More important, Romantic literature strongly influenced the ideals of these young, would-be knightly crusaders for honest, unbiased and effective justice; V.V. Stasov indeed writes that his class learned more from Gogol, Pushkin, Sir Walter Scott, Victor Hugo and each other than from all their lectures.[93]

Nevertheless, K.K. Arsen'ev, at the School ten years after Stasov, makes the following comparison between *pravovedy* and Lycéens in the 1850s: 'I knew well many boys of the same age as myself who were studying at the Lycée and clearly recall that they were much more interested in politics and literature than the *pravovedy*.... The traditions which came down still from Pushkin's time, even if having lost their strength, sustained among Lycée boys well beyond the period I am describing an intellectual ferment which was entirely alien to those studying at the School of Law'.[94]

The significance of role-models may indeed partly explain differences of atmosphere in the Lycée and the School of Law. The latter was a specialist school whose 'official saints' were *pravovedy* who had brought honesty to Russian justice and made a vital contribution to the success of the Judicial Statutes of 1864. The Lycèe's 'official saint' was A.S. Pushkin, a great literary figure, with Prince A.M. Gorchakov, an international statesman, as his understudy. A respect for humanism, literature and the individual personality was part of the Lycée's tradition, and a school which produced M. Saltykov-Shchedrin, N.Ya. Danilevsky and Ya.K. Grot, together with every Foreign Minister but two in the half-century before 1914, could well be described as continuing, at least to some extent, in the tradition of its founding fathers. Even in the late nineteenth and early twentieth century, though of course a basically conservative and monarchist institution, the Lycée still had a tolerant, cultured and, by the norms of the Russian élite, liberal atmosphere.[95]

The Lycée's atmosphere may even have owed something to its broad and humanist curriculum, which put a great stress on foreign languages. Though some critics complained that the study of French, German and English declined somewhat after the reform of the curriculum in 1877, Thomas Darlington still considered the proficiency in modern languages to be 'wonderfully good' at the end of the century. Nevertheless the Lycée curriculum from the 1840s onwards was something of a battleground between two, or perhaps two and a half, warring concepts and traditions. The 'half' was represented by the effort in the late 1840s to turn the Lycée into a training school for future officials of the Ministry of Internal Affairs, mirroring the role that the School of Law played for the judicial department. This effort encountered opposition from staff, boys and the Ministry, and was soon abandoned, though, as we have seen, I.I. Shamshin remained convinced that Lycée graduates' complete lack of acquaintance with chancellery procedures was a weakness for which later generations of Lycéens suffered.[96]

The two main conflicting schools of thought were, however, what might be described as on the one hand jurist-political and on the other generalist-humanist. Before 1877 the two co-existed in a somewhat unhappy tandem, but the 1877 reform of the curriculum represented a triumph for the jurists, while the 1901 changes were the revenge of the humanists. The first school of opinion, of which V.P. Bezobrazov and N.M. Korkunov were leading lights, argued that the Lycée's course was too diffuse and that future officials required above all a thorough grounding in law. The 1877 reform therefore gave a majority of hours to legal studies in the senior classes – though, sensibly, it reserved spots for political economy and finance, and was never able to push back literary and linguistic studies beyond a certain point. Unfortunately, too, history was taught inadequately in the Lycée until the 1880s.[97]

The counter-attack was led by G.N. Vyrubov, a former Lycéen and a professor at the Collège de France, and was linked explicitly to a defence of the Lycée's humanist traditions. The complete man must be educated, argued Vyrubov. No major branch of human knowledge could be ignored. Short courses did not need to be superficial, especially if tough entrance examinations ensured high intelligence among the pupils. Vyrubov complained that 'the present-day Lycée is an entirely unnatural unification of an incomplete gymnasium with an incomplete judicial faculty', adding that Lycéens of the new type stand lower than School of Law men, whose educational programme is at least fully rationally adapted to a definite goal'. Legal training might need to be the norm for most officials, but, argued Vyrubov, 'there ought to be officials of another sort, able to direct the state apparatus, to diagnose the country's true needs and decide in a disinterested way the political problems which lie before it. Such people need not a legal but a general education, encompassing all the functions of social life. The present Lycée doesn't in any sense provide such an education'.[98] Here indeed was an aristocratic cry for a ruling élite of generalists with broad horizons and much of the culture on which the civilized, humanist Russian nobleman had long prided himself. Here too was a call for the Lycée to be different and to stand out defiantly from the common ruck and the trends of the times.

* * *

The most obvious conclusion to be drawn from this chapter is that the education of the Russian ruling élite was distinctly varied. There was a very great difference indeed between the intellectual standards of a cadet corps and of Moscow University in the 1840s, and when distinctions between eras are added to variations among educational institutions the picture becomes even more mixed. Moreover, most of the institutions studied here aimed to form personalities as well as intellects. Closed educational establishments, they had powerful means of moulding the individual in accordance with the desires of the collective, the latter being themselves manipulated to a greater or lesser degree by the authorities.

Of course, the formation of both the intellect and the personality of an individual is a delicate process and crass generalizations about the influence of a particular school must be avoided. L.S. Birkin, a Lycéen in the late 1860s, felt that the school had done little to develop his intellect. He believed that he really only began to think when he became a JP, ten years after his graduation. Nor did the Lycée do much to shape his character or moral sense. In this respect out-of-school influences, and particularly his selfless and humane elder brother, were of much greater importance. The contrast between Birkin and Yu. Yu. Belenkov, both products of the Lycée's 31st graduating class, underlines the general point that even in a boarding school noted for putting a distinct stamp on its inmates, the degree and manner in which a boy is influenced by his schooling differs enormously according to his personality, his family background and ethos, the level of maturity at which he enters the school, and a number of other factors.[99]

The Lycée with its civilized respect for a certain degree of individuality was not so 'totalitarian' an education as Nicholas's cadet corps. Certainly, it is possible to find among the members of the Council examples of the firm, tough, resolute personality that the corps are said to have produced. Among individuals whom we will encounter later, Victor Wahl and Peter Durnovo spring to mind. Here certainly were hard and unsentimental men, whose notions of politics and of the good society bore the mark of their military-authoritarian training. In Durnovo's case, as we shall see, to a personality and basic convictions shaped in the cadet corps was added an intellect not only of a high natural order but also honed by further legal education when Durnovo was already an adult.

An entire chapter of this book has been devoted to Peter Durnovo, another to Anatol Kulomzin, not just because of the intrinsic interest and importance of the two men, but because, in terms of personality, opinions and upbringing, they represent opposite poles within the élite. In each case the link between the man's education on the one hand and his personality and opinions on the other is reasonably clear. In the quality of its intellectual training, in the broadening of horizons, in the models of group life and activity and in the social ideals it offered, Moscow University was barely on the same planet as the Naval Cadet Corps in the 1850s. The liberal, humane, sensitive and 'westernizing' Kulomzin was as surely a product of the former institution as Durnovo was of the latter.

Nevertheless, when we come to look at Kulomzin's career in detail it will be clear that much more than his life at university went into the shaping of his personality and opinions. Indeed, the reason he was at Moscow in the first place, rather than at a cadet corps like most of his peers, was precisely the particular nature of his domestic environment, the domination of female influences and other wholly individual factors. Moreover, if Moscow University shaped Kulomzin's world view, so too, as we shall see, did his two years of travel in Western Europe after graduation.

Though the precise balance between domestic, school and other influences in shaping a man's personality is a complex puzzle which can often only be guessed at, the contrasts among some of the members of the State Council seem clear from their memoirs. One can only speculate as to the damage the Naval Cadet Corps may have done to A.N. Mosolov's personality, but his basic character and certainly his political views seem to have been shaped by his conservative if cultured upper-gentry family. The family influence seems to have been reinforced by that of M.N. Murav'yov, whom Mosolov encountered early in his service career, while in fact not much more than a schoolboy. P.P. Semyonov, on the other hand, though gaining intellectually from his education, seems to have been a mature adult on entering the School of Guards Sub-Ensigns because of harrowing experiences in his earlier life.

In contrast, V.N. Kokovtsov, though stressing his love for his father and family, goes out of his way to underline the influence on his personality exerted by the Lycée. Interestingly, in discussing people and events which subsequently exerted a powerful intellectual and moral influence on him, Kokovtsov emphasizes the fact that two key individuals, D.M. Sol'sky and Ya.K. Grot, were former Lycéens. A fundamentally lonely man, not much inclined to warmth in his relationships, Kokovtsov unquestionably derived a good deal of emotional succour from the Lycée family to which he felt very strongly that he belonged.[100]

With all the necessary reservations and all due respect for the complexities of the human character and its formation, one can still see, to take but one example, the shadowy outline of a family resemblance among the Council's Lycéens. Very often there was a genuinely civilized and humane outlook, a cosmopolitanism linked to excellence in foreign languages. There was too a strong monarchism, combined, however, with a commitment to European standards of behaviour and distinctly liberal-conservative political ideals and hopes. There was also a polish and an elegance, a consciousness in many cases of having come from a 'good' family and of possessing powerful connections. Of course this is chasing shadows, for all these characteristics can be found in non-Lycéens as well – most of whom were, after all, products of the same Russian upper-class world as were the Lycéens. Though the men were very different in personality and by no means alike even in their political views, a common thread nevertheless runs through – to take but a few examples at random – from D.F. Kobeko and M.P. Kaufmann, efficient, liberal senior officials and intelligent amateur historians, to Andrei and Peter Saburov, members of an ancient Muscovite boyar family but linked closely to the most humane and civilized circles in Petersburg society; the thread runs on through Lobanov-Rostovsky, Izvol'sky and Sazonov, for the Lycée's traditions and world-view were suited to the production of European diplomats, on to Kokovtsov himself and to a number of others. It was possible to emerge from the Lycée as an uncivilized, narrow-minded brute, but there was not much excuse for doing so.[101]

What can be said more generally about the training members of the State Council received at educational institutions for their future professional roles? The professional training of officers is of no concern to us here, which is why I have passed over in silence the higher military academies, which served this function exclusively.[102] Little more can be said, however, about professional training for future civil servants at the educational institutions studied, since this barely existed save for future jurists. As we have seen, Torke concludes that, at least before the foundation of the School of Law, legal studies in Russia provided a very inadequate professional training even for the latter, who emerged from university with no practical grasp of jurisprudence or of how the Russian judicial system functioned. Indeed in Torke's view the future bureaucratic élite's lack of a proper grounding in law was one of its key weaknesses.[103]

Without at all wishing to rule Torke's objections out of court, they do need to be put in context. Torke writes in the distinctly Prussian, or perhaps Prusso-German, tradition as regards the proper education of officials. The British tradition, combining a general, usually classical or humanist, education with on-the-job apprenticeship, is distinctly different and closer by far to the Russian imperial model. As we shall see, Russian higher officials were divided as to the proper pre-entry training for high officials. Meanwhile Serge Witte, for one, put forward arguments about the specific and distinctly anti-legalist training requirements of officials in underdeveloped Russia which would be grist to the mill of latter-day theorists of 'development administration'.[104] Nor should G.N. Vyrubov's comments be forgotten. As he rightly stated, the graduates particularly of privileged schools were being trained to become not just ordinary civil servants but a political governing élite, the only one Russia possessed. Wide horizons were a requirement for such people. It may well be that a broad understanding of history, anthropology, political economy, finance and foreign cultures and languages was more valuable for such an élite than a purely legal training.

In conclusion, two general points: The first is that, although the professional training of future members of the ruling élite may well be judged inadequate, they had nevertheless been brought up to serve something beyond their own self-interest and more abstract than the mere person of their sovereign. Among the military cadets, regiment and country ranked alongside the sovereign, while at the privileged schools and the universities service to the common good and to abstract ideals of progress, national prosperity and justice were strongly stressed.

Secondly, as regards intellectual and cultural education, one must remember that in the nineteenth century the rather small Russian upper class, from which most of the 215 members of the State Council were drawn, made a contribution to world culture incomparably greater than any of its European equivalents. If one looks at the British or the German aristocracy and gentry, where is one to find in the sphere of literature figures on the scale of Pushkin, Lermontov, Turgenev, Tyutchev or Tolstoy? In music no Western élite produced a Mussorgsky, a Borodin, a Rimsky-Korsakov, a Rachmaninov or even a Taneev. Moreover it is worth stressing that this Russian group is drawn from a narrow circle, not from the whole hereditary noble or even hereditary noble landowning estate, a wider body which would immediately include Dostoevsky, Tchaikovsky and indeed most other significant figures in nineteenth-century Russian culture.[105] It would be very strange indeed if the 215 members of the ruling élite, drawn from the same world as these cultural figures, virtually all at the same educational institutions as them,[106] and in some cases their friends or even close relatives, turned out *en bloc* to be an uneducated, uncivilized or intellectually lifeless group. In fact, as we shall see, this was very far from being the case.

CHAPTER 4

THE ROADS TO POWER

In late imperial Russia the most important governmental positions were generally held, as we have seen, by career civil servants. A few key figures in government were military or naval officers, or even indeed professors and businessmen. Others were landowning nobles, much of whose lives had been devoted to private activities rather than affairs of state. Many even from these latter groups had, however, spent part of their lives in the bureaucracy. Thus the path to political power lay through the civil service in the last decades of the Old Regime, and an attempt to see how bureaucratic careers influenced mentalities, values and opinions should tell one a good deal about the nature of the Russian governmental élite.

I

The civil service regulations, contained in volume III of the Code of Laws, set out in seemingly great detail a host of rules covering, amongst other points, entry to the civil service, promotions and appointments, and pensions. But the impression of the Russian bureaucracy these regulations convey is not only inadequate but extremely misleading. Senior officials in the late nineteenth century were unanimous in stressing that the regulations were a patchwork of often vague and contradictory rules, never adequately codified and by that time largely unworkable.[1] Few would have disagreed with Vladimir Kokovtsov's comment that, 'among the parts of the existing Code of Laws one could scarcely find a section more outdated than volume III, "The Statute Concerning the Service of Those Appointed by the Government". If someone were set the task of depicting the civil service of contemporary Russia on the basis of the regulations laid down in this volume one would get a picture which very far from coincided with the truth'.[2]

Kokovtsov's comment is relevant when one studies conditions for entry to the civil service. At first glance, even at the end of the nineteenth century large sections of the population appear to be excluded from an official career on the basis of their membership in 'non-privileged' estates.[3] In practice, however, exemptions from the rules were so widespread and evasion of the law so common that privileged access to the bureaucracy had largely become a myth.[4] Thus Article 146 of the 1896 regulations alone exempted 33 categories of posts, covering 73,003 jobs, from the rules covering officials' social origins, a figure which is all the more remarkable given the existence of other similar, albeit less all-encompassing, articles.[5] Indeed in Kokovtsov's view, legally established noble privilege, previously of real importance as regards civil service careers, was by the turn of the century 'without any practical significance'.[6] This had indeed long been the case for civilian officials who aspired to hold top governmental posts. Though the regulations never required those occupying senior jobs to have had a higher education,[7] in practice by Nicholas II's reign the overwhelming majority of top officials educated at civilian schools had been to universities or other institutions of higher education.[8] Even in the reign of Nicholas I, however, any graduate of such an institution, regardless of his social origins, enjoyed the unrestricted right to enter the civil service, beginning his career at a rank much senior to that of a less well-educated nobleman.[9]

Though the young graduate of a Russian institution of higher education had the right to become a civil servant, to enter a specific department and to occupy a particular post, he needed to gain the approval of the chiefs of the branch of the civil service in which he wished to work.[10] Precisely whom he had to petition varied from ministry to ministry, and depended on whether the young man wished to serve in Petersburg or the provinces.[11] The basic principle was, however, always that, in Witte's words, senior officials who bore the responsibility for the correct functioning of a department must have the right to select the candidates whom they considered suitable to fill subordinate posts in 'their' ministries.[12]

Inevitably, since departmental chiefs possessed this right of co-option, they could reject candidates whom they considered unsuitable not only for professional but also for social reasons. The most flagrant example of this was the diplomatic service, ironically one of the few branches of the Russian bureaucracy for which a specific 'professional' examination had since 1859 denied automatic access to anyone with a higher education. Memoirs make it clear that this examination was sometimes used to exclude the socially undesirable rather than the stupid candidate from a diplomatic career.[13] Using an argument dear to all heads of Russian civil service departments, N.K. Giers, the Foreign Minister, could, however, confidently defend his ministry's selection procedures, stressing that the Foreign Ministry 'better than any other institution can judge to what extent a given candidate, by his general level of knowledge and education, as well as in other respects, meets the demands of service in this department and especially in embassies, missions and consulates'.[14]

Even had they wished to emulate the Foreign Ministry, most Russian departmental chiefs would, however, have been unable to do so. Nor, if they wanted to have well-educated staffs in their offices, could they afford to be nearly as selective as their Prussian counterparts.[15] The reason for this was simply supply and demand. In Russia the supply of educated candidates was so small even in 1900 that the Peretz Commission could not think of demanding a complete secondary education as a qualification for entry into ranked officialdom.[16] It is true that, with four-fifths of officialdom serving in the provinces, the central bureaucracy could afford to set relatively high standards for young entrants, especially since most graduates wished to avoid provincial service, where conditions and pay were poor and career prospects far worse than in Petersburg.[17] This fact, coupled with the development of Russian higher education, meant that by 1900 even assistant desk officers' posts could generally be filled by recruits with a higher education. Two generations earlier, when the 215 members of the State Council entered service, matters had been distinctly different.[18]

With the exception of the judicial department and a number of smaller technical branches, jobs in the civil service were open to graduates from all university faculties and many other institutions of higher education. The regulations' failure to link special types of education to future career paths was strongly criticized by I.D. Delyanov and S.A. Taneev in the 1880s.[19] Proposals to demand a 'relevant' educational background for entry to a specific department were, however, greeted without enthusiasm by other ministers, particularly the heads of the 'generalist' departments of internal and foreign affairs.[20] Thus, objecting to Delyanov's proposals, I.N. Durnovo argued that 'people who have successfully passed through higher education and who have not taken any special administrative examination are willingly accepted into service in all departments because thanks to their wider vision and greater sharpness they can cope easily with any administrative activity, regardless of the faculty in which they studied'.[21]

The young graduate entrant could in general expect no formal in-service training or probationary period before taking up his post.[22] He must learn his job as he went along, in the style of an apprentice, though usually he had, at least formally speaking, no master assigned to teach him his trade. It is true that, in an effort to ensure that well-educated young officials had a training in Russian provincial realities, Nicholas I had stipulated that a graduate entrant should spend his first three years' service outside the capitals under the supervision of

the provincial governor.[23] After Nicholas's death, however, this rule
went 'completely unobserved',[24] and, except in the judicial department, no other system of in-service training replaced it. Moreover,
although the judicial department's system of 'candidates', formally
established in 1864, came in for much attention from the Peretz
Commission, the comments of senior judicial and procuratorial
officials make it clear that this system had many gaps, and had indeed
only really got started in the 1880s and 1890s.[25] The lack of an effective system of in-service training was owed in part to the fact that
senior officials formally responsible for the training of juniors were
overburdened by other tasks. Above all, however, as a comparison
with the Prussian system of in-service training makes clear, neither
the parents of prospective officials nor the Russian state could afford
to support young men in the Prussian style through a lengthy period
when they would be working without pay to master their future
profession.[26]

Comparisons between Russia and Prussia are indeed of interest
across the whole range of the formal education and in-service training of prospective officials. By contrast with the Prussian pattern of
strictly defined university courses and many years of closely supervised and examined in-service probationary training, the Russian
regulations seem extremely loose and undemanding. Whether the
strict parameters, the duration and the thoroughness of the Prussian
administrator's preparation were unmitigated blessings is, however,
a moot point. Prussian critics of their own administration stressed
that a largely legal education and training was a poor preparation
either for political leadership or for understanding contemporary
social and economic realities. Moreover, the great expense of supporting young men through years of unpaid training made it necessary that graduate entrants to the civil service come from wealthy
families, something that was not necessarily true in Russia.[27] Such
arguments would not, however, have been echoed by most Russian
senior officials, who on the whole looked up to 'Prussia, which
beyond question enjoys an excellent officialdom and a model civil
service system'.[28]

The sharp differences between Russian and Prussian civil service
procedures extended not only to recruitment and training but also to
many other aspects of an official's career. Thus D.M. Sol'sky, contrasting Russia with the other major European states, noted that
Russian civil service regulations did not lay down 'detailed rules
about the requirements and qualifications which people appointed to
specific jobs have to meet'.[29] P.L. Lobko stated that

> only in the specialist departments – in the ministries of war and
> Justice – has the principle of gradual advancement and the require-

ment of specified qualifications for appointment to specific jobs, with rare exceptions, been applied. In the administrative sphere one does not know whether even the possibility of establishing such a system in appointments has seriously been considered at any time. All that has existed are different tendencies in appointments policy, which emerged under the influence of the individuals who exercised power at particular times.

Lobko contrasted Russian procedures with those existing in 'Prussia and generally in Germany, where a strict system as regards career patterns adequately ensures that jobs are occupied by people who are fully trained for them'. In Lobko's view an even greater rigour existed in France, which helped to explain why the French administration functioned with such speed and efficiency despite the instability of its political masters.[30]

Lobko's enthusiasm for tighter rules governing appointments to jobs was not shared by all high officials.[31] Had his opponents possessed foreknowledge of the immediate future they could well have argued that the performance of Russian generals on the battlefield scarcely justified Lobko's pride in the army's rigorous appointments policy. In fact Lobko's critics maintained that the bureaucracy was so diverse in its functions that it was useless to establish specific qualifications for types of jobs through general civil service regulations. Efficiency demanded that each minister be trusted to decide for himself what experience and skills were required for positions in his department.[32] Senior officials differed as to just how much leeway ministers should be given. V.N. Kokovtsov, the most effective spokesman for ministerial discretion, argued that unqualified persons would rarely be appointed, 'for the simple reason that this would not be in the interests of the chief himself, who is responsible for the correct management of affairs in the part of the administration entrusted to him'. He added that 'the need to fill jobs with persons qualified for them is so great that even in those departments for which no regulations exist on this point, definite principles have been worked out, because of the evident need for them, which are accepted as guidelines in appointing men to posts which become vacant'.[33]

The traditional Russian method of seeking to ensure that posts were filled by men of the requisite skill and experience was the rank (*chin*) system; indeed in theory this system provided the key to all promotions and appointments procedures in the civil service. The main nineteenth-century legislation on promotions and appointments was Nicholas I's laws of 25 June 1834[34] and 20 November 1835.[35] Nicholas inherited Peter I's Table of Ranks, whereby each civil servant (save for the horde of messengers, watchmen and junior clerks) held a rank which was directly equivalent to that of an officer in the armed forces. To match the 14 ranks into which civil servants were divided, Nicholas's government categorized all posts in the civil service according to 14 classes.[36] Henceforth an official was to have the right to occupy only those posts whose class was more or less equivalent to his own rank. Nor could he be promoted in rank unless he held a job of a roughly appropriate class. Fixed terms were established to regulate the speed at which officials could be promoted in rank. Under Nicholas I these terms differed according to an official's education and social status, but the law of 9 December 1856 abolished those distinctions.[37] Henceforth officials in ranks 14 to 8 were promoted at the rate of one step every three years. Promotion in ranks 8 to 5 came every four years, and movement above rank 5, as one approached the apex of the civil service, depended on imperial good will.[38] By law all such promotions were supposed to happen only if an official showed diligence and efficiency. In practice, however, unless he actually committed a crime an official could expect regular promotion in rank, so long as no flagrant divergence between his rank and the class of his job drew the attention of authorities outside his ministry.[39] For an official who showed special ability and zeal the fixed term for promotion in rank could be reduced by one year.[40]

The practical effect of these regulations was that a university student aged twenty-two who entered the civil service at rank 10 could by law not be a candidate for the directorship of a department or the governorship of a province before he reached the age of forty, unless of course he had been promoted on one or more occasions for reasons of special zeal and ability.[41] The best students of the Alexander Lycée and the School of Law, however, entered the civil service at rank 9 and were moreover usually younger than university students. For them the law by no means excluded reaching a directorship or governorship in their mid-thirties, which, by the standards of most modern European civil services, was a tender age to bear the heavy responsibilities that governorships and directorships entailed.[42]

The Table of Ranks and the system of promotions and appointments with which it was closely associated have come in for much criticism both in nineteenth-century Russia and subsequently.[43] In particular, automatic promotion in rank and the legal requirement of senior rank for candidates for political office have at times been seen as breeding a spirit of routine and mediocrity in the governing class. Indeed, immortalized by Gogol, the *chin* has come to embody, even in the eyes of some to cause, the distasteful essence of Russian bureaucracy. Thus Count I.I. Vorontsov-Dashkov wrote in the 1890s that when in 1885 I gave it as my opinion that ranks ought to be abolished, I saw in this a means to a radical cure of bureaucracy. A closer acquaintance with civil institutions has, however, forced me to alter my original view. In reality there is no reason to suppose that the harmful side of bureaucracy, namely chancellery red tape, lack of connection with reality and with the true interests of the country, will disappear with the abolition of ranks.[44]

Vorontsov-Dashkov's opinion came close to the truth, for the *chin* system, imposing from a distance, seems ever less important the closer one gets to the reality of civil service operations. In the first place, even Nicholas I's initial legislation had allowed the appointment to a post of an official one rank above or below the post's class. In provincial jobs much greater flexibility was allowed.[45] After Nicholas I's death the entire judicial department, all provincial posts, and sections of every ministry secured exemption from the rules governing promotions and appointments.[46] Moreover, it is clear both from Daniel Orlovsky's study of the Ministry of Internal Affairs[47] and from the complaints of Vorontsov-Dashkov, K.K. Rennenkampf, V.A. Neporozhnev and A.S. Taneev[48] that enormous evasion of the legal regulations was practised by ministries after 1858, when Alexander II abolished the civil service inspectorate[49] established by his father as a private watchdog over the bureaucracy.

It is nevertheless true that members of the Peretz Commission believed that *chin* requirements still caused problems, especially where senior appointments were concerned.[50] In this context it is no doubt relevant that only at the senior levels could the monarch and his Personal Chancellery keep any watch on appointments and interfere with ministers' full freedom of action. There is no evidence, however, that at those levels the theoretical need for a man's rank to coincide with a post's class caused major difficulties. Indeed even for senior officials the coincidence of rank and class seems in practice to have been a matter of chance. Thus in 1892, of the 2,536 men who held the rank of Senior Civil Counsellor (rank 4), only 283 (11 per cent) occupied jobs of the 4th class.[51] Moreover, study of the published service records of late nineteenth- and early twentieth-century ministries confirms the complaints of senior officials that the system of ranks was in chaos, with ministers and desk officers sometimes holding the same rank, jobs of the 5th class being held by officials of rank 10, and junior officials often having no rank at all.[52] Finally, in my own study of the 215 members of Nicholas II's State Council I have encountered marked evasion of the civil service regulations and not a single example of a man failing to be appointed to a job because of his lack of the correct rank.[53] The evidence derived from a study of actual bureaucratic careers seems therefore to bear out the comment by Prince P.D. Svyatopolk-Mirsky that 'difficulties stemming from the need for rank and job to correspond are hardly felt at all in reality, and service practice yields no examples of cases where a capable man was not appointed to a job only because he lacked the necessary rank'.[54]

On the other hand the need, under the regulations, to get the Emperor's consent each time a non-official was appointed to any significant post may well have limited the government's ability to draw on men with experience and abilities different from those of civil servants. Even I.L. Goremykin, the Minister of Internal Affairs, who was not very dissatisfied with the civil service regulations, believed that the rules were obstructing his desire to draw zemstvo and municipal government officials into his department's service.[55] It was, however, the Ministry of Finance that was most outspoken in its determination to open its ranks to qualified non-officials. Arguing that the Russian financial administration fulfilled many functions which in the West were performed exclusively by private enterprise, Witte stated that his department must, where necessary, be allowed to recruit senior personnel from the private sector, since these 'outsiders' were often better qualified than officials to run certain branches of the Finance Ministry.[56]

In attempting to open middle-ranking and senior positions in the civil service to outsiders, Witte encountered obstacles which were, however, much more basic and formidable than volume III of the Code of Laws. The papers of the Peretz Commission show that most top officials were unwilling to make access to the civil service easier for outsiders, and were insistent that such 'invasions' should be kept to the strictly necessary minimum. Most ministers and senior officials argued that considerable administrative experience was essential for those occupying high governmental posts, and were determined to preserve a proper hierarchy and career structure within the civil service. They looked with jealousy on any incursion of non-officials into top administrative posts, a jealousy that was in part fuelled by the feeling that their own monopoly of such positions recompensed them for the (by the standards of the private sector) inadequate salaries they received.[57] Such attitudes, probably inevitable in any professional bureaucracy, obviously have a serious effect on the nature and mentality of the governing élite when, as was the case in Russia, access to top political positions lies in large part through the ranks of the civil service. Yet even here a certain balance is required. As we have already seen, however much it may have disliked outsiders' incursions, the civil service never monopolized top political positions. Moreover, as I have already noted, the two most important domestic departments, namely Internal Affairs and Finance, were particularly open to 'outsiders' from the landowning nobility and the financial–industrial world respectively.

The evidence presented thus far, drawn overwhelmingly from the minutes of the Delyanov and Peretz special commissions and the comments made by ministers and senior officials on the commissions' findings, cannot of course tell one everything one would like to know about the reality of promotions and appointments procedures in the Russian civil service. The careers of the 215 members of the State Council spanned the years between the 1840s and the eve of the Revolution, a period in which, inevitably, much changed in the civil service. Moreover, even if one could come to firm judgements about promotions and appointments in one ministry it would be unwise to imagine that such judgements must apply to the civil service as a whole. As the Emperor's Own Personal Chancellery rightly stated, in the second half of the nineteenth century the looseness of the regulations, added to the lack of any central institution which could force departments to observe them, meant that ministries went their own way as regards promotions and appointments procedures.[58] Finally, a point of common sense, appointments in any organization reflect the views and capabilities of the individuals and groups who run that institution: generalizations about the 'quality' of appointments have to take this factor into account.

For these reasons it would be foolish to make self-confident generalizations about promotions and appointments procedures throughout the whole period and across the whole range of the bureaucracy. Equally, given our lack of empirical evidence it would be premature to indulge in theoretical debates as to whether 'the Russian bureaucracy' adhered to 'rational-legal', 'patron-client' or any other of the models beloved of political scientists. Nevertheless, before being too carried away by the stress placed here on the gaps and loopholes in Russia's civil service regulations, we should remember R.F. Kaufman's warning that the 'tendency to dismiss formal rules and norms as "façades" which disguise the reality of personal rule is much over-emphasized in analysis of clientelist organizations'. It was after all the law which legitimised the real hierarchy of the Russian bureaucracy, granting senior officials the power to appoint, promote, reward or punish their juniors. Secondly, despite evidence of the importance of cliques and personal relationships, one should not forget K.R. Legg's comment that 'given the complexity of bureaucracies and the problems of information flow and evaluation, recruitment and career advancement (in both government and the private sector) can rarely be determined on achievement criteria alone. Rather the accidents of opportunity and friendship loom large'.[59]

As regards appointments policy only one branch of the late

nineteenth-century bureaucracy, namely the provincial governors, has been subjected to detailed study. Unfortunately, the two works on appointments of governors, by Werner Mosse[60] and Richard Robbins,[61] come to almost diametrically opposite conclusions. Mosse stresses the unsystematic, varying and haphazard nature of the appointments, which were in his view much influenced by candidates' personal connections. Robbins, on the other hand, states that 'while favouritism and patronage continued to play a role in determining advancement to gubernatorial positions, training and expertise became ever more important in decisions on appointments'. The Ministry attempted with increasing success to ensure that governors would not be appointed unless they possessed administrative expertise and considerable experience of the problems of governing Russia's provinces.[62]

Both scholars' opinions have something to recommend them. Mosse's view is, for instance, precisely that of P.L. Lobko and was shared by other contemporaries.[63] Moreover it might be reasonable to suspect that jobs filled usually by upper-class generalists were more likely to be the subject of backstairs intrigues and court connections than more specialized jobs in less 'aristocratic' departments. On the other hand, Robbins's study of the governors not only utilizes extensively the records of the Ministry of Internal Affairs' personnel administration, but also combines this with deep knowledge of the actual performance of governors when facing various crises 'in the field'. For this reason his conclusions, which like Mosse's can also find support from other sources,[64] deserve particular respect.

Moving beyond gubernatorial appointments into other areas of the civil service, one finds great differences existing among the various ministries as regards the professionalization of their appointments procedures. At one extreme is the Ministry of State Properties, which between losing control over the state peasants in the 1860s and becoming a genuine Ministry of Agriculture in the 1890s was the Cinderella among the departments of state. According to Kulomzin, who as assistant Minister of State Properties between 1879 and 1882 ran personnel policy, there was a total absence of any system or logic as regards promotions and appointments in this ministry in the 1870s.[65]

The wife of one senior official claimed that matters were not much better in the Ministry of Communications even at the turn of the century. 'No definite lines of policy and no lists of candidates are kept', she complained. 'Everything depends on personal connections or on the ability to keep reminding people about oneself' – something most easily achieved of course by an official stationed in Petersburg.[66] Moreover, according to Witte, cliques of old boys from the School of Communications Engineers tended to dominate the appointments and promotions system in that ministry and to use their power for the benefit of their comrades.[67]

Yet it would be wrong to imagine that such procedures invariably prevailed in other departments. At the opposite extreme of the civil service, for instance, one had the State Chancellery and Chancellery of the Committee of Ministers. In both these élite institutions, at least from the 1860s, highly efficient cadres were selected on a professional basis by dedicated, hard-working and intelligent chiefs.[68]

For our purposes the most interesting department is, however, the Ministry of Justice. This is partly because, as we have seen, so many members of the State Council were former procurators or judges, but also because the evidence to hand as regards promotions and appointments in this ministry is more plentiful than that available for any other department. For a number of reasons one might expect promotions and appointments procedures in the Ministry of Justice to have been more efficient than those operating in the rest of the civil service. As we have seen, the judicial department was unique in the degree of specialized professional training, both at university and during probationary service, which it demanded from young officials. Its rigorous and detailed specification of the qualifications needed by candidates for any judicial or procuratorial post won even Lobko's approval and, according to M.V. Murav'yov, the Minister of Justice, worked well and caused few problems.[69] Moreover, as we shall see, after the influx of able young men in the 1860s and 1870s the judicial department's cadres formed one of the élites of the civil service. Given the generally high quality of senior judicial personnel in the last decades of imperial Russia, it may seem strange to suggest that there were very serious problems in promotions and appointments procedures in this ministry.

Nevertheless difficulties existed. As always, some criticisms of judicial promotions and appointments procedures may have been biased and fuelled by personal motives. When, for instance, A.V. Lyadov stated that I.G. Shcheglovitov ignored professional advice and criteria in appointing men to judicial posts, considering instead their political views and personal connections,[70] he may have been attempting to revenge himself on his former chief and to curry favour with his new masters in the Provisional Government. It is, however, also possible that Lyadov's criticisms of Shcheglovitov were justified and that they reflected not only the minister's personal failings but also the increasing politicization of the bureaucracy as a whole in the constitutional period, together with the diminished autonomy of the judicial department given the existence since 1905 of the Council of Ministers.

Certainly the complaints of S.E. Kryzhanovsky about judicial appointments procedures are difficult to dismiss as the product of personal bias. He argued that the relatively small size of the judicial department made cliques and 'personal relations' much more significant as regards promotions and appointments than was the case, for instance, in the larger and more impersonal Ministry of Internal Affairs. In Kryzhanovsky's view this factor had an influence that was wholly harmful on the way appointments were made.[71] Given the clear evidence presented earlier that former pupils of the School of Law appear to have exercised considerable influence on the judicial department's appointments system, Kryzhanovsky's comments take on a redoubled significance.

Much the most valuable source on promotions and appointments procedures in the judicial department is, however, the minutes of a conference of senior judicial officials held in Petersburg in the winter of 1894–5 under the chairmanship of the Minister, N.V. Murav'yov. Complaining that in Western Europe 'the rules about service careers are much fuller and more precise', Murav'yov reported that he had been studying new French legislation for further perfecting their system of judicial promotions and appointments. As regards the defects of the present Russian system, he stated,

> what above all draws one's attention is the considerable predominance [*znachitel'noe preobladanie'*] of the element of chance, which it is, however, very hard to combat. . . .the picture available to the high-level institutions and officials who direct the appointments system is of necessity extremely limited; some of these officials put forward only those people who are, so to speak, to hand, while others appoint only candidates recommended to them or people who are by chance known to the central authorities. . . . Aside from protection and politicking [*iskatel'stvo*], which are completely unacceptable in such an important and sacred affair as that of justice, even when the leadership fulfils its obligations in the most honest manner when making appointments to judicial positions, it cannot be free of the injustified fear that in the given case a truly worthy person will be forgotten, and that in different circumstances the given appointment would not have been made. The lack of information about all suitable candidates for appointment to judicial posts is felt both in the Ministry of Justice and in the judicial instances.[72]

Murav'yov's solution to this problem lay in the annual composition by conferences of top judicial personnel of a complete, and subsequently published, list of candidates for each job along the lines proposed by the new French legislation.[73] Not all the senior judges, procurators and officials attending the conference agreed with Murav'yov's solutions, but there was almost general recognition of the problem he had defined and a common belief that it needed to be tackled. Interestingly, the senior judges and procurators at the conference shared Murav'yov's doubts on the system of collective, collegial making of judicial appointments which at that time existed in the district courts and judicial chambers. In the opinion of E.F. de Rossi, for instance, where colleges of judges made appointments, 'two or three people, knowing by chance a given individual, will put forward his candidacy, and the remainder, trusting their colleagues, will agree to this'.[74] In addition, the chairman of the Petersburg Judicial Chamber, I.I. Vlezkov, stated that if collegiate bodies were given the task of drawing up lists of candidates, then, unless the jobs concerned were solely in their own institutions, 'in the final analysis the colleges will be governed almost exclusively by seniority'.[75]

Although a study of promotions and appointments procedures in the various departments of the Russian bureaucracy yields many insights, if one wishes to understand how in practice men reached the top of the imperial civil service one has to investigate the careers of particular officials and attempt to distil from their experience what were the most significant ingredients of their success. Fortunately, the careers of the 215 members of the State Council provide ample evidence for such a study.

One member of the State Council, Fyodor Terner, wrote in his memoirs that 'the life of a young man whose father has connections is much easier than that of a young man who has to carve out his own way for himself, to do which is not easy'. The careers of many top officials bear out this emphasis on family connections. In Terner's own case, for instance, his family was of humble origins, as we have seen, and his father, a doctor, died when Fyodor was still an adolescent. Nevertheless many of Dr Terner's friends and former patients helped Fyodor Terner in his career. Although he graduated first among the students of cameralism at Petersburg University, it was the support of his father's former patient, Count Alexander Borch, which won Terner a junior post in the Foreign Ministry in 1851. Subsequently, when it became apparent that his connections were much too weak to enable him to advance in this most aristocratic of government departments, it was Borch again who helped to ease Terner's transfer into another ministry.[76]

If family connections could prove vital, particularly at the outset of a young man's career, so too could links forged in élite schools or regiments. Whereas for ordinary mortals entry into the Foreign Ministry was extremely difficult, P.S. Botkin records that 'no obstacles hindered Lycéens. . . . Young people from this privileged institution moved into the Ministry directly from the school bench as if from one room to another'.[77] Equally, A.N. Trubnikov was introduced to the Minister of Internal Affairs at a Life Guards Lancers celebration, a meeting which resulted in a lucrative appointment as a Special Duties official in the Ministry.[78] Frequently, of course, membership in exclusive schools and regiments implied impressive family connections,[79] and it was often a combination of all three that secured young men plum jobs. A.N. Mosolov's career was, for example, decisively influenced by his first posting to the staff of M.N. Murav'yov, Governor-General of Vilno, who not only taught his young subordinate basic administrative skills but also established him as a junior member of the Russian nationalist tendency within the ruling élite. Mosolov's position on the Governor-General's staff was secured through the friendship of his brother, a former cadet of the School of Guards Sub-Ensigns and an officer of the Life Guard Hussars, with Murav'yov's grandson. Moreover, Mosolov was saved from obscurity among the many members of Murav'yov's staff by the patronage of the Governor-General's wife, who had him transferred to her husband's private office, frequently invited him to lunch, and in other ways brought him to the attention of the formidable Murav'yov. Mosolov gained the patronage of Madame Murav'yov in part through private letters of introduction, but this intelligent, sensitive and, at this stage in his life, slightly lost young man seems also to have had a way with the elderly wives of senior officials.[80]

Yet for all the importance of school, regimental and family connections, by themselves they could never guarantee a successful career, unless of course one were a member of the imperial family itself. As Table N of chapter 2 shows, no member of the State Council was better connected than Prince Aleksei Dimitrievich Obolensky. Moreover, what the table cannot reveal, Aleksei's brother Nicholas was a close friend of the Emperor Nicholas II. In the mid-1890s Obolensky leaped from being a mere district marshal of nobility to key positions in the central government, within three years becoming assistant Minister of Internal Affairs. Yet even here, although Obolensky's connections were a necessary cause of his rise, they were not a sufficient one. I shall be dealing later in more detail with Obolensky and his brother; suffice it to say here that this in some ways 'remarkably gifted'[81] man succeeded for many years in greatly impressing such hard-headed politicians as A.A. Polovtsov and S.Yu.Witte. Moreover, since both statesmen were, in their somewhat different ways, on the lookout for articulate and intelligent aristocrats knowledgeable about rural conditions, once Aleksei Obolensky came to the attention of high political figures his seemingly excellent qualifications in this respect contributed greatly to his rapid advance.[82]

Although family, school and regimental connections could remain important throughout a man's career, once established in the service he above all needed official 'patrons'. All sources confirm, however, that the support of these patrons had to be earned. Even in A.N. Mosolov's case, family connections secured the possibility of M.N. Murav'yov's patronage but not its certainty. As Prince V.P. Meshchersky rightly stated, 'to be able to win the trust of such a strict chief as Murav'yov it was necessary to show immediately that one was a gifted person', which Mosolov achieved by dint of self-discipline, hard work, and by showing his ability to think with clarity and precision.[83] Similar qualities won for F.G. Terner the support of V.I. Tengoborsky, though Terner also secured the attention and sympathy of other leading officials through publishing a number of books and articles on economic affairs.[84] Among the members of the State Council, N.V. Shidlovsky and P.M. Kaufmann had A.A. Polovtsov as their patron, and Polovtsov's diaries reveal what factors influenced the bureaucratic patron in pushing the interests and careers of his clients. Polovtsov liked both Shidlovsky and Kaufmann, a feeling which no doubt owed something to his preference for men from upper-class families rather than 'mere bureaucrats'. Moreover, like most patrons, as his clients rose in seniority and importance Polovtsov would have hoped thereby to widen his own circle of informants and of influence in high governmental circles. Much more important, however, particularly when he first forged his links with these two promising young officials, was Polovtsov's conviction that he had discovered intelligent, efficient, scrupulously honest and very diligent civil servants among his subordinates whose future advance was very much in the interests of the state.[85]

Of course, intelligence, hard work, writing skills and other professional virtues could not on their own secure a man's advance in the Russian civil service. As in any bureaucratic hierarchy, success required one to bend one's will and adapt one's opinions, values and manners to those of one's superiors.[86] F.G. Terner, for instance, tells the cautionary tale of V.P. Bezobrazov, the able, energetic and efficient head of the Land Credit Commission. Bezobrazov had strong opinions which he hated having to accommodate to those of his chiefs. Nor was this proud man willing to efface his own personality or to hide his ambition, not to mention his resentment at being given tedious work, behind a meek and obedient façade when facing his superiors.[87] Such personalities as Bezobrazov have difficulty in flourishing in any civil service, but the traditionally hierarchical and authoritarian Russian bureaucracy was, at least in some of its branches, particularly inimical to them.

Certainly the power which a chief exercised over his subordinates was very great. The subordinate official with a hostile boss had no sympathetic personnel department to which he could appeal for a transfer, though if the man in question had powerful connections, or if his reputation for excellence was widespread, he might himself arrange to switch to another department. Unless he did so, however, he was very much at his boss's mercy. Under Articles 761 and 762 of the Civil Service Regulations a chief indeed possessed the right to dismiss a subordinate from the bureaucracy without providing any reasons for so doing; but this power was not often used and virtually never in the central civil service.[88]

Much more to the point was the great influence possessed by an official's superior, not only as regards evaluation of his performance and recommendation for promotion, but also as concerned pay and pensions. Basic civil service salaries were generally low and the special subsidies and bonuses given out, in an almost wholly uncontrolled manner, by chiefs on special occasions could be crucial for an official's well-being. Prince V.P. Meshchersky, admittedly no lover of the bureaucracy, complained that 'even in Petersburg and in the same institution one official receives, because of his chief's good will, a full year's salary as a special reward, and another, who has worked harder, receives a quarter of that sum'.[89] Even if, as should probably be done, one discounts part of Meshchersky's complaint and believes those high officials who asserted that rewards were generally distributed in the interests of efficiency and on the basis of merit,[90] it nevertheless remains true both that merit was determined solely by the chief himself, and that even wholly honest and public-spirited officials such as F.G. Terner felt no shame in using their powers to be especially generous to deserving friends.[91] Moreover, the situation as regards pensions was even worse. The basic rate, fixed in 1827, had by the end of the century long since been overtaken by inflation. No one could live on such a pension and by 1894 about half the number of retiring officials received supplementary awards. As the Peretz Commission stated, however, his chief's recommendation was usually vital in deciding whether a man's pension was sufficient to live on; moreover 'the intercession of influential persons to whom certain of the petitioners have access is sometimes exceedingly important'.[92] In the light of such facts it is scarcely surprising that, to quote P.N. Durnovo, 'a sense of dependence and an inclination to pliability' towards higher officials were traditionally more highly developed in the Russian than in other civil services.[93]

For most Russian officials ambitious to reach the top of the bureaucracy some element of 'pliability', not to mention tact and caution, was required in dealing with superiors. The career of A.N. Mosolov, for instance, provides a spectacular example of what could happen if this rule was ignored. Joining the Chancellery of the Ministry of Internal Affairs in 1869 on the invitation of L.S. Makov, a friend and former official colleague, Mosolov made rapid progress in the 1870s by clinging to the coat-tails of his patron, who became Minister of Internal Affairs in 1878. Director of the department of Foreign Faiths, which was the bureau within the Ministry of Internal Affairs responsible for policy towards the Empire's non-Orthodox religions, at the extremely early age of thirty-four, Mosolov had every reason to hope that he would one day occupy a key position in the government. Political inexperience and incaution, combined with overdependence on a single patron, ruined his chances, however. By nature a stubborn, strong-minded and public-spirited man, Mosolov had firm views on Russian religious policy, including Russia's relations with the Vatican, which was the major topic of importance during his incumbency as director of the department. In inter-ministerial committees debating the restoration of relations with the Vatican Mosolov expressed his views with determination, clashing strongly first with K.P. Pobedonostsev and subsequently with Count D.A. Tolstoy. When Makov was dismissed and Pobedonostsev and Tolstoy became the chief figures in Alexander III's government, Mosolov's hopes of rising to the top of the Ministry of Internal Affairs were doomed.[94]

Tolstoy's treatment of Mosolov illustrates practices not uncommon in the Russian civil service. The Minister had no intention of dismissing or even, in formal terms, of demoting his director of a department. This only happened in the Russian bureaucracy if one were exceptionally unfortunate, corrupt or incompetent, or, more likely, were the particularly bitter enemy of the very powerful. Mosolov was moved sideways, being appointed governor of a province. Transfer to provincial service was, however, rightly seen by him as a near-fatal blow to his ambitions, his vanity and to his desire to play a key role in formulating governmental policy. Demoted from the staff to the line and with 'any wide field of activity...closed to me', the ambitious Petersburg official bitterly bemoaned his provincial exile, in which he remained for over a decade.[95]

Tolstoy did of course have other alternatives than to dismiss Mosolov or despatch him to the provinces. Had the Minister wished to treat Mosolov more harshly he might have offered him a place on the ministerial council, which, in A.N. Kulomzin's words, was where one tended to place vice-directors, heads of sections or senior desk officers who for one reason or another could be promoted no further.[96] On the other hand, if Mosolov had been older and more senior, and if he had possessed powerful friends, Tolstoy might have tried to push for his 'promotion' out of the Ministry of Internal Affairs into the Senate or even, just possibly, the State Council. Not for nothing did A.A. Saburov's special commission on senatorial reform complain in 1904 that ministers often foisted on to the Senate

unsuitable officials whom they wished to remove, reward or sometimes merely rest.[97] Nor was the State Council always immune from
the appointment of men whose failure, decrepitude, or political
disagreements with ministers could be clothed in a decent, kindly or
perhaps politically opportune manner by nomination to this most
dignified and somnolent of state institutions.[98] Thus in 1904 Prince
Alexander Obolensky wrote to his wife that the new Minister of
Internal Affairs had 'already dropped two of his assistants, Stishinsky
and Zinov'ev, and both are the State Council, which is becoming a
storehouse for unwanted objects'.[99]

Once one begins to discuss the fate of members of the State Council,
or even indeed of senators and directors of departments, one is frequently moving beyond the world of administration and into that of
politics. Thus, for instance, the collapse of A.N. Mosolov's career in
1881 was owed not to his failings as an official but rather to political
circumstances. No longer a mere executor of policy, he was now
participating in its formulation, admittedly in a relatively narrow
sphere, at the highest levels of government. In addition, his future
depended less on his efficiency as a bureaucrat than on changing
currents of opinion and shifting personnel in court and ministerial
circles. When Mosolov lost the political battle in 1881–2 he was
removed, as a provincial governor, out of the political sphere back to
the largely administrative world whence he had come.

Defining precisely where the sphere of politics ends and that of
administration begins is difficult. Unlike in constitutional Prussia,
Russian law made no distinctions between 'political' and 'administrative' posts in the civil service.[100] Theoretically all executive officials
were mere servants of the will of the monarch, who alone formulated policy. In practice the world of administration shaded off
into that of politics, but how deeply political ripples spread down the
ranks of the bureaucracy varied from period to period and from
department to department. Inevitably, the Ministry of Internal Affairs, which 'directs the course of almost the whole of Russian
life',[101] was in general the most politicized of governmental departments. Even in his twenties Mosolov had been in the thick of
political controversy because of his known Russian nationalist views
and his role in the russianization of the Baltic provinces. At the age of
twenty-five he was already facing a smear campaign orchestrated by
P.A. Valuev and Baltic German circles that alleged he was a 'red' in
his attitude to noble–peasant relations and a secret correspondent of
Moskovskie vedomosti.[102] Subsequently instability at the top of the
Ministry and the rapid succession of Ministers with differing personal followings and political beliefs greatly increased this department's politicization.

On the other hand, an excellent contrast to Mosolov is provided by Edward Pleske, a wholly apolitical fiscal and financial specialist whose rise through the ranks of a Finance Ministry dominated for decades by a handful of masterful chiefs was due to his skill as an official and his technical expertise. Unlike Mosolov, Pleske did not truly become even a semi-politician until he burst on to the political scene by succeeding Serge Witte as Minister of Finance in 1903. A.N. Kuropatkin described the new Minister as a 'good man of very honest and firm principles, without a particularly broad mental outlook but an excellent worker with a fine knowledge of credit affairs .... He gives the impression of being a conscientious and precise bureaucrat'. Pleske himself was, not surprisingly, alarmed by his sudden appearance on the wider political scene, especially in the wake of the formidable Witte. Kuropatkin reported: 'Pleske told me that he has absolutely no acquaintances at court. That he lives like a marmot, completely shut away in Petersburg. That he has a circle of his personal friends. That the prospect of relations with the grand dukes and the various court officials terrifies him but that he'll attempt to keep himself far from all this'.[103]

Unfortunately for the shy and conscientious specialist, as a minister one had no option but to play a role at court and in Petersburg society if one was to defend the interests of one's department and maintain one's own position. Especially if he headed a key department, the minister who retained the attitudes of an official and the habits of a marmot would, like the unfortunate Vladimir Lambsdorff, gradually lose influence over policy in the face of the contempt of Petersburg society and the court intrigues that would follow in its wake. Not for nothing did Count Paul Benckendorff report to his brother in June 1904 that Lambsdorff had long since been widely regarded in Petersburg society as being of 'no weight'. 'His *manière d'être* and his whole personality have got people used to ignoring his advice.... One [i.e. Nicholas II] has grown accustomed to treating him like a secretary who executes orders and no more. Unfortunately he is the type of minister which one prefers'.[104]

For a minister or senior official, holding one's own in Petersburg society or at court was an exhausting and dispiriting business. The capital's political and social 'world' was a village. For a start, it was physically small. From Sergeevskaya, Furstatskaya or Mokhovaya streets, in or around which most of the bureaucratic élite lived, a half-hour walk would take the senior official past much of the history of his life. The flats or houses of his friends; his clubs; the government departments in which he had worked; the Guards barracks in which he had served as a young man; the privileged schools, cadet corps or university at which he had been educated: most of these were to be found a short walk on either side of the Nevsky

С. Петербургъ - St.-Pétersbourg.
Невскій проспектъ - Perspective Nevski.

The Nevsky Prospekt, Petersburg's main street; and (*right*) the block of flats in which P.N. Durnovo and P.A. Saburov lived; it was typical of the Petersburg accommodation of senior officials without large private incomes.

Prospekt. As one would expect from the evidence presented earlier about the closeness of family, school and service links, most of the colleagues, friends and acquaintances whom the high official would encounter in this area would be people whom he had known for decades, or their friends and relations. In this tight-knit community, which had all a village's love of gossip and all its knowledge of the intimate details of one's neighbours' affairs, there was, however, concentrated almost the whole political life of a highly centralized empire. The ambitious, not always scrupulous, types usually attracted to politics congregated within this village's confines. The Petersburg village, and by no means only its male inhabitants, was absorbed by politics, careers and power. In this jealously competitive environment rapid promotion was likely, in Nicholas Basily's words, to 'provoke envy and calumny', Field Marshal Prince Baryatinsky adding that unless you were an official lucky enough to have 'extremely powerful connections in Petersburg you are a dead man, they peck you to death'.[105] The village's speciality was usually mendacious but generally malicious gossip. An outsider recalled that Petersburg society women, 'often more intelligent than the men, almost always of a finer spirit and a more observant nature, are ambitious for their husbands and at the same time for themselves. They are all more or less tormented by the desire to play some sort of role, above all a political role'.[106]

Long immersion in this society could breed an obsession with the outward signs of status and power. D.P. Golitsyn illustrates this through the life of his fictional hero, Peter Rezhaninov,[107] but one can find enough real examples of the same process.[108] All this, together with the influence of the capital's freezing, dark and damp winters, caused one member of the State Council, Prince Alexander Obolensky, to describe Petersburg as the headquarters of 'futility, sadness, gossip, and cold'.[109] Obolensky's father-in-law, A.A. Polovtsov, reflecting on the life of the much admired former minister, Admiral Shestakov, wrote that 'it is curious how such a clever, enlightened, honest man in the midst of work in Saint Petersburg weakens spiritually, falls in love with honours at court, and becomes distrustful and even malicious. There is not a good word about anyone in his notes'.[110] For the sensitive and fundamentally pure-hearted Nicholas II the intrigues of this society, which inevitably often reached whirlwind velocity in the presence of the ultimate source of power and honour, were utterly distasteful and it was this distaste quite as much as fear of assassination which drove him into isolation at Tsarskoe Selo. Not for nothing did the Empress Alexandra remark in October 1900 that she and the tsar 'saw few people' and, when advised by a well-wisher to go out more in society, retorted: 'Why? So as to hear still more lies!'[111]

The Evropeiskaya (Hotel d'Europe), Petersburg's most exclusive hotel, and (*below*) the view from its restaurant, setting for many intrigues and cabals.

For a man anxious to retain his footing in Russian top-level politics and thereby to influence the Empire's fate, not only ambition and toughness, but also subtlety, finesse and tact were required to survive in this world. In the 1890s, for instance, it did not take much insight to realize that Victor Wahl, a straightforward military type to whom the very meaning of the word 'tact' or 'finesse' was incomprehensible, would not last as Petersburg's city governor (*Gradonachal'nik*). Sure enough, having trod in his customary blunt manner on many influential toes, Wahl was dismissed in disgrace, though his career was rescued from disaster by the intercession of the Empress Marie.[112] Subtler and more experienced Petersburg figures such as A.A. Polovtsov and A.N. Kulomzin on the other hand realized that the sympathies of the influential must not be alienated, that useful information as to political currents and 'coming personalities' must be culled from Petersburg's drawing-room conversations, but that a very sharp guard must be kept on one's tongue.[113] Thus V.K. Plehve, one of the smoothest and most seasoned of Petersburg operators, in Polovtsov's words made use of the 'evasiveness of anyone with pretensions to a service career in Petersburg'.[114]

Inevitably, the nature of Russian political life influenced the relations between ministers and officials. The latter, lacking security of tenure, generally dependent on their salaries, without alternative possibilities of employment and faced with the prospect of an inadequate pension, were bound to temper their advice and their professional loyalty to chiefs according to the winds which seemed to be blowing in court and ministerial spheres. It was indeed precisely because of fears about 'service discipline' that A.N. Schwartz, the Minister of Education, was so alarmed by direct contact between the monarch and lower officials, or indeed by public displays of the Emperor's disagreement with a minister's policy. Nor, given the vulnerability of a minister's position, can it have reassured Schwartz to hear a comment from S.V. Rukhlov, 'who in a moment of sincerity said to me, God preserve you from relying on the Emperor over anything even for a second; he can't support anyone over any matter'.[115]

Uncertain of their positions at court, subject after 1906 to criticism in the Duma and the press, it is not surprising that in the intrigue-ridden world of Petersburg politics ministers should put a strong stress on loyalty among their deputies and senior advisors. Moreover, since, as with any large-scale organization,[116] a Russian ministry committed many errors and contained minor scandals which its chief did not want publicly exposed, it was doubly important for him to be surrounded by men whom he could trust, or who at the very least would not be dangerous rivals. In this context it is easy to understand why 'in general ministers take as assistants people who are not capable of being dangerous deputies, that is people who are not outstanding in their abilities'.[117] Moreover, since 'close friendships formed in the schools, the regiments, and even in the administration were often so strong that they constituted a powerful defence' against the 'intrigues and slander campaigns' which 'abounded',[118] one can also grasp why, in particular, insecure ministers in the more 'political' ministries were likely to strengthen the elements of 'cliquishness' and 'factionalism' in high administrative circles by appointing friends to key positions.[119]

Nevertheless the influence of politics on the quality of high-level administrative appointments should not be exaggerated. Some assistant ministers might well be chosen more for their reliability than their brains, but no minister with any ambition to retain his position could afford to appoint low-quality personnel to key executive posts, since he himself would inevitably take the blame for their failures and would in addition prove unable, owing to their inadequacies, to prevail in conflicts with other departments over policy.[120]

Nor should one underestimate the extent to which most ministers and senior officials were committed both to the efficiency of their own departments and to Russia's well-being. A strong sense of public service imbued much of the higher bureaucracy and kept considerations of personal advantage in check. Often surrounded from their early years of service – as is indeed the case in many professions – by careerism and personal intrigues, and realizing that merit is not always rewarded on earth, officials in many departments, but particularly the financial and judicial ones, were also well aware that their salaries were a fraction of what they could earn in the private sector.

A.F. Koni, for instance, wrote in 1868 that far higher salaries were to be earned by former colleagues who had opted for private legal practice, but he added that he could never have reconciled himself to the game-playing and defence of one-sided private interests which was the essence of work as an advocate in the civil and commercial field. The government's service provided 'the authority and the official influence which give one the possibility energetically and productively to act in the various "darker corners" of Russian life'. In addition, Koni believed that '*in corpore* the government is more liberal and more energetic than society.... In Russia one must expect everything from the government...and therefore serving and honourably defending, to the extent possible, the judicial reforms from the attacks of enemies within and without is a genuinely useful task'.[121]

Of course decades of service might dampen the optimism and the faith in governmental enlightenment expressed by the young Koni, but it by no means necessarily killed a sense of commitment to public service. Ambition, love of power and a desire for status inevitably moved some high officials, but there was also truth in Peter Bark's response to Nicholas II, when asked why he had returned to the upper ranks of the Ministry of Finance from the chairmanship of a private bank, accepting a 90 per cent drop in salary in the process. Bark replied that he had never attached overriding importance to money, and preferred 'the wider field of state service devoted to the country's good...to service in private interests'.[122] Of course in the Russian upper bureaucracy, as in any other human institution, it was only exceptional men such as N.Kh. Bunge or Alexander Knirim who were so wholly devoted to state interests and the efficient completion of their own professional tasks that questions of personal status, salary and promotion faded into relative insignificance. Nevertheless the upper ranks of the Russian civil service did produce a number of men of this calibre.[123]

Inevitably as we come to focus on the final stages of senior officials' careers, the word 'court' has cropped up ever more frequently. In an absolute or semi-absolute monarchy this is indeed to be expected. Until the 1870s high-level politics in Russia still at times had what one might describe as a tinge of Versailles, with the status of individual aristocratic families at court waxing and waning with sometimes decisive implications for the political fortunes of members of these families and their clients.[124] A late example of this sort of aristocratic politics was provided by the career of Prince A.A. Lieven, whose spectacular fall from grace in 1881–2 was almost certainly eased by the fact that deaths in his family and conversion of some members to Radstockist evangelicalism had in the preceding months radically reduced the influence of, and imperial good will towards, what had for three generations been a powerful court family very close to the Romanovs.[125] In the following decades, however, this aspect of politics greatly decreased in importance, partly because Alexander III and, even more, Nicholas II distanced themselves from Petersburg high society and lived in rural semi-isolation.[126]

This increasing isolation was an important factor as regards top-level appointments, since it greatly reduced the number of prospective candidates whom the monarch knew personally. Since the Russian emperors also lacked a Prussian-style Civil Cabinet to advise them on matters of bureaucratic personnel,[127] their control over even top-level appointments was bound to be very limited and spasmodic. In most cases a minister or other top official suggested candidates for a top position to the monarch, though the recommendations of his relatives and of unofficial advisers such as Prince V.P. Meshchersky could also be decisive.[128] Only occasionally, as for instance in the case of N.A. Maklakov,[129] did Nicholas II personally take the initiative in selecting a candidate for a key position.

The Minister of Internal Affairs (in this case Prince P.D. Svyatopolk-Mirsky) and his staff.

Given the immense importance of the top-level appointments made by Nicholas II, the manner in which such appointments were sometimes made could be alarming. The nomination, for instance, of Prince P.D. Svyatopolk-Mirsky as Minister of Internal Affairs in 1904 after Plehve's assassination was a decisive moment in Nicholas II's reign and contributed significantly to the onset of the 1905 revolution. As the *Oberhofmarschall*, Count Paul Benckendorff, reported to his brother, the intention had been that the hard-line authoritarian 'Wahl was going to be appointed Minister of the Interior', the implication being that Plehve's policy would be continued, if not toughened. 'A *scène de famille* during which one almost threw oneself at his [i.e. Nicholas II's] knees, stopped this nomination.' Instead Peter Svyatopolk-Mirsky was appointed, without any deep thought being given to the radical shift in internal policy that this would entail. How, as Benckendorff pertinently remarked, was Mirsky to cope, given the 'tremendous opposition' which his views would arouse among entrenched members of the higher bureaucracy currently pursuing, with Nicholas II's public support, policies wholly contrary to the new Minister's beliefs? Moreover, 'the poor boy has neither the health nor the personality for this position'. Complaining that the Emperor and his wife had a trivial and superficial grasp of current events, wholly failing to think deeply or systematically,

Benckendorff complained that 'one can't change absolutely one's political colour just to give one's mother pleasure'.[130]

The incompetence with which top-level appointments were sometimes made meant that the best available talent in the higher bureaucracy was frequently not employed in key positions. Still more to the point, even where high officials were able they were often too old for the positions they held. Thus in 1904 the average age of Russian ministers was sixty-two, while that of the members of the State Council was over sixty-nine. Understandably, S.E. Kryzhanovsky complained in his memoirs that 'the dominance of old men at the centre of power' was 'the basic evil of our old bureaucratic set-up.... Both physically and spiritually exhausted, these men lived in the distant past, were incapable of creativity or bursts of activity and were indifferent to almost everything except anxiety about preserving their own positions and their peace and quiet'.[131] The events of 1904–6 shocked the monarch and his advisers into appointing much younger and more vigorous men to some key posts.[132] Nevertheless, to take but three major examples, in the Great War I.L. Goremykin, B.V. Stürmer and Prince N.D. Golitsyn were appointed to crucial positions whose burdens they were far too old to bear.

How does one explain this tendency towards gerontocracy? In part it simply reflects the fact that most ministers and members of the State Council were career civil servants who had progressed up the bureaucratic ladder at roughly the speed one would expect of successful officials in Europe in a system where no major mechanisms for accelerated promotion exist.[133] The 215 members of the State Council had, for example, on average become vice-directors of departments aged 34.7 and directors aged 42.5, subsequently making the next move up the ladder to the Senate or an assistant ministership shortly before reaching the age of fifty. Seen in these terms, an average age of 53.7 for the final step to ministerial office seems unremarkable.

There were other factors, however, behind the existence of a gerontocracy. We have already noted the bureaucracy's tendency to respect the rights of seniority, and the manner in which rapid promotion excited jealousy and set off intrigues to unseat the successful official. Nor should we be surprised at these men's unwillingness to retire upon reaching the summit of their profession, since this is a natural and common human weakness. The absence of a strict upper age limit, imposed from outside on the civil service, was moreover only a reflection of the degree to which senior officialdom ruled Russia, the ability of the monarch or of his Personal Chancellery to impose rules on the bureaucracy being distinctly limited. Probably, however, the most important single reason why elderly officials clung to office was simply the inadequacy of the pension they would receive on retirement and their uncertainty up to the last moment as to just what this pension would amount to.[134] It was this issue, cited by every senior procurator and judge, which dominated the discussion of gerontocracy and compulsory age limits in the Ministry of Justice in January 1895, for instance.[135] Equally, Count V.N. Lambsdorff, noting in his diary the presence of elderly and ill officials in key posts, blamed this on the fact that 'the majority of honourable dignitaries and officials, going into retirement after half a century of service, find themselves in a deplorable material position'.[136]

II

What influence did their bureaucratic careers have on the mentalities and political opinions of the Russian ruling élite? Was there such a thing as a general bureaucratic mind-set or political viewpoint? Before answering either question in the affirmative, one must note that the 215 members of the State Council were individuals, each one of them a complex product of inherited and assimilated influences to which only a full-scale biography could do true justice. Moreover if one is seeking to generalize about the impact of their careers on the whole group of 215, it is important to remember just how diverse these careers were. Among the 215 men one finds generals, landowning nobles, judges and procurators, experts on local government and peasant affairs, policemen, financial and fiscal experts, diplomats, professors, experts on drafting legislation, and railway managers and engineers. All were in one sense bureaucrats, but their career experience and its impact on their views was by no means identical. Both the biographical and the departmental approach are, however, the subjects of later chapters; for the moment, let us concentrate on making what generalizations we can about the bureaucratic élite as a whole.

In the first place it should be remembered that a man entering the civil service from a civilian school or university in general possessed a trained memory, and relatively sophisticated analytical and writing skills. As we have seen, he had been educated in rational and logical thinking. To succeed in the civil service he needed usually to build on skills acquired at school by becoming an expert in particular facets of administration, by developing his capacity for disciplined, systematic and diligent work, and by learning to write clear, brief, precise, logical and thorough reports.[137] The overwhelming majority of the civilian members of the State Council were in these respects professional and competent civil servants.

Useful testimony to this effect comes in the memoirs of Prince Boris Vasil'chikov, an aristocrat whose career was largely spent in

High officials of the Ministry of Internal Affairs gather to celebrate their department's centenary. The Minister (standing at the front in the centre of the carpet) is V.K. Plehve; to his right is V.V. Wahl, to his left N.A. Zinov'ev, and (on the step next to the plant) P.N. Durnovo.

zemstvo and noble estate activism. Vasil'chikov writes that before seeing Petersburg administrators at close range he shared the contempt for bureaucrats that was general both in his class in particular and in Russian society as a whole. Subsequently his opinions changed. He comments that

> during the two years of my service as a minister I gained a very high opinion of the qualities of Petersburg officialdom. The level of the personnel of the Petersburg chancelleries and ministries was extremely high as regards knowledge, experience and fulfilment of official duties. In these officials' work, it is true in the purely chancellery and limited sphere of their speciality, was felt the influence of a common school, of professional traditions, and in some cases very great gifts were evident. Besides this I was struck by their immense capacity for hard work.[138]

Some bureaucratic virtues and vices were merely opposite sides of the same coin. A top official was, for instance, deeply knowledgeable about the workings of the government system. He was expert in the rapid and efficient execution of administrative tasks. Faced with the intractable problems of actually governing Russia he was likely to be more realistic than most other elements in educated society about the limited range of possible courses of action open to the government. Realism was likely to be allied to rational calculation and to pragmatism. Grand ideological visions, even if once cherished by the young official, would have disintegrated, faced by the need to confront the multiplicity of problems that flowed over his desk every day. Of course, realism and pragmatism did not simply obliterate the deeply-held instincts and commitments of senior officialdom. The strong Russian nationalist beliefs of A.N. Mosolov, A.A. Saburov's absolute commitment to the rule of law, or V.K. Plehve's deeply ingrained anti-Semitism – such political values shaped the goals of these and many other high officials and influenced, indeed sometimes wholly distorted, their conception of reality.[139] Nevertheless, for the official who wished his policies to be effective, reality was always likely to intrude and to temper fervent convictions. Nor in any case was an official, forced for over twenty years to accommodate his own views to the opinions of his chiefs and the changing currents in the government's policies, likely to emerge as a fervent ideologue deeply committed to some sweeping vision of Russia's future.

The problem was indeed that as he emerged on to the political scene the veteran official might not be deeply committed to anything at all. Years of seeing both sides of the case, accommodating his views to those of his boss, or assimilating the values and opinions current in his ministry, could sap independent views or will power – as, of course, quite simply, could age itself.[140] Moreover, his expertise in showing political tact, avoiding pitfalls and cultivating the influential, which had often been the key to his acquiring high office, might well prevail over other considerations in his desire to enjoy the comforts and status of his hard-won eminence. Prince D.P. Golitsyn's fictional hero, Peter Rezhaninov, travelled this path[141] and a number of his contemporaries believed the same was true of I.L. Goremykin.[142]

Moreover, even if, as was generally the case, a top official retained his commitment to more than merely personal ends, his specialist career might well have unfitted him for a political role in the higher reaches of the government. Thus Polotsov wrote of Aleksei Kuropatkin that he was an 'extremely clever and noble man but educated only as regards military topics; he doesn't have a clue about internal or international law or about political economy, and is therefore not only useless but also dangerous in the discussion of general political matters'. Kuropatkin in fact, as minister, struggled to educate himself more broadly in politics and economics by reading books, but amidst the strains of running a large department this was not easy.[143]

Of course most civilian specialists were not quite so remote from political and economic affairs, in their education and careers, as was the case with a professional soldier. Not merely the specialist, however, but every official had certain key limitations when promoted into the political arena. His experience in the loosely regulated and partly factionalized and politicized Russian bureaucracy probably toughened him, in preparation for the world of bureaucratic politics, to a greater degree than would have been the case in a more rule-governed and apolitical civil service. Moreover, once released from the constraints of bureaucratic subordination and allowed to exercise his initiative as a departmental chief, some Russian officials showed not only great drive and energy but also sometimes a genuinely statesmanlike vision. Even the most intelligent official, however, was ill trained to gauge the public mood, appeal to public sympathies or mobilize mass support for himself or the regime he served. Indeed the traditional official might not only fail to grasp the full need for such activity, and himself be incompetent to direct it, but be likely also to feel a deep aversion to such 'one-sided', political, 'demagogic' and 'populist' attitudes, so alien to the calm and rational contemplation of the 'general interest' to which he was accustomed.[144]

As regards the political opinions of members of the State Council, it should come as no surprise that these were informed by a strong sense of élitism. These men were, after all, in Mill's phrase, 'governors by profession'.[145] As seasoned experts in governing society, many of them not surprisingly felt themselves better equipped than ordinary mortals to run Russia. Moreover the traditions not only of the imperial bureaucracy itself but also of most of these men's own families could only strengthen their sense of having a historical claim to rulership. Like members of the upper and upper-middle classes throughout Europe, senior Russian officials were convinced that the progress of civilization demanded that societies be led by their educated and cultured élites. The backwardness of most of the Russian peasant population could only reinforce officialdom's sense of itself as the guardian both of civilization and of the untutored masses. No member of the State Council, and least of all of its liberal wing with its commitment to culture, law, economic development and property rights, believed for a moment in universal suffrage or the rule of the masses. Indeed Andrei Saburov, one of the élite's most selfless and outstanding liberals, was also unmatched in his outspoken opposition to universal suffrage in 1905–6.[146] Conservatives who retained their faith in peasant traditionalism, Orthodoxy and monarchism might well in a sense be more 'populist' than the liberals, but none would have disagreed with Kireev's belief that 'one cannot govern Russia with the help of the peasants. One cannot be guided by them', for the people, sound though their instincts might be, 'cannot determine the state's complex and delicate cultural tasks'.[147]

Moreover if some conservative officials might allow a non-speaking role in Russian politics to the patriotic Russian masses, they were by no means inclined to extend speaking parts to non-official members of educated society. A.N. Schwartz's contempt for Duma amateurs, 'too ignorant' to be allowed to poke their noses into educational affairs,[148] struck the authentic note of bureaucratic absolutism. Fourteen years earlier Schwartz had written that the future of intermediate education must be decided by expert and experienced pedagogues, who would study the efforts of their peers in other European countries and combine their own professional knowledge with a sense of the state's long-term needs. The invasion of the classroom by the shifting currents of public opinion would in Schwartz's view have ruinous consequences.[149] An if anything still more complete mandarin was P.N. Durnovo, for whom the representatives of landowning and educated society in the third Duma tended to be 'young people who are carried away' by all sorts of enthusiasms and theoretical fantasies since they lacked serious grounding in the profession of government.[150]

The belief that senior officialdom possessed to a unique degree the experience, the expertise and the breadth of political understanding to govern Russia was widespread within the higher bureaucracy. Nor, of course, given the Russian political tradition, was such a belief wholly misplaced. The suspicion of outside 'amateurs', evident in the Peretz Commission's objections to the appointment of non-officials to top bureaucratic posts, is easily visible in senior bureaucrats' comments about, to take but two examples, Prince Aleksei Obolensky and Prince Peter Syvatopolk-Mirsky.[151] Peter Bark, the Minister of Finance from 1914 to the fall of the monarchy, was not only a relatively liberal member of the upper bureaucracy but also a man who had served for a number of years in private banks. Nevertheless he makes clear that the failings of a number of key figures such as Prince N.S. Shcherbatov, Count A.A. Bobrinsky and A.D. Protopopov when appointed to top executive office had much to do with their lack of administrative experience, as well as, in some cases, the fact that they did not possess the seriousness of purpose, the diligence or the brains necessary to rise to the higher ranks of the civil service. And if such criticism was largely directed by Bark at gentry politicians with seats in the legislature, his opinion of the competence in governmental posts of Russia's professors was also not high. Not for nothing did Bark express admiration for the Prussian-German political system, where all candidates for ministerial office 'had passed through the serious school of the state administration'.[152]

Nevertheless, it would be a mistake to imagine that the higher bureaucracy was united in resolute opposition to any participation by society in government. In the first place, driven as it was by departmental and personal rivalries, the higher bureaucracy was in practice never likely to unite on anything. Secondly, given the num-

ber of semi-constitutional projects which were put forward by leading ministers in Alexander II's government, it is clear that much of
top officialdom favoured representative institutions at that time.[153]
No minister would of course have been stupid enough to put forward a constitutional project between 1882 and 1904, but liberal
sympathies remained very strong in the upper bureaucracy, Alexander
III calling Dmitri Tolstoy the 'last of the Mohicans' because of his
genuine belief in the autocratic principle.[154] By the period 1900–4,
according to A.A. Kireev, the great majority of high officials believed Russia was heading towards constitutionalism in the near
future and very many welcomed the move.[155]

The lack of any self-confident, united bureaucratic front against
the introduction of representative institutions owed much, in the
first place, to the fact that the bureaucracy by no means lived on an
island divorced from society as a whole. Most members of Nicholas
II's ruling élite, by birth members of the noble landowning class,
were by no means opposed to the claim of this group in particular to
participation in government, not only at the local level through the
zemstvos but also often through central consultative institutions as
well. Though crude attempts should not be made to equate high
officials' origins with their views for or against constitutionalism, the
papers of many members of the ruling élite show how a purely
bureaucratic and mandarin mentality was often tempered by the
nobleman's respect for the interests and opinions of the landowning
class and the zemstvo. In the period immediately prior to 1905, for
instance, the state's relations with the zemstvo movement, led by
D.N. Shipov, reached their nadir. Yet the imperial state was not
exclusively embodied by V.K. Plehve. Indeed at the very moment
when Dmitri Shipov was being humiliated by Plehve, his brother
Nicholas and his cousin Ivan, both subsequently to be appointed
members of the State Council, were senior state officials.[156]

The second major factor in the lack of opposition to reform is that
many senior officials were well aware of the need for the regime to
win back the support of elements of educated society alienated by
being denied the right to participate in government. This awareness,
evident enough in Alexander II's reign, was by the early twentieth
century very widespread. Thus in April 1903 Kireev recorded a
conversation with the 'good-natured' Fyodor Terner, whom, as he
rather sweetly put it, was scarcely 'a Red'. 'Even he, however,
recognizes that we have come to the crossroads and that our police
state is coming apart at the seams. He says correctly that the sovereign must turn to the nobility and to the zemstvos and that with
very few exceptions they will both answer him with love and trust,
but that in ten years' time this will be very difficult and in twenty
years impossible'.[157]

Finally, it must be remembered that top Russian officials and the educated society to which they belonged were but one component part of a broader world of European dimensions. Indeed the Russian élite was probably closer in many respects to the mainstream of continental culture than was true of its British peers. Meanwhile European currents were flowing strongly in the direction of civil rights, the rule of law, and parliamentary institutions – principles which seemed indeed to be coming to dominate much of the world outside Europe as well. Of course there had always been voices raised in Russia which strongly criticized Western society, argued for a special Russian path, or – much more frequently in late nineteenth-century high official circles – maintained on practical and pragmatic grounds either that the Empire was unready for a parliament or that because of its multi-ethnic nature it was unsuited for one.

Such arguments were, however, bound to lose some of their force as the level of discontent in Russian society rose, in the late nine-teenth and early twentieth centuries, and as the failings of Nicholas II's version of imperial absolutism became increasingly evident. Thus Serge Witte, no admirer of parliamentary government, wrote in his memoirs that 'constitutional liberalism is apparently the in-evitable historical law in the present position of things on our planet', and since it expressed 'the political psychology of the people' there 'is no escaping it'. He added that when critics told him that constitu-tionalism was an impossible form of government, it was 'as if I heard that human life, based on the breathing of air, is rotten, that such life is impossible for the air infects the organism by the bacteria it breeds'.[158]

CHAPTER 5

THE MANY FACES OF THE BEAST

In this chapter I hope to illustrate some of the types of men to be found within the upper reaches of Russian government in the last years of the Old Regime, and to provide some clues as to the links between their backgrounds, personalities, careers and opinions. Initially I will investigate the extent to which differing social backgrounds determined specific mentalities and political views. Next I will study ethnic distinctions and their influence, before moving on to an attempt to link career patterns to personalities and opinions. As we shall see, the borders between one group and another were always blurred, and every group contained within it individuals who did not conform to the normal pattern of their peers' opinions and personalities. A fundamental aim of the chapter is therefore to make what generalizations are possible about types of officials while never forgetting that the 215 members of the State Council were distinct individuals.

I

In the group I have called 'aristocratic magnates', for example, members did commonly share certain values, attitudes and weaknesses. It is fair to say that their political views were often strongly tinged by Whiggish and oligarchical liberal-conservatism. The line I drew earlier, however, between 'aristocratic magnates' and other aristocrats cannot of course be seen as a chasm dividing fundamentally different types of men. Inevitably one finds members of the State Council such as Ananiy Petrovich Strukov, a successor to Count Aleksei Bobrinsky as leader of the United Nobility (the pressure group founded in 1906 to defend noble interests). Strukov's outlook and opinions were similar to those of most of the magnates.[1] Equally important, at the heart of the group of magnates one finds anomalies such as Count S.D. Sheremetev, whose habits and opinions were influenced more by his conceptions of Muscovite boyardom than by any hankering after English-style Whig principles.[2] Nor should one forget the case of Prince M.S. Volkonsky, an aristocratic magnate by any definition, but also a man whose untypical bureaucratic career, personal insecurity, and hunger for political and social eminence may well have been shaped by a childhood and adolescence spent in Siberia as the son of a Decembrist exile, stripped of rank and title and deprived of the chance of a higher education.[3] One safe generalization about the aristocratic magnates ought to be that they were resolutely opposed to any compulsory expropriation of private land during the revolution of 1905. Needless to say, this generalization holds good for most of them. Even so it was a magnate, Prince Boris Vasil'chikov, whose seeming willingness as Minister of Agriculture to accept some measure of expropriation threw the United Nobility into a panic in the spring of 1907.[4]

If Whiggism was a powerful influence on most of the Council's aristocratic magnates, it is important to define what exactly Whig principles were in the Russian context. The aristocratic Whigs within the ruling élite usually combined a firm commitment to private property and landowning interests with a belief in a greater political role for the aristocracy in Russian politics. Disliking governmental arbitrariness and illegality, they criticized the bureaucracy's increasing monopolization of power, and welcomed the idea of society's representatives being given a say in governmental decision-making. Though at heart monarchists, and sensitive to appeals from the crown to their patriotism and sense of public duty, they were often by no means wholly satisfied with the pre-1905 Russian political system, still less with the last two Romanov emperors and their grand-ducal relatives.

An interesting, relatively typical, and extremely important Whig magnate among the Council's members was Count Aleksei Bobrinsky, whose subsequent role as chairman of the United Nobility was foreshadowed by his efforts, even in the reign of Alexander II, to become a leader of the landowning class and to make the nobles assume the direction of all social forces in what he hoped would be an increasingly liberal and constitutional Russia. The sophisticated, cultured and cosmopolitan Bobrinsky criticized the superficiality and vulgarity of Alexander III and his brothers, while sharing the subsequent despair, even contempt, felt by the bulk of the ruling élite for Nicholas II. Frustrated in his political ambitions before 1905, Bobrinsky had every reason to rejoice in the constitutional reforms of 1905–7. Not only did the latter greatly increase the political influence of the landowning class, but the institutions created in these years proved to be stepping-stones which took Bobrinsky to a position of great power and eminence, firstly in the United Nobility and subsequently in the state legislature and in the Council of Ministers.[5]

Many factors help to explain widespread discontent among magnates with the absolutist regime existing before 1905. Of course, some causes of discontent, such as bureaucratic arbitrariness and the government's failure to maintain Russia's international power and prestige, were shared by other members of educated society. As Boris Vasil'chikov's comments about his father's Whiggism make clear, however, specifically aristocratic factors were also important.[6] Some great landowners were highly disgruntled by the fact that in Russia, unlike in other European monarchies, the aristocracy's social status was not reflected in political power. Not surprisingly, some Russian aristocrats envied their English counterparts not only for their political power and independence but also because the English path to power seemed so attractive, so free and so inherently noble. Certainly, by comparison with the daily grind of Petersburg bureaucratic life, which was the usual path to political office in Russia, the attractions of the Oxford Union, of the parliamentary game, and of London's intertwined worlds of politics and high society are very obvious.[7]

But aristocratic discontent with absolutism reflected more than Russia's lack of a House of Lords or Prussian *Herrenhaus* where great magnates could slumber with becoming dignity. Aristocratic members of the State Council could learn to their cost that even a magnate's civil rights and personal dignity were not completely secure against the operations of the police state. The aristocracy's letters were opened by the police at will,[8] some magnates suffered from the state's religious intolerance,[9] while no one however highly placed could be quite sure that the police were not recording his links with 'suspicious persons'.[10] Not surprisingly, as the diary of Princess E. A. Svyatopolk-Mirsky records, anti-bureaucratic feeling was widespread among magnates interested in political matters.[11] Concern with the effects of bureaucratic arbitrariness on Russia's society and political stability combined easily with a sense of the aristocracy's rights and a resentment of those who had replaced society's 'natural rulers' as governors of the Empire.

Moreover, although dislike of bureaucratic absolutism was partly offset by close links to the monarchy, even attitudes to the later Romanovs were equivocal. A member of the Petersburg aristocracy could be too conscious of his own family's history and status, too highly cultured and critical, above all too familiar with court life and the Romanovs, to regard the latter with any great awe. As Prince S. M. Volkonsky noted, Nicholas II's charm, alluring when the Emperor was infrequently encountered; scarcely compensated for the frustrations of having to move in court circles or work in close proximity to the monarch.[12] Equally, the letters of Paul Benckendorff, the last *Oberhofmarschall*, not only contain frequent evidence of the inadequacies and pettiness of the imperial couple and members of their family, but also somewhat qualify the criticism *ad hominem* by admitting that 'there is something ridiculous in any and every monarchy'.[13]

Study of the lives of the Council's magnates throws light on many of the frustrations faced by the Russian aristocrat in politics. Essentially the problem was a vicious circle. The main path to political power in Russia lay through decades of service in the central bureaucracy. In common with their European peers, and indeed with the children of the very rich in any modern society, few Russian aristocrats desired to spend their lives in the civil service. Moreover, the boring, mechanical and sometimes humiliatingly subservient nature of the work done by most Russian junior bureaucrats made this career option even less attractive,[14] especially given the sense of independence, power and even, sometimes, satisfaction a great magnate could feel in running his own or his father's estates.[15]

Certain side alleys by which aristocrats could reach important governmental posts did, it is true, exist. Diplomatic life was much more attractive than the bureaucratic grind and required the high-society polish that was the aristocrat's hallmark. Moreover the Foreign Ministry treated its junior and middle-level officials in a much more gentlemanly and easygoing manner than was the case in most domestic departments.[16] Apart from this narrow and specialized opening, however, the only aristocratic route to political power lay through service as a marshal of the nobility. However, conscientious service as a marshal usually meant working in boring provincial towns, and was in itself a very inadequate preparation for high office in the central government.[17]

Not surprisingly, none of the magnates who held top posts in the domestic central administration distinguished themselves; Boris Vasil'chikov spoke for more than just himself when he wrote that he 'was no good as a minister' and felt completely lost in the Petersburg political and administrative jungle.[18] Even Aleksei Bobrinsky, politically more ambitious than many of the magnates and, as veteran marshal of the capital's nobility, also no stranger to Petersburg politics, was taken aback when he finally achieved ministerial office. 'My role is exhaustingly hard labour', he wrote to his daughter in September 1916. 'I work from morning until night. . . . I had imagined this post differently. There is the appearance of power but in fact thousands of plots, conferences and discussions.'[19]

As Bobrinsky's letter suggests, most aristocrats found it neither pleasant nor easy to accustom themselves to the high work-rate usually required of senior officials. Theirs had after all in many cases been a leisurely existence. The diary of Prince N.V. Repnin, for instance, who many decades later was appointed to the State Council, reveals that he spent the early part of 1869 in Marienbad, the summer in Paris and Biarritz, returned to Russia in September, but was back in Brussels and Paris in January and February 1870.[20] The need to work in an unprecedentedly hard and regular manner was, however, by no means the worst problem facing the ambitious aristocrat. As the Russian governmental apparatus became larger, more complex and more specialized, its requirements and values inevitably drew it further away from the aristocracy. The latter, like their peers throughout Europe, had seldom had technical or professional training and tended rather to value 'character', manners, a broad cultural education, and the ability to be entertaining in drawing-room conversations.[21] Aleksei Bobrinsky, who combined decades of activity in noble politics with an interest in archaeology, patronage of the arts and scholarship, charitable work and other voluntary activity, lived in the mainstream of the European aristocratic tradition, but he was seen by many senior officials as charming, superficial and incapable of running a department of state.[22]

Above all, however, the magnates tended to lack the temperament to survive in Russian politics. Both P.D. Svyatopolk-Mirsky and Boris Vasil'chikov rightly stressed that they had the wrong personalities to be successful ministers, for survival in Petersburg politics required toughness, ambition, love of power, willingness to flatter and play the courtier, and a taste for battle.[23] There was not much room in this world for a man like Svyatopolk-Mirsky who could say that it was 'not in his character continually to fight' and that he far preferred to be independent outside Petersburg than a mere 'secretary of the sovereign' as Minister of Internal Affairs.[24] Unless indeed there was something distinctly unusual in his character and background, a magnate's life had not remotely prepared him for the strains of high office. Rich, independent, proud, supremely confident of his social status, the magnate had little incentive to submit himself not only to the strains and dangers of a high official post but also to the fierce competition among colleagues, generally his social inferiors, for the power and rewards of high office. Moreover, if he did enter this competition such a man, frequently very honourable, was likely to find himself at a thorough disadvantage when dealing with often less scrupulous colleagues with decades of experience in Petersburg bureaucratic politics.[25]

Judging by some of the secondary literature, one might expect there to be a clear and consistent contrast between the political views of aristocrats and commoners within the ruling élite. Thus for instance S.S. Oldenburg speaks of aristocratic-oligarchic and bureaucratic-populist tendencies within the ruling élite and Yu.B. Solov'yov identifies K.P. Pobedonostsev and P.L. Lobko as the leaders of the latter camp.[26] A.A. Polovtsov had no doubt either of the existence of these two camps, or that membership was determined by a man's social origins. In his view 'the priests' sons under Pobedonostsev's leadership are united and represent nothing but rejection, prohibition and pleasing one's own ambition'. This 'gang of bureaucratic proletarians', 'alien to any cultural inclinations' and 'ignorant in their evaluation of states' political ideals', sought to destroy any independent, aristocratic forces in society in order to consolidate their monopoly of political power.[27]

No student of Russian ruling circles would deny that tensions existed between 'aristocrats' and 'bureaucrats' within the élite, the former often regarding the latter as unprincipled and servile careerists, while officials frequently saw aristocrats in high office as arrogant and superficial amateurs. Sometimes these feelings were informed by tension between men of very unequal birth, as was the case, for instance, with the battles between N.K. Giers, Count V.N. Lambsdorff, I.A. Zinov'ev and Count D.A. Kapnist which bedevilled the Foreign Ministry in the 1890s.[28] Nevertheless the impact of differing social origins should not be exaggerated. As has been made clear earlier, the great majority of top officials were not 'priests' sons' but rather children of the gentry. The comment of one indignant noble landowner in 1909 that 'it is our brothers who by the will of fate have got into the administration's feeding trough and are betraying us' is very much to the point.[29] As the memoirs of V.I. Gurko and D.N. Lyubimov illustrate, high officials did not need to be 'parvenus' to have a patronizing, even on occasion somewhat contemptuous and resentful, attitude to aristocratic outsiders in top positions. Gurko was after all the son of a field marshal, and Lyubimov, anything but a parvenu, closely connected to Aleksei Bobrinsky. What their memoirs illustrate is not the self-made man's resentment of the aristocrat but rather the professional administrator's and politician's attitude towards amateurs encroaching on his supposed field of expertise.[30]

Certainly study of the political views of those members of the State Council who came from bourgeois or minor gentry backgrounds does not support Polovtsov's thesis that this group was in any sense united or committed to some general political programme. On the contrary, though harder-working than the magnates and less enamoured of the idea of oligarchical Whiggism, the bourgeois and minor gentry covered the whole spectrum of political views which existed within the Russian ruling élite. To the extent that the opinions of members of this group can be related to their biographies, it is clear that political loyalties followed past occupations rather than social origins, generals and professors tending towards the Council's authoritarian and conservative right, while financial and judicial officials were inclined to belong to the Council's more reformist and compromising centre.[31]

N.A. Zinov'ev

Of the relatively few commoners in the State Council, the one who perhaps most closely approximated to Polovtsov's stereotype of the bureaucratic parvenu was N.A. Zinov'ev. In every way, including even his physical appearance, Zinov'ev was a strong contrast to the aristocratic element within the ruling élite. The aristocratic ideal was the tall, elegant and handsome Guards officer, always well-mannered and at his ease in society. Some members of the State Council, such as the Dolgoruky brothers or Vladimir Frederycksz, came close to this ideal.[32] Nicholas Zinov'ev emphatically did not. An unkind contemporary described him as 'tall, thin as a skeleton, with a small wrinkled head which reminds one of a dried-up lemon on which a few greying hairs have grown'.[33] Describing himself as 'perhaps an old bureaucrat' and admitting that 'I always was a pedant and a formalist',[34] Zinov'ev notably lacked the lightness of touch, the wit or the conversational brilliance on which the aristocracy tended to pride itself. Short-tempered, often rude and extremely combative, he was seen by contemporaries as a typical bureaucrat, though his background and decades of provincial service combined to make him a rather more crude variation on the bureaucratic theme than most of the purer products of the Petersburg chancelleries.[35] The immensely hard-working, thorough and precise Zinov'ev complained incessantly that the State Council lacked the time or information to go into legislative proposals in the proper detail and seriousness, and he sought to correct this failing by lengthy and dense speeches packed with statistics, which were notorious for emptying the chamber.[36]

Zinov'ev, however, embodied Polovtsov's conception of the

bureaucratic parvenu not only through his ambition, his pedantry, his slavishness towards his seniors, his seeming lack of fixed principles, and his relative narrowness of vision, but also in some of the political views he espoused. In some ways Zinov'ev was the naïve official, in his conviction that administrative excellence could solve complex issues of education, religion and nationality so long as 'politics' was not allowed to intrude.[37] Along with this naïvety, however, went a genuine sense that the state bureaucracy should act to defend the masses from exploitation by the social élites which dominated local government and owned Russia's factories and estates.[38] Zinov'ev on many occasions denounced the unfair burden on the poor of Russia's inequitable tax system, remarking *vis-à-vis* rural servitudes that although the state must of course rely on the strong, 'one ought not to forget about the very weak and it is necessary that the weak should know that their rights can be defended in the legislative institutions'.[39]

Indeed in February 1916, in a rare burst of political theorizing, Zinov'ev came close to an open defence of socialism. 'What is socialism in its Russian translation?', he asked, answering that

> it is community feeling...an attempt to improve the position of society.... One must improve things in such a way that what was in the past the property of the few becomes the property of the broad mass.... It speaks for itself that everything depends not on the doctrine but on the means of its application. If we preach that the introduction of this principle should be by violence that truly becomes criminal; but it would be equally criminal if we, by means of violence, begin to return to serfdom and turn free men into slaves.... Consequently the whole question revolves around how precisely the socialist idea is realized, whether it is realized by force or legally. In the latter case all of society will move towards a better condition.[40]

Between the 'aristocratic magnates' and the bourgeois and 'minor gentry' stood approximately 60 per cent of the appointed members of the State Council. Whether or not they themselves owned estates, the overwhelming majority of these men came, as we have seen, from well-established landowning families. The extent to which their social origins coloured their political views, however, depended both on their occupations and on their personal experience and loyalties.

A handful of this central bloc among the 215 men not only owned estates of from 1,000 to 10,000 *desyatiny* but also devoted most of their lives to agriculture and local affairs. Although, as with the aristocratic magnates, these provincial activists often disliked the bureaucracy's increasing power under the absolutist regime and opposed some governmental policies, they were on the whole one of the most conservative groups within the ruling élite, often being closely aligned with the views of Prince V.P. Meshchersky.[41] Thus even in November 1904, A.A. Arsen'ev, a member of a prominent Tula family, told Nicholas II that another speech about 'senseless dreams' was needed to put the zemstvos in their place.[42]

S.S. Bekhteev was somewhat less obscurantist and, in addition, was a genuine expert on Russian agriculture. He nevertheless fully shared the conservative provincial nobleman's suspicion of the bureaucracy, together with his conviction that the noble landowner, uniquely capable of maintaining order and culture in the countryside, also best understood the peasant masses and their needs, and was therefore better qualified than the state's officials to fulfil the functions of a ruling class. A speech made by Bekhteev to the annual conference of the United Nobility in February 1909 gives one an accurate sense of his overall political conceptions. 'At a time of general shakiness', complained Bekhteev, expressing his opposition to reformist currents within the government, 'when everything is unsteady, all authorities shaken – God, Tsar, laws, obedience – when everything is being rejected, everything subjected to doubt, at this moment one cannot undertake the reconstruction of institutions according to recipes dictated not by life but by the desire to realize abstract doctrines, to imitate the West and to seek an example there'.[43]

The Council's most complete Junker was, however, P.A. Krivsky, who served for many decades as the noble marshal of Saratov province, where he owned 4,000 *desyatiny*.[44] As regards his wealth, his commitment to local affairs, and his outlook, Krivsky was very much the representative of the provincial gentry. Saratov's aristocratic magnates, who owned more than half the province's noble land, were on the contrary seldom numbered among the province's local activists.[45] Krivsky had the blinkered provincialism, the obstinately self-confident conservatism, and the blunt tactlessness of much of Prussian Junkerdom.[46] Polovtsov described him as 'an ardent representative of class and every other kind of reaction' and 'a violent supporter of noble interests', while Count A.A. Uvarov, admiringly, remarked that he was 'a public figure about whom no one can say that he ever took the road of concession or compromise'.[47] Convinced that the nobility was too weak in defending its own interests and that 'it too often...hides its personal convictions in a cowardly way', Krivsky's longest-lasting political campaign was for stricter labour discipline and enforceable work contracts among agricultural labourers.[48]

Krivsky's background and life were typical of the richest layer of the provincial gentry. His father, an officer, had been crippled in the Napoleonic wars. Krivsky himself, trained in the School of Guards

Sub-Ensigns and the Chevaliers Gardes, perhaps developed his equi-vocal attitude towards Nicholas I's regime because of the setbacks to his own military career. Though anything but a liberal, Krivsky was a supporter of the zemstvos' independence from the bureaucracy because 'whatever else we may be we are nevertheless local men and the governors are newcomers'. Absolutely committed to the no-bility's leading role in politics and society, Krivsky loathed 'self-seeking and servile' elements in the bureaucracy and utterly despised the newly emerging rural 'aristocracy' of 'rich merchants, tradesmen and kulaks, whom he remembered as coachmen and cattle-dealers and whom he continued to treat in the old way'.[49]

Tough, insensitive, arrogant and unsentimental, Krivsky had the provincial nobleman's virtues of independence, personal generosity and hospitality. The blunt crudity with which he expressed his po-litical opinions tells one, however, much about the nature both of the man and of the particular ultra-conservative strain he represented in the Russian provincial gentry. 'I love Russia above all else', said Krivsky in December 1902.

> I love its greatness, its power, in which I take pride before all for-eigners. I am devoted with all my being to the Autocratic Tsar. I love the whole Russian people and within it I love above all the nobility. I love the nobility for the fact that by its faithful service to the Tsar and the country it has helped our Tsars raise Russia to such a position of greatness. I believe in the nobility and am sure that despite everything it has borne in the last forty years, united in the interests of the state, it is a force before which, whether it likes it or not, any untruth will be forced to stop and reckon.[50]

Non-official provincial landowners such as Arsen'ev, Bekhteev and Krivsky were, however, a very small minority among the ap-pointed members of the State Council. A much larger and, from our point of view, more interesting group is made up of men who, al-though owning between 1,000 and 10,000 *desyatiny*, nevertheless devoted much of their lives to the paid service of the state. Among this group one finds, to cite just a few of the better-known names, M.G. Akimov, A.G. Bulygin, S.S. Goncharov, I.L. Goremykin, M.P. Kaufmann, P.A. Kharitonov, A.N. Kulomzin, A.I. Lykoshin, S.A. Mordvinov, Prince Aleksei Obolensky, A.A. Saburov, P.P. Semyonov, I.I. Shamshin, I.G. Shcheglovitov, D.S. Sipyagin and P.A. Stolypin. Merely to list these names is to make the point that inherited property and social status did not in general determine views on specific issues, for there can have been few questions facing Nicholas II's ruling élite on which this group was not seriously divided. Nevertheless in many cases the fact that these high officials were at the same time considerable landowners with roots in provin-cial society could influence their outlooks.

As one would expect, men who had served as noble marshals and provincial governors most often diverged from the mandarin 'ideal type'. A.G. Bulygin, for instance, was an almost exaggerated example of the noble landowner in bureaucratic disguise. D.N. Lyubimov writes of Bulygin as newly-appointed Minister of Internal Affairs that

> it was clear to me that Bulygin hated the cares, the fuss and the increased work. The main thing that he valued was peace and calm. Moreover, his was by no means an affected or olympian calm, donned for the sake of appearance, as was for instance the case with Plehve, but a real calm linked organically to Bulygin's mind and habits. He was a typical noble landowner of bygone days, very much one of Goncharov's Oblomovs, but in new circumstances, deprived of his serfs, having flourished in the service, where a blind fate had raised him to the very summit. Here he took on the external appearances of an administrator but in the depth of his soul he remained the same old balanced and dignified big landowner – an ideal man to be a provincial marshal of the nobility, even an excellent governor in a quiet province, but entirely unsuited for the political struggle with all its intrigues at the centre of which, by the will of fate, he found himself. Such was my impression after my first meeting with A.G. Bulygin. It scarcely changed after ten months of service under his leadership.[51]

It was, however, not only high officials who had served as marshals and governors whose purely mandarin outlook was tempered by their links to rural society and the landowning gentry. As we shall see, even a pure-bred State Chancellery official such as A.N. Kulomzin could know a lot about running gentry estates and peasant farms, and could moreover both sympathize with and feel a part of the zemstvo and provincial world, whose views and interests he wished the central government to listen to and defend.[52] A similar case was that of Evgeni Turau, a lifelong jurist who, together with his wife, owned 2,750 *desyatiny* in Volhynia. Turau, an honorary JP in his district, was active both in the district zemstvo assembly and in the sessions of the local JPs. In addition, he played a major role in the encouragement of cottage industries, organizing a number of major *Kustar'* exhibitions.[53]

Among officials who came from landowning families but who themselves owned little or no land, one can find both pure bureaucratic mandarins and individuals who still felt part of the landed gentry and defended its interests. Among the former group there is, for example, V.N. Kokovtsov, a member of an old noble family, some of whose relatives were still considerable landowners and who himself still owned a small estate. Educated in Petersburg and never having served outside the central bureaucracy, Kokovtsov's manner and sympathies were, however, entirely those of a professional élite official. Reacting in horror in 1904 to the idea that non-official amateurs might have some role in influencing the arcane secrets of the state's budget, even after the establishment of the Duma Kokovtsov was capable of thanking God that Russia had no parliament. Here indeed, in the words of Kokovtsov's son-in-law, N.N. Fliege, was a man whose 'faith in the official apparatus was unlimited' and who 'treated sceptically everything that originated from people not dressed in *viz-mundiry* [i.e. civil service uniforms]'.[54]

Quite different were the views and loyalties of A.N. Mosolov, who came from a prominent gentry family rendered landless and bankrupt after the emancipation of the serfs. In his memoirs Mosolov writes that, although deprived of his own 'nest', he sought always to retain the habits and loyalties of an old-style nobleman because it was in the landed gentry, not among Petersburg officialdom, that there grew up 'Russia's best sons'. Though himself an ambitious central government official, Mosolov defended the landowners' cause, opposing Witte's policies in the 1890s and in 1897 writing a memorandum which 'pointed to a series of entirely just and harmless measures which would by natural means strengthen the Russian nobility and make it again the most useful cementing force in the future growth and internal development of Russia'.[55] Study of figures such as Kulomzin, Turau and Mosolov therefore warns one that although a gap was developing between bureaucracy and gentry in late imperial Russia the two worlds were as yet by no means wholly divided or distinct, at least as regards officialdom's upper ranks.

In many cases, inevitably, 'mandarin' and gentry characteristics conflicted within a single individual, the final balance being influenced by personal factors not susceptible to generalization. Count Vladimir Lambsdorff, for instance, the son of an Aide-de-Camp General, was born into the centre of the court aristocracy. His father's bankruptcy, whose worst consequences were alleviated by the generosity of Alexander II,[56] meant, in Lambsdorff's own words, that 'I possess no private fortune.... Brought up on habits of luxury and independence, I was suddenly reduced, at the commencement of my career, to carving out my own path against great difficulties'.[57] For all his private criticisms of Alexander III and Nicholas II, Lambsdorff retained not only a genuine reverence for the memory of Alexander II but also a deep and self-sacrificing loyalty to monarchs for whose folly he was often held to account in society. Lambsdorff, who retained the exquisite manners of an old-fashioned courtier, once remarked in his diary that 'I like aristocratic principles'.[58] On another occasion, commenting on a conversation between M.N. Ostrovsky, I.A. Vyshnegradsky and I.N. Durnovo, Lambsdorff's aristocratic origins reasserted themselves as he noted bitterly that 'the Great

Russian landowners evidently don't amount to anything of importance in the eyes of our ministers-cum-bureaucrats and parvenu speculators'.[59]

Yet, above all, Lambsdorff was a servant of the state and a professional diplomat. For him the court had 'the character of a café', the Yacht Club was a 'temple of idleness' and much of the aristocracy was a 'little clique, owing its position to the accident of birth, a clique of which the court and the circle of profligates and idlers called "society" is largely composed'.[60] Phenomenally hard-working, Lambsdorff had not only most of the virtues of an efficient administrator, but also a broad and intelligent understanding of the realities underlying contemporary currents in international relations. His comments on the arms race, chauvinism, the balance of power and true Russian interests indeed show not only wisdom but also humanity and foresight.[61] To understand Lambsdorff's failings as a minister, and indeed his whole mind-set and loyalties, one must, however, grasp something of the exceptionally sensitive and insecure personality of this homosexual recluse. The Foreign Ministry absorbed Lambsdorff's whole being and gave his life the only sense of security it ever possessed, for outside the Ministry, as he wrote in 1889, there existed only 'the unknown and the uncertain'.[62] As he wrote to Valerian Obolensky-Neledinsky-Meletsky in November 1902, 'what would life offer me if one removed from it my work, which alone can give it sense, ennoble it and bind all the wounds that bleed at the bottom of one's heart'.[63] The Foreign Ministry was indeed not only the focus of Lambsdorff's professional skills and energies but also his home and his 'fatherland', whence he drew most of his personal friendships, including his long-standing, loyal but deeply jealous and possessive friendship with his chief, N.K. Giers.[64] Inevitably, as one plunges deeper into the diary and private correspondence of Lambsdorff, generalizations about the 'class nature' of the Old Regime fade into the background and it is the complex personalities and conflicting loyalties of the individual members of the ruling élite which most absorb one's interest.

II

To attempt to link a man's ethnic background to his mentality or political opinions is by no means simple. For a high official of foreign origin, retaining non-Russian values, attitudes or habits might or might not entail attempting to use one's official position to protect one's own community from pressure for russification. Moreover, assessing the influence of non-Russian parentage is complicated by the fact that the whole Russian educated class had been saturated with Western influences since the early eighteenth century. Especially before 1850 and, above all, in the aristocratic élite, these influences had sometimes been so strong as completely to divorce individual Russians from their own language and culture. Thus N.P. Balashov, one of the Council's aristocratic magnates, was brought up in a family whose women did not even speak Russian, a phenomenon which, in the opinion of Balashov's brother Ivan, was typical of the high aristocracy in the era of Nicholas I.[65] Spending much of their childhood abroad, and educated by a series of non-Russian tutors, the Balashovs were brought up in eighteenth-century style. Fluent in foreign languages and fully conversant with ancient mythology and contemporary Western culture, the Balashov boys as adolescents could barely speak Russian and had carefully been kept away from the Orthodox Church for fear of contamination by its ignorance and superstition.[66] Reflecting on his childhood, Ivan Balashov records that 'the education of children of our circle was absurd in those days'. Many of his peers, whose national culture was wholly alien to them and who were only too aware of Russia's 'weakness and relative backwardness in everything', in Balashov's view fell an easy prey to russophobia.[67]

Influenced by their own sympathies and by changing currents in Russian society under Alexander II, both Balashov brothers ultimately ceased to be 'Russian foreigners in Russia',[68] but the same was not true of all the Council's aristocrats. A contemporary wrote of the princes Alexander and Nicholas Dolgoruky that, 'brought up by an English tutor, they were quite English in their ways and customs and spoke the language like natives'.[69] Linked to the ultra-exclusive high society set of 'Russian-bred lords', which prided itself on its wholly English character, two of the four Dolgoruky brothers ended up living permanently in London.[70]

If 'in manners and breeding' the Petersburg aristocracy was of all groups in Russian society 'the least national', cosmopolitan influences were also extremely strong among the wealthier elements of the provincial landowning gentry. Though inevitably exposure to Western influences differed according to individual families' circumstances and traditions, the memoirs of members of this group born around the mid-nineteenth century[71] are full of descriptions of foreign tutors and governesses, and of childhoods surrounded by Western cultural influences.[72] Not only were trips to Western Europe frequent, they also sometimes had a specifically educational purpose, being designed to open the eyes of young noblemen to the world beyond Russia's borders.[73] Moreover even in upper gentry circles, the children of the '50s and '60s might well still converse with their parents exclusively in French.[74] Such habits became less frequent the further one progressed down the social scale, but foreign influences nevertheless remained strong. In the first place many Russian and Orthodox landowning or official families had intermarried with the daughters of Protestants in the imperial service. As we shall see, for instance, in the case of A.N. Kulomzin, the influence of a distinctly un-Russian mother on a son could be considerable. In addition, even for the son of a wholly Russian family with no foreign blood, to pass through a Russian civilian institution of higher education was, as we have seen, to encounter many basically Western ideas about history, justice and politics. Nor should one forget that, as adults, future members of the State Council did not travel to the West merely to gamble on the Riviera or take the waters at Carlsbad; service records and memoirs are replete with accounts of lengthy assignments to Central and Western Europe to study foreign institutions and governmental procedures.[75] Close acquaintance with the life and culture of the rest of Europe was indeed the mark of a member of the imperial ruling élite regardless of his social origin. Moreover, the fact that in official circles Western methods and institutions were often seen as models Russia would do well to follow made this acquaintance all the deeper and more serious.

Of course, the fact that Russian educated society was highly westernized did not mean that no differences existed between Russians and men of non-Russian backgrounds within the ruling élite. Non-Russians were, however, very much in a minority, as we have seen, the only significant non-Russian groupings being 'German bourgeois', Protestants from Finland, and Baltic nobles. In the largest of these groups, the 'German bourgeois', most of the members were well on the road to complete russianization. Nevertheless, the most obvious means to measure this process, namely allegiance to the Orthodox Church, could on occasion provide a crudely distorted sense of an individual's cultural identity.

F.G. Terner was, for example, Orthodox, but three of his grandparents had been German Protestants, and the culture which dominated his home and childhood was German. He also chose his wife from Russia's German community. Even in the state gymnasium he entered in 1840, the director and inspector were German. Not surprisingly, there were strongly un-Russian elements in Terner's character. He himself puts his 'consistency and restraint' down to his German upbringing. To these one might add a slightly self-righteous sense of bourgeois propriety, a moderation, and above all a strong Protestant, pietist streak. These traits, by no means typical among the Russian ruling class, influenced not only Terner's personality and religious views but also his attitude to public office.[76] In his memoirs he remarks that 'my attitude has always been to treat the Russian and German nationalities with equal justice and sympathy, and this can be considered a consequence of my mixed Russian and German blood'.[77] Here clearly was an outlook which saw state and nation as distinctly different entities, and a state official as to some extent belonging to a community of guardians standing outside and above social groups, all of which had to be treated with an impartial hand. Such an outlook, though to some extent part and parcel of the imperial administrative tradition, was more easily held by a 'semi-German' high official than by his Russian peers in the early twentieth century.

If Fyodor Terner was, in his outlook and loyalties, in some ways more a servant of the state than he was either a Russian or a German, the same was true, though in a rather different manner, of Vladimir Frederycksz. The Minister of the Court, a Protestant Finn of Swedish ethnic origin, married to a Roman Catholic Pole, belonged to no nationality and felt no allegiance to any ethnic group. His outlook and loyalties were those of a Horse Guard and a courtier. To such an extent was the Horse Guards Regiment his fatherland that even as a minister he refused to move from his private house, since this afforded him an unobstructed view of his old regiment's parade ground. The son and nephew of Guards colonels who became ADC generals, Frederycksz 'had for the Emperor the devotion of an old servant who had grown up in the Court, and for the Empress a sort of chivalrous cult'. Frederycksz's tact, trustworthiness and discretion made him a useful arbiter of high-society quarrels, but his deep kindness and sense of honour were exceeded only by his stupidity. Holding himself aloof from all political questions, he never became involved in disputes over russification or the rights of the Empire's non-Russian minorities.[78]

Of the non-Russian groups represented in the ruling élite, the Baltic German nobility, more homogeneous than the 'German bourgeois' and more numerous than the Finns, had traditionally exercised much the greatest influence. Information about religion, landowning and education has suggested that the State Council's 'Baltic barons' were less russianized than most of the 'German bourgeois', but much more so than the bulk of the Baltic gentry's elected local leaders. Closer knowledge of the men in question confirms that this was the case.

By the turn of the twentieth century most Baltic noble landowners, resentful of russification, were more hostile to Russia and less knowledgeable about Russian life than had been the case half a century before. Narrowly provincial in outlook, they were for the most part convinced of the superiority of German culture and of the Protestant religion. Their intense pride in their ancient provincial institutions and traditions, combined with an arrogance derived from centuries of domination over the Latvian and Estonian peasantry, often made it difficult for them to comprehend contemporary social and intellectual currents. Indeed, not only was compromise with the Russian government or the local peasantry and intelligentsia difficult to achieve;

at times the three provincial nobilities found it hard to collaborate even among themselves. In this sometimes rather narrow, blinkered and stuffy world, Baltic noblemen whose outlook had been broadened by service in the Russian upper bureaucracy were a valuable but distinctly minority voice.[79]

Even in adolescence the path of Balts with their eyes on careers in the imperial service diverged from those of noblemen aiming to spend their lives within the Baltic provinces. Whereas the latter were for the most part educated at Dorpat University, the former, according to Baron Eduard von Dellinghausen, well realized that it was more sensible to cultivate different connections and loyalties by attending one or other of Petersburg's major educational institutions.[80] It is therefore very much to the point that even the State Council's most unreconstructed Balt, namely Oscar von Ekesparre, the marshal of the Osel nobility, had attended a Russian cadet corps.

Ekesparre, a landowner on Osel and a veteran Baltic marshal, had only served ten years in the Russian state service before devoting himself to his estates and elected noble office. Prominent in the latter capacity as a defender of the Lutheran Church and the Baltic self-governing institutions against the centralizing and russifying tendencies of the Petersburg authorities, of all the Balt members of the State Council Ekesparre was the most wholly and unequivocally rooted in his native soil and the Baltic gentry milieu.[81] Yet just as Ekesparre, with his Russian education, was not quite the typical Balt marshal, so, to take but one example, at the other end of the spectrum of the Council's Balts Vladimir Lambsdorff, for all his Orthodoxy and Russian patriotism, was nevertheless not entirely divorced from his Baltic roots. In 1904, for instance, Lambsdorff, the first cousin of the Estland marshal (*Ritterschaftshauptmann*), was a potentially useful source of information for Dellinghausen on decisions taken in the Committee of Ministers as regards plans to extend the use of Russian in Baltic administration.[82]

Between Ekesparre and Lambsdorff stood most of the Balt members of the State Council. Just exactly how their loyalties were divided depended from individual to individual and family to family. The Uxkull brothers, landless Protestants whose father had been a general in the Russian service, stood in statistical terms about midway on the path to russianization. Alexander Uxkull-Güldenbandt made himself thoroughly unpopular with the Livonian gentry in 1881 when, as governor of the province, he showed what seemed to them a criminal degree of sympathy for Latvian and Estonian peasant demands, and great laxness in suppressing rural disorder. On the other hand, Alexander's younger brother, Julius, was in the twentieth century to become the Baltic marshals' invaluable ally and source of information in Petersburg high official circles. A highly efficient senior official in the State Chancellery, Julius Uxkull was well placed to render this assistance. Thanks to him, neither the reports and plans of the Baltic governors, nor ministerial deliberations on Baltic affairs, remained a secret to the marshals, whose interventions with ministers or even the monarch owed much to Uxkull's advice as to the best timing and procedure to adopt. In Julius Uxkull's case this activity reflected his wholehearted loyalty to the Balts' cause and his conviction that the superior civilization of the Baltic provinces must be preserved intact from russification.[83]

The opinions of V. V. Wahl, another Protestant Baltic nobleman, were roughly similar to Julius Uxkull's, though, because of Wahl's personality and military background, rather cruder and less well disguised. Serving under Count Berg, the Viceroy of Poland, in the wake of the 1863 rising, Wahl shared his chief's dislike for N. A. Milyutin's policy of winning the loyalty of Polish peasants by backing their socio-economic claims against the landowners. Baltic noblemen like Berg and Wahl loathed on principle the 'levelling' tendencies behind such assaults on property and the social hierarchy; in addition, a Russian bureaucracy which played this game against Poles could, and indeed sometimes did, use the same tactics to win the loyalty of Latvian and Estonian peasants.[84] For Wahl, therefore, the Russian nationalist tendency within the ruling élite, 'guided by principles tinged with socialist ideas', was both a social and a national threat.[85] Nor did he share any of the affection commonly felt by Russian officials for the peasant commune, which he saw as an encouragement to socialist ideas and a brake on agricultural progress.[86] When a fellow 'German' official once argued the advantages of acting as a 'slav' in one's official capacity, Wahl replied, 'I'm not a hermaphrodite and can't turn into one'.[87] For him emperor, state and nation would always remain distinct.

The focus of his loyalty, as was traditional in the Baltic gentry, was less the state, let alone Russia, than the person of the monarch. Moreover in Wahl's case this feeling was reinforced by the rather naïve awe he felt during his service as an aide-de-camp at court in the 1860s.[88] The Russian Empire was for him something of a private Romanov estate, whose managers were duty bound to do everything possible to ensure their master's well-being. Thus on first taking over as city governor of Petersburg, Wahl informed his subordinates that their supreme task was 'to prevent anything that could in any way disturb our adored monarch or call forth the slightest displeasure of His Majesty'.[89] The anachronistic and sycophantic language in part reflected a mind devoid of political sophistication, but it also stemmed from a real dilemma facing non-Russian high officials, especially when they were serving in politically sensitive posts. In the late nineteenth and early twentieth centuries Romanov dynastic absolutism was forced increasingly to take on the mantle of Russian nationalism in order to survive. For Wahl, who felt himself to be non-Russian and detested many Russian nationalist policies, this was bound to create problems. Although he personally might avoid these difficulties by stressing his purely dynastic allegiance and loyalty, such an attitude was bound to seem increasingly threadbare and ana-chronistic when coming from a top official in the politically all-important Ministry of Internal Affairs.[90]

III

One would expect the different branches of the governmental service each to leave a specific mark on individuals who served within them for a number of years. As we have seen, some branches of the govern-ment recruited men from particular backgrounds and educated them in specific attitudes and values. In addition, long experience of using different professional skills and ways of thinking, not to mention decades of viewing overall state policy through the prism of an indi-vidual department's interests and purposes, was likely to colour an official's attitudes even after he had moved outside his own branch of service. To what extent did this happen and to what degree can one gauge such effects through a study of the members of the State Coun-cil? In the first place, the greater the number of individuals who served in a specific department the surer and better informed are one's gene-ralizations about the influence of that department on their attitudes. In addition, the longer men served in a single department, the greater, obviously, are one's chances of ascribing to them a specific ministerial mentality or point of view. The separateness and corporate spirit of the department itself also affected the influence it could exert on those who served in it, as did its internal homogeneity and the extent to which it controlled its own educational institutions through which it could indoctrinate future entrants in their adolescence.

On most of these counts the Council's 58 generals were likeliest to bear the mark of their careers. The regiment was a little world apart, its members often even living physically removed from the civilian population in isolated garrisons, generally retaining their own values and attitudes. In addition, the Council's generals had, with few excep-tions, attended military schools throughout their adolescence and indeed sometimes even earlier. As we saw, the purpose of such mili-tary education, especially under Nicholas I, had been less to broaden intellectual horizons and develop critical minds than to foster the military values of obedience, discipline, courage and apolitical patri-otism. Nor was the constricted, isolated and determinedly apolitical community of an officers' mess likely to fill the gaps left by a mili-

Three authoritarian generals: Count A.P. Ignat'ev (*above*), V.V. Wahl (*right*), Baron A.N. Meller–Zakomel'sky (*below*).

tary education.[91] Most of the Council's members were, it is true, members of the army's intellectual élite who had graduated from higher military colleges, but the education one derived from the artillery, engineering or General Staff academies was of a purely technical nature. All in all there was much truth in Polovtsov's comment that some generals in key political posts were much better equipped to command and obey than to discuss, understand or reason, while even an intelligent senior officer often lacked the education or political sense to make a useful contribution outside his own narrow field.[92]

The Council's generals and admirals, to the extent that they thought about politics at all, belonged in the great majority of cases to the authoritarian and conservative tendency within the ruling élite.[93] In their relationship to the monarch they also on the whole felt themselves bound by a particularly rigid interpretation of the military code of obedience. The combination of this code with political naïvety could produce odd results. Thus Admiral A.A. Birilyov, who signed the Treaty of Bjorkoe unread, stated subsequently that 'if he should find himself in the same position a second time he would do the same, considering that his duty as an officer of the navy obliged him to obey without question any order given him by his Sovereign Lord'.[94]

Of all the sections of the administration concerned with domestic affairs the Gendarmerie, or political police, was the one most dominated, indeed in its case monopolized, by former army officers. It therefore provides a test case for the impact of the officer on the civil service. The memoirs of Russian security chiefs make it abundantly clear that most of the ex-officers who joined the Gendarmerie were extremely incompetent political policemen. Often attaching undue importance to correct forms and to military spit and polish, their rigidity and obsession with rank and seniority were constant thorns in the flesh of the Okhrana. Not only did these ex-officers on the whole lack political knowledge or understanding, they also did not possess the intelligence, subtlety or psychological insight to exploit the secret agents within revolutionary organizations who were the key to the effectiveness of the security police. Of course not all Gendarmerie officers shared these failings. The often highly effective Okhrana officers were themselves recruited from the Gendarmerie. Moreover, incompetence as a security policeman could reflect not so much political naïvety or lack of intelligence as a moral shrinking from the methods the Police Department employed. Nevertheless the extreme ineffectiveness of ex-officers in the political police in their struggle against terrorism in the 1870s was a major factor in the state's inability to contain the revolutionary movement without destroying the bases of the legal order, and thereby alienating important sections of the community.[95]

Among the members of the State Council, V.V. Wahl provides a good example of the limitations of an army officer who transferred into the domestic administration. Wahl was not wholly without his virtues, some of them military. He was a loyal subordinate, and a man who could be trusted to follow his superiors' orders rather than his own inclinations. He was conscientious, efficient and not devoid of a sense of responsibility towards those he governed. But he combined in a dangerous manner tactlessness, lack of political sophistication and a penchant for violence.[96] His first service experience was in Poland in the 1863 rising, and he writes in his memoirs that the only possible response to guerrilla warfare and the underground gangs who murdered Russian soldiers was counter-terror and the public execution of arrested guerrillas.[97] Beyond a simple 'law and order' policy, however, Wahl seems to have had no conception of political approaches to the Polish problem, confining himself to denunciations of the socialist tendencies in the policies of N.A. Milyutin.[98] Not surprisingly, Wahl, by then a key figure in the Ministry of Internal Affairs, had no intelligent response to offer to the rise of mass discontent, and particularly of the proletariat, at the end of the nineteenth century. Gurko states, 'Wahl did not comprehend the Zubatov programme. To him it seemed fantastic in conception and harmful in results'.[99] Even in 1907 Wahl was wholly opposed to the legalization of trade unions, which he considered 'extremely harmful and corrupting'.[100] In thus closing off all legal outlets, in the form of either autonomous or state-directed unions, through which the proletariat could express its discontent, Wahl remained true to character. He was indeed, in Kireev's words, *'un homme à poigne* and nothing more'.[101]

Nevertheless to conclude a section on the Council's generals with the implication that all of them tended to share Wahl's views on society and politics would be a mistake. This is not only because, of course, the Council's 58 generals included many strikingly contrasting personalities, but also because the army was an enormous and by no means homogeneous organization which offered a number of very different career patterns. The group of 58 men was, therefore, by no means homogeneous. At one extreme was A.I. Kosych, a general noted as a provincial governor for his humanity, effectiveness and liberalism, and, according to Klyachko, the only appointed member to attach himself to the Left Group in the State Council after 1906.[102] At the other pole comes General Baron A.N. Meller-Zakomel'sky, who in 1905–6 applied the savage methods of colonial warfare he had developed in Central Asia to the suppression of revolution in Russia. Reflecting on Meller-Zakomel'sky's character and employment prospects, Witte not unjustly commented that this 'rather dark man... would be a very good gaoler, especially in those gaols where corporal punishment is practised'.[103]

The contrasting backgrounds, careers and opinions of General Prince P.D. Svyatopolk-Mirsky and General P.L. Lobko usefully illustrate the degree of diversity within the group of 58 generals. The prince was an 'aristocratic magnate', Lobko a scion of the minor gentry. For all his military rank, Mirsky was in many ways a mere show soldier, his service being confined to a few comfortable years in the ultra-exclusive Life Guard Hussars followed by a series of mostly political postings. Lobko was equally far from being a 'fighting general', his experience of command of military units being even more limited than Svyatopolk-Mirsky's. In an army whose officers spent an inordinate amount of time on administrative chores, Lobko was the king of military administrators, his whole career being devoted to this area. It is therefore probably correct to state that in both Mirsky's and Lobko's cases the two generals' careers had more in common with those of some of their civilian counterparts than with senior military officers sitting in the Council whose lives had mostly been a preparation for high command in the field.[104]

The political opinions of Svyatopolk-Mirsky and Lobko were also poles apart. The former was a liberal with distinct oligarchical tendencies. It was not out of character for him to have been one of the few members of the Peretz Commission to support the principle of privileged noble access to civil service posts. His dislike of bureaucratic authoritarianism is a thread running through his wife's diary.[105] Lobko on the other hand was, even in the early twentieth century, a firm believer in absolute monarchy and authoritarian bureaucracy. He was also a statesman of strong populist leanings. Polovtsov records Lobko's determination in 1900 that state lands rich in oil deposits should be granted as far as possible to the poorer classes rather than to rich entrepreneurs. The State Controller was a firm opponent of Witte's policy of state-induced industrialization, complaining in 1901 that 'the chief burden of that system has undoubtedly fallen upon the agricultural masses, seriously impairing their purchasing power. They have to bear almost the entire burden of direct and indirect taxes'. Arguing in 1905 that peasant disturbances arose out of economic misery caused in part by the state's economic policies, Lobko stressed that the rural masses were still loyal to the monarchy and the existing political order. Insisting that the peasants should be well represented in the Duma, he contrasted their loyalty with the untrustworthiness and liberalism displayed by much of the landowning gentry.[106]

Of the civilian ministries it was the judicial department which put the strongest mark on its officials. This was in part simply because, as we have seen, many high officials had served in this ministry for all or most of their careers. In addition, however, almost all these men had studied for a number of years either in the universities' law faculties or in the School of Law. In the latter case they had passed their adolescence in an institution strongly influenced by the judicial department and geared to its needs and values. Moreover, whether at the School or at university, the future jurists had been exposed to the teachings of law professors committed to the creation of a legal order in Russia, not to mention the provision of fair, equal and incorruptible justice for all Russian subjects. For Russians sharing this faith, the judicial statutes of 1864 were a bible, and it was in defence of this bible and the values it embodied that the specifically departmental outlook of top judicial officials was formed. This outlook was in its purest form the property of a specific generation, namely those who had entered the judicial department in the years around 1864, and it was this generation which made up the overwhelming majority of jurists within Nicholas II's State Council. A.F. Koni, himself one of the Council's leading liberal jurists, writes that his comrades of the 'generation of 1864' were

> full of faith in the worth and durability of the matter which had been entrusted to them, and looked on their work not as service in one of the many ministries but as a vocation which called them to indefatiguable creative work. The new legal system served in their eyes not just as one of the forces for improvement within the general state organism, but as a school of respect for human dignity and as one of the best means for the development in the people of a consciousness of law.[107]

Here, uniquely among the members of the State Council, one finds a group of men of whom some at least fitted Anthony Downs's definition of the bureaucratic zealot, in their passionate and single-minded devotion to a single departmental goal.[108]

Of the State Council's liberal jurists in the late nineteenth and early twentieth centuries, 'the most outstanding', in V.I. Gurko's view, was A.A. Saburov.[109] Saburov's old friend, Anatol Koni, described him as 'tall, with a face which had strong features and big expressive eyes', remarking that 'he seemed somewhat absent-minded because he was constantly submerged in his inner thoughts and removed from the trifling conventions of everyday life'.[110] Not only physically, but also in his character and views, Saburov was one of the most striking members of the State Council. A fine judge, noted for his 'remarkable, compressed, clear and always meaty summings-up' before juries, Saburov was nevertheless also a man of great and not always wholly practical idealism.[111] This set him somewhat apart from the bulk of his more pragmatic and down-to-earth peers, whose realism was no doubt typical of most senior civil servants the world over. Few other top officials, however, enjoyed such respect and affection as did Saburov in the last two decades of his life. Even V.P. Meshchersky, who had no time for liberal jurists, described Andrei Saburov as a man of an 'outstandingly good nature, completely forgetful of himself'.[112] Extremely high-minded and humane, Saburov was deeply involved in a string of charitable organizations. Among members of the imperial ruling élite he was surely unique in receiving, among the normal felicitations from leading individuals and institutions on his completion in 1907 of fifty years of state service, a letter from the body set up for the protection and rehabilitation of Jewish prostitutes, saluting him as 'a humane unprejudiced man with broad views who loves his country as one single fatherland and wishes good to all his fellow citizens without exception'.[113]

Andrei Saburov's personality is one more individual portrait to add to our gallery. He also embodied an important tradition within the imperial ruling élite not sufficiently recognized by historians. Russian liberalism and the imperial legal tradition, though defeated in 1917 and pulverized by Stalin, have, it is true, had their historians but such accounts have seldom concentrated on the place those traditions held within the government or ruling élite.[114] Andrei Saburov's whole career was devoted to the two causes. His appointment in 1904 as chairman of the special commission on senatorial reform was the culmination of a lifetime devoted either to implementing the 1864 statutes as a judge, or to defending their content in countless inter-departmental skirmishes. Demoted to the Senate from a ministerial post in 1881, Saburov did not hesitate to use his senatorial position to check the arbitrary actions of Alexander III's government – in the process courting and suffering further demotion.[115] The principles established by Saburov's special commission were in line with the beliefs that guided the whole of his career, namely that politically inspired disturbances only 'deepened the need to create an authoritative institution which would firmly and undeviatingly preserve legality in administration and would re-establish the people's weakened conception of the need to obey authority acting on the basis and within the limit of the law'.[116] That the senatorial reform to which he had devoted such energy failed ultimately to materialize is merely one example of the tremendous frustrations Saburov faced in the course of his long crusade for legality; that failure was at the same time a vital factor in the inability of the Old Regime to establish a firmly based legal order guaranteeing civil rights in the wake of the 1905 revolution.

For Saburov legality was the essential basis for a civilized, prosperous, humane and free society. Gladstonian even in his wholehearted commitment to the rescue of prostitutes, Saburov was indeed in both moral and political terms the embodiment of European Victorian liberalism. Religious toleration, moral improvement, political freedom, economic advance, the triumph of reason and of education – all these in his view were inextricably connected with the protection through law of civil and property rights. Deeply fearful of the impact of mass democracy on his ideals, at the Tsarskoe Selo conference in June 1905 he argued in classically liberal terms that 'universal suffrage in my view is always a weapon for despotism in the hands of that party which is the strongest'. To accept mass democracy would be to hand over Russia 'to that party which is best organized – that is to the revolutionaries'. It would mean that 'all the cultured elements of the population will be devoured by the overwhelmingly greater numbers of the remaining uneducated elements, and the fate of Russia will thus be given over to those least capable of political activity'. In Saburov's view 'the franchise ought to be widened little by little, as happened in England, according to the degree of development of the masses'.[117]

Already a minister in the reign of Alexander II,[118] Andrei Saburov was a relatively well-known figure in Russian political life throughout the last four decades of the Old Regime. The name of Alexander Knirim, on the other hand, was known only to the relatively small circle of experts in the field of civil and commercial law. As with most Petersburg civil servants, Knirim's career was pursued out of the glare of publicity and within the confines of a particular field of expertise. Never one to seek the limelight, the stroke he suffered shortly after appointment to the State Council deprived him of any chance to make his mark in broader political and social affairs. Knirim had the essential qualities of the outstanding jurist. He possessed 'a sharp, clear brain, which allowed him to analyse with ease the most complicated legal questions, . . . an astonishing capacity for work and a devotion to jurisprudence which made the discussion of legal issues for him not a heavy burden but a task he loved. To this was added a deep acquaintance with Russian and foreign legal literature and legislative sources, a remarkable memory and the ability to distinguish the important from the trivial and not to lose himself in details'. Calm, restrained and balanced, never prone to self-advertisement or empty eloquence, Knirim 'carefully pondered and weighed his every step...but once he came to believe in an idea, once he became enthused by it, he unwaveringly and firmly moved forward, undismayed by obstacles, forgetting personal interests, bending all the strength of his outstanding mind and abilities to the attainment of the designated goal'.[119]

For much of Knirim's life this 'designated goal' was the creation of an up-to-date civil code for the Russian Empire. First mooted by him publicly in 1874, the task absorbed the last quarter-century of his career. The existing civil code was based in part on the wholly antiquated Volume X of Speransky's *Svod Zakonov* (1833) and in part on laws scattered throughout other volumes. Internally contradictory and almost comically out of tune with the realities of contemporary economic and social life, the existing civil code confused even the best jurists and led to constant uncertainty and wavering in judicial procedures and judgements. Knirim's commitment to modernize the code was, however, a formidable undertaking, as a comparison with parallel German efforts makes clear. As A.I. Lykoshin states, whereas the German criminal code was the product of two years' work, their civil code took from 1874 to 1896 to compile and even then, unlike the Russian, did not include commercial law. Moreover German jurists working on the civil code were far better funded, had much superior past civil codexes to draw on, could fall back on the richest legal literature in the world, and in addition were on considerably closer terms with academic lawyers than was generally the case with senior Russian jurists. Starved of money and for long largely ignored by legal scholars, Knirim's committee on the civil code had to struggle too with other major obstacles. Higher authority was inclined suddenly to demand the completion of work on a specific area of civil law, such as for instance the codex on illegitimate children, thereby upsetting Knirim's timetable and endangering consistency among the various sections of the new code. Politically motivated attacks, together with complaints about apeing foreign legislation, were frequent, and not always rebuffed by those who headed the Ministry of Justice. With the future of the committee often hanging by a thread, the morale of Knirim's assistants was vulnerable and some inevitably thought that another area of activity and a different patron might better advance their careers.[120]

In the face of these difficulties Knirim mustered all his administrative and political skills, his capacity for managing people and his knowledge of the inner workings of Russian bureaucratic politics. The committee's operations were meticulously and efficiently planned. Knirim encouraged the pride and enthusiasm of his juniors by organizing informal seminars to discuss the committee's latest projects, allowing them to publish their work under their own names, fighting relentlessly in defence of their interests, and above all by communicating to them some of his own deep commitment to the task in hand. He struggled, ultimately with success, to interest the academic and non-official legal world in his code, inviting rigorous outside criticism of his committee's drafts. Promotions and appointments within the committee were made purely in the interests of business, Knirim's personal feelings, let alone his career prospects, playing no role. Acting on this principle, Knirim refused to take the chairmanship of the committee, realizing that his project's success would be better served if a more senior official with diplomatic skills and with greater weight in top governmental circles held the job.

Having engineered the appointment of N.I. Stoyanovsky, a man chosen because his skills complemented those of Knirim, the latter then shielded Stoyanovsky from most of the strains of running the committee in order to free him for the vital task of conducting external relations with other bureaucratic institutions and statesmen. Here, in other words, is an example of a senior official so wholly absorbed in his work, so convinced of its vital importance for Russian economic and social development, that personal considerations were more or less lost to view. Lykoshin records how Knirim, a Balt and a Protestant, would pace up and down on the beach while on holiday at his summer dacha in Estland, admiring the sunset and plotting how best the work of his committee could be advanced when the wasted weeks of holiday were over.[121]

Neither Saburov nor Knirim was wholly typical of the 'generation of 1864' within the State Council's jurists. More selfless and less career-minded than the majority, they were also more other-worldly, Knirim, for instance, being once described as a man 'completely foreign to a noisy social life, wholly buried in his books, his work and his family, reminding one by his whole appearance more of a learned professor than of a top state official'.[122] Certainly the pronounced liberal views on general political matters of A.A. Saburov were exceptional, as was indeed inevitably the case, given the fact that neither jurists nor open liberals enjoyed great popularity in the Winter Palace, whence came all appointments to the State Council. In general the Council's jurists were professional men of the law rather than liberals, but of course an official holding the view that no circumstances could justify the violation of the law was bound at some point to come into conflict with authoritarian tendencies dominant in the Ministry of Internal Affairs and to acquire a certain liberal reputation.

Strict allegiance to every comma of the law, exercised without concern for political reality, could indeed to many of the jurists' critics seem to be less liberal than merely pedantic. Not only bureaucratic conservatives took this view. A.N. Naumov criticizes P.P. Kobylinsky, 'a precise and strict lawyer', for the minute and petty scrutiny to which he subjected all bills reaching the State Council from the Duma. In Naumov's view, Kobylinsky, 'not a stupid man but narrow, dry and extremely intolerant', forgot the political need for collaboration with the Duma amidst a lawyer's joy in dissecting the weaknesses of a legal document. Such views were, however, commonest among conservative officials, particularly those serving in the Ministry of Internal Affairs. For the latter, jurists appeared to lack common sense or a true grasp of the complex and chaotic realities of Russian life. Obsessed by formal rules and logical formulae which had little relevance in Russian conditions, even 'an outstanding lawyer' such as I.Ya. Golubev not only lacked 'even a trace of broad views' but also had 'petty' opinions on matters outside his narrow field. Certainly, if one were looking for a caricature of a jurist's obsession with form over substance, one would find it in Golubev's intense concern, amidst the social revolution of 1917, that Russia preserve a bicameral legislature.[123]

Nevertheless, the overall intellectual level of the Council's jurists was very high, a fact acknowledged even by those within the bureaucracy who disliked the goals to which the 'generation of 1864' was committed.[124] The task set themselves by these jurists, namely the imposition of law, justice, predictability and system on Russian life, was, however, one of appalling difficulty. Knirim's ultimately only partially successful efforts in the field of civil law provide scarcely a hint of the tremendous problems entailed in integrating scores of millions of peasants, to a considerable extent untouched by the 1864 reform, into the imperial legal order.[125] Moreover, the policies of the Ministry of Internal Affairs, indeed the whole ever-sharpening political and social crisis faced by the imperial regime, conspired to frustrate the jurists' efforts. Even so, at least until 1917, all was far from failure and for this the 'generation of 1864' must take considerable credit.[126] Even a source as hostile to the ruling élite as Klyachko admits that many senior jurists, and not necessarily only those who were politically liberal, were educated 'in a spirit of respect for the law' and 'preserved sufficient independence sometimes to dare to say the truth to the autocrat'. Klyachko mentions in this respect legally minded conservatives such as E.V. Turau, Count K.I. Pahlen and I.Ya. Golubev, but other leading lights of the 'generation of 1864' such as S.S. Goncharov, I.I. Shamshin and E.Ya. Fuchs could also easily be included in this list.[127]

A good sense of the values and preoccupation of senior jurists, many of them subsequently members of the State Council, is provided by the minutes of a conference of chairmen and senior procurators of Judicial Chambers summoned to Petersburg in December 1894 to discuss the present state of Russian justice. Among the future members of the Council attending the conference the political spectrum encompassed A.F. Koni on the 'left', P.M. Butovsky and N.E. Schmemann in the 'centre', and N.N. Schreiber, V.F. Dietrich and M.G. Akimov on the 'right'. From the minutes of the conference one has, however, the sense that, whatever their subsequent political disagreements, here was a group of highly trained professionals, committed to improving the quality of Russian justice and the role of legality in Russian life.[128]

Nevertheless, before becoming too euphoric about the virtues of the Council's jurists and their impact on Russian life, one must make certain qualifications. It was difficult to maintain the full crusading

Two conservative jurists: M.G. Akimov and (*right*) I.L. Goremykin.

spirit of 1864 throughout a lifetime's service in the face of the low priority given to legality by key elements in Russian government and society. Still harder was it to pass on the torch to a younger generation. Viewing the judiciary and procuracy from very different political angles in the early years of the twentieth century, Prince V.P. Meshchersky and A.F. Koni concurred that jurists were ceasing to be crusaders and becoming in their attitudes more like normal officials. Koni bemoaned the weakening of the old fire, the independence, the breadth of vision and the generosity of spirit.[129]

Among the jurist members of the State Council there are too few members of the post-1870 generation to allow systematic comparisons with the 'men of 1864'; nevertheless one key representative of the younger group, I.G. Shcheglovitov, came to be seen as betraying, as Minister of Justice, the cause for which the fathers had toiled.[130] To some extent this sense of betrayal stemmed from the desertion of a former legal liberal to the authoritarian camp after appointment as Minister. Nor did the unsavoury and demagogic exploitation of popular anti-Semitism endear him to most of the 'men of 1864', for whom there must have been bitter irony in the fact that, as regards the Beilis affair, even Meshchersky, the judiciary's old scourge, wrote of Shcheglovitov's *cause célèbre* as a 'nightmarish medieval play', a defilement of Russian justice, and 'a new stimulus for turning the Russian people into animals' and the Russian courts into the playthings of politics.[131] Above all, however, as Shcheglovitov's interrogation by the Provisional Government revealed, it was the sense that the Minister of Justice had undermined the rule of law and subordinated justice to administrative convenience that infuriated those true to the traditions of the judicial statutes.[132]

It was, however, not only younger jurists who stood in the authoritarian camp, accepting a measure of illegality as the price of preserving order in a backward and turbulent society. As we have seen, former jurists occupied key positions throughout much of the central government. Above all they tended to dominate the Ministry of Internal Affairs and its Police Department, which were the centres of arbitrariness and anti-liberalism in Russian politics. Among the former jurists who held top posts within the Ministry of Internal Affairs under Nicholas II the names of V.K. Plehve, P.N. Durnovo, I.L. Goremykin, S.E. Kryzhanovsky, A.I. Lykoshin and A.A. Makarov stand out. This is scarcely a list of names associated with the defence of legality, civil rights or liberalism. Though it would not be true to say that a legal education and career had had no impact on the political views of these authoritarians,[133] these names are a warning against glib generalizations about the political leanings of jurists within the Russian imperial ruling élite.

Although 65 of the 215 members of the State Council had previously served in the Ministry of Internal Affairs, it is difficult to gauge the impact of that service on their attitudes. Men tended to serve for a much smaller proportion of their careers in that ministry than, for instance, in the judicial department. Moreover the Ministry of Internal Affairs was a large and amorphous department, many of whose branches had little in common with each other. Among the former officials of this ministry who reached the State Council there were, however, two, admittedly overlapping, groups which stand out. One included former governors, usually upper-class and very often, as we saw, with experience in the armed forces or as noble marshals. The other, a smaller group, had had considerable experience in the Ministry's central offices; many of them were former jurists. Though different in career experience, personality and expectations, most members of both these groups were nevertheless at the conservative end of the ruling élite's political spectrum. Indeed, speaking of the Right Group in the State Council after 1906, Klyachko states that 'in this party were all the reactionaries, all the representatives of the Russian police and of the policy of the Ministry of Internal Affairs'.[134]

One explanation for the, of course by no means universal, tendency towards conservative and authoritarian views among former officials of this department was that these men had reached the summit of the Ministry of Internal Affairs between 1881 and 1905. In this period the domestic policy pursued by Alexander III and later by Nicholas II had been in general anti-liberal. Since outside the economic or purely technical realm the Ministry of Internal Affairs dominated domestic policy,[135] anti-liberal tendencies among its former senior officials are scarcely surprising. One would not, after all, expect too many liberals in the ranks of a ministry run for over two decades by D.A. Tolstoy, I.N. Durnovo, D.S. Sipyagin and V.K. Plehve.

Nevertheless important additional reasons existed for the illiberal attitudes current in this ministry. A provincial governor, forced to make political bargains with local élites in order to run his province effectively, could not easily remain within the letter of the law. Nor did the latter mean much to the peasants with whom, equally, compromise and conciliation were necessary if order was to be maintained with the minimum of force. Moreover 'strict legality' in administration was easier to demand from Petersburg than to impose on the *ispravniki* and *uryadniki* (low-ranking police officials) who long remained the government's only effective agents in the countryside. Nor on the whole did those who ran the Ministry of Internal Affairs wish to see their agent, the governor, tightly controlled by laws and regulations which might inhibit the speed and effectiveness of his response to the multiform and unpredictable problems thrown up by local life, let alone to the disorders becoming increasingly frequent as modernization's influence spread into the provinces.[136] V.P. Meshchersky was indeed right to say that no other minister faced as difficult a task as the head of the Ministry of Internal Affairs, particularly if the minister wished to pursue a policy of liberalization. Faced with an increasingly conflict-ridden and fragile society, containing many elements whom no concessions would satisfy, a Minister of Internal Affairs unsurprisingly feared to appear weak or to put constraints on the freedom of action of the repressive organs of the state.[137]

A difficulty in generalizing about the former governors on the Council, let alone about the influence of governorships on attitudes, is that some men were governors for one year, as we have seen, and others for decades. Moreover, the local groups with whom a governor was dealing, the types of problem he faced and therefore the lessons he was likely to draw from his experiences could differ enormously from province to province. On the whole, however, the governors on the Council do not appear to have been as intelligent as were the men who had risen to the top of the State Chancellery, the Chancellery of the Committee of Ministers, or the departments of justice or finance. In part this was simply because Nicholas II was particularly anxious to have former governors in the Council and therefore held the door open for entry rather more widely than was the case with other groups of high officials.[138] Perhaps, too, where ap-

pointments to the Council were concerned, the direct involvement
of the monarch increased the extent to which unofficial links and
backstairs patrons influenced the selection process.[139] Nor should
one forget when reading Petersburg officials' comments about former governors, the element of superiority assumed by such men
towards anything provincial.[140]

A.N. Naumov, in general a fair and clear-sighted witness, was,
however, not a central official but rather a provincial nobleman who
felt himself much more at home amidst governors and marshals than
among the veterans of the Petersburg bureaucracy. Even so, his
memoirs on the whole portray the latter group as more impressive
than the former. About A.S. Bryanchaninov, for instance, a wealthy
ex-officer of the Chevaliers Gardes from an old Vologda family who
served for many years as governor of Samara, Naumov commented
that he was not particularly intelligent, had rather simplistic and
stubborn views on politics, particularly as regards the zemstvos,
and was weak-willed. As befitted a former Guards officer, he was a
great stickler for form and correct appearances. In Naumov's view,
Bryanchaninov himself was to some extent a figurehead, the brains
and backbone of the local administration being provided by his wife.
On the other hand, and this was of vital importance if a governor
was to be effective, Bryanchaninov was a good diplomat, much liked
by local élites, trusted for his honesty and kindness, and possessing
good relations with the powers-that-be in Petersburg, which made
him a useful link between the centre and his province. Not only for
Bryanchaninov, but also for governors in general, these attributes
may have been at least as important as outstanding brains, which
may explain why the Council's former governors sometimes appear
intellectually inferior to senior officials from other parts of the civil
service.[141]

Nevertheless, because of his provincial service a former governor
enjoyed significant advantages over veterans of the central administration. In the first place his field of activity, to some extent covering
all aspects of provincial life, was much broader than that of a central
official, with the possible exception of a man serving in the State
Chancellery or Chancellery of the Committee of Ministers. In addition, a governor was much closer to the population, still overwhelmingly provincial and rural, than an official in Petersburg, better able
to assess its needs, and more in a position to judge the applicability
or otherwise of governmental policy in the context of rural social
realities. The governor was also forced to be a politician in a sense
that was not true of an official in a Petersburg ministry. At provincial
level problems had to be solved and policies implemented not on
paper but in practice. Local institutions and élites had to be wooed,
for the provincial bureaucracy on its own was much too small and

inefficient to implement policies without them. Moreover a governor, particularly if he had previously served as a marshal, might well have experience in public speaking before large assemblies, which central officials generally lacked. As Peter Bark makes clear in his memoirs, the absence of this experience and skill could become very important for ministers in the Duma period.[142]

As we have seen, the top posts in the central offices of the Ministry of Internal Affairs were generally held either by former governors, or, rather more often, by veteran Petersburg officials, some of whom had considerable experience as jurists. Usually the leadership of what one could term the authoritarian tendency in Russian government came from political heavyweights presently or previously holding one of these posts. The views of the most intelligent of these authoritarians, Peter Durnovo, will be discussed in a later chapter; nevertheless the role of two others, V.K. Plehve and N.A. Maklakov, was so important that their opinions cannot be ignored.

A sense of Plehve's views in 1902–4 is conveyed by conversations he had in this period with A.A. Kireev and S.Yu. Witte. According to Kireev, even in the spring of 1904 Plehve did 'not believe in the imminence' of revolutionary disturbances, comforting himself with the thought that 'I have lived through more than one moment like the one we are living through now'. Plehve made this somewhat glib comparison with the crisis of 1880–1 in part because he believed that 'in the event of things going to extremes, the government will find support in the peasantry and *meshchanstvo*'.[143] Though making due obeisance to the importance of regaining public support, Plehve was wholly unwilling to see the state's leading role in society weakened. Old bureaucrat that he was, he still to some extent counted on 'winning the country's confidence by good and honest administration'.[144] Though he did not believe that repression on its own would solve the country's ills, nor would 'wholesale concessions' to public opinion's demands. There was not yet a mass base for revolution, but matters would get out of control if liberals gained a hold on central power. In Plehve's words, ordered reform, 'in tune with modern needs', could only be initiated by the government, which possessed experience, realism and the ability to keep the fast-moving current of a changing society within its banks. Liberal leaders were, as he put it, so 'led away by utopias' and had given so many 'hostages' to fortune that they would never be satisfied by anything less than a share in power, nor be competent or willing 'to maintain the state's authority' in the face of the demands for further concessions which would undoubtedly be presented by the left.[145]

After 1905 authoritarians were much less sanguine about the regime's ability to tap mass support, and therefore even less inclined to see the state's repressive apparatus weakened. Other aspects

V.K. Plehve's carriage after the explosion of the bomb that killed him.

of Plehve's views still, however, found an echo. In the autumn of 1916 N.A. Maklakov, for instance, wrote to Nicholas II denouncing the absurdity of those who believed Russia's social and political crisis could be solved by the establishment of a constitutional system based on liberal principles. Maintaining that the groups represented within the Progressive Bloc were inconsistent in their ideas, divided and weak, Maklakov argued that even the strongest bulwark of Russian liberalism, namely the Kadets, had no support outside the professional middle class. In contrast, the revolutionary parties represented 'a serious danger and a real strength'. They were backed by the masses, particularly by the working class but also by the peasantry. Conservative as regards their own customs and property, as the events of 1905–6 showed the peasants became socialists once revolution offered them the opportunity to expropriate the property of others. If conservative liberals, Octobrists and Kadets gained power, they would never be able to hold their ground against the left and the result would be 'a social revolution, ...communes, ...the end of the monarchy and of the propertied class and the triumph of the peasant, who will turn into a bandit'.[146]

Thirty members of the State Council had previously served in the State Chancellery or the Chancellery of the Committee (subsequently Council) of Ministers. For a number of reasons it is much easier to type-cast these men than was true of the former officials of the Ministry of Internal Affairs. In the first place both chancelleries were far smaller and more homogeneous than the ministry. Existing at the very centre of the Petersburg bureaucracy, neither chancellery had provincial offices. The two chancelleries' function was to act as secretariats, one to the State Council, the other to the Committee (later Council) of Ministers, and both to the various special commissions which attempted to co-ordinate governmental policy-making and legislation. The chancellery officials researched, prepared and edited all papers coming to the three bodies, took the minutes of their sessions and provided expert advice on matters under discussion. Both Korkunov at the time and Yaney today stress the crucial role played by the two chancelleries in the Russian system of government,[147] and all sources confirm that the officials of these two institutions represented the élite of the Russian bureaucracy. Thus A.N. Kulomzin could write in 1902 about the Chancellery of the Committee of Ministers that 'I have such a good Chancellery that outside it [i.e. when serving elsewhere] even our average people are found to be brilliant'.[148] Six years later P.N. Durnovo stated that 'as a result of its traditions, its experience and its editorial skill with laws the State Chancellery stands higher than all the other departments which exist in Saint Petersburg', adding that in general only the cleverest young men with the most brilliant career prospects entered either it or the Chancellery of the Committee of Ministers.[149] Count V.N. Lambsdorff defined the essential skills of the aspiring central government official as being the capacity tactfully to grasp political and personal currents within the system of government, and the ability to write clear, concise and logically constructed reports.[150] In these arts the officials of the two chancelleries were masters.

Nevertheless, service in the two great central chancelleries could have some ill effects on officials. Conscious of their status as an élite, some men developed an arrogant conviction about their own omnicompetence. This could have dangerous results, since work in the chancelleries was far removed from the 'life of the people' and based only on studying papers.[151] Although most chancellery officials had considerable experience in other departments, they could at times prove ill prepared if faced with direct executive responsibility for concrete policies. V.N. Kokovtsov, for instance, writes the following about N.V. Shidlovsky, an able long-serving official of the State Chancellery who was appointed in 1905 to head a commission studying the causes of working-class discontent in Petersburg: 'Shidlovsky had a high opinion of his own powers and was very critical of everything and everybody, but was quite ignorant of administrative affairs. He had had no practical business experience, having given himself up, after a long career in the [State] Chancellery, to the subtleties of the editor's art. He was completely at sea in his new position'.[152]

Together with a certain type of inexperience and arrogance, one also sometimes found in the two chancelleries a degree of world-weary cynicism and a marked lack of strongly held convictions. As Kulomzin's memoirs illustrate, this was in part the product of the chancellery official's uniquely close view of the political manoeuvrings, the errors and at times even the corruption existing at the top levels of nineteenth-century Russian government.[153] It was partly too the result of the long experience any civil servant knows of bending his own will and convictions to accommodate those of his chiefs. More rapidly than most officials, those serving in the chancelleries learned the lesson that it was not only competence and hard work, but also cultivation of the influential, prevarication and subtlety that helped one along the road to success. Moreover, Gurko argues that the constant writing of minutes of conferences and committees which was the chancellery official's lot had its bad sides, since 'to a well-informed editor with a mind of his own, it was a difficult and disagreeable task to state in a convincing way two diametrically opposite opinions, and it could not fail to exert a pernicious influence upon him. While it gave training in dialectics and, to a degree, in impartiality, it also developed a sceptical, indifferent attitude and an inclination to compromise'.[154]

If one were to seek a model official of the two chancelleries one could find none better than P.A. Kharitonov. The son of a top civil servant and himself a long-serving State Chancellery official, Kharitonov is described by Witte as 'an intelligent man and an able bureaucrat, complacent, cultured and unprincipled...a good jurist of great experience but the product of an education in the Petersburg chancelleries and especially in the State Chancellery'. Such products, in Witte's view, revealed themselves by never hesitating to change their opinions to accord with those of a new chief or altered circumstances.[155] On the other hand, a less hard-bitten cynic and – the two often being connected – an outsider to Petersburg official life, might well be far more impressed by the professional skill, the brains, and the experience of a senior official of the chancelleries. Thus Naumov writes, about Kharitonov:

As regards his abilities, his reasonableness, his experience and his immense professional training, Peter Alekseyevich was one of our outstanding statesmen. Possessing the gift of being able to express his thoughts accurately, logically and in detail both orally and in particular on paper, calm, equable and thoughtful, Kharitonov was an irreplaceable helper in the many-sided labours of the Council of Ministers, always giving productive and intelligent advice and the means to the successful solution of the most tangled and confused questions.[156]

B.V. Ananich, the leading contemporary Soviet scholar on pre-revolutionary state finance, writes that the Ministry of Finance was an exception to the generally low quality of the Russian bureaucracy in the second half of the nineteenth century.[157] Though one might challenge his condemnation of the rest of the civil service, Ananich's compliment to the financial department is certainly deserved. In part the quality of financial officials reflected the fact that between Emancipation and the 1905 revolution the Ministry of Finance had been dominated by four men, M.Kh.Reutern, N.Kh.Bunge, I.A. Vyshnegradsky and S.Yu.Witte, all ministers of high calibre. In this period the financial department was very much associated with 'new' rather than 'old' Russia, with the world of banks, railways and factories rather than the realm of landowners, priests and peasants. The establishment and highly profitable operation of the huge vodka monopoly reflected the efficient honesty of this department's staff. The increasingly sophisticated and detailed involvement in a wide range of financial and economic questions, which allows even one cautious economic historian to describe Witte's department as something close to a ministry of 'national development', further underlines the professional skill and knowledge of the senior officials in this department.[158]

All the more surprising therefore is the fact that only 19 former financial officials were appointed to the State Council. One explanation for this may be that, to the extent that financial officials had defined political views, they tended to find themselves towards the liberal end of the ruling élite. Another relevant point is that, unlike jurists and State Chancellery officials, senior members of the finance department did not have the long experience in drafting or scrutinizing laws which was so useful for members of the State Council. Also, unlike the governors, they did not enjoy strong imperial backing. Undoubtedly, however, a major reason why the financial group in the State Council is relatively small lies in the fact, mentioned earlier, that by Nicholas II's reign some senior financial officials had chosen upon leaving the Ministry to enter the world of private business and finance, thus debarring themselves from appointment to the Council. The material advantages of such a shift could be enormous. Peter Bark, for instance, moving from the vice-directorship of the State Bank to the top position in the Volga-Kama Bank, received a salary more than ten times greater than that of some appointed members of the State Council,[159] a differential which becomes even more

P.Kh. Schwanebach

impressive when one remembers that imperial Russia had no income tax even in 1914. The departure to private employment of leading financial officials of the calibre of A.I. Putilov, A.I. Vyshnegradsky, I.V. Kovalevsky, P.L. Bark and M.M. Fyodorov is therefore scarcely surprising.[160]

Among the Council's financial officials P.Kh. Schwanebach and F.G. Terner belonged to what one might describe as the 'pre-Witte' school. Schwanebach was unique among the financial officials in enjoying close relations with the imperial family, a tie to some extent inherited from his father. He had the courtier's talent for frivolous but amusing chatter. A strong and by no means unintelligent critic of Witte's economic policy, Schwanebach is, however, notable above all for being the only financial official in the Council to stand clearly in the authoritarian and conservative camp within the ruling élite. His opinions on controls over education and the press, not to mention greater rights for Jews, place him squarely in this camp. His comments on Russia's political situation in May 1907 suggest, moreover, that he had failed to learn much from the events of the previous three years. Assuring Nicholas II that Kadets and revolutionaries were less important than 'the great mass of the population which is fed up with revolution and political agitation', Schwanebach urged the Emperor to believe that 'Russia's fate will not be decided by political intriguers but by the at present silently slumbering forces of the country's elemental conservatism'. Though his views may have been sincerely held, this combination of superficial judgement with telling the monarch precisely what Nicholas longed to hear has a courtier's ring to it.[161]

Fyodor Terner was very different from Schwanebach both in his personality and his political views. Among his peers Terner's reputation for honesty, public spirit and diligence stood higher than respect for his brains. Polovtsov describes him as 'an exceedingly decent, modest, not very gifted hard worker who dedicated himself exclusively to the study of the science of finance...never in any way outstanding or brilliant...he won the fully deserved respect of people who knew him'.[162] Always full of moral purpose, and in his later life strongly influenced by Radstock's religious revivalism, Terner remained very much an 1860s liberal. He had the Victorian liberal's belief in the benefits of economic advance based on free trade and self-help. Convinced that 'the development of factory industry has everywhere served to develop the well-being and wealth of the people', he argued that 'the high feeling of brotherly love and Christian charity ...ought to be limited to its natural sphere.... To transform charity from the area of personal private activity into an official obligation, means to humiliate both him who receives it and him who gives help, to harm them both materially and morally, and at the same time throws into confusion the general state organism by the addition of a principle, which, although generous, is alien to it'.[163] Nor did Terner in 1860 see any benefits in the rural commune. A disaster as regards the development of agriculture, its egalitarian and redistributive tendencies provided 'a security for all' which was 'equivalent to the exploitation of the good and hard-working in the interests of the lazy and careless'.[164] As regards the labouring classes, Terner's view in 1860 was that the way forward lay through cheap bread, education, a sense of self-reliance and the construction of producers' voluntary co-operatives.[165] Though in his later years Terner came to accept the commune as a necessary institution of social welfare during a transitional period of economic development,[166] he never dropped his commitment either to liberal economic principles, particularly free trade, or to the extension of the political and legal reforms carried out by Alexander II.[167]

The remaining financial officials within the State Council can all, to somewhat varying degrees, be defined as belonging to what V.N. Kokovtsov once described as a 'family' of 'fellow workers from that old and splendid school of finance which gained its experience working under Serge Yulevich [i.e. Witte]'.[168] Close acquaintance with these men very much confirms Gurko's comment that Witte 'assembled a fine group of assistants and other officers in the Ministry of Finance'.[169] By universal consent, what one finds here is a group of intelligent, conscientious and highly skilled professionals. The sphere in which these men were used to operating was, however, necessarily narrow and technical. By comparison with their peers in the two great central chancelleries or the Ministry of Internal Affairs, their acquaintance with broad issues of domestic politics was slight.

The same was true, to a considerable extent, as regards personal experience of bureaucratic politics. As technical specialists somewhat removed from the political battlefield, these men had also risen in a stable ministry little affected by changing political currents or the rapid rise and fall of ministers, indeed dominated by masterful chiefs for many decades. The calm and internally united atmosphere within Witte's ministry no doubt owed much to the fact that 'our director was a man whose authority we all revered. Under his supreme control we all carried on the state's business without waverings or friction, and there were no annoying discordant notes in our complicated work'.[170] If there was no room for bureaucratic politics within Witte's ministry, it may also be true that the department's autocratic chief discouraged the development of very strong, independent-minded or abrasive subordinates. Certainly modesty and self-effacement were prominent characteristics of some of Witte's former close associates, P.M. Romanov, E.D. Pleske and I.P. Shipov being obvious cases in point.[171]

When N.N. Pokrovsky emerged into the ministerial world from the ranks of financial officialdom, Paul Benckendorff wrote that 'he has an excellent reputation as a man of intelligence and knowledge of his speciality, that is to say finance...he has never been able to show any political independence'.[172] Not only, however, could the same have been said of all the Council's financial officials; some of them showed little appetite for politics even after acquiring ministerial rank. A glaring example of this was I.P. Shipov, one of whose outstanding traits as a minister was a distinct unwillingness to act independently or take direct responsibility for policies. If in 1905–6 Shipov's total dependence on Witte, his former chief, is unsurprising, his relations with Nicholas II caused the latter some bewilderment. The Emperor once remarked that 'I cannot get used to his [i.e. Shipov's] manner of reporting; he tries to explain every little detail and as soon as I do not agree with a suggestion he abandons it and adopts my idea, although I sometimes express it quite casually just to hear his opinion'.[173] Witte, who knew Shipov well, summed up his characteristics:

> He is a very able, even gifted, bureaucrat, an official who not just knows how to work hard but also knows the right sources to read and how to study a subject through books; an extremely conscientious official, able to analyse any material; he can analyse any issue without making a single error. Shipov is, however, a man who doesn't have strong political views, indeed I can almost say that he doesn't have any political views at all.[174]

To the extent that financial officials did have political leanings they tended, however, to belong to the liberal wing of the ruling élite.[175] One discerns a distinctly humanitarian strain in the personalities and opinions of many members of the financial group. A good example of this is M.D. Dmitriev's rather horrified reaction when some of the State Council's authoritarians took a harsh view of the possibility of improving conditions in gaols and borstals. Stressing that the state's prisoners were human beings and had to be treated as such, Dmitriev remarked that at present they were often deprived of everything that made life bearable. Arguing in a manner that his opponents considered sentimental and impractical, he stated that poor conditions of life for impoverished non-criminal labourers had to be improved, not used as an excuse to deny prisoners the bare rudiments of human existence.[176]

Apart from humanitarianism, however, close contact with the expanding world of capitalist industry and finance probably had a certain liberalizing influence. A sense of Jews' importance in the international financial community as well as a closer and more sympathetic knowledge of that world often tempered anti-Semitism, for instance, as Peter Bark's memoirs make clear.[177] Moreover, the Finance Ministry was accustomed to collaborate with the leaders of Russian finance and industry, and sensitive to their needs and interests. The world of foreign bankers and Russian industrialists or railway tycoons might not be liberal in its political sympathies, but its goals, needs and ways of thinking were far removed from those of traditionally-minded landowners, peasants and priests who formed, along with the army and parts of the civil service, the social base of Russian conservatism.

The only remaining group of officials sufficiently large and cohesive to deserve study in itself is the 13 long-service veterans of the Foreign Ministry. As we have seen, of the 13 men there were only 2, I.A. Zinov'ev and A.P. Vlangali, who did not come from aristocratic or well-established gentry families. As mentioned earlier, Zinov'ev's success was owed in part to resolute ambition but also to brains and deep expertise in a vital geographical area without attractions for many of the diplomatic service's aristocrats. Vlangali's ascent, by contrast, was largely a matter of luck and carefully forged connections in society.

Of the 11 remaining men, a number had comfortable private incomes, for it was not easy to meet the expenses of diplomatic life in a major European capital without some addition to one's official salary.[178] The Russian diplomat's life-style had something of the easy-going quality of a gentry 'nest'. Nor was it always very much more hard-working. To some extent the stress on a diplomat's ability to move comfortably and with elegance in society made sense in a European world whose social and political élites were still, in the major monarchies, both closely united and drawn from traditional ruling groups. The importance of the externally glittering representative functions of a diplomat could, however, be overemphasized, as was indeed the case in Britain and Germany as well.[179] Strict obedience to the instructions of one's bureaucratic chiefs was not always the hallmark of the Russian diplomat. Consciousness of one's own independent social status, together with geographical remoteness from one's chief in Petersburg, contributed to this weakness, but so too could the fact that the standing of the Minister of Foreign Affairs was at times undermined by the close interest taken in diplomatic activity by his imperial master. The link between the Foreign Ministry and the court indeed contributed neither to the inner cohesion and discipline of the diplomatic service, nor to the quality of some top appointments.[180]

Diplomats' views on domestic politics ran the risk of superficiality since these men's careers had been exclusively spent in missions outside Russia. Izvol'sky's attitude of 'what will Europe say?' angered some officials of the home departments in 1905–7.[181] Nor did Serge Sazonov's grasp of Russia's domestic political crisis, even after the 1917 revolution, run very deep. In his view the Russian people were not politically ambitious, 'and merely desired a satisfactory arrangement with regard to land, something like that which Stolypin had in view, and liberation from a peculiar and archaic system of administrative tutelage'.[182] Remoteness from Russian domestic concerns hampered the Russian diplomat from grasping the overall balance of state interests and strengthened a tendency on the part of many civil servants to don departmental blinkers. Amidst concern for balance-of-power theory and concentration on the struggle for national pride and pre-eminence in the international sphere, it was not always easy to remember Russia's internal weakness. In early 1908, for instance, Izvol'sky demanded impatiently whether on Near Eastern questions he could again 'speak with the firmness that was proper for the Minister of Foreign Affairs of a great power', needing to be sharply reminded by P.A. Stolypin of the realities of Russia's domestic crisis.[183] Nevertheless, recklessness was not the norm in the Foreign Ministry. It was after all a Foreign Minister, Prince A.M. Gorchakov, who coined the phrase that Russia was 'a great powerless country'[184] and his successors were in general well aware of Russian weakness. They were equally aware, however, that in an imperialist world weak countries were likely to go to the wall, and that how other nations perceived one's military power and strength of will was a vital factor in one's ability to defend one's interests and security. Sitting on the side-lines of international relations might be desirable for reasons of internal security and prosperity, but, as happened in the 1860s, one ran the risk of some fundamental shifts occurring to one's disadvantage in the international order.[185]

If the position of Russian diplomacy was unenviable, its prospects were certainly not improved by the quality of some senior Russian diplomats. Most of the Council's ex-ambassadors were, it is true, able and intelligent men. Baron R.R. Rosen, Baron G.G. Staal, I.A. Zinov'ev, Count Paul Shuvalov and P.A. Saburov certainly deserve this compliment.[186] The six men who actually headed the Foreign Ministry between 1895 and 1914 were, however, much more of a mixed bag. If Count M.N. Murav'yov was decidedly lightweight for so vital a post,[187] he was nevertheless much superior to N.P. Shishkin,[188] who temporarily headed the ministry after Prince A.B. Lobanov-Rostovsky's death in 1896. S.D. Sazonov was distinctly inexperienced when he took over the ministry in 1910, and lacked either great intelligence or a calm temperament.[189] Vladimir Lambsdorff, though far cleverer and more experienced than Sazonov, to an even greater degree had the wrong personality for the job, while Alexander Izvol'sky's great intelligence was in part vitiated by excessive concern for fame and popularity.[190]

Indeed the only one of Nicholas II's Foreign Ministers in whom Russians could take real pride was Aleksei Lobanov-Rostovsky. One of the Council's oldest members (born 1824) and a true (albeit state-supported) *grand seigneur*, Lobanov had something of the spirit of pre-1789. Here was an ambassador who sparkled in salons, collected mistresses, attended church in his dressing gown, and assembled a library of 8,000 books during his embassy in Vienna. Regular attention to diplomatic correspondence, on the other hand, was not his forte. Lobanov-Rostovsky was a brilliant conversationalist, a fine linguist competent even in Hebrew, and a great dilettante. His Old Regime leanings, set forth in a number of published works on eighteenth-century France, were reflected in a more serious manner by his dislike of Panslavism and Balkan adventures, and his commitment to good Russo-Austrian relations.

Lobanov was a man bored by details, somewhat selfish and much inclined to an easy life. Like most veteran continental statesmen, he had few clues about extra-European affairs. Nevertheless even Witte, not on the whole favourable to Lobanov, believed that he had sufficient experience and grasp of affairs to have avoided the disasters which later befell Russian policy in the Far East. Realism, common sense, intelligence and judgement Lobanov had in abundance. Even his charm, his sense of humour and his aristocratic style had their relevance to his effectiveness as Foreign Minister, for they contributed to his good relations with Nicholas II. Since controlling the latter, particularly before the Russo-Japanese war and Bjorkoe, was one of a Russian Foreign Minister's major headaches, Lobanov's ability to impose his personality on the young monarch was a valuable asset. Nor, as the Panslav A.A. Kireev admitted with some surprise, did Lobanov as Foreign Minister justify the forebodings of those who had predicted a reign of superficial charm combined with lazy inattention to matters of state.[191]

Inevitably, a number of men do not fit easily into any of the groups, social, ethnic or professional, into which I have divided the members of the State Council. In some cases this is simply because the individuals in question did not serve in any of the major departments so far discussed in this chapter. In other cases one is dealing with highly original and unusual personalities, untypical of any sub-group within the ruling élite.

Prince M.I. Khilkov, for instance, one of the Council's five civilian engineers, in background, personality and career was set sharply apart from all other members of the State Council. A scion of one of Russia's oldest aristocratic families and the son of wealthy parents well placed at Nicholas I's court, Khilkov was educated in part at the Corps des Pages and entered service in the Guards. Unique among the Council's aristocrats in pursuing a career as a railwayman, not only his background but also his lack of formal engineering training set Khilkov apart from other engineers, civilian and military, within the ruling élite. He was truly a self-taught engineer, having learned his trade through a number of years' work as an engine-driver in South America and as a shipwright in Liverpool. This 'totally extraordinary character' then returned to Russia, served in ever-increasingly important posts in the Russian railways until finally, owing to a combination of professional skill and the patronage of the Empress Marie Fyodorovna, becoming Minister of Communications. Witte describes Khilkov as a 'fine railwayman...a practical technician, the kindest of men but in no way an administrator'.[192]

To a considerable extent Khilkov was simply a unique phenomenon. Certainly one would be hard pressed to fit him into any social, ethnic or professional stereotype. On the other hand, Mikhail Khilkov was very much a product of the late 1850s and early 1860s, sharing with some other members of the Council who belonged to this generation a strong dose of liberal idealism. One of the first generation of peace arbitrators, Khilkov is said to have given much of his own land away to the local peasantry. Subsequently he remained on the left of the ruling élite, enthusiastic about trade unions' defence of workers' rights and overcome with emotion when Nicholas II agreed to the creation of representative institutions in 1905. A man of the 1860s in his generosity of spirit, his fascination with scientific and technological advance, and his commitment to the people's welfare, Khilkov shared too some of his generation's naïvety and its shock when the great gulf that divided it from the masses was revealed. Faced with disaffection among railway workers in 1905, Khilkov assured his fellow ministers that the railway union was politically loyal and was only pursuing the cause of its members' material well-being. Sallying forth to Moscow to negotiate with striking railway-men, Khilkov perched on an engine and attempted to rally the workers around him, assuring them that he too was an engine-driver. According to Witte the railwaymen merely 'laughed at his naïvety'.[193]

By comparison with Khilkov, V.P. Cherevansky seems distinctly ordinary, at least at first glance. Though he was the only long-serving official of the State Control to be appointed to the Council between 1894 and 1914, 'decent, honest, hard-working Cherevansky'[194] seems in many ways typical of the efficient professional senior civil servants from a number of other ministries whom we have already encountered. Perhaps this by no means wealthy man stands out a little for the generosity with which he endowed scholarships in institutions of higher education.[195] He was also unusual, though far from unique, in combining an official career with writing novels, his best-known work, *Pod boevym ognyom* (1898), being a tale of romance, intrigue and adventure set in Russian Central Aisa.[196] Cherevansky's non-fiction writing had an overtly political aim. Though, as we have seen, the ruling élite contained a considerable number of experts on Russia's European borderlands, Cherevansky was the only civilian member of the Council whose field of expertise was Central Asia, where much of his career had been spent, and Russia's relations with the Empire's Moslem minority. It was on these subjects, and particularly on the significance of Russia's imperial mission in the Islamic world, that Cherevansky concentrated most of his literary attention.

His views were rather those one might expect of a European colonial administrator in the Victorian era. He had no doubts about the superiority of European culture to that of Asia. For Cherevansky, European civilization rested on the humane principles of Christianity and the advancement of education, technology and economic prosperity. Russians should take pride in the fact that they were Europe's sentinels in Asia. To Russia went the major credit for pushing Islam's power back from the borders of Central Europe to the Pamirs and the Mongolian frontier. To weaken Islam was to reduce the world-wide influence of a culture that was by its very nature obscurantist, inhumane and determined to close as much of the world as possible to the spiritual and material benefits that Europe had to offer. The Islamic threat was, however, by no means dead, for not merely were Moslems largely proof against Christian influences, their own missionary efforts among pagan and Buddhist peoples in Asia and Africa were often much more successful than those of the Christian Churches. Moreover, in response to the advance of Christianity and progress in the world, reactionary Islam was beginning to reassert its old militancy and to attempt to unite against its common enemy.

Russians, said Cherevansky, should garner confidence in themselves and their world-wide role from their empire's huge extent, its power, and the great difficulties they had surmounted in rising from a vassal state of the Mongols to one of the world's leading civilized powers. Writing in the wake of the 1905 revolution, Cherevansky stressed that a major cause of Russia's internal demoralization was the shock to her people's self-confidence and their faith in the power and sense of purpose of the state, brought about by defeat at the hands of Japan. For Cherevansky, Russian national pride, built on an awareness of the heroism and suffering of earlier generations and on a consciousness of Russia's majestic imperial mission, was the best antidote to internal divisions, socialist fantasies and the decline in Russians' pride and self-confidence.[197]

Though Cherevansky was an intelligent and well-read observer of Moslem affairs, as a scholar he was not in the same league as most of the State Council's professors. The latter were, as one would expect, distinctly to the right of most of their Russian academic brethren. This was particularly true of professors who also served as officials in the Ministry of Education, whether in the ministry's central offices or, more often, as curators of educational districts. The latter group included some of the most generally unpopular members of the ruling élite, one of whom undoubtedly was A.N. Schwartz.

Schwartz himself, aware of how deeply he was disliked in society, wrote in his memoirs, 'to speak the truth I could never understand this'. In part the unpopularity of any senior educational official of that time stemmed from the fact that his job made him a central figure in the government's troubled relations with the intelligentsia, the professorate and with Russia's students. To impose order and the government's educational priorities on these groups was not conducive to a man's popularity. Since the educational department was also in the forefront of the government's campaign to impose the Russian language in the borderlands, a Russian nationalist like Schwartz, who served as curator in both Riga and Warsaw, was bound in addition to acquire non-Russian enemies.

Schwartz was in many ways a sad figure. He had an international reputation as a classical scholar, and was offered a chair both at the Sorbonne and in Oxford. His relatively meagre list of publications owed much, however, to his having sensed, correctly, that classical scholarship was little read or respected in Russia. Scholarship and teaching were always for him of pre-eminent interest; he became an educational administrator in order to support his family of five children. As a top educational official, and especially during his two-year stint as Minister, Schwartz succeeded in antagonizing a remarkable number of people of widely differing persuasions. This was in part because he was determined to defend education from, as he saw it,

A.N. Schwartz

political influences, whether from the right, with its desire that the schools should inculcate military-patriotic values, or from the intelligentsia, with its wish for broad and 'socially relevant' courses in gymnasia. A great élitist, determined that Russian schools should be as rigorous and intellectually demanding as their best European counterparts, Schwartz had no time for what he saw as the unstable, ignorant, impractical and self-contradictory wishes of Russian society *vis-à-vis* the state's educational system. Children must be taught to work hard, think systematically and develop analytical skills. Courses must be designed by professional educators in accordance with European principles of pedagogical science. Such views, combined with a nature 'not inclined towards close relations with other people', an inflexible personality stronger in its adherence to principle and the letter of the law than in its sensitivity to political currents, and an unconcealed intellectual arrogance, did not win Schwartz many friends.[198]

A.N. Schwartz was both a professor and a Muscovite. As such he felt himself to be wholly different from Petersburg bureaucrats, towards whom in general he felt a deep antipathy. Above all he loathed the veteran Petersburg political officials spawned in the cold and intrigue-ridden world surrounding the State Chancellery and Chancellery of the Committee of Ministers, a world that in Schwartz's view bred slipperiness, ambition, compromise and cynicism, and which, he believed, refused to accept anyone not sharing those values.[199]

Also somewhat removed from the Petersburg bureaucratic norm, though not so distant from it as Schwartz, were certain civilian officials whom one might also describe as courtiers. V.I. Mamantov, for instance, spent his entire career in institutions attached to the person of the Emperor, emphasizing in his memoirs that he was in the service of the Sovereign (*gosudarevaya sluzhba*) and not that of the state (*gosudarstvennaya sluzhba*).[200] The distinction was a real one, affecting both the path taken by Mamantov's career and the outlook he developed during its course.

Mamantov was one of the many members of the State Council who benefited immensely from his father's connections. I.S. Mamantov, head of the Petitions Chancellery, died when his son was on the point of starting his career, but old friends of the father, notably O.B. Richter and Baron A.A. Budberg, patronized the son of their dead comrade and speeded his promotion. V.I. Mamantov thereby became assistant head of chancellery of Imperial Headquarters in 1895, a plum position because it brought one into very close proximity to the imperial couple. Only five years later, at age thirty-six, Mamantov was appointed assistant head of the Petitions Chancellery, a job of the same class as an assistant ministership. The key to this appointment, which 'stunned' everyone and meant that Mamantov had leap-frogged over many of his seniors, was that Nicholas II had personally declared that the formal impediments to Mamantov's promotion were unimportant, thereby emphasizing that although imperial control over the civil service was no longer a reality, when the monarch's eye lighted on a particular official that person could benefit enormously.[201]

Mamantov appears to have been a conscientious and well-meaning official, though nothing in his memoirs suggests that his mind was particularly original or exciting. Of his service in the upper reaches of the Petitions Chancellery, which handled personal petitions sent to the monarch, he writes that 'one needed considerable thoughtfulness, hard work and caution so that, without undermining the law or harming the interests of third parties, one could attain results consistent with the demands of higher moral justice and with the realities of life, which often went beyond the law's constraints'. In Mamantov's view, his one-time chief, Count P.A. Heiden, 'a strict man of the law and a formalist', was quite the wrong person to head an institution which aimed to succour 'the wretched and the wronged' when they turned personally to the supreme source of power, but also of mercy and of benevolence, for aid and protection. In Mamantov's views one sees preserved the old, patriarchal and personal aspect of monarchy, as distinct from the cold, impersonal and 'objective' rule of bureaucracy and of law.[202]

In the course of his career, Mamantov came into conflict on a number of occasions with another of the Council's courtiers, A.S. Taneev.[203] Even more than Mamantov, Taneev held his post at the

top of the Emperor's Own Personal Chancellery almost by hereditary right, his father and grandfather having preceded him in this
position. Taneev had the smooth tongue, the suppleness and the pettiness of a true courtier. Witte's comment that Taneev's 'single merit
was that he was a nothing' is a trifle harsh, for Taneev was not without cleverness and cunning of a somewhat insipid sort. In A.A.
Mosolov's view, Taneev, the father of Anna Vyrubov, Alexandra
Fyodorovna's bosom friend, was 'very close to their Majesties,
though he carefully hid his influence on them'. If so this did
not reflect very well on the imperial couple, for Taneev lacked the
independent-mindedness, the knowledge and experience which a
true head of the monarch's private office should have possessed.[204]

Unimpressive as a courtier–cum–official, Taneev was, however,
the composer of a number of symphonies, operas and chamber
works which enjoyed an international reputation. Though not a
musical figure of the first rank, his compositions are still sufficiently
valued to warrant an entry in the short and distinctly exclusive *New
Dictionary of Music* (1975), where, one hardly needs to add, his position as a top-ranking state official sets him apart from all his musical
peers. Taneev's peculiar combination of talent with weakness is of
concern only to a biographer, but the fact that this very senior civil
servant, living at the heart of the imperial court, could at the same
time be a central figure in the Russian musical world is of more than
anecdotal interest.

The point was made earlier that the Russian imperial bureaucratic élite was very much part of the highly cultured world of pre-
revolutionary educated society. In no field was that more true than in
that of music. A.S. Taneev was the first cousin of Serge Taneev
and a close friend of P.I. Tchaikovsky. The latter was educated
alongside future members of the State Council, at the School of
Law, just as N.V. Rimsky-Korsakov was a product of the naval
cadet corps and M.P. Mussorgsky of the School of Guards Sub-
Ensigns. The Taneevs, Rimsky-Korsakov and Mussorgsky, along
with Serge Rachmaninov, himself a good friend of Nicholas II's
brother Mikhail, all came from families of the Russian traditional
landowning gentry. In the light of this, the idea that a chasm divided
the imperial ruling élite from Russian culture, embodied in the
radical and radical-liberal intelligentsia, seems remarkable.[205]

The same point emerges emphatically from the life of P.P. Semyonov, a product of the old Ryazan gentry, the School of Guards
Sub-Ensigns and Petersburg University, who was unquestionably
one of the leading figures in Russian cultural life of his times. Only a
full-length biography could do justice to Semyonov's outstanding
personality and varied life, but merely to list his major offices and
achievements is to stress the leading role he played in both Russian

cultural and governmental affairs. An expert botanist and geologist, the first European ever to discover and explore the Tyan-shan area of Central Asia, the founder of Russia's finest private collection of sixteenth- and seventeenth-century Flemish and Dutch paintings, Semyonov's published works stretch from a book on the fossilization of Siberian limestone to a study of the history of Dutch painting. Vice-president of the Geographical Society, member of the Imperial Academies of both Arts and Science, active in a string of Russian charities and a member of many foreign learned bodies, Semyonov was also a key figure in the Russian bureaucracy. Of all the 'bureaucratic liberals' in Nicholas II's ruling élite who drew their inspiration from Alexander II's Great Reforms, it was Semyonov who, as secretary to Rostovtsev's Editorial Commission, played the most important role in the reform era. Subsequently, presiding for 17 years over the State's Central Statistical Committee, Semyonov did much to put Russia's statistical studies on their feet. From 1882 an active member of the Second Department of the Senate, which handled appeals from peasant courts, Semyonov remained closely involved in the work of the statistical committee and was the guiding hand behind Russia's first universal census of 1897. A member of the State Council from 1897, Semyonov was given the ultimate accolade for a bureaucrat when appointed a Knight of Saint Andrew in 1911.[206]

Of course it would be absurd to claim that Peter Semyonov was typical of the imperial ruling élite, as absurd indeed as to make a similar claim for the appalling Baron A.N. Meller-Zakomel'sky. The two men occupy the extreme ends of the spectrum along which one finds the members of the State Council. Between them, as we have seen, is a whole range of individuals many of whom can, to a greater or lesser extent, be fitted into one or other of the sub-groups into which the ruling élite can be divided. To attempt to break down the body of 215 men into these sub-groups is to impose some degree of order on what would otherwise be a chaotic and unstructured set of individual biographies. Yet to attempt to create too much order would be disastrous, for the untidy accumulation of detailed individual portraits gives an overall sense of the ruling élite more akin to an impressionist painting than to a structured analytical exercise.

In such an approach anecdote too has its role. One learns something of the nature of the imperial ruling élite when one reads tales, perhaps legendary, of A.N. Meller-Zakomel'sky amusing himself by skilfully beheading Turkoman prisoners in Central Asia, while absorbing too a description of Semyonov in Petersburg's Alexander Market, crawling on the ground in full-dress senatorial uniform in order to look at a painting by a Dutch master from the best possible angle. Peter Durnovo's use, as head of the Police Department, of secret agents to raid the office of a foreign diplomat suspected of a

liaison with Durnovo's *inamorata*; Andrei Saburov's crusades to rescue prostitutes; 'Gramophone' Kokovtsov's love of his own 'loud
well-rounded phrases';[207] Fyodor Terner's dedicated preaching of
the Bible in the homes of Petersburg workmen; Khilkov on his loco-
motive; even Ivan Goremykin's lovingly nurtured glossy whiskers,
habitually stroked by their somewhat feline and cynical owner as he
resignedly contemplated the world's folly – all these contribute to
our sense of what the imperial ruling élite was actually like.

Moreover, to stress the ruling élite's diversity is not merely to
emphasize the banal point that in this group of human beings, as
with most others, one finds the good, the bad and the ugly. The
great differences between the various individuals concerned not only
deter one from confidently ignorant generalization about 'tsarist
bureaucracy', they also say something fundamental about the imperial
regime and the old Russian ruling class. Here on the one hand was a
state which treated its subjects in a more arbitrary and at times brutal
manner than was true of any of the other major European states in
the Victorian and Edwardian eras – if, that is, one ignores the suppression of the Paris Commune and turns a blind eye to goings-on in
some at least of the European powers' colonies. Yet here too was a
traditional upper class whose nineteenth-century contributions in the
fields of literature and music were far more impressive than those of
any of their European peers. The radically differing personalities to
be found within Nicholas II's State Council reflected not only normal
contrasts between individual humans or even simply departmental
differences, but also something of the dual face of the Russian old
nobility and the state officialdom with which, at the summit of the
bureaucracy, it was still very closely linked.

CHAPTER 6

P.N. DURNOVO:
THE POLICEMAN AS
SAGE AND PROPHET

Peter Nikolaevich Durnovo was born in 1845 into an old gentry family. The Durnovos were a large family, as was typical of this milieu, with many branches of widely varying wealth and status. Among those appointed to the State Council under Nicholas II there was, for instance, Peter Pavlovich Durnovo, a distant cousin of Peter Nikolaevich, whose fortune and inherited status placed him at the heart of Petersburg aristocratic society. Whereas, however, Peter Pavlovich's grandfather and great-grandfather had risen to the top of the service hierarchy, and the former had married a fabulously wealthy heiress, Peter Nikolaevich's ancestors had made the run-of-the-mill careers and marriages typical of the middle stratum of the landowning gentry. Among P.N. Durnovo's direct ancestors and their brothers there is a uniform pattern of careers pursued up to the rank usually of captain but occasionally of colonel, together with ownership of estates of between 100 and 150 serfs. Durnovo's own father, Nicholas Sergeevich, was a middle-ranking civil servant, his highest position being acting vice-governor of Vilno.

N.S. Durnovo owned no property but his wife inherited 153 serfs in Vologda province in the far north, an estate of limited value before 1860 but whose land is unlikely to have been of much worth after Emancipation. P.N. Durnovo therefore had to make his own way in the world, finding in the full-time service of the state an alternative to the traditional life of the rural nobleman. Throughout his career P.N. Durnovo's major source of income was his salary, but through his wife, who inherited 1,400 *desyatiny*, he also had an interest in landed property.[1]

In line with the traditions of his family and class, P.N. Durnovo had a military education, attending the Naval Cadet Corps in the second half of the 1850s. According to A.N. Mosolov, Durnovo's contemporary at this institution, the intellectual training it provided in the mid-1850s was 'pitiful, pretty beggarly and repulsive', living conditions very rough, the cadets 'semi-savage' and the Corps au-

P.N. Durnovo

thorities often crude and brutal in their treatment of the boys.[2] Durnovo, who came from a poorer, less cultured and probably less sheltered background than Mosolov, was no doubt less shocked by the Corps, but it is unlikely that his education did much to advance his intellect or sensibilities, though it no doubt encouraged in him a rugged patriotism.

Graduating from the Corps in 1862, Durnovo spent the rest of the decade in the navy, much of it at sea. Thus when the political views of many of his future peers in the State Council were being formed by the enthusiastic liberal currents predominant in the early years of Alexander II's reign, Durnovo was confined in the narrow, disciplined and anti-intellectual atmosphere of the Naval Cadet Corps and a man-of-war. Significant also for his world view was the fact that he loved military service and always remained intensely loyal to the Russian navy.[3] Indeed it would not be too much to say that, at least in the last decade of his life, Durnovo's vision of the perfect Russian community was a distinctly military one, spiritually united in a common patriotic cause and with the potentially wayward lower orders kept under strict discipline by their social and professional superiors. Yet in 1870, for reasons which can only be surmised, Durnovo broke away from the simple career pattern of the naval officer by entering the Military Judicial Academy. Two years later he parted company entirely with the armed forces by joining the judicial department. Among the State Council's former 'jurists' he was unique in having been a professional officer and the product of a military legal education.

It is possible to see a number of important ways in which Durnovo's background, adolescence and military career shaped his views and his personality. Family background, education and early career all contributed to a sense of pride in the Russian armed forces, to military values and a military mentality, and to a commitment to service and sacrifice[4] in the cause of Russian power and greatness. In addition, the bluntness, even crudity, with which Durnovo subsequently expressed his views and which sometimes alienated his more refined colleagues in the upper ranks of the civil service, can to a considerable extent be ascribed to the fact that, in S.D. Sazonov's words, he had 'the education of a navigating officer and little general culture'.[5] Nevertheless, Durnovo's remoteness in his youth and early manhood from the dominant currents of Russian intellectual life was probably not an unmitigated loss. As an autodidact, his opinions were largely shaped by a sharp brain and varied experience of life. At the same time, the legal training and experience through which he passed as a mature ex-officer not only taught him the art of public speaking but also the ability to analyse problems and organize his thoughts. His genuinely independent and even sometimes original ideas may well have owed something to his unusual – by the standards of the imperial ruling élite under Nicholas II – mixture of military and legal training. Indeed, if in later life Durnovo was to understand how ill-founded was the faith of many of his compatriots, liberal and socialist alike, in the inevitable onset of a bourgeois-liberal phase of Russian development, the correctness of his insight may ironically have owed something to his very lack of an orthodox education in political science, philosophy or history.

Between 1872 and 1881 he served as a state prosecutor in the judicial department, where, according to Witte, amidst many able contemporaries Durnovo's 'energy and efficiency' stood out.[6] In 1881 came a crucial shift into the Ministry of Internal Affairs as head of the judicial section of the Police Department. Two years later Durnovo became vice-director of the department and in 1884 its chief, a post he held for nine years. The directorship of the Police

Department gave him command over all the Empire's police forces and was a position of immense power and significance. In purely career terms Durnovo's shift to the Ministry of Internal Affairs had yielded handsome rewards, which was no doubt exactly what he had intended. Nevertheless, his transfer to the Police Department was not only a statement of ambition but also of political views. No liberal would have wished, or been able, to hold the top job in the headquarters of the Russian police in the repressive reign of Alexander III. According to A.I. Ivanchin-Pisarev, a friend of Durnovo described the Police Department's chief in the following terms: 'He is a direct, sharp and stubborn man. If he says something is impossible, then no arguments will change his decision. He is opposed to all efforts, which other officials love to flaunt, to display pretensions to liberalism, to hand out promises or seek to reassure people.'[7]

Other accounts of Durnovo in this period, admittedly by political enemies, are less flattering. Thus, for instance, for all his legal training and the respect he sometimes showed for elements of legality in subsequent periods of his career, arbitrariness and contempt for certain civil rights were the rule in Durnovo's department. Responding to criticism of his wide use of administrative exile, he argued that political suspects were often better off in his hands than before the courts. 'You think the courts are proof against personal influence? They are made up of human beings just like other humans...believe me, they would deal with you more harshly than we do.'[8] Always susceptible to pretty women, Durnovo wrote that when a beautiful female paid attention to him he wished to free all the prisoners in the Empire: one source insists, perhaps unfairly, that female intercessions were indeed effective in the liberation of prisoners.[9] In Yaroslavl in 1886, when a revolutionary group with terrorist links was discovered, Durnovo ordered the arrest of anyone against whom there was 'the least suspicion'. Some 50 people were subsequently held in gaol for two years while the 'preliminary investigation' lasted.[10] Still more unpleasant in a way were the Police Department's efforts to cultivate informers in Petersburg student circles. Durnovo put pressure on one girl, stressing that 'I regard youth with great good will and don't allow arrests for trifles', and insinuating that it was very much in the interests of the young that he should know what was going on in their discussions. Subsequently, the girl in question, under pressure from Durnovo to divulge information and abandoned by her friends because she was suspected of having police links, had a nervous breakdown.[11]

Measured against the activities of a Himmler, a Beria or even a Dzerzhinsky, such methods no doubt seem distinctly innocent. Aldanov is right to suggest that Durnovo's cynicism was tempered by the moral code of the Victorian élite to which he belonged. The torture of political prisoners or the total absence of moral scruples of a Beria or Himmler were unimaginable to Durnovo, who was by nature in any case by no means a cruel or sadistic man.[12] Perhaps even more important, though a fervent Russian nationalist, Durnovo lacked the ideological blinkers which could shut out reason and turn mass murder into the salutary cleansing of society of its racial or class enemies. Nevertheless, it is not difficult to understand the revulsion felt at police methods in imperial Russia, nor to realize that, like most men who directed the Police Department, Durnovo was bound to be tainted by the means he employed and the information about individuals' hidden lives at his disposal. In his case, already somewhat sceptical by nature, he was undoubtedly further encouraged in his cynicism by a job in which one scarcely saw human nature at its most attractive.

In 1893 scandal brought Durnovo's career as head of the Police Department to a close. He sent police agents to search the office of a foreign diplomat whom he considered to be a rival for the affections of a certain woman, enemies in the bureaucracy reported the matter to Alexander III, and the Emperor, in a rage, 'promoted' his police chief to the First Department of the Senate – in other words to precisely the institution designed to enforce legality in the civil service.[13] Though Alexander's gesture undoubtedly said something about his attitude both to the Senate and the rule of law, in fact Durnovo seems to have performed creditably as a senator. Supervising matters far removed from the struggle with the revolutionary movement, he showed no sympathy for unnecessarily arbitrary treatment of the population by bureaucrats and, in Witte's view, stood out in particular as a defender of the Jews against illegal administrative persecution.[14]

D.S. Sipyagin brought Durnovo back into the Ministry of Internal Affairs in 1900 as one of his three deputies, ensuring however that Durnovo kept away from political affairs by entrusting him with control over the Empire's postal service. Two rather conflicting aspects of Durnovo's career under Sipyagin are of interest. On the one hand, as was always true with him, he displayed great energy, administrative ability and strength of purpose in radically improving the efficiency of the post office.[15] On the other hand, equally typically, Durnovo lost money on the stock exchange and was in dire need of rescue, which came in the form of 60,000 roubles supplied by Sipyagin from the funds of the Police Department.[16] Here we have two aspects of Russian senior officialdom on display: on the one hand its professional efficiency in fulfilling useful public functions, and on the other its ability on occasion to exploit its position as an unchecked and largely irresponsible ruling clique. The possibility under an absolute monarchy for one high official to do another a good turn and to use the state exchequer, generally with imperial consent, as a means of rescuing a colleague from financial embarrassment[17] provides one cynical explanation for the affection in which many senior civil servants held autocracy. It also illustrates how in the higher and more politicized echelons of the civil service, inevitably linked to the intrigues and the 'family atmosphere' of the court, the ideal of strict regulation of officials' behaviour and a sharp separation of private and public lives was never fully attainable. Yet, as with all such comments on Russian senior officialdom, a *caveat* is required here. To imagine that the activities either of Durnovo or the Police Department were typical of the civil service as a whole would be mistaken, for both the man and the department were notorious in high official circles for their lack of scruple.

In 1902 the Ministry of Internal Affairs acquired a new chief in the person of V.K. Plehve, like Durnovo a product of the procuracy and the Police Department. Since the two men had had the same schooling in the Police Department's ruthless form of bureaucratic politics, neither for instance shrinking from using perlustration of the posts to acquire information on personal rivals or sources of potential support,[18] it is scarcely surprising that Plehve and Durnovo thoroughly distrusted each other. Nevertheless, the way in which Durnovo effectively distanced himself from Plehve's policies may well have reflected more than mere personal dislike or careerist calculation. Bureaucratic absolutism was manifestly not operating very effectively in the period 1900–4, Plehve's policies were proving counterproductive, and a man of Durnovo's intelligence may quite genuinely have come to believe that the measures of police repression successful in the 1880s were an inadequate answer to the much more broadly-based discontent evident in early twentieth-century Russia.

Two comments about Durnovo in the period 1901–3 by other senior officials illustrate not only some of his opinions at this time but also the way in which he was viewed by his peers. Prince V.M. Golitsyn, the former governor of Moscow, wrote in 1901 that 'P.N. Durnovo rightly said to me that everything here [i.e. in Petersburg] is based on paper and that all the government's activity boils down to this. Rules, regulations and theories are drawn up but nothing more is done and in this way what has been created in theory is entirely undermined by practice. I never expected such a view from him and thought he was first and foremost infected by the general Petersburg bureaucratic spirit or disease.'[19]

The highly conservative A.N. Mosolov, at the time close to the end of his career in the central offices of the Ministry of Internal Affairs, in 1903 described Durnovo as small, nimble as a monkey and similarly sensual. P.N. Durnovo is undoubtedly a man of lively mind, quick wits and neither bad nor complacent. Nevertheless, for all that he is somewhat callous, not very balanced even at his advanced age and very frivolous. Unreliable in relations and prone to betray people, he looks lightly on all worldly ties. It is the same with him in political matters. Everything in his view is a matter of trifles and unnecessary delays. He is willing to abolish and build anew at a stroke. I used to be like him in many ways, with the same hatred of the bureaucratic view of life and human society. He is an enlightened man, liberal in the Petersburg manner, but wholly incapable of creating anything stable.[20]

Armed with this reputation for a certain degree of liberalism, Durnovo was the only one of Plehve's deputies to retain his post under Prince P.D. Svyatopolk-Mirsky. Acting as the new Minister's closest aide, it was in the period 1904–5 that Durnovo went furthest in criticizing the methods of the Russian police state. In February 1905 a commission was set up to study the effects of the Emergency Laws of 1881, on which Durnovo sat as the Ministry of Internal Affairs' representative. Arguing in a way that would later be cited against him, Durnovo urged that the system of administrative exile should be abolished or at least radically changed. He justified this by saying that governors' misuse of the power to send individuals into exile meant that dangerous elements merely got dumped from one province into another, with no advantage to the state. Moreover, whether or not exile was imposed differed from province to province according to individual governors' political views and the strength of their nerves. The use of emergency laws against people who, however annoying, were in no sense a threat to the security of the state merely alienated society from the government and brought the use of police powers against genuinely dangerous enemies into disrepute. Equally unacceptable was the frequent recourse to emergency legislation in order to avoid working through the often slow-moving channels of the legal system. In Durnovo's view the answer to this problem was more courts and judges, not recourse to fines and regulations imposed under cover of laws designed to combat subversion and terrorism.[21]

As one might expect, sympathy for some aspects of liberalization did not blind Durnovo to an intelligent grasp of how repression should be applied as and when it became necessary. Commenting on the chaotic and brutal response to Gapon's demonstration in January 1905, Durnovo stated: 'it is in many circumstances possible to avoid battles with the troops...the mistake had been to summon infantry

Cossacks during the 'pacification' of the Baltic provinces in 1905–6.

units whereas it would have been more appropriate to limit oneself
to cossacks and cavalry, who could disperse the crowd with whips,
especially since the demonstrators were not armed'.[22] After the
fall of Svyatopolk-Mirsky in January 1905, Durnovo stayed on as
Assistant Minister under A.G. Bulygin, but D.F. Trepov took over
the direction of the state's response to growing internal disorder, and
dominated the Ministry. In October 1905, however, Durnovo's
chance came and, in the face of dangers and challenges which would
have deterred a less self-confident and determined man, he seized
with both hands the opportunity to take over the Ministry of Internal
Affairs.

The situation he faced on assuming office was little short of catastrophic. Far from restoring calm and regaining wide support by
issuing the October manifesto, the government had signalled to its
many potential enemies that it was weak and on the run. It was in
November and December of 1905 that the imperial regime came
closest to collapse. Urban strikes, riots and even rebellions, not to
mention peasant disorders, reached their peak in this period, while
the government, and specifically its apparatus of repression, was all
but disintegrating. As the Gendarme general, A.V. Gerasimov,

commented, the revolutionaries 'almost crushed us' in 1905.[23]

At the top, in the Ministry of Internal Affairs, according to D.N. Lyubimov, all was chaos by mid–October 1905. The post and telegraph strike had cut off communications with the provinces, leaving each governor to his own devices. Nervous officials wandered round the ministry with no information and no means of doing anything but repeat rumours. The upper levels of the Police Department were split between the factions of N.P. Garin and P.I. Rachkovsky, while the secret agents on whom the Internal Agency crucially depended were being uncovered, murdered, or inspired to desert in droves. According to Gerasimov, the Petersburg Okhrana was close to collapse. Meanwhile in the provinces, governors, caught by surprise by the manifesto and usually with very limited means of repression at their disposal, could exercise little control over events.[24] Most dangerous of all, the armed forces, on which the regime's survival now clearly rested, were in the view of a recent historian, John Bushnell, wholly unreliable as a force for internal repression. By November and December of 1905, Bushnell argues, the great majority of units even of the army were in a state of actual or incipient mutiny and no one could be sure how even the most trustworthy units would react to confrontation with rioting crowds.[25]

Bushnell's analysis of the roots of military and peasant rebellion in 1905 is not so different from the one held by Durnovo. Bushnell argues that under the Old Regime peasants, whether in or out of uniform, were in a permanent state of potential rebellion against authority from which they were deterred partly by inertia, and partly by fear in the face of the seemingly solid position of the established authorities and the massive force they could bring to bear against rebels. In Bushnell's view, therefore – to express a relatively complex argument in simple terms – peasant soldiers rebelled when authority seemed seriously shaken, but returned rapidly to discipline once a powerful and self-confident hand was felt from above.[26]

Durnovo believed this too, and set out to provide the strong and ruthless hand. As Gurko puts it, 'Durnovo had a way of impressing on people his own firmness and the inflexibility of his decisions'.[27] 'Without petty pride and vindictiveness' as regards his many personal enemies in the Ministry, Durnovo successfully restored to it his own energy, sense of purpose and self-confidence. In Lyubimov's words, as Minister Durnovo radiated authority to a degree that astonished those who had known him in his previous incarnation.[28] Compromise was spurned and any official who wavered or showed weakness was replaced. The all-important railway and telegraph network was saved for the government as a top priority by immediate and determined action against strikes. Exploiting the growing fear in propertied circles of mass anarchy and rebellion, Durnovo was also prepared to use force ruthlessly to bring peasants and workers back into line. Fearful of exposing soldiers' loyalty to the strain of long drawn-out 'peaceful' confrontation with urban crowds, Durnovo ordered in February 1906 that groups refusing to disperse must be fired on immediately. Even less pretty were the means of repression in the countryside where relatively small detachments of reliable troops restored authority over huge areas by collective punishments and making brutal examples of suspected rebels.

At the pinnacle of this system of repression stood Durnovo, who in these critical months showed not only great energy and courage in the face of ever-present threats to his life, but also a clear grasp of what needed to be done if the government was to remain in control of the situation. In retrospect it seems that while Durnovo's policies left an evil legacy of hatred in Russian society and made compromise between the regime and the liberals more difficult, without a man of his rare calibre and toughness at the head of the Ministry of Internal Affairs the state might well have collapsed in the winter of 1905–6. Among conservative groups Durnovo henceforth enjoyed great prestige as the saviour of the regime and social order. Nicholas II clearly shared such views at least in part, loading down Durnovo, for whom he had no personal affection, with rewards upon his retirement as Minister on the eve of the first Duma's convocation.[29]

After leaving the Ministry of Internal Affairs Durnovo became a major figure in the State Council, leading the latter's conservative wing, the so-called Right Group, from 1907 until 1915, the year of his death. In his speeches in the Council, which are the major source for much of what follows, can be found the influence of many elements of his biography. By the last decade of his life Durnovo was very much the senior mandarin, with decades of experience in government behind him, and firmly convinced that it was the right and duty of the expert official to run society. The very language of his speeches, with their appeals to 'cold reason', experience and realism, their condemnation of the sentimentality and inexperience of elected parliamentarians, breathes the conviction that the experienced governmental élite should stand above 'transient political factors' and rule in the long-term interests of state and society. Durnovo was, however, as we have seen, not only an official but also a former officer, and his military values and loyalties are reflected very clearly in his political thinking. So too was his past service as a police chief, in which post he had been forced to contemplate the nature of Russian revolutionary organizations and the threat they posed to the imperial state. A policeman's professional concern with the prevention of revolution and subversion was inevitably, in Durnovo's case, much strengthened by his experience of 1905–6. His memory of how close the imperial regime had come to disaster in these two years seems to have convinced Durnovo that nothing must be done to weaken the state's repressive apparatus, obliterating in the process the doubts he had expressed, in the years immediately prior to the revolution, about the effects of the Emergency Laws.

Central to Durnovo's political ideas was the belief that only the existing state apparatus held the Russian Empire together and that Russian society had not developed to a point where it could generate institutions of its own capable of uniting and directing the community. He once explained that

> everyone considers me an inveterate monarchist, reactionary defender of autocracy, incorrigible obscurantist... and doesn't realize that in my views I am the most convinced of republicans. In fact I consider best for a people the situation where the people itself can have at the head of the administration as president the most worthy citizen chosen by themselves. For certain countries such an ideal, through one fortunate circumstance or another, is becoming a possibility. But this it is by no means possible to say about our immense and very varied Russian Empire, where because of purely practical considerations the machinery of administration and the Empire's unity demand the existence of the imperial banner woven by history. If it goes Russia will disintegrate. That is the immutable law of nature in Russia's political order.[30]

This imperial banner could not moreover afford to be merely a monarchical symbol of unity covering a constitutional and parliamentary regime. The monarchy had to be the legitimizing principle and source of authority for the centralized, authoritarian bureaucracy required to govern the state and enforce some degree of cohesion and direction on society. It was of vital importance that this state, and in particular its repressive apparatus, stand outside society's control and possess the means and the self-confidence to rule if necessary in the teeth of public opinion. Where necessary, as Durnovo stressed to the State Council on a number of occasions, this state's rulers must be prepared to be ruthless. 'Governing a state', he said in 1910, 'is a harsh business. Justice itself yields to the demands of higher state interests. It is not for nothing that according to the ideas of our people the tsar has to be terrible but gracious, terrible first and foremost and gracious afterwards. ...in deciding legislative questions I have never been guided by sentiment.'[31]

Among the threats to this authoritarian state's effectiveness bureaucratic paper-shuffling, evasion of responsibility and rule by the book loomed large. In his last speech to the State Council, in July 1915, Durnovo had the following to say about the wartime failings and predicament of the imperial government: 'We had an obligation to remember firmly that in Russia one can and must give orders, that the Russian Sovereign can command everything that his reason tells him is useful and necessary for his people, and that no one, illiterate or literate, will dare to disobey him.... We fear to give orders, feared in the past to give orders, and instead of taking command we wrote circulars and published laws without number. Authority, which dislikes living in the homes of the weak, flew off in search of a stronger embrace.'[32]

In the State Council Durnovo fought a rear-guard action to defend the state's independence, and especially the freedom of action of the police apparatus, from the encroachments of public opinion and the institutions through which it was represented. First and foremost among these came the Duma. In part Durnovo's hostility to the Duma simply reflected a mandarin's view that elected members of a representative institution, especially a new one, lacked the political wisdom or experience to govern. In January 1912 he spoke of the Duma's members as 'young people who get carried away', having stressed earlier that 'the state Duma, as a young legislative institution, is clearly inclined to hand out money without careful consideration, for charitable, educational and other agreeable purposes'.[33] Beyond this, however, he feared that any expansion of the Duma's power would set up conflicting loyalties and alternative centres of patronage within what, as he fully recognized, was already a partly factionalized and politicized civil service.[34]

Very conscious of the fact that the survival of the imperial regime rested on the support of the armed forces, Durnovo regarded it as of the utmost importance to halt any legislative encroachment in military affairs, particularly in these early years of parliamentarism, when precedents were being set for the future. In March 1909 he attacked the Duma's encroachment on imperial prerogatives in the matter of the establishment of a naval general staff, asserting that

such intervention, however insignificant, creates dangerous precedents for the direction of the state's defence and gradually entangles the military and naval ministries, all their establishments and ultimately the army and the fleet in civilian attitudes which are alien to them. It introduces discord into military relations and as a result, slowly and quietly but none the less inexorably, undermines the foundations on which the military power of the Russian state rests. Such results will occur because by these impatient interventions the military administration will be transferred into the hands of the State Council and state Duma which is contrary to the Fundamental Laws, to our basic beliefs, and to our conception of the high significance of that power which created Russia and personifies her strength and might. We consider it our duty to defend these political principles in general, and in particular in questions of military administration, with all the means at our disposal.[35]

Not only the legislature but also the legal system in Durnovo's eyes threatened political stability by paralysing the executive branch's freedom of action. In May 1907 he criticized plans initiated by A.A. Saburov designed to give the First Department of the Senate the power to impose strict legality on the executive, including the right to declare states of emergency and martial law null and void. 'One cannot', argued Durnovo, 'in the course of a few weeks introduce North American or English systems into Russia'. The attempt to subject the whole executive branch to 'irresponsible' judicial control was 'almost revolutionary' and would be exceptionally dangerous. 'The administration and the police are still the major force restraining raging passions and it is therefore impossible to put their every step under the control of an irresponsible institution.' As Minister of Internal Affairs his view had been as follows: 'governors allowing themselves even an excess of authority for the sake of the urgent preservation of order were doing their duty and those who instead of taking energetic action searched in the law for appropriate articles or for suitable circulars – they were not doing their duty'. He had come to the conclusion that 'in the sphere of administration administrative discretion outside the control of any administrative justice ought to be allowed to exist. . .I am far from preaching lawlessness – but the discretionary power realizes political tasks in conformity with the demands of expediency and in this area no one can hinder it.'[36]

Holding such views, it was logical that Durnovo should be opposed to trying officials before juries. In March 1913 he argued that 'the transfer of crimes committed by officials into the hands of ordinary jurymen threatens our civil service with very real dangers'. In such cases jurors would require 'not only maturity and lack of bias. . .but also the ability and the skill to evaluate from the political point of view the expediency and necessity of the various orders of the administrative power'. In Durnovo's view, however, nothing that had happened in recent years had increased the chances of jurors adequately meeting this need. On the contrary, with the booming yellow press constantly denigrating officials and sowing distrust of the authorities, political sense and maturity would be even harder to come by than in the past.

This matter is not about the percentage of convictions and acquittals; it concerns the destruction of our civil service in its entirety. I don't say that the personnel of our civil service has achieved any sort of perfection, but at the present time Russia cannot produce anything else. On us lies the obligation of preserving that which exists and arranging justice in such a way that officials can be confident that no one will condemn them unless they are guilty, thanks to dislike, revenge or political calculation.[37]

In Durnovo's view it was precisely the failings of the civil service which made the expansion of legislative or judicial power so dangerous. In a country of Russia's immense size it was difficult enough for the central authorities to control the action of local officials or to galvanize them into energetic activity. In the face of hostile public opinion expressing itself through a press freed from preliminary censorship, it would become even harder. If on top of this local police and officials were held legally responsible before a jury for acts committed in the course of carrying out their duties, there was every reason to fear that they would refuse to act. Even as it was, the temptation to use laws and circulars as an excuse for not taking risky, energetic or unpopular action was very strong. Faced with insistent demands in April 1906 that civil rights must be guarded through strictly enforced laws prohibiting arbitrary official actions, Durnovo retorted that laws must also force officials to act and to obey instructions from their superiors. 'It is necessary', he argued, 'to state in the law that in certain circumstances the police are obliged to arrest people'.[38] Convinced even in April 1911 that the revolutionary threat was far from being definitely scotched and sure that the legal system was too slow and weak to repress subversion, Durnovo was determined to keep the police apparatus from crumbling in the authorities' hands.[39] He would certainly have agreed with A.N. Kulomzin's comment about Loris-Melikov, the head of government in 1879–81, that 'by his constant demands that it [i.e. the police] should always act legally in all its undertakings, one can with truth say that he caused its collapse; this is a strange statement but it's true; our police never knew anything about laws and when threatened with responsibility for infringing the law it becomes lost and prefers to sit and do nothing'.[40]

As we have seen, Durnovo was so insistent that the administration's power remain unchecked because he felt that without it Russia would disintegrate. In part this simply reflected his very low opinion of the population's capacity for self-government. The man who called the gentry's representatives in the Duma 'young people who get carried away' was not likely to have great faith in peasants' capacity for democratic government. More important, however, was Durnovo's belief that the existing political and social order faced great dangers from a revolution of the masses. In part his fears centred on the risks of separatist movements in the non-Russian borderlands, though, judging by his famous memorandum of February 1914, he seems to have felt that this threat was a potential rather than present danger.[41] A much more immediate danger came, however, from the Russian people, peasants and workers, themselves.

Peter Durnovo was totally committed to the world of Russia's propertied and, as he put it, cultured élite. He saw the interests and values of this élite to be under severe threat from social revolution. As regards gentry land, he argued that 'at the present time the state's interest boils down to the fact that large and medium-sized estates should remain, as far as possible, firmly in the hands of those people to whom they at present belong'.[42] Durnovo was just as clear about the property rights of industrialists. Speaking on the issue of workers' sickness insurance, for instance, he argued, in April 1912, that 'one ought in this question to grasp one point firmly, namely that private institutions, such as the [factory] hospitals at present are, cannot be disposed of by anyone save their owners'. Summing up his speech on this issue, he expressed his fear that Russia's propertied élite was increasingly living in a state of siege. 'In our eyes with a threatening gradualness the demands of the propertyless class, egged on by various theoretical teachings up to and including those of a social-revolutionary nature, are growing little by little, and where this will end no one knows.'[43] Still more stark in its fears of a social catastrophe was the Durnovo memorandum of February 1914. 'An especially favourable soil for social upheavals', wrote Durnovo, 'is found in Russia, where the masses undoubtedly profess, unconsciously, the principles of socialism. . . . The Russian masses, whether workmen or peasants, are not looking for political rights, which they neither want nor comprehend. The peasant dreams of obtaining a gratuitous share of somebody else's land; the workman of getting hold of the entire capital and profits of the manufacturer.'[44]

In Durnovo's view the conflict between the élites and the masses was at present irreconcilable and the former's interests could only be maintained by a significant dose of coercion. He argued that it was madness to believe that introducing constitutional-liberal principles into contemporary Russia would solve its social crisis. On the contrary, in his view it would merely make the élites' position untenable. Already, institutions introduced because of the reformist currents of recent years, from workers' insurance funds, through the free press, up to and including the Duma itself, had seriously weakened the state's authority. Educated public opinion constantly pressed for the extension of such reforms. In Durnovo's view to agree to this would be fatal. 'Even though it may sound like a paradox, the fact is that agreement with the opposition in Russia positively weakens the government. . . . the Russian opposition is intellectual throughout, and this is its weakness, because between the intelligentsia and the people there is a profound gulf of mutual misunderstanding and

distrust.' The workers and peasants were committed to socio-
economic not political goals, and were far more likely to follow
socialist rather than liberal leaders. The latter's major role lay in
weakening the imperial regime, but should the latter ever collapse
Russian moderates would be unable to put anything of their own in
its place. On the contrary, anarchy and social revolution of the most
extreme sort would be inevitable, for 'the legislative institutions and
opposition parties, lacking real authority in the eyes of the people,
will be powerless to stem the popular tide'.[45]

If political reform could not solve the conflict between élite and
masses, the same was true in Durnovo's view as regards socio-
economic changes. The essential reasons for this were that Russia
was still too poor and undeveloped, lacking the solid middle strata
which were the best guarantee of social stability. Only time and
economic development could create a situation in which large sections of the population shared with the élites a vested interest in the
existing order. Until that time it was an illusion to imagine that any
kind of consensus could be created in Russian society which would
not jeopardize the élites' survival. As regards, for instance, plans to
create an all-class *volost'* [at parish level] zemstvo, Durnovo had the
following to say in May 1914:

I find it risky to create self-governing units combining a great
number of propertyless people with a very small number of propertied, completely different in education, way of life and customs, and finally and most important when all the thoughts of the
non-propertied are directed towards taking away the land of the
propertied. . . . the majority will fall under the influence of the least
honest people and will blindly obey him who most satisfies the
half-savage instincts of the crude mob. This of course is very sad
but not hopeless. The new forms of landownership, one may
hope, will help to form a class of small but solvent property-
owners which will serve as the basis on which our descendants will
build the all-class *volost'*.[46]

In Durnovo's attitude to *volost'* reform is to be found a theme which
runs throughout his political thinking. Very much a materialist,
Durnovo always stressed that it was pointless to create institutions
before socio-economic conditions were ripe for them, a principle he
applied not only to 'hot' political issues such as the *volost'* zemstvo
but also to much less sensitive questions such as the proposal to
hand over supervision of released convicts to committees of prison
guardians. His views on the Stolypin peasant reform shifted somewhat in the last decade of his life. Initially condemning the injustice
and potential social discontent that 'the destruction of the peasant's

nest' would entail, Durnovo subsequently accepted the need to move towards individual ownership of allotment land. Nor was he opposed to small changes in favour of the peasantry such as taking *starostas* [peasant headmen] on to the state's payroll. Fundamentally, however, he was committed to protecting private property and maintaining strict controls over the rural population until economic development had turned peasants into prosperous conservative farmers.[47]

His attitude towards the workers' question was not essentially different. Speaking, for instance, on workers' sickness insurance, he of course conceded that 'good relations between workers and entrepreneurs are in the highest degree desirable', and agreed that, although is most ways workers were distinctly better off than the bulk of the peasantry, 'the accumulation of a great number of people in one place, the obligation to work, in the great majority of cases, in closed premises and perhaps under other unpleasant conditions without doubt oblige one to treat the factory workers differently from the rest of the population'. At the same time, Durnovo argued, it was unrealistic and foolish to imagine, as the insurance bill's supporters in his opinion did, that one could simply borrow German legislation, make it more generous towards workers, and apply it to Russia. In Durnovo's view Russian capitalism was still too undeveloped to afford such a welfare burden. No amount of legislation could alter the fact that the great mass of the Russian population would for the moment have to reconcile itself to much worse living conditions than its peers in other major European states, for 'we are at the very least fifty years behind Germany and all the rest of Europe both industrially and in every other sort of development'. As regards the workers, Durnovo stressed that 'I by no means shut my eyes to the imperfections and the mess of the existing position, but unfortunately the extremely backward conditions and interrelations in our life don't allow many sharp changes'. Certainly, such changes should not be attempted in a fearful attempt to appease the masses, still less to assuage the intelligentsia's inferiority complex towards Europe, or 'the passion, unfortunately common among Russians', for self-flagellation.[48]

As is generally the case, Durnovo's sense of priorities as regards governmental policies was best reflected in his view of how the state's limited financial resources should be expended. Accepting, though no doubt with some misgivings, that a very rapid expansion of primary education was needed, Durnovo nevertheless argued that the Duma's enthusiasm for this cause was diverting its attention from a more balanced view of how the interests and prosperity of the peasantry could be increased. 'I don't deny', he said in May 1910, 'that the need to build schools in Russia is very great, but it's also impossible to deny the fact that in general the need for various buildings and organizations is immense.'[49] In a manner central to the Russian imperial tradition, Durnovo believed that resources should first and foremost be concentrated on securing internal order and external military power. With good reason bewailing the poor quality and, by European standards, small size of the uniformed police force, Durnovo argued that the shortcomings of the police were both a threat to internal stability and, because of the frequent need to deploy troops in support of the civil power, to military training as well.[50]

Above all, however, it was the armed forces which in Durnovo's eyes had first claim on the exchequer. On many occasions pointing to deficiencies in the army and navy, and stressing too the dangers of the contemporary international situation, Durnovo summed up his general position in June 1908. 'In my eyes', he said, 'all so-called cultural needs retire into second place before the urgent necessities on which depend the very existence of Russia as a great power.' Here spoke not only the realistic statesman of the age of imperialism, aware that in this era weak states were liable to be exploited or even destroyed by their stronger rivals, but also the true representative of the imperial ruling class, which had always drawn a large part of its sense of self-confidence and legitimacy from the belief that the alliance between crown and gentry had created a great, powerful and respected Russia.[51]

In Durnovo's view Russia faced major international challenges and dangers with a highly polarized society ruled by an élite which could only maintain its position, at least in part, by coercion. How much did he appreciate the need to reunite and re-integrate Russian society? By what means did he propose to achieve this?

In part Durnovo's age, not to mention his military-bureaucratic experience, militated against his fully appreciating the extent of the problem, let alone the possible means of solving it. A mandarin, conditioned to giving and taking orders, accustomed to rational calculation of state interests and to the world of bureaucratic politics, Durnovo was unused to thinking of how to 'sell' policies to the public, how to mobilize public opinion, or how to open paths to some kind of popular participation in politics. In part too, of course, he shared the common arrogant belief of Europe's élite that workers, not to mention peasants, should defer to their traditional and better-educated social superiors. The backwardness of the Russian people, particularly in the 1860s and 1870s when Durnovo's instincts about politics were formed, could only reinforce this élitist attitude. Durnovo spoke of the 'cultural weakness of the Russian people', feared that agitators could easily appeal in the countryside to 'the half-savage instincts of the crude mob', and argued that beyond an instinctive radical egalitarianism Russian workers and peasants had no real political aspirations.[52] Gurko is quite right to say that Durnovo 'could not fathom the psychological depths of the people'[53] – for here, certainly, was not a man who could give peasants or workers a sense that the ruling élite valued their contribution to society, understood their needs or aspirations, or indeed was willing to make sacrifices to accommodate peasant or worker demands. The latter point is of course very important. One possible way in which the dangerously narrow basis of support for the existing regime might have been widened successfully was by allowing a degree of expropriation of private land in favour of the peasantry. To Durnovo such a plan was anathema. It would impoverish the élites, himself included, undermine fundamental principles of civilized life and, save in the very short run, do nothing to improve the peasant's lot. To make concessions on such a matter to 'ignorant peasants' would in any case have stuck in Durnovo's gullet; instead he preferred to trust in force, which he once described as 'one of the most reliable means of government, especially in Russia'.[54] Finally, of course, it needs to be stressed that, given his view of human nature, the idea of uniting society behind some great utopian vision would have inspired Durnovo to irony.

His understanding of the values and institutions which might bind together Russian society was indeed traditional and unoriginal. 'The valorous spirit of true warriors' united officers and troops who had endured danger together in defence of their country.[55] The Orthodox Church too was crucial as a focus for national unity, and Durnovo devoted very great attention in the State Council to defence of its prerogatives against advocates of increased rights for other churches or for individuals wishing to abandon Orthodoxy, or indeed the priesthood. 'I think', said Durnovo in May 1910, 'that the cultural weakness of the Russian people does not yet allow the preaching and propaganda of all dogmas to be permitted without distinction. If we want to preserve the unity of the Russian state it would be madness to weaken the force binding it together – that is the Orthodox Church.'[56]

In a thoroughly traditional manner, influenced by a conservative's belief in original sin, Durnovo argued that

> as I see it, in each man's conscience or around it, in the depths of the human spirit, there exist restraining elements created by education, life and the conditions of social existence or, which is the same thing, a notion of moral discipline. This discipline through the promptings of religion, laws and tradition puts, as it were, sentry posts on all those many paths along which move passion, weak will and human feebleness. Before these sentry posts conscience halts. The disciplined conscience reflects and the man moves over

to the path of duty, honour, loyalty to oaths and the inviolability of promises.[57]

In his usual blunt manner Durnovo made no bones about the fact that the Church 'teaches the people not only Christ's truth but also the need for obedience to the imperial power'. The religious and national significance of the monarchy was for Durnovo axiomatic. Yet it would be quite wrong to call him a 'dynastic nationalist', as if he were a courtier or some Baltic baron of the era of Nicholas I. For Durnovo the monarch was very much the servant of the nation. 'It is not', he argued in May 1910, 'that the Orthodox Church is pre-dominant because the Emperor confesses the Orthodox creed; on the contrary, the Emperor confesses the Orthodox creed because the Orthodox Church is the predominant church, and Orthodoxy is predominant because in it there has lived from ancient times the spiritual consciousness and the spiritual ideals of the Russian nation.'[58]

In the course of debate on the Orthodox Church Durnovo commented nostalgically that 'ancient and medieval peoples were strong in spirit, they were not confused by theories or by the various considerations of the Social Democrats, *Trudoviki* [worker-peasant party] and such people, but marched firmly down the road of the creation of a realm and the consolidation of their power'.[59] In this yearning for a monolithic community, insulated from dissidents, critics and foreigners, and united in pursuit of national power, one finds a theme running through much of Russian history and linking Durnovo to both Ivan IV and Stalin. Nevertheless, too much should not be made of such comparisons. By the late nineteenth and early twentieth centuries Russian imperial society was very different indeed from the monolithic and state-dominated worlds of medieval or Stalinist Russia. This was particularly true of the upper and middle classes, a point illustrated by some of Durnovo's own speeches.

In December 1911, for instance, insisting that the pre-eminence of the Orthodox Church must be maintained, Durnovo argued that the Russian state must not officially establish and recognize ecclesiastical hierarchies for other religious groups, such as the Old Catholics. The Orthodox Church and the imperial state were organically linked elements around which the Russian national community was formed; all other churches were simply 'private civil societies' enjoying the rights that the civil law conferred on such bodies. Durnovo thus made a clear distinction in his mind between the realm of the state and that of the individual; he firmly believed that this distinction between public and private must be embodied in the law. However opposed, for instance, to official recognition of the Old Believers, whatever his fears about the effects of their rituals and processions on the Orthodox masses, Durnovo did not deny that the dissenters had the right, along with other private organizations, to own property, set up schools, and within their own houses and churches to hold services and preach. Only if their activities were a threat 'to the state or to public morality' did the government have the right to intervene. Given this distinction between the public and private spheres, the absolute domination of society by the state was impossible. Speaking about the 'Old Catholic' bishop Koval'sky, Durnovo argued that although the state could not officially recognize his ecclesiastical title, he could of course 'be called Bishop by courtesy, for example in drawing-rooms'. So long as Russia was governed by a European élite in whose private drawing-rooms due courtesy could be extended to Polish bishops, heretical or not, Russian society was not going to be monolithic nor the Russian state all-powerful.[60]

It was, however, by no means only the values of the Edwardian drawing-room which divided Durnovo's world from Soviet Russia. At the centre of society's autonomy from the state in late imperial Russia was the institution of private property. Moreover, conservative members of the ruling élite such as Durnovo, who very much advocated the existence of a strong state, were also in general among the greatest defenders of private property not only against the radical left but also against 'governmental socialism'. As we have already seen in relation to legislation on workers' sickness insurance, Durnovo was a firm opponent of the state's infringing on the rights of private property. Because civil rights and the autonomy of society from the state were firmly rooted in the material interests of the most powerful elements in politics and society, they were by no means easy to uproot. On this question there is great interest in a speech made by I.G. Shcheglovitov, one of Durnovo's successors as leader of the Right Group, who argued that 'with each day that passes the state is drawing new and various sides of human life into its path of development, and the concept of subjective civil law of which the civil jurists used to boast is now in great danger'.[61]

For Durnovo, as was indeed the case for most European conservatives by the early twentieth century, nationalism was the most effective force for integrating the community and parrying the socialist threat. Although Durnovo was a wholehearted nationalist, by comparison with his British or German peers, any Russian leader was bound to have major problems in utilizing nationalism as a means to legitimize the existing regime or to integrate imperial society. In the first place, the Russian Empire was a multi-ethnic community. In theory Durnovo was prepared almost to ignore this fact and to treat the non-Russians in a ruthless manner. In April 1912, for instance, he argued that 'we have taken over the non-Russian peoples not in order to give them pleasure but because we need them and we will organize them as the interests of our country demand'.[62] Four years earlier Durnovo had stated that 'the sense and content of our nationalities policy is a persistent and careful movement towards a strictly defined goal, thought out and projected in advance. . . . such a policy demands firmness and even severity, but it's impossible to be firm if one wants to please everyone and make one's bow in four directions, to Poles, Lithuanians, Germans, etc.'[63] Nevertheless, Durnovo accepted that on occasion considerations of prudence required that deviations be allowed from a strict Russian centralist line. Moreover, he was quite sufficiently intelligent to realize that in a multi-ethnic empire wild appeals to Russian chauvinism were as likely to weaken the regime as to gain it support. Over the 1910 Finnish legislation he intervened only to speed matters along, and thus, as he put it, to choke off agitation in the press and public as quickly as possible. As regards the Cholm issue he remained silent and, so it seems, unimpressed.[64]

The second reason why a Russian leader had less chance than his German or British equivalent to exploit nationalist feeling was very simple. As regards her foreign policy, Russia was not powerful enough to run the risks or win the victories that might have satisfied nationalist yearnings, or consolidated the prestige and legitimacy of the imperial regime. The most obvious way to seek nationalist support through one's foreign policy was aggressively to assert Russia's position in the Balkans, the area in which Russian traditions, national interest and sentiment all combined in a potentially heady brew. The problem here, however, was that a forward policy in the Balkans would bring Russia into collision with the Central Powers, which were both a formidable military bloc and the main bulwark of European monarchical conservatism. As he made clear in his memorandum of February 1914, Durnovo was convinced that the consequences of such a collision would be catastrophic.

Durnovo's memorandum, by now quite well known, is undoubtedly a remarkable document.[65] Predicting that the next war between the great powers would be long drawn-out, Durnovo rightly stressed that it would be a test of the economic strength and political unity of the societies taking part at least as much as of the prowess of their armies. Convinced that Russian industry, finance and communications would not be able to stand the strain of a long conflict against so formidable an enemy as Germany, Durnovo also believed that war would tear apart Russia's society and government. The Duma politicians and educated public opinion would as always blame all disasters on the government, whose authority they would help to undermine. Meanwhile the peacetime army, the state's most reliable bulwark, would be destroyed. If, as was likely, the imperial regime collapsed, then 'the legislative institutions and opposition parties, lacking real authority in the eyes of the people, will be powerless to stem the popular tide, aroused by themselves, and Russia will be flung into hopeless anarchy, the issue of which cannot be foreseen'. Given the immense dangers of war with Germany, conflict must be avoided at almost any cost. In Durnovo's view this was by no means impossible since Russia and Germany had important political and economic interests in common and were divided by no irreconcileable conflicts.[66]

No one who reads Durnovo's memorandum today could reasonably doubt that its author was a man of exceptional intelligence and far-sightedness. Durnovo combined great originality of thought and clarity of vision with a deep knowledge of military, geopolitical, economic and political realities. The result was brilliant, but from the point of view of a supporter of the imperial regime, deeply alarming. Durnovo's proposed solution to the dangers he foresaw, namely escape from the Triple Entente and reconciliation with Germany, was not as easy as he imagined and was, in the event, not achieved. Thus the strains of war were imposed on top of the domestic political crisis – which itself, as he had pointed out, was by no means soluble by any procedure as simple as giving in to liberal demands and conceding a constitutional regime. On the contrary, the government was caught between the conviction that only a repressive police state could avert social revolution and the knowledge that retention of this police state would alienate most sections of educated society from the regime. Moreover, although in February 1914 Durnovo might argue that the liberal opposition 'represents no real force', it nevertheless remained true that, as he himself had put matters only eight years before, 'educated Russia governs the state. One must try to have as many loyal people as possible among the educated.'[67]

Historians have, perhaps foolishly, tended to divide into 'optimistic' and 'pessimistic' camps as regards imperial Russia's chances of survival. Durnovo tended to belong in the latter camp. Indeed in 1912 he himself said, 'we are in a blind alley.... I fear that we all, along with the tsar, won't succeed in getting out'.[68] For Durnovo, as for many other members of the ruling élite, Nicholas II himself was a major part of the problem. Prince Boris Vasil'chikov, a former minister and a member of the State Council, records in his memoirs that in the spring of 1914 the Emperor spoke to Durnovo about the possibility of the latter heading a government. Durnovo responded. 'Your Majesty, my system as head of the government and Minister of Internal Affairs cannot provide quick results, it can only tell after a few years and these years will be a time of complete rumpus: dissolution of the Duma, assassinations, executions, perhaps armed uprisings. You, Your Majesty, will not endure these years and will dismiss me; under such conditions my stay in power cannot do any good and will bring only harm.'[69] Vasil'chikov's account of this conversation may be open to question, but the sentiments he ascribes to Durnovo accurately reflected the views of a man who in 1906 complained that the Emperor was 'the kind of man who, if you asked him for his last shirt, would take it off and give it to you'.[70]

Durnovo died in September 1915, some 17 months before the beginning of the revolution he had predicted. The liberal newspaper *Rech'* commented in its obituary:

> The Old Regime did not value Durnovo so highly and was not so sincerely attached to him for nothing, for he was the most outstanding example of the ruling bureaucracy. . . . One could never say about him that he deceived himself in his line of behaviour: on the contrary he understood perfectly and spoke openly about where this line would lead, and nevertheless boldly continued to pursue it. . . . the late Durnovo always completely ignored public opinion. . . . He was not afraid of newspaper disclosures; he himself understood what he was doing and remained true to himself until his last day.

As obituaries go, it was a not inaccurate statement of Durnovo's personality and views.[71]

CHAPTER 7

A.N. KULOMZIN:

A RUSSIAN VICTORIAN

Anatol Nikolaevich Kulomzin was a major figure in Russian political life in the last decades of the Old Regime. As secretary of the Committee of Ministers from 1883 to 1904 he worked at the very centre of the imperial government, few of whose secrets were hidden from him. Kulomzin's role as secretary was in part to attempt to co-ordinate governmental activity and reconcile warring departments. In addition, however, he bore direct executive responsibility for the colonization of Siberia. Subsequently he sat in the State Council, briefly serving as its president during the First World War. The advantage of studying Kulomzin's biography in some detail lies, however, not only in the man's importance or even in the interest to a historian of his unpublished letters and memoirs. His values and political opinions can to some extent be regarded as typical of the more liberal wing of the imperial ruling élite. A study of his biography provides, therefore, a basis for understanding the cultural and intellectual sources of bureaucratic liberalism, as well as the ways in which liberal values could be shaped by an individual's background and experiences.

The Kulomzins, ultimately Tartar in origin, were an old noble family but by no means a great one. Though Count Alexander Bobrinsky's genealogy notes that the family was ennobled only in 1616, clearly there were Kulomzins who owned land in Kostroma in the sixteenth century. Ikonnikov states that, prior to Anatol Nikolaevich, 'the Kulomzins, a provincial family, never produced individuals of high rank', even colonels being rare. The Kulomzins' history seems typical of that of much of the Russian landowning gentry. Virtually all adult males in the eighteenth and nineteenth century were officers, a great many of them serving in the navy. Such information as exists on the ownership of property shows that members of the family never owned more than 450 serfs, in northern Russia a distinctly more realistic guide to wealth before 1861 than possession of large areas of land. In the great majority of cases the Kulomzins married into families similar to their own; noble, of Russian rather than Western origin, of middling wealth and connections, but in general

A.N. Kulomzin

with old and well-respected gentry names. A.N. Kulomzin had deep roots in the Kineshma district, his estate, Kornilovo, having by 1913 been in his ancestors' possession for over 300 years.[1]

The wooden house in which the Kulomzins lived at Kornilovo was certainly not grand. Built originally by A.N. Kulomzin's grandmother, it had new wings added as and when the growth of the family demanded enlargement. Kulomzin writes that his was a typical house of the middle layer of the northern gentry in the mid-nineteenth century. Painted ochre, during Kulomzin's childhood the house boasted a red wooden roof, a hall and seven rooms. Almost all the furniture was made by peasant craftsmen, and the paintings which hung on the drawing-room walls were mostly reproductions of masterpieces, painted by a peasant artist. Kulomzin adds that even in the eighteenth century his was in general a simple family with few pretensions to culture. In that era the house possessed no library, a very small garden and not even the barest outlines of a park. Though among the nobles of Kineshma district on the eve of Emancipation there were some men of wealth and culture, in general the Kulomzins' traditions and outlook were typical of their milieu. Anatol Kulomzin recalls that among local nobles 'men who had not in one way or another served in the army were a rare exception; still rarer were nobles with a higher education, and in my own family I was the first representative of the civilian element'.[2]

It was probably also somewhat typical that the expenditure of Kulomzin's grandfather and father had considerably exceeded their incomes. In particular, the passion for cards of Kulomzin's father, a former lieutenant of the Finland Guards Regiment, meant that on the latter's death in 1838 the estate was in a very bad way. A.N. Kulomzin, an only child, was eight months old when his father died, and the whole burden of rescuing the estate and bringing up her young son fell on his mother's shoulders. It was a burden that Isabella Kulomzin showed herself more than competent to bear. Her background was quite different from that of the Kulomzins. Her father, Peter Grek, came from a German professional family and was ennobled in the early nineteenth century. Isabella Grek was excellently educated, spoke five languages fluently and loved music and painting. Her circle of friends shared her intellectual and cultural interests. In addition, Kulomzin's mother, a Calvinist with a distinct puritan strain in her character, was a woman of great resourcefulness, efficiency and strength of will. She had an immense influence on her son, who adored her. Brought up to speak four languages and to appreciate music and the arts, as a child Kulomzin spent a number of months in the Rhineland and a considerable time both in Moscow and the Crimea. He writes that all these journeyings bred in him a strong intellectual curiosity and a passionate interest in the areas and peoples he visited. Whenever possible, Isabella took her son on Sundays not only to Orthodox services but also to Protestant ones where, he records, he heard a great many sermons, 'for the most part very edifying'. The strong prejudices inculcated into him by his mother were, Kulomzin remembers, proof against any interest he might have developed as a young man in either drink or cards, and on occasion cut him off somewhat from his peers.[3]

It is certainly legitimate to trace key elements of Kulomzin's personality to his mother's influence and the 'Protestant ethic' which she embodied and which dominated his childhood. His later devotion to 'improvement' and moral causes, his capacity for disciplined work and his determination to succeed can all plausibly be ascribed to maternal influence. The humanity and sensitivity which he was to display in later life can in part be attributed to the influence of the highly cultured, intelligent and sensitive women who were responsible for his upbringing and in whose company he spent his childhood and early adolescence. The harsh military education provided for most of his peers and indeed the influence of fathers often steeped in the disciplinarian values of Nicholas I's Russia were blessings he was fortunate to avoid. A nervous child, prone to migraines, who burst into tears through nervousness while taking his university examinations, Kulomzin would, if the experience of his peers is anything to go by,[4] have been seen as a prime target for fatherly toughening. Maybe his critics would have argued that with a less sheltered upbringing and a bit more paternal influence Kulomzin might have been a better comrade in student gambling sessions and, perhaps, a tougher and less obsequious senior official.

It was Isabella Kulomzin who decided that her son should break with the tradition of his class and family by shunning a military education and instead attending Moscow University. To achieve this goal she sold jewellery and silver, and even moved temporarily to Moscow in order to hire the best teachers available in the Empire.[5] Taught by such luminaries as Mulhausen and Römer, Kulomzin passed the university's entrance examination with ease and went on to be a model student. Successful and highly motivated in his academic work, Kulomzin was also greatly influenced by the general intellectual liveliness of Moscow University even in the last, bleak years of Nicholas I's reign. The major debate at the time in the university was still that between 'Westerners' and slavophils, and both camps influenced Kulomzin. He writes that he was so impressed by the slavophils' justifications of the commune – so flattering, as he puts it, to Russian national pride – that neither visits to Western Europe, nor the study of economics, nor the evidence of his own eyes convinced him of its falseness until 1905–6: '. . .only the troubles of 1905–6 which pointed to the socialist spirit which the commune had bred in the life of the peasantry finally sobered me'. On the whole, however, although the slavophils served a useful purpose in making students search for the roots of their own national culture, 'I could never have been inspired by the narrowness of their views of our contemporary development'.[6]

More interesting were the opinions of the Westerners, particularly Granovsky and Solov'yov, who pointed to the West as the source of conceptions of service to the community. Kulomzin indeed states that what most students got from university was not so much positive factual information as, rather, a 'large slice of general intellectual development, drawn by us from the lectures of the humanities professors, and especially of idealism'.[7] Above all, for Kulomzin study at Moscow University ensured that the intellectual curiosity and the humane, cultured and liberal values inculcated into him at home were broadened and deepened by his formal education. Kulomzin writes that on leaving university he and his friends, monarchists to a man and wholly untouched by socialist ideas, nevertheless believed strongly in emancipation of the serfs, honest, legal and open government, a free press, and the gradual development of representative institutions which might lead in the more distant future to a constitutional order.[8]

On finishing university Kulomzin completed his education by spending two years in Western Europe, between 1858 and 1860. True to his Victorian upbringing, Kulomzin kept hard at work during his Grand Tour. His study of Western society and of the European economy was thorough and systematic to a degree that was truly Gladstonian. He concentrated on three areas in particular: financial, and in particular fiscal, systems; education in the West; and legal systems and penology. In these areas he read all the available literature, consulted experts and visited personally an astonishing range of institutions. In Britain alone, for instance, he toured Scottish banks, the Liverpool and London docks, numerous factories, Eton, Mechanics' Institutes, the universities, stock exchanges, law courts, congresses of statisticians and a variety of private homes. Kulomzin records that it was for him a 'solemn moment' when he first attended a session of the British Parliament; but he also took care to visit working men's debating societies and succeeded in being thrown out of a private radical-Chartist meeting. Typically, while in theory having a holiday on the Isle of Wight, Kulomzin spent much of his time in learned discussions of the British financial system.[9]

Quite apart from its general effect in broadening Kulomzin's horizons, the Grand Tour of 1858–60 also contributed materially to his career. Articles he wrote on financial and educational issues while studying in the West were published in Russian learned journals and won the attention of influential figures in Petersburg on the lookout for young talent.[10] Much more important, however, was the impact of the Grand Tour in crystallizing Kulomzin's values and aspirations. Though by no means uncritical of some aspects of European life, Kulomzin in general admired Western, and in particular British, society enormously. To a very great extent, what he saw in 1858–60 became for him a model for Russia's future development. In the early years of the twentieth century he wrote in his memoirs, 'that which we are just in the process of acquiring now was already in full flower with them fifty years ago'.[11]

In Germany, and even more so in Britain, it was above all the vigour and self-disciplined effectiveness of private initiative and activity which struck him most forcefully. For Kulomzin, it was 'the powerful independent activity which distinguishes its highly cultured public elements' which was 'the most brilliant side of English life'.[12] In education he admired the British training in independent thinking and character-formation, the Prussian stress on developing patriotism, and the Belgians' insistence that children, the citizens of the future, must understand their rights. In contrast, he abhorred French clericalism's stress on rote-learning and sadly acknowledged that, even at the turn of the century, Russian school books, 'designed for the ordinary people, are so filled with details, so overburdened, that the main point – the cult of love for one's motherland – has been lost'.[13] Kulomzin associated freedom with the tremendous power and dynamism of the industrial revolution, which he had experienced at first hand in these two years of travel, in a variety of forms. Moreover, freedom brought in its wake not only economic advancement but also political self-education and discipline. Commenting that he had heard highly intelligent speeches on politics in English working men's clubs, Kulomzin stressed 'the remarkable political development of the masses' in Britain, 'as a consequence of the long-established custom of freedom both of expression and of the press'.[14] Among the advantages of liberalism, he argued, was the development of conservative ideas and groups capable of defending themselves in a vigorous manner.[15] One example of this was the great strength of British religious life, expressed most powerfully for Kulomzin in the custom of morning and evening prayers for family and servants in many of the houses he visited.[16] Having seen in the Britain of the late 1850s a society at the peak of its power and self-confidence, in which freedom and social discipline were fruitfully combined, Kulomzin remained heavily influenced by his experience in the West for the rest of his life.

Kulomzin returned to Russia on the eve of Emancipation. Despite plans to write a thesis and take up a post at Moscow University, he was swept up in the atmosphere of the time and agreed to become a peace arbitrator in the Kineshma district.[17] He wrote afterwards that at such a time he could not bear to stand aside writing a dry thesis which no one would ever read. His decision to become a peace arbitrator, as he records, owed much to the influence of English ideas about the role of the landowner as JP and unpaid servant of the local community.[18] For all the Kulomzins' deep roots in the Kineshma district such a conception of local service had not yet developed in Russian soil.

As an arbitrator Kulomzin worked extremely hard, travelling the length and breadth of his district and reckoning that in this period he covered some 4,000 versts a year on horseback. He writes that he and his colleagues regarded their duty to be fair as something sacred and were infuriated by landowners' attempts to twist the law or to influence the administration in their own favour. Much effort had to be expended on parrying the attacks in the noble assembly of the more conservative members of the local gentry. The arbitrators' task was not easy since both nobles and peasants felt, with some truth, that the settlement was unjust and would lead to major losses to themselves. Nevertheless in the great majority of cases Kulomzin eventually succeeded in reconciling the two sides and achieving an agreed settlement. He recalls that he was determined not to wax sentimental about the peasants and to carry out the law firmly, but was nevertheless filled with the sense that he was the defender of the weak against the strong. In addition, he said, when he saw how intelligently the peasants coped with the problems of Emancipation, 'my heart was full of the most triumphant impressions, of a deep feeling of satisfaction and love for this marvellous people and of faith in the possibility of productive activity among them. . . . The ideals with which I had been imbued during my journeyings abroad after finishing university gave me no rest'. He was inspired to great efforts to found schools and to set up an effective fire insurance, to ensure fairness in the military recruitment system and to protect peasant elders from police pressure.[19]

Kulomzin's service as an arbitrator had an important influence on his subsequent political views, stamping him indelibly as a man of the 1860s. For the rest of his life he looked back happily to the early 1860s as a period of great hope and optimism in which considerable good will and co-operation between classes was achieved. He associated himself, his efforts and his ideals with the era of Alexander II, 'my deeply loved tsar-liberator, whom I served with such passion and complete selflessness in the execution of the Emancipation reforms'.[20] Those who attempted to chip away at the reforms of the 1860s were always his political foes. In addition, however, service as an arbitrator made Kulomzin very knowledgeable about his local district, its economic situation and the life of its peasantry. A man who knew that peasant customs, farming methods and problems differed from village to village in a bewildering manner, an official who had himself on many occasions ridden round all the settlements in his district, could never become a mere Petersburg dignitary remote from rural life. In fact the knowledge and interest built up during his service as an arbitrator was the foundation for much of Kulomzin's later activity in the spheres of agriculture and peasant life, not to mention as a local historian.[21]

By the autumn of 1863 Kulomzin was beginning to pine for city life. He writes, 'I feared to become lifeless and to lose any connection with the educated world'. In addition, he felt that the task of the arbitrators was largely completed, their heroic days as selfless intermediaries between classes having been succeeded by an era in which they were superior policemen, concerned above all to ensure that peasants fulfilled their obligations to landowners and the state. Kulomzin believed too that the institutions of peasant self-administration and justice were by late 1863 securely founded. Subsequent events, he admits, showed him how mistaken was his optimism. Police and administrative pressure on the *starshiny* [peasant elders] ruined their authority among their fellow peasants, while vodka played an ever-greater role in village affairs. The decline in their number and calibre meant that the peace arbitrators became ineffective, while the combination of administrative and judicial functions ruined the JPs' chances of effectively supervising peasant affairs. Reflecting early in the twentieth century on his decision to switch from local to Petersburg service forty years before, Kulomzin wrote that he had made the wrong choice, but that at the time he had felt isolated and lonely in the countryside.[22]

Service in the central administration by no means meant that Kulomzin had severed all his links with the Kineshma district. He remained a big landowner, owning in the 1880s, together with his mother and wife, over 15,000 *desyatiny* in Kostroma and Ufa. Moreover, unlike the bulk of Kostroma's gentry, particularly in the province's northern districts, Kulomzin's estates ran profitably after Emancipation. This was in part, as was true of a number of landowners in southern Kostroma, because increased profits from forestry made up for lost income from serf labour. In addition, Kulomzin's exploitation of his estates was diversified. Cattle-rearing was more important than grain production, and a horse stud contributed to profits, as did a starch mill. Kulomzin was well known, moreover, as a pioneer in the exploitation of the phosphorus deposits lying under his estates. Though day-to-day management of the properties rested with his mother and subsequently with one of his sons, Kulomzin spent part of every year on the estates. His private interest in the affairs of the Kineshma district and his public activity in the spheres of agriculture and peasant affairs went hand in hand. In the early

1880s, for instance, Kulomzin spent some time investigating the operations of the commune and the failings of peasant agriculture in Kineshma at a time when he was serving as Assistant Minister of State Properties.[23]

In the 1870s Kulomzin played a considerable role in the Valuev Commission on the rural economy. À propos of that Commission, V.V. Kalachov, a Yaroslavl landowner and later member of the State Council, asked Kulomzin's advice about a paper he had written on the problems of farming in 'the non-Black Earth region, since you both know the theoretical side well and are also well acquainted with our northern economies'.[24] The remark was justified, as was Kulomzin's own satisfaction on hearing that he had been appointed a member of Witte's Commission on the state of the rural economy. 'I'm very pleased by this', Kulomzin informed his wife, 'because this is a field of activity I have thought about all my life. I have done one or two things in this area in the Chief Administration of State Properties and the work of the earlier Valuev Commission passed through my hands. Three years ago I presented a note to the Emperor about this question.'[25] Looking forward to work on the Witte Commission, Kulomzin rejoiced in February 1902 that influenza gave him the excuse not to pay calls and to get on with his research quietly at home. Before the Commission met, he added, he must consult with his son, who was managing their estates, about agriculture in Kostroma.[26]

Kulomzin's memoirs and correspondence show not only that he knew a good deal about rural conditions but also that to a considerable extent he felt himself to be a member of the landed nobility, respected its role and shared its concerns. In April 1902, for instance, he wrote with pride that his family had always maintained its links with the local community; at present one of his sons was running the estate and another working in the zemstvo.[27] Warned two months later that his daughter-in-law was becoming frustrated with rural life and putting pressure on her husband to return to Petersburg, Kulomzin said that such a move would cause him real concern, 'for at the present moment the only salvation for the landowners is to exert an influence on the people by their presence, to cultivate that influence, to interest themselves in the details of the people's life and tone down the savagery of their customs. Perhaps then revolution in the distant future will pass us by'.[28] Frequently in Kulomzin's writings one encounters his view that power in Russia must be decentralized, local autonomy encouraged, and zemstvo and provincial opinion consulted about political questions.[29]

For all his interest in local affairs, however, from 1864 on Kulomzin's life centred on service in the Petersburg bureaucracy, almost four decades being passed by him in the State Chancellery and the Chancellery of the Committee of Ministers. Entering the State Chancellery in February 1864 presented few problems. Kulomzin's publications had won him a reputation in Petersburg and his friends, the Kalachov family, also smoothed his path into the holy of holies of the central bureaucracy. In the first years of his service Kulomzin forged important connections and acquired some powerful patrons. A paper delivered to the Geographical Society on the administration of Vienna and Berlin brought him to the attention of N. Kh. Bunge, under whom he was subsequently to serve. In July 1865 Kulomzin married Ekaterina Zamyatin, the daughter of the Minister of Justice, through whom he met numerous top officials. Probably more important, however, was the patronage offered by his chiefs in the State Chancellery and Chancellery of the Committee of Ministers. These two officials, F.P. Kornilov and A.P. Zablotsky-Desyatovsky, taught him a good deal about the art of writing papers and, clearly impressed by his intelligence and diligence, promoted him at great speed in the teeth of the regulations about ranks. Aged only thirty, Kulomzin was appointed head of the third, or financial, section of the Chancellery of the Committee of Ministers, in which post he was responsible for the statutes of railway companies and the defence of the national interest when bids were made for the construction of new lines.[30]

This was a daunting task, for these bids were decided in the Committee of Ministers, some of whose members had a private interest in seeing that fair bidding did not take place. Kulomzin's job demanded in part the skilful drafting of minutes, a knowledge of financial matters, and a minute and careful dissection of the terms offered in the bids of the railway companies. By temperament, training and long-held interest in financial questions Kulomzin was well equipped to master these essentially technical and professional skills. There was, however, from the start a strongly political element to his job as well, for if the state's interests were to be protected one needed to reckon with ministers' personalities and ambitions, to manoeuvre and to intrigue. Kulomzin was, for instance, determined to ensure that railway companies' accounts should be open for inspection, and annual general meetings of shareholders not just a formality dominated by tycoons who were the majority holders. Carefully and slowly he manoeuvred legislation to this effect through the Committee, secretly providing his old patron, K.V. Chevkin, with information and using him as the Chancellery's mouthpiece, while concealing this fact from Prince Gagarin, the Committee's chairman and Chevkin's enemy and brother-in-law. With the help of Chevkin and consistent pressure from the Chancellery, the number of scandals in bidding for railway concessions was reduced, but the task was uphill and the glimpses Kulomzin gained of ministerial morals in the course of this campaign for honesty were often depressing.[31]

In 1873 Kulomzin was appointed assistant chief of the Chancellery of the Committee of Ministers and was drawn ever more deeply into the world of high politics. His sympathies were with Alexander II's more liberal ministers, M.Kh. Reutern and D.A. Milyutin, who stood for honesty and efficiency in administration and were responsive to public opinion. The greed, amateurism and corruption of some ministers and courtiers appalled Kulomzin. So too did the task of writing the minutes of some sessions of the Committee of Ministers. 'There is nothing more difficult', wrote Kulomzin to his mother, 'than the art of expounding opposed opinions on paper', especially at the end of four hours of argument among ministers which one was supposed to transform into a resolution confirming general harmony and agreement. Still more ticklish was having to draw up minutes to disguise the fact that ministers were ignoring an imperial command, a task Kulomzin records having to carry out on one occasion in connection with railway concessions. Initially fascinated by his job, by 1875 Kulomzin had become dispirited by Petersburg paperwork, writing to his wife, 'how many years have passed without trace in boring and pointless Saint Petersburg activity'.[32]

An opportunity for change came from an unexpected quarter. In 1879 Count P.N. Ignat'ev died and was succeeded as chairman of the Committee of Ministers by P.A. Valuev. The latter wanted his own protégé, N.P. Mansurov, to head the Committee's Chancellery, but realized this would be unjust since Kulomzin's claims on the job were better. Valuev therefore persuaded his successor as Minister of State Properties, Prince A.A. Lieven, to take Kulomzin as his deputy.[33] In transferring from the Chancellery of the Committee of Ministers to the Ministry of State Properties Kulomzin was moving from one of the bureaucracy's most efficient institutions to a department which was notoriously ineffective, corrupt and out of date. As Assistant Minister Kulomzin attempted to rationalize the deployment of officials to accord with the ministry's present tasks rather than the ones it had fulfilled before Emancipation. He also tried to galvanize the ministerial apparatus into increasing the benefits to the peasantry of the state forests, institutes and model farms which it ran. Unfortunately, Kulomzin was to run up against a problem endemic in nineteenth-century Russian administration, namely the incompetence and untrustworthiness of subordinate officials, especially in the provinces. This made decentralization of decision-making very difficult; it also meant that a minister's intelligent schemes for the benefit of the rural population could be circumvented by the lazy, incompetent or corrupt officials who bore the responsibility for their implementation. As Kulomzin himself stressed in his memoirs, 'once the surveillance of public elements was removed' it was extremely difficult for the chief to discover, let alone overcome, such local bureaucratic conspiracies.[34]

The years 1879 to 1882 were difficult both for the Ministry of State

Properties in particular and for the government as a whole. The ministry was rocked by the Bashkir lands scandal, which poisoned relations between Kulomzin and his Minister and led to the latter's fall.[35] The replacement of Lieven by M.N. Ostrovsky did not, however, greatly improve Kulomzin's position. The new Minister distrusted Kulomzin, who in turn wrote about Ostrovsky that 'one can to a certain extent say that he looked on private property with a socialist attitude'; greatly disliking the rich, Ostrovsky believed employers were generally rogues and felt (according to Kulomzin) that all land should be granted by the state in usufruct rather than owned as outright property.[36]

Uncertain of his position within his own ministry, Kulomzin watched with dismay the course taken by governmental policy in 1881–2. In March 1881 he expressed the hope to his mother that the new monarch, Alexander III, would summon elected representatives from the zemstvos to sit in the State Council, mount a campaign against corruption in high places, and end top-level intrigues by hearing 'ministers' reports only in the Council, in the presence of all the ministers'.[37] Subsequently he wrote that economic reforms were also badly needed. The productivity of peasant agriculture must be improved, greater freedom given for colonization and state land sold to peasants at low prices. As regards private land, however, 'supplementary allotments cannot of course be granted' to the peasantry.[38]

Later in 1881 Kulomzin told his mother of the desperate position in which the state found itself and of his gloomy forebodings about the future. No one in the government was confident, Alexander III was locked away in Gatchina and the peasantry was likely to explode into rebellion at the slightest rumour.[39] In his memoirs, written in 1903, Kulomzin says that it was a disaster that Alexander III's elder brother died, and describes D.A. Tolstoy, Pobedonostsev and Meshchersky as Russia's evil geniuses. Educated Russians would, in Kulomzin's view, have been satisfied with very limited representation in a consultative assembly, but were alienated by the state's refusal of all compromise. Pobedonostsev had a purely negative mind, capable of destroying others' schemes but without having ideas of his own as to how to bring tsar and people together. Meanwhile D.A. Tolstoy's rigid authoritarianism was tailor-made to turn loyal moderates into enemies of the regime.[40]

Whatever his views on governmental policy in the 1880s, Kulomzin's own career flourished in this period. In December 1882 the chairman of the Committee of Ministers, M.Kh. Reutern, who had not in the past been a particular patron of Kulomzin, informed him that the secretaryship to the Committee was about to fall vacant. Kulomzin records Reutern's statement that 'he has looked through the entire list of senior officials of the first four ranks and finds there is no one better than me'. Kulomzin wavered as to whether to accept the post, because 'however flattering my recall was, I understood that it meant returning from activity connected with real life to pure paper work, even if the job was more independent'.[41] In the end Kulomzin took the secretaryship, partly because his relationship with Ostrovsky was so unsatisfactory.

The fundamental purpose of the Committee of Ministers was to co-ordinate the administrative activities and, to some extent, the policies of the various branches of the executive. Much of the secretary's energy went into arranging compromises between ministers. The position was a powerful one, as Kulomzin himself makes clear. It was the secretary to the Committee who was responsible for its minutes, which he presented to the Emperor in regular private audiences. This undermined the chairman's power, making it impossible for him to dominate the Committee and silence the voices of those members with whom he disagreed. The secretary and the chairman could easily come into conflict and a good personal relationship was necessary. Even more frequent were clashes with ministers, who were acutely sensitive to the way their opinions were portrayed in the minutes and reported to the monarch. Indeed Kulomzin states that one essential function of the secretary was to make it unnecessary for the Emperor to have to arbitrate between wrangling ministers.[42] Only a past master at Petersburg bureaucratic politics could have survived in this job, as Kulomzin did, for twenty years. Madame Bogdanovich, for instance, recorded in December 1896 that 'Kulomzin came. He is extremely careful, said nothing in an affirmative way but touched on everything by means of questions'.[43]

Certainly Kulomzin possessed the smooth and flattering tongue of a courtier. Typically, he remembered in April 1898 to advise D.M. Sol'sky that Nicholas II would be chairing a session of the Siberian Committee on the seventh anniversary of the attempt at his assassination in Japan. 'Forewarned by me', wrote Kulomzin, Sol'sky 'expressed in the name of all those present our salutations and our joy that God had preserved HIS valuable life'.[44] Four years later, when the Emperor enquired whether Kulomzin had recovered from an illness, the latter was quick to answer that the monarch's sympathy and kindness had been responsible for his cure.[45] When Polovtsov described Kulomzin as 'extremely obsequious' and A.A. Polivanov remarked that he 'cleverly...combined...readiness for political progress with the manners of court courtesy', neither was wide of the mark.[46]

As secretary to the Committee of Ministers, Kulomzin served under three chairmen, M.Kh. Reutern, N.Kh. Bunge and I.N. Durnovo. The first he respected, the second he liked and admired, and the third he despised. On hearing of I.N. Durnovo's appointment Kulomzin wrote, 'you can't imagine how much the appointment of Ivan Nikolaevich sickens me...not for my own sake but for that of business. But, God knows, it could have been much worse (Pobedonostsev, Ostrovsky).... There will be a lot of rethinking that I'll have to do. The Siberian railway is the one thing I mustn't drop but the two jobs are linked to one another'.[47] The 'railway' was the Siberian Railway Committee, established in 1891, chaired by the tsarevich Nicholas but directed by Kulomzin. If part of the Committee's charm was the close proximity into which it brought one to the heir and subsequently Emperor, its real attraction for Kulomzin lay elsewhere.

The result of energies expended on Siberian affairs would be not the ephemeral triumphs, the frustrations and the intrigues of Petersburg life, but vast new regions settled and flourishing, roads, churches and schools built. Here with a vengeance was the 'real life' for which Kulomzin yearned rather than the paper-shuffling of the Committee of Ministers. Russia's future seemed to lie in Siberia, and a man who played a major role in its early development could feel that he had made a real and lasting contribution to his country's prosperity and greatness. Kulomzin's interest in Siberia had indeed been aroused long before the formation of the Railway Committee. In 1875 he had written to his wife: 'Today all morning I read the reports of the Siberian governors. What a terrible place! How much one would wish to go there and work for Russia's good. That's where enlightened people are needed and how much good one could do there!'[48]

The high point of Kulomzin's stewardship of the Siberian Committee was the three-month tour of inspection which he undertook in 1896 in order to study on the spot how colonization was developing.[49] Inevitably, where such a huge area and so many people were involved, Kulomzin's impressions were mixed. Some Siberian districts were more prosperous, their officials more conscientious and their peasant farmers more flexible and efficient than was the case in other areas. On the whole, however, Kulomzin emerged from Siberia with a number of clear conclusions. Overpopulation, land shortage and high rents were the main cause of emigration from European Russia. The colonists left with bitterness in their hearts against the landowning gentry, to an extent that surprised and scared Kulomzin. Great suffering occurred in the course of emigration, partly because the peasants did not plan their movements sufficiently or send out scouts in advance to find where good land was available. In general, peasants adapted themselves well to Siberian agricultural conditions, though their efficiency as farmers varied to an interesting degree according to the province in which they originated. The spirit and determination of the colonists was strong. They were taking advantage of ownership of their own farms and were undoubtedly becoming more prosperous than if they had stayed in Europe. Watching the effects of peasant independence and enterprise unleashed persuaded Kulomzin that 'in this respect the communal system in Russia has huge defects'.[50] The colonists' desire for self-improvement led to repeated requests by them that churches and schools be built to meet their needs.

Kulomzin's account of his expedition to Siberia, and particularly the letters he wrote at the time, tell one a good deal about both the man and the official. He clearly revelled in the possibility of escaping from Petersburg and studying affairs at first hand. Often working from early in the morning until late at night, Kulomzin invested in his administration of colonization an energy and enthusiasm which comes through very strongly. The letters show him as well able to forget the sense of his dignity as a high official, and as anxious to talk to anyone, peasant-colonist or junior bureaucrat, who could give him information about the problems faced by the colonization administration and the best ways of increasing its usefulness to the colonist. His genuine and practical humanity, together with a real though unsentimental admiration for the courage of the peasant-colonist, are also very much in evidence.

In the aftermath of the agrarian troubles of 1905 the Siberian Committee was sometimes criticized for not having acted with sufficient energy to thin out the population of the Central Russian provinces by colonizing Asiatic Russia. Speaking in the State Council in May 1908, Kulomzin defended the Committee's record, arguing that the problems had been much less simple than his critics imagined. As regards both funds and authority, the Committee had needed to struggle constantly against powerful ministries resentful at any incursion into what they saw as their domain. The Ministry of Internal Affairs had, for instance, attempted to conduct its own, highly restrictive, colonization policy, while (Kulomzin might have added) Witte's attitude towards the Committee was scarcely more constructive. Undoubtedly, Kulomzin admitted, the Committee had made mistakes, as for instance over its road-building programme, but these had to be balanced against the many successes it had achieved. Before 1891 governmental policy on colonization had been neutral or even hostile, peasant emigration to Siberia being conducted in a chaotic and wasteful manner. This the Committee had changed. A network of officials had been created in Siberia which had spared many colonists much suffering, directed them to the best areas for settlement, and given them loans and grants to help to develop their farms. Nevertheless, 'the business was new and it was necessary to act carefully'. The interests of the indigenous tribes had to be protected against land-grabbing by colonists. In addition, absurd rumours about a land of milk and honey in Siberia had been current among the peasants in European Russia, and unless these had been checked the colonization administration risked being swamped by floods of immigrants. Had this happened it was the colonists themselves who would have suffered, for even as it was emigration often entailed tragic losses for peasant families.[51]

Together with his private interests as a landowner and his official work for the Siberian Committee and the Chancellery of the Committee of Ministers, Kulomzin had also by 1900 established a reputation for himself as an author, his works covering financial, fiscal and railway matters, as well as purely historical issues. Above all, however, he concerned himself with questions of education, which was a source of great interest to him throughout his life. His major work on this subject, *Dostupnost' nachal'noy shkoly v Rossiy*, came out in 1904 and was an appeal for universal primary education to be established immediately as a top governmental priority. Stressing that Russia was very far behind the rest of Europe in the provision of primary schools, Kulomzin argued that until the whole Russian population was at least literate, intermediate and higher education for relatively small sections of the community was 'to a certain extent a luxury'.[52]

Kulomzin linked the need for primary education to the demands of economic prosperity and modernization. 'It is difficult', he wrote, 'to implant agricultural skills and technical knowledge of crafts in a dark and illiterate environment which distrusts any knowledge. It is important to give a push to the peasant's mind while it is still young and receptive, to awaken his inquisitiveness and desire to live better, his ability to struggle against poverty, drunkenness and misfortune. The education of the people is a key factor from the point of view of the general interests of the state'.[53] From the political point of view, whatever might be said about the dangers of crash programmes to educate the masses, the risks of not ensuring that they were educated by the state rather than in other ways were obvious. Putting forward arguments clearly designed to outflank conservative opponents of reform within the government, Kulomzin reminded his readers that in practice, through 'schools of literacy' and private tuition, education was beginning to reach peasants and workers in large quantities. 'There can be no disputing the fact that once the population is being educated, it's better that it should be taught at properly organized government schools than in any old place, by chance, on the side.' Not merely would the technical quality of the government's schools be much higher: 'teaching here is combined with a religious and moral upbringing, with the study of the dogmas of the faith in which the pupil was born, and this gives him the rudiments of a certain discipline of mind and character. Nothing similar can be said of the literacy which percolates through outside the schools'. The risks of leaving popular education to chance and in private hands were even more evident in the borderlands than in Russia proper.[54]

As regards the type of education required, Kulomzin argued that the top priority was to bring basic literacy to all children. Arguments over curricula or disputes between church or state education were luxuries which Russia could not at present afford. For the moment one should stick to three-year, single-class schools with a minimum of 1 teacher for every 50 children, and give top priority to spreading such schools throughout the Empire. Once this had been achieved, attention should be turned to establishing two or more classes and adding technical education to the basic curriculum.[55] Once uniform standards were imposed it would be an illusion to imagine that church schools would be cheaper than state ones, nor would they better guarantee a child's morals. Indeed, in practice, even 'at the present time the church-parochial and secular schools are almost identical in their programmes, their general character and as regards the average length of study'.[56] In Kulomzin's view secular schools should pay much more attention to church singing lessons, 'so important for the religious development of children', but in general, over the longer run, he favoured the creation of a uniform 'state school'.[57] Denying that priority should be given to boys, Kulomzin argued that literate families required educated mothers and stressed that peasant opposition to girls' education had been much exaggerated.[58]

Above all, Kulomzin stressed the need for speed and for decisive action by the government. This was not the moment to indulge in dreams about high standards of education or to bewail the obvious and no doubt severe failings of the single-class three-year school. At present Russia could afford no more and, moreover, as yet had not even achieved what it could afford. Teachers' salaries must be raised substantially to avoid the scandal of widespread defection of teachers from rural schools into the excise service and even the police.[59] Of course financial constraints had to be recognized, but the central government's contribution to rural primary schools should be raised from its present paltry level of less than 25 per cent of total costs to at least 37 per cent, in other words to double the zemstvo investment. As far as possible the burden of supporting schools should be removed from the communes.[60] Nor was rural education the only problem. Urban primary schools were packed and turned many children away, in large part because the deputies of the town Dumas, drawn from the middle and upper classes, preferred to devote funds to gymnasia and *Realschule* which their own children were far more likely to attend than humble primary schools. The central government should insist on norms which would mean that at least half a town's educational budget should be spent on the nine-tenths of the urban population who would not get beyond a primary schooling.[61] On the other hand, where local institutions of self-government were concerned, the government should remember that it was essential to establish zemstvos in the Western Provinces if the miserable educational levels there were to be improved.[62]

A further interest of Kulomzin lay in social conditions in the towns, and in particular in the provision of cheap housing for workers. The flowering of this interest in the early twentieth century owed something to purely personal experiences and sufferings. To the extent that one can judge from a man's letters, Kulomzin seems to have loved his wife and was certainly very upset by her serious illness in 1900 and 1901. In early 1902 he wrote to her in the following terms:

> I have always deeply loved Katenka and now more than ever, I hope you don't doubt this. But the sadness which I went through in the last few months, your illness, taught me to love God, to give him thanks and to pray to him. . . . In my opinion our sufferings or those of people close to us are sent to us to bring us close to Christ, that is so that we should become indulgent, good or at any rate just to our neighbours. . . . I wanted to say to you *à propos* this that it was precisely so that there should be at least some strain of service to my neighbour that I, at the height of your illness, joined the Kostroma Charitable Society and took upon myself the working out of how to find bearable homes for people from our Kostroma; this was after I had personally investigated their flats in the summer and had seen the stinking dens in which they live. . . . Hence the brochure, but I've long since been interested in the question of flats and have worked on the subject when I could and preached about it in the highest places.[63]

The 'brochure' to which Kulomzin referred was written by him in 1901. It stated that the aim behind the construction of cheap housing was 'to reduce the mortality rate amongst the working-class population of the major cities, to arrest the physical and moral degeneration of the working class, protect the family and reduce social discontent', arguing that 'all these distant and complicated goals cannot be achieved without, first of all, elementary sanitation in workers' housing'.[64] Kulomzin had investigated the activities of building societies in the West with typical thoroughness and financial acumen. Workers, he wrote, invested small sums every week in these societies, in which they received shares and the right to rent flats in the societies' homes. He had inspected German and British accommodation provided by such societies in 1901 and had been impressed by their good order and the scale of the amenities they offered. It was, he wrote, true that without governmental help many of the German societies could not have started, 'nevertheless, it is impossible to deny that the partici-

A.N. KULOMZIN

pation of the workers themselves in the enterprise, the application, even if partial, of the principle of self-help, is something in the highest degree important and attractive'.[65]

Kulomzin underlined that proper housing for workers was in its infancy even in the West. Even in Britain and Germany, where thousands of workers were well housed, tens of thousands were still living in the old abominable conditions. In Russia as yet virtually nothing had been done, and Kulomzin reported his impressions from inspecting Petersburg housing, where workmen 'huddle together often in rooms which give one the impression of being disgusting God-forsaken boxes'.[66] The Kostroma Society's plans for workers' housing would be 'the first experiment in this type of help for the poorest elements of the working population, occupied in physical labour'. Kulomzin's initial plan was to house some 215 Kostroma emigrants in a building which would cost roughly 63,000 roubles; both the layout of the rooms and the economics of the accommodation's construction and upkeep were gone into with Kulomzin's usual care and precision.[67]

In the first years of the twentieth century, when Kulomzin's term as secretary to the Committee of Ministers was nearing its end, the Russian state was lurching towards disaster. Kulomzin's correspondence with his wife is too fragmentary to give one a sense of his shifts of mood and views, as crisis succeeded crisis and one minister followed another into retirement or the grave, though occasional insights are possible. Thus in April 1902 he records his disgust at Petersburg's cold-heartedness at the news of Sipyagin's assassination.[68] On 5 April he writes:

> Today I finally calmed down when I read, this morning in *Pravitel'-stvennyy Vestnik*, about V.K. Plehve's appointment as Minister of Internal Affairs. This was the only sensible appointment, but rumours were going round about Bobrikov. Plehve knows the governors, knows police business, and will put everything in order. This is the general, calming feeling which has seized everything and everyone.... What is needed is a clever man who won't hound the zemstvos, who won't be in agreement with Witte in everything...who won't forbid voices from the provinces speaking about the conditions of the poor or impede humane people from helping the unfortunate hungry.[69]

In the following weeks Kulomzin's hopes of Plehve were realized. On 3 May 1902, for instance, he wrote that Plehve was running the police in a much more efficient manner than Sipyagin. Under the latter the Police Department, acting in an uncontrolled and arbitrary manner, had arrested innocent suspects right and left without carefully checking their credentials, while the real terrorists went free.

Now a professional hand was felt at the wheel and many innocent people were being released.[70] How long Plehve's popularity with Kulomzin lasted is impossible to say, but whatever credit the Minister still possessed was dissipated by his refusal to confirm D.N. Shipov as chairman of the Moscow zemstvo, a move which in Kulomzin's view played a key role in precipitating the 1905 revolution.[71]

Much the fullest statement of Kulomzin's political views is contained in a memorandum submitted to Nicholas II in May 1905, authored by six top officials: Kulomzin himself, Andrei and Peter Saburov, Count K.I. Pahlen, O.B. Richter and Fyodor Terner. Of course the memorandum was strongly influenced by the revolutionary turmoil threatening to engulf Russian society at the time it was written, and expresses views in a manner which would have been considered unacceptably sharp and radical only months before; it can nevertheless be seen as reflecting rather accurately the basic convictions held by A.N. Kulomzin throughout his political life.[72]

The memorandum starts by saying that for the third time in their lives the authors were living through a period of ferment in Russia and on each occasion domestic instability had been linked to failure in war or diplomacy. Noting the discontent which had existed in educated society as a result of the failures and weaknesses revealed in the Crimean war, the memorandum states that the nobility's best representatives had aided Alexander II in his reform programme and that, despite fears to the contrary, the peasantry had behaved with great intelligence, good will and calm during Emancipation. The second period of ferment had erupted after the Russo-Turkish war when general discontent arose out of the failure of diplomacy to retain the fruits of military victory for Russia. In addition, during the war, it goes on, 'all our defects once again manifested themselves clearly: extortion in matters concerning military supplies, general lack of internal and external readiness, and the lack of tact of the internal administration, which sharply opposed the timid manifestation of zemstvo independence in matters concerning the local economy'. Amidst failing self-confidence and terrorist outrages an exhausted and confused educated society fell into the strong arms of Alexander III with a sigh of relief. Attempts by the revolutionaries to infiltrate the peasantry were, moreover, wholly unsuccessful.

Alexander III's advisers had, however, made a fatal error. This was based, says the memorandum, on the belief that

the events of 1 March 1881 which cast a pall on our history were the consequence of the policy of liberation of the reforming tsar who had died so prematurely. The consequence of this fatal misconception was the government's attempt, which has prevailed for the last 25 years, to limit the rights and privileges which were given to Russia in the era of great reforms of the Emperor Alexander II. Thus the universities were deprived of that autonomy in their internal administration which they had long enjoyed and which was confirmed by the statute of 1864, the zemstvo was reorganized on a class basis, was in its economic activity largely deprived of the independence granted it by the law, and also saw the range of its activities considerably limited. Its best elements left zemstvo service.

The idea behind the establishment of land commandants (*Zemskie nachal'niki*) had been a good one and certainly no one could doubt the need for an agent of the authorities standing closer to the peasantry. Nor was there anything wrong in principle in giving the land commandants both administrative and judicial powers, as was done with English JPs. Nevertheless, the land commandants lacked the security of tenure possessed by Russia's peace arbitrators and JPs, both of whom could be dismissed only by the Senate, and in addition their judicial powers were entirely beyond the control or surveillance of any higher judicial body. Moreover, the land commandants were given the right to interfere in the intimate details of peasant economic life, a right 'which no civilized administration should possess'. Matters became worse when land commandants increasingly were appointed from outside the area, and by now the office no longer enjoyed any respect in peasant eyes. Before 1890 the nobility had remained somewhat aloof from the zemstvo, but in the following decade nobility and zemstvo drew together and the nobles were antagonized by anti-zemstvo measures.

Turning to the government's nationalities policy, the memorandum notes that

> linking our borderland to the centre is an unchanging condition for the very existence of our huge empire. Beyond question knowledge of the language of state amongst the various elements of the population serves as a powerful means towards the achievement of this goal. But even here those who carried out imperial wishes deeply annoyed all elements among the various nationalities populating Russia by their one-sided tendencies. The attempt to russify nationalities like the Poles, Finns, Georgians and Armenians, who have their own distinctive literary language, was entirely without a firm basis.

Moreover, religious measures often aroused the fanatical opposition of the non-Russian clergy.

Meanwhile as regards the Russian masses, says the memorandum, the government had done too little in the last twenty years to improve the conditions of the peasantry. The tax burden undoubtedly weighed too heavily upon them. In addition, 'the state did not attach to the education of the masses the significance it deserved and, because of this, even those weak measures which were taken to develop the agricultural skills of the peasantry, to instil into them improved methods of using the land they own, could not yield significant results'. This failure greatly contributed to the crisis which beset the regime by the early twentieth century. Noting the string of political assassinations that had occurred in 1901 to 1904 and remarking that the murder of ordinary policemen had now reached epidemic proportions, the memorandum nevertheless lays most stress on the rising tide of rural disorder. The mass of the peasantry, 'lacking any culture, knowing no respect for private property, educated on the communistic principles of the *obshchina* [peasant commune] and not trained to any strict fulfilment of the law, is becoming an obedient weapon in the hands of the enemies of order'.

Kulomzin and his peers emphasized the fact that sedition, superficial in the 1850s and only somewhat more deeply rooted in the 1870s, had now spread far and wide into the mass of the population:

These facts ought, it would seem, to refute the arguments of those who say that the present troubled period is only something superficial and transient and even that it could quickly disappear in the event, for example, that fortune favoured us in the Japanese war. On the contrary, we deeply believe that the adverse criticism and condemnation which reigns in our educated and semi-educated society and which even extends to hysterical hallucinations, combined with total ignorance of the nature and difficulties of legislative work, in alliance with the instinctive striving of the lower classes to overthrow private property, which expresses itself in riots and mass pogroms – that together these two forces are eating away the roots of our political system. All the forces of political reason and will must be directed towards the struggle to avert this calamity.

The memorandum's authors strongly rejected the view that concessions would merely be interpreted as weakness, encourage further demands and lead to the ultimate collapse of the state. They greeted the decrees of 12 December 1904 and 18 February 1905 as indicating a will to reform, and stated that the edict on religious toleration had been met with joy throughout the country. After 18 February there had been a tendency for local activists in public organizations to swing away from mere ranting and towards constructive criticism. Time was, however, of the essence for, with every day that went by, demands were becoming more extreme. The various classes of society were vastly different in their levels of education and many of the demands wholly failed to recognize this fact. By now the desire for representative institutions had put down deep roots even among the semi-educated, and the constitutional reforms promised by the government were awaited with 'feverish excitement'. If this excitement was not given an outlet in the near future, demands would become still more extreme and might herald calamity for the state. The government should act quickly and should take the swiftest means to setting up a representative assembly.

As regards the new body's sphere of competence and power, the best approach, says the memorandum, would simply be to give it the same rights as the State Council. In other words it would be a consultative assembly devoted largely to domestic affairs which would submit recommendations to the monarch in the form of majority and minority opinions. It should, however, have two rights not possessed by the Council, namely the power to interpellate ministers and to initiate legislation. This was not the moment to indulge in debates about the best theoretical models for a newly constituted legislature to follow. 'At the present critical moment when the government must above all rely, for the struggle with the Social Democratic party, on that part of society which is interested in the preservation of the state', the key point was to set up a representative institution as soon as possible.

As regards the franchise, the memorandum's authors were true not only to their backgrounds but also to the European Victorian principles of political development which they had absorbed ever since the days of their youth.

The question about the relationship which should exist between the elected deputies and various numerical assessments of the population by class or category of job is an evidently meaningless issue in Russia, for it would be impossible to give the dominant position amongst the deputies to those uneducated elements which in humerical terms far outweigh all the rest. This is both because those elements lack intellectual and moral development or stability and because of their complete ignorance as to the workings of a political system. to allow these elements a dominant role would threaten the complete destruction of any culture in our country. In no West European state have the lower classes received from the outset the right to elect public representatives; everywhere the broadening of the electoral base has been the work of centuries, and it is sufficient to remember that in England before the electoral reform of Lord Grey in 1831 the number of electors to the English Parliament did not exceed 165,000 people.

Of course, the memorandum continues, if the dominant weight in an assembly were given to nobles and merchants a howl of rage would go up from those who were concealing their own aims behind slogans of the people's rights, but this was a fact which would have to be lived with.

The simplest method of getting an assembly on its feet quickly was to revert to the 1864 zemstvo franchise. District marshals should chair electoral meetings and, given the terms of the 1864 law, few extremists would be elected. In zemstvo and similar milieux socialist ideas would soon lose their charm when exposed to the open air. It was unnecessary persecution which gave such ideas their prestige. The expanded zemstvo, which should be extended to as many areas as possible, must be made the focus for the government's counter-attack against subversion. More power to the zemstvo would mean more effective local government and the diversion of activists into practical activity to improve Russian society. Once they came face to face with the difficulties of this task, they would be less inclined to indulge in utopian visions about political change.

Kulomzin's letters from rural Kostroma in July 1905 record his dismay at the increasing radicalization of society, but if anything this only strengthened his belief that a representative assembly should be established at top speed. Very scared by the spreading influence of the Union of Unions in Kostroma and elsewhere, he wrote that 'only the realization of the expected reforms will tear men of order away from this circle which is moving strongly in the direction of Social Democracy. At present all are united by the aim of winning a representative system. You can't imagine the lunacy which has seized everyone. People whose interests are entirely contrary to these ideas, leap into the ravine and drag in others'. Meanwhile the Kostroma working class had been influenced by socialist currents spreading from Ivanovo-Vosnesensk, one effect of which had been that they had turned against religion and hurled icons out of their houses. Kulomzin commented that 'a dead and stifled church has killed the religious spirit in our people'.[73] There is no evidence as to Kulomzin's immediate reaction to the October manifesto, but in April 1906 Madame Bogdanovich says he told her that 'he is now a constitutionalist...previously, before 17 October, he wasn't one but from that day he has become one and doesn't want a return to the past'. In Kulomzin's view P.N. Durnovo had initially performed a useful task in restoring order, but subsequently his senseless repression had merely caused trouble and stirred up anger.[74]

In the period after 1906 Kulomzin devoted much of his time to private interests, including writing works of history. He spoke rarely in the State Council, though, as one might expect, he was an enthusiastic supporter of extra funds for education, railway-building on the Amur River, and local historical museums.[75] His attitude towards the Duma, rather like that of Alexander Obolensky, was one of relative benevolence coupled with a desire to avoid unnecessary conflict.[76] In a letter to his son, while condemning the endless passions and squabbles in the Third Duma, he nevertheless described it as a '*chambre introuvable*' and wrote that 'a return to the former system is impossible not only *de iure* but also *de facto*', since the government lacked the power to face the Duma's wrath in the event of such an attempt.[77]

During the summer of 1915, when the government was putting out feelers to the moderate opposition, Kulomzin was appointed president of the State Council, a post in which, according to Naumov, he was too gentle and kindly to exercise a firm control over overlengthy and irrelevant debates.[78] Initially a member of the Centre Group, Kulomzin abandoned it for Neidhardt's Right-Centre in disapproval of the course pursued by the Centre under the leadership of Baron V.V. Meller-Zakomel'sky. In the summer of 1915 he thoroughly disapproved of the Centre's adherence to the Progressive Bloc. 'All these blocs and secret conferences are entirely unfitting for the House of Lords and the people involved don't themselves know where they are headed. How unpatriotic, not to say foul, to seize a share of political power on the grounds of the country's misfortune when in fact they are completely forgetting their country. All this is terrible and I dislike it.'[79] In such terms, perhaps suitable for a man whose 57 years of service in the state bureaucracy ended with him as president of the State Council and a Knight of Saint Andrew, Kulomzin concludes the last letter to be found among his private papers. He was to survive the revolution and die in emigration in 1921, though one of his sons was killed in the civil war.[80]

CHAPTER 8

Aristocrats in Politics:
THE BROTHERS ALEXANDER
AND ALEKSEI OBOLENSKY

By comparison with Peter Durnovo neither Prince Alexander Obolensky nor his brother Aleksei was a key figure in Russian politics, though neither was a political nonentity. Both Obolenskys were members of the State Council, and Aleksei, previous to this, held important executive positions within the central government. In addition, both men played an active role at the provincial level, partly though not entirely as noble marshals and in the zemstvo, while Alexander was also a big industrialist and a leading figure in Russian industrial and commercial organizations. As was seen in Table N of chapter 2, the Obolensky brothers were at the heart of the Russian aristocracy. Their connections with Nicholas II's court were strong. Among many reasons why it is worthwhile devoting a chapter to the two brothers is the existence of their large private correspondence, never previously studied, which provides valuable insights into the Obolenskys' personalities and the world in which they lived. Moreover, the brothers represent a somewhat different strain within the ruling élite from Peter Durnovo and Anatol Kulomzin, both of whom were, for all their links to the landowning nobility, full-time central government officials. Alexander and Aleksei Obolensky belonged to the less powerful but still very important noble group in top governmental circles whose lives had been devoted partly to private affairs and only in part to the paid service of the state.

The Obolenskys were of course one of the oldest and most aristocratic of Russian families. They were also, however, one of the most numerous. Inevitably therefore, among the 88 princes and princesses Obolensky listed by Ikonnikov in the generation of Alexander Obolensky's father, some were extremely rich and well-connected, while others were penniless and without status. Alexander's and Aleksei's branch of the family belonged in general in the former category. Their grandfather's elder brother, Andrei, had for instance owned 6,851 male 'souls', while a glance at the brothers' family tree shows numerous relatives in good positions in service and at court. On the other hand, to offset these advantages, Alexander's and

Prince Alexander Obolensky

Aleksei's grandfather had been one of 10 children and their father one of 12.[1] Even the most princely inheritance was unlikely to stand the strain of such numbers in a society where primogeniture and entail barely existed.

Alexander's and Aleksei's father, though a comfortably-off land-owner with 500 'souls', was not a rich magnate. Nor did he start his career with powerful connections at court. On the contrary, Dimitri Aleksandrovich Obolensky came from a distinctly Muscovite milieu, his mother being the daughter of Yuri Neledinsky-Meletsky, a relatively well-known poet from a prominent gentry family. D.A. Obolensky was on very good terms with the Moscow slavophils, being for instance a close relation of Yuri Samarin. He also, as a young official in the 1840s, moved in Petersburg literary circles, as well as belonging to the society of enlightened bureaucrats so ably described by Bruce Lincoln. If within this world of youngish and well-educated officials Obolensky stood out for his title, his relative wealth and his, albeit not very strong, high-society links, his mental outlook, life-style and interests stamped him much more as an enlightened bureaucrat than as the product of a court and aristocratic environment. It is very likely that Dimitri Aleksandrovich's serious-mindedness, his interest in literary, musical and cultural affairs, his long and successful civil service career, and his commitment to enlightenment, liberalism and progress all influenced his sons.[2]

Contemporaries' comments about Dimitri Aleksandrovich's eldest son, Alexander, are relatively scarce. In his biographical notes on members of the Senate M.L. Levinson, untypically, deviates from providing facts about A.D. Obolensky's career to stress his virtues as a man and a statesman. In the State Council 'it was for the most part his acquaintance with peasant and zemstvo questions which was of the greatest use, as well as his knowledge of the legal conditions of peasant life and of administration.... Everywhere where Prince A.D. served, his sensitivity to local needs, the simplicity with which he treated people and his good relations with all his comrades won him general sympathy'.[3] No one seems to have had any doubts as to Alexander Dimitrievich's personality, though on occasion contemporaries could be less impressed by his brains. Prince P.D. Svyatopolk-Mirsky, for instance, considered Alexander Obolensky a good candidate for top political office, 'if one pays more attention to decency than to brain'.[4] Polovtsov on the other hand said of his son-in-law: 'He is a clever man who had a good education...an extremely calm man, with firm, defined views worked out on many questions as a result of many years' experience'.[5]

Polovtsov's stress on Obolensky's calm and even temperament is certainly borne out by Alexander Dimitrievich's correspondence. The sudden enthusiasms and dramatic shifts in mood experienced by some at least of his children, not to mention his brother Aleksei, were alien to him.[6] Less well read in literature or philosophy than either his brother or his wife, he had a more practical temperament, and enjoyed running his estate and business interests, while involving himself deeply in the management of local affairs. When Alexander Obolensky wrote about others, the words 'solid', 'careful', 'balanced', 'deliberate' and 'unextravagant' were always compliments.[7] His relaxations were those of a quiet and to some extent self-contained man. He enjoyed solitary rural walks, reading books of history and, above all, music. On the latter subject he was a genuine expert, serving for many years as a member of the board of the Imperial Musical Society and in 1909–13 as its vice-chairman. Prone to bouts of loneliness and insomnia when away from his wife, Obolensky wrote to her in 1886 from his estate, Nikol'skoe: 'even when I'm alone I'm better here than anywhere else...for me Nikol'skoe is the only place where loneliness is somehow bearable'.[8] Dislike of the bustle, self-importance and intrigue of Petersburg life, together with the contrast he draws between the capital and the busy, productive and yet tranquil existence he leads at Nikol'skoe, are constant themes in A.D. Obolensky's letters.

In 1913, for instance, he wrote shortly after returning to the capital, 'I have already become completely immersed in the Petersburg atmosphere. I don't say that I'm feeling bad, but somehow living is a burden. It's as if one isn't doing anything special but in general feels tired...a sort of sad, heavy atmosphere'.[9] Nine years earlier he had commented in a letter from the capital, 'here there is futility, sadness, gossip and cold – to sum up, it's foul'. The countryside in contrast had its 'own atmosphere and interests. Petersburg with all the tragic, busy and disturbed times it's going through seems something far away – so that one only thinks about what's going on there but doesn't feel about it.... Everyone has got plenty of bread and so they are all satisfied, and when one is here and is plunged into the local atmosphere and interests one forgets quite a bit about matters concerning the war and internal politics'.[10] The worst torture of all was when, to the burdens of coping with political questions was added the need to play a representative role in society. To many officials the prestige of acting as temporary governor-general in the borderlands would have been recompense for any inconvenience. Alexander Obolensky, however, merely records that 'it was rather boring and unpleasant for me to play the role of chief of a vice-royalty'.[11]

To understand Alexander Obolensky's attitude to official service one has to remember that he was a man who had inherited both high social status and considerable personal wealth. His father was both a prince and a member of the State Council while his mother was born a princess Trubetskoy. A.D. Obolensky's wife was the daughter of the Imperial Secretary, A.A. Polovtsov, and, still more to the point, one of the two granddaughters of Baron Stieglitz, a multi-millionaire banker. Anna Obolensky owned 7,000 *desyatiny* in Tambov province, urban properties, and had large holdings of stocks and bonds.[12] It is nevertheless a moot point whether she was richer than her husband.

Alexander Obolensky had not inherited a great fortune from his father, who, as we have seen, was comfortably-off rather than rich; but, when still a boy, he had been nominated as sole heir to the Nikol'skoe estate in Penza by his childless great-uncle, A.N. Bakhmetev. Along with the estate of 16,000 *desyatiny* went a very extensive glass factory.[13] Though in the two decades after Emancipation the factory had gone through hard times, giving Alexander Obolensky little income in the 1880s and 1890s, by the twentieth century it was once again very profitable. In the period of Alexander Obolensky's ownership production increased five-fold, turnover by 1912–13 being worth 775,000 roubles.[14] On 8 August 1911 Obolensky wrote to Anna: 'I went round the whole factory. Work is racing along and my heart really rejoiced to see how well this business is now going. In the last year up to 1 April the factory gave a clear profit of 76,000 roubles', a result Obolensky called 'brilliant'.[15] Still better was to come, for two years later annual profits for the whole estate were reckoned at 200,000 roubles. In the face of sums such as these, the 10,000 roubles that Alexander Obolensky earned as a member of the State Council was not very significant.[16]

Alexander Obolensky's extensive private concerns represented, however, not only an alternative source of income to the state's service but also a rival field of activity. Life at Nikol'skoe may have spelt tranquillity for Obolensky but it certainly did not imply laziness. In June 1903 he wrote to his wife from the country that he got up at 7 a.m. every day, inspected the demesne farms and worked in the office until noon, rested after lunch and then returned to work in the office at 5 p.m., finishing each day by riding round to inspect different parts of the estate.[17]

Nikol'skoe was a little kingdom of which Alexander Obolensky was undisputed ruler. By the eve of the First World War the glass factory alone employed 1,300 people, the estate as a whole many more. The glass factory, moreover, was not only large and profitable but also unique, being Russia's oldest and most famous glassworks. Conditions of factory life at Nikol'skoe were, by the standards urban Russian industrial capitalism had attained by 1914, distinctly patriarchal, with strong remnants of the pre-1861 social order. The great majority of workers at the factory were the children and grand-children of those who had laboured in the glassworks for the Bakhmetevs. Most owned allotment land in the neighbourhood. The majority even of the managerial and technical staff also came from the district. All those employed in the factory had free access to the school, hospital, orphanage and old people's welfare fund set up by the estate's owners.[18]

Alexander Obolensky took a very close interest in the affairs of both the welfare services and the factory itself. Because it was the former which most interested his wife, he reported on them to her in greatest detail. In 1883, for instance, his letters are full of information about the new estate school he was building: on 30 November 1883, to take but one example, he wrote to Anna to say that he had spent all morning listening to lessons at the school.[19] Frequently there are references to his giving encouragement to or sorting out quarrels between the teachers, doctors, managers and other employees on the estate.[20]

When possible Obolensky involved himself in the technical details of the glass industry, in which some of his Bakhmetev relatives had been experts. In May 1898, for instance, he spent almost a whole day in Petersburg watching the work of a skilled craftsman whom he intended to employ at Nikol'skoe.[21] On other occasions the factory's business took him as far afield as Finland and even Paris, where in 1900 his glass won a gold medal at the International Exposition. Obolensky's fellow glass manufacturers may have looked a little askance at conditions in his factory, feeling for instance that workers were spoiled and inclined to regard the works almost as their own property, but other manufacturers clearly respected his business acumen.[22] He was perpetually re-elected chairman of the All-Russian Congress of Glass Manufacturers, was a member of the council of the Congress of Representatives of Trade and Industry, and in addition headed one of the key legislative sub-committees preparing for the renegotiation of the Russo-German trade treaty in the immediate pre-war years.

Given the great interest and energy he invested in his estate, not to mention the wealth and recognition it brought him, Obolensky's willingness to work as a state official is rather surprising, and was owed in part at least to his wife's dislike of Penza and her wish to spend a good deal of the year in the capital. In the autumn of 1889, when Anna Obolensky's efforts to find her husband a suitable post in Petersburg were bearing fruit, Alexander wrote that he would accept the job if offered, 'although frankly speaking this is awful servitude and having been accustomed to complete freedom in this respect it's rather difficult to put on the yoke of an official'. In addition, he said, 'when you see how everything here livens up when I'm around and how useful in general my presence is here, it is sad to abandon all this. But if one has to live in Petersburg it's better to have work and a job than to be idle'.[23]

The presence in the countryside of figures such as Alexander Obolensky, wealthy, public-spirited and with excellent connections in Petersburg, had many advantages for rural society. To some extent the Obolenskys represented the interests of the local community in its relations with the higher state authorities. In June 1914, for instance, one finds Obolensky pressing the Minister of Education about the construction of a school in the local town,[24] on other occasions a grant for church-building, or support for the career of some individual member of the local community was requested.[25] In times of emergency Alexander Obolensky helped both the workers on his estate and the wider community as well. Reservists called up for service in the Russo-Japanese war retained part of their pay if their families were in need.[26] Fellow glass manufacturers used to the more impersonal and purely owner-employee relationships in their factories looked somewhat askance at the Nikol'skoe set-up, in which younger members of the community were regarded as having almost an inherited right to jobs in the glassworks.[27] Moreover, at least in this particular case, gentry claims that their houses were islands of culture which a poor and still relatively primitive rural community badly needed had some foundation: a major local figure such as Alexander Obolensky, willing to throw his weight behind the expansion not only of railways and roads but also of musical evenings and literacy in his local area, was a valuable asset.[28]

Alexander Obolensky's correspondence with his wife contains interesting information about his activities in the famine year of 1891–2. In April 1891 he wrote that 'I still can't gather reliable information about the people's need for bread'. Some areas seemed threatened by hunger, others had plentiful supplies, and the reports coming to him were contradictory. Still, he had purchased grain against any eventualities that might arise. In October, he reported that there was as yet no famine in the area, 'but there will of course be great need in the winter' and he had successfully pushed the zemstvo into establishing a grain reserve. He himself had bought extra supplies of grain 'so as to have the possibility in the spring when one must expect special need and high prices to give some help to the population'.

On 16 December 1891 Obolensky reported to his wife that 'I bought six wagons today which will make it fully possible for us to increase our charitable work and probably to realize my dream about selling cheap bread'. Nevertheless reports coming in from local areas were 'less terrible and appalling than I had expected'. The consensus seemed to be that there was no actual starvation and that if the zemstvos and charities did their work properly it could be avoided. Obolensky was not sanguine that such efficiency could be attained. 'There's no unity or sensible organization. . . . There's no lack of funds and without doubt not only starvation but even great need could be avoided, but the whole issue depends on people and on the organization of the matter'. He himself had set up a *stolovaya* [canteen] at Nikol'skoe and had, largely with the help of money given by Count Kutuzov but partly with his own grain, fed the starving in two other areas as well. In July 1892, back at Nikol'skoe, he reported to his wife that thus far the cholera had only reached the town of Penza. 'I feared cholera much more', he wrote, 'when it was further away and now have somehow grown accustomed to thinking about it and the possibility of its appearance and don't fear it at all'.[29]

Obolensky's service to the local community was, as one might expect, expressed in part through activity in the zemstvo and as the Penza provincial marshal of nobility. On leaving Moscow University he had served for a decade in the judicial department, to which he returned in the 1890s as a chief procurator in the Senate. Among the State Council's jurists he was the only landowning magnate. For much of the 1880s, however, Obolensky remained in retirement from the civil service and worked as marshal of Penza province, a job he could combine with close supervision of Nikol'skoe, which inherited in this period. Although, inevitably, most able to play an active role in zemstvo affairs in the 1880s, even later as a top official in the central government Alexander Obolensky attended zemstvo assemblies and busied himself with local affairs.[30]

From 1902 a member of the State Council, Obolensky attended the zemstvo assembly in the winter of the following year. He reported to his wife that he had been impressed by the detailed and serious discussion of local affairs, as well as by the absence of 'empty chatter' or of debate on 'useless but fashionable topics' of a political nature.[31] A year later Obolensky was again at the provincial zemstvo assembly, in which, he wrote to his wife, 'my authority is very very great. . .a big group of real local grass-roots zemstvoists always take their lead from me'. In these years immediately prior to the 1905 revolution, Obolensky was distinctly unhappy with the political line pursued by D.S. Sipyagin and V.K. Plehve. In addition, 'in my opinion the entire Penza state administration are worse than the worst of cretins'. Nor was Obolensky impressed by the December 1904 imperial manifesto promising civil rights and religious toleration, which, he wrote, 'smacks of insincerity, of an act which was forced on them by the need to promise something in the saving quality of which they don't themselves particularly believe'. Nevertheless he fought hard to counter the politicization of the Penza zemstvo and to keep it loyal to the central government. Alexander Obolensky wrote to his wife that of course the assembly had to reply to the imperial manifesto's concessions to zemstvo feelings, and that he and the then provincial marshal had drawn up a telegram 'which we sent by the most legal means possible, through the governor and the Minister of Internal Affairs. . .thanking him [i.e. Nicholas II] for his trust in the zemstvo and his call for it to undertake a broader and more independent activity. I put forward the notion which I am always urging, that one must not look on the zemstvo as something quite separate from all other state institutions but that on the contrary the zemstvo must and can act only in full accord with them'. The zemstvo assembly accepted the draft 'without incident' thanks to the prestige enjoyed by the provincial marshal and Obolensky himself, though there were deputies who found the tone of the document too moderate.[32]

Alexander Obolensky's own work as a provincial marshal in the 1880s had followed predictable patterns. His time was spent in conferences with the governor, attendance on provincial administrative boards and dealing with the affairs of the nobility, including a host of issues concerned with individual nobles' inheritances. Much energy also went into attending functions as the nobility's representative – including, so it seems, a never-ending series of appearances in full uniform at special occasions in Penza's schools. With some justice Anna Obolensky commented on 8 March 1882 that 'judging by your letters you have to do a lot of boring work in your official position'.

For Alexander Obolensky the worst period of the year came in December when the zemstvo assembly met. 'In itself', he wrote, 'the assembly is not particularly unpleasant; I will manage this work well enough and it is genuine work. What is appallingly boring are the visits of all the deputies, which one has to return – and, worst of all, the dinners'.[33]

For A.D. Obolensky, however, the main problem about service as Penza's marshal was his wife. Whether for reasons of illness, pregnancy or boredom Anna Obolensky, as noted, loathed living in the town of Penza. This meant that her husband had to live there alone from 'January right through to the end of May', something which after five years of service as a marshal began to be unbearable. On occasion sharply critical of other marshals' dereliction of duty, Alexander Obolensky wrote that people already criticized him for not living enough of the time in Penza and if family reasons made it impossible to fulfil a marshal's functions he would have to give up the job.[34] When Anna heard of his intention to resign as marshal she wrote approvingly, but added, 'It's easier for you yourself to judge to what extent all this is good and convenient and how people will view this'. Perhaps it would be thought that 'you wish only to think about yourself and shrug your shoulders about everything else.... though I must say that for me the thought of spending this spring with you quietly somewhere in Italy and then having a peaceful summer at Nikol'skoe without any of the marshal's duties is very pleasant'.[35]

As we have seen, the solution finally reached was Alexander's transfer into the central government. He served from 1892 to 1897 as a chief procurator in the Senate, for the next two years as assistant governor-general of Warsaw, then for three years as a senator, before being appointed to the State Council in 1902. Apart from these official posts, Obolensky played a major role in the Imperial Musical Society, in which he followed in his father's footsteps as vice-chairman, as well as in the Red Cross Society, of which, again, he was deputy chief. In 1905 crisis came to both these organizations, as indeed to the Russian state itself. With the Conservatoire on strike and problems with both teachers and students mounting, Obolensky was beset as well with furious personal battles and reciprocal accusations of corruption which wracked the Red Cross. In September 1905 Obolensky's usual conscientiousness, coupled with his sense that 'I do believe that from him to whom much has been given, much is also demanded',[36] fought a losing battle with the desire to escape temporarily from Petersburg at almost any cost. Writing to his wife from Biarritz, later in that month, he admitted that 'to tell you the truth my conscience is beginning to gnaw at me and I'm feeling a little uneasy at the fact that I left.... Here I am living alone, doing nothing and enjoying nature while in Petersburg there's... work, state business, Red Cross business and Conservatoire business, and in addition I don't know what is happening on the estates since I have no news from Ushakov'.[37]

Alexander Obolensky's political views were, as one might expect, conservative, though he was never a true *ultra*. In addition, of course, as an aristocratic magnate and a provincial activist he found some aspects of bureaucratic absolutism not to his taste. In the 1880s Obolensky clearly felt that the Emancipation settlement had gone too far in freeing the peasantry from all noble supervision, and he welcomed Alexander III's counter-reforms.[38] The best source for his opinions in this period are the records of the Kakhanov Commission on local government, of which he was an active member.[39]

On most matters before the commission Obolensky sided with provincial noble activists led by A.D. Pazukhin and S.S. Bekhteev against the opinions of the majority of central government officials. He upheld the estate (*soslovie*) tradition in local affairs, the peasant commune, the exclusion of Jews from zemstvo assemblies, and the need to create a local authority drawn where possible from the local nobility which would combine judicial and administrative functions, and supervise peasant affairs.[40] He joined in the attacks on bureaucrats too prone to undermine local institutions and customs on the basis of theoretical considerations derived from outside Russia and inappropriate to provincial conditions. Alexander Obolensky defended *volost'* institutions as simple, practical and understood by the peasants, complaining that even if the reforms of communal and local administration desired by liberal bureaucrats were introduced, much would in practice remain the same given the conditions of rural life and the tenacity of peasant customs.[41]

On the other hand, on a number of issues, particularly where questions of legality were concerned, Obolensky diverged from Pazukhin and Bekhteev and tended to express views similar to those of the commission's other jurists. Thus he opposed Pazukhin's and Bekhteev's efforts to strengthen the commune's right to expel undesirables at will, and also voted against their proposal to increase the powers of the *starshina* (i.e. the zemstvo mayor) *vis-à-vis* the *volost'* court. Still less was Obolensky willing to see disputes between zemstvos over property settled by the administration rather than the courts, since it had been a firm principle established by the 1864 Judicial Statutes that questions concerning property must be resolved by due legal process.[42]

Within the State Council Alexander Obolensky's was a voice for moderate conservatism. After 1906 he belonged to the Council's 'Centre Group' which in general supported Stolypin's policies, did not share the Right Group's antagonism towards the Duma, and was on the whole a force for compromise and moderation. From his two-year stint in Warsaw Obolensky had acquired both knowledge of and interest in Polish and Belorussian affairs, and on the rare occasions he spoke in the Council, it was almost always on these subjects. Speaking on the Cholm issue in June 1912, Obolensky argued that it was of course absurd to imagine that one could turn Poles into Russians; all that could be hoped for was that a *modus vivendi* would be found through which Poles would become loyal subjects of the imperial state. Cholm was, however, wholly different from the other territories administered by the governor-general in Warsaw and was indeed already at least half Russian. In Obolensky's view it would be a mistake not to encourage it to make the rest of the journey.[43] Equally, on issues of education and language, Obolensky's stance was moderate conservative. State-supported schools must teach their pupils in Russian, with necessary exceptions made for religion and the teaching of the local language.[44] On the other hand, Polish municipal councils must be allowed to debate in Polish, and it was 'very stupid' of the State Council to throw out a Polish municipal reform bill because of dislike of this self-evident necessity.[45]

Alexander Obolensky's wartime letters to his wife provide some clues as to his political attitudes towards the end of his life. In Petersburg at the outbreak of the war, Obolensky wrote that in the Duma session 'one felt in general a very great enthusiasm... and a sort of calm confidence in final victory'. Instead of the 'usual Duma chatter and abuse' there was genuine unity, 'which is something really surprising'.[46] When the internal political crisis broke in the summer of 1915 Obolensky shared the intense general alarm at Russia's military setbacks, fear at Nicholas II's assumption of the supreme command and surprise that the ill effects of the latter were less than expected. When the Progressive Bloc was formed in the Duma and the State Council Centre Group's leader wished to join it, Obolensky recorded his dissent in a letter to his wife dated 29 August 1915. 'The Bloc's programme...is entirely unacceptable for many, and amongst others for me – I can, for example, in no way believe that to defeat the Germans it's necessary to release all political prisoners in administrative exile – I and certain others protested against the resolution of Meller [the Centrist leader] and I will probably leave the Centre Group'. At the same time Obolensky had little sympathy for Goremykin and his policies. Commenting on the government's attitude to the Duma, which Obolensky commended for its 'tact' and 'patriotism', he stated in September 1915: 'Here everyone is expecting a decision to dissolve the Duma. Like virtually everyone I think that this would be a great and dangerous political mistake – it is in my opinion an extremely important safety valve and things will be worse if all these people go off home dissatisfied and

Prince Aleksei Obolensky in emigration, and (*right*) at an earlier date, with his wife, *née* Saltykov.

resentful – but evidently they don't understand this'. Feet firmly planted in the conservative wing of the Centre Group, in which he remained despite the doubts expressed in the summer of 1915, Alexander Obolensky avoided the purge of the more liberal Centrists carried out on 1 January 1917, and sat in the State Council until the revolution.[47]

It would be difficult to imagine two human beings more different in personality than Alexander Obolensky and his younger brother Aleksei. Of the two, the latter was cleverer and more interested in ideas, but also much more unstable, nervous and excitable. In December 1867 the father of the two men, Dimitri, wrote to Alexander Obolensky, 'I'm convinced...that you will always act sensibly'. He would certainly not have dared say the same about Aleksei.[48] Alexander himself, attempting to calm his wife as regards their own children's antics, wrote in December 1903, 'if you knew what my brother Alyosha was like aged sixteen to twenty then you would be horrified', though he added that in the end Aleksei's good and unspoiled nature had triumphed over the worst sides to his character.[49] By then Anna had first-hand experience of Aleksei which went back over twenty years. In 1884, in a rather typical letter, she remarked to her husband that his brother 'is bustling about, losing control of himself and talking all sorts of rubbish'.[50] The unfortunate Aleksei was himself not unaware of some of his deficiencies, once writing to his sister-in-law that 'I don't have in my character this trait of keeping on a straight line down the middle of the road and I waver like a pendulum: I either boil or freeze and feel myself to be either a jester or a monk'.[51]

This trait did not of course endear Aleksei Obolensky to Petersburg high officialdom. Pobedonostsev once described him as a man in whose head two cocks were constantly crowing at the same time. Kryzhanovsky, speaking of the drafting of the October manifesto in 1905, wrote that 'as usual with Prince Obolensky one fantasy rapidly got jumbled together with another in the most contradictory combinations'. Gurko adds that 'under Obolensky's chairmanship no conference could ever have arrived at any definite decisions'.[52] Witte describes Aleksei Obolensky more kindly, as indeed one might expect since he was for a number of years the latter's main 'patron' in top governmental circles. In his view Obolensky was 'by no means stupid, well-educated, a convincing talker and honest but extremely light-minded and impressionable'. Witte added that when Obolensky 'talks he does so with conviction and convincingly but he changes his convictions as often as cleanly people change their underclothes'.[53]

Whereas Alexander Obolensky attended Moscow University, Aleksei followed his father to the School of Law, his parents quite possibly feeling that his character made him vulnerable to the freedoms of university life. After brief service in the judicial department he retired to his estate in the Kozyol district of Kaluga province, serving as district marshal from 1883 to 1894. As marshal Aleksei's financial position and – the two being closely connected – ambitions were very different from those of his older brother. Aleksei inherited 1,400 *desyatiny* in Kaluga, though after his mother's death a further 3,400 *desyatiny* in Saratov came his way. In October 1889, struggling along on his 1,400 *desyatiny*, Aleksei admitted to his brother that 'my financial affairs are not in a brilliant state' and that he was in need of a 6,000 rouble loan. He blamed partly bad harvests, partly the interference of their mother. Responding to Alexander's question as to why he had not been tougher with the peasants, Aleksei answered: 'I didn't do so because Mama came and wailed about the fate of these villains to such an extent that for the sake of calm in the house I had to give way to the peasants'.[54]

Typically, with his immediate financial problems solved Obolensky's imagination once again began to roam. In the last week of October 1889 Aleksei reported to Alexander that there were good prospects of his becoming Kaluga province's marshal. The only problem was financial. As a district marshal he could live off 200 roubles a month, but as marshal of the province, even in 'cheap' Kaluga, this would be completely impossible. There were, however, in Aleksei's view many advantages to taking the job of provincial marshal. For a man of only thirty-four it would of course be a great honour to serve as a province's marshal; but beyond that Aleksei Obolensky believed that the job might well open up excellent career prospects for him in the future. It was absolutely true, he wrote, no doubt replying to a nudge from Alexander, that 'the sooner I get a paying job the better'. Nevertheless, 'having served almost ten years without, so to speak, having "done any petitioning at court", wouldn't it be better to serve three more and immediately request something bigger?' He could at present obtain a vice-governorship but this would not bring him an income sufficient to live, even as a single man, part of the year in Petersburg with his mother. It would also leave his estate unsupervised.

> At present I have no chance at or claims on any job higher than a vice-governorship.... What, however, would the position be after three years as a provincial marshal? I might, as you say, turn out to be in a still worse position. A vice-governorship would be too small for me and yet they might still not give me a governorship. Of course this is possible but it seems to me to be improbable. Would I really have no chance of being given a vice-directorship or something of that sort? It seems to me that all this would more or less depend on me. I can say straight out at the elections that I'll only stand for three years. I can begin to try for a place in the second year. In the course of three years' service I will probably have an opportunity for personal contact with the ministers and will thus at least to some extent put myself in view.[55]

Alexander, destined to foot the bill for this adventure, vetoed his brother's plans and Aleksei remained a district marshal until 1894. Thereafter, however, his rise was spectacular. In 1894 he was offered a major post in the central offices of the Ministry of Agriculture. A year later he became director of the Noble and Peasant Bank and only two years subsequently was Assistant Minister of Internal Affairs, a position he held until a disagreement with D.S. Sipyagin led him to accept a senatorship in 1901. Within a year, however, Aleksei was back in a key executive position as Assistant Minister of Finance, and in 1905–6 served as chief procurator of the Holy Synod, thence retiring into the State Council where he was a prominent member of the Centre Group until the revolution.

Gurko, an old enemy of Obolensky, claimed that the latter's meteoric rise was owed to the close friendship between his brother Nicholas and the Emperor.[56] The explanation is, however, insufficient, for a man who could persuade both Witte and A.A. Polovtsov that he was 'remarkably gifted' owed his rise to more than mere connections, however powerful these were.[57] In part Obolensky's success stemmed from the fact that key figures in Petersburg, Witte included, were on the look-out for able aristocrats, competent to fill public office and knowledgeable about rural life. Moreover, the Minister of Finance was probably drawn to Aleksei Obolensky, at least initially, because of his need to find a suitable candidate to head the Noble Bank. The bank's chief was by custom an aristocrat, since only a man with powerful connections and status could survive the intrigues and accusations of indignant landowners whose appeals he had been unable to satisfy.[58] As director of the bank Aleksei Obolensky served Witte well. On 11 May 1897, for instance, Aleksei wrote to his brother indignantly about the nefarious schemes of noble marshals seeking to 'use state funds for class goals'. Allying themselves with Witte's enemies in the Ministry of Internal Affairs, wrote Aleksei, some of the marshals had devised a scheme 'in which money was unceremoniously ladled out from the state treasury'.[59]

Aleksei Obolensky's letters and his speeches in the State Council do not provide enough evidence for a comprehensive study of his political views. He was, it is clear, always on the liberal wing of the ruling élite. Witte, though stressing that Obolensky was basically a good and honest man, wrote that 'the prince is the very type of high-society titled liberal, who, for all his liberal views, never forgets his own comfort and convenience...he was troubled by the conflict between his own 1880s-style liberalism, which he took for granted, and the emergence of many of these liberal principles from democratic soil'.[60] The observation rings true. In 1905, for instance, Obolensky pressed for more seats in the Duma to be given to landowning representatives of 'society', and accepted a broad franchise for the Duma 'presuming that the peasants will choose predominantly the better landowners'.[61] When this failed to happen and the first two Dumas assaulted not only the state but also landed property, Obolensky came to the conclusion that it was necessary to change the franchise and supported Stolypin's 'coup' on 3 June 1907.[62]

In the era of the Third and Fourth Dumas, however, Obolensky was consistently on the left of the State Council, which he urged not to pick quarrels with the Duma and not to block reforms unless it was strictly necessary.[63] Representative institutions, he reminded the Council in June 1908, had been created to restore moral authority to a political system shaken not only by the revolution but also 'perhaps' by bureaucratic absolutism as well.[64] It was important not to clash with the Duma over trifles and to give the latter every opportunity to work effectively. In March 1908 he underlined his conviction that society must be given room to flex its muscles, arguing, 'I am convinced that the strength and the future development of the Russian state lies in the greatest possible degree of independence in the action of local self-governing institutions'.[65] Six years later, speaking on plans to introduce a *volost'* zemstvo, he attacked the views of members of the upper house who opposed the bill on the grounds of peasant backwardness and the threat peasant domination of an all-class *volost'* would entail for landowners' interests. Aleksei Obolensky argued that the new bill adequately protected noble interests and was essential to the efficiency of rural local government. Nobles should not block such reforms but rather use their superior culture and education to help to guide peasant communities towards a realistic grasp of local needs. The task of conservatives was, he added, to show the way to necessary and practical reforms 'while the decision is still in our hands'.[66]

Aleksei's letters to his brother and sister-in-law during the First World War illustrate his despair at governmental policy. On 4 January 1915 he wrote that Goremykin seemed genuinely to think he was performing a useful function by presiding over the Council of Ministers and stopping any strong and active person from running the government. In addition, by draping himself in a special mystique of devotion to the monarch and obedience to his will he was failing to protect the Emperor from criticism and undermining the crown's prestige.[67] On 12 June 1915 Aleksei wrote to Alexander that at least military disasters had forced the government to wake up. 'The real danger has at last forced them to get rid of the jokes in the internal administration and evidently the reform of the ministry is well under way. After this change they propose to summon the Duma and to give us genuine unity. – In a word they are doing everything they should have done ten months ago.' In Aleksei's view Rodzyanko and the Duma members were striving with genuine patriotism to work with the government, but influential figures were still attempting to put brakes on concessions to public opinion and the autonomous actions of society. Meanwhile time was not standing still.[68] Six days later Aleksei was more pessimistic. 'I fear even more than previously that the government will again, by delaying, fail to take advantage of the wave of good feeling with which society responded to our failures. Then we will have to await disaster, from which God protect us.'[69]

By the autumn and winter of 1915 Aleksei's mood had turned to despair. 'Society' was now wholly alienated from the state, he wrote in September 1915. He had just attended the Kaluga zemstvo assembly which had become completely unrecognizable. 'It has swung to the left to such an extent that I have turned out to be a member of the extreme right!' Recognizing that 'agitation is in general harmful and at present criminal', Aleksei nevertheless blamed the situation squarely on the government. 'The heroic activity of Goremykin has borne its fruit.'[70] On 17 December 1915 he wrote that he had composed some rubbish for the provincial nobility to send to Nicholas II. 'In general', he added, 'it's not only difficult but also unpleasant nowadays to write things full of agreed-on criticism when the unconditional truth is so severe, pitiless and decisive.' Commenting on the home front and the 'mania for profits' that the war had unloosed, Obolensky asked: 'Can one be victorious given such conditions? The deeper one goes into this question the more irreparable our situation seems to be. There remains only to live from day to day'.[71]

Aleksei Obolensky was interested not only in political issues on the surface of contemporary life, but also in deeper questions of politics, philosophy and religion. He was an acquaintance of both Konstantin Leont'ev and Vladimir Solov'yov, and had tremendous admiration for the latter's philosophical writings and for his commitment to the reconciliation of the Christian churches.[72] As regards his own personal beliefs, Aleksei was convinced of God's necessity for man. He once wrote, 'believe me, there is no other way to live than by subordinating oneself in everything, one's thoughts, feelings and will, to an external authority. It's impossible to live otherwise'.[73] In Aleksei Obolensky's view, however, religion was also vital for Russia, for it alone gave Russian society whatever originality and strength it possessed. This was in part because Russia lacked the institutions and attitudes which made Western society strong. Take away the religious link between tsar and people and what, for instance, did autocracy mean save the population's inability and 'unwillingness to rule itself'? An aristocratic sense of family pride was missing in Russia despite assiduous attempts to cultivate it. So too, in Obolensky's view, was the powerful and self-confident egoism of Western bourgeois man. In addition, 'the conceptions which are the cornerstones of European civilization', the faith in freedom, education and progress which was absorbed with one's mother's milk in the West, 'are easily rejected in Russia, just as easily as they were accepted'. For all these reasons the Church must be of vital importance for thinking Russians. 'If the slavophils had any significance in our country it was only from the ecclesiastical point of view of their teaching, and not of course because of their abstract ideas about a mysterious Russian culture or their exaggerated sentimental patriotism'.[74]

Certainly an overdose of 'sentimental patriotism' was not a fault of which one could easily accuse Aleksei Obolensky, who was always suspected on the right for his lack of nationalist fervour. Meshchersky, for instance, wrote in 1910 that 'Prince A. Obolensky is a pleasant man and a very intelligent statesman, but he is infected with the *idée fixe* that for a statesman there is something higher than God, tsar and country, that this is liberal progress and that, when necessary, the interests of the first three ought to be sacrificed to the latter'.[75] In part Obolensky's lack of aggressive nationalism was owed to his clear understanding of superior Western efficiency and power. Russian nationalist dreams about the decay and disintegration of the West were, he wrote in 1890, nonsense. Noting after a visit to Germany that 'the Germans have a calm, even attitude to business, they are orderly both within and without, disciplined in their habits, their minds and their hearts', Obolensky added that their 'chauvinism is truly staggering'. Contrasting German order and purpose with Russian lethargy and inconsistency, he wrote, 'if, which God forbid, there is a war they will smash us for certain'.[76] Sometimes Aleksei's consciousness of Russia's backwardness and failings in comparison to the West assumed an acute form. Always highly impressionable, his close acquaintance with the cold-blooded and intrigue-ridden world of Petersburg politics and high society at times drove him to despair. On one occasion, overwhelmed by depression at the mess which he saw at the centre of Russian political and social life, he commented that were it not for the Russian language he would feel Russians were no good at anything. Since, however, the language was one of the finest in the world, it should follow that the Russian people ought to be able to do something well.[77]

In the State Council after 1906 Obolensky spoke often on topics linked to Russian nationalist issues. Interestingly, he shared the commitment of most European liberal-conservatives to sea power. Arguing for the rebuilding of a Russian battle fleet, he said that it was wrong to be so disheartened by defeat in the Japanese war that one altogether forgot about national honour. 'I personally am not among those who continually put forward the need to develop national pride. Pride is a vice even if it is a national one. But national dignity, a state's dignity and honour, these must be preserved.' Running through Obolensky's speech is a sense that the most civilized and cultured nations in the world had great navies, through which they asserted their right to play a role in human progress. Russia must not allow itself to drop out of the club of civilized leading powers. 'The state which truly wishes to be global and to play a role cannot be deprived of those naval methods of communication which the whole world possesses.' Navies were a great force for cultural as well as political influence. 'If Russia is called upon to play a role in the world, it must have the possibility of realizing definite tasks there and in practical terms it can only realize those tasks by one means: by carrying its flag and its significance to any place across the globe'.[78]

In general, however, Aleksei Obolensky's speeches in the State Council were anathema to the fierier brand of Russian nationalist. He repeatedly stressed that the imposition of Russian nationalist policies on a multi-ethnic empire could only lead to disaster. All citizens must be recognized as equal subjects of the Emperor; allowing national *curiae*, for instance, in zemstvo elections, thereby both recognizing that nationalities must be separately represented and tilting the franchise in favour of Russians, was quite simply an anti-state principle. Obolensky told the State Council in May 1909 that whatever else might be said of the Russians, they had succeeded in bringing one-sixth of the world's surface and 140 different peoples into one state. These peoples could not simply be kept down by force. The Russian state must have high and great principles and they must be above nationalism. All peoples must be equal before the monarch because 'the Emperor is the head of the state, standing outside and above all parties, all nationalities, all groups and all classes'. The Russians had not been and must not become like the Western colonial powers. They had always treated other races as equals, assimilated them and united all peoples under the imperial banner. 'It is completely impossible to solve the national question in Russia by following the example of Western European colonial policy...the Russian state's attitude to the national question must be completely *sui generis*'.[79]

Three years later over the Cholm issue, Aleksei Obolensky denounced those who argued that Russians 'must be motivated by healthy national egoism'. The Russian nation, stressed Obolensky, 'is not one of those nations...struggling with each other within the state, it is the central, state and ruling nation and its dominion rests precisely on the fact that it isn't one of the many nations but is the only state nation and that its interests are closely bound up with those of the Empire as a whole. Imperial interests are the interests of the Russian people because this is the Russian Empire. It is a misunderstanding to separate the Russian nation from the imperial ideal'. If the Russians merely became the largest of the Empire's warring tribes then the various races of the Empire could never be reconciled and in the long run the Empire was doomed.[80] Obolensky's 'solution' to the nationalities problem was therefore not so much to recognize the political rights of the minorities as to deny political rights to any nationality as such, Russians included, and to stress that all had equal cultural and civil rights in a to some extent supra-national, imperial state. Behind this attitude lay a deep and sincere loathing for Russian chauvinism and a commitment to civilized principles which stood above national boundaries and prejudices.

This attitude is strikingly illustrated in two of Aleksei's letters to his sister-in-law in the first months of the Great War. On 12 September 1914 he wrote to Anna about 'this insane catastrophe' that had befallen Europe and the crazy views of those who had convinced themselves that Germany was at the root of all evil in the world and that its destruction would bring some kind of bliss to mankind. Such ideas were of little comfort to him. He had two sons at the front and perhaps they too would 'prove to be a sacrifice to that nice European paradise which must ensue after the mutilation of the best young elements of the civilized world'. Reflecting on the dangers of envisioning a happy utopia when human obstacles had been cleared aside by violence, Aleksei Obolensky wrote that

when mankind begins to busy itself about the creation of bliss on earth this bliss is extremely doubtful but beyond question blood-shed results. All socialist utopias are like this, all plans to introduce bliss on this planet will lead without fail to evil and bloody actions. And the higher the bliss towards which people strive the more blood will be poured out and it will extinguish any bliss. All this is a consequence of sinning against the Second Commandment. The idol of nationalism has been put before God and there now re-mains only the cult of hatred towards the Germans – how this came about it's too late now to discuss but there only remains to us to try in every way to conquer the Germans, which is possible, however, without any hatred towards them. Defeating them will be a long drawn-out business, however, even if we abandon such idiocies as wanting completely to destroy Germany.[81]

In a second letter to Anna Obolensky, written on 20 October 1914, Aleksei commented that the war was taking place not only on the battlefield, but was leading to all sorts of horrors and excesses against civilians. He added that 'these pictures of destruction, grief, suffering and the death of women, children and everything alive in the vicinity removes all that poetry which did still exist in former wars'. Moreover, as regards the much-trumpeted German atrocities, 'in many cases we are not inferior to them in such matters. For exam-ple both we and the Germans torment and hang our Jews'. As for German civilians within Russia, they were being persecuted in all sorts of ways and he was doing his best to help them. As regards the war's causes he admitted that Germany might have been responsible for pouring in the last drops which caused the vessel to overflow, but all the powers had played their part in filling that vessel to the brink.

I think that the discrepancy between material and technical pro-gress and the spiritual condition and development of civilized man-kind could only produce the result it has produced. Equilibrium has been lost and everything has collapsed. And to the degree to which the achievements of material culture are destroyed, and they are being destroyed, there is being revealed on the one hand the savagery which was hidden beneath that culture, and on the other are appearing signs of that returning spirituality in the form of astonishing acts of selflessness, courage and real valour. And in the end, *ne vous en deplaise*, will be restored a true faith in the living God without which everything is dust and ashes.

To expect, however, that mere Russian victory would bring this transformation would be a huge illusion. 'As a Russian I of course ardently long for this result [i.e. victory], but here the nature of the spiritual baggage with which we enter Berlin, if we are fated to do so, is important.' If victory were merely to lead Russians to trumpet their own virtues and their superiority, tested in battle, over other nations, 'then what will the world gain from this?...the triumph of the ideals of *Novoe Vremya*, utterly repulsive in Russia, will not become better in Berlin. But most important, this triumph can't happen – it would be completely senseless'.[82] In the midst of the nightmare by which he was surrounded Obolensky sought to find some purpose, some grounds for optimism, some hint of light and progress in contemporary events. His correspondence does not reveal whether he was able to maintain this search and this optimism amidst the trials of revolution and emigration. Fortunately, he was dead before his son fell a victim to German National Socialism, a movement which embodied almost everything that Aleksei Obolensky loathed.[83]

CHAPTER 9

AUTOCRACY, BUREAUCRACY, CATASTROPHE

The aim of the previous chapters of this book has been to understand the nature of the Russian ruling élite in the last years of the Empire. To this end I looked first at the historical development of this élite and the relationship over the centuries of its various component parts. Next I attempted a statistical study of the social, ethnic and educational backgrounds of the appointed members of Nicholas II's State Council, of their wealth and connections, and the paths taken by their careers. The remaining chapters of the book represented an attempt to put flesh on the skeleton, as well as to grasp something of his heart and soul. I tried to do this in part by general studies of the education and socialization of the élite as a whole at home, in school and in the state's service. I also, however, sought to understand élite mentalities by looking more closely at the personalities, opinions and biographies of individual members of the State Council.

In this, the book's last chapter, I have attempted to draw together a number of strands. In doing so, I have allowed the shadow of impending revolution to spread across my work. The élite studied in this book was to be totally destroyed in an exceptionally violent and important revolution by which the government and society of Russia were transformed. How does one account for the failure and demise of the Empire's governing élite? Three types of explanation exist, and I have tried briefly to encompass them all in this chapter. Firstly, one might argue that the imperial élite fell because of the failings of the institutions through which it governed and of their interaction. Of these institutions the single most important one was the monarchy itself, and I have therefore attempted to comment briefly on the nature of monarchical absolutism under Nicholas II. Secondly, however, one might assume that it was the very nature of the ruling élite which was the key factor in its demise. I have therefore briefly discussed the nature of this élite, together with its strengths and weaknesses. Finally, one could take the line that the imperial élite was destroyed less by the weaknesses inherent in its own nature and in the institutions through which it ruled than by a combination of external, 'objective' circumstances over which it had little control and which would have doomed almost any regime to destruction.

Sketching what these circumstances were, I conclude with an attempt to sum up how the members of the ruling élite understood the political crisis through which they were passing and what basic policies they advanced in the effort to survive it.

In recent years there has been considerable debate among historians of the German *Kaiserreich* as to the significance of the imperial institution within the governmental system, and the importance one should attach to the personality of the last Hohenzollern ruler, William II.[1] Historians of late imperial Russian have been less inclined to touch upon such matters. Much intelligent work has been done on politics and a little even on government under Nicholas II. The sad and spectacular fate of the last Russian emperor has encouraged the writing of a large number of usually rather sentimental popular studies of his life and personality, but in recent decades no one has attempted a serious political biography of Nicholas II, nor indeed to provide a clear picture of the monarchy's role within the institutional framework of Russian government.[2] In my opinion, however, a study of Russia's ruling élite cannot simply pass over in silence the place of the monarch within that élite or his role in the politics and government of the Empire. In seeking to illuminate these questions some comparisons with the role of Prussia-Germany's last monarch can be of use.

Of course in all respects Russia, particularly before 1905, was more of an absolute monarchy than was Germany. It is true that after 1864 the considerable degree of autonomy possessed by judicial and local-government institutions placed some constraints on the Russian emperor's absolute power. Even in these two spheres, however, the tsar's prerogatives were much less limited than those of the Kaiser. The latter had no emergency powers which he could invoke on a regular basis when he wished to circumvent the rule of law in political cases. Moreover, he faced not semi-autonomous zemstvos but fully-fledged federal states, whose almost complete control over many aspects of domestic policy was enshrined in a constitution, protected by the states' representation in the empire's upper house, and rooted in an age-old sense, at least in some of the states, both of a separate identity and of anti-Prussianism. Nor of course did the German monarch by the 1890s rule over a largely illiterate peasant population. Instead he faced a highly articulate and organized working-class movement, and a huge middle class. Social groups in Germany had every opportunity to organize themselves and to articulate their views, using *inter alia* a parliament which possessed a veto over all legislation and all financial bills. Even after 1905, when Russia acquired a parliament, the powers of that body were not as wide or as deep-rooted as those of the Reichstag. Bismarck and

The tsarist myth. Tsar and people meet for the celebrations over the canonization of St Seraphim of Sarov.

William II might for instance dream of *coups d'état* to limit their parliament's franchise: Nicholas II carried out such a coup in June 1907. Even during the First World War Nicholas II enjoyed appreciably more independent political power than his German cousin. The latter was to a considerable extent the captive of generals and nationalist politicians, becoming the figurehead for the Hindenburg-Ludendorff dictatorship. Nicholas II, on the other hand, manœuvring quite craftily to avoid capture, remained the key figure in Russian politics until the Empire's demise in March 1917.

On the whole, however, the similarities between Hohenzollern and Romanov monarchy are more obvious than the differences. Nicholas II may not have pestered his relatives with letters about the divine right of kings, but he believed in the principle as firmly as did his German cousin. George Katkov is undoubtedly correct to stress Nicholas II's conviction that God had placed on him personally a moral responsibility for governing the Empire which he could never shed.[3] An uplifted sense of the moral and religious nature of his office helps to explain the Emperor's attempt in his actions to follow the pure dictates of conscience and conviction. Perhaps not surprisingly, the monarch was the first to fall victim to the tsarist myth as regards his relationship both to God and to the Russian people. Combining considerable distaste for the Petersburg and Moscow élites with his own paternalist brand of populism, Nicholas undoubtedly felt himself to be the necessary guide, protector and friend of the Russian peasant, in whose values and interests he believed his regime to be rooted.[4]

In all of this there was of course a great deal of naïvety and ignorance. The Emperor was very far removed from Russian realities and somewhat disinclined to allow mere empirical evidence to spoil his vision of the harmonious and trusting relationship between the tsar and his people.[5] Since of course he never personally encountered criticism, hatred or disharmony directly, this was all the easier. Yet it would be wrong to ascribe all Nicholas II's views to mere mysticism, naïvety and ignorance. In both Russia and Germany absolutism also had its rational justifications, believed in not only by naïve monarchs but also by clever and hard-headed officials.

In the Russian case there was good reason to fear that society could never spontaneously generate a consensus on which the various ethnic groups, not to mention the Russian élites and masses, could agree as a basis for peaceful co-habitation. Stable and coherent government, capable of running foreign and defence policy and of considering the overall long-term interests of the community, must, it could easily be argued, be imposed on society rather than derived from it. On the surface, the German case for absolutism seems less convincing. The *Kaiserreich* was after all a rich and successful state, much of whose population had good reason for satisfaction with the existing order. Unlike in Russia, the working class was not on the whole revolutionary, peasants tended to vote conservative and ethnic minorities comprised a relatively small proportion of the empire's population. Yet for all that, consensus in the *Kaiserreich* was hard to obtain, save that is in condemnation of external enemies. The Hohenzollern empire was after all the product of the German civil war of 1866, which itself could in part be seen as an episode in an internal conflict which had existed, at least in the form of clashes between confessional camps, for centuries. The empire was a conglomerate of parochial groupings bequeathed by history and sometimes intensely resentful of their exposure to the modern world. Over time these parochialisms were weakening, but a society of ghettos, Prussian-agrarian, liberal, Catholic and socialist, was in the making. The activities of these ghettos' representatives in the Reichstag did not promise much in the way of coherent or far-sighted government should the Old Regime surrender executive power into their hands.[6]

For those, especially among high officials, who rejected parliamentary democracy as an effective means of governing their societies in the contemporary era, there was no alternative either in Germany or Russia but to vest supreme authority in the traditional monarchical state. This had, however, many undesirable consequences, not the least of which was that within the traditional political framework great power remained in the hands of hereditary monarchs whose activities could throw senior officialdom into despair.

Yet it is possible to sympathize with the Russian as with the German emperor as each tried to exercise some of the power which fate had entrusted to him. No doubt it would have been better had both monarchs acted as the mere symbol and source of legitimate sovereign authority, leaving the actual business of ruling to a grand vizier of the type of a Richelieu or Bismarck. To act in this way required, however, a conscious admission that another individual could fulfil the role of ruler more effectively than one could oneself. Such modesty is not natural to human beings and should not perhaps be expected of an hereditary absolute monarch. Moreover, one had first to find one's Richelieu or Bismarck and indeed to recognize that one had done so amidst the storm of opposition the policies of a grand vizier would undoubtedly arouse. For the monarch it was particularly difficult to remain inactive when opposition to a Caprivi, Witte or Stolypin came from the crown's traditional allies on the right, who appealed directly to the sovereign to exercise his prerogatives on behalf of causes and values with which he was likely to feel considerable sympathy.[7]

Nor did family traditions and myths help. It was not easy for the descendant of Frederick II or Peter I, brought up on the dynasty's heroic legend, to play the *roi fainéant* and abandon all control over policy to some mayor of the palace. The Russian tradition demanded that the tsar not only reign but rule. The monarchy's most devoted adherents, not the least important of whom was the Empress Alexandra, held up before Nicholas II the models of Ivan the Terrible and Peter the Great, judging him by their standards of authority and resolution.[8] Yet at the same time as playing the role of the ruthless and Machiavellian prince, the Russian emperor was also expected to be guided by the highest principles of a Christian Orthodox conscience, thus providing his people with spiritual leadership and inspiration.[9] In the midst of these impossible burdens it would have been surprising had Nicholas II not drawn strength from his dynasty's past triumphs over adversity. Even in the dark days of 1915–17, as pressure on his government mounted, the Emperor could have recalled how Aleksei Mikhailovich emerged strengthened from seemingly insuperable domestic and foreign crises in the 1660s, how Peter I recovered from defeat and rebellion in the Northern wars, and how an unpopular Alexander I faced the disasters of 1812 before the victory of 1814. In the light of family history the truth seemed to be that confronted by war and potential rebellion the solution was not to show weakness or abandon sovereign power, but rather to display resolution, suppress discontent by force, and trust that military victory would ultimately justify one's stance and strengthen the legitimacy of one's dynasty.

The very language in which political discourse was conducted in Russia made it difficult for a monarch to stand aside while his officials ruled. The bureaucracy was widely disliked in Russian society, on the right as much as anywhere else, and frequently denounced as the source of all the Empire's ills. As tends to be the case in a political system, however, the myth of the essential goodness and wisdom of the sovereign, in Russia's case the emperor, was always maintained at least in public. Since the emperors did indeed tend to see themselves as virtuous champions of their people's welfare whose benevolent policies were sabotaged by bureaucratic incompetence, they were much inclined to accept the rules of political discourse at face value. Appealed to frequently to save their nation from the wiles and corruption of a selfish bureaucracy, they were extremely unlikely to abdicate their powers in favour of the civil service's senior representatives.[10]

Nevertheless, the attempt actually to exercise this power was the cause of many difficulties. In part the problem was simply that the emperor bore the burdens of supreme power throughout his reign, which when one ascended the throne in one's twenties, as did both Nicholas II and William II, entailed many decades of rulership. Modern democratic politicians are likely to be temperamentally far better equipped than a hereditary ruler to stand the strains of top office, yet few could continue to bear its burdens for more than a decade. With both William II and Nicholas II one can see evidence of a flight from the burdens of supreme political power. In the case of the former, the regular routine of official business was soon abandoned as the restless Kaiser indulged his taste for travel, easily became bored by affairs of state, and sought relaxation and entertainment among his personal entourage.[11] Nicholas II was steadier and more conscientious than William II, but even he took long holidays in Livadia and Hesse which could seriously disrupt the business of government.[12] More to the point, in order to cope with the burdens and worries he shouldered, Nicholas seems to have adopted a policy of refusing to see the gloomy or threatening side of political developments. On one occasion indeed the Emperor told S.D. Sazonov that only by means of such resolute optimism could a Russian ruler remain sane. It is certainly possible to agree with Father George Shavel'sky that the Emperor's search for peace of mind was sometimes pursued at the expense of the state's interests. A refusal to listen to the unpleasant and threatening scarcely contributed to a realistic grasp of changes in Russian society. On the other hand, it is legitimate to see Nicholas II's attitude as the psychologically necessary response of a

Nicholas II *en famille*. His daughters, from left to right, are Tatiana, Anastasia, Marie and Olga.

shy and sensitive man faced with the duty of bearing for life the burdens of supreme political office in a huge and complex state going through a period of rapid change and increasing crisis.[13]

Both Nicholas II and William II suffered from the fact that their personalities were unsuited to the roles they were forced to play. Though neither man was particularly deep or cultured, in terms of intelligence neither was inferior to a great many contemporary leaders of democracies. Temperament was a different matter. The attempts of the in some ways brilliant but distinctly unbalanced and neurotic William II to act the role of stern and self-confident Prussian military monarch would have been almost comic, had they not had such dire political effects. In Nicholas II's case one had a man who, while not without inner resources of determination and firm ideals, loathed the hurly-burly of the political world and the tough, often unscrupulous characters who inhabited it. Basically a kind, extremely sensitive and, initially, naïve man, Nicholas shrank from personal confrontations and lacked the aggressive and even bullying personality needed if tough but competent statesmen were to be cudgelled into working together under his leadership, in pursuit of policies in whose formulation he himself played a leading role. The last Russian monarch combined the values of an easygoing and polite patriarchal landowner with those of an army officer. Exceptionally self-controlled and very delicate in his treatment of his immediate entourage, he placed a high value on the traditional military values of simplicity, honesty, loyalty and obedience to constituted authority. The very different ethics of political life were alien to him.[14]

Nicholas II's basic dislike of politics provides one explanation for the joy with which he retired into family life and the deep resentment with which he met any attempts by outsiders to intervene in this sphere. It was of course the Emperor's tragedy that his son's haemophilia and his wife's increasingly neurotic and hysterical personality made his family life anything but serene and also had fatal consequences in the political sphere. The wish to pacify his wife, added to resentment at political intrusion in his personal affairs, helps to explain Nicholas II's failure to end the scandal of Rasputin's presence at court – though a certain contempt for public opinion also figured in this. If on the one hand that contempt was part and parcel of the absolutist inheritance, it can be said in the Emperor's defence that those in Petersburg who revelled in the Rasputin affair had previously lapped up rumours that Nicholas was a drunkard and his wife a lesbian.[15]

Even leaving Rasputin aside, however, Alexandra's influence was disastrous, for she reinforced her husband's naïve faith in peasant monarchism and his isolation and alienation from almost all elements in Russian society. To project the monarchy directly into the hearts and minds of the Russian masses was, for all the imperial couple's naïve populism, an almost impossible dream. Nicholas II attempted through, for instance, the ceremonies surrounding the canonization of Seraphim of Sarov to play on traditional sentiments linking Orthodoxy and patriotism to the monarchy. He genuinely enjoyed talking to his peasant subjects and, particularly after 1905, used festivities such as the Poltava and Borodino celebrations to this end. He was quick to encourage the schoolboy *Poteshnie* [paramilitary, patriotic boy scouts] or to spot the advantages of modern colour photography for developing patriotic feelings among Russian schoolchildren.[16]

Truly to 'sell' the emperor to his people would have required more modern mass-communications technology, however, not to mention a more realistic and ruthless sense of how to put propaganda to good effect. Moreover, the sort of policies, beginning with land reform and extending into the spheres of social mobility and education, which might have put meat on the populist bones were well beyond the imagination and tolerance of relatively ordinary and unoriginal members of Victorian European royalty such as Nicholas and Alexandra. Indeed if one focused merely on the question of the expropriation of gentry estates in 1905–6 and left out all economic and political considerations, one would still be forced to conclude that Nicholas lacked the toughness or ruthlessness to break with the traditional social élite and to withstand the accusations of disloyalty and injustice which would have been levelled at him by those aristocratic elements with whom he had been surrounded throughout his life.

If it was too much to expect the monarch to devise original and radical policies to bridge the growing gulf between his regime and the masses, one might have expected that the court could be used as a focus for the wooing of key élites. Quite the opposite happened. The

Nicholas II driving through Riga; with him (at right) is Baron V.B. Frederycksz.

court as such virtually ceased to function and the monarch was increasingly disliked by all the élites, both traditional and new, whether in Petersburg or Moscow. In the latter city the Romanovs' cause was not helped by the arrogant and unattractive personality of the governor-general, the Grand Duke Serge Aleksandrovich, who failed to understand the changes which were occurring in Muscovite society or to build bridges to the growing industrial, commercial and professional élites who were bound to be of key importance in the new Russia that was emerging.[17] In this respect the Romanovs compared poorly with their German peers, whose courts were often used to win the loyalty of the upper bourgeoisie for the Old Regime by judicious helpings of honours, flattery and attention. If one thinks of the links which Bavaria's Prince Regent Luitpold forged, not only with financial–commercial–industrial but also artistic élites in Munich, the complete absence of such efforts in Petersburg or Moscow is all the more depressing. Indeed even William II, with his fascination with modern technology and his friendship for a figure such as the Jewish shipping magnate, Albert Ballin, in this respect stands head and shoulders above his Russian cousin.[18]

Nicholas II's failure on this score not only weakened his regime's support among Russia's élites but also closed off to him potentially useful sources of information about what was happening in Russian society. This permitted the monarch to retain dangerous though no doubt psychologically satisfying illusions about the extent to which his regime enjoyed mass support. It also, however, weakened him in his dealings with the bureaucracy, since he lacked intelligent sources of information alternative to those provided by his ministers. The figure of Prince V.P. Meshchersky is often paraded as one of the evil geniuses of late imperial Russia, and indeed the Prince was an unabashed if intelligent reactionary. Yet in many ways the pity was that Nicholas did not know more figures like Meshchersky, intelligent and independent observers who could have represented the viewpoints of various strands in Russian society and thought. Instead the Emperor's household and personal circle was a narrow one, dominated by Guards officers who, though personally decent and honourable men, knew little about the new Russia, held stereotyped opinions similar to those of the monarch, and in any case were resolutely discouraged from discussing politics with him.[19]

The Emperor's choice of personal entourage reflected his sense that such a circle impinged on his domestic life, in which peace and comfort were all-important. Yet most of even that entourage was not wholly trusted and was kept at arm's length, a matter on which General A.A. Mosolov reflects in his memoirs with understandable frustration.[20] Somewhat illuminating is the case of V.A. Mamantov, a household official whom Nicholas had known quite closely for years. When the Emperor complained in 1898 that he lacked the time even to glance at his preferred newspapers, *Novoe Vremya* and *Russkie Vedomosti*, Mamantov began to organize an early-morning press summary. Initially greeting this with delight, Nicholas rapidly abandoned support for the project, in Mamantov's view because of whispers that the new 'press secretary' might be relaying to the Emperor only a biased selection suiting his own point of view. Such was the Emperor's suspicion and fear of falling into any official's hands that he allowed an essential service to lapse. With such attitudes it was very difficult for him to build up a loyal band of personal supporters, to be properly informed, or to hold his own against the ministerial bureaucracy.[21]

Mamantov's memoirs indeed convey a sense of how the Emperor's personality, together with the institutional framework surrounding 'autocracy', in practice combined to make genuine monarchical absolutism impossible. For the monarch to be an effective head of government he required an efficient private office capable of keeping trivia off his desk, providing him with alternative, condensed briefs to those submitted by ministers, and checking to see that his orders were actually implemented by the bureaucracy. None of this seems to have been done. Certainly, the Emperor's Own Personal Chancellery signally failed to fulfil the functions of a private office. The history of Alexander III's attempt to turn the Chancellery into something of a private watchdog over the civil service is illuminating, demonstrating the weakness of the monarch when he tried to exercise any close control over bureaucratic practice.

Alexander's effort, launched in 1894, was fuelled by the usual imperial suspicion of the bureaucracy, strengthened in this instance by a sense that the latter's growth, complexity and professionalism was placing it increasingly beyond monarchical control. When he reestablished the civil service inspectorate in his Own Personal Chancellery, Alexander intended to give it relatively modest powers. Nevertheless his project was denounced and ultimately emasculated by ministers. In the first place ministers, running a bureaucracy politicized at the top and extending over a huge area, argued that any imperial intervention in appointments and promotions would undermine service discipline and impede a chief's ability to get his subordinates to obey orders. Secondly, it was hinted broadly that the monarch's intervention in the bureaucracy's internal affairs was amateur and too ignorant to be of value. When it came to the final confrontation in the Committee of Ministers, the 'household officers', V.B. Frederycksz and A.S. Taneev, found themselves ranged against the entire bureaucratic élite. If the Romanovs hoped to prevail in such disputes with their ministers they clearly needed political heavyweights at the court, rather than comfortable personalities such as the stupidly amiable Frederycksz and the flatteringly trivial Taneev.[22]

The weakness of the institutions surrounding the supposed chief executive provides many hints as to the true nature of 'autocracy' in late imperial Russia. To draw certain comparisons: How effectively, without a White House staff, could a US President control his administration or exercise personal power? Where are the Russian equivalents to the Prusso-German monarch's civil cabinet, in J.C.G. Röhl's view a more than adequate institution to buttress genuine monarchical absolutism, with a breadth of jurisdiction and a flow of memoranda to rival any governmental office?[23] Of course possession of an effective civil cabinet by no means ensured the effectiveness of absolutism, but it did contribute to its possibility.

In Russia most business between the monarch and his ministers was conducted in weekly one-to-one sessions. Only in exceptional circumstances did the monarch personally chair committees of his ministers or top officials. According to A.N. Naumov, personal audiences were extremely pleasant and distinctly frustrating. Nicholas II invariably agreed with a minister's ideas, but equally invariably could not be relied on subsequently to support them against other advisers or if they ran into trouble.[24] The reason for this state of affairs seems relatively clear. Particularly where, as in Naumov's case, the audiences concerned technical economic questions, the monarch was hopelessly ill-equipped to challenge his minister's suggestions. Nor was he briefed in advance by his Chancellery on the issues his minister would be raising. Subsequently, however, another minister, adviser or acquaintance might well express an alternative viewpoint to which the impressionable and inexpert monarch might also agree. The result was disharmony between governmental ministries and policies, together with frustration and ineffectiveness among ministers.

Possible remedies for this weakness were obvious enough. The monarch himself could have chaired ministerial cabinet meetings, where final co-ordinated policies could be hammered out. This, however, would have exposed the Emperor to the possibility of direct semi-public confrontations with individual ministers or groups of them on matters on which many of them were likely to be much better informed than he was. The chances of his being coerced into rapid acceptance of policies of which he disapproved would have been greatly increased. Nor indeed was it conceivable that the monarch could match the work rate of a senior minister in briefing himself for cabinet meetings, or that he could subsequently defend governmental policy in the legislature. The other obvious possibility was for the monarch to remove himself from day-to-day affairs of government, leaving the co-ordination of policy in the hands of a chief minister and giving the latter his full support. Such an abdication of power and responsibility was, however, unacceptable to Nicholas II. There is therefore real truth in the criticism that, unable himself to impose co-ordinated policies on the governmental machine, the last Russian emperor was unwilling to allow anyone else to do it for him – thus fatally weakening his regime.[25]

Looked at from a minister's perspective, the business of government, especially after 1906, was undoubtedly fraught with difficulties. To be effective a minister had to steer his legislation through the Duma and the State Council – a challenge, since it required a talent for public oratory to which an old bureaucrat was unaccustomed. Since the two houses, formed on very different electoral principles, were constantly at loggerheads, the minister's problems multiplied. In the face of legislative or public opposition the minister could not necessarily rely on the support of his 'cabinet' colleagues. The latter, less united in their political views even than a contemporary Western parliamentary cabinet, were also not bound together by common ties of self-interest. Intra-ministerial intrigue did not risk the fall of the cabinet, the onset of a general election, the possible victory of the opposition and the almost inevitable blow to an individual's ambitions of a clear break with the party line. On the contrary, the successful intrigue which led to the removal of an unfriendly minister and his replacement by a client or ally could greatly improve one's influence in overall policy-making. Intrigue was therefore inevitably rife and the one man who might have suppressed it, namely the chairman of the Council of Ministers, could not do so because he could not rely on imperial support in attempts to discipline recalcitrant ministers or impose policies upon them. Much confusion ensued. Moreover, intrigue in ministerial circles continued as in the past to send its ripples down the ranks of the upper civil service, so that the unfortunate minister could not even be assured of the loyalty of his subordinates. In many respects the Russian system of government was therefore even more confused than its German counterpart, since at least in the latter the chancellor exercised a considerable degree of coordinating power over all aspects of civilian government.[26]

The disorganization in institutions caused, above all, by remaining elements of monarchical absolutism is therefore a significant element to be taken into account in balancing the factors that led to the Old Regime's demise. Certainly, any attempt to 'blame' the bureaucratic élite for the collapse of imperial Russia has to reckon on the fact that this élite governed in an institutional context largely dependent on the survival of absolutism, while general policy goals, the parameters of possible reform and the selection of ministers remained prerogatives of the emperor. Monarchs were frustrated at their inability to govern effectively, suspected bureaucratic sabotage, and played with their ministers at divide and rule.[27] Russian ministers, however, like their Prusso-German counterparts, learned how difficult it was to force major policies upon the monarch or to drive him out of the political arena. If Russian ministers had ever doubted these facts then the events of 1915 would have sobered them, as Nicholas II rejected compromise with the Duma on a 'ministry of public confidence', assumed command of the army and rapidly removed members of the Council of Ministers of whom he disapproved. For all their fears and their protests about the onset of 'personal rule', however, there was little that senior officialdom could do to thwart their imperial master, against whom they had no other weapon but to warn of the probable collapse of the government and of impending revolution. No more effective had been the opposition of Marschall von Bieberstein and his colleagues to the onset of 'personal rule' in Germany almost two decades before.[28] The lesson in both cases was clear. In the existing semi-absolutist system senior officialdom was in the last resort suspended between parliamentary institutions and hereditary monarchs, neither of which they fully trusted or could control.

Let us turn from the institutions through which Russia was governed to the ruling élite itself. The most obvious general point to make is that this was indeed a bureaucratic ruling élite, with all that this implies. It was not, to take various other types of élite at random, an aristocratic élite based on heredity, an elected ruling group constituted through success on the hustings and membership of a political party, and of course it was not a moneyed or business élite. With a number of exceptions, usually partial, those who governed the Russian state had spent most of their adult lives in its service, ascending the official ladder because they won the approval of their bureaucratic superiors. In some respects the civil service through which they had risen approached the Weberian ideal type. The bureaucracy functioned on the basis of detailed rules laying down procedures, functions and hierarchies. Its various departments were divided on rational grounds of functional specialization, and in most cases staffed by experts in specific aspects of state policy. The basic prerequisite for entry to the service was education, the main criteria for promotion were experience and personal merit, the main reward a regular salary.

Inevitably, as has been the case with all organizations in all societies since the beginning of history, practice often diverged from Weberian norms.[29] Moreover, different Russian ministries strayed from these norms to a greater or lesser extent, as a comparison between the departments of Finance and Internal Affairs make clear. The former operated largely in a world whose rules were those of the capitalist market. This was true both of the Russian domestic economy and in the area of international finance. Moreover, by comparison with the Ministry of Internal Affairs, the Finance department was somewhat removed from politics and the realm of the imperial court. The department of Internal Affairs on the other hand was not only highly politicized but also operated in areas where externally imposed rules often counted for relatively little. This for instance was true of many of the ministry's important activities in rural society, since the peasantry to a great extent lived outside the imperial legal order created by the statutes of 1864. Still more subject to 'administrative discretion' was the handling by the Ministry of Internal Affairs of 'subversion', a category whose boundaries were broad and ill-defined in imperial Russia.

Be that as it may, with all due deference to departmental distinctions, the Russian bureaucracy could never in any case have adhered fully to Weberian norms unless a transformation had occurred in the way the Empire was governed. Above all else this was because the imperial civil service not merely executed policy in accordance with fixed laws, it also both played a major part in formulating policy and laws, and in addition exercised considerable discretion in deciding when such laws should be dispensed with in the name of the more effective, efficient or just solution to a specific problem. It is true that one might imagine imperial Russia moving to a position in which junior and middle-level officials operated strictly within the confines of rules controlling both their relations with society and the inner workings of the bureaucracy itself. Admittedly some top officials, as we have seen, believed that any further moves in this direction would have paralysed the bureaucratic machine and made lower officialdom ineffective agents of ministers' policies. This, however, is a debatable point. What cannot be contested is that the strict sub-ordination of top officialdom to a regime of externally imposed laws and rules would have entailed a political revolution, for it would have meant the transfer of ultimate political power from its erst-while possessors, namely the monarch and the upper bureaucracy, to other individuals and groups selected according to some alternative method.

The politicization of the upper bureaucracy clearly had an impor-tant impact on civil service promotions and appointments, an area to which much attention has been devoted in this book. Since senior officials in practice formulated policy, disputes over that policy inevit-ably divided the bureaucracy's ranks. Probably more important, the bureaucracy's chiefs were often forced to fill key positions with sub-ordinates who were not only efficient but also loyal to themselves and their policies. Selection according to Weberian criteria of merit would have been not merely ineffective but positively dangerous. Equally, lacking security of tenure, subordinates were bound up to a point to temper their loyalty and advice to their chiefs in the light of political considerations and the advancement of their own careers. In addition, the majority of élite officials lived in the Petersburg village, as had their families for generations. Most of the inhabitants had known each other and each other's families for decades. In such circumstances the regulation of promotions and appointments by strict impersonal norms was never likely. Connections, personal re-lations and face-to-face contacts were bound to count for a good deal. Moreover, where clear rules governing promotions and appoint-ments did exist they were sometimes subverted and might indeed prove counter-productive. One example of this was the manner in which the diplomatic exam was used more as a means of sifting out socially undesirable candidates than incompetent ones. Similarly, the attempt to require sea-going experience as a qualification for promo-tion in the navy ended by having an adverse effect on naval officers' career patterns and the fighting efficiency of the fleet.

It would nevertheless be a great mistake to imagine that nepotism triumphed over merit in bureaucratic promotions, resulting in a senior officialdom dominated by incompetents and fools. A simple-minded equating of Weberian norms with effectiveness and efficiency is certainly wrong. Given the world in which a top official might well have to operate, a nose for politics and a talent for bureaucratic manoeuvring might be at least as valuable as possession of the whole range of professional official skills. In any case, study of officials' careers convinces me that for all the influence of chance, connections and factional allegiance, merit was not only in theory but also in practice the single most important factor in ensuring one's rise to the top of the Russian civil service.

As in any bureaucracy, however, merit as judged by one's superiors included not only skilful, systematic and conscientious professional work but also tact in not treading on influential toes or deviating too obviously from official norms. Bureaucratic merit also definitely did not mean the possession of political skills, in so far as these are defined by the ability to gauge public moods, appeal to popular instincts or sentiments, or create institutions whereby the mass of the population can have at least the illusion of participation in politics. However hard they might strive as governors and guardians to be just and to serve the long-term interest of the community, the imperial bureaucratic élite was bound to find it difficult to communicate its good intentions to the masses or to satisfy the peasants' and workers' pressing desire to see their dignity and self-esteem given adequate recognition by the country's leaders.

Having described the ruling élite as bureaucratic, one does, however, immediately need to qualify one's statement. Some members of that élite were academics, businessmen or, much more often, landowners rather than full-time civil servants. As we have seen, the relationships among bureaucracy, aristocracy and gentry were complicated and by no means static. Most of the ruling group sprang from the aristocracy and gentry, and the values, loyalties and interests of the traditional social élite still to a considerable extent permeated much of the upper bureaucracy. However, the bureaucratic élite itself was by no means uniform. The functions performed by the many sectors of the civil service were highly varied and departmentalism was rife. Among the members of the State Council were landowners of varying degrees of wealth and status whose careers had largely been spent as Guards officers, noble marshals and provincial governors; highly trained specialists in aspects of the law, finance or technology (e.g., railway engineers), who had never served outside their own particular field of expertise; an élite group of officials of the central co-ordinating chancelleries, often with experience in a number of departments and generally very sensitive to political currents running in court and ministerial circles. One might add to these three groups any number of smaller ones, ranging from security police chiefs, through diplomats and army officers, to judges, experts on questions of religion and nationality, professors and a number of other specialists as well. When one adds to such differences of career, distinctions in social origin, education and generation, it is clear that the 'bureaucratic élite' came in a number of shapes and sizes, some of which were closer to the ordinary man's vision of bureaucracy than others.

Inevitably, the calibre of these men varied. In some cases very powerful connections, chance or bureaucratic politics propelled to the top of the government service individuals of limited talent or merit. Count S.D. Sheremetev, for instance, came about as close as anyone could to sitting in the State Council by hereditary right, while the strange paths by which two of N.K. Giers's former assistant ministers, A.G. Vlangali and N.P. Shishkin, reached the Council have already been described. Some men of rather ordinary ability and limited originality plodded their way to the summit of the bureaucratic slope, aided generally by a marked capacity for hard work. N.A. Zinov'ev and F.G. Terner would fit this category. Nor can one ignore the fact that an honourable, conscientious and reliable personality such as Terner's could provide very useful fireproof 'padding' in the upper reaches of a politicized bureaucracy where clashes between highly ambitious and determined men often caused sparks to fly. Count V.N. Lambsdorff and I.P. Shipov on the other hand were not only conscientious but also intelligent and talented officials, who nevertheless lacked the temperament for top political office. I.L. Goremykin may have shared some of Shipov's narrowness of vision, though in the case of the former an exaggerated dose of the somewhat world-weary cynicism of the veteran onlooker on Petersburg high politics was a major disincentive to effective action, as was indeed an affection for the perks of ministerial office.[30]

Among the members of the State Council there were, however, many men of rare intelligence, energy and public spirit, who combined broad views with the veteran official's political realism and knowledge of how the state apparatus functioned. In some cases, of which D.F. Kobeko and M.P. Kaufmann are good examples, whether through chance, political circumstances or the constraints of monarchical absolutism, a man's potential for statesmanship was not realized. In others, advancement came too slowly and an official no longer possessed the health or energy to be effective when he reached top office. Nevertheless the idea that the veteran civil servant, conditioned by years of obedience to regulations and deference to his seniors, was of necessity incapable of initiative, energy or vision on reaching top office is certainly incorrect, a point brought out in the chapters on A.N. Kulomzin and P.N. Durnovo.

Of course 'political office' imposed new challenges and insecurities on the civil servant, from which some shrank. Others, however, thrived on their new-found freedom, independence and room for creative effort. Parts of the civil service, precisely because of the extent to which they were politicized, bred men of rather greater political nous, entrepreneurial independence and flexibility than the average product of an apolitical and rule-guided bureaucracy. The skills, for instance, which A.V. Krivoshein had cultivated in forging connections and building coalitions in order to boost his career as an official, stood him in very good stead as Minister of Agriculture. His ability to woo key elements in the Duma and in society, not to mention the imperial couple, were vital political ingredients in his success. Coupled with the vision and drive he showed in his campaign for rural modernization, not to mention his sure grasp of how to manage a large and complicated ministry, these political skills made Krivoshein an exceptionally effective minister.[31]

All in all, the calibre of Russian senior officialdom was not in my view the key element in the collapse of the Old Regime; in that, it ranked well below the institutional framework in which the élite governed and, notably, the objective circumstances with which it was faced. Most top officials were efficient civil servants and some had the makings of statesmen. Where, as for instance in the First World War, the leadership provided by ministers was distinctly inferior, that generally had less to do with the fact that talent was unavailable than with the monarch's unwillingness to use it. As I have maintained, it is certainly a mistake to see the upper bureaucracy as a caste united against any involvement of society in government. Senior officialdom contained many men with liberal sympathies, and more who understood the dangers of alienating educated society from the state.

At the same time top bureaucrats, who largely monopolized political experience in Russia, had good reason to feel both that the existing administrative system was the essential fundament of any viable authority, and that they themselves possessed a political realism much superior to that of the bulk of the intelligentsia. It would certainly be a great mistake to swallow whole the latter's condemnation of blind and reactionary tsarist officialdom. Russia's problems were too complicated and contradictory to be solved by naïve moral nostrums or indeed by simple adaptation of Western principles and political practices. It is a complete illusion to imagine that the replacement of the imperial bureaucratic élite by the leaders of the Octobrist, Kadet or even of the moderate socialist parties would have ensured effective solutions to the Empire's problems, or the integration of élite and masses into a community capable of living at peace with itself. Some of the 'blindest' and most 'reactionary' tsarist officials were indeed to prove more effective governors and better prophets than their self-confident critics in the liberal and radical intelligentsia.

The main weakness of top officialdom lay less in what it was than in what it was not. Here one returns to the point made earlier about the narrow social and ethnic base from which the ruling élite was drawn. Not that that élite was a caste, subject in Pareto's interpretation to degeneration for lack of new blood.[32] The Russian hereditary nobility, in absolute terms a large group, was by no means a closed order, and those of its members who survived a rigorous competitive process to become rulers of the state were unlikely to be degenerate. On the other hand these rulers were, unequivocally, the offspring of a single group, in relative terms small, in Russian society, a group which had ruled Russia since time immemorial. In the changing conditions of late nineteenth- and early twentieth-century Russia this was extremely dangerous. For Russian peasants and workers, not to mention non-Russians, the state was inevitably associated with the traditional social élite. Empathy, mutual understanding or trust between rulers and ruled was hard to expect, given the cultural gap between the élite and the masses, not to mention the sharply escalating social and ethnic tensions existing in the Empire. The values, aspirations and often the material interests of the governmental élite were very different from those of the bulk of the state's population. Even had top officials had a clear sense of the need for and means to mass mobilization behind the state's goals, the gap between rulers and ruled would have rendered the success of such an effort dubious.

Social origins and bureaucratic careers combined here to contribute to the élite's vulnerability. The young, relatively well-off nobleman, brought up in a cultured European family and educated very possibly in a school for nobles only was far removed from the ordinary Russian. Links between élite and mass did of course exist. The nobleman might have fond memories of his peasant nanny, love the Russian countryside and be moved by the music of certain composers springing from the social élite but who often drew their inspiration from the songs of the peasantry. Russian nationalism was a powerful potential factor for integration in the half of the Empire which was Russian, though one which could scarcely be utilized unless the peasants were both educated and preserved from the clutches of counter-élites preaching some nationalist variety of socialism. State officials were not, however, suited either by their training or their values to turn into charismatic figures or to mobilize popular emotions, even had such activity been possible within the confines of a semi-absolutist state. Moreover, in a way that was genuinely somewhat tragic, the higher the ideals, the humanity and the level of culture of members of the ruling élite, the further removed they were in many ways from the kind of demagogic techniques which might have made the mobilization of mass support more feasible.

In such circumstances the flowering of counter-élites, themselves excluded from power and able to appeal to mass values and instincts inherently hostile to the state's traditional rulers, was dangerous, but also, given the history of Russian nineteenth-century society, inevitable. Parts of the intelligentsia already constituted, by the 1870s, a counter-élite with its own irreconcilable sub-culture. Moreover the rapid modernization of society in the century's last decades ensured the growth of education and therefore of potential leaders in sections of the population traditionally wholly excluded from positions of authority and status. Of course, given time, the Empire's rulers might have had the wisdom to integrate some of these counter-élites into the governing and privileged stratum, though pressure on state jobs from sons of an impoverished gentry limited the extent to which this could easily be achieved. In time too the regime might have succeeded both in modifying mass values and in adapting itself to them. In the period of transition, however, the existing élite was likely to be isolated and distinctly vulnerable.

It would be difficult to deny that the 'objective circumstances' in which the Russian ruling élite found itself in the late nineteenth and early twentieth centuries were extremely difficult. In part problems stemmed from Russia's geography and earlier history. The huge size of the Empire and its multi-ethnic nature bred fears of disintegration unless tight central control was maintained. The spread of nationalism from west to east in Europe and the existence on Russia's borders of states which might encourage separation increased such fears. Meanwhile within the Russian heartlands a traditionally deep gap separated the élite from the masses. Of course a wide division between rulers and ruled was not only true of Russia, nor was hostility between landowner and peasant. The enserfment of a previously free peasantry had come late to Russia, however. Moreover, serfdom had probably been harsher than in most of Central and Eastern Europe and had survived somewhat longer. Agrarian discontent on a small scale had been endemic. In the 1770s it had burst out on a truly grand scale in the Pugachov rebellion, whose outbreak may have owed something to a peasant sense that social justice had been infringed by the continuation of serfdom alongside the ending of the gentry's obligation to serve the state. Nor of course was understanding between élites and masses increased by the former's westernization. Russia therefore entered the period of modernization with a tradition of conflict between the two major social groups which was exacerbated by the inevitable battles and resentment resulting from the very recent Emancipation settlement.

Modernization itself of course imposed great strains on Russian society. One of its effects was to undermine the position of groups which had been traditional bulwarks of the imperial regime. The economic strength and social influence of the landowning gentry were much reduced in large areas of the Russian countryside. Literacy, urban work and the spread of communications began to change the mentality of the peasants and the balance of power between generations in the villages.[33] Rapid population growth increased pressure on the land, pushed up rents and increased conflict between gentry and peasantry. Meanwhile in the cities the early phase of industrialization created a working class subjected to the usual combination of low wages, bad conditions and demeaning labour discipline. Nor were the greatly expanding commercial, industrial and professional categories of the middle class likely to remain satisfied with their position under an Old Regime which denied these groups the status, rights and freedoms which many of their members increasingly came to desire.

The situation was exacerbated by the fact that capitalism, with its ugliness and naked inequalities, stuck in the gullets of many members of the élite, reared in a tradition of service and culture rather than in respect for the private accumulation of wealth. Still less did modern capitalism's stress on individual enterprise, differentiation and absolute property rights square with the customary habits and deeply entrenched collectivism of the Russian masses. For the Empire's rulers the dangers of the situation were greatly increased by the existence at the outset of the period of modernization of an alienated radical intelligentsia and a revolutionary tradition committed to the destruction of the imperial state and the immediate reconstruction of society on an egalitarian and collectivist basis. In addition, unlike in the early years of industrialization in Britain or Germany, a body of untested but attractive socialist doctrine existed as a blueprint for a modern society alternative to the one provided by liberal political economy. The imperial state struggled to keep the masses and radical intellectuals apart by a combination of repressive police measures against the latter and a mix of tight control and concessions to welfare collectivism (e.g. the commune) among the former. By the twentieth century, however, it was clear that, particularly in the cities, this policy had failed and that the working class was coming under the sway of counter-élites drawn from the radical intelligentsia and organized in revolutionary parties.

The link-up of revolutionaries with the masses greatly increased the threat to Russia's propertied classes. Russia was too poor for large sections of the population to share a strong common interest in private property or the existing economic order. In particular, the suppressed conflict between the communal peasantry and the landowning gentry was an immense source of weakness for Russian conservatism. Nor, given the very different cultures and value systems of the élites and the masses, did the latter have any great respect for the principles on which the former's world was based. Where property rights and law were concerned, the defection of some of the élite's most articulate and determined members to the cause of revolutionary socialism could only reinforce the masses' alienation from the society of their 'betters'. Nor did Russia's élites have the means to buy off discontent. Given Russian agrarian realities and the agricultural crisis of the last quarter of the nineteenth century, the Russian gentry was often involved in a hand-to-mouth struggle for survival.[34] Nor were the conditions of early capitalist industrialization propitious as regards generous wages, comfortable working conditions or relaxed systems of labour discipline.[35] Because Russia was a poor society, its élites did not have the room for concessions and compromise of their richer British or German peers. The cultural gap between élite and masses, the defection of part of the educated classes, and the weakness of the educational system, the clergy or even the army as means of inculcating élite values into the masses, removed possibilities of influence possessed by the ruling élites of some other European states. Into the gap stepped violence as a means of social control in the interests of Russia's élites. Not merely was forceful repression of the masses a Russian tradition, it was in many ways the only effective weapon to hand in early twentieth-century Russian conditions.

It is important to remember that the Russian ruling and propertied élites were very much part of Victorian and Edwardian Europe and shared their European peers' values, interests and assumptions. If, however, one wished to preserve all these in a poor society undergoing the strains of rapid modernization whose burdens were largely being borne by peasants and workers, one was unlikely to do so with a regime guaranteeing civil rights and moving towards liberalism and liberal-democracy. The logic of the situation pointed more in the direction taken by twentieth-century Spanish élites, who first used terror to keep the masses in check while the economic bases of a bourgeois society were being constructed, and then conceded liberal-democratic political institutions because in the changed social conditions the latter posed little threat to their own essential interests. A 'Spanish' solution was indeed to some extent the goal to which P.A. Stolypin was heading with his combination of repression, social engineering and the encouragement of capitalism. It was also the key to P.N. Durnovo's view that it would be fatal to weaken the repressive apparatus of the police state in any way until Russian society had developed economically to the point where the values and interests of the élites would enjoy widespread support in the population.

In pre-1914 Russia, however, the situation was distinctly less clear-cut than in the Spain of the 1930s. There had as yet been no Bolshevik revolution to terrify all anti-communist elements into a united front of repression. Nor had the monarchy fallen, or legal socialist and anarchist parties garnered huge public support, or working-class militancy been in threatening and uncontrolled evidence on the streets. If, as seemed reasonable to assume, 1905 had been Russia's 1848, then from the perspective of 1910–14 the immediate demise of the Romanov regime was by no means to be expected.

Moreover, the analysis so far has been too crudely materialist.

Man does not live by bread alone and the Russian educated classes before 1914 certainly did not do so. On the contrary, many members of these classes held with deep sincerity to various ideals and values. In some cases of course this merely reinforced their fear of the Russian masses. Indeed the events of 1905–6 convinced even some former radicals and liberals that should political power be transferred to the Russian people at the present time, not only would the élites' property disappear, but all respect for law, individual rights, freedom of speech and cultural values as well.[36]

The spiritual values and ideals of the Russian élites led in other political directions too. A deep strain of humanitarianism and concern for social justice ran through parts of Russian educated society, one element of which went into the making of the revolutionary movement. A number of members of leading gentry families played major roles in Russian socialism's development. Of Russia's two best-known anarchists, one was born into the heart of the court aristocracy and the other into the top layer of the provincial gentry. Humanitarianism was not the sole source of these men's inspiration. On the contrary, the deep resentment of civilized members of a Victorian élite at the petty tutelage, the absurdity and sometimes the crassly incompetent cruelty of imperial bureaucratic absolutism played a major part in precipitating them into the revolutionary movement.[37] By the early twentieth century the absolute number of well-educated would-be members of a free society in Russia was very great, greater indeed than in many states in Western Europe. By 1905–14 the pressure of Russian urban and educated society on the imperial state was heavy, too heavy for the Old Regime fully to resist.[38] Among the goals most desired by this society were precisely the creation of the civil rights and the dismantling of the police state that Durnovo and his ilk most feared. From the perspective of Durnovo, the Russian educated classes were pulling down the scaffolding which alone could support their Russian house in order, very temporarily, to secure a bit more light in their living rooms.

Durnovo's opinions are of interest, in part for the inherent value of the insights they provide. Unless one grasps that the so-called 'reactionary' line was not simply the product of closed minds and short-sighted self-interest, but could be supported by intelligent men with often convincing arguments, neither the dilemma facing the Empire's rulers nor the onset of revolution make much sense. To understand this often conflicts with the prejudices and stereotypes of Western historians, as well as with inflexibly held 'scientific' theories of modernization and suchlike. In Durnovo's defence, it needs to be remembered that in his own era as well the Russian intelligentsia regarded opinions such as his as hopelessly out-of-date and laughably inferior to their own 'scientific' grasp of how societies became modern. In retrospect, however, he seems in many respects no less acute an observer of Russian politics and certainly no less intelligent a prophet than they.

Durnovo's views are also of interest because of the manner in which he integrates domestic and foreign policy. Few top officials could achieve so intelligent a synthesis and very few contemporaries indeed could have predicted so brilliantly how events were to develop in 1914–17. Introducing into a discussion of Russia's domestic political crisis considerations of international relations inevitably focuses one's attention even more sharply on the scale of the difficulties facing the imperial ruling élite in the Empire's last years. The deep and contradictory strains in Russian society were in themselves hard enough to manage. When one adds to these the impact on Russia of the threatened breakdown of the balance of power and of international security, then the extent of the government's difficulties becomes clear. Yet Russia could not abdicate from international society. Neither the élite's pride, the regime's legitimacy nor domestic political pressure would allow this. Still more important, in an imperialist world the threat to Russian security should she simply stand aside from great-power politics would have been immense. Nevertheless, though it is not at all inconceivable that the imperial regime, granted luck and wise leadership, might have surmounted the domestic political crisis, when war with the Central Powers was added to the equation the odds against the imperial government rose very steeply.[39]

In a sense Durnovo represented the quintessence of the traditional noble and absolutist state. On the one hand he was the resolute defender of the position of the established social élite, from whose lower reaches he himself sprang. On the other hand he was the state official, the guardian of a political structure which to a considerable extent wished to stand outside and above society, had little trust in the wisdom of social groups and exploited all of them in the cause particularly of its own external military power and prestige. For Durnovo himself, the concepts of state, dynasty, gentry and nation were inextricably linked because of his own background and education. The threat of revolution was a danger to the property and status of the social élite. It was also a danger to the imperial state which had, over the centuries, succeeded in organizing, disciplining and exploiting the Russian people in the name of military power and economic progress, only now to be threatened by a new *Pugachovshchina* in which, in his view, the instinctively socialist and anarchical tendencies of the masses would be exploited by leaders from the intelligentsia pursuing hopelessly impractical ideals. Add to this the feeling general in the European upper and middle classes before 1914 that, supposedly for the good of all their members, societies must be governed by their educated and rational élites rather than by workers, let alone semi-literate peasants, and one has more or less summed up the roots of Durnovo's thinking.

It would of course be ludicrous to claim that this thinking was particularly deep or in many respects original, let alone that it attained philosophical heights. Durnovo was a shrewd and realistic down-to-earth politician, capable of seeing through some of the shibboleths and illusions of his contemporaries and of avoiding stereotyped, 'scientific' conceptions of where the world was heading. Quite clearly, however, his thinking contained important gaps. In the twentieth century there were obvious dangers in regarding the Russian people as unruly children to be held down by force. This was at best a doctrine for a temporary military dictatorship or for an élite which had won respite for a generation by pulverizing its enemies in civil war. Thought had to be given to methods whereby the sentiments and interests of the masses might be appeased, flattered and channelled in ways acceptable to the regime. Nor was simple resistance to the encroachments of upper- and middle-class Russia on the institutions of the police state a sufficient answer to the problem of how to cope with the demands of the increasingly sophisticated world of Russia's cities. The fact that basically there were still two Russias, mass and élite, made life exceptionally difficult for Russia's rulers. Durnovo's speeches and writings convey some very interesting insights on this point. They by no means, however, provide an adequate answer as to how the ruling élite was to emerge unscathed from the problems it faced. Moreover, Durnovo's views on war and international relations more or less closed off, through their very realism, one obvious escape route, namely the Bismarckian path of 'White revolution' through the capture of nationalist sentiment via a triumphant foreign policy.

Durnovo serves well as the right-hand marker within the ruling élite. He represented, at least in the last decade of his life, in a clear, intelligent and articulate manner the authoritarian and conservative wing among Russia's rulers. A.N. Kulomzin serves almost as well as a left-hand marker. Certainly, within the élite there were men more 'to the left' than Kulomzin, some of whom were highly intelligent. A.F. Koni and D.F. Kobeko would be good examples of this tendency. Kulomzin, however, comes closer to typifying the liberal wing of the ruling élite.

As I have mentioned, a comparison of the lives of Kulomzin and Durnovo is of great interest because it reveals not only the different viewpoints of the two wings of the ruling élite but also how these were shaped by men's backgrounds, educations and careers. The feminine, cultured and sensitive influences which dominated Kulomzin's childhood and adolescence were totally different from the rough, masculine, anti-intellectual world of the Naval Cadet Corps. Nor does one need to emphasize the contrast between the service of one as a peace arbitrator and of the other as a front-line naval officer, or between their subsequent careers, in the security police apparatus on the one hand and the State Chancellery and Chancellery of the Committee of Ministers on the other. More fundamentally, Durnovo and Kulomzin were men of completely different personality, the former being much tougher, harder and more cynical. It would by no means be completely wrong to describe Durnovo, in Pareto's terms, as a lion and Kulomzin as a fox. Certainly one can see Durnovo as tough-minded and Kulomzin as tender-hearted.

If one applies these categories to the 'left' and 'right' of the ruling group as a whole, problems emerge: where does one place Nicholas II, undoubtedly a conservative authoritarian in his convictions and yet scarcely lion-like or tough-minded in his personality? Moreover the Council's liberals are not to be equated with the wider-eyed naïvety of some of the liberal-radical elements populating the Provisional Government in 1917. Within the imperial ruling élite the application of liberal principles could be a distinctly stern affair. Andrei Saburov noted in 1905–6 that he by no means objected to determined repression, merely to its arbitrary aspect which undermined all respect for law, order and regularity in the eyes of the population.[40] Categorizing individuals according to psychological types inevitably has its problems too, if only because attitudes can change with time and circumstances. N.A. Zinov'ev, for instance, Plehve's assistant minister, would certainly have been considered an authoritarian in 1905 and joined the Right Group in the reformed State Council. Not only, however, were his speeches often distinctly humane, but he came in time to have a much friendlier attitude towards the autonomy of civil society than he had ever shown as a ministerial official. Finally, one might question the whole validity of categorizing officials by psychological types, and offer alternative definitions. One such might well be departmental: the Council's authoritarian 'right' was after all centred around former top officials of the Ministry of Internal Affairs who in their time had been responsible for relations with the peasantry, the maintenance of the state's coercive apparatus and the struggle against revolutionary socialism.

Nevertheless the tough-minded : tender-hearted contrast is too appropriate to be completely abandoned. Its relevance is unmistakable, to take but one example, when one compares the cold, logical ruthlessness of Peter Durnovo's views on the treatment of prisoners with the far more humane, Christian and sentimental attitude of Mikhail Dmitriev, a leading light of the State Council's less hard-line Centre Group.[41] If, as is legitimate, one takes the authors of the collective memorandum to Nicholas II of May 1905 as representatives of 'establishment liberalism', one would certainly not go 'amiss in stressing the humane, tender-hearted nature of this group. Fyodor Terner was a man with a sensitive Christian conscience who used much of his meagre spare time to preach the gospel in the houses of the Petersburg poor, while Andrei Saburov rescued prostitutes and worked for charities without pay and Anatol Kulomzin devoted his leisure to schemes for educating the masses and, off and on, for providing the working classes with decent housing. These were not attitudes or activities one could easily imagine ascribing to, to take but three examples, Peter Durnovo, Aleksei Ignat'ev or Victor Wahl. In the camp of the Council's liberals one finds a much greater shrinking from violence than among the authoritarians, a greater humanity and a firmer faith in human nature, including the nature of the Russian people. When one knows something of the personalities and world-views of liberals such as Kulomzin, Andrei Saburov, Anatol Koni, Peter Semyonov and Mikhail Khilkov, it is difficult not to feel that the period of optimistic, idealistic populism of the late 1850s and early 1860s made a lasting impact on them. Progress was achievable, ideals could be realized, the Russian people could to some extent, at least in the longer term, be trusted and need not simply be subjected to coercion.

There is no doubt that if one intended to ascend to heaven in company one would not only be much happier travelling with the Council's 'left' than with its 'right', but also more firmly convinced that the whole group would arrive at the correct destination. That is not, however, necessarily a comment on the relative merits of the two groups' political programmes. We have already seen what Durnovo had to offer; let us now turn briefly to the viewpoints of his colleagues towards the left of the ruling élite.

On the whole it is fair to describe these men as both liberals and Westerners. They were liberals in the sense that they believed in the essential principles of the Victorian liberal world. They attached a high importance to the rule of law and believed that education was a vital force for progress. Private property was for them an essential basis both for economic prosperity and for civil rights. They believed that the state must allow civil society space to breathe and develop. As the level of education and maturity of that society rose, political rights should be granted it. Not for one moment, however, did they endorse democratic principles at Russia's current level of development. Like their opposite numbers throughout Europe but, because of Russia's relative backwardness, to an even greater degree, they were convinced that premature devolution of power to workers and peasants would result in the triumph of an ignorant, reactionary collectivism in which popular prejudice and short-term material greed would wreck the institutions that made economic development, individual rights and indeed civil society possible. They had few doubts that in a country at Russia's level of development it was the right and duty of the educated and cultured to rule. Undoubtedly, they saw the political hegemony of workers and peasants as heralding the end of European civilization in Russia, and the demotion of the latter from the ranks of the leading world powers to the level of an Egypt or a China.

As was evident from the May 1905 memorandum, the élite's liberals were also quite explicitly Westernizers, drawing their model of modernization from earlier Western, and in this specific case English, practice. This of course did not mean that the élite's liberals lacked pride in their country or that they were blind to some ways in which Western principles might have to be adjusted on Russian soil. Kulomzin, for instance, accepted the commune, which was anathema to principled liberals, partly because in this case he was influenced by Russian nationalist sentiment, and even Terner came to see the commune as a necessary, albeit temporary, safety net amidst the strains of modernization. Basically, however, economic, cultural and political modernization was expected to follow Western paths. In this the 'left' within the ruling élite were in line with most of the liberal intelligentsia, as represented in the Kadet party, and with most Russian Marxists. Nevertheless, in the light of twentieth-century political developments outside the English-speaking democracies, Scandinavia and the Low Countries, it is difficult not to feel that the liberals' optimism about Western-style modernization was perhaps not firmly rooted in an understanding of the dynamics of their own society.

Against this point of view certain quite powerful arguments can be advanced. A simple-minded equation of Russia with the underdeveloped societies which emerged from de-colonization in post-war Asia and Africa is seriously misleading.[42] *Inter alia* it radically underestimates the sophistication of the Russian economy, state apparatus and ruling élite in the pre-1914 era. One certainly cannot disregard the chance of a Western-style political development taking place in Russia. An élite which had carried out one massive infraction of property rights in 1861 might in the end either itself have sanctioned land reform or been forced to do so in the wake of the monarchy's overthrow. With the peasantry bought off and the conflict between peasant and landowner removed from the agenda, the chances of survival for Western-style political institutions, if scarcely brilliant, would undoubtedly have been better than had previously been the case.

Moreover the historical context in which the Russian Old Regime was operating was very different from the era of the 1950s, 1960s and 1970s, on the study of which most theories of underdevelopment are based. Before 1914, although socialist ideas and ideals existed and were beacons of hope for much of the working class, they were not on the whole blueprints for modernization but rather based on models of already industrialized societies. Nor of course had any of these ideas yet been put into practice. The dominant model of modernization was still overwhelmingly the Western liberal one. This was sustained in part by the successes of Western societies, and by the dominance acquired over men's minds by having the field, at least as regards practice, more or less to oneself. In addition, however, the power of the Western model owed a great deal to what one might pompously describe as the correlation of forces in the world in the nineteenth and early twentieth centuries. To put it more bluntly, the world's leading powers all subscribed to the Western model; moreover they exercised direct political power over much of the globe and had great economic and strategic interests in the rest. Not for one moment were they likely to allow any major portion of the world to secede from the 'Western model', let alone a portion in which the other great powers had such a vast economic and strategic interest as Russia. In still more concrete terms, had the Russian revolution of 1905 succeeded and the country swung far to the left, threatening to remove itself from the 'Western' road, European intervention would have been a certainty. Moreover, this would have been not the disjointed, self-critical intervention of Western liberal democracies exhausted by years of war but a much more purposeful affair, spearheaded by the peacetime German army. There is no good reason to doubt that such intervention would have been just as successful in restoring Russia to a path acceptable to its neighbours as had been the case with the Russian Empire's own involvement in Hungarian affairs in 1848–9.

Nevertheless it is as impossible to ignore the holes in the arguments advanced by Kulomzin and his peers, if not more so, than was the case with the views put forward by Durnovo. The élite's liberals had their eyes fixed largely on Russian educated society. They stressed, fairly enough, the dangers of ignoring and alienating this society and the great difficulties of governing in the teeth of public opinion. They also believed that to deny the educated public a responsible role in politics was to encourage unrealistic dreams and irresponsible actions on its part. Convinced that if educated society was given room to breathe and to participate in government it would become more sober and conservative, the authors of the May 1905 memorandum argued that socialist ideas were too inherently unrealistic to flourish long if exposed to the light of day, and that the popularity they enjoyed in Russia was largely because they were forbidden and repressed.

The obvious weakness of the liberal programme of modernization was that, though it might go a long way towards satisfying educated society, it had little to offer the masses and very much played down their importance or capacity for independent thought and action. Conservative–liberals such as Andrei Saburov, Anatol Kulomzin and Aleksei Obolensky had as little intention of allowing gentry estates to be confiscated as their more ruthless and authoritarian peers. Nor were they willing or indeed able to do much to change the face of Russian industrial capitalism. The logic of liberal modernization was indeed that the remaining collectivist institutions, in particular the commune, would be weakened if not destroyed. This policy, foreshadowed in the May 1905 memorandum, was subsequently embodied in Stolypin's assault on the commune. Though from the élite's point of view the necessity for this assault is clear enough, the need to create a strong capitalist peasant class being both politically and economically essential, the policy was bound to antagonize the bulk of the communal peasantry and in the short-to-medium term to exacerbate mass disaffection and political instability.

Nor was there any reason for the Russian masses to rejoice in a political reform which increased the state's dependence on the social élites by giving the latter an explicit role in government while virtually excluding workers and peasants from effective representation. This was the aim of the authors of the May 1905 memorandum, and it was the reality of the constitutional regime established after June 1907. In this context, citing the precedent of the pre-1832 British Parliament as the authors of the May 1905 memorandum did, was not good enough. British institutions were sanctioned by traditions very different from those of the tsarist myth and the Russian service state. The explicit and unprecedented linking of political power to criteria of wealth and property ownership was unlikely to strike Russian peasants or workers as other than a further development of unjust class politics. Moreover – to return to a point made earlier – Britain's constitution had not excluded the mass of the population from the dignity of a vote at a time when socialist theories and political parties existed, supported by elements of the educated classes, that were on the lookout for any opportunity to undermine the legitimacy of the existing order. To sum up, there was little reason to believe that the liberal programme set out in the 1905 memorandum would reduce the disaffection of the Russian masses – if anything quite the opposite. Moreover, the obviously and explicitly foreign provenance of this programme was likely in the long term to contribute to its unpopularity.

Yet, as I have argued, if liberal reform was to mean anything and to restore the regime's credibility with educated society, it had to establish civil rights firmly and to tackle the police state. So long as personal rights and freedom could simply be abrogated at will by invoking the 1881 emergency laws, the rift between state and edu-

Twilight of the Old Regime. P.A. Stolypin and his family.

cated society was bound to remain wide. Officialdom, particularly police officialdom, had to be subject to the rule of law and to the glare of publicity as expressed through interpellations in parliament and the criticism of a free press. Moreover, it was inevitable that the representative bodies expressing public opinion would seek further and further to extend their control over the state apparatus. In addition, pressure to extend the franchise, to shift power from the gentry to the educated classes as a whole, was bound to mount.

It was precisely these trends that so scared Durnovo, Nicholas Maklakov and other members of the élite's authoritarian wing. They were convinced that the gradual retreat of state power and the growing freedom of Russian society would increase the room for manoeuvre of revolutionary socialism while by no means lessening its popularity. As the state apparatus came more and more under the sway of the courts and of public opinion, the feebler became its chances of displaying self-confidence, energy and, where necessary, ruthlessness in the defence of an unpopular cause. As the traditional organs of police power and of authoritarian bureaucracy came under ever-increasing pressure from public opinion, the 'last of the Mohicans' in the State Council began to predict the forthcoming destruction of 'bourgeois society' in Russia. They had a point.[43]

NOTES

Published sources are cited in full at the first instance, and thereafter by author's surname and short title only. The following abbreviations are used throughout:

ARCHIVES

CUBA	Columbia University (New York), Bakhmetev Archive
RO	Otdel Rukopisey Biblioteki imeni Lenina (Moscow)
TsGAOR	Tsentral'nyy Gosudarstvenyy Arkhiv Oktyabr'skoy Revolyutsii (Moscow)
TsGIA	Tsentral'nyy Gosudarstvennyy Istoricheskiy Arkhiv (Leningrad)

PERIODICALS AND WORKS OF REFERENCE

AHR	American History Review
ASRGD	Almanakh sovremennykh russkikh gosudarstvennykh deyateley
CMRS	Cahiers du monde russe et soviétique
DBL	Deutschbaltisches Biographisches Lexicon
FzGO	Forschungen zur Geschichte Osteuropas
GHdbR	Genealogisches Handbuch des baltischen Ritterschaften
IZ	Istoricheskie Zapiski
JfGO	Jahrbücher für Geschichte Osteuropas
KA	Krasnyy Arkhiv
PSZ	Pol'noe sobranie zakonov
RR	Russian Review
RS	Russkaya Starina (SPB)
SEER	Slavonic and East European Review
SOGS	Stenograficheskiy otchot Gosudarstvennogo Soveta
SR	Slavic Review
SZ	Svod zakonov Rossiyskoy Imperii

(SPB = St Petersburg)

Dates in Russian sources are according to the Julian calendar unless otherwise indicated.

CHAPTER 1

[1] E.g., in electoral Bavaria, part of long-settled western Germany, only five families still extant in 1900 could trace their ancestry back to the early Middle Ages. See Erwin, Freiherr von Aretin, 'Vom Adel in Bayern', *Suddeutsche Monatshefte* 23 (Feb 1926), pp. 385–91.

[2] The figure of 10 princes is not entirely clear-cut. Among the 215 members of the Council were two princes Svyatopolk-Mirsky, who claimed descent from Rurik. The claim is accepted by N.I. Ikonnikov, *La Noblesse de Russie*, 2nd edn., vols. A1–Z2 (Paris, 1958–66), here vol. P: 541–7, but rejected by Prince P.P. Dolgorukov, *Rossiyskaya rodoslovnaya kniga*, 4 pts. (SPB, 1854–7), here pt. I: 128. Whatever their ultimate origins, however, from the fourteenth to the nineteenth centuries the Svyatopolk-Mirsky family was Polish and had a history wholly different from the Russian Rurikids. The Tatishchevs were also descendants of Monomakh, like the Vyazemskys tracing their ancestry through the princes of Smolensk, but they abandoned their princely title in the Middle Ages. On the Tatishchevs' history see S.S. Tatishchev, *Rod Tatishchevykh* (SPB, 1900).

[3] Dolgorukov, *Rodoslovnaya kniga*, pt. I: 78–86 (Obolensky), 86–109 (Dolgorukov), 139–58 (Vyazemsky), 212–17 (Lobanov-Rostovsky), 250–5 (Khilkov), 255–70 (Volkonsky). In strict genealogical terms Prince N.V. Repnin should be included among the Volkonskys since his grandfather, Prince N.G. Volkonsky, married the daughter of the last Repnin and took that family's name (ibid., 273–4).

[4] On these struggles see, e.g., a useful survey by J. Fennell, *The Crisis of Medieval Russia 1200–1304* (Harlow, 1983).

[5] See n. 3 for the histories of these families. Ch. 4 of R.O. Crummey, *The Formation of Muscovy 1304–1613* (Harlow, 1987), provides an up-to-date and lucid discussion of the period 1462–1533 when these territorial gains were made by Moscow's princes.

[6] Among useful recent works concentrating in part at least on the fall of the Patrikeevs are those by N. Shields Kollmann, 'Consensus Politics: The Dynastic Crisis of the 1490s Reconsidered', *RR* 45 (1986), pp. 235–67, and G. Alef, 'Aristocratic Politics and Royal Policy in Muscovy in the Late Fifteenth and Early Sixteenth Centuries', *FzGO* 27 (1980), pp. 77–109. On the élite in this period see, e.g., A.A. Zimin, 'Knyazheskaya znat' i formirovanie sostava Boyarskoy dumy vo vtoroy polovine XV–pervoy treti XVI v', *IZ* 103 (1979), pp. 195–241, and G. Alef, 'Reflections on the Boyar Duma in the Reign of Ivan III', *SEER* 45 (1967), pp. 76–123. On the genealogies of the Golitsyns and Kurakins see Dolgorukov, *Rodoslovnaya kniga*, pt. I: 285–319.

[7] On the 'service princes' see in particular A.A. Zimin, 'Sluzhil'ye knyaz'ya v russkom godudarstve kontsa XV – pervoy treti XVIv', in N.I. Pavlenko et. al., eds., *Dvoryanstvo i krepostnoy stroy Rossii XVI–XVIIIv* (Moscow, 1975), 28–56, and ch. 2 of M.E. Bychkova, *Sostav klassa feodalov Rossii v XVIv*, (Moscow, 1986).

[8] Dolgorukov, *Rodoslovnaya kniga*, provides details of the families' boyars and *okol'nichie*. A number of works cover the boyar élite in the sixteenth and seventeenth centuries, often providing lists of those who held this rank. See, e.g., A.A. Zimin, 'Sostav Boyarskoy dumy v XV–XVI vekakh', *Arkheograficheskiy ezhegodnik za 1957 god* 41 (1958), pp. 41–87; A.M. Kleimola, 'Patterns of Duma Recruitment, 1505–1550', in D.C. Waugh, ed., *Essays in Honour of A.A. Zimin* (Columbus, O., 1985), 232–58; Bychkova, *Sostav*; Ya. E. Vodarsky, 'Pravyashchaya gruppa svetskikh feodalov v Rossii v XVIIv', in Pavlenko, *Dvoryanstvo*, 70–107; R.O. Crummey, *Aristocrats and Servitors: The Boyar Elite in Russia, 1613–1689* (Princeton, N.J., 1983).

[9] The Romanov dynasty itself came quite close to dying out in the seventeenth and eighteenth centuries and many old Russian families did so. Nor

was Russia special in this respect. Adolph Christoph Graf zu Dohna (1683–1736), for instance, had 15 children, of whom 9 boys reached adulthood; however, only two of his great-grandsons produced heirs. *Genealogisches Handbuch der gräflichen Häuser*, Band X (Marburg, 1981), 62ff.

[10] H. Reif, *Westfälischer Adel, 1770–1860* (Göttingen, 1979), discusses a group of Catholic nobles whose tradition of primogeniture, entail and self-sacrificing celibacy by younger sons was so strictly enforced that the families in question risked extinction (see esp., e.g., pp. 58–9, 79–81, for the origins of this tradition). On this see also H. Kleine, *Der Verfall der Adelsgeschlechter* (Leipzig, 1879), where *inter alia* German Catholic and Protestant families' reproduction rates, marriage and inheritance patterns are compared.

[11] A.A. Kurakin's service record is in TsGIA, Fond 1162, Opis 6, Ed. Khr. 272, pp. 85ff. On his family see Ikonnikov, *Noblesse*, vol. H: 199–221.

[12] TsGIA, Fond 1162, Opis 6, Ed. Khr. 128, pp. 28ff (service record). Ikonnikov, *Noblesse*, vol. D: 518–40.

[13] TsGIA, Fond 1162, Opis 6, Ed. Khr. 100, pp. 13ff (service record). Dolgorukov seems to omit this branch of the Vyazemsky family altogether. For L.D. Vyazemsky's line, see *Annuaire de la Noblesse de Russie* (SPB, 1892), 245.

[14] L.M. Minarik, 'Proiskhozhdenie i sostav zemel'nikh vladeniy krupneyshikh pomeshchikov Rossii kontsa XIX–nachala XXv', *Materialy po istorii sel'skogo khozyaystva i krestyanstva CCCP*, sbornik 6 (Moscow, 1965), 375–95, on the origins of the estates of Russia's biggest landowners in the early twentieth century. On seventeenth- and eighteenth-century land grants and their recipients, the comments of Vodarsky in 'Pravyashchaya gruppa' (e.g. p. 84) are very much to the point.

[15] For Kurakin and Vyazemsky see nn. 11 and 13 respectively. Ikonnikov, *Noblesse*, vol. W: 235–70 (Dolgoruky); vol. K: 426–567 (Obolensky); vol. S: 342–99 (Volkonsky and Repnin); vol. F:

293–311 (Khilkov); vol. I: 422–36 (Lobanov-Rostovsky). The size of Lobanov's estate is unknown but judging by the extent of his parents' possessions and the fact that Lobanov himself was a bachelor with four brothers he is unlikely to have been very rich.

[16] B. Meehan-Waters, *Autocracy and Aristocracy: The Russian Service Elite of 1730* (New Brunswick, N.J., 1982), 76, mentions this point with reference to the reign of Peter I. S.M. Troitsky, *Russkiy absolyutizm i dvoryanstvo v XVIIIv* (Moscow, 1974), 303, 315, 322, e.g., makes the same point.

[17] There has of course been an endless debate on the 'class nature' of Russian absolutism and the relationship between the state and social classes under the Old Regime. Much Soviet writing on this subject is silly and wooden, but some is not. I have for instance no quarrel with Troitsky's view, in *Russkiy absolyutizm*, that the nobility was not uniform, that gentry–bureaucratic relations were complex and shifting, and that some historians have exaggerated the power of the Russian state and its domination of society (see esp. his pp. 3–16). For Western views on Soviet interpretations of absolutism see H.J. Torke: 'Die Entwicklung des Absolutismus – Problems in der sowjetischen Historiographie seit 1917', *JfGO* 21 (1973), no. 4, pp. 493–508, and 'Die neuere Sowjethistoriographie zum Problem des Russischen Absolutismus', *FzGO* 20 (1973), pp. 113–33. Also A. Gerschenkron, 'Soviet Marxism and Absolutism', *SR* 30 (1971), no. 4, pp. 853–69.

[18] In their different ways both J.P. LeDonne's articles on the eighteenth-century political élite and L.M. Minarik's work on the formation of Russia's greatest aristocratic estates strongly underline these points; so too do the histories of the families represented in Nicholas II's State Council. Minarik, 'Proiskhozhdenie'; J.P. LeDonne: 'Appointments to the Russian Senate 1762–1796', *CMRS* 16, no. 1 (Jan–Mar 1975), pp. 27–56; 'Catherine's Governors and Governors-General', *CMRS* 20, no. 1 (Jan–Mar

1979), pp. 15–42.

[19] E.g., A.A. Kurakin's wife, a Princess Volkonsky: Ikonnikov, *Noblesse*, vol. H: 221, or V.S. Obolensky-Neledinsky-Meletsky's mother, who on the eve of Emancipation owned almost 2,000 serfs in her own right: ibid., vol. K: 521.

[20] I discuss the Obolenskys' case in more detail in ch. 8.

[21] Volkonsky's wife was Elizaveta Grigorevna *née* Volkonsky, the granddaughter of Field Marshal Prince P.M. Volkonsky: see Minarik, 'Proiskhozhdenie', 383–4, for her properties, and 378–9 for those of the Dolgorukys. The estates of Volkonsky's father, a Decembrist, were confiscated in flat contradiction of the spirit of the 1785 charter. M.S. Volkonsky rebuilt his fortune at dizzying and maybe not wholly honest speed after 1856. See A.A. Polovtsov, *Dnevnik gosudarstvennogo sekretarya A.A. Polovtsova*, ed. Zayonchkovsky, 2 vols. (Moscow, 1966), here II: 255.

[22] Ikonnikov, *Noblesse*, vol. D: 499. This was almost certainly a major reason why D.P. Golitsyn was so poor. One of his Golitsyn great-uncles, for instance, owned 5,795 serfs in 1860, though another great-uncle and aunt, like his grandfather, became Catholics and lived abroad.

[23] Opinions differ as to the extent to which the nobility responded to the challenge to increase production on their estates. Arcadius Kahan, for instance, wrote that eighteenth-century 'agriculture was probably not so unresponsive to new opportunities and stimuli as some of the older histories would have us believe', and went on to discuss noble industrial entrepreneurship as well. See A. Kahan, 'The Costs of "Westernisation" in Russia: The Gentry and the Economy in the Eighteenth Century', in *The Structure of Russian History: Interpretive Essays*, ed. M. Cherniavsky (New York, 1970), 224–50. M. Confino, however, has stressed the inefficiency of gentry agriculture and in particular its inability even to achieve proper accounting methods in order to gauge profit and loss on its estates: *Domaines et seigneurs en Russie vers la fin du XVIIIe Siècle. Études*

de structures agraires et de mentalités économiques (Paris, 1963).

[24] For Alexander Obolensky see ch. 8. One slightly gushing contemporary described Anatol Kurakin as having 'a wonderful head for business. Under his able management his fortune has considerably increased': see Anon., *Russian Court Memoirs 1914–16* (London, 1917), 297. Princess Lydia Vasil'chikov, the daughter of L.D. Vyazemsky, is of course not an unbiased source in her description of how he ran their estate of Lotarevo in Tambov province. Nevertheless ch. 4 of her memoirs, *Verschwundenes Russland*, ed. Tatiana Metternich (Vienna, 1980), is of considerable interest.

[25] There are frequent references to this in the secondary literature: see, e.g., V.M. Kabuzan and S.M. Troitsky, 'Izmeneniya v chislennosti, udel'nom vese i razmeshchenie dvoryanstva v Rossii, 1782–1858 gg', *Istoriya CCCP* 4 (1971), pp. 153–68; Minarik, 'Proiskhozhdenie'.

[26] TsGIA, Fond 1162, Opis 6, Ed. Khr. 585 (service record), pp. 80ff. and a minute on the small value of Khilkov's estate in Tver (p. 63).

[27] Kleimola, 'Patterns', covering the period 1505–50, illustrates the balance between princes and others within the ruling élite. Among works on the early Muscovite élite and state, S.B. Veselovsky, *Issledovaniya po istoriy klassa sluzhilykh zemlevladel'tsev* (Moscow, 1969), deserves pride of place. Useful surveys of early Muscovite politics include H. Rüss, *Adel und Adelsoppositionen im Moskauer Staat* (Wiesbaden, 1975), and N. Shields Kollmann, *Kinship and Politics: The Making of the Muscovite Political System, 1345–1547* (Stanford, Calif., 1987).

[28] S.B. Veselovsky, *Issledovaniya... Klassa*, 465–516.

[29] The first chapter in Rüss, *Adel*, entitled 'Einführende Vorbemerkungen' (pp. 1–30), is an excellent introduction to this subject. Kollmann, *Kinship*, puts a very heavy stress on the hereditary nature of membership in the boyar élite and on the latter's power *vis-à-vis* the sovereign (e.g., p. 55: 'The overwhelming majority of men who became boyars

did so because they were the men next in line in their family's succession system'). S.B. Veselovsky, *Issledovaniya... Klassa*, stresses (e.g., p. 472) that the prince did have customary obligations towards his aristocratic servitors.

[30] On the early Muscovite bureaucracy see A.A. Zimin, 'D'yacheskiy apparat v Rossii vtoroy poloviny XV–pervoy treti XVIv', *IZ* 87 (1972), pp. 219–86; P.B. Brown, 'Muscovite Government Bureaus', *Russian History* 10, pt. 3 (1983), pp. 269–330.

[31] On the relationship between state, magnates, service gentry and serfdom, see particularly R. Hellie, *Enserfment and Military Change in Muscovy* (Chicago, 1971). He stresses the domination of politics by the magnates and the powerlessness of the middle-service gentry save in moments of dire emergency when the state's rulers, fearing for the social order, went some way grudgingly to accommodate pressing gentry concerns.

[32] Crummey, *Formation*, 176. An essay by Crummey entitled 'Ivan The Terrible', in S.H. Baron and N.W. Heer, eds., *Windows on the Russian Past* (Columbus, O., 1977), 57–74, is a useful guide to recent literature on Ivan IV. S.B. Veselovsky, *Issledovaniya po istorii oprichniny* (Moscow, 1963), is a vital work on this period. Alef, 'Reflections', and Kleimola, 'Patterns', provide information about the make-up of the boyar élite in the period 1462–1550.

[33] Crummey, *Aristocrats*; Vodarsky, 'Pravyashchaya'. Another useful article is by A.M. Kleimola, 'Up Through Servitude: The Changing Conditions of the Muscovite Elite in the Sixteenth and Seventeenth Centuries', *Russian History* 6, pt. 2 (1979), pp. 210–29.

[34] Crummey, *Aristocrats*, chs. 1 and 2.

[35] Ibid., 27.

[36] Ibid., 27–8, 70–4, 164–7; Vodarsky, 'Pravyashchaya', pp. 76–83 and *Prilozhenie*, pp. 105–7; G.C. Weickhardt, 'Bureaucrats and Boiars in the Muscovite Tsardom', *Russian History* 10, pt. 3 (1983), pp. 331–56.

[37] On the governmental system in the seventeenth century see, e.g.,

N.V. Ustyugov, 'Evolutsiya prikaznogo stroya Russkogo gosudarstva v XVIIv', in *Absolyutizm v Rossii (XVII–XVIIIvv)* (Moscow, 1964), and B. Plavsic, 'Seventeenth-Century Chanceries and their Staffs', in W.M. Pintner and D.K. Rowney, eds., *Russian Officialdom: The Bureaucratization of Russian Society from the Seventeenth to the Twentieth Century* (Chapel Hill, N. Car., 1980), 19–45. Hellie, *Enserfment*, explains the paradox of a redundant service class acquiring extra powers over the peasantry. P. Longworth, *Alexis, Tsar of All the Russias* (London, 1984), is an interesting survey of the man, his regime and his times.

[38] See the author's introduction to vol. I of D, Schakhovskoy, *Société et Noblesse Russe. Collection fondée par Nicholas Ikonnikov sous le titre, 'La Noblesse de Russie' pursuivie et complétée* (Rennes, 1978), for information on the Velvet Book and (here p. 51) families listed in it still extant in the early twentieth century.

[39] Ikonnikov, *Noblesse*, vol. C: 49–122; Minarik, 'Proiskhozhdenie', pp. 372–3. TsGIA, Fond 1162, Opis 6, Ed. Khr. 610, 611 (service records).

[40] Ikonnikov, *Noblesse*, vol. G: 31–50; *Almanakh sovremennykh russkikh gosudarstvennykh deyateley (ASRGD)* (SPB, 1897), 377–80. TsGIA, Fond 1162, Opis 6, Ed. Khr. 583, 584 (service records).

[41] Ikonnikov, *Noblesse*, vol. O: 87–130; A. Romanovich-Slavatinsky, *Dvoryanstvo v Rossii* (SPB, 1870), 243. TsGIA, Fond 1162, Opis 6, Ed. Khr. 483, 484 (service records). *Spisok grazhdanskim chinam pervykh tryokh klassov* (SPB, 1895), 202.

[42] I have discussed this point at length in *Russia and the Origins of the First World War* (London, 1983), ch. 4. TsGIA, Fond 1162, Opis 6, Ed. Khr. 536 (service record). Tatishchev's eldest son did own a rather small estate in Kursk. Ikonnikov, *Noblesse*, vol. Q: 104; S.S. Tatishchev, *Rod, passim*.

[43] Anon., *Russian Court Memoirs*, 288–9; Ikonnikov, *Noblesse*, vol. E2: 433–59; A.A. Ignatiev, *A Subaltern in Old Russia* (London, 1944), 9–13. TsGIA, Fond 1162, Opis 6, Ed. Khr.

210 (service record).

[44] Ikonnikov, *Noblesse*, vol. O: 253–80. TsGIA, Fond 1162, Opis 6, Ed. Khr. 489 (service record). I touched on this Moscow circle in my *Origins*, 91–2. Of recent works on the business community of Moscow, see particularly J.A. Ruckman, *The Moscow Business Élite: A Social and Cultural Portrait of Two Generations, 1840–1905* (De Kalb, Ind., 1984), and P.A. Buryshkin, *Moskva kupecheskaya* (New York, 1954).

[45] Ikonnikov, *Noblesse*, vol. W: 481–90; *ASRGD*, 191–2; A.P. Tyrtov, 'Istoricheskaya zametka o rode dvoryan Tyrtovykh', *RS* 48 (1885), pp. 679–86.

[46] Ikonnikov, *Noblesse*, vol. X: 1–23.

[47] TsGIA, Fond 1162, Opis 6, Ed. Khr. 1918, p. 100 (service record), and Ed. Khr. 527 (grandfather's service record). V.N. Stroev, *Stoletie Sobstvennoy Ego Imperatorskogo Velichestva Kantselyarii* (SPB, 1912).

[48] Ikonnikov, *Noblesse*, vol. J: 533–70. The Murav'yovs were transferred from Ryazan to Novgorod in 1488.

[49] Ibid., vol. M: 184–218.

[50] Ibid., vol. Y: 91–106.

[51] CUBA, MSS V.N. Kokovtsov, 'Vospominaniya detstva i litseyskoy pory grafa V.N. Kokovtsova'.

[52] Ikonnikov, *Noblesse*, vol. S1: 127–36.

[53] Ibid., vol. G: 241–51. Though Shirinsky-Shikhmatov himself had no land his wife inherited 700 *desyatiny* in the Vyazma district of Smolensk.

[54] Ibid., vol. T2: 363–88. TsGIA, Fond 1162, Opis 6, Ed. Khr. 202, p. 76 (service record).

[55] See ch. 7.

[56] Ikonnikov, *Noblesse*, vol. V1: 141–50 and TsGIA, Fond 1162, Opis 6, Ed. Khr. 55 (Bryanchaninov). Sipyagin's service record was not to be found in TsGIA. *Spisok grazhdanskim chinam* (1895), 588, states that he inherited 4,970 *desyatiny* in Saratov and bought 803 *desyatiny* in Moscow.

[57] TsGIA, Fond 1162, Opis 6, Ed. Khr. 565, p. 31 (service record). Ikonnikov, *Noblesse*, vol. X: 431–54.

[58] TsGIA, Fond 1162, Opis 6, Ed. Khr. 511, p. 60 (service record). Ikon-

nikov, *Noblesse*, vol. P2: 367–75.

[59] P.P. Semyonov, *Detstvo i yunost'* (Petrograd, 1917); Ikonnikov, *Noblesse*, vol. O2: 461–6. TsGIA, Fond 1162, Opis 6, Ed. Khr. 496, p. 210 (service record).

[60] TsGIA, Fond 1162, Opis 6, Ed. Khr. 349, p. 92 (service record). Ikonnikov, *Noblesse*, vol. J: 277–91.

[61] TsGIA, Fond 1162, Opis 6, Ed. Khr. 18 (service record). Ikonnikov, *Noblesse*, vol. A1: 107–228. Apart from A.A. Arsen'ev, who owned land in Tula, the Council also contained his distant cousin, the landless D.S. Arsen'ev, whose wife, however, owned 5,000 *desyatiny* in Kursk and Oryol: see his service record in TsGIA, Fond 1162, Opis 6, Ed. Khr. 19, p. 21. General N.N. Sukhotin also shared a small estate with his brother, a noble marshal, in the Chernzh district of Tula in 1900, a district in which their family had owned land since a direct ancestor had been a *voevoda* there in 1649. The Sukhotins had been Tula landowners in the sixteenth century. Ikonnikov, *Noblesse*, vol. P1: 110–47.

[62] TsGIA, Fond 1162, Opis 6, Ed. Khr. 39, p. 82 (service record). *Almanach de Saint Petersbourg. Cour, Monde et Ville* (SPB, 1910), 26.

[63] See, e.g., the case of S.S. Bekhteev, who owned 2,689 *desyatiny* in Oryol, had a salary from the state for many years, was a noted agricultural expert and yet still, according to his wife, could not make ends meet. See a letter from Bekhteev's widow in TsGIA, Fond 1162, Opis 6, Ed. Khr. 39, p. 70.

[64] See n. 47. A.A. Mosolov writes that in the early twentieth century the Taneev family 'was none too well off' and the strain of constantly dressing to be in attendance on the Empress told heavily on the pocket of Anna Vyrubova, A.S. Taneev's daughter. Times and habits had changed, however. The notoriously mean Empress Alexandra Fyodorovna gave her friend £200 per annum to cover her expenses at court. A.A. Mosolov, *At the Court of the Last Tsar* (London, 1935), 41.

[65] Ikonnikov, *Noblesse*, vol. C: 271–

81. TsGIA, Fond 1162, Opis 6, Ed. Khr. 626, p. 7.

[66] On the Durnovos see Ikonnikov, *Noblesse*, vol. C: 569–98; on the Balashovs, vol. A2: 325–31; also Minarik, 'Proiskhozhdenie', pp. 368, 383. The latter, however, wrongly states that M.V. Durnovo (née Kochubei) was P.P. Durnovo's mother; she was actually his wife.

[67] See Meehan-Waters, *Autocracy*, *passim*.

[68] It is impossible to list here even the major works on the eighteenth-century Russian nobility. As always, much wisdom is to be drawn from I. de Madariaga, *Russia in the Age of Catherine The Great* (London, 1981), here 79–89 and 556–7 in particular. Kabuzan and Troitsky, 'Izmeneniya', provide the best information available on the make-up of the late eighteenth-century nobility. The histories of some of the families represented in the State Council are often illuminating. Tauride province was, for instance, very much virgin land open to Russian colonization in the early nineteenth century. One family which rooted itself there as part of the Crimean nobility were the Olives. They were descended from William Olive, an officer in Napoleon's army who remained in Russia after 1812, became an aide-decamp to the Grand Duke Constantine, bought land in the Crimea and was the province's marshal 1848–53. His son, the future member of the State Council, entered service in the exclusive Life Guard Hussars and his grandchildren married into old aristocracy and held positions at court. Obviously the Romanovs' patronage was important in the Olives' rise and it is always conceivable that there was some private, unspoken link between the two families. Even so, the Olives' ability to implant themselves so quickly in the Crimean nobility was in a sense the mark of a relatively open, 'frontier' society. On the other hand, among the biggest landowners in the Crimea were the Dolgoruky family, who had bought a large estate there in the 1830s. See Minarik, 'Proiskhozhdenie', pp. 378–9. For the Olives see Ikonnikov, *Noblesse*, vol. O; 115–17.

[69] Romanovich-Slavatinsky, *Dvoryanstvo*, 155–62.

[70] I.P. Kutaysov was a young Turkish prisoner given by Catherine II to her son Paul. The latter took a liking to Kutaysov, and – partly no doubt to spite the nobility – made him a count and a Knight of Saint Andrew, granting him three estates in Courland, the most aristocratic of the Baltic provinces. After Paul's murder Kutaysov was immediately dismissed, but his family nevertheless took root in the Russian nobility. One son, a general, was killed at Borodino, the other became a member of the State Council, married a princess Lopukhin, and died in 1840. I.P. Kutaysov's grandson married a princess Urusov, the daughter of a senator, while his great-grandson, P.I. Kutaysov, was an appointed member of Nicholas II's State Council. Ikonnikov, *Noblesse*, vol. E: 247–9.

[71] E.I. Indova, 'K voprosu o dvoryanskoy sobstvennosti v Rossii v posdniy feodal'nyy period', in Pavlenko, *Dvoryanstvo*, 272–92, provides (283–5) a list of land grants for the first half of the eighteenth century. The article itself is somewhat naïve and misleading.

[72] LeDonne, 'Catherine's Governors', p. 30.

[73] See n. 17.

[74] D. Ransel, *The Politics of Catherinian Russia* (New Haven, Conn., 1975), has much of interest on this topic.

[75] On these points, R.E. Jones, *The Emancipation of the Russian Nobility 1762–1785* (Princeton, N.J., 1973), is wholly convincing.

[76] Alexander I's use of Colonel Schwartz, a German of humble origin, to control the aristocratic Russian officers of the Semyonovsky regiment in the years after 1815 is a useful illustration of the tension between imperial absolutism and elements of the Russian aristocracy with a particularly dangerous institutional base, namely a Guards regiment united by a common social background, mess life, and triumphant past campaigns against Napoleon. See V.I. Semevsky, *Politicheskiya i obshchestvenniya idei Deka-*

bristov (SPB, 1909).

[77] On these coups see, e.g., S.M. Troitsky, 'Istoriografiya "dvortsovykh perevorotov" v Rossii XVIIIv', in *Voprosy Istorii* 41 (1966), no. 2, pp. 38–53; M. Raeff, 'The Domestic Policies of Peter III and His Overthrow', *AHR* 75 (1970), no. 5, pp. 1289–1310.

[78] J.J. Kenney, 'The Politics of Assassination', in H. Ragsdale, ed., *Paul I: A Reassessment of His Life and Reign.* (Pittsburgh, 1979), 125–46; 133, 135 quoted here. A good sense of the atmosphere surrounding the coup is provided by Anon. [Sablukov], 'Reminiscences of the Court and Times of the Emperor Paul I of Russia, Up to the Period of his Death', *Fraser's Magazine* 72 (1865), no. 427, pp. 222–41.

[79] J.H.L. Keep, 'Paul I and the Militarization of Government', in Ragsdale, *Paul I,* 91–103; here pp. 92–3. In my view, for all the good work done in recent decades on the Decembrists, Semevsky, *Politicheskiya,* is still the best single source on this subject. W.B. Lincoln, *Nicholas I: Emperor and Autocrat of All the Russias* (London, 1978) is an attempt at a sympathetic understanding of the Emperor's mentality, aims and achievements.

[80] The fullest all-round survey is still that by H.J. Torke, published in 1967: 'Das russische Beamtentum in der ersten Hälfte des 19 Jahrhunderts', *FzGO* 13 (1967), pp. 7–345. At the core of Torke's work is a sometimes explicit comparison of the Russian bureaucracy with its German counterparts, of which he takes an extremely favourable view.

[81] Walter Pintner, for instance, has shown that although the social origins of the bureaucratic élite did not change radically between 1750 and 1850, levels of education, administrative experience and professional expertise rose considerably. Bruce Lincoln's work somewhat qualifies this view as regards Nicholas's actual ministers, landed magnates or generals for the most part, but supports it fully as regards the group of younger officials manning key positions in the bureaucracy, from directors of departments down to desk officers. For Pint-

ner's excellent work see in particular his 'The Evolution of Civil Officialdom, 1755–1855' (pp. 190–226), and 'Civil Officialdom and the Nobility in the 1850s' (pp. 227–49), in Pintner and Rowney, *Russian Officialdom*; also his 'The Russian Higher Civil Service on the Eve of the Great Reforms', *Journal of Social History,* Spring 1975, pp. 55–68. W.B. Lincoln: 'The Ministers of Nicholas I: A Brief Inquiry into their Backgrounds and Service Careers', *RR* 34 (July 1975), pp. 308–23, and *In the Vanguard of Reform. Russia's Enlightened Bureaucrats 1825–1861* (De Kalb, Ind., 1982); D.T. Orlovsky, *The Limits of Reform* (Cambridge, Mass., 1981); R.S. Wortman, *The Development of a Russian Legal Consciousness* (Chicago, 1976); S.F. Starr, *Decentralization and Self-Government in Russia 1830–1870* (Princeton, N.J., 1972).

[82] See, e.g., A.P. Korelin, *Dvoryanstvo v poreformennoy Rossii* (Moscow, 1979); S. Becker, *Nobility and Privilege in Late Imperial Russia* (De Kalb, Ind., 1985); Yu.B. Solov'yov: *Samoderzhavie i dvoryanstvo v kontse XIX veka* (Leningrad, 1973), and *Samoderzhavie i dvoryanstvo v 1902–1907gg* (Leningrad, 1981); R. Manning, *The Crisis of the Old Order in Russia: Gentry and Government* (Princeton, N.J., 1981); V.S. Dyakin, *Samoderzhavie, burzhuaziya i dvoryanstvo v 1907–1911 gg* (Leningrad, 1978).

[83] E.g., P.A. Zayonchkovsky, *Pravitel's-tvennyy apparat samoderzhavnoy Rossii vXIXv* (Moscow, 1978); G.L. Yaney, *The Systematization of Russian Government: Social Evolution in the Domestic Administration of Imperial Russia 1711–1905* (Urbana, Ill., 1973); N.P. Eroshkin, *Ocherki istorii gosudarstvennykh uchrezhdenii dorevolyutsionnoy Rossii* (Moscow, 1965).

[84] D.T. Orlovsky, 'High Officials in the Ministry of Internal Affairs, 1855–1881', in Pintner and Rowney, *Russian Officialdom,* 250–82.

[85] R.G. Robbins, *The Tsar's Viceroys,* in the press as I write (1988).

[86] H. Whelan, *Alexander III and the State Council* (New Brunswick, N.J., 1982).

[87] D.K. Rowney: 'Organizational Change and Social Adaptation: The Pre-Revolutionary Ministry of Internal Affairs' in Pintner and Rowney, *Russian Officialdom*, 283–315; 'Higher Civil Servants in the Russian Ministry of Internal Affairs: Some Demographic and Career Characteristics, 1905–1916', *SR* 31 (Mar 1972), pp. 101–10; 'The Ministry of Internal Affairs in the Light of Organizational Theory', in R. Kanet, ed., *The Behavioral Revolution and Communist Studies* (New York, 1971), 209–31.

[88] W.E. Mosse, particularly 'Aspects of Tsarist Bureaucracy. Recruitment to the Imperial State Council 1855–1914', *SEER* 57, no. 2 (Apr 1979), pp. 240–54; 'Russian Bureaucracy at the End of the Ancien Regime: The Imperial State Council 1897–1915', *SR* 39, no. 4 (Dec 1980), pp. 616–32. On these see in particular Appendix A, n. 1.

[89] E.g., my own 'The Russian Civil Service under Nicholas II: Some Variations on the Bureaucratic Theme', *JfGO* 29 (1981), no. 3, pp. 366–403, is an effort to provide basic information about those holding the four senior ranks in the civil service and about officials in key departments in the reign of Nicholas II.

[90] LeDonne, 'Senate', p. 40.

CHAPTER 2

[1] J. Blum, 'Russia', in D. Spring, ed., *European Landed Élites in the Nineteenth Century* (Baltimore, Md., 1977), here p. 81.

[2] K.A. Krivoshein, *A.V. Krivoshein, 1857–1921, ego znachenie v istorii Rossii nachala XX veka* (Paris, 1973), ch. 1. A.V. Krivoshein married into the Moscow business élite, thereby maybe setting a trend.

[3] On the eighteenth century see, e.g., Troitsky, *Russkiy absolyutizm*, esp. 122–3, 129–30, 137. In the nineteenth century, Nicholas I's law of 25 June 1834 established formal links between an official's estate and the speed with which he could be promoted in rank, but these links were abolished by Alexander II's law of 9 Dec 1856; see *Pol'noe sobranie*

zakonov (PSZ), 2nd ser. (SPB), vol. 9/1, no. 7224 and vol. 31/2, no. 31237.

[4] A. Besançon, *Éducation et société en Russie dans le second tiers du XIXᵉ siècle* (Paris, 1974), 83.

[5] I discuss education in ch. 3. Besançon, *Éducation*, 73. Even in 1900 68.4 per cent of the students at Petersburg University were the sons of nobles and officials; see Brockhaus and Efron, *Entsiklopedicheskiy slovar'*, 43 vols. (SPB, 1890–1906), here XXVIIIa: 287–90. On distinctions between students of Petersburg's various faculties see, e.g., V.O. Zherebtsov, *Vospominaniya o Saratovskoy pervoy muzhskoy gymnazii, SPB' om universitete* (Saratov, 1912), 96.

[6] M. Mayzel, 'The Formation of the Russian General Staff, 1880–1917. A Social Study', *CMRS* 16, nos. 3–4 (July–Dec 1975), pp. 297–322, here p. 302.

[7] To what extent the up-and-coming generation in the civil service and officer corps was different in origin from its seniors is difficult to answer. In the army's élite one gets the impression of considerable changes in social origins. To reach a top military command birth counted for far less, by the end of the imperial period, than having graduated from the General Staff Academy. The Academy's graduates, only 48 per cent of whom were nobles in the class of 1913, were a genuine meritocracy. See in particular Mayzel, 'Russian General Staff'. Many of the military leaders of the White counter-revolution were anything but aristocrats. In the civil service, there were great differences from ministry to ministry. In 1913–14 fewer of the younger officials of the Ministry of Justice were noble than they had been 20 years before, and the Ministry of Education's top officials were largely non-noble. In the Ministry of Internal Affairs, and still more in the Foreign Ministry, it was a very different matter. See my 'Russian Civil Service'.

[8] On professional groups and the growth of the educated class in the second half of the nineteenth century, see V.R. Leykina-Svirskaya, *Intelligentsiya v Rossi vo vtoroy polovine XIX veka* (Moscow, 1971), esp. p. 70: in 1860

there were only *c.* 20,000 imperial subjects with a higher education. On the merchant estate, see in particular ch. 1 of T.C. Owen, *Capitalism and Politics in Russia: A Social History of the Moscow Merchants, 1855–1905* (Cambridge, 1981); A.J. Rieber, *Merchants and Entrepreneurs in Imperial Russia* (Chapel Hill, N.Car., 1982); Ruckman, *Moscow Business Elite*, ch. 1, pp. 15–48. On the clergy see, e.g., J.S. Curtiss, *Church and State in Russia: The Last Years of the Empire, 1900–1917* (New York, 1940), esp. pp. 62–3: 'The man who assumed the cassock of a village priest...usually came from an ecclesiastical family, and his father, who had been a priest before him, almost certainly lacked the means to give his son a costly university training'. See also G.L. Freeze, 'Revolt from Below: A Priest's Manifesto on the Crisis in Russian Orthodoxy (1858–59)', in R.L. Nichols and T.G. Stavrou, eds., *Russian Orthodoxy under the Old Regime* (St Paul, Minn., 1978).

[9] See M.L. Bush, *The English Aristocracy: A Comparative Synthesis* (Manchester, 1984).

[10] H. Schissler, *Preussische Agrargesellschaft im Wandel, Kritische Studien zur Geschichtswissenschaft no. 73* (Göttingen, 1978), 73, 83. See also W. Goerlitz, *Die Junker. Adel und Bauer im deutschen Osten* (Limburg, 1964), here esp. pp. 159–60, 217. The classic work on assimilation is H. Rosenberg, 'Die Pseudodemokratisierung der Rittergutsbesitzerklasse', in H.U. Wehler, ed., *Moderne deutsche Sozialgeschichte* (Düsseldorf, 1981), 287–308.

[11] On Bavaria see K. Möckl, 'Hof und Hofgesellschaft in Bayern in der Prinzregentenzeit', in K.F. Werner, ed., *Akten des 18 deutschfranzösischen Historikerkolloquiums Darmstadt von 27–30 September 1982* (Bonn, 1985), 220; on Württemburg, a paper delivered by Dr. F. Freiherr Hiller von Gaertringen, 'Hof und Hofgesellschaft Wurttemburgs in der zweiten Hälfte des 19 Jahrhunderts', in the 24th *Budinger Vorträge, Hof und Hofgesellschaft in den deutschen Staaten, des 19 und beginnenden 20 Jahrhunderts*, 2 Teil; also G. Herdt, *Der württemburgische Hof im 19 Jahrhundert. Studien über das Verhältnis zwischen Königtum und Adel in der absoluten und konstitutionellen Monarchie* (Göttingen, 1970).

[12] N. von Preradovich, *Die Führungsschichten in Osterreich und Preussen 1804–1918* (Wiesbaden, 1955), 7.

[13] J.A. Armstrong, *The European Administrative Élite* (Princeton, N.J., 1973), 10, 73–103. In Britain the would-be entrant usually required an education at public school and Oxbridge. Neither was cheap. Whatever his Prussian equivalent saved during gymnasium would be spent many times over in his years of unpaid probationary service prior to appointment as a tenured administrative or judicial official.

[14] F.M.L. Thompson, *English Landed Society in the Nineteenth Century* (London, 1963), 22–3, 287–9; J. Pellew, *The Home Office 1848–1914* (London, 1982), 5–10, 33–6.

[15] Z. Steiner, *The Foreign Office and Foreign Policy 1894–1914* (Cambridge, 1969), 10–23, 173–85. P.E. Razell, 'Social Origins of Officers in the Indian and British Home Army: 1758–1962', *British Journal of Sociology* 14 (1963), pp. 248–60, here p. 253.

[16] Preradovich, *Führungsschichten*, 111–14.

[17] Ibid., 153; Goerlitz, *Junker*, 298.

[18] L. Cecil, *The German Diplomatic Service 1871–1914* (Princeton, N.J., 1976), here pp. 58, 76.

[19] Even the Prussian House of Deputies in 1909 was only 28.4 per cent noble. The last British House of Commons in which landowners were a majority was that elected in 1880; see Thompson, *English Landed Society*, 276. On the British political élite see W.L. Guttsman, 'Aristocracy and the Middle Class in the British Political Élite 1886–1916. A Study of Formative Influences and of the Attitude to Politics', *British Journal of Sociology* 5 (1954), no. 1, pp. 12–32. On Prussian ministers in 1911 see Preradovich, *Führungsschichten*, 114. On the general theme of persistence of élites, see A.J. Mayer, *The Persistence of the Old Regime* (London, 1981).

[20] The Frenchmen were V.I. Guerrier

(Ger'e), the only member of the Council to be born a citizen of a foreign state, and S.V. Olive: on the latter see Ikonnikov, *Noblesse*, vol. O: 115–17; on Guerrier, see his memoirs in RO, Fond 70, Opis 32, Delo 15, especially here pp. 1–4. A.G. Vlangali and A.S. Kostanda were of Greek origin: on Vlangali see Polovtsov, *Dnevnik*, here II: 351–2; on Kostanda see TsGIA, Fond 1162, Opis 6, Ed. Khr. 251, where his service record states, most unusually, that he was from the Greek nobility; this suggests that his father was probably the first member of his family to come to Russia. Baron I.O. Velho was the grandson of a Portuguese banker and the son of a full general who was the palace commandant at Tsarskoe Selo. Dolgorukov, *Rodoslovnaya kniga*, pt. II: 284; *ASRGD*, 124–5.

[21] Admirals F.K. Avelan and O.K. Kremer, Generals Count V.B. Frederycksz, O.K. Grippenberg and A. Roediger, and K.K. Linder.

[22] In a number of cases families immigrated to the Baltic provinces from German communities outside the Empire, stayed in the region for one or two generations, and then moved on to Russia proper. Examples of this are provided by the Terner and Unterberger families: see vol. I, ch. 1, of F.G. Terner, *Vospominaniya zhizni F.G. Ternera*, 2 vols. (SPB, 1910, 1911); also *Deutschbaltisches Biographisches Lexicon* (*DBL*) (Vienna, 1970), 829–30.

[23] The three of which I know are the Heidens (Dolgorukov, *Rodoslovnaya kniga*, pt. III: 104–5), the Kaufmanns (Ikonnikov, *Noblesse*, vol. F: 259–63), and Schaffhausen (ibid., vol. O2: 429–30).

[24] To pick almost at random: the first Härbel (the name was russianized to Gerbel') in Russia was a Swiss architect, the first Gerhard (russianized to Gerard) an architect-cum-communications engineer (*Russkiy biograficheskiy slovar'*, 20 vols. [SPB, 1900–13], here IV: 492–3, 467). Baron A.P. Mohrenheim's grandfather was the 'originally Austrian' court doctor of Catherine II; see Brockhaus and Efron, *Entsiklopedicheskiy slovar'*, here XIX: 845.

[25] For Röhrberg's family see *DBL*, 637.

[26] The best general sources on the Baltic Germans and their nobility are R. Wittram, *Baltische Geschichte, Die Ostseelande. Livland, Estland, Kurland 1180–1918* (Munich, 1954), and A. von Taube, *Die Deutschbalten* (Lüneburg, 1973).

[27] Dolgorukov, *Rodoslovnaya kniga*, pt. III: 179–80, pt. II: 87 respectively, on the Medems and Lievens; *Genealogisches Handbuch des baltischen Ritterschaften* (*GHdbR*), Teil *Estland* (Gorlitz, 1930–6), I: 475, on the Uxkulls.

[28] Ikonnikov, *Noblesse:* vol. I: 1 (Lambsdorff); vol. G: 525 (Korff); *GHdbR*, Teil *Livland* (Gorlitz, 1929–43), II: 643 ff. (Budberg).

[29] Goerlitz stresses this correctly in *Die Junker;* for his relatively brief comments on the Balts, see pp. 18–20, 56, 123–5. 259–60, 339–41.

[30] *GHdbR*, *Estland*, II: 188 (Staal); *Livland*, II: 776 (Rennenkampf).

[31] On the Wahls see *GHdbR*, *Livland*, I: 227–34. Wahl's title of nobility had to be recognized in Russia (as it was in 1816) before he could acquire full proprietorship of estates on which he held mortgages. See Wittram, *Baltische Geschichte*, 209, for Baltic laws on noble estates. The contrast between the agrarian societies described in Schissler, *Preussische Agrargesellschaft*, and Confino, *Domaines et seigneurs*, is considerable.

[32] See Guerrier's service record in TsGIA, Fond 1162, Opis 6, Ed. Khr. 117, p. 129. Guerrier himself was a Protestant.

[33] The three were O.K. Grippenberg, A.F. Roediger and K.K. Linder. The latter was married twice, but only once to a Russian. TsGIA, Fond 1162, Opis 6, Ed. Khr. 152, 445 and 293.

[34] All this information comes from service records. Medem's is in TsGIA, Fond 1162, Opis 6, Ed. Khr. 332. It was possible between 1865 and 1885 for children of mixed marriages to remain Protestant; see Wittram, *Baltische Geschichte*, 185, 217.

[35] The statistics on the Baltic marshals and *Landrats* are drawn from *Spisok litsam*

sluzhashchim po vedomstvu Ministerstva Vnutrennykh Del (SPB, 1914).

[36] The statistics on the imperial population are from J.N. Westwood, *Endurance and Endeavour: Russian History 1812–1980* (Oxford, 1981), 492–5.

[37] Rogovich's service record is in TsGIA, Fond 1162, Opis 6, Ed. Khr. 458, p. 19. See also V.L. Modzalevsky, *Malorossiyskiy rodoslovnik*, 5 vols. (Kiev, 1908–14), here IV: 279–94.

[38] See S.Yu. Witte, *Vospominaniya*, 3 vols. (Moscow, 1960), I: 167–9, 171–4.

[39] One would search in vain in the memoirs of Shebeko's son for any mention of the Ukraine or of Little Russia: N.N. Schebeko, *Souvenirs* (Paris, 1936). On Poltoratsky, see Ikonnikov, *Noblesse*, vol. M: 267–81.

[40] On salaries see in particular *Smeta raskhodov Gosudarstvennogo Soveta na 1909 god*, which I found in the Library of Congress under *Gosudarstvennyy Sovet. Pechatnye materialy* (SPB, 1908). Pensions and, even more, irregular but not uncommon gifts of money to high officials, designed to stave off financial crisis or embarrassment, were decided on a more arbitrary basis than salaries and therefore made officials more dependent on the Emperor's favour. Polovtsov, *Dnevnik*, is an interesting source on this point. His conversation with Alexander III on Valuev's debts is enlightening: see his vol. I: 406.

[41] For aristocratic shareholding see A.M. Anfimov, *Krupnoe pomeshchishchee khozyaystvo evropeyskoy Rossii* (Moscow, 1969), 270–88; Korelin, *Dvoryanstvo*, 101–3, 106–14; L.P. Minarik, *Ekonomicheskaya kharakteristika krupneyshikh zemel'nykh sobstvennikov Rossii kontsa XIX – nachala XXv* (Moscow, 1971). A few archival documents relate to ownership of stocks and bonds; see, e.g., TsGIA, Fond 1650, Opis 1, Ed. Khr. 122, p. 50, for Prince Alexander Obolensky. General Count I.D. Tatishchev, who came from an aristocratic and well-connected family, was educated at the School of Guards Sub-Ensigns, commissioned into the Preobrazhenskys, and whose maternal grandfather was a millionaire businessman, is a striking example of a man who owned no land but must surely have had a private income (Ikonnikov, *Noblesse*, vol. Q1: 101–4). See also, e.g., the letter of A.V. Ivanov's widow dated 26 Feb 1909 to M.G. Akimov for evidence of Ivanov's private means (TsGIA, Fond 1162, Opis 6, Ed. Khr. 207, p. 53). More often Fond 1162 reveals officials' complete dependence on their salaries, though sometimes the men in question belonged to great or well-placed families: see, e.g., M.D. Dmitriev (Ed. Khr. 176, p. 144), Prince M.I. Khilkov (Ed. Khr. 585, p. 63), Count V.N. Lambsdorff (Ed. Khr. 280, p. 41), A.P. Salomon (Ed. Khr. 487, p. 43), N.N. Schreiber (Ed. Khr. 622, p. 144). And see Becker, *Nobility*, 53, for Petersburg nobles' bond- and shareowning.

[42] According to the service records the only men who owned more than one stone house in or near a town were S.M. Dukhovsky, Count V.B. Frederycksz, A.A. Makarov, N.N. Maslov, Count P.A. Shuvalov, and L.P. Sofiano. Anfimov, *Krupnoe*, 276–7, states that Count S.D. Sheremetev and P.P. Durnovo were large urban landowners.

[43] Holding a directorship or founding a company was illegal after 1884 for a high official on active service. Those members of the Council who held directorships were, as far as I have been able to discover, either landowning magnates or officials, usually in the Ministries of Finance or Communications, acting on the government's behalf in private companies in which the state owned shares. In the former category were Prince A.S. Dolgoruky, Prince Alexander Obolensky and Count Aleksei Bobrinsky. Among the latter was D.F. Kobeko. Korelin, *Dvoryanstvo*, 102–3, discusses this point. Kokovtsov writes that Witte wanted, while a member of the State Council, to become an adviser to the Russian Bank for Foreign Trade at a salary of 75,000 roubles a year plus a share in the bank's profits. He needed permission for this step, which was refused since 'his acceptance would be a direct violation of the law'; see V.N. Kokovtsov, *Out of my Past. The Memoirs*

of Count Kokovtzov (Stanford, Calif., 1935), 331.

[44] The two novelists were Prince D.P. Golitsyn and V.P. Cherevansky; A.P. Nikol'sky was probably the most consistent 'journalist'. On the latter see Levinson, *Pravitel'stvuyushchiy Senat*, 73–4. According to the same source (pp. 17–18), Cherevansky donated 10,000 roubles 'of his limited means' to scholarships at establishments of higher education to celebrate his fiftieth anniversary in the state's service.

[45] *GHdbR, Livland*, I: 232–4, for Wahl. For Verkhovsky see Ikonnikov, *Noblesse*, vol. S1: 134–6, 144. It would be tedious to list (even if one could find out) all the members of the Council who themselves owned no land but whose brothers possessed estates. The list would include N.N. Shipov, whose brother Dimitri was the well-known Moscow zemstvo activist; S.D. Sazonov (whose wife, however, owned land); and A.A. Polivanov. The father of V.N. Kokovtsov undertook to support his son during his lengthy training for a university post, but the father's sudden death forced Kokovtsov to join the civil service instead; see CUBA, V.N. Kokovtsov MSS: 'Vospominaniya', pp. 256, 265.

[46] Anfimov, *Krupnoe*, 345, writes that hereditary nobles sold land at a rate of 700,000 *ds.* per year between 1895 and 1905, and 1.5 million *ds.* in the seven subsequent years. In the latter period 34.7 per cent of this land was bought by other hereditary nobles.

[47] T. Shanin, *The Awkward Class* (Oxford, 1972). Shanin's thesis, derived from Chayanov, is that peasant landholding was determined by the peasant family's life-cycle, in other words by how many mouths a family had to feed and how many arms it could mobilize for labour in the fields.

[48] E.g., Peter Saburov, who in 1908 is recorded as owning 470 *ds.* of inherited land in Tambov; in 1895 Saburov, a member of an ancient landowning family, had 5,800 *ds.* Some of this land may of course have been sold; but it is surely suspicious that in 1908 at least one of Saburov's sons was a landowner and

marshal of the nobility. See *spiski* for 1895 and 1908 and Ikonnikov, *Noblesse*, vol. O: 126. There is an even greater variation in the statistics given by the *spiski* for A.N. Kulomzin's landowning between 1881 and 1914. Kulomzin himself complained in 1909 that the 1908 *spisok* was inaccurate, since he had in fact sold 4,000 *ds.* and given even more to his two sons. See TsGIA, Fond 1162, Opis 6, Ed. Khr. 269, for a letter from the State Chancellery to the Civil Service Inspectorate dated 17 Jan 1909. Prince Aleksei Dimitrievich Obolensky, on the other hand, owned only 1,400 *ds.* in Kaluga in 1900, subsequently inheriting another 3,400 *ds.* in Saratov from his mother: see the *spisok* for 1908 and Ikonnikov, *Noblesse*, vol. K: 567.

[49] P.M. Kaufmann was the man in question. His service record is in TsGIA, Fond 1162, Opis 6, Ed. Khr. 228.

[50] None figure on Anfimov's list of great landowners.

[51] Figures drawn from N.A. Proskuryakova, 'Razmeshchenie i struktura dvoryanskogo zemlevladeniya evropeyskoy Rossii v kontse XIX – nachale XX veka', *Istoriya CCCP* I (1973), pp. 55–75, here *prilozhenie* 3.

[52] Among these estates were N.I. Shebeko's 15,352 *desyatiny* in Kherson, Prince N.S. Dolgoruky's estate in Tauride (average value per *d.* 150.49 rs.) and the Bobrinsky properties in Kiev.

[53] E.g., S.N. Härbel (Gerbel), who owned 924 *ds.* in Kherson.

[54] E.g., Princess Elizaveta Grigorievna Volkonsky (*née* Volkonsky): see Ikonnikov, *Noblesse*, vol. S2: 398, and TsGIA, Fond 1162, Opis 6, Ed. Khr. 92.

[55] See Anfimov, *Krupnoe*, ch. 3, for a discussion of the various regions; Proskuryakova, 'Razmeshchenie', Table 7, for the distribution of noble land.

[56] E.g., the Tyrtovs' estate in Tver: see ch. 1, n. 45.

[57] *Vsya Rossiya, Russkaya kniga promyshlennosti, torgovli, sel'skogo khozyaystva i administratsii. Adres-kalendar' Rossiyskoy Imperii* (SPB, 1897, 1900), II: 115–352.

[58] Anfimov, *Krupnoe*, 267; M.L. Levinson, *Gosudarstvennyy Sovet* (SPB,

1907; Petrograd, 1915), 72. Minarik, *Ekonomicheskaya*, 111, stresses that, as regards the biggest estates, profits very often came from industrial enterprises rather than agriculture.

[59] The lists are to be found at the front of pt. I of Dolgorukov's *Rodoslovnaya kniga*.

[60] Princes A.S. and N.S. Dolgoruky, D.P. Golitsyn, M.I. Khilkov, A.A. Kurakin, A.B. Lobanov-Rostovsky, Alexander and Aleksei Dimitrievich Obolensky, V.S. Obolensky-Neledinsky-Meletsky, N.V. Repnin, M.S. Volkonsky and L.D. Vyazemsky, together with Count I.D. Tatishchev. All these men and families are covered by Ikonnikov and Dolgorukov with the exception of Prince L.D. Vyazemsky, for whom see ch. 1, n. 13.

[61] A.A. and N.A. Khvostov; A.A. and P.A. Saburov; A.D. Samarin; Count A.P. Ignat'ev; S.A. and Count S.D. Sheremetev. Again, Ikonnikov and Dolgorukov are reliable sources for all these men and families.

[62] *M.N. Anichkov, A.A. and D.S. Arsen'ev, A.S. Bryanchaninov*, S.S. Bekhteev, A.G. Bulygin, *P.N. and P.P. Durnovo*, A.P. and P.P. Izvol'sky, *V.V. Kalachov, P.M. Lazarev*, A.N. Mosolov, S.A. Mordvinov, *Count M.N. Murav'yov, N.A. Myasoedov, A.A. Polivanov*, S.D. Sazonov, N.N. Selifontov, *Count P.A. Shuvalov*. D.S. Sipyagin, *N.N. Sukhotin, A.N. Trubnikov, P.P. Tyrtov, I.F. Tyutchev, Prince B.A. Vasil'chikov, V.V. Verkhovsky, A.D. Zinov'ev, Prince A.A. Shirinsky-Shikhmatov, N.V. Shidlovsky*. It is in tracing the family origins of these men that I had my worst problems. In the case of the 21 names italicized, Ikonnikov was my salvation. The Brockhaus and Efron encyclopaedia contributed the names of two families; *ASRGD*, Levinson and the *Almanach de Saint Petersbourg* one apiece. Four other names came from contemporary memoirs. For the precise page references for all the men and families listed in nn. 60, 61, and 62, see my 'Russian Civil Service', pp. 377–8.

[63] Baron A.A. Budberg, Baron E.F. Hoyningen-Huene, Baron A.F. Korff, Count V.N. Lambsdorff, Prince A.A. Lieven, Count O.L. Medem, Baron E. Yu Nol'de, Baron R.R. Rosen, Barons Alexander and Julius Uxkull von Güldenband, Baron M.A. Taube, Count S.A. Toll. Access to the volumes of the *Genealogisches Handbuch der baltischen Ritterschaften* has led me to alter some of the statements in my article, 'The Russian Civil Service'. Neither the Staals (*GHdbR, Estland*, II: 188–96) nor the Rennenkampfs (*GHdbR, Livland*, II: 776–85) were noble before 1600, though both can trace their origins to the sixteenth century as bourgeois families. I have therefore dropped both families from my list; see 'Russian Civil Service', n. 55. My only other addition to this note concerns the Nol'de family, whose genealogy is to be found in *GHdbR*, Teil *Kurland* (Gorlitz, 1930–44), I: 417–44, Baron E. Yu Nol'de himself emerging on p. 433.

[64] See Ikonnikov, *Noblesse*, vol. P: 541–7. The other old Polish family was that of P.P. Kobylinsky, whose archival *fond* (TsGIA, Fond 961, Opis 1, Delo 2, p. 1) has a note on his family.

[65] Ikonnikov, *Noblesse*, vols. O: 429–31 and F: 259–63, on the Schaffhausens and Kaufmanns respectively. Dolgorukov, *Rodoslovnaya kniga*, pt. III: 103–5, on Count L.L. Heiden.

[66] Romanovich-Slavatinsky, *Dvoryanstvo*, 24.

[67] E. Amburger, *Geschichte der Behordenorganisation Russlands von Peter dem Grossen bis 1917* (Leiden, 1966), 502–19; Meehan-Waters, *Autocracy and Aristocracy*, particularly ch. 2 and conclusion.

[68] Bobrinsky, *Dvoryanskie rody*, II: iii–xlii. On the Stolypins see Ikonnikov, *Noblesse*, vol. P2: 367–75.

[69] E.g., as regards P.A. Krivsky, a thoroughly obscurantist large landowner from Saratov, who was educated at the School of Guards Sub-Ensigns and Cavalry Junkers and commissioned into the Chevaliers Gardes. With this background there are long odds on Krivsky's membership of the gentry family of that name, which goes back to 1619. There were, however, other less ancient gentry families called Krivsky and it is conceiv-

able that he belonged to one of them.

[70] Ikonnikov is once again much the best source: see *Noblesse*, vol. A2: 325–9 (N.P. Balashov); vol. Fl: 141–2 (V.V. Kalachov); vol. H1: 163–81 (A.N. Kulomzin); vol. O2: 461–6 (P.P. Semyonov); vol. Pl: 231–4 (I.G. Shcheglovitov); vol. Y: 91–105 (I.P. and N.N. Shipov); vol. X: 497–503 (N.A. and S.A. Voevodsky). See P. de Gmeline, *Dictionnaire de la noblesse russe* (Paris, 1978), 226 (D.E. and I.E. Shevich); 390 (A.I. Lykoshin); 497 (A.P. Rogovich), for whom see also Modzalevsky, *Malorossiyskiy*, IV: 279–95. For V.N. Kokovtsov see Levinson, *Gosudarstvennyy Sovet* (1915), 52–3 and the first chapter of Kokovtsov's 'Vospominaniya' in CUBA. For Taneev see Stroev, *Stoletie*, 247. For the Stolypins see n. 68. A.P. Strukov was the only man about whose membership of the group I had any doubts. Strukov's family were, however, already great landowners in the eighteenth century, and his brother, educated at the Corps des Pages, was commissioned into the Horse Guards. It would be very surprising therefore if this Strukov family was not the same as the one ennobled in the seventeenth century. See Minarik, *Ekonomicheskaya*, 68; also *ASRGD*, 1215.

[71] The fullest source on this family is D.G. Williamson, *The Counts Bobrinskoy – a Genealogy* (Middlesex, 1962).

[72] *GHdbR, Estland*, II: 188–96.

[73] The group of 85 is made up of old Russian and Baltic nobles plus Count L.L. Heiden and P.M. Kaufmann.

[74] In my article 'The Russian Civil Service' I recorded only 11 barons. Baron E.F. Hoyningen-Huene, whose family received the title nine years before he was born, seems to have been omitted. *GHdbR*, Teil *Oesel* (Dorpat, 1935–9; Hamburg, 1968), 155–64.

[75] Korelin, *Dvoryanstvo*, 31: Thompson, *English Landed Society*, 49–50. In 1883 there were 443 hereditary members of the House of Lords, 7 peeresses in their own right, 38 Scottish peers and 97 Irish peers without British titles.

[76] Minarik, *Ekonomicheskaya*, 19.

[77] A.A. Davydov, *Vospominaniya* (Paris, 1982), 59–70 and 81–91, contains useful information on this branch of the Lieven family. Lieven's extremely rapid rise – e.g., Governor of Moscow aged thirty-two, Assistant Minister aged thirty-three, Minister aged forty – is a reflection, at least to some extent, of his powerful connections.

[78] On the Golitsyns see Ikonnikov, *Noblesse*, vol. D: 518–40. See also D.P. Golitsyn, *V Peterburge* (SPB, 1892).

[79] On Budberg see *GHdbR, Livland*, II: 643–62. There are only 7 fathers in this group of 8 because it includes the Uxkull-Güldenbandt brothers, whose father was the lieutenant-general: see *GHdbR, Kurland*, II: 475–520.

[80] The fathers of V.B. Frederycksz (Ikonnikov, *Noblesse*, vol. D: 201–4) and Meller-Zakomel'sky (ibid., vol. J: 164–7) were ADC generals. Mohrenheim's father was ambassador in Constantinople: see Brockhaus and Efron, *Entsiklopedicheskiy slovar'*, XIX: 845. The father of Baron I.O. Velho was a full general and palace commandant: see *ASRGD*, 124–5.

[81] On Kutaysov's family see Ikonnikov, *Noblesse*, vol. H: 247–9.

[82] A.A. Shirinsky-Shikhmatov was descended from a Crimean noble who entered the Russian service in the sixteenth century. Although his father was a senator, none of his other forebears was particularly distinguished, and his family history is more that of the gentry than of the aristocratic élite. Shirinsky-Shikhmatov's grandfather owned only 113 serfs, and he himself inherited no land. See Ikonnikov, *Noblesse*, vol. E: 241–9, and TsGIA, Fond 1162, Opis 6, Ed. Khr. 1278 (service record).

[83] See the lists in the appendices to Crummey, *Aristocrats and Servitors*, and Meehan-Waters, *Autocracy and Aristocracy*. It is easy at this level of the Russian nobility to trace such men's ancestors through either Ikonnikov or Dolgorukov.

[84] For the sources on these four men's families see n. 80. Velho and Mohrenheim were both the third generation of their family in Russia, each generation having produced very prominent figures.

The founder of the Meller-Zakomel'sky family's fortunes, an artillery general, was created a baron in 1789 and killed the following year. One of his sons was an ADC general and another a General of Artillery and Minister of War. The generation of A.N. Meller-Zakomel'sky's grandfather produced no major figures, but not only A.N. Meller-Zakomel'sky's father but also his brother were generals. Apart from Ikonnikov, Dolgorukov, *Rodoslovnaya kniga*, pt. II: 283–4, discusses this family. Vladimir Frederycksz's father and all three of his uncles were generals, one of the latter also being an ADC general. Frederycksz's grandfather was a brigadier, his great-grandfather being a banker granted a barony. Ikonnikov, *Noblesse*, vol. D: 199–204.

[85] Ikonnikov, *Noblesse*, vol. V2: 547–9. Of the four sons of F.F. Trepov the elder, three became members of the State Council and one was Commandant of the Palace and a close adviser to Nicholas II. Of Trepov's five daughters, two married counts Nieroth, one married a Hofmeister and senator and one married Frederycksz's deputy, General A.A. Mosolov. Two of Trepov's sons-in-law held important posts at court.

[86] On Salomon's family see TsGIA, Fond 1162, Opis 6, Ed. Khr. 487. After A.P. Salomon's death Prince Alexander of Oldenburg praised the dead man's 'outstanding natural gifts, a rare degree of erudition' and also his 'lively and sympathetic nature'. He wrote to the chairman of the State Council about the Salomon family's 'still very unstable financial position, since the dead man maintained his family only on what he earned through service and could not have left any capital or valuable property' (p. 43). See also *ASRGD*, 68, 1198.

[87] *Annuaire de la Noblesse de Russie*, 3ᵉ Année (1900), 91–5; *Russkiy biograficheskiy slovar'*, II: 630–3; *ASRGD*, 155–6; *Almanach de Saint Petersbourg* (1910), 34. Bezak's eldest son married the daughter of General N.N. Shipov, one of the 215 members of the State Council.

[88] On the Kharitonovs and Kaufmanns see Levinson, *Gosudarstvennyy*

Sovet (1915), 104; TsGIA, Fond 1162, Ed. Khr. 582, p. 319; and Ikonnikov, *Noblesse*, vol. F: 259–63. The Kaufmanns were an old Austrian noble family but started again more or less from scratch after breaking their links with their homeland and entering the Russian service nobility.

[89] See Brockhaus and Efron, *Entsiklopedicheskiy slovar'*, XXII: 588–9, for the Corps des Pages; XVII: 859–60 for the Alexander Lycée; and XXIV: 922–3 on the School of Law. The Lycée's requirements not only fluctuated across the years but also differed as regards various categories of students. In 1847, for instance, most boys had to be the sons of colonels or civil counsellors, or to stem from families entered in the fifth (titled nobles) or sixth (nobles belonging to families ennobled before 1685) sections of the provincial noble registers. On the other hand, half the scholarships which enabled boys to attend the Lycée free of charge were reserved for sons of major-generals, rear admirals, senior civil counsellors or above. See I. Seleznev, *Istoricheskiy ocherk Imperatorskogo byvshego Tsarskosel'skogo, nyne Aleksandrovskogo litseya za pervoe ego pyatidesyatiletie s 1811 po 1861 god* (SPB, 1861), 420–3. According to K.K. Arsen'ev, the School of Law's requirements were the same as the Lycée's, but most of the boys did not come from rich or prominent, let alone aristocratic, families. See K.K. Arsen'ev, 'Vospominaniya Konstantina Konstantinovicha Arsen'eva ob Uchilishche Pravovedeniya 1849–1855 gg', *RS* 50 (1886), pp. 199–220, here p. 219. The School of Guards Sub-Ensigns and Cavalry Junkers (reconstituted as the Nicholas Cavalry School in 1864) was extremely expensive, especially for cadets destined for the cavalry. See V. Potto, *Istoricheskiy ocherk Nikolaevskogo Kavaleriyskogo Uchilischa 1827–1873* (SPB, 1873), 105, 163. According to cadets present in the school in the late 1840s, the boys were almost all well off, often rich, and drawn much more from old landowning families than from service families. See Anon., 'Shkola Gvardeyskikh Podpraporshchikov i Yunkerov v vospominaniyakh

odnogo iz eya vospitannikov', *RS* 41, (1884), pp. 203–16 and 441–54, here p. 205. Also Semyonov, *Detstvo i yunost'*, 161.

[90] Among the many memoirs of life in the Guards regiments, those by Count A.A. Ignat'ev, who subsequently became a Soviet general, are among the most amusing. For all his inevitable bias, a good deal of nostalgia shines through. See Ignatiev, *Subaltern*, esp. 14 and 66. Entry into one of the four regiments depended above all on the wishes of the colonel and officers of the unit in question. As Ignat'ev rightly stresses, service in one of these regiments was a tradition in many great families. Between 1829 and 1908, 11 Sheremetevs, 9 Arapovs, 7 Hendrikovs, 6 Zvegintsevs, 7 Rodzyankos, 5 Gagarins, 5 Pashkovs, 5 Kurakins and 4 Shebekos served in the Chevaliers Gardes. See S. Panchulidzev, *Sbornik biografiy Kavalergardov, 1826–1908* (SPB, 1908), here Table of Contents.

[91] The three are P.A. Krivsky, S.V. Markov and A.I. Panteleev.

[92] Once again, P.A. Krivsky and A.I. Panteleev are the two possible additions to this total.

[93] Polovtsov, *Dnevnik*, II: 381–2.

[94] See Preradovich, *Führungsschichten*, 3–74, for what is almost a hymn of hate towards the Austrian aristocracy for its failure to participate in politics, the bureaucracy, the army or even diplomacy. The indictment is exaggerated because Preradovich is so exacting and so obsessed with genealogy that for him the category 'Austrian' becomes distinctly limited – amazingly, he defines the Habsburgs as non-Austrian and the Hohenzollerns as non-Prussian because of the ultimate origins of the two families. Gollwitzer argues that the Austrian aristocracy was very exclusive but not entirely inactive. See esp. pp. 304–6, 317–21, 334–6, in H. Gollwitzer, *Die Standesherren. Die politische und gesellschaftliche Stellung der Mediatisierten. 1815–1918* (Stuttgart, 1957). He prints on pp. 389–92 an attack on the aristocracy by Karl Menger and Crown Prince Rudolph entitled 'Die Lebensweise und die Soziale

Gewohnheiten unserer Aristokraten'.

[95] Prince A.B. Lobanov-Rostovsky and Count Alexander Bobrinsky.

[96] The memoirs of Princess Radzivill, alias Count Paul Vasili, provide useful insights into Petersburg high society: see *La Société de Saint Petersbourg* (Paris, 1886).

[97] Ikonnikov, *Noblesse*, vol. C: 89–91.

[98] Vasili, *Société*, 215–16.

[99] The *Almanach de Saint Petersbourg* for 1909–13 lists the Club's members. By 1913 the Shebekos were full members of the Russian aristocracy, and both N.I. Shebeko's sons, one an ambassador, the other a general, became members of the Club. So did the son of P.A. Saburov, who was the son-in-law of Count S.D. Sheremetev, and those of P.M. Lazarev.

[100] Gollwitzer, *Standesherren*, 259–62. He states, however, that in practice quite a number of *Standesherren* did marry wealthy non-nobles. One must, of course, remember that not all German great nobles were *Standesherren*, i.e. formerly sovereign but now mediatized princes and counts.

[101] Stolypin's social status is, for instance, shown not only by the fact that he was the son of an ADC general, a considerable landowner, and a member of an old noble family, but also through his connections: the mother-in-law of Count S.D. Sheremetev and D.S. Sipyagin was a first cousin of Stolypin's father, and another of Marie Arkad'evna Stolypin's daughters married the brother of Count V.N. Lambsdorff. Ikonnikov, *Noblesse*, vol. P: 369–71; vol. I: 8–9.

[102] Aleksei Bobrinsky's brother Andrei was an elected member. On Polovtsov and his wife see the introduction by P.A. Zayonchkovsky to Polovtsov's published diary, *Dnevnik*, I, esp. pp. 6–8.

[103] The four members of the group of 'magnates' not included in Table N were all in some way related. L.D. Vyazemsky's daughter married Boris Vasil'chikov's first cousin. A.A. Kurakin married a Princess Volkonsky, a distant cousin of M.S. Volkonsky. Prince M.S. Volkonsky himself not merely married a Princess Volkonsky but was also a first

cousin of Prince N.V. Repnin. To confuse matters utterly, not merely was Repnin himself really a Volkonsky, his great-grandfather Volkonsky having married the last Repnin heiress, he also married a Princess Volkonsky. As one might imagine, attempting to trace relationships in the huge Volkonsky family is a nightmare. See Ikonnikov, *Noblesse*, vol. S., and Dolgorukov, *Rodoslovnaya kniga*, pt. I.

[104] Vasili, *Société*, 246–8.

[105] Repnin and his wife together seem only to have owned 6,500 *ds.* by the early twentieth century, but by then their son and daughter already owned *c.* 6,800 *ds.* in their own right. Their daughter married Duke George of Leuchtenberg, a distant relative of the Romanovs. Ikonnikov, *Noblesse*, vol. S2: 397–8. Svyatopolk-Mirsky and his wife owned over 7,000 *desyatiny* of land, mostly in provinces where land prices were high. Their connections are evident from Table N. Svyatopolk-Mirsky was in addition a page, an officer of the Emperor's Own Life Guard Hussar Regiment, a junior ADC to Alexander II, and an ADC general. His service record is in TsGIA, Fond 1284, Opis 52, Ed. Khr. 77, p. 33.

[106] See Ikonnikov, *Noblesse*, vol. Z: 1–3 (Akimov); vol. Y: 197–200 (Goncharov); vol. E: 169–71. (Goremykin); vol. V: 249–50 (Gudim-Levkovich); vol. M: 267–81 (Poltoratsky); vol. B: 577–9 (Shebeko); vol. O: 579–80 (Sofiano); vol. Q: 535–6 (Timashev). The Poltoratsky, Shebeko and Sofiano families were Ukrainian in origin. For Ganetsky see *Russkiy biograficheskiy*, vol. Gaag-Gerbel: 211–13, where the life and background of General Ivan Stepanovich Ganetsky is described. N.S. Ganetsky has the same patronymic, and was born five years subsequently (he is referred to as Ganetsky 2, his putative brother being called Ganetsky 1); both men were educated at the First Cadet Corps, commissioned into the Finland Guards and stemmed from the Smolensk landed nobility. It would be a tremendous coincidence if they were not brothers. On Makhotin see *ASRGD*, 1,000. For Sukhomlinov's

family, see V.A. Sukhomlinov, *Vospominaniya* (Berlin, 1924), ch. 1. Gmeline, *Dictionnaire*, 286, dates the Gudim-Levkovich family back to the fifteenth century, but Ikonnikov states that P.K. Gudim-Levkovich's ancestors only go back to the 1700s.

[107] *Russkiy biograficheskiy*, vol. Gaag-Gerbel: 482–5, 492–4, contains a full account of the Härbel family's activities in the eighteenth and nineteenth centuries.

[108] Dmitriev was the son of a chancellery official (TsGIA, Fond 1162, Opis 6, Ed. Khr. 357, p. 20). Witte describes S.V. Rukhlov as being of 'simple peasant origin' (*Vospominaniya*, I: 260), but Rukhlov's service record says he was the son of a junior-ranked official (Provincial Secretary), and that he had inherited 636 *desyatiny* – though admittedly in Vologda, where land was only worth 13.02 roubles per *d.* in 1905. See TsGIA, Fond 1162, Opis 6, Ed. Khr. 480.

[109] The service record will often merely record that a man was the son of a commissioned officer – e.g., as regards N.P. Bogolepov (TsGIA, Fond 733, Opis 122, Ed. Khr. 961), who, however, by the sound of his name seems likely to have sprung from a clerical family. S.S. Manukhin (TsGIA, Fond 1162, Opis 6, Ed. Khr. 314) was the son of a 'personal noble'. K.P. Yanovsky was another 'commissioned officer's son'; see TsGIA, Fond 1162, Opis 6, Ed. Khr. 638. N.N. Pokrovsky was the son of a Senior Civil Counsellor; see TsGIA, Fond 1162, Opis 6, Ed. Khr. 424.

[110] TsGIA, Fond 1162, Opis 6, Ed. Khr. 475.

[111] TsGIA, Fond 1162, Opis 6, Ed. Khr. 417.

[112] Koni's service record says he was the son of a junior ranked official (Collegiate Counsellor); see TsGIA, Fond 1162, Opis 6, Ed. Khr. 244. His father's non-official career is described in *Russkiy biograficheskiy*, vol. Kna-Ku: 104–8.

[113] Nikol'sky was the son of a priest and himself a journalist; see TsGIA, Fond 1162, Opis 6, Ed. Khr. 365, and Levinson, *Gosudarstvennyy Sovet* (1915), 70–1. See, for Tagantsev, TsGIA, Fond

1162, Opis 6. Ed. Khr. 526, and N.S. Tagantsev, *Perezhitoe* (Petrograd, 1919), 4–6; Tagantsev's father was a *meshchanin* who inscribed himself as a 3rd guild merchant to save his son from having to do 25 years' military service (required of the sons of peasants and *meshchane* in the era before Alexander II's reforms). On Pikhno, see TsGIA, Fond 1162, Opis 6, Ed. Khr. 415, p. 33, and Witte, *Vospominaniya*, I: 167–9. Zverev (TsGIA, Fond 1162, Opis 6, Ed. Khr. 200) was, according to V.I. Gurko, *Features and Figures of the Past* (Stanford, Calif., 1939), 188–9, educated at the expense of a local landowner. Gurko calls Zverev a peasant, but his service record says he was a *meshchanin*.

[114] Ikonnikov, *Noblesse*, vol. Y: 197–201.

[115] The Kobeko family is an example of the latter. Interestingly, D.F. Kobeko, son of a new noble of modest status and only relatively senior rank, was able to attend the Alexander Lycée. *Russkiy biograficheskiy*, vol. Kna-Kyu: 19.

[116] Krivoshein, *Krivoshein*, ch. 1.

[117] N.N. Schreiber and F.G. Terner, for instance, were the sons of doctors, P.F. Unterberger the son of a vet. See TsGIA, Fond 1162, Opis 6, Ed. Khr. 622, p. 116 (Schreiber); Terner, *Vospominaniya*, I: ch. 1; *DBL*, 830 (Unterberger).

[118] Ikonnikov, *Noblesse*, vol. Bl: 103–4; *Russkiy biograficheskiy*, vol. Be-Bya: 111–12.

[119] On Bobrikov's family see Ikonnikov; on his career see TsGIA, Fond 1162, Opis 6, Ed. Khr. 43. The Grand Duke Vladimir, GOC of the Guards, was Bobrikov's most important patron; see, e.g., A.V. Bogdanovich, *Tri poslednikh samoderzhavtsa* (Moscow, 1924), here 81, 220. In 1902, recording that Hesse, the Palace Commandant, had pushed Bobrikov's candidature for the post of Minister of Internal Affairs, Polovtsov wrote: 'This wild, in every sense sordid non-commissioned officer, to Finland's misfortune, remains her tormentor; probably not for long'. Bobrikov was assassinated two years later.

[120] On the Zinov'ev family see Ikonnikov, *Noblesse*, vol. T2: 391–3; *ASRGD*, 659–61.

[121] The only exception was Count A.P. Ignat'ev, who acquired 11 points. Though far poorer than my 'aristocratic magnates', Ignat'ev had been at the 'right' school and in the 'right' regiment, and, above all, possessed exceptionally powerful parents and relatives. His family indeed stood at the centre of Russian politics from the 1870s until the Revolution. Nevertheless, according to Vasili (*Société*, 213), in the 1880s the Ignat'evs still lacked the right of entry into the exclusive Petersburg drawing rooms of my 'aristocratic magnates'. I have arbitrarily reduced Ignatev's total to 9 points because his social status and even his connections were distinctly inferior to those of my landowning magnates.

[122] I was wrong to suggest in my article, 'The Russian Ruling Élite under Nicholas II. Career Patterns', *CMRS* 25 (1984), no. 4, pp. 429–54, that soldiers and civilians were almost equally likely to be landowners; since writing that article I have discovered a number of 'concealed' civilian landowners.

[123] The source of virtually all my information on careers is the service records.

[124] There was a strong tendency for the technical branches to be filled by those who passed out with the best marks from their cadet corps, many of whom later entered the various higher military academies. See, e.g., Ignatiev, *Subaltern*, 40–1, 102–3. On various élites within the army see 'Osnovy podgotovki komandnogo sostava armii', in P.P. Ryabushinsky, ed., *Velikaya Rossiya*, 2 vols. (Moscow, 1910–11), I: 188–93, II: 155–73.

[125] See my 'Russian Civil Service', n. 43. The statistics on generals in 1908 were derived from *Spisok generalam po starshinstvu* (SPB, 1908).

[126] In the military group 3 men had entered service in one of the four most exclusive Guards regiments, 12 in other Guards units and 17 in units of the line. The relevant numbers for the civilian group were 12, 5 and 9.

[127] Mayzel, 'Russian General Staff',

passim.

[128] The officers of the Border Guards (which came under the jurisdiction of the Ministry of Finance), Gendarme officers and governors were all much better paid, e.g., than army officers of equivalent rank. P.A. Zayonchkovsky, *Samoderzhavie i russkaya armiya na rubezhe XIX–XX stoletiy* (Moscow, 1973), 219–24; A.P. Martynov, *Moya sluzhba v otdel'nom korpuse zhandarmov* (Stanford, Calif., 1972), 7, 16, 214.

[129] TsGIA, Fond 1162, Opis 6, Ed. Khr. 252.

[130] TsGIA, Fond 1162, Opis 6, Ed. Khr.

[131] On the extent to which the army's energy was absorbed in self-administration, see J. Bushnell, *Mutiny and Repression: Russian Soldiers in the Revolution of 1905* (1985).

[132] Lobko's service record is in TsGIA, Fond 1162, Opis 6, Ed. Khr. 298. See also Polovtsov's comments in *Dnevnik*, ??: 211–12, and in 'Iz dnevnika A.A. Polovtsova', *KA* 3 (1923), pp. 100–1; and Witte's comments in *Vospominaniya*, II: 150.

[133] According to G.M. Hamburg, 'Portrait of an Élite: Russian Marshals of the Nobility 1861–1917', *SR* 40 (1981), p. 67, in 1895 22 provincial marshals for whom evidence exists owned on average 5,500 *desyatiny*, 125 district marshals averaging 3,500 *desyatiny*. The Council's 18 former district marshals averaged 10,058 *desyatiny*, the 16 provincial marshals 36,241 *desyatiny*. These averages are a little deceptive, since they are inflated by the colossal estates of a handful of individuals. Even so the median figures for the district and provincial marshals are 5,700 *desyatiny* and 14,528 *desyatiny* respectively. The zemstvos at the turn of the century were dominated by men owning between 500 and 5,000 *desyatiny*.

[134] The provincial marshals were elected at an average age of thirty-seven and served an average term of 12 years. All but one of these men had considerable service experience prior to their election as provincial marshals. The exception was A.D. Samarin, who after finishing his compulsory service in the army had been active only in local affairs (e.g., as a land commandant). TsGIA, Fond 1162, Opis 6, Ed. Khr. 489.

[135] On the marshals see Hamburg, 'Portrait of an Elite'; also Korelin, *Dvoryanstvo*, 220–34. Marshals, for instance, held officials' ranks (*chin*).

[136] Bobrinsky, Krivsky, Arsen'ev and Ekesparre are all discussed in ch. 5, q.v.

[137] This reflects the ministry's importance and the scale of its activities. These were so broad that *Novoe Vremya* in 1915 claimed that the ministry 'directs the course of almost the whole of Russian life' (28 Sept 1915, p. 3).

[138] On the contrasts between the centre and the provinces, see the comments of the Peretz Commission on civil service reform (TsGIA, Fond 1200, Opis 16ii, Ed. Khr. 1 & 2, pp. 12–13); also the comments of V.N. Kokovtsov (ibid., p. 771) and of A.N. Kulomzin (p. 668.)

[139] Their service records are in TsGIA, Fond 1162, Opis 6, Ed. Khr. 204 (Zinov'ev) and 458 (Rogovich).

[140] Most of the vice-governors were ex-marshals and officers. Of the 27 marshals, for instance, 16 (59.3 per cent) subsequently served as vice-governors or governors.

[141] Many of the officers were present or former imperial aides-de-camp.

[142] Five men (of whom two were judicial officials) had been serving in other ministries.

[143] See nn. 12 and 14 above.

[144] Four governors became assistant ministers, 10 headed departments, etc., of the Ministry of Internal Affairs, 8 became senators and 6 were appointed straight to the State Council. Both Alexander III and Nicholas strongly approved of having former governors in the Council, which explains in part why there were so many of them.

[145] See Maklakov's comments about his appointment as minister in *Padenie tsarskogo rezhima*, 7 vols. (Leningrad, 1925), III: 85–6.

[146] It is worth remembering that some officials switched departments more than once.

[147] So too was S.E. Kryzhanovsky,

who also made this move. See his comments in *Vospominaniya* (Berlin, n.d. [1938]), 28.

[148] See, e.g., Anon. ('P.T.'), *Obshchestvennoe vospitanie i obrazovanie v Rossii: zapiski ob Uchilishche Pravovedeniya* (SPB, 1869), xvi–xvii. RO, Fond 126, K. 11, p. 39 (Kireev's diaries).

[149] See D. Christian, 'The Supervisory Function in Russian and Soviet History', *SR* 41 (1982).

[150] On this first generation of judicial officials A.F. Koni, *Otsy i dety sudebnoy reformy* (SPB, 1914), is very useful. So too is the correspondence between A.N. Kulomzin and his friend A. Popov from the late 1850s and early 1860s. This correspondence expresses well an idealistic young man's disgust with the existing civil service and his hope that the reform of the judiciary will provide an opening for young men of his type. TsGIA, Fond 1642, Opis 1, Ed. Khr. 178, pp. 2, 3, 7.

[151] Gurko, *Features and Figures*, 178.

[152] RO, Fond 178, Opis 1, Karton 9803, Ed. Khr. 3, p. 6.

[153] A typical instance was when Prince Alexander Obolensky (himself a 'jurist'), looking for a candidate to appoint as head of chancellery to the Governor-General of Poland, wrote to his wife, 'I'll search in the judicial department and I want to write to Kapnist so that he can recommend someone to me'. TSGIA, Fond 1650, Opis 1, Ed. Khr. 242, p. 67 (a letter to Anna Obolensky from the late 1890s).

[154] See also Kryzhanovsky, *Vospominaniya*, 28.

[155] The Committee of Ministers was abolished in 1905. The newly created Council survived until 1917. Both were designed to provide top-level co-ordination of the executive branch of government, but the Council had more teeth.

[156] This is especially true since, firstly, the statistics include officials belonging to the administration of the Empress Marie's institutions; and, secondly, those working closest to the monarch ought to have had a better than normal chance of securing appointment to the State Council.

[157] N.M. Korkunov, *Russkoe gosudarstvennoe pravo*, 2 vols. (SPB, 1901), 94; Yaney, *Systematization*, 257–8.

[158] Ivone Kirkpatrick, *The Inner Circle* (London, 1959), x.

[159] For the five men's service records see respectively TsGIA, Fond 1162, Opis 6, Ed. Khr. 582 (Kharitonov), 119 (Uxkull), 371 (Nolde), 449 (Rennenkampf), 88 (Voevodsky).

[160] Twenty-two transfers were divided equally among the ministries of Justice, Internal Affairs and Finance, 8 among all other government departments. In addition, 11 officials from the chancelleries were promoted thence to the State Council.

[161] Gurko, *Features and Figures*, 29; N.P. Eroshkin, *Istoriya gosudarstvennykh uchrezhdeniy Rossii do velikoy oktyabrskoy sotsialisticheskoy revolyutsii* (Moscow, 1965), 241–3.

[162] Cherevansky's service record is in TsGIA, Fond 1162, Opis 6, Ed. Khr. 597.

[163] See, e.g., Ya. I. Livshin: 'K voprosu o voenno-promyshlennykh monopoliyakh v Rossii v nachale xx veka', *Voprosy istorii* 7(1957), pp. 55–70; 'Predstavitel'nye organizatsii krupnoy burzhuazii', *Istoriya CCCP* 3/11 (1959), pp. 95–1117.

[164] See, for instance, Witte's memorandum of early 1895 on this issue in TsGIA, Fond 1200, Opis 16/i, Delo 2, pp. 54–8. Kokovtsov's comments are in his thoughts on the recommendations of the Peretz Commission on civil service reform, also in Fond 1200, Opis 16/ii, Ed. Khr. 1 and 2, pp. 747–83.

[165] Service records in TsGIA, Fond 1162, Opis 6, respectively Ed. Khr. 242 (Kokovtsov), 424 (Pokrovsky), 81 (Verkhovsky), 338 (Mordvinov), 614 (Shipov).

[166] See D.C.B. Lieven, 'Russian Senior Officialdom under Nicholas II: Careers and Mentalities', *JfGO* 32 (1984), no. 2, p. 216.

[167] Prince A.A. Kurakin worked off and on as an unpaid special-duties official in the department of State Properties in the 1870s and 1880s, and became a member of the ministerial Council in 1899.

But Kurakin, a landowning magnate who devoted most of his time to running his own huge estates, was in no sense a genuine full-time official. TsGIA, Fond 1162, Opis 6, Ed. Khr. 272 has his service record.

[168] I feel J.A. Armstrong, in *European Administrative Elite*, 176 ff., exaggerates the prestige and significance of transport engineers before 1917. There is of course absolutely no comparison with their role in the Soviet élite.

[169] Of the 6 Ministers of Education among the 215, 3 were professors, 1 was a 'jurist', 1 was a chancellery official and 1 was a general. The latter 2 had some experience in running educational institutions outside the Ministry of Education. Drafting in these men may suggest that the Emperor and those from whom he took advice lacked confidence in the department's own officials. A.N. Schwartz, for instance, complained to Nicholas II that the talented officials in his ministry were almost all 'Kadet either by conviction or by imitation'; RO, Fond 338, Opis 3, Delo 2, p. 15.

[170] See my *Russia and the Origins of the First World War*, ch. 4, sec. 2.

[171] Service records in TsGIA, Fond 1162, Opis 6, Ed. Khr. 181 and 626 respectively.

[172] For Lambsdorff's and Obolensky-Neledinsky-Meletsky's service records, see TsGIA, Fond 1162, Opis 6, Ed. Khr. 280 and 376 respectively. I.V. Bestuzhev, *Bor'ba v Rossii po voprosam vneshney politiki 1906–10* (Moscow, 1961), writes that men generally served their whole careers either in Petersburg or abroad. The same was true of the British Foreign Office in those days; see Steiner, *Foreign Office*, 16–23, 167–70, 185.

[173] I have included the Imperial Secretary (*Gosudarstvennyy Sekretar'*) and the Secretary to the Committee/Council of Ministers among the ministers. They were formally speaking, members of the bodies they served.

[174] E.g., V.B. Frederycksz, who served longest (20 years), and A.N. Kulomzin second longest (19 years). No one else came near this length of time in office.

[175] I have not yet mentioned the Council's 11 admirals. They were all specialists whose careers were spent within the navy, though F.V. Dubasov played a role in suppressing the Moscow uprising in 1905 and D.S. Arsen'ev was tutor for a time to the Grand Duke Serge and his brother Paul.

[176] See, e.g., W.B. Lincoln: 'The Ministers of Alexander II', *CMRS* 17 (1976); 'Ministers of Nicholas I'.

CHAPTER 3

[1] A small number of individuals attended both a cadet corps and, e.g., a university. P.P. Semyonov was an example.

[2] Orlovsky, 'Ministry', p. 264, suggests this connection.

[3] The only full study of the noble family is J. Tovrov, *Action and Affect in the Russian Noble Family from the Late Eighteenth Century Through the Reform Period* (Ph. D. diss., Univ. of Chicago, 1980). See also Manning, *Crisis*, 39–43, for a brief discussion of the subject. Many of the ideas discussed in following paragraphs are covered by Tovrov. Even more came from the outstanding work of Heinz Reif, *Westfälischer Adel*, whose discussion of changing upbringing, education and mentality in the Westphalian gentry up to 1860 is of exceptional interest.

[4] Tovrov, *Action*, 168–70, stresses that actual physical violence, beating, etc., was not encouraged, as it was in some other European societies.

[5] This is a major theme in Reif's *Adel*. Interestingly, as a study of the family histories of the Prussian gentry reveals, the East Elbian gentry was closer to Russia than to Westphalia in this respect.

[6] Ch. 7 of Tovrov, *Action*, and pp. 40–3 of Manning, *Crisis*, discuss the impact of some of the changes in child-rearing in the 1850s and 1860s.

[7] See Reif, *Adel*, 166ff.

[8] *Grazhdanin* (SPB), no. 22 (20 June 1910), pp. 5–7. 'Vol'nyy' was the newspaper's most intelligent occasional columnist.

[9] Terner, *Vospominaniya*, I: 2, 5.

[10] The paragraphs on Mosolov are based on the first section of his memoirs, 'Kratkoe zhizneopisanie Aleksandra Nikolaevicha Mosolova (1844–1865). Vospominaniya', contained in two exercise books in RO, Fond 514, Karton 1, Ed. Khr. 4.

[11] Among the unpublished memoirs of Council members only those of A.N. Mosolov, A.N. Trubnikov, A.N. Kulomzin, I.P. Balashov and V.N. Kokovtsov discuss their childhood, and all lost at least one parent before they were grown – although admittedly Mosolov was seventeen when his father died. Of the published memoirs, only those of Terner, Semyonov and V.I. Mamantov say anything at all about childhood. Of these three men, Semyonov effectively lost both parents and Terner one, while even Mamantov's father only survived until the age of forty-seven, when his twenty-three-year-old son was on the point of entering the civil service.

[12] See the first 146 pages of Semyonov's autobiography, *Detstvo*.

[13] See the first, unpublished, volume of Kokovtsov's memoirs in CUBA, 'Vospominaniya detstva i litseyskoy pory grafa V.N. Kokovtsova', esp. the first 100 pages.

[14] Major-General Lalaev, *Istoricheskiy ocherk voenno-uchebnykh zavedeniy* (SPB, 1880), 129; the same point is made by M. Maksimovsky, *Istoricheskiy ocherk razvitiya glavnogo inzhenernego uchilishcha 1819–1869* (SPB, 1869), 117. Alan Sked makes very much the same point in his study of the Wiener Neustadt Academy in this era: *The Survival of the Habsburg Empire; Radetsky, the Imperial Army, and the Class War* (London, 1979), 2–9. Virtually everything Sked says could indeed be applied to the Russian cadet corps of Nicholas I's reign.

[15] The fullest study of Nicholas's cadet corps is the multi-volume work by Colonel N. Mel'nitskoy, *Sbornik svedeniy o voenno-uchebnykh zavedeniyakh Rossii*, 4 vols. (SPB, 1857–60); see esp. II: pt. 3, pp. 8–13, 66–7, 71–80; pt. 4, pp. 7, 12, 14, 15, 20, 23–4, 27, 29–31, 109, 149; III: pt. 1, pp. 15–21, 23ff.

Lalaev, *Voenno-uchebnykh*, 6–93.

[16] Mel'nitskoy, *Sbornik*, II: pt. 3, p. 72 (for the formal requirements for entry); pt. 4, pp. 64, 125 (for complaints that illiterates were still entering the Noble Regiment).

[17] Ibid. IV: 95–7, and *prilozhenie*, 1–3.

[18] Lalaev cites Lelyukhin on p. 87 of *Voenno-uchebnykh*. Although D.M. Lyovshin, *Pazheyskiy ego Imperatorskogo Velichestva korpus za sto let* (SPB, 1902), is mostly about the Corps des Pages, pp. 371–97 are an intelligent summary of aspects of cadet corps education under Nicholas I.

[19] Mel'nitskoy, *Sbornik*, III: pt. 2, p. 261.

[20] J.K. Zabel, *Das Preussische Kadettenkorps* (Frankfurt, 1978). See n. 14 for Sked, *Survival*. The memoirs of J. Masters, *Bugles and a Tiger* (London, 1973), say much about the attitudes of Sandhurst in the inter-war years; see esp. p. 4.

[21] On Ignat'ev see Lyovshin, *Pazheyskiy*, 427. See Zabel, *Kadettenkorps*, for the thinking behind this truly totalitarian education. Almost every work on nineteenth-century Russian military education has some references to bullying. On the Artillery School see N. Firsov, 'Novichki', *RS* 116 (1903), pp. 49–59. The Corps des Pages was not far behind. See P.A. Kropotkin, *Zapiski revolyutsionera* (London, 1902), 69–70.

[22] For Lelyukhin see Lalaev, *Voenno-uchebnykh*, 89.

[23] Anon., 'Shkola Gvardeyskikh', esp. pp. 214–16, 443–5.

[24] See, e.g., Lyovshin, *Pazheyskiy*, 433–4, on the fate of some pages in the Nicholas era, particularly under one cruel and incompetent Corps director. Lyovshin is citing here the memoirs of N.A. Borovkov.

[25] RO, Fond 514, Karton 1, Ed. Khr. 4, pp. 14–20.

[26] Lyovshin, *Pazheyskiy*, 529–30.

[27] Maksimovsky, *Ocherk*, 99–102, 119, 150.

[28] Lyovshin cites Denisov's view in *Pazheyskiy*, 386.

[29] Polovtsov, *Dnevnik*, II: 174, 415.

[30] See in particular N. Hans, *The Russian Tradition in Education* (London, 1963), 45-64.

[31] Lalaev, *Voenno-uchebnykh*, 104; Maksimovsky, *Ocherk*, 118-20, 150.

[32] Maksimovsky, *Ocherk*, 128.

[33] Lyovshin, *Pazheyskiy*, 560-4. See also Major-General Lalaev, *Istoricheskiy ocherk obrazovaniya i razvitiya pervogo Moskovskogo kadetskogo korpusa 1778-1878* (SPB, 1878), 109-14.

[34] Lalaev, *Voenno-uchebnykh*, 122-3.

[35] On the educational reforms see esp. ch. 6 of P. Zayonchkovsky, *Voennye reformy 1860-70 godov v Rossii* (Moscow, 1952); also Lalaev, *Voenno-uchebnykh*, 122-5, and Maksimovsky, *Ocherk*, 117-20.

[36] See Zayonchkovsky, *Reformy*, esp. 247-50; Lalaev, *Voenno-uchebnykh*, 245-9; Lyovshin, *Pazheyskiy*, 549-61. See also Zabel, *Kadettenkorps*.

[37] RO, Fond 514, Karton 1, Ed. Khr. 4, pp. 14, 19-20.

[38] Maksimovsky, *Ocherk*, 99.

[39] Lalaev, *Voenno-uchebnykh*, 90, gives the number of cadets per institution for 1854. Since he does not include the artillery and engineering schools, the disproportionate number of pages and graduates of the School of Guards Sub-Ensigns is more striking than ever.

[40] Lyovshin, *Pazheyskiy*, is an excellent source on the Corps; see esp. pp. 405-10, 467-9, 513. On awe at the court, see e.g. the memoirs of A.N. Trubnikov (TsGIA, Fond 1112, Opis 1, Ed. Khr. 5, pp. 4-6) and M.M. Osorgin (RO, Fond 215, Opis 1, Ed. Khr. 6, pp. 187-8). See also Meshchersky's statement in *Grazhdanin*, no. 98 (19 Dec 1902), p. 23.

[41] Lyovshin, *Pazheyskiy*, 437-65; Kropotkin, *Zapiski*, 67-8.

[42] Lyovshin, *Pazheyskiy*, 565-77; Kropotkin, *Zapiski*, 71-109. Osorgin's unpublished memoirs are in RO, Fond 215, Opis 1, Delo 6, pp. 173, 188.

[43] See RO, Fond 514, Karton 1, Ed. Khr. 4, p. 21, where Mosolov records that in 1857 a shift in behaviour occurred after one new boy was cruelly persecuted; his parents intervened and a senior cadet was arrested.

[44] Semyonov, *Detstvo*, 161; Potto, *Ocherk*, 174.

[45] Ibid., 288.

[46] Ibid., 245-307. Semyonov, *Detstvo*, 151-4. TsGAOR, Fond 542, Opis 1, Ed. Khr. 352, p. 105 (Wahl).

[47] For a useful survey, in particular of the government's educational policies, see P.L. Alston, *Education and the State in Tsarist Russia* (Stanford, Calif., 1969). In 1909 Thomas Darlington made an excellent all-round study of Russian education for the British Board of Education, published as *Special Reports on Educational Subjects*, vol. 23: *Education in Russia* (London, 1909). On Nicholas I's gymnasia sections of Besançon, *Éducation et société en Russie*, are extremely useful. On D.A. Tolstoy's gymnasia see A. Sinel, *The Classroom and the Chancellery: State Educational Reform under Count Dmitry Tolstoi* (Cambridge, Mass., 1973).

[48] See in particular Besançon, *Éducation*, 16-40, and Sinel, *Classroom*, 16-17, 154, 173-6 and 197.

[49] General conclusions here are drawn in part from the sources listed in n. 47. See Darlington, *Education*, 70 and 121, for the timetables of Russian gymnasia in 1819 and 1871. A.N. Schwartz is quoted from a private letter in RO, Fond 338, Opis 5, Delo 12, p. 5. His papers convey a good sense of the thinking of senior government officials in the educational sphere; see in particular his memorandum of June 1890 entitled, 'K voprosu ob organizatsii sredno-uchebnykh zavedeniy', in RO, Fond 338, Opis 5, Delo 9; also ibid., Opis 4, Delo 1/3, 'Otchot A.N. Shvartsa o poezdke za-granitsu dlya osmotra sredneuchebnykh zavedeniy Germanii i Frantsii' dated 1894.

[50] Delyanov's comments (TsGIA, Fond 1200, Opis 16ii, Ed. Khr. 1 and 2, p. 434) occur in the midst of a discussion about the links between education and service.

[51] Sinel, *Classroom*, 208, 212.

[52] F. Uspensky, *Petersburgskiy universitet v 1867-71 gg* (Petrograd, 1920), 171-2, blames the classical gymnasia for poisoning pupils' attitude towards edu-

cation, with dire effects subsequently for the universities.

[53] Darlington, *Education*, 78, 363.

[54] V.V. Mavrodin, ed., *Leningradskiy universitet v vospominaniyakh sovremennikov*, vol. I: *Peterburgskiy universitet* (Leningrad, 1963), 119, 120; V.O. Zherebtsov, *Vospominaniya*, 96; F.N. Ustryalov, 'Vospominaniya o S. Peterburgskom Universitete v 1852–1856 godakh', *Istoricheskiy Vestnik* 16 (1884), p. 602; Armstrong, *European*, 165–6; Darlington, *Education*, 100.

[55] Zherebtsov, *Vospominaniya*, 96–7.

[56] Mavrodin, *Leningradskiy*, 68–73, 195–9, 220; P.A. Zayonchkovsky, ed., *Moskovskiy universitet v vospominaniyakh sovremennikov* (Moscow, 1956), 167, 251; Ustryalov, 'Vospominaniya', *Istoricheskiy Vestnik* 17 (1884), pp. 128–30, 372; Zherebtsov, *Vospominaniya*, 96. See Kulomzin's memoirs in TsGIA, Fond 1642, Opis 1, Ed. Khr. 172, p. 56, for a description of his gentry circle. Terner, e.g. (*Vospominaniya*, 37–8), spent his student days in a close circle of former gymnasium friends.

[57] Anon., 'Universitet i korporatsiya', *Istoricheskiy Vestnik* 1 (1880), pp. 779–802.

[58] Terner, *Vospominaniya*, I: 33–7.

[59] Ustryalov, 'Vospominaniya', *passim*.

[60] Besançon, *Éducation*, 65–78; V.I. Sorokin, 'Vospominaniya starogo studenta', *RS* 60 (1888) and 128 (1906).

[61] Torke, 'Beamtentum', pp. 140–5.

[62] V.V. Grigorev writes that lawyers were required to study religion, Latin literature, medieval and modern history, Russian history, political economy and statistics, since 'without this addition to the specialized legal course the council, quite correctly, found it impossible to educate either learned jurists or officials fully competent to serve the state'; see his *Imperatorskiy S. Peterburgskiy Universitet v techenie pervykh pyatidesyati let ego sushchestvovaniya* (SPB, 1870), 112.

[63] B.N. Chicherin, 'Vospominaniya' (pp. 136–49) and A.N. Afanasev, 'Moskovskiy universitet v vospominaniyakh A.N. Afanaseva 1843–1849' (pp. 151–68), in Zayonchkovsky, *Moskovskiy*;

Darlington, *Education*, 82; Wortman, *Development*, 223–9. TsGIA, Fond 1642, Opis 1, Ed. Khr. 178, p. 1 for Kulomzin's statement.

[64] Wortman, *Development*, is good on the intellectual background to the legal reform. See also a number of classic works, e.g., G.A. Dzhanshiev, *Osnovy Sudebnoy reformy* (Moscow, 1891) and I.V. Gessen, *Sudebnaya reforma* (SPB, 1905).

[65] Eg. V. Lind, who entered Moscow's law faculty in 1860, wrote that its courses were less effectively organized than in Petersburg: see Zayonchkovsky, *Moskovskiy*, 248.

[66] Besançon, *Éducation*, 64. Grigorev, *Peterburgskiy*, provides very useful information on the law department and its professors: see esp. here pp. 236–43. For later appointments (i.e. post-1869) see *Biograficheskiy slovar' professorov i prepodavateley Imperatorskogo S. Peterburgskogo Universiteta, 1869–1894* (SPB, 1896). One would for instance be hard pressed to study late imperial administration without Korkunov, *Russkoe gosudarstvennoe pravo*.

[67] Zherebtsov, *Vospominaniya*, ch. 2.

[68] The best starting-point as regards the two schools is A. Sinel, 'The Socialization of the Russian Bureaucratic Elite 1811–1917', *Russian History* 3, no. 1 (1976), pp. 1–33. The best history of the Lycée (up to 1886) is by N.I. Kareev, 'Kratkiy ocherk istorii Litseya, sostavleniy professorom N.I. Kareevym', in *Pamyatnaya knizhka Imperatorskogo Aleksandrovskogo Litseya* (SPB, 1886), 1–277. In the *Pamyatnaya...Litseya* for 1898–9 (SPB, 1899), the history is carried on to the end of the century: see 'Istoricheskiy ocherk uchebnogo i vospitatel'nogo dela v litseye za posledniya dvenadsati let', pp. 3 ff. Anon., *Istoricheskiy ocherk imperatorskogo Aleksandrovskogo Litseya* (Paris, 1936) and Seleznev, *Ocherk*, are both valuable sources. For the period relevant to the late imperial ruling élite, A.A. Rubetz, *Kratkaya istoricheskaya pamyatka Imperatorskogo Aleksandrovskogo, byvshego Tsarskosel'skogo Litseya* (SPB, 1911), is a short survey by the Lycée's Inspector of Classes. Memorial

volumes published by the 31st and 40th courses at the Lycée are useful: *XXXI kurs Imperatorskogo Aleksandrovskogo Litseya cherez 25 let posle vypuska, 1871–1896* (SPB, 1896) and *Imperatorskiy Aleksandrovskiy Litsey, XL kurs* (SPB, 1909). Many memoirs contain comments on the Lycée, but two are wholly or mostly devoted to it: P. Knyazhnin (pseud. P. Popov), *Shest' let v Imperatorskom Aleksandrovskom Litseye* (SPB, 1911), and the first, unpublished, volume of Kokovtsov's memoirs in TsGIA. On the School of Law the fullest general work is G. Syuzor, *Ko dnyu LXXXV yubileya Imperatorskogo Uchilishcha Pravovedeniya 1835–1910* (SPB, 1910). For a sense of the celebrations and rituals at the School see *Semidesyatipyatiletie Imperatorskogo Uchilishcha Pravovedeniya 1835–1910* (SPB, 1911). An interesting source, part memoir and part analysis of the School's educational system, is 'P.I.', *Obshchestvennoe vospitanie i obrazovanie v Rossii: zapiski ob Uchilishche Pravovedeniya* (SPB, 1869). Wortman, *Development*, 204–20, discusses the contribution of *pravovedy* to the growth of a Russian legal ethos. Among the memoirs are K.P. Pobedonostsev, *Dlya nemnogikh – otryvki iz shkol'nogo dnevnika* (SPB, 1885); Prince V.P. Meshchersky, *Moi vospominaniya*, vol. I (SPB, 1897), 3–91; V.V. Stasov, 'Uchilishche Pravovedeniya sorok let tomu nazad, 1836–42', *RS* 29 (1880), pp. 1015–42, 30 (1881), pp. 393–422, 573–602, and 31 (1881), pp. 247–82; K.K. Arsen'ev, 'Vospominaniya Konstantina Konstantinovicha Arsen'eva ob Uchilishche Pravovedeniya, 1849–1855 gg', *RS* 50 (1886), pp. 199–220; I.A. Tyutchev, 'V Uchilishche Pravovedinya v 1847–1852 gg', *RS* 48 (1885), pp. 436–52. See also V.A. Andreev, *Po povodu vospominaniy ob Uchilishche Pravovedeniya V.V. Stasova* (SPB, 1889).

[69] Arsen'ev, 'Vospominaniya', p. 215.

[70] For a quick quide to the prevalence of Lycéens and *pravovedy* in government posts see Table 12, p. 400, of my 'Russian Civil Service'.

[71] For Grot's comment see *Pamyatnaya...Litseya, 1856–1857* (SPB, 1856),

[40]. Syuzor, *Ko dnyu*, 153–6, compares present-day (1910) freedom in the upper classes of the School of Law with the nineteenth-century regime. 'Freedom' meant, however, that the top classes were allowed out on Saturdays and Sundays without having to say where they were going, though very strict rules were still in force as to how they should behave themselves out of school.

[72] *Pamyatnaya...Litseya, 1886*, 195–8; 'P.I.', *Obshchestvennoe*, xiv, 83, 92. See, e.g., Kokovtsov's comments on his classmates' shock, at age sixteen to seventeen, at suddenly being confronted with university lectures, and on the professors' simplification of their courses: CUBA, 'Vospominaniya', pp. 216–17.

[73] 'P.I.' *Obshchestvennoe*, 67–72; *Pamyatnaya...Litseya, 1886*, 184, 198, 200. Kokovtsov writes that in 1872 long essays were introduced for those seeking gold medals at the Lycée and that within a few years they became much more serious pieces of work. He comments that he was too busy at the Lycée reading his notes to do much supplementary reading: CUBA, 'Vospominaniya', pp. 251, 254. The 1880 *Pamyatnaya knizhka* published, e.g., S.I. Timashev's long essay entitled 'The Relationship of the State to the National Economy'. *XXXI kurs*, 16–17. Syuzor, *Ko dnyu*, 173–7.

[74] On the School of Law's military regime see esp. Meshchersky, *Vospominaniya*, I: 3–91; Arsen'ev, 'Vospominaniya', pp. 201–4. Tyutchev, 'Uchilishche', pp. 361–70, seems not to have minded the military regime too much. Kokovtsov: CUBA; 'Vospominaniya', pp. 180–228; Knyazhnin, *Shest'*, 29–31, 48–105; *XL kurs*, 32–9.

[75] Witte's comment is in *Vospominaniya*, I: 79–80. Andreev, *Po povodu*, wrote (p. 10) that 'for a student who intends to enter the civil service our universities right up to the present day are precisely the same kind of preparatory school as the School of Law; for students not limiting themselves to following a course and passing exams to get a diploma, the university offers means for a further scholarly education which the

School of Law doesn't give'.

[76] For an interesting Third Section report on moods among the student body and the reasons for disaffection dating from 1869, see 'Revolyutisonnoe i studencheskoe dvizhenie 1869g v otsenke Tret'ego Otdeleniya', *Katorga i ssylka* 10 (1924), pp. 106–21.

[77] N. de Basily, *Memoirs: Diplomat of Imperial Russia: 1903–1917* (Stanford, Calif., 1973), p. 10; CUBA. papers of N.N. Fliege, 'Litsey', p. 3.

[78] Even in the early twentieth century, as Basily (*Memoirs*, 9) writes, 'among my friends there were many sons of impoverished nobles'.

[79] In the case of the School of Law, by Prince Peter of Oldenburg, but he was effectively a Romanov.

[80] When for instance the very young and newly appointed N.V. Charykov was first presented to the Minister of Foreign Affairs, Prince A.M. Gorchakov, the veteran statesman immediately said: 'We are school-fellows, you and I'. Charykov records that 'by these words he at once won my heart'. Subsequently Gorchakov showed great friendliness to Charykov. See N.V. Tcharykow [Charykov], *Glimpses of High Politics* (London, 1931), 101.

[81] Kokovtsov records in his memoirs how he, his cousin and classmate E.D. Pleske, and P.M. Kaufmann, another Lycéen, worked with A.P. Salomon and D.M. Sol'sky, both old boys, to secure extra funds for the school in the early twentieth century: CUBA: 'Vospominaniya', pp. 278–9.

[82] See for instance A.N. Kulomzin's comments in his article, 'Dmitri Nikolaevich Zamyatin', *Zhurnal ministerstva yustitsii*, no. 9 (Nov 1914), pp. 234–331, here pp. 236–67 and esp. pp. 266–7.

[83] Grot's comment is cited with enthusiasm, e.g. by Yu. Yu. Belenkov in *XXXI Kurs*, 21, where he writes that, 'in this precept of one Lycéen to other Lycéens it seems to me lies the great strength which gives our Lycée that "brilliant lustre"...which not one Lycéen would willingly wish to lose'. For Grot's speech, see n. 71 above, and *Pamyatnaya...Litseya, 1856–57*, 23–47.

V.A. Andreev wrote, with justice, that the School of Law's authorities, unlike those of some schools, had always been carefully chosen, were 'totally clean and honest', had never been accused of any bias in judging students' work or behaviour, utterly repelled any attempts at obsequiousness, and provided an example of honesty and conscientiousness: *Po povodu*, 14–15. The list, for instance, of Inspectors of Classes at the School (Syuzor, *Ko dnyu*, 159) includes some very well-known and admirable names, and the same is true at the Lycée. On the whole, memoirs from the 1860s on speak very highly of the authorities, tutors sometimes excepted. See e.g. Knyazhnin, *Shest' let*, 24–31.

[84] See Wrangel's 'Obyasnitel'naya zapiska', reprinted in *Pamyatnaya... Litseya, 1886*, 263–70.

[85] Syuzor, *Ko dnyu*, 156, 214–15; 'P.I.', *Obshchestvennoe*, xxxii–xxxiii; *Pamyatnaya...Litseya, 1886*, 265–6; Rubetz, *Kratkaya*, 15–16.

[86] F.K. Neslukhovsky, cited in Anon., *Istoricheskiy...Litseya*, 136.

[87] E.g., Stasov, 'Uchilishche', *RS* 30, pp. 398, 408–9, and 31, pp. 276–9. Arsen'ev, 'Vospominaniya', pp. 218–19; Knyazhnin, *Shest'*, 23, 32–4.

[88] A. Orlova, 'Tchaikovsky: The Last Chapter', *Music and Letters* 62 (Apr 1981), pp. 125–37.

[89] Syuzor, *Ko dnyu*, 206. Rubetz, *Kratkaya*, 15, comments that the senior class at the Lycée sometimes called for a boy's expulsion for a dishonourable act. More often it interceded for junior boys in trouble.

[90] Kokovtsov: CUBA, 'Vospominaniya', pp. 168–75.

[91] Arsen'ev, 'Vospominaniya', p. 209.

[92] Syuzor, *Ko dnyu*, 189. In the last years of the nineteenth century, practical training became much fuller and more rigorous. 'P.I.' *Obshchestvennoe*, 60. The quote is from a letter of I.I. Shamshin, a Lycéen who later became a member of the State Council, to M.G. Akimov, dated 15 Dec 1908; see TsGIA, Fond 1162, Opis 6, Ed. Khr. 599, p. 125.

[93] Syuzor, *Ko dnyu*, 216–30; Stasov, 'Uchilishche', *RS* 29, pp. 1021–4, and

30, pp. 581–600; Wortman, *Development*, 211–12.

[94] Arsen'ev, 'Vospominaniya', pp. 201, 217–18.

[95] See for instance Knyazhnin's discussion in *Shest'*, 81, of his classmates' favourite poets and the comment of Lycée class representatives that 'members of the Lycée always treated each other's views with full respect and always avoided any grounds for disagreement among themselves of a political nature': see TsGAOR, Fond 1074, Opis 1, Ed. Khr. 402, p. 3. Basily, *Memoirs*, 9–10, writes that most Lycée teachers did not hide their liberal sympathies and that although his own dissertation on Speransky had a 'clearly liberal tone' this did not stop him being awarded the Pushkin prize.

[96] Darlington, *Education*, 233; Seleznev, *Ocherk*, 281–7, 468, 479. See n. 92 above for Shamshin's comment.

[97] Kareev is the best source for this first current of opinion. He quotes frequently from the arguments of Korkunov and Bezobrazov: *Pamyatnaya... Litseya, 1886*, 228–39 (e.g.). See also 'Istoricheskiy ocherk', ibid., *1899*, 1–4. On history teaching, which until the 1880s avoided the nineteenth century, see Kokovtsov: CUBA, 'Vospominaniya', p. 218; Knyazhnin, *Shest'*, 49–73; *XL kurs*, 32.

[98] G.N. Vyrubov, *Zapiska ob ustroystve Imperatorskogo Aleksandrovskogo Litseya i programmakh prepodavaniya v nyom* (SPB, 1901), *passim*.

[99] For, e.g., Birkin's and Belenkov's very different evaluations of the Lycée's influence, see *XXXI kurs*, 16–19, 21–3.

[100] Kokovtsov: CUBA, 'Vospominaniya', pp. 161, 174, 234, 283–6, 294.

[101] For comments on most of these men see ch. 5. On Kobeko see in particular Witte, *Vospominaniya*, I: 346. On Kaufmann, see Polovtsov, *Dnevnik*, II: 425. A.N. Naumov, *Iz utselevshikh vospominaniy*, 2 vols. (New York, 1955), esp. vol. II.

[102] On the General Staff Academy, see Mayzel, 'Formation'.

[103] Torke, 'Beamtentum', ch. 3, sec. 3.

[104] For Witte's views see a memorandum written in early 1895 in TsGIA, Fond 1200, Opis 16i, Delo 2, pp. 54–8. On the general issue of 'development administration' see, e.g., J. La Palombara's 'Overview' in La Palombara, ed., *Bureaucracy and Political Development* (Princeton, N.J., 1963), 3–33.

[105] A good source here is Gmeline, *Dictionnaire*, where most of these families are listed. Of the composers, Mussorgsky (pp. 416–17) and Rimsky-Korsakov (pp. 493–4) came from genuinely ancient families, while Rachmaninov (pp. 488–9) was from an old family entered in the sixth book of the Tambov noble rolls.

[106] E.g., Lermontov and Mussorgsky were at the School of Guards Sub-Ensigns, Pushkin and Saltykov-Shchedrin at the Lycée, Rimsky-Korsakov was a naval officer, Tchaikovsky at the School of Law, and numerous other figures of course at the universities of Moscow and Petersburg.

CHAPTER 4

[1] See, e.g., a Resolution by the Committee of Ministers dated 20 June 1895 (TsGIA, Fond 1409, Opis 4, Delo 14817, p. 162i). N.V. Murav'yov's views on the regulations are contained in pp. 70–3 of the same file. The Peretz Commission, set up in 1895 to review the civil service regulations, stated that 'the Civil Service Statute... is nothing other than a series of legislative acts issued at various times, in part outdated, in part contradictory and not answering the needs of contemporary service activity and quite often actually incapable of being fulfilled in practice, as a consequence of which, in some circumstances, the need to allow deviations is inevitable and is required both by the demands of life and by the good of the service' (TsGIA, Fond 1200, Opis 16ii, Ed. Khr. 1 and 2, p. 118ii).

[2] TsGIA, Fond 1200, Opis 16ii, Ed. Khr. 1 and 2, p. 747i (Kokovtsov's comments on the Peretz Commission's report).

[3] I discuss this point in 'Russian Senior

Officialdom', p. 202. *Svod zakonov Rossiyskoy Imperii* (*SZ*) (SPB, 1896), vol. III, esp. Art. 5, lists those groups with a right to enter the civil service. Women were wholly banned from the service save in certain medical and secretarial jobs (ibid., Arts. 156, 157); so too were the great majority of Jews (ibid., Art. 9). The exemptions and evasions which benefited most other groups did not extend to these two.

[4] See the comments of the majority of the Peretz Commission in TsGIA, Fond 1200, Opis 16ii, Ed. Khr. 1 and 2, pp. 135–40. S.A. Taneev wrote to Peretz in February 1897 that of the 4,132 men who joined the civil service between 1 Nov 1894 and 1 Aug 1895, 1,656 (40.1 per cent) did not have the right to do so by social origin (p. 920). The Peretz Commission commented that exemptions and exceptions to the regulations were becoming the general rule (p. 132).

[5] The figure comes from the report of the Peretz Commission (p. 132), which stated that, in all, the ministries of the Interior, Finance, Justice, Education, Agriculture, State Control, Communications and court (Apanage Dept.) had only 126,174 ranked officials.

[6] TsGIA, Fond 1200, Opis 16ii, Ed. Khr. 1 and 2, p. 748ii.

[7] S.A. Taneev argued in 1887 that the top ranks of the civil service should be closed to those without a higher education. The Delyanov Commission's report of 30 Sept 1884 took the same line, as did Delyanov's later report of 25 Nov 1892. Between these two dates Delyanov's efforts to restrict the inflow of impoverished students into education had led him to attempt to end the legal advantages (seniority on appointment) gained by graduates in the civil service. His efforts were ridiculed by most senior officials. (TsGIA, Fond 1200, Opis 16ii, Ed. Khr. 1 and 2, pp. 396–8 [Taneev] and 387–96, 399–403, 424–39 [Delyanov]; the State Council's views in 1887 are on pages 398–9, the ministers' comments on pp. 404–24.) The Peretz Commission, disinclined to lumber all branches of the civil service with restrictive rules, confined itself to stressing the importance of higher education without making it obligatory.

[8] See section III of this chapter, and my 'Russian Civil Service', pp. 375–6 and 386–99.

[9] *SZ* (SPB, 1842), Arts. 81–2; *SZ* (1896) Art. 57.

[10] Arts. 390–4 of the 1842 regulations cover the procedure for entry into the civil service. See also Arts. 168–78 of the 1896 regulations.

[11] For most entrants acceptance legally depended on the heads of ministerial departments [*departamenty*] in Petersburg or equivalent provincial chiefs. The Ministry of Finance was, e.g. in 1858, exceptional in making the appointment of all but 'chancellery officials' depend formally on the Minister's own sanction (*PSZ*, 2nd ser., vol. 33/2, no. 33261, pp. 715–16, 6 June 1858). In the provincial offices of the mid-nineteenth-century Ministry of Internal Affairs, only the counsellors of provincial boards and senior officials of charities were centrally appointed. See Seleznev, *Istoricheskiy ocherk*, 468–9.

[12] See Witte's letter to A.N. Kulomzin dated 27 Mar 1895 in TsGIA, Fond 1409, Opis 4, Delo 14817, p. 154.

[13] See, e.g., P.S. Botkin, *Kartinki diplomaticheskoy zhizni* (Paris, 1930), 25–6; D.I. Abrikossow, *Revelations of a Russian Diplomat* (Seattle, Wash., 1964), 80–1.

[14] Undated report originating in the mid-1880s, in TsGIA, Fond 1200, Opis 16ii, Ed. Khr. 1 and 2, p. 424.

[15] See, e.g., J.R. Gillis, 'Aristocracy and Bureaucracy in Nineteenth-Century Prussia', *Past and Present* 41 (1968), pp. 121–2; Armstrong, *Administrative Elite*, 204–5.

[16] TsGIA, Fond 1200, Opis 16ii, Ed. Khr. 1 and 2, p. 129ii.

[17] Kokovtsov wrote that 'there can be no question that at present a very great difference exists between the conditions of life and service in the centre and in the provinces, and that this difference is felt especially hard by those with higher education. The desire of young people who are finishing at institutions of higher education not to enter service in the provinces is not just quite common,

as the Commission's minority supposes, but general.... Many do in fact enter service in the provinces, but they decide on this only as a last resort, having first exhausted all ways of arranging for themselves a job in the centre'. (Ibid., p. 771i.)

[18] Ibid., p. 1178, for P.L. Lobko's comments.

[19] For Taneev's views and proposals see ibid., pp. 396–9; for Delyanov's, ibid., pp. 435–6.

[20] Ibid., p. 424, for N.K. Giers's comment that the Foreign Ministry 'needs educated and gifted people, irrespective of which faculty they studied in. Many of our outstanding diplomats studied in various specialist educational establishments; amongst them were and still are former soldiers, mathematicians, engineers and Orientalists, and experience has shown that their specialized education has in no way had a harmful effect on their activity'. M.N. Ostrovsky, the Minister of State Properties, was also particularly unimpressed by Delyanov's proposals. He argued that no pre-service training could teach men to be useful officials and that linking education to future departmental service would be at odds with the practice of transferring between departments, which was a hallmark of the Russian civil service (ibid., p. 411).

[21] Ibid., p. 416.

[22] For the discussion on this matter in the Peretz Commission see ibid., pp. 191–7.

[23] Ibid., pp. 12, 771.

[24] TsGIA, Fond 1409, Opis 4, Delo. 14817, pp. 27–8: a report from the Emperor's Own Personal Chancellery to Alexander III in 1894. P.L. Lobko (Fond 1200, Opis 16ii, Ed. Khr. 1 and 2, p. 1180) regretted the demise of Nicholas I's rule, which fell into abeyance partly because young officials disliked provincial service and strove to evade it.

[25] See the minutes of a conference of senior judicial and procuratorial officials held under the chairmanship of N.V. Murav'yov in December 1894 and January 1895: *Soveshchaniya starshikh predsedateley i prokurorov sudebnykh palat po* *nekotorym voprosam sudebnoy praktiki v svyazi s peresmotrom zakonopolozheniy po sudebnoy chasti* (SPB, printed for internal governmental circulation, 1895). Two sessions were devoted to the system of candidates, on 2 and 3 Jan 1895; see pp. 244–89.

[26] Ibid. (*passim*), also TsGIA, Fond 1200, Opis 16ii, Ed. Khr. 1 and 2, esp. pp. 193–6.

[27] On the Prussian civil service and its critics, see, e.g., J.C.G. Röhl, 'Higher Civil Servants in Germany, 1890–1900', in *Imperial Germany*, ed. J.J. Sheehan (New York, 1976); G. Bonham, 'State Autonomy or Class Domination: Approaches to Administrative Politics in Wilhelmine Germany', *World Politics* 35 (1983), pp. 631–51 (esp. pp. 635–6); also Gillis, 'Aristocracy and Bureaucracy'. See L.W. Muncy, *The Junker in the Prussian Administration Under William II, 1888–1914* (Providence, R.I., 1944), 119–20, on the great expense borne by the parents of prospective civil servants, which was more than four times as great as the cost of educating a future officer.

[28] TsGIA, Fond 1200, Opis 16ii, Ed. Khr. 1 and 2, p. 125i. Report of the Peretz Commission.

[29] Ibid., p. 417ii, undated but written in 1887.

[30] Ibid., pp. 1180 i and ii, dating from the early twentieth century.

[31] Ibid., pp. 208–17.

[32] Lobko's line was not echoed within the Peretz Commission, probably in part because it was not considering statutes for individual departments and the detailed job requirements that would accompany them. The five members of the Commission most inclined towards ministerial autonomy were A.I. Ivashchenkov, P.M. Kaufmann, A.N. Bryanchaninov, P.M. Romanov and Prince V.S. Kochubei.

[33] TsGIA, Fond 1200, Opis 16ii, Ed. Khr. 1 and 2, pp. 749, 771.

[34] *PSZ*, 2nd ser., vol. 9/1, no. 7224.

[35] Ibid., vol. 10/2, no. 8594.

[36] The list of posts so classified is attached to the law of 20 Nov 1835.

[37] *PSZ*, 2nd ser., vol. 31/2, no. 31,237.

[38] This was according to Article 623 of the *Svod Zakonov* of 1842. In 1892 long fixed terms were established for promotion to ranks 4 and 3. See *SZ* (1896), vol. III, Art. 328. At this level, however, the Emperor's personal intervention could be invoked to nullify any regulations.

[39] See TsGIA, Fond 1200, Opis 16ii, Ed. Khr. 1 and 2, e.g. p. 2, for the Peretz Commission's comments on this.

[40] Article 571 of *SZ* (1842), vol. III. Para. 4 of the law of 9 Dec 1856, *PSZ*, 2nd ser., vol. 31/2, no. 31,237.

[41] The calculation is based on the time it would take to rise from rank 10 to rank 5, since para. 18 of the law of 25 June 1834 allowed appointment to jobs one class above or below one's rank: *PSZ*, 2nd ser., vol. 9/1, no. 7224.

[42] J.A. Armstrong, 'Tsarist and Soviet Elite Administrators', in *SR* 31 (1972), pp. 1–28, here p. 12.

[43] A.A. Polovtsov, for instance, was a strong enemy of the *chin*, as frequent outbursts in his diary make clear: see, e.g., *Dnevnik*, I: 184, 362, 407, 467. Influential general surveys of imperial Russian history often stress the *chin*'s key role: see, e.g., A. Leroy-Beaulieu, *The Empire of the Tsars and the Russians*, tr. Z.A. Ragozin, 3 vols. (New York and London, 1893–6), here II: 92–3; R. Pipes, *Russia under the Old Regime* (London, 1974), 134–7. For recent works by a specialist on the *chin* system, see H.A. Bennett: 'Evolution of the Meaning of *Chin*', *California Slavic Studies* 10 (1977), pp. 1–43, and '*Chiny*, *Ordena* and Officialdom', in Pintner and Rowney, *Russian Officialdom*, 162–89.

[44] Undated paper entitled 'Po voprosu ob izmenenii zakonopolozhenii o chino-proizvodstve' in TsGIA, Fond 1200, Opis 16i, Delo 1 and 2, pp. 937–41.

[45] See para. 2 of *PSZ*, 2nd ser., vol. 10/2, no. 8594.

[46] See Arts. 142–6 of *SZ* (1896), vol. III. For a short published account of procedures in the judicial department, see Brockhaus and Efron, *Entsiklopedicheskiy* XXV: 403–4 and XXXI: 929–30.

[47] Orlovsky, 'Ministry', pp. 266–71.

[48] See in particular pp. 29–30 of their report to Alexander III in TsGIA, Fond 1409, Opis 4, Delo 14817 (2 May 1894).

[49] See *PSZ*, 2nd ser. vol. 33/2, no. 33261, for the law of 6 June 1858..

[50] See my 'Senior Officialdom', nn. 48 and 49.

[51] Figure cited by Vorontsov-Dashkov in the report cited in n. 44 above.

[52] See my 'Russian Civil Service', p. 370 and n. 16.

[53] One can choose more or less at random. Even the tighter military regulations were, e.g., in 1901 ignored so that Major-General Prince P.D. Svyatopolk-Mirsky, assistant minister and GOC of the Gendarmerie, could be promoted '*vne pravil*' to lieutenant-general: see TsGIA, Fond 1284, Opis 52, Ed. Khr. 77, p. 21. V.K. Plehve's career also 'took off' when his merits came to the Emperor's attention. Promoted to rank 5 in 1880 in the teeth of the regulations, three years later he had jumped two more ranks to become a Privy Counsellor. TsGAOR, Fond 1568, Opis 1, Ed. Khr. 2.

[54] TsGIA, Fond 1200, Opis 16ii, Ed. Khr. 1 and 2, p. 728: a note dating from the early twentieth century.

[55] Letter from Goremykin dated 20 Apr 1897, TsGIA, Fond 1200, Opis 16i, Delo 3, pp. 19–25.

[56] TsGIA, Fond 1200, Opis 16i, Delo 2, p. 56; report undated, but originating early in 1895.

[57] TsGIA, Fond 1200, Opis 16ii, Ed. Khr. 1 and 2, pp. 9–13, 28, 209–16, 223, and also Kokovtsov's comments on pp. 773–4.

[58] See an unsigned report originating in early 1894 and almost certainly written either by Vorontsov-Dashkov or Rennenkampf, stressing, for instance, that no effort had been made by departments to give similar jobs the same class or pay. So diverse and autonomous had ministerial procedures become that there was a risk this would turn 'servants of the state and of the Emperor into the hired workers of individual men and departments'. TsGIA, Fond 1409, Opis 4, Delo. 14817, esp. pp. 37–9.

[59] R.F. Kaufman, 'The Patron-Client

Concept and Macro-Politics: Prospects and Problems', in *Comparative Studies in Society and History* 16, no. 3 (1974), pp. 291–3; K.R. Legg, *Patrons, Clients and Politicians. New Perspectives on Political Clientelism* (n.p., 1975), 47.

[60] W.E. Mosse, 'Russian Provincial Governors at the End of the Nineteenth Century', *Historical Journal* 27, no. 1 (1984), pp. 225–39.

[61] R.G. Robbins, 'Choosing the Russian Governors: The Professionalisation of the Gubernatorial Corps', *SEER* 58 (1980), pp. 541–60.

[62] Ibid., pp. 542, 544–5, 554–6.

[63] TsGIA, Fond 1200, Opis 16ii, Ed. Khr. 1 and 2, pp. 1180–1. Prince V.P. Meshchersky in *Grazhdanin*, no. 49 (15 Dec 1913), p. 17; Ignatiev, *Subaltern*, 94.

[64] S. Bensidoun, *L'Agitation paysanne en Russie de 1881 à 1902* (Paris, 1975). 456–7.

[65] RO, Fond 178, Karton 9803, Ed. Khr. 6, p. 41 (A.N. Kulomzin's memoirs).

[66] TsGAOR, Fond 1729, Opis 1, Ed. Khr. 479, pp. 1–3, from a letter to Prince P.D. Svyatopolk-Mirsky.

[67] Witte, *Vospominaniya*, I: 90, 199.

[68] See, e.g., Kulomzin's comments in RO, Fond 178, Karton 9803, Ed. Khr. 3, p. 26; Ed. Khr. 4, pp. 9–11; Gurko, *Features*, 36.

[69] For Lobko's views see TsGIA, Fond 1200, Opis 16ii, Ed. Khr. 1 and 2, p. 1180. For Murav'yov's comment see *Soveshchaniya starshikh predsedateley i prokurorov*...(unpub.; printed SPB, 1895), session of 4 Jan 1895, p. 290.

[70] *Padenie tsarskogo rezhima*, VII: 256–80.

[71] Kryzhanovsky, *Vospominaniya*, 28.

[72] *Soveshchaniya*, p. 291.

[73] Ibid., pp. 292–5.

[74] Ibid., p. 303.

[75] Ibid., p. 299.

[76] Terner, *Vospominaniya*, I: 30, 67–8, 103–5.

[77] Botkin, *Kartinki*, 17.

[78] TsGIA, Fond 1112, Opis 1, Ed. Khr. 5, p. 25 (Trubnikov's memoirs).

[79] See ch. 2 above; this was more true of exclusive Guards Regiments and the Corps des Pages than of the Alexander Lycée, still less of the School of Law.

[80] RO, Fond 514, Karton 1, Ed. Khr. 4 (Second Book), pp. 29–31.

[81] The words quoted here regarding Obolensky are from an entry in Polovtsov's diary, dated 5 May 1901.

[82] Polovtsov was always a determined advocate of increasing the aristocratic and landowning element in government, as a counterbalance to the growing power of the bureaucracy. This is a theme that runs throughout his diaries. According to Gurko, Witte regarded Obolensky as an oracle on Russian agriculture and was greatly under his influence in the early twentieth century (*Features*, 207). Obolensky's initial appointment in the Ministry of Finance (1895) was, however, as director of the Noble and Peasant Bank. This institution, always under intense pressure and criticism from the landowning nobility, was generally headed by well-connected aristocrats, since the latter's social credentials, together with their court and high society connections, secured them in part from attacks which could prove fatal to the careers of ordinary officials unlucky enough to hold this post. Terner, *Vospominaniya*, II: 171–2.

[83] *Grazhdanin*, no. 38 (13 May 1904), p. 21.

[84] Terner, *Vospominaniya*, I: 69–74.

[85] Polovtsov, *Dnevnik*, I: 324; II: 75, 179, 425, 441–2, 445; *KA* 4 (1923), p. 105.

[86] See, e.g., A. Downs, *Inside Bureaucracy* (Boston, 1967), 230.

[87] Terner, *Vospominaniya*, I: e.g., 187, 203.

[88] *SZ* (1896), vol. III, Arts. 761, 762. The articles were designed to deal with corrupt officials against whom it was impossible to find sufficient evidence to satisfy a court of law. According to the journal *Nedelya*, these articles were 'actually quite often misused...this of course gives scope to arbitrariness but the law was only intended to be applied in completely exceptional cases. In practice, even in recent years, there have been examples of dismissals resulting from an official's conscientious attitude to his work, that is when he suffered for not

aiding some particular wish of his chief'. That issue of the journal is among the papers of the Peretz Commission in TsGIA, Fond 1200, Opis 16ii, Ed. Khr. 1 and 2, p. 525. A.S. Taneev wrote that 'the right to dismiss officials not at their own request on the basis of Point 3, which is possessed by the person appointing the official in question to the post he holds, still has real significance in the provinces both as a means of maintaining the quality of officials and especially as a means of stopping officials from acting in ways that are not susceptible to investigation by normal channels. Nevertheless this regulation is applied much more rarely than might seem the case to someone standing outside the service. The wrongness of this rule lies above all in the principle it enshrines. Statistical data would probably confirm this statement.' (Ibid., p. 1189i.) As effective head of the Civil Service Inspectorate, Taneev was best placed to know about such matters.

[89] *Grazhdanin*, no. 48 (19 Dec 1910), pp. 10–11.

[90] See, e.g., the comments in the State Council by P.N. Durnovo, backing up A.P. Nikol'sky's arguments on this point: *Stenograficheskiy otchot Gosudarstvennogo Soveta* (*SOGS*), Session 5 (29 May 1910), cols. 3401–5.

[91] Terner, *Vospominaniya*, I: 47.

[92] TsGIA, Fond 1200, Opis 16ii, Ed. Khr. 1 and 2, pp. 37–8.

[93] *SOGS*, Session 2 (19 May 1907), col. 406.

[94] See Mosolov's memoirs: TsGAOR, Fond 1463, Opis 1, Ed. Khr. 1115, pp. 24–8, 76, 82–5; RO, Fond 514, Karton 1, Ed. Khr. 6, 'Ob udalenii', pp. 28–9; Ed. Khr. 7, 'Vospominaniya' (1902–3), p. 16 (the latter for V.K. Plehve's comment on Mosolov's glittering prospects in the late 1870s).

[95] RO, Fond 514, 'Ob udalenii', pp. 41–2; TsGAOR, Fond 1463, Opis 1, Ed. Khr. 1115, pp. 88, 158.

[96] RO, Fond 178, Karton 9803, Ed. Khr. 5, p. 21 (Kulomzin's memoirs).

[97] The commission's report (and some of its papers) are in Saburov's fond (1074, Opis 1, Ed. Khr. 1105) in

TsGAOR; see esp. p. 27. Meshchersky made a similar comment in *Grazhdanin*, no. 8 (23 Feb 1913), pp. 21–2.

[98] Cf., e.g., the appointment to the Council of the thoroughly mediocre N.P. Shishkin. On the latter's career see my 'Senior Officialdom'. n. 139.

[99] TsGIA, Fond 1650, Opis 1, Ed. Khr. 234, p. 26.

[100] On the politicization of the Prussian bureaucracy in the early constitutional period, see, e.g., H. Fischer, 'Konservatismus von unten. Wahlen in ländlichen Preussen 1849–1852. Organization, Agitation, Manipulation', in D. Stegmann, ed., *Deutscher Konservatismus im 19 und 20 Jahrhundert* (Bonn, 1983), 69–128. Also J.R. Gillis, *The Prussian Bureaucracy in Crisis 1840–1860. Origins of an Administrative Ethos* (Stanford, Calif., 1971), esp. ch. 8. See also M.L. Anderson and K. Barkin, 'The Myth of the Puttkamer Purge and the Reality of the Kulturkampf: Some Reflections on the Historiography of Imperial Germany', *Journal of Modern History* 54, no. 4 (1982), pp. 647–86; see esp. p. 655: 'It was 1848, and the accompanying politicization of public life', that made the Prussian civil servant's traditionally rather independent position 'between crown and people in the long run untenable'.

[101] *Novoe Vremya*, 28 Sept 1915, p. 3.

[102] TsGAOR, Fond 1463, Opis 1, Ed. Khr. 1115, p. 24.

[103] A.N. Kuropatkin, *Dnevnik* (Nizhniy Novgorod, 1923), 72–3.

[104] Letter of 28 May/11 June 1904, to his brother, Count Alexander Benckendorff: Brooke MSS.

[105] Basily, *Memoirs*, 24. TsGAOR, Fond 542, Opis 1, Ed. Khr. 352, p. 20.

[106] Vasili, *Société*, 210.

[107] D.P. Golitsyn (pseud. Muravlin), *V Peterburge* (SPB, 1892), e.g. 312–13, 320–4, 329. Golitsyn's novels bring out well the atmosphere and smell of Petersburg bureaucratic life.

[108] E.g., Polovtsov's record of the decline of the 'brilliant' and 'noble' P.A. Markov into an increasingly lazy high official, indifferent to major issues but increasingly concerned with petty rituals

and triumphs at court: see Polovtsov, *Dnevnik*, I: 107; II: 133–4, 243; *KA* 3 (1923), p. 87.

[109] TsGIA, Fond 1650, Opis 1, Ed. Khr. 234, p. 86 (in a letter to his wife).

[110] Polovtsov, *Dnevnik*, II: 136.

[111] RO, Fond 126, K. 13, 31 Oct 1900, p. 57 (A.A. Kireev's diary).

[112] Bogdanovich, *Tri poslednikh*, 3, predicted Wahl's fall. Sure enough he soon aroused a hornets' nest by his blunt words and actions. For his self-justification see TsGAOR, Fond 542, Opis 1, Ed. Khr. 334, pp. 1–9, a note dated 27 Sept 1898; and see Ed. Khr. 364, pp. 18–23, for the appeals from Wahl and his wife to the Emperor and Dowager Empress after his dismissal, and pp. 12ff. for a draft letter expressing gratitude to Marie Fyodorovna for her intervention.

[113] Bogdanovich, e.g. *Tri poslednikh*, 208 (3 Dec 1896): 'Kulomzin came. He is extremely careful, said nothing in an affirmative way but touched on everything by means of questions'.

[114] Polovtsov, *Dnevnik*, II: 41.

[115] RO, Fond 338, Opis 3, Delo 4, 'Moi vospominaniya o gosudare', pp. 3–4.

[116] Downs, *Bureaucracy*, 71–2.

[117] Polovtsov, *Dnevnik*, I: 477.

[118] Basily, *Memoirs*, 124.

[119] E.g., A.P. Izvol'sky and S.D. Sazonov both appointed former classmates at the Alexander Lycée as assistants. N.K. Giers, constantly insecure and under pressure in the 1880s, appointed A.K. Vlangali and N.P. Shishkin as his deputies, which helps to explain how such relatively unimpressive individuals later reached the State Council.

[120] The rule that to be effective chiefs had to build up competent staffs is for instance witnessed to by Serge Witte's appointments. Gurko writes (*Features*, 67) that Witte 'assembled a fine group of assistants and other officers in the Ministry of Finance'.

[121] See *Vozrozhdenie*, no. 24 (Nov–Dec 1952), pp. 161–6, for 'Pis'mo A.F. Koni', introduced by Vladimir Butchik.

[122] For Bark's comments see 'Vospominaniya P.L. Barka', *Vozrozhdenie*, no. 157 (Jan 1965), ch. 4, pp. 58–64, here p. 62.

[123] On Bunge see A.N. Kulomzin's comment to his wife about Bunge's selflessness: as regards appointments and promotions, Bunge 'never thought about himself' (letter dated 15 Oct 1895 in TsGIA, Fond 1642, Opis 1, Ed. Khr. 217, p. 132). On A.A. Knirim see the article by A.I. Lykoshin entitled 'Pamyati A.A. Knirima', in *Zhurnal ministerstva iustitsii*, no. 10 (Dec 1905), pp. 1–29.

[124] Count Aleksei Bobrinsky, for instance, records the unpopularity of the Shuvalov and Bobrinsky families at court in 1880–1, partly because of their attitude to Catherine Dolgorouky and to the financial corruption that surrounded her. Aleksei Bobrinsky's uncle, Vladimir, lost his ministerial post as a result. See Bobrinsky's diary, pp. 7–9, 55, in TsGIA, Fond 899, Opis 1, Ed. Khr. 32.

[125] On Lieven see Terner's comments in *Vospominaniya*, II: 184–5.

[126] The divorce between monarchy and aristocracy is a major theme of Polovtsov's diaries.

[127] See ch. 9, nn. 21 and 22.

[128] A.N. Mosolov's appointment to the State Council was, for instance, influenced by Meshchersky. P.A. Krivsky and S.F. Platonov were other members of the Council appointed on Meshchersky's recommendation. Polovtsov, *KA* 3 (1923), 6 May 1902, p. 146. See also Mosolov's memoirs in TsGAOR, Fond 1463, Opis 1, Ed. Khr. 1115, p. 364; RO, Fond 514, 'Vospominaniya' (1902–3), pp. 48–9.

[129] 'Dopros N.A. Maklakova', *Padenie tsarskogo rezhima*, III: 85–6.

[130] Letter to Count Alexander Benckendorff, 31 Aug/13 Sept 1904, no. 2703, Brooke MSS.

[131] Kryzhanovsky, *Vospominaniya*, 46–7.

[132] In the years between 1906 and 1914 a number of men became ministers in their early and middle forties, e.g. P.A. Stolypin, N.A. Maklakov, I.P. Shipov, P.P. Izvol'sky, A.V. Krivoshein, I.G. Shcheglovitov, Prince B.A. Vasil'chikov and D.A. Filosofov.

[133] Armstrong: *Administrative Elite*, 239–41; and 'Tsarist and Soviet Elite Administrators', pp. 14–19.

[134] Pensions of members of the State Council were much better than those of most top officials, which was in itself a major incentive for the decrepit to want to enter the Council. The Council's members' pensions were, however, individually fixed by the Emperor, and some were twice the size of others. See TsGIA, Fond 1162, Opis 6 (service records).

[135] *Soveshchaniya*, X Protocol, 4 Jan 1895, pp. 290–312.

[136] Count V.N. Lambsdorff, *Dnevnik V.N. Lamzdorfa*, 2 vols. (Moscow, 1926, 1934), II: 11.

[137] Ibid., 221, for Lambsdorff's catalogue of essential bureaucratic skills.

[138] Vasil'chikov, 'Vospominaniya', ch. 6, p. 1; ch. 7, p. 85 (MSS, private).

[139] An excellent example of this is V.K. Plehve's dislike of the Jews, which in 1903 seems to have clouded his perception of Russia's internal political realities. On 29 May 1903, for instance, Plehve told Kireev that 'the Jews were much more dangerous than any constitutionalists', which made Kireev ask himself, 'does he really think that.... He is a Judophobe. Perhaps he thinks he'll make himself popular by this means'. (RO, Fond 128, K13, p. 235.)

[140] Gurko writes (*Features*, 38) that 'a skeptical, indifferent attitude and an inclination to compromise' were 'characteristics of our governing class even at its best'. P. Woodruff (pseud.), in *The Men Who Ruled India*, 2 vols. (London, 1971), vol. II, *The Guardians*, makes similar comments about the British administration in India, as does Downs, *Bureaucracy*, 230, about officialdom in general.

[141] Golitsyn, *V Peterburge*, 162, 192, 235, 246, 280, 283, 306, 312–13, 317–24.

[142] See, e.g., Polovtsov's comments about Goremykin in 1897: 'He thinks only about holding on to his state apartments' (*KA* 46 (1931) p. 121), and 'he is a clever and honest man but limitlessly idle and has fallen in love with the riches and comforts of a high position about which he had never dared to dream' (ibid., p. 124).

[143] Ibid., p. 120, entry for 17 June 1897. See also Polovtsov's entry in 'Dnevnik', *KA* 3 (1923), p. 83, entry for 11 Mar 1901.

[144] A.V. Krivoshein was one official who showed himself an expert politician in the Duma period, enjoying simultaneously the backing of the Duma, the Moscow business community, the Empress Alexandra and most of his ministerial colleagues. Even for him, however, the idea of mobilizing support among the masses was remote. See *Grazhdanin*, nos. 39–40 (1 June 1908), p. 12; Gurko, *Features*, 192–4; K.A. Krivoshein, *Krivoshein, passim*.

[145] Quoted by M. Albrow, *Bureaucracy* (London, 1970), 22.

[146] See for instance a long draft letter written by Saburov in early 1906 discussing the political situation and addressed to a member of the imperial family. Among other points, Saburov stresses that universal suffrage would mean 'that all the cultured elements of the population will be devoured by the overwhelmingly greater numbers of the remaining uneducated elements, and the fate of Russia will thus be given into the hands of those least capable of political activity'. (TsGAOR, Fond 1074, Opis 1, Ed. Khr. 1116, here p. 14).

[147] RO, Fond 128, K. 13, pp. 235, 238.

[148] RO, Fond 338, Opis 1, Delo 4, p. 23, a letter dated 19 July 1908. The same sentiments are expressed in Delo 70, pp. 5–13, in which Schwartz writes to his daughter in April 1909 of his contempt for the Duma.

[149] RO, Fond 338, Opis 4, Delo 1/3: 'Otchot A.N. Shvartsa o poezdke zagranitsu dlya osmotra sredneuchebnykh zavedeniy Germanii i Frantsii', p. 19.

[150] See *SOGS*, Session 7 (26 Jan 1912), col. 1259.

[151] See, e.g., Gurko's comments in *Features*, 207–9, 213, 292–302; Kryzhanovsky, *Vospominaniya*, 54; Kokovtsov, *Out of My Past*, 31, 34.

[152] Bark, *Vozrozhdenie*, no. 160 (Apr

1965), p. 78; no. 165 (Sept 1965), p. 92; no. 179 (Nov 1966), p. 103.

[153] See in particular V.G. Chernukha, *Vnutrennaya politika tsarizma, s serediny 50-kh do nachala 80 kh gg XIX veka* (Leningrad, 1978), pt. 1.

[154] Cited in Polovtsov, *Dnevnik*, II: 151.

[155] E.g., Kireev wrote in October 1900 that 'I have seen a lot of intelligent people recently and they all, in one voice, say, some with joy...others with horror, the same thing: the present state system has outlived its era and we are heading towards a constitution. This is clearer than daylight'. Pobedonostsev agreed. RO, Fond 128, K. 13, p. 51; see also ibid., p. 100, 'a constitutional order is, in the eyes of the great majority, the only salvation'.

[156] Ikonnikov, *Noblesse*, vol. Y: 102–5.

[157] RO, Fond 128, K. 13, p. 232.

[158] Witte, *Vospominaniya*, II: 305–6. His *Samoderzhavie i zemstvo* (Stuttgart, 1903) was probably the best-known statement for absolutism in the immediate pre-1905 era.

CHAPTER 5

[1] On Strukov see, e.g., the comment of A.P. Naumov in *Iz utselevshikh*, II: 165, that he was a true aristocrat in the best sense of the word.

[2] For Sheremetev see Vasil'chikov, *Verschwundenes*, 203–7.

[3] See esp. Prince Serge Volkonsky, *My Reminiscences*, 2 vols. (London, 1924), here II: 50–60, on his father's undeviating conformism to official norms and insecurity, neither of which was typical of aristocratic magnates.

[4] See Manning, *Crisis*, 297.

[5] Bobrinsky's Fond in TsGIA (899) contains his diary for 1880–1, a number of documents related to his activity in the United Nobility, and a collection of letters to his daughter from 1913–16. His comments on Alexander III and his brothers date from January 1881 and are from his diary (Ed. Khr. 32, p. 40), as is his description of a speech he made to the Petersburg nobility on 19 Feb 1881

(pp. 50–1). See, e.g., Princess E.A. Svyatopolk-Mirsky's diary entry of 22 Nov 1904 on Bobrinsky's distrust of Nicholas II: 'Dnevnik', *IZ* 77 (1965), p. 259.

[6] Vasil'chikov, 'Vospominaniya', ch. 1, pp. 2–4 (MSS, Private).

[7] See, e.g., the views of N.V. Charykov, from the richest layer of the provincial gentry and with aristocratic connections. Charykov contrasts English freedom with Russia, 'a bureaucracy-ruled and police-ridden country', and comments that 'had there been in Russia a Constitutional Government, I should certainly have tried to enter parliament': Tcharykow [Charykov], *Glimpses*, 81, 90.

[8] In fact a desire to know what aristocratic courtiers were saying about him behind his back was one motive for Alexander III's sanctioning of the so-called 'black cabinets'.

[9] E.g. the wife of Prince M.S. Volkonsky, though the embarrassment she suffered was, as she well knew, nothing to the suffering of less highly placed people with views similar to her own: Volkonsky, *Reminiscences*, II: 45–56. See also E. Heier, *Religious Schism in the Russian Aristocracy 1860–1900. Radstockism and Pashkovism* (The Hague, 1970).

[10] E.g., when Prince L.D. Vyazemsky, already a member of the State Council, got into trouble in 1900 for intervening to protect protesting female students from being beaten by police and cossacks, he was not only exiled to his estate but was also reported on by the police department, who stated that their only previous cause to suspect him was that he had been 'in close relations' with Countess Sophie Panin in 1880 at a time when the security police were keeping the latter under surveillance. See a letter of 9 Mar 1900 from D.S. Sipyagin, in TsGIA, Fond 1162, Opis 6, Ed. Khr. 100, p. 10. Vyazemsky's behaviour underlines the fact that a Russian aristocrat with political ambitions might be forced to swallow part of the pride and independence usually associated with his status in Europe. After falling out of favour as a result of his intervention in

1900 he wrote a grovelling letter to V.K. Plehve, stating that the police had been giving the students 'a harsh but fully deserved lesson': ibid., undated letter, pp. 11ff.

[11] The Princess's whole diary is spattered with criticism of the bureaucracy: e.g., the defeat at the hands of Witte and Kokovtsov of her husband's schemes for representative institutions is described as 'the complete triumph of the bureaucracy' ('Dnevnik', p. 260).

[12] Volkonsky, *Reminiscences*, II: 89, 96–7, 105–7.

[13] See particularly his letter of 12/25 March 1905 in Brooke MSS.

[14] On this see, e.g., A.N. Kulomzin's comments about his friends' despair in the late 1850s at the tedium of official work and the sometimes humiliating attitudes of their chiefs: TsGIA, Fond 1642, Opis 1, Ed. Khr. 178, pp. 2–7. Also Semyonov, *Detstvo*, I: 177–9, 188.

[15] On Alexander Obolensky, a magnate deeply involved in running his estates, see ch. 8. Prince A.A. Kurakin also devoted much of his energy to managing his own business affairs: see Anon., *Russian Court Memoirs*, 279.

[16] See my *Origins*, ch. 3, n. 24, and Tcharykow, *Glimpses*, 100.

[17] The letters of Alexander Obolensky and his wife provide useful material on the travails of an aristocratic marshal in the 1880s. See ch. 8.

[18] Vasil'chikov, 'Vospominaniya', ch. 7, pp. 57–60.

[19] Letter dated 22 Sept 1916: TsGIA, Fond 899, Opis 1, Ed. Kh. 50, p. 12.

[20] Fragments from Repnin's diary; see TsGIA, Fond 1035, Opis 1, Ed. Khr. 748, p. 14.

[21] Gollwitzer, *Standesherren*, 287ff., is good on this point. For an interesting view of the values and life-style of the Austrian aristocracy in the early and mid-nineteenth century see H. Steckl, *Osterreichs Aristokratie im Vormärz* (Munich, 1973).

[22] *ASRGD*, 867, and Levinson, *Sovet* (1915), 14, list Bobrinsky's many non-official activities. S.D. Sazonov, *Fateful Years, 1909–16* (London, 1928), 307, comments on Bobrinsky's ignorance and superficiality as a minister. Naumov (*Iz Utselevshikh*, II: 299), himself a big landowner not an official, records that Bobrinsky was charming but was not taken seriously in business-like circles. Even so A.N. Schwartz, disgusted by the liberalism of his officials, suggested Bobrinsky to Nicholas II as a possible Minister of Education: TsGIA, Fond 338, Opis 3, Delo 4, p. 4.

[23] Vasil'chikov, 'Vospominaniya', ch. 7, pp. 57–60. Svyatopolk-Mirsky, 'Dnevnik', p. 248 ('No, I am no minister').

[24] Ibid., pp. 257, 266.

[25] On this see Vasil'chikov, 'Vospominaniya', ch. 7, pp. 57–9, and Gurko's comments on Vasil'chikov and Svyatopolk-Mirsky in *Features*, 292ff., 500. D.N. Lyubimov, CUBA MSS, 'Russkaya smuta nachala devyatisotykh godov, 1902–1906. Po vospominaniyam, lichnym zapiskam i dokumentam', chs. 9 and 10, is kinder than Gurko about Mirsky, stressing the latter's 'complete honesty and great decency' (p. 185). Nevertheless, Svyatopolk-Mirsky emerges from Lyubimov's memoirs as a rather ineffective minister who lost control of events.

[26] S.S. Oldenburg, *Last Tsar: Nicholas II, His Reign and His Russia*, 4 vols. (1975), I: 11–13; Leroy-Beaulieu, *Empire of the Tsars*, II: 382–3, 399–402; Solov'yov, *Samoderzhavie i dvoryanstvo*, 281–6.

[27] Polovtsov, *Dnevnik*, II: 20, 431–2, 446.

[28] Lambsdorff's diary: *Dnevnik*, e.g. I: 342, on I.A. Zinov'ev: 'he is at all times an extremely ambitious parvenu; there's always the desire to push oneself forward, to ascribe everything to oneself. ...all this type of behaviour and petty vanity repels my minister' (i.e. N.K. Giers). Subsequently Giers also clashed with Zinov'ev's successor, the aristocratic Count Dimitri Kapnist. 'I am a free man,' shouted Kapnist after one argument in January 1892. 'Of course you are a great lord and we are all rogues', responded Giers (ibid., II: 264). Even here, however, differences in social background worsened but did not cause the major problems. Giers, after all, came from an anything but aristocratic

background, but feared Zinov'ev's intelligence and ambition.

[29] *Trudy chetvyortogo s'ezda upol'nomochennykh dvoryanskikh obshchestv 32 gubernii* (SPB, 1909), 259.

[30] See ch. 4, n. 152.

[31] On political affiliations in the State Council after 1905, two theses are of use: A.P. Borodin, *Gosudarstvennyy Sovet v 1911–14 gody* (Candidate's thesis, Moscow Univ., 1977), and A. Shecket, *The Imperial State Council and the Policies of P.A. Stolypin, 1905–11* (Ph.D. thesis, Columbia Univ., 1974). Even when a member of the Council seldom spoke, one can trace in *SOGS* his membership of a faction through his voting for or against key 'party' motions.

[32] Vasili, *Société*, 243–6; Anon., *Court Memoirs*, 282.

[33] L. L'vov, *Byurokraticheskie Siluety* (SPB, 1908), 30.

[34] *SOGS*, Session 7 (25 Nov 1911 and 23 Feb 1912), cols. 612 and 2056.

[35] On Zinov'ev's character see Gurko, *Features*, 184–5; D.N. Shipov, *Vospominaniya i dumy o perezhitom* (Moscow, 1918), 227–8. On his background and education see *ASRGD*, 659–61. My comments are also based on reading all Zinov'ev's long and numerous speeches in the State Council from 1906 to 1917.

[36] L'vov, *Siluety*, 30–1. *SOGS*, e.g. Session 7, col. 589, when Zinov'ev, typically, opened his speech on the government of Baku by complaining that far more statistics were needed before the State Council could decide on this issue.

[37] Zinov'ev early expressed his hope that the reformed State Council would not fall prey to a 'narrow party spirit' (*SOGS*, Session 1 (24 June 1906), p. 5). See also, e.g., Session 3 (26 Mar 1908), col. 727: 'I am completely and deeply convinced...that one ought not to introduce politics into schooling, just as one should not introduce it into religious questions'.

[38] See, e.g., *SOGS*, session 3 (2 Apr 1908), cols. 913–22 (on the need for bureaucratic supervision to ensure that the élites who ran the zemstvos did not exploit the masses; subsequently Zinov'ev became more pro-zemstvo); Session 5 (29 May 1910), cols. 3422–5 and Session 7 (14 Dec 1911), cols. 774–84 and (8 Feb 1912) 1466–71 (on the need to extend the municipal franchise in order to undermine selfish, entrenched urban élites); Session 8 (5 June 1913), cols. 2177ff. (on landowners' efforts to secure the advantages of ownership while shifting the land tax to the peasants).

[39] *SOGS*, Session 8 (5 June 1913), col. 2132; Session 9 (20 May 1914), col. 2378; Session 12 (18 Feb 1916), col. 258.

[40] *SOGS*, Session 12, cols. 255–8.

[41] See, e.g., Meshchersky's enthusiastic comments about Krivsky in *Grazhdanin*, no. 97 (15 Dec 1902), p. 18, and the warm obituary of S.S. Bekhteev published in *Grazhdanin*, no. 28 (24 July 1911), pp. 3–4.

[42] Bogdanovich, *Tri poslednikh*, 308.

[43] The speech is in *Trudy*, 181–8, the extract cited on p. 187. My comments on Bekhteev are also based on a letter written by him to Prince Alexander Obolensky on 5 July 1885 (TsGIA, Fond 1650, Opis 1, Ed. Khr. 49, pp. 1–8), which is notable particularly for its defence of noble landowners' qualifications as a ruling class. The obituary noted in n. 41 above is also of interest, as is Bekhteev's book, *Khozyaystvennye itogi istekshago 45-letiya; mery k khozyaystvennomu podyomu* (SPB, 1902).

[44] Krivsky's service record is in TsGIA, Fond 1162, Opis 6, Ed. Khr. 265.

[45] See the comments of 'N.P.' in *Grazhdanin*, no. 98 (19 Dec 1902), p. 8.

[46] On the Junkers see in particular Muncy, *Junker*, esp. 33–40, also Goerlitz, *Junker*, and ch. 5 of O. Graf von Stolberg-Wernigerode, *Die Unentscheidene Generation. Deutschlands konservative Fuhrungsschichten am Vorabend des Ersten Weltkrieges* (Munich, 1968). S. Wehking, 'Zum politischen und sozialen Selbstverständnis preussischer Junker, 1871–1914', *Blätter für deutsche Landesgeschichte*, Band 121 (1985), pp. 395–447, is a useful survey of the Junkers' role in Prussian central politics under the Second Reich. Astonishingly, there is no modern scholarly book dedicated to the social history

of Prussian Junkerdom in the nineteenth and twentieth centuries.

[47] Polovtsov, *Dnevnik*, II: 130, and 'Dnevnik', *KA* 3 (1923), p. 146. Uvarov's views are quoted in *Grazhdanin*, no. 97 (15 Dec 1902), p. 8.

[48] The fullest study of Krivsky is contained in Panchulidzev, *Sbornik*. See also the useful article of T. Mixter, 'Of Grandfather-Beaters and Fat-Headed Pacifists. Perceptions of Agricultural Labor and Hiring Market Disturbances in Saratov, 1872–1905', *Russian History/Histoire Russe* 7, pts. 1–2 (1980), pp. 139–68.

[49] Panchulidzev, *Sbornik*, 161–5.

[50] From a speech made by Krivsky at a dinner given in his honour by the Saratov nobility on 6 Dec 1902 and cited in *Grazhdanin*, no. 97 (15 Dec 1902), p. 18.

[51] CUBA: Lyubimov MSS, 'Russkaya smuta', p. 223.

[52] See ch. 7.

[53] Levinson, *Senat*, 44–5. TsGIA, Fond 1162, Opis 6, Ed. Khr. 560 (service record).

[54] For Fliege's comment see his MS in CUBA entitled 'Gr. V.N. Kokovtsov', here p. 3. On Kokovtsov's attitude to the budget see Svyatopolk-Mirsky, 'Dnevnik', p. 263.

[55] On Mosolov's background and adolescence see RO, Fond 514, Opis 1, Ed. Khr. 4. TsGAOR, Fond 1463, Opis 1, Ed. Khr. 1115, pp. 152, 162, 260.

[56] See TsGAOR, Fond 568, Opis 1, Ed. Khr. 892, p. 86. Alexander II gave 150,000 roubles to pay off Lambsdorff's debts on the condition that his creditors made no attempt to recover their money through the courts.

[57] A letter from Lambsdorff to Princess E.A. Saltykova-Golovkina, whom he was proposing to marry, dated 15 Apr 1889. TsGAOR, Fond 568, Opis 1, Ed. Khr. 287, p. 8ii.

[58] Lambsdorff, *Dnevnik*, II: 101.

[59] Ibid., I: 350.

[60] Ibid., I: 78, 146; II: 101.

[61] Lambsdorff's diary, letters and dispatches provide ample evidence for this comment. I discuss his views briefly in 'Pro-Germans and Russian Foreign Policy 1890–1914', *International History Review* 2, no. 1 (Jan 1980), pp. 34–54; here pp. 35–6.

[62] Lambsdorff, *Dnevnik*, entry for 9 Mar 1889.

[63] Letter dated 28 Nov 1902, extract on p. 44i of TsGIA, Fond 568, Opis 1, Ed. Khr. 280.

[64] See the extraordinary letter of resignation, replete with offended jealousy and insecurity, which Lambsdorff wrote to Giers on 12 July 1886 and the Minister's kindly reply, in which he stressed that his only desire had been to take some of the burden of work off Lambsdorff's back: TsGIA, Fond 568, Opis 1, Ed. Khr. 422, pp. 236–42.

[65] TsGIA, Fond 892, Opis 3, Delo 1 (memoirs of I.P. Balashov), p. 21i.

[66] Ibid., pp. 22, 29, 33, 56, 89.

[67] Ibid., pp. 58ii, 91i–91ii.

[68] Ibid., pp. 91i–91ii.

[69] Anon., *Russian Court Memoirs*, 282.

[70] Ibid. Ikonnikov, *Noblesse*, vol. W: 269–70. Ignatiev, *Subaltern*, 97.

[71] See, e.g., the memoirs of M.M. Osorgin in RO, Fond 215, Opis 1, Delo 5; of A.N. Kulomzin in TsGIA, Fond 1642, Opis 1, Ed. Khr. 172, 173, 174, 178 and 179; P.P. Semyonov, *Detstvo*; A.P. Izvols'ky, *Memoirs of Alexander Iswolsky* (London, n.d.), ch. 5; and N.V. Charykov [Tcharykow], *Glimpses*.

[72] See, e.g., A.P. Izvol'sky's comments about the life of this stratum, which 'was quite remarkable in its adoption of the forms of Western Europe.... As far back as I can remember, there was in my parents' house a permanent staff of cosmopolitan instructors: English maids, and French, English and German tutors and governesses; this was also a common custom in other houses of the same standing': *Memoirs*, 159–60.

[73] N.V. Charykov was, e.g., partly educated in Scotland, his sisters in Germany: *Glimpses*, 77, 86. For A.N. Kulomzin's 'grand tour' and its influence see ch. 7.

[74] Izvol'sky, *Memoirs*, 161. M.M. Osorgin, born in 1861, recalls his own shift towards fluency in Russian because of the influence of his teacher, Yakovlev. 'Before his appearance I, encouraged by

my mother, always took pride in my flowing French conversation and in my knowledge of foreign languages, and spoke Russian like a foreigner': RO, Fond 215, Opis 1, Delo 5, p. 61.

[75] To pick at random among many examples in the service records: P.N. Durnovo was, as we shall see, a Russian nationalist from a relatively poor family and with a narrow military education. How much 'general enlightenment' he derived from an assignment to Paris in 1884 to study French police methods one cannot say, but a man of his intelligence is unlikely to have kept his eyes shut during a lengthy stay in the French capital. His service record is in TsGIA, Fond 1162, Opis 6, Ed. Khr. 190. M.N. Galkin-Vrasskoy, e.g., was dispatched to the West in 1862 to investigate foreign use of tariffs: see TsGIA, Fond 1162, Opis 6, Ed. Khr. 105.

[76] Terner, Vospominaniya, I: 3–13, 315, 328–46.

[77] Ibid., 4.

[78] The quote is from Izvol'sky's Memoirs, 289. On the family see Ikonnikov, Noblesse, vol. D: 199–204: on Frederycksz's personality and political inactivity the best sources are Volkonsky, Reminiscences, II: 96, and Mosolov, Court, 102–5, 108–10.

[79] The most thorough all-round survey of the position of the Baltic nobility at the turn of the century is Georg Hermann, Der Strukturwandel des baltischen Adels in der Zeit vor dem Ersten Weltkrieg, in Wissenschaftliche Beiträge zur Geschichte und Landeskunde Ost-Mitteleuropas, Band 41 (Marburg, 1959). The memoirs of Eduard Freiherr von Dellinghausen, Im Dienst der Heimat (Stuttgart, 1930), provide much useful information about the mentality of the Baltic gentry in this period. Alexander von Tobien, Die Livländische Ritterschaft und ihre Verhältnis zum Zarismus and Russischen Nationalismus, 2 vols. (Riga, 1925), is a partisan but thorough defence of the gentry's position. Gert von Pistohlkors, Ritterschaftliche Reformpolitik zwischen Russifizierung und Revolution (Göttingen, 1978), is an excellent revisionist work illustrating the narrow limits to which the gen-

try's reformist inclinations were confined unless heavy pressure was applied from Petersburg. Pistohlkors, for instance, draws attention (pp. 194–7) to the broader and more politically sophisticated approach to the gentry's problems adopted in 1904–6 by Baron Alexander Meyendorff and Baron Boris Wolff, who stood out among the Livonian Ritterschaft because of the insights they had gained through imperial bureaucratic service.

[80] Dellinghausen, Dienst, 15.

[81] Ekesparre's service record is in TsGIA, Fond 1162, Opis 6, Ed. Khr. 633. See also Tobien, Ritterschaft, I: 194–5, 424–5. Ekesparre's spoken Russian was e.g. much better than that of the other marshals. Wittram, Baltische, 221, says Ekesparre enjoyed considerable prestige in Petersburg.

[82] Pistohlkors, Ritterschaftliche, 124–5; Dellinghausen, Dienst, 93.

[83] On the Uxkull family background see GHdbR, Teil Estland, 1: 475–520. Tobien, Livländische, I: 21, 68, 495, on Alexander Uxkull and I: 301 on Julius. On the latter see also Pistohlkors, Ritterschaftliche, 124, 127, 169. It was Julius Uxkull who suggested to Nicholas II that Ekesparre be appointed to the State Council: Dellinghausen, Dienst, 178. On Julius Uxkull's views see also Gurko, Features, 27, 39.

[84] TsGAOR, Fond 542, Opis 1, Ed. Khr. 352, pp. 197, 216 (Wahl's memoirs).

[85] Ibid., p. 197.

[86] Ibid.

[87] Ibid., p. 23ii.

[88] Ibid., pp. 70, 131.

[89] Ed. Khr. 270, p. 1, document dated 8 May 1892.

[90] Gurko, Features, 190–2, makes roughly this point.

[91] On the political naïvety of most imperial officers, see P. Kenez, 'The Ideology of the White Movement', Soviet Studies (Glasgow) 32 (1980), pp. 58–82.

[92] Polovtsov has a good deal to say in his diaries about the political role of army officers. See, e.g., Dnevnik, II: 174 and 'Dnevnik', KA 3 (1923), p. 125. In his view, General Staff officers, poli-

tically no less ignorant than their military brethren but more self-confident and arrogant, could be the greatest menace of all. 'Dnevnik', *KA* 3 (1923), p. 101, and 46 (1931), p. 125.

[93] E.g., after 1906 the great majority of the Council's generals and admirals belonged to the Right Group: see Naumov, *Iz utselevshikh*, II: 151. Also V. L'vov, 'Zvyozdnaya palata', *Minuvshie Dni* (Moscow-Leningrad) 3 (1928), pp. 13–38, whose description of the personalities and roles of the members of the Council after 1906 shows that the upper house's military members were much less important than their civilian counterparts. See also n. 31 above.

[94] Izvol'sky, *Memoirs*, 60.

[95] I have written on this subject in 'The Security Police, Civil Rights, and the Fate of the Russian Empire', in O. Crisp and L. Edmondson, eds., *Civil Rights in Imperial Russia* (Oxford, 1988).

[96] My major source for these comments are Wahl's rather revealing memoirs in TsGAOR, Fond 542, Opis 1, Ed. Khr. 352, as well as letters, memoranda and other documents also contained in this Fond. Gurko, *Features*, 190–2, discusses Wahl, and there are also comments on him in other memoirs and diaries.

[97] TsGAOR, Fond 542, Opis 1, Ed. Khr. 352, p. 139.

[98] E.g., ibid., p. 197.

[99] Gurko, *Features*, 191.

[100] Bogdanovich, *Tri poslednikh*, 415.

[101] RO, Fond 126, K. 13, p. 70, diary entry for September 1902.

[102] On Kosych, see, e.g., *ASRGD*, 953–4, and Lvov, 'Zvozdnaya', p. 24.

[103] Witte, *Vospominaniya*, III: 395. Gurko, *Features*, 445, writes 'this general was noted for his firmness and ruthlessness'. The comments of V.G. Kiernan on the effects on the European metropolises of colonial military mentalities are relevant here: see Kiernan, *European Empires from Conquest to Collapse, 1815–1960* (Leicester, 1982), 160–7, 201–5.

[104] For the two men's service records see (Lobko) TsGIA, Fond 1162, Opis 6, Ed. Khr. 298, p. 129ff., and (Mirsky) TsGIA, Fond 1284, Opis 52, Ed. Khr.

[77]. Gurko, *Features*, 295, calls Mirsky a show soldier. For a sense, perhaps a little exaggerated, of the time invested by officers in administration see Bushnell, *Mutiny*, ch. 1.

[105] On the diary see n. 11 above. For Mirsky's comments on noble privilege see TsGIA, Fond 1200, Opis 16ii, Ed. Khr. 102, e.g. p. 727, where he argued that the removal of class barriers to entry to the civil service would further encourage members of the peasantry and lower middle class to seek to rise out of their natural environment.

[106] The fullest expression of Lobko's political opinions is his speech on the composition of the Bulygin Duma, at a conference held at Peterhof in June 1905 under Nicholas II's chairmanship. The record of the conference is published in Eberhard Frowein, ed., *Petergofskoe soveshchanie o proekte Gosudarstvennoy dumy* (Berlin, 1905). Lobko's speech is discussed by Solov'yov in *Samoderzhavie... 1902*, 180–2, as well as by P. Sh. Ganelin in Akademiya Nauk SSSR, *Krizis Samoderzhaviya v Rossii, 1895–1917* (Leningrad, 1984), 199–211. His opposition to Witte's policies, evident from these sources, is confirmed in Lobko's own *Vsepodanneishiy otchot gos. kontrolera za 1901*, parts of which are cited (p. 55) by A.P. Mendel, *Dilemmas of Progress in Tsarist Russia. Legal Marxism and Legal Populism* (Cambridge Mass., 1961). The comment on oil concessions is from Polovtsov, 'Dnevnik', *KA* 46 (1931), p. 129.

[107] A.F. Koni, 'Pamyati Andreya Aleksandrovicha Saburova', *Na zhiznennom puti*, 5 vols. (Berlin, n.d.), IV: 399.

[108] For a definition of the term 'zealot' see Downs, *Bureaucracy*, 88–9.

[109] Gurko, *Features*, 99–100.

[110] Koni, 'Pamyati', IV: 410.

[111] Ibid., 400, 409. See, e.g., Saburov's enthusiastic comment about Nicholas II's decisions on the Duma franchise: 'He swept to the side all worry about the practical consequences of the proposed measure and asked himself the only important question for a Russian tsar: where does my duty lie?' The extract is from a draft undated letter written in the

winter of 1905–6 and found among Saburov's papers in TsGAOR, Fond 1074, Opis 1, Ed. Khr. 1116, p. 15i.

[112] Meshchersky, in *Grazhdanin*, no. 43 (6 Nov 1911), p. 1. Polovtsov called Saburov a 'very decent man in all respects, a very noble character', on 26 May 1906: 'Dnevnik', *KA* 4 (1923), p. 113.

[113] Most of the greetings to Saburov are in Ed. Khr. 1109, 1111 and 1119, but the letter cited is from TsGAOR, Fond 1074, Opis 1, Ed. Khr. 1132, and is dated 28 Dec 1907.

[114] An exception here is V. Leontowitsch, *Geschichte des Liberalismus in Russland* (Frankfurt, 1957).

[115] Koni, 'Pamyati', IV: 407.

[116] TsGAOR, Fond 1074, Opis 1, Ed. Khr. 1105, p. 102. This is the key passage in the explanatory note attached to the record of the special commission.

[117] *Byloe* 3 (1917), pp. 245–6. TsGAOR, Fond 1074, Opis 1, Ed. Khr. 1116, p. 11 (see n. 111 above). The newspaper *Slovo*, issue no. 338 (23 Dec 1907), p. 3, has a piece on Saburov and his career.

[118] Polovtsov wrote in 1886, 'looking at this good and decent man one can't understand how it would be possible to appoint him a minister': *Dnevnik*, I: 380. V.M. Golitsyn, though motivated in part by political feelings, also criticized Saburov as a minister for talking too much, paying too much attention to zemstvo chatter, and lacking system or consistency of purpose: RO, Fond 75, diary of Prince V.M. Golitsyn, GBM 10 (covering 1880–1), e.g., pp. 140, 281, 298, 331, 347, 412.

[119] A.I. Lykoshin, 'Pamyati A.A. Knirima. K istorii sostavleniya proekta grazhdanskogo ulozheniya', *Zhurnal ministerstva yustitsii* (SPB), no. 10 (Dec 1905), pp. 1–29; here pp. 4, 5, 7.

[120] Ibid., pp. 1–3, 8–11.

[121] Ibid., pp. 13–25.

[122] Ibid., p. 7, on Knirim.

[123] Naumov, *Iz utselevshikh*, II: 153, 212 on Kobylinsky. Polovtsov, *Dnevnik*, II: 41, and Gurko, *Features*, 94–6, on Golubev. For Meshchersky's views on this, see an interesting piece in *Grazh-*

danin, no. 46 (27 Nov 1911), p. 16.

[124] I have never heard a senior jurist described as stupid, an epithet quite often used against high officials in other departments by their enemies and critics. Gurko, *Features*, 178, and Kulomzin in his memoirs (TsGIA, Fond 1642, Opis 1, Ed. Khr. 178, pp. 2, 3, 7) agree that the cream of the young entrants to the civil service in the 1860s tended to enter the judicial department.

[125] For all the somewhat tortured language he employs, George Yaney has a good deal that is sensible to say on these topics. See esp. his *Systematization*.

[126] This was particularly true in the Duma era of course.

[127] L'vov, 'Zvyozdnaya', pp. 21, 22. A.F. Koni: *Na zhiznennom Puti*, IV: 371–7, and *Otsy*, 282; Witte, *Vospominaniya*, III: 547; *Grazhdanin*, no. 14 (17 Apr 1911); Polovtsov, 'Dnevnik', *KA* 3 (1923), p. 111.

[128] *Soveshchaniya*, passim, but the debate on the procuracy's role, on 21 Dec 1894 under the chairmanship of P.M. Butovsky, is perhaps of particular interest. Among future members of the State Council, V.F. Dietrich, A.N. Shcherbachev, E.G. Turau and N.N. Schmemann participated in this discussion (see Protocol XIII). My comments about jurists' political allegiances are based on study of support for motions in the reformed State Council, as recorded in *SOGS*.

[129] *Grazhdanin*, no. 2 (10 Jan 1902), p. 2. Koni, *Otsy*. 15–17.

[130] Shcheglovitov would be an interesting, if unpleasant, subject for a biography. Among the useful sources for this would be his relatively frequent scholarly articles in the *Zhurnal ministerstva yustitsii* before 1905, his subsequent speeches in the State Council and the record of his interrogation by the Provisional Government in 'Dopros I.G. Shcheglovitova', *Padenie*, II: 337–439. A speech delivered by Shcheglovitov to the chairmen of JPs' sessions, reprinted in *Grazhdanin*, no. 48 (8 Dec 1913), pp. 5–6, and Shcheglovitov's *Vliyanie inostrannykh zakonodatel'stv na sostavlenie sudebnykh ustavov, 20 noyabr 1864* (SPB,

1914), are also of interest.

[131] *Grazhdanin*, no. 39 (6 Oct 1913), pp. 11–12; no. 42 (27 Oct 1913), p. 14; no. 43 (3 Nov 1913), p. 10. On Shcheglovitov and anti-Semitism, see in particular H. Rogger, *Jewish Policies and Right-Wing Politics in Imperial Russia* (London, 1986), esp. chs. 2, 3 and 4.

[132] See *Padenie*, II: 337–439.

[133] For, e.g., P.N. Durnovo, see ch. 6. It may be significant that Shcheglovitov, brazen under interrogation about his anti-Semitism, was shamefaced about illegal acts he had condoned: 'Dopros Shcheglovitova' in *Padenie*, II: 397. In contrast to Ministry of Internal Affairs officials, Shcheglovitov was also in favour of abolishing the so-called administrative guarantee (i.e., officials could only be prosecuted with their boss's consent) on the ground that it encouraged wanton illegality by officials: *SOGS*, Session 12 (6 June 1916), cols. 1588–96.

[134] L'vov, 'Zvyozdnaya', p. 24.

[135] In 1915 *Novoe Vremya* stated that the Ministry of Internal Affairs 'directs the course of almost the whole of Russian life' (28 Sept 1915, p. 3), while four years earlier Meshchersky argued that 'the direction taken by governmental policy is decided not by the Council of Ministers and not by its chairman but by the Minister of Internal Affairs, in whose hands at present lies control over all rights and freedoms, over everything appertaining to the realization of the act of 17 October 1905': *Grazhdanin*, no. 10 (13 Mar 1911), p. 12.

[136] R.G. Robbins, *The Tsar's Viceroys* (forthcoming, 1988) makes all these points in a lucid way. See in particular chs. 3, 4, and 5.

[137] See Meshchersky's thoroughly realistic comments on the dilemma faced by Prince P.D. Svyatopolk-Mirsky in *Grazhdanin*, no. 69 (29 Aug 1904), p. 20; no. 73 (12 Sept 1904), pp. 19–20.

[138] E.g., A.N. Mosolov's appointment to the State Council in 1903. V.K. Plehve told Mosolov that during an audience, 'the Emperor had a sheet of paper in the left-hand drawer of his desk. Saying that he knew much that

was good about you, he added that he wished primarily to have deserving governors in the Council'. The source from whom Nicholas 'knew much' about Mosolov was V.P. Meshchersky: TsGAOR, Fond 1463, Opis 1, Ed. Khr. 1115, p. 364i.

[139] See n. 138 above, and also M. G. Akimov's comment that the Emperor didn't always agree with Akimov's choice of candidates for the State Council and insisted on his own judgement of people over Akimov's objections: Naumov, *Iz utselevshikh*, II: 217.

[140] Gurko, *Features*, 198, makes the classic statement about the superior quality of central officialdom to those active in local society's organizations. See also, e.g., n. 152 of ch. 4 above.

[141] Naumov, *Iz utselevshikh*, I: 237, 244; II: 151–3. On Bryanchaninov's background and career see TsGIA, Fond 1162, Opis 6, Ed. Khr. 55 (service record) and Ikonnikov, *Noblesse*, vol. V1: 149.

[142] On the general point about governors see n. 136 above. This is a point to which P.L. Bark often returns in his memoirs: see, e.g., his ch. 13, *Vozrozhdenie*, no. 168 (Dec 1965), p. 93: 'Old bureaucrats with a good service past had no experience as regards public speaking'. In Bark's view, few were good orators and this caused them real trouble in the Duma. Lack of oratorical talent was one reason why, in Bark's view, A.V. Krivoshein refused the chairmanship of the Council of Ministers in 1914: see Bark's ch. 14, *Vozrozhdenie*, no. 205 (Jan 1969), p. 71. Krivoshein was by no means alone in this weakness. Kokovtsov in *Past*, 202–4, writes that General N.K. Schaufuss, the Minister of Communications, 'was a military engineer and little suited to the new conditions of legislative work. He was a poor speaker, totally unprepared to defend in public the interests of his ministry against the unceremonious attacks of his opponents; every rude criticism of his work threw him into such confusion that he answered it with unconcealed irritation', ultimately deciding that the Duma's existence made his continued presence at the head

of his ministry impossible.

[143] RO, Fond 126, K. 13, pp. 312–13 (a conversation with Plehve of 2 Apr 1904).

[144] Ibid., p. 258, from a letter to Kireev of September 1903.

[145] From a conversation with Witte in October 1902, recorded by D.N. Lyubimov in CUBA MSS: 'Russkaya smuta', pp. 48ff.

[146] Maklakov's letter is cited by Bark in ch. 23 of his memoirs: Vozrozhdenie, no. 180 (1966), pp. 72–4. See also a speech made by Maklakov in the State Council on 6 June 1916: SOGS, Session 12, cols. 1566–82.

[147] Yaney, Systematization, 257–8; Korkunov, Pravo, II: 94.

[148] Letter to his wife dated 7 Feb 1902: TsGIA, Fond 1642, Opis 1, Ed. Khr. 220, pp. 22–3.

[149] SOGS, Session 3 (25 June 1908), col. 2047. Lyubimov describes the State Chancellery as incomparable and its officials as 'entirely exceptional in their knowledge of affairs and their capacity for hard work'. He echoes Durnovo's comments about their career prospects. CUBA MSS: 'Smuta', pp. 12–13.

[150] Lambsdorff, Dnevnik, II: 221.

[151] Gurko, Features, 38–9.

[152] Kokovtsov, Past, 40. Gurko, Features, 97.

[153] See ch. 7.

[154] Gurko, Features, 38.

[155] Witte, Vospominaniya, III: 294, 460.

[156] Naumov, Iz utselevshikh, II: 376. Other, distinctly similar, comments on chancellery officials are Witte, Vospominaniya, III: 127, on Baron E. Yu Nolde, and I: 260–1, on S.V. Rukhlov. For the latter see also Gurko, Features, 42–3, and ibid., 39, on Baron Julius Uxkull.

[157] Akademiya Nauk, Krizis, 30.

[158] O. Crisp, Studies in the Russian Economy Before 1914 (London, 1976), 24.

[159] Bark received over 120,000 roubles a year: see his memoirs, ch. 4, in Vozrozhdenie, no. 157 (Jan 1965), pp. 58–60. In the Smeta raskhodov for 1909, the majority of the Council's appointed members received, after deductions, less than 15,000 roubles a year, and nine

men, admittedly all of them with private means, received less than 10,000.

[160] Ya. I. Livshin discusses the role of these men in his two articles, 'K voprosu' and 'Predstavitel'nye'.

[161] The quotation comes from pp. 132 and 135 of 'Zapisky sanovnika', a document dated 31 May 1907 and published in Golos Minuvshego, nos. 1–3 (Jan–Mar 1918), pp. 115–36. For comments on Schwanebach see Witte, Vospominaniya, III: 453–5; Izvolsky, Memoirs, 94–5; Kryzhanovsky, Vospominaniya, 110 (the first two very and the third rather critical). The comments of Gurko, Features, 232, and Polovtsov, 'Dnevnik', KA 4 (1923), p. 87, are much friendlier. A.A. Polivanov records Schwanebach's opposition to opening a new university in 1907: 'This means to organize another hotbed of revolution'. See Iz dnevnikov i vospominaniy po dolzhnosti voennogo ministra i ego pomoshchnika (Moscow, 1924), 25.

[162] For Polovtsov's comment see 'Dnevnik', KA 4 (1923), p. 121. Also Gurko, Features, 97; Witte, Vospominaniya, I: 287–9, and Lambsdorff, Dnevnik, I: 30.

[163] F.G. Terner, O rabochem klasse i merakh k obespechenie ego blagosostoyaniya (SPB, 1860), 16, 20.

[164] Ibid., 35–9.

[165] Ibid., 23–9, 31–2, 141–5, 304–11.

[166] This is the key point in his detailed Gosudarstvo i zemlevladenie, 2 vols. (SPB, 1896, 1901). The work more or less sits on the fence as regards the commune's effects on agriculture.

[167] See Terner's memoirs, e.g., Vospominaniya, I: 116–17, 169, 310; II: 110–15, 190–1, 229, 291–2.

[168] A speech by Kokovtsov of 10 Feb 1904 reproduced in Grazhdanin, no. 13 (12 Feb 1904), p. 19.

[169] Gurko, Features, 67.

[170] See n. 168.

[171] On Pleske see Witte, Vospominaniya, I: 345, and II: 244–6; Kuropatkin, Dnevnik, 72–4; Terner, Vospominaniya, I: 45; Polovtsov, 'Dnevnik', KA 3 (1923), p. 143; Grazhdanin, no. 35 (2 May 1904), p. 17. On Romanov see Witte, Vospominaniya, I: 210–11; S.S. Manukhin in

TsGAOR, Fond 564, Opis 1, Ed. Khr. 701, p. 4 and Kokovtsov, *Past*, 8. For Shipov see below, nn. 173, 174.

[172] Letter to Alexander Benckendorff dated 20 Dec 1916 from his brother Paul: Brooke MSS.

[173] Kokovtsov, *Past*, 90.

[174] Witte, *Vospominaniya*, 1: 361–6.

[175] One way of measuring this is to study membership of the State Council's groupings after 1905. Of the financial officials among the 215 men, only Sch-wanebach belonged to the Right Group.

[176] SOGS, Session 4 (28 Mar 1911), col. 1653.

[177] Bark, 'Vospominaniya', ch. 15, *Vozrozhdenie*, no. 171 (Mar 1966), pp. 92–3.

[178] Ministerstvo Inostrannykh Del: Kommissiya po reorganizatsii zagrani-chnoy sluzhby, *Svod otchotov zagrany-chnykh ustanovleniy ministerstva na vopro-snik kasatel'no organizatsii zagranichnoy sluzhby* (SPB, n.d.), here 148–53.

[179] Cecil, *German*, 68–74. The British Embassy in Petersburg frequently stress-ed the significance of diplomats playing a role in Petersburg high society and looked with some scorn on France's envoys' inability to do this: see, e.g., the British Annual Report on Russia for 1912, which is reprinted as document 135 in K. Bourne and D.C. Watt, gen. eds., *British Documents on Foreign Affairs: Reports and Papers from the Foreign Office Confidential Print*, Part I. Series A: *Russia, 1859–1914*, ed. D. Lieven (1983), VI: 283–306. Count V.N. Lambsdorff com-plained in the following terms of efforts to 'foist *grands seigneurs* such as Prince A.S. Dolgoruky, on the Foreign Minis-try as ambassadors. 'An impressive ap-pearance is a good thing but in the final analysis what's important is not so much that an ambassador be an imposing fi-gure as that he does his job well, and one rarely sees this with amateurs drawn from the side': 'Dnevnik', *KA* 46 (1931), p. 34, entry for 5 Feb 1895.

[180] See my *Origins*, 61–2.

[181] See, e.g., Gurko, *Features*, 481, and Kokovtsov, *Past*, 142, 159–60. Also Schwanebach, 'Zapisky', p. 126.

[182] Sazonov, *Fateful Years*, here p. 282.

[183] E.A. Adamov, *Konstantinopol' i prolivy* (Moscow, 1925), 8–10.

[184] See an entry in P.A. Valuev's diary for 11 Jan 1876: *Dnevnik P.A. Valueva*, 2 vols. (Moscow, 1961), II (1865–1876): 326.

[185] I have discussed all these issues at much greater length in my *Origins*, es-pecially chs. 1 and 4ii.

[186] Many of these men left memoirs or collections of letters. See, e.g., R.R. Rosen, *Forty Years of Diplomacy*, 2 vols. (London, 1922); J.Y. Simpson, ed., *The Saburov Memoirs* (Cambridge, 1929); Baron A. Meyendorff, ed., *Correspon-dence diplomatique de M. de Staal* (Paris, 1929). The latter is described by Basily, *Memoirs*, 11–12, as 'The perfect model of the old-school diplomat. His sharp mind went along with his exquisite cour-tesy'. Respect for Zinov'ev's talent was general: see, e.g., Witte, *Vospominaniya*, III: 525–6; Rosen, *Forty Years*, I: 134; Charykov [Tcharykow], *Glimpses*, 20. P.A. Saburov was rare in combining diplomatic and financial expertise. A useful memorandum by him on the links between Russia's economic and financial situation on the one hand and her foreign policy on the other is in TsGIA, Fond 1044, Opis 1, Ed. Khr. 224. I have quoted extracts from this in my 'Pro-Germans', pp. 37–8. Russian high officials concur-red that Shuvalov was a man of con-siderable cunning and an ambassador who enjoyed exceptionally high respect in Berlin. Charykov, e.g., in *Glimpses*, 265, writes of Shuvalov's 'extraordinary personal prestige' in Berlin and on his retirement from the Embassy in Berlin he was, according to Lambsdorff, 'com-pletely engulfed by the moving farewells of court and society. This is a demonstra-tion which has no precedents or limits': 'Dnevnik V.N. Lamzdorfa', *KA* 46 (1931), p. 19, entry for 1 Jan 1895.

[187] See, e.g., Polovtsov, 'Dnevnik', *KA* 3 (1923), p. 82; 46 (1931), p. 123. Rosen, *Forty Years*, I: 174–5.

[188] See, e.g., Lambsdorff, *Dnevnik*, II: 31–2, 73, 319, 332; Rosen, *Forty Years*, I: 127; Witte, *Vospominaniya*, II: 28.

[189] See my *Origins*, esp. ch. 5 and the

conclusions.

[190] This is not the place to discuss the controversial personality and achievements of A.P. Izvol'sky. Of his intelligence few had any doubts. Rosen, who thoroughly disapproved of the policy pursued by Izvol'sky as Minister, nevertheless calls him 'by long odds the ablest man in our service'. *Forty Years*, I: 172–3.

[191] After Lobanov's death Kireev wrote that, contrary to expectations, he had turned out to be clever and to know his job, though, in the diarist's opinion, no Austrophile could truly be suitable as a Russian Foreign Minister: RO, Fond 126, K. 12, p. 8li, entry for 21 Aug 1896. For other views on Lobanov see Rosen, *Forty Years*, I: 104–5; Izvol'sky, *Memoirs*, 165–6; Polovtsov, 'Dnevnik', *KA* 67 (1934), p. 177, and Witte, *Vospominaniya*, II: 28–32, 44, 79–80. For a posthumous semi-hagiography, see V. Teplov, *Knyaz' Aleksei Borisovich Lobanov-Rostovsky. Biograficheskiy ocherk* (SPB, 1897).

[192] On Khilkov's family see Ikonnikov, *Noblesse*, vol. F2. His parents between them owned over 1,000 serfs. *ASRGD*, 186–90, has considerable information on Khilkov's background, upbringing and career. Witte, *Vospominaniya*, II: 24–7, and III: 122.

[193] Ibid. and also Witte, *Vospominaniya*, II: 376, 547, 553. Stolypin's daughter records a conversation with Khilkov: M. von Bock, *Reminiscences of My Father* (New York, 1970), 193–4. Kireev wrote on 17 Jan 1905 of Khilkov's popularity with Maxim Gorky and other figures of the far left: see RO, Fond 126, K. 14, p. 7 i.

[194] The quote is from Polovtsov, 'Dnevnik', *KA* 3 (1923), p. 168, entry for 4 Jan 1903.

[195] Levinson, *Senat*, 17–18.

[196] *ASRGD*, 429–31. V.P. Cherevansky, *Pod boevym ognyom. Istoricheskaya khronika* (SPB, 1898).

[197] My comments are based on a reading of three of Cherevansky's major works: *Mir Islama i ego probuzhdenie*, 2 vols. (SPB, 1901); *Dve volny. Istoricheskaya khronika*, 2 vols. (SPB, 1898); *Tvorchestvo russkoy sily* (SPB, 1911).

[198] These paragraphs are a most inadequate summary of the conclusions I drew from reading all of Schwartz's letters to his family and to fellow officials in the Ministry of Education. There are also reflections on his relations with Nicholas II, Stolypin, his ministry and the public (Opis 3, Dela 1–5). The RO Fond also contains the useful 'Otchot A.N. Shvartsa o poezdke zagranitsu dlya osmotra sredneuchebnykh zavedeniy Germanii i Frantsii' (Opis 4, Delo 1/3). The TsGIA collection contains only official papers written by Schwartz between 1902 and 1911, some of which, however, are of considerable interest. The biography *Aleksandr Nikolaevich Shvarts* (Moscow, 1916), written by Schwartz's former student, Serge Sobolevsky, is also of great interest not only on Schwartz himself but also on Russian education in the late nineteenth and early twentieth centuries.

[199] See in particular RO, Fond 338, Opis 3, Delo 2, 'Zametki. Moya perepiska s Stolypinym', esp. pp. 5 ii, 6 i. Schwartz wrote that his chief enemies in the Council of Ministers were veteran Petersburg officials, and in particulär V.N. Kokovtsov, I.P. Shipov and P.A. Kharitonov, men 'who saw in me above all a man new to Saint Petersburg and in addition a man not inclined to forge any strong links with them, as well as a man of principle daring to look into the future and not occupied only with day-to-day compromises'. In Schwartz's view most of his fellow ministers were subtle political operators concerned above all with hanging on to their portfolios and contemptuous of what they viewed as a professor's concern for legality and scholarly pedantry.

[200] Mamantov entitled his memoirs *Na godudarevoy sluzhbe* (Tallin, 1926).

[201] Ibid., 6–9, 19, 32, 37, 162–5.

[202] Ibid., esp. 10–11.

[203] Ibid., 143, 199–201.

[204] A.A. Mosolov, *Pri dvore imperatora* (Riga, n.d.), 28. Witte, *Vospominaniya*, I: 311.

[205] See ch. 3, nn. 105, 106. A. Jacobs, ed., *A New Dictionary of Music* (London, 1975), 317. See also Stroev, *Stoletie*, 322.

A. Vyrubova comments on her father and his musical circle in her *Memories of the Russian Court* (London, 1923), 1–2.

[206] Semyonov's autobiography exists in two parts: *Detstvo* and *Memuary: Epokha osvobozhdeniya krestyan v Rossii* (Petrograd, 1915). The collection of essays entitled *Pëtr Petrovich Semyonov-Tyan-Shansky, Ego Zhizn' i tvorchestvo*, ed. A.A. Dostoevsky (Leningrad, 1928), provides a lively rounded picture of Semyonov's life and work. For an English-language biography see W.B. Lincoln, *Petr Petrovich Semenov-Tian-Shanskii: The Life of a Russian Geographer* (Newtonville, Mass., 1980).

[207] The nickname 'Gramophone' was apparently pinned on Kokovtsov by Moscow business circles: Polovtsov, 'Dnevnik', *KA* 4 (1923), p. 104.

CHAPTER 6

[1] For details of Durnovo's service, education and property the best source is his record in TsGIA, Fond 1162, Opis. 6, Ed. Khr. 190. On the Durnovo family see Ikonnikov, *Noblesse*, vol. C: 570–98.

[2] For Mosolov's comments see his memoirs in RO, Fond 514, Karton I, Ed. Khr. 4, pp. 13–14, 20.

[3] On Durnovo's love of the navy and his own comments on his naval career see *SOGS*, Session 3 (13 June 1908), cols. 1712–15.

[4] One of his ancestors was killed at the siege of Ochakov in the 1730s, another at the siege of Azov under Peter I: Ikonnikov, *Noblesse*, vol. C: 574, 576.

[5] Sazonov, *Fateful Years*, 289. Lyubimov, CUBA MSS: 'Smuta', p. 358.

[6] Witte, *Vospominaniya*, III: 74.

[7] A.I. Ivanchin-Pisarev, 'Vospominaniya o P.N. Durnovo', *Katorga i ssylka* 68 (1930), pp. 40–60; here p. 51.

[8] Ibid., p. 57. At the Tsarskoe Selo conference of April 1906 Durnovo stated that 'administrative measures were introduced because judicial punishments turned out to be too harsh and weren't applied', *Byloe*, no. 4 (Oct 1917), pp. 225–6.

[9] Ivanchin-Pisarev, 'P.N. Durnovo', pp. 55, 59.

[10] A.V. Godeonovsky, 'Yaroslavskiy revolyutsionnyy kruzhok 1881–1886', *Katorga i ssylka* 24 (1926), pp. 105–6.

[11] Ivanchin-Pisarev, 'P.N. Durnovo', pp. 43–7.

[12] M. Aldanov, 'P.N. Durnovo. Prophet of War and Revolution', *RR* 2 (1942), pp. 39–40.

[13] Ibid.; Gurko, *Features*, 179.

[14] Witte, *Vospominaniya*, III: 75; Gurko, *Features*, 182.

[15] See, e.g., Meshchersky's comment in *Grazhdanin*, no. 34 (29 Apr 1904), p. 23.

[16] Witte, *Vospominaniya*, III: 75.

[17] One comes across a few examples of this in memoirs (which in this matter should be treated with some suspicion) and even in service records. In October 1906, for instance, D.F. Kobeko was granted 6,000 roubles for some private purpose, after which Nicholas II felt he had no claims to any special recognition of the fiftieth anniversary of his entry into the state's service: TsGIA, Fond 1162, Opis 6, Ed. Khr. 237, p. 133. Polovtsov's comment on the case of P.A. Valuev, who admittedly reached the very pinnacle of the state's service, is useful evidence of high officials' sense that, in emergency, they had a right to such subsidies. See *Dnevnik*, I: 406: 'a man who served your father for 20 years in eminent positions has a right, Your Majesty, to be rescued by you from such a dishonourable position as being declared bankrupt'.

[18] F.E. Zuckerman, *The Russian Political Police at Home and Abroad (1880–1917): Its Structure, Functions and Methods* (Ph.D. diss., New York Univ., 1973), 77, 78. Gurko, *Features*, 404 ff.

[19] RO, Fond 75, 'Dnevnik', book 23, entry for 16 Nov 1901.

[20] TsGAOR, Fond 1463, Opis 1, Ed. Khr. 1115, p. 316.

[21] W. Santoni, *P.N. Durnovo as Minister of Internal Affairs in the Witte Cabinet* (Ph.D. diss, Univ. of Kansas, 1968), 430–7, discusses Durnovo's comments in this commission.

[22] Lyubimov, CUBA MSS: 'Smuta',

p. 196. I have myself discussed the general issue in question in 'Security Police'.

[23] 'Dopros Gerasimova' (26 Apr 1917), p. 3, in *Padenie*, III.

[24] Lyubimov is an excellent source on moods within the Ministry of Internal Affairs; see in particular CUBA MSS: 'Smuta', pp. 296–8, 327. Also Gerasimov in 'Dopros', p. 3, and Zuckerman, *Political Police*, 169.

[25] Bushnell, *Mutiny*, esp. chs. 4 and 5.

[26] Ibid., 226–9 for a summary of the book's argument.

[27] Gurko, *Features*, 438–9.

[28] Lyubimov, CUBA MSS: 'Smuta', pp. 351–2; Gurko, *Features*, 413–14.

[29] Santoni, *Durnovo*, is much the most detailed study of the planning and execution of counter-revolution in 1905. Ch. 17 of Lyubimov, 'Smuta' (CUBA MSS), is also of great value. A further source on Durnovo's views at the time are his numerous comments during the special conferences studying constitutional reform and the franchise in the winter and spring of 1905–6. See in particular the April 1906 conference, whose minutes are printed in *Byloe*, no. 4 (Oct 1917), pp. 184–246, where Durnovo's comments on pp. 208, 210, 212, 223, 225–7, 231, 243, are of particular interest.

[30] Naumov, *Iz utselevshikh*, II: 150.

[31] SOGS, Session 6 (17 Dec 1910), col. 595.

[32] SOGS, Session 11 (19 July 1915), cols. 35–6.

[33] SOGS, Session 7 (26 Jan 1912), col. 1259; Session 5 (28 May 1910), col. 3287.

[34] Durnovo's comments on the Duma chancellery are probably to be explained by this concern. See SOGS, Session 3 (25 June 1908), cols. 2047–9. He was afraid that if the best young officials were drawn into the chancellery and subsequently went on to senior positions in other parts of the service they would carry with them the bacillus of new and divided loyalties. For his comments on factionalism in the civil service, see SOGS, Session 2 (19 May 1907), cols. 406–8, 414.

[35] SOGS, Session 4 (19 Mar 1909),

col. 1350. Durnovo's firmness on this point was evident too in the discussions on the Fundamental Laws in the April 1906 conference at Tsarskoe Selo: 'If doubt exists that the military department can be hampered in the organization of the army then this is a danger which is far greater than any other'. See *Byloe*, no. 4 (Oct 1917), p. 243.

[36] SOGS, Session 2 (19 May 1907), cols. 404, 410, 413–15.

[37] SOGS, Session 8 (29 Mar 1913), cols. 1292–4.

[38] *Byloe*, no. 4 (Oct 1917), p. 231.

[39] In April 1911, for instance, Durnovo argued strongly against an amnesty, stressing that the revolutionary threat was by no means destroyed and the need for repression still therefore very real. His memorandum on this is quoted by N.A. Rubakin in RO, Fond 358, Karton 143, Ed. Khr. 5, p. 100. See also SOGS, Session 2, cols. 404–5.

[40] RO, Fond 178, Karton 9803, Ed. Khr. 5, p. 23.

[41] T. Riha, ed., *Readings in Russian Civilization* (Chicago, 1964), prints an English translation of Durnovo's memorandum to Nicholas II of February 1914. Discussion of the threat from the non-Russians comes on pp. 462, 464.

[42] SOGS, Session 6, col. 1122.

[43] SOGS, Session 7, cols. 3490, 3497.

[44] Riha, *Readings*, 469.

[45] Ibid.

[46] SOGS, Session 9 (19 May 1914), col. 2300.

[47] Durnovo's main statements on the peasantry and rural affairs are in SOGS, Session 5, cols. 1640–2; Session 6, cols. 1120–3; Session 9, cols. 2297–2302.

[48] The main speech on the workers' question is in SOGS, Session 7 (20 Apr 1912), cols. 3483–98. See also Session 9, col. 2301, and Session 7, col. 264.

[49] SOGS, Session 5, col. 3309. Durnovo's major statements on education and other budgetary needs were in Session 5, cols. 3283–90, and Session 7, cols. 1255–66.

[50] SOGS, Session 3, cols. 1287–91; Session 7, cols. 1260–61.

[51] SOGS, Session 3, col. 1711.

[52] See, e.g., SOGS, Session 5, col. 2013; Session 9, col. 2300. Riha, *Read-*

ings, 469.

[53] Gurko, *Features*, 415.

[54] Lyubimov, CUBA MSS: 'Smuta', p. 358.

[55] *SOGS*, Session 3, col. 1713.

[56] *SOGS*, Session 5, col. 2813.

[57] *SOGS*, Session 6, col. 595.

[58] Ibid., col. 598; Session 5, col. 2797.

[59] *SOGS*, Session 6, col. 596.

[60] On the Old Believers see in particular Durnovo's comments in *SOGS*, Session 5, cols. 2800–3; on the Old Catholics see Session 7, cols. 1255–66.

[61] *SOGS*, Session 12 (6 June 1916), col. 1589.

[62] *SOGS*, Session 7, col. 2955.

[63] *SOGS*, Session 3, col. 667.

[64] *SOGS*, Session 7, col. 2956; Session 5, cols. 3926–7. He certainly showed no enthusiasm for the Cholm issue in December 1905: see Tsarskoe Selo conference in *Byloe*, no. 3 (1917) p. 264.

[65] I have discussed the memorandum in my *Origins*, ch. 4, sec. 1.

[66] See Riha, *Readings*, 470.

[67] Ibid., 469. *Byloe*, no. 4 (Oct 1917), p. 208.

[68] Naumov, *Iz utselevshikh*, II. 215.

[69] Vasil'chikov, MSS. Private: 'Vospominaniya', ch. 7, p. 82. He states that his source for this conversation is 'fully reliable' and was very close to Durnovo.

[70] Kryzhanovsky, *Vospominaniya*, 75.

[71] *Rech'* (SPB), 12 Sept 1915, p. 2.

CHAPTER 7

[1] Ikonnikov, *Noblesse*, vol. H: 163–81, provides details of the Kulomzins' family tree. A.N. Kulomzin himself wrote about his estate and the surrounding area in *Arkhiv sel'tsa Kornilova* (SPB, 1913), ix. In his memoirs (TsGIA, Fond 1642, Opis 1, Ed. Khr. 172, pp. 2–5) he notes that in the seventeenth and eighteenth centuries most Kulomzins had very small estates.

[2] Ibid., Ed. Khr. 172, pp. 8, 18, 22; Ed. Khr. 174, pp. 2–3; Ed. Khr. 180, p. 2. Nevertheless, thanks to generous scholarships endowed by local aristocrats much of the Kostroma nobility had at least a cadet corps education rather than – as was often the case in other provinces at the time – simply entering the army in the ranks and subsequently being promoted into the officer corps.

[3] Ibid., Ed. Khr. 172, pp. 9–13; Ed. Khr. 174, pp. 18–19, 21, 28; Ed. Khr. 173, p. 59.

[4] E.g., A.N. Mosolov: see RO, Fond 514, Karton 1, Ed. Khr. 4, pp. 3–14.

[5] See TsGIA, Fond 1642, Opis 1, Ed. Khr. 172, p. 16; Ed. Khr. 174, pp. 19–20; Ed. Khr. 173, pp. 31–6 for Kulomzin's preparation for university.

[6] Ibid., Ed. Khr. 172, pp. 52–3.

[7] Ibid., Ed. Khr. 178, p. 1.

[8] Ibid., Ed. Khr. 175, p. 25; Ed. Khr. 178, pp. 8–9.

[9] The main source on Kulomzin's foreign travels is Ed. Khr. 179.

[10] Ibid., Ed. Khr. 179, pp. 1, 10, 62, 66; Ed. Khr. 181, pp. 87–8.

[11] Ibid., Ed. Khr. 179, p. 12.

[12] Ibid., p. 2.

[13] Ibid., pp. 21, 33–4, 56–9.

[14] Ibid., Ed. Khr. 178, p. 32.

[15] Ibid., Ed. Khr. 179, p. 50.

[16] Ibid., Ed. Khr. 179, pp. 22–3.

[17] Ibid., Ed. Khr. 180, describes his district on the eve of Emancipation, and Ed. Khr. 181 gives an account of his own activities as an arbitrator.

[18] Ibid., Ed. Khr. 181, p.26.

[19] See in particular ibid., pp. 35, 83.

[20] RO, Fond 178, Karton 9803, Ed. Khr. 5, p. 4ii.

[21] Kulomzin commented, e.g., that 'my continual journeyings around the district, both within my own section and to help verify the statutory charters of my neighbouring arbitrators, not to mention my visits to my own estates which were scattered around the districts, gave me the possibility of going quite deeply and closely into the various types of peasant economy we had in different corners of one and the same province': TsGIA, Fond 1642, Opis 1, Ed. Khr. 182, p. 61.

[22] Ibid., Ed. Khr. 181, pp. 94–5.

[23] For basic information about the extent of Kulomzin's landholdings, which differed greatly over the decades, see the *Spiski* of the first three ranks of officials for 1881, 1908 and 1914. *Vsya Rossiya* for 1900 lists the ways in which the Kulomzin estates were exploited, and

ASRGD, 199–200, discusses Kulomzin's role as regards phosphorus deposits. In TsGIA, Fond 1642, Opis 1, Ed. Khr. 181, p. 40, Kulomzin talks of his investigations into Kostroma agriculture in the early 1880s.

[24] Ibid., Ed. Khr. 311, p. 3, letter dated 25 Aug 1878.

[25] Ibid., Ed. Khr. 220, p. 14, letter dated 30 Jan 1902.

[26] Ibid., pp. 15 and 27, letter dated 16 Feb 1902.

[27] Ibid., p. 72, letter to his wife dated 13 Apr 1902.

[28] Ibid., p. 146, letter to his wife dated 10 June 1902.

[29] E.g., as regards the Witte Commission's decision to summon experts from all corners of Russia to discuss the question of rural credit: 'We will learn the wishes of the provinces and I rejoice at this', Ibid., p. 54, letter to his wife dated 30 Mar 1902.

[30] RO, Fond 178, Karton 9803, Ed. Khr. 3, pp. 1–3, 8, 26, 33. Kulomzin was, for instance, promoted 'Court Counsellor' (*Nadvornyy Sovetnik*) after only six months in the previous rank.

[31] Ibid., Ed. Khr. 4, pp. 26–49.

[32] The latter quote comes from a letter dated 11 Sept 1875 in TsGIA, Fond 1642, Opis 1, Ed. Khr. 216, p. 57. For the rest, see RO, Fond 178, Karton 9803, Ed. Khr. 4, particularly pp. 15–18 (a section out of place in Kulomzin's papers in RO), 30–1, 38.

[33] Ibid., Ed. Khr. 5, p. 4.

[34] See, esp., ibid., Ed. Khr. 5, pp. 5, 43; Ed. Khr. 6, pp. 25, 41.

[35] See ibid., Ed. Khr. 5, pp. 15, 27, 38, 40; Ed. Khr. 6, pp. 17, 21.

[36] Ibid., Ed. Khr. 5, pp. 39–40; Ed. Khr. 6, p. 46.

[37] Ibid., Ed. Khr. 5, pp. 25 and 26, letters of 3 and 15 Mar 1881.

[38] Ibid., pp. 26, 30, a letter of 26 Mar 1881 and a later comment in the memoirs.

[39] Ibid., p. 38 (no date ascribed to this letter save 1881).

[40] Ibid., Ed. Khr. 6, pp. 18–19, 32, 38. In TsGIA, Fond 1642, Opis 1, Ed. Khr. 178, p. 64, Kulomzin states that Tolstoy's treatment of B.N. Chicherin was a typical example of his inability to see the difference between the government's friends and its dangerous enemies.

[41] RO, Fond 178, Karton 9803, Ed. Khr. 6, pp. 46–7.

[42] RO, Fond 178, Karton 9803, Ed. Khr. 4, pp. 11–15.

[43] Bogdanovich, *Tri poslednikh*, 208.

[44] RO, Fond 178, Karton 9803, Ed. Khr. 9, p. 29.

[45] TsGIA, Fond 1642, Opis 1, Ed. Khr. 220, p. 22, letter to his wife dated 7 Feb 1902.

[46] Polovtsov, 'Dnevnik', *KA* 3 (1923), p. 162; Polivanov, *Iz dnevnikov*, 168–9.

[47] TsGIA, Fond 1642, Opis 1, Ed. Khr. 217, pp. 91–2, letter to his wife dated 7 Aug 1895.

[48] Ibid., Ed. Khr. 216, p. 51, letter dated 6 Sept 1875.

[49] All the following comments are drawn from Kulomzin's description of his expedition in his unpublished memoirs (RO, Fond 178, Karton 9803, Ed. Khr. 8). This gives a livelier and more rounded picture than his official report, *Vsepoddaneyshiy otchot Shtats Sekretarya Kulomzina po poezdke v Sibir' dlya oznakomleniya s polozheniem pereselenskogo dela* (SPB, 1896). The chapter of his memoirs was written in 1905–10, but is based to a great extent on letters written by Kulomzin during his visit and reproduced in whole or part in Ed. Khr. 8.

[50] RO, Fond 178, Karton 9803, Ed. Khr. 8, p. 20.

[51] The speech, made on 12 May 1908, is in *SOGS*, Session 3, cols. 1177–88. It should be read together with Kulomzin's memoirs (Ed. Khr. 7 and 8 of RO, Fond 178, Karton 9803) as his retrospective view of the problems and achievements of the Siberian Committee under his leadership. For an excellent account of the whole process of colonization, see D.W. Treadgold, *The Great Siberian Migration: Government and Peasant in Resettlement from Emancipation to the First World War* (Princeton, N.J., 1957).

[52] *Dostupnost' nachal'noy shkoly v Rossiy* (SPB, 1904), 58.

[53] Ibid., 5.

[54] Ibid., 6–7.

[55] Ibid., 9–16.

[56] Ibid., 28.

[57] Ibid., 28–9.

[58] Ibid., 17.

[59] Ibid., 30–5.

[60] Ibid., 45–7.

[61] Ibid., 53–9.

[62] Ibid., 68.

[63] TsGIA, Fond 1642, Opis 1, Ed. Khr. 220, pp. 13, 40: two letters dated 30 Jan and 10 Mar 1902.

[64] *Doma s deshyovymi kvartirami dlya rabochikh* (SPB, 1902), 5.

[65] Ibid., 6–15.

[66] Ibid., 20.

[67] Ibid., 17, 21–5.

[68] TsGIA, Fond 1642, Opis 1, Ed. Khr. 220, p. 57, letter of 3 Apr 1902. Others also commented on the heartlessness of Petersburg society as regards assassinations. On 4 Apr 1902 Alexander Obolensky wrote about the dead Sipyagin, 'how few people feel sorry for him – as a minister almost no one regrets his passing and even this tragic event evidently made little impression even in the very highest spheres on which the appointment of ministers depends' (TsGIA, Fond 1650, Opis 1, Ed. Khr. 233, p. 12). Two years later Aleksei Obolensky, in the country at the time, wrote about how he imagined Petersburg would react to Plehve's death: 'I can imagine what a degree of sham coupled with abuse is going on, how people are rejoicing at the event and pretending to be indignant' (ibid., Ed. Khr. 249, p. 8).

[69] TsGIA, Fond 1642, Opis 1, Ed. Khr. 220, p. 59, letter of 5 Apr 1902.

[70] Ibid., p. 95, letter of 3 May 1902.

[71] Bogdanovich, *Tri poslednikh*, 369.

[72] What follows is simply a précis of the memorandum, which is to be found in TsGIA, Fond 1044, Opis 1, Ed. Khr. 233, and is 14 pages long.

[73] TsGIA, Fond 1642, Opis 1, Ed. Khr. 727, pp. 4–6, 9–12, letters to Baron E. Yu. Nol'de dated 25 June and 27 July 1905.

[74] Bogdanovich, *Tri poslednikh*, 380.

[75] *SOGS*, Session 3 (30 May 1908), cols. 1455–61; Session 4 (20 May 1909), cols. 2063–73; Session 5 (20 May 1910), cols. 3192–3.

[76] E.g., 'On me falls the very unpleasant duty of making small corrections to a bill which has already passed through the Duma, but the fact is that there was no avoiding this': *SOGS*, Session 3, col. 1628, in a speech dated 11 June 1908.

[77] The letter is undated but probably written in 1909: TsGIA, Fond 1642, Opis 1, Ed. Khr. 221.

[78] Naumov, *Iz utselevshikh*, II: 298.

[79] RO, Fond 70, Opis 3, Delo 7, p. 12, letter to V.I. Guerrier (Ger'e) dated 24 Aug 1915.

[80] Ikonnikov, *Noblesse*, vol. H: 181–2.

CHAPTER 8

[1] Of numerous sources on the Obolensky family, Ikonnikov (*Noblesse*, vol. K) is the most thorough. In D.A. Obolensky's generation one finds, for instance (pp. 526–7) Prince Dimitri Petrovich, who in 1853 seems to have owned only four serfs and who served five years as a private after dismissal from a cadet corps for bad behaviour. D.A. Obolensky's father was a Privy Counsellor, a senator, the owner of 680 serfs, a paper factory and a sugar mill. Dimitri himself rose to be a Senior Privy Counsellor and a member of the State Council. His wife was a Princess Trubetskoy (ibid., 505, 522).

[2] On D.A. Obolensky see in particular Prince D.A. Obolensky, *Moi vospominaniya o velikoy knyagine Elene Petrovne* (SPB, 1909), *passim*, but esp. pp. 37ff, Also Lincoln, *Vanguard*, esp. 152–4. F.G. Terner in *Vospominaniya*, I: 227–8, discusses D.A. Obolensky's personality.

[3] Levinson, *Senat*, 43.

[4] Svyatopolk-Mirsky, 'Dnevnik', p. 270.

[5] Polovtsov, 'Dnevnik', *KA* 3 (1923), p. 126.

[6] Typical is a letter of 20 Aug 1911 complaining that his son Dimitri is always disorganized and changing his plans: TsGIA, Fond 1650, Opis 1, Ed. Khr. 236, p. 51.

[7] E.g., his fiancée (and later wife) Anna Polovtsov wrote in April 1881 that she had always lived an entirely

inner, spiritual life and him a practical and active one: ibid., Ed. Khr. 106, p. 3. Anna discussed philosophical issues with her brother-in-law, not her husband. She read literature, he history.

[8] See ibid., Ed. Khr. 228, p. 35 (18 July 1886), and also, e.g., Ed. Khr. 229, p. 19 (13 June 1887).

[9] Ibid., Ed. Khr. 237, p. 89 (12 Nov 1913).

[10] Ibid., Ed. Khr. 234, pp. 73, 86 (18 July and 1 Sept 1904).

[11] Ibid., Ed. Khr. 231, p. 80 (2 June 1897).

[12] On Anna's property see Obolensky's service record in TsGIA, Fond 1162, Opis 6, Ed. Khr. 373. In the correspondence are scattered references to Anna's stocks and bonds – e.g., on 13 May 1914 Alexander refers to dividends on some shares owned by his wife whose value was 140,000 roubles (Fond 1650, Opis 1, Ed. Khr. 238, p. 18). These may or may not have been her industrial stocks held by the Azov Bank (ibid., Ed. Khr. 237, p. 89) in November 1913.

[13] Bakhmetev was afraid that on his death the old and famous glass factory, on which he had showered love and attention, would be shared out among the children of his three sisters. He therefore chose to leave his entire estate to one of his great-nephews, Alexander Obolensky. See the 'Istoricheskiy ocherk Nikol'sko-Bakhmetevskogo zavoda' in Anon., *150 let Nikol'sko-Bakhmetevskago khrustal'nago zavoda knyaz'ya A.D. Obolenskogo* (SPB, 1914), here p. xxviii.

[14] Ibid., xxix–xxxii.

[15] TsGIA, Fond 1650, Opis 1, Ed. Khr. 236, p. 36.

[16] Ibid., Ed. Khr. 122, p. 50.

[17] Ibid., Ed. Khr. 234, p. 22.

[18] On the factory's history see the 'Istoricheskiy Ocherk' in Anon., *150 let*, and an article in *Novoe Vremya*, no. 13638 (1/14 Mar 1914), p. 13. All comments about the Nikol'skoe estate, unless otherwise cited, come from these two sources.

[19] TsGIA, Fond 1650, Ed. Khr. 227, p. 56.

[20] E.g., in the letter cited in n. 19, Alexander Obolensky wrote that he had been paying close attention to the priest, encouraging him to give up some of his 'silly escapades' (?), sending him books, drinking tea with his wife and influencing the way he taught children at the school.

[21] Ibid., Ed. Khr. 232, p. 1 (letter dated 12 May 1898).

[22] Anon., *150 let*, xxxii–xxxiii.

[23] TsGIA, Fond 1650, Opis 1, Ed. Khr. 229, pp. 75–6.

[24] Ibid., Ed. Khr. 238, p. 35 (letter of 5 June 1914).

[25] E.g. in 1887 A.D. Obolensky intervened on behalf of a young man attempting to become a doctor. Ibid., Ed. Khr. 229, p. 37; Ed. Khr. 122, p. 25 (church building); Ed. Khr. 234, p. 53 (paying for a local girl's education).

[26] Ibid., Ed. Khr. 234, p. 52: in a letter dated 17 June 1904 Alexander Obolensky wrote that he had sent between one-half and one-quarter of the reservists' pay to their families depending on how much they had earned and the extent to which their families were in need. On 4 Sept 1882 Anna Obolensky wrote that two peasants had had their horses stolen and 'of course they will have to be helped'. She added, 'a lot of people come to me and if I helped them all the whole of Nikol'skoe would have to be reorganized'. Ibid., Ed. Khr. 107, p. 96.

[27] Anon., *150 let*, xxxiii ff.

[28] He played a major part in developing musical education in Penza, and held musical evenings at Nikol'skoe (see, e.g., his letter of 1 Jan 1914: TsGIA, Fond 1650, Opis 1, Ed. Khr. 238, p. 1). Ed. Khr. 227 (Mar 1883–Oct 1885) contains much information about the foundation of the Penza Music School – e.g., pp. 26–8, 38, 47, 50. See Ed. Khr. 230, p. 29, on public literacy.

[29] Ibid., pp. 27, 29, 67, 77–9, 84–5, 98–9, 107.

[30] For details of Obolensky's career see his service record in TsGIA, Fond 1162, Opis 6, Ed. Khr. 373.

[31] TsGIA, Fond 1650, Opis 1, Ed. Khr. 239, p. 115, letter dated 12 Dec 1903 but, confusingly, placed in a package containing letters from 1915–16.

[32] Ibid., Ed. Khr. 227, p. 88. All the quotes are from a single letter dated 18 Dec 1904 but placed in a package containing correspondence from 1883–5.

[33] Ibid., Ed. Khr. 107, p. 39; Ed. Khr. 227, p. 60.

[34] Ibid., Ed. Khr. 228, p. 38, letter of 18 July 1886. In the Kakhanov Commission Obolensky denounced the apathy shown by some marshals. 'Materialy Kakhanovskoy kommissii', no. 9 (Jan–Feb 1885), p. 8.

[35] TsGIA, Fond 1650, Opis 1, Ed. Khr. 106, p. 61, letter from Anna of 24 Nov 1886.

[36] Ibid., Ed. Khr. 227, p. 29.

[37] Ibid., Ed. Khr. 235, letter of 22 Sept 1905.

[38] On 25 Apr 1881 Anna, at that time his fiancée, wrote to Alexander that she had been upset by his view that the Emancipation settlement's failings were the cause of peasant misery because the peasantry had been left wholly free; ibid., Ed. Khr. 106, p. 7. Commenting on Alexander III's call to peasant mayors and elders attending his coronation to listen to local noble leaders, Alexander Obolensky commented that the Emperor 'made a short but very good speech... which will have a great significance': ibid., Ed. Khr. 227, p. 24.

[39] For the records of this Commission, to which I was fortunate in securing access in the Harvard Law Library, see n. 34 above.

[40] Pazukhin, Bekhteev and Obolensky argued that in its essentials the division between noble and peasant had existed for thousands of years and was still at the core of rural realities. 'Materialy', no. 4 (Oct 1884), p. 21; no. 9 (Jan–Feb 1885), p. 49; no. 17 (Mar 1885), p. 11. On the need for something close to the subsequently established land commandant (zemskiy nachal'nik) see no. 5 (Oct–Nov 1884), pp. 7–12. On the commune, see no. 4 (Oct 1884), pp. 21–4.

[41] Ibid., no. 4 (Oct 1884), pp. 9–10, 12; no. 5 (Oct–Nov 1884), pp. 7–13.

[42] Ibid., no. 4 (Oct 1884), p. 63; no. 6 (Jan 1885), pp. 10–13; no. 9 (Jan–Feb 1885), p. 80.

[43] SOGS, Session 7 (14 June 1912), cols. 5088–97.

[44] Ibid. (6 Apr 1912), cols. 2982–86.

[45] SOGS, Session 9 (27 Nov 1913), cols. 128–33, and TsGIA, Fond 1650, Opis 1, Ed. Khr. 238, p. 17, letter to Anna dated 17 May 1914.

[46] Ibid., Ed. Khr. 238, p. 47, letter of 26 July 1914.

[47] Ibid., Ed. Khr. 239, pp. 13, 28–31, 46, 49–50; letters of 20 June, 5, 27, 29, 31 Aug, 2, 4 Sept 1915.

[48] Ibid., Ed. Khr. 99, p. 1, letter dated 5 Dec 1867.

[49] Ibid., Ed. Khr. 234, p. 27, letter of August 1903.

[50] Ibid., Ed. Khr. 109, p. 16.

[51] Ibid., Ed. Khr. 249, p. 72, undated letter.

[52] Kryzhanovsky, Vospominaniya, 54; Gurko, Features, 209, 213.

[53] Witte, Vospominaniya, II: 39.

[54] For details of Obolensky's property, his marriage to a Princess Saltykov, etc., see his service record in TsGIA, Fond 1162, Opis 6, Ed. Khr. 374. Ikonnikov, Noblesse, vol. E: 522, 545, mentions that in 1900 his mother still owned the land in Saratov. See TsGIA, Fond 1650, Opis 1, Ed. Khr. 95, pp. 1–9 for Aleksei's letter of 15 Oct 1889.

[55] Ibid., pp. 11–18, letters of 23 and 25 Oct 1889.

[56] Gurko, Features, 207. Nicholas was indeed very close to the Emperor. See, e.g., Svyatopolk-Mirsky, 'Dnevnik', in which Princess Mirsky writes (p. 250) of N.D. Obolensky: 'he is very close to the sovereign and loves him, to the extent that anyone loves him'.

[57] Gurko, Features, 207, writes that Witte was under Obolensky's influence in the early twentieth century; the quote is from Polovtsov's diary for 5 May 1901: KA 3 (1923), p. 91.

[58] Terner, Vospominaniya, I: 170–2.

[59] TsGIA, Fond 1650, Opis 1, Ed. Khr. 95, pp. 23–5.

[60] Witte, Vospominaniya, II: 39; III: 124.

[61] The quote is from an entry in Polovtsov's diary dated 26 Oct 1905: KA 4 (1923), p. 81. See also a letter from

Anna Obolensky to Alexander dated 12 Nov 1905, in which she states that Aleksei and her father were fighting to increase the representation of landowners in the State Council: TsGIA, Fond 1650, Opis 1, Ed. Khr. 119, p. 102.

[62] *SOGS*, Session 6 (4 Mar 1911), col. 1249; a comment made during a speech on the Western Zemstvo bill.

[63] E.g., *SOGS*, Session 4 (30 Dec 1908), col. 463: 'I think the State Council should not enter into conflict with the Duma unless there is an extreme need to do so'.

[64] *SOGS*, Session 3 (18 June 1906), col. 1786.

[65] *SOGS*, Session 3 (2 Apr 1908), col. 893.

[66] *SOGS*, Session 9, cols. 2247–58.

[67] TsGIA, Fond 1650, Opis 1, Ed. Khr. 249, p. 22, letter to Anna.

[68] Ibid., Ed. Khr. 95, pp. 30–2.

[69] Ibid., Ed. Khr. 249, p. 26, letter to Anna.

[70] Ibid., Ed. Khr. 95, pp. 38–40, letter to Alexander dated September 1915.

[71] Ibid., Ed. Khr. 249, pp. 27–9, letter to Alexander.

[72] Ibid., Ed. Khr. 247, pp. 100–1, letter to Anna dated 14 Nov 1889.

[73] Ibid., Ed. Khr. 247, p. 37, letter to Anna dated 3 June 1890.

[74] These ideas are drawn from two letters which Aleksei wrote to Anna on 14 May 1888 and 14 Nov 1889: ibid., pp. 48–57 and 100–4. As usual with Aleksei Obolensky one has sometimes to pan for gold in a sludge of words and ideas. In the State Council he rejected religious intolerance or persecution but stressed that the state had (e.g., as regards former priests or the recognition of Old Believer hierarchies) the duty to protect the uniqueness and prestige of the Church in the face of any possible threat: *SOGS*, Session 5 (13 May 1910), cols. 2900–10 and Session 7 (4, 11, 16 Nov 1911), cols. 99–106, 220–8, 361–4.

[75] *Grazhdanin*, no. 16 (9 May 1910), p. 18.

[76] TsGIA, Fond 1650, Opis 1, Ed. Khr. 248, pp. 58–60, letter to Anna dated 11 Nov 1890.

[77] Ibid., Ed. Khr. 249, p. 86, letter to Anna, undated but probably from the mid- or late 1890s.

[78] *SOGS*, Session 3 (18 June 1908), cols. 1779–89.

[79] *SOGS*, Session 4 (8 May 1909), cols. 1944–9.

[80] *SOGS*, Session 7 (13 and 14 June 1912), cols. 5019–21, 5102–7.

[81] TsGIA, Fond 1650, Opis 1, Ed. Khr. 249, pp. 11–14.

[82] Ibid., pp. 15–18.

[83] Ikonnikov, *Noblesse*, vol. K: 567.

CHAPTER 9

[1] The best introduction to this debate is a review article by G. Eley, 'The View from the Throne: The Personal Rule of Kaiser Wilhelm II', *Historical Journal* 28, no. 2 (1985), pp. 469–86. J.G.G. Röhl, *Germany without Bismarck* (London, 1967), played a large part in originating the debate. I. Hull, *The Entourage of Kaiser Wilhelm II, 1888–1918* (Cambridge, 1982) and J.C.G. Röhl and N. Sombart, eds., *Kaiser Wilhelm II: New Interpretations* (Cambridge, 1982), are recent works by historians convinced of William II's political significance. For H.U. Wehler, however, Röhl's is a 'purely personalistic approach which minimizes structural conditions and thus totally misses the importance of non-individual processes': see Wehler, *The German Empire 1871–1918* (Leamington Spa, 1985), 274.

[2] S.S. Oldenburg still provides the best work of this nature. His *Tsarstvovanie Imperatora Nikolaya II*, 2 vols. (Belgrade, 1939; Munich, 1949), is, of course, an apologia for Nicholas II, but a serious work requiring careful attention for all that. The 4-vol. English translation, *Last Tsar* (1975), is cited above, ch. 5, n. 26.

[3] G. Katkov, *Russia 1917: The February Revolution* (London, 1967), 352–8.

[4] Comments on the personality and views of Nicholas II are of course legion among the primary sources. One work surprisingly often ignored by historians is the memoirs of Peter Bark. His chapter on Nicholas II combines sympathy

with insight. See 'Glava iz vospominaniy', *Vozrozhdenie*, no. 43 (July 1955), pp. 5–27.

[5] Some of Nicholas's comments during the First World War provide damning evidence as to his ignorance of Russian realities and public moods. See, e.g., a letter to his wife of 9 Sept 1915 stressing how much better he could gauge public opinion than ministers who were confined to Petersburg: *The Letters of the Tsar to the Tsaritsa, 1914–1917*, ed. C.E. Vulliamy (London, 1929), 85. For his belief, expressed to General A.A. Mosolov on 14 Feb 1917, that his excellent reception by troops and crowds of civilians when on tour made it unthinkable that a threat could exist to his dynasty, see Mosolov, *Pri dvore*, 99.

[6] This is of course to risk generalizations on modern German history which I am not qualified to make. On the fragmentation of politics in the *Kaiserreich* under the strains of modernization and democratization, see a useful summary in D. Blackbourn and G. Eley, *The Peculiarities of German History* (Oxford, 1984), 264–76. On parochialism, see M. Walker, *German Home Towns: Community, State and General Estate, 1648–1871* (Ithaca, N.Y., 1971). For a view from the right of officialdom and its beliefs under the *Kaiserreich*, see Stolberg-Wernigerode, *Generation*, ch. 7 (pp. 250–74). For an equally brief but useful summary of the views of the Junker ghetto, see Wehking, 'Junker'.

[7] Not always, of course. William II had very limited sympathy with agrarian interest-group politics and felt that these reflected not only one-sided and unpatriotic tendencies but also a disloyal attitude on the part of traditional Prussian élites towards his person, dynasty and government. See, e.g., Hull, *Entourage*, 84, and H.J. Puhle, *Agrarische Interessenpolitik und preussischer Konservatismus im Wilhelminischen Reich, 1893–1914* (Bonn–Bad Godesberg, 1975), esp. 207–8, 237, 274–8. The Russian United Nobility was still a more old-fashioned, magnate-dominated 'estate' pressure group and its relationship with Nicholas II was correspondingly much

better. See, e.g., G.W. Simmonds, *The Congress of Representatives of the Nobles Associations, 1906–1916. A Case Study of Russian Conservatism* (Ph.D. diss., Columbia Univ., 1964), esp. 14, 242–3. Also G.A. Hosking and R.T. Manning, 'What was the United Nobility?', in L.H. Haimson, ed., *The Politics of Rural Russia* (Bloomington, Ind., 1979), 142–83, esp. here 160.

[8] See, for instance, the letters of the Empress during the First World War, e.g. 14 Dec 1916: 'Be Peter the Great, John the Terrible, Emperor Paul': *Letters of the Tsaritsa to the Tsar, 1914–1916*, introd. B. Pares (London, 1923), 455–6.

[9] Andrei Saburov, for instance, wrote apropos of the debate over the suffrage, in the winter of 1905–6, that Nicholas II 'swept aside all care about the practical consequences of the proposed measure and asked himself the only important question for a Russian tsar: *where does my duty lie?* Having decided this question he did not hesitate before the dangers facing him': draft of a letter written early in 1906, p. 14, in TsGAOR, Fond 1074, Opis 1, Ed. Khr. 1116.

[10] See, for instance, Kireev's diary. On 15 Dec 1897, e.g., he wrote that Nicholas II had a low opinion of his ministers (a theme constantly repeated in the diaries), and on 13 Dec 1904, Kireev himself wrote to the Emperor saying, 'Everybody knows, Your Majesty, that you have no great trust in the bureaucracy and all rejoiced and rejoice in this fact'. In February 1904 the Empress Marie had said, *vis-à-vis* top officialdom, 'C'est eux qui empêchent tous': RO, Fond 126, K. 12, p. 171; K. 14, pp. 303, 367.

[11] See Hull, *Entourage*, esp. ch. 2.

[12] See I. Nish, *The Origins of the Russo-Japanese War* (London, 1985), 189, on Nicholas II's absorption in personal affairs at one key stage in the Empire's negotiations with Japan. Count V.N. Lambsdorff complained in a letter dated 10 Dec 1900 that the tsar took inordinately long semi-holidays at Yalta, from which business suffered. TsGAOR, Fond 568, Opis 1, Ed. Khr. 280, p. 16i.

[13] See G. Shavel'sky, *Vospominaniya*

poslednego protopresvitera russkoy armii i flota, 2 vols. (New York, 1954), here I: 334–5, 338.

[14] Bark, 'Vospominaniya', *Vozrozhdenie*, no. 43, pp. 9–12, 22–3. Mamantov, *Sluzhbe*, is another rarely cited source on Nicholas II, although the two men worked closely together for many years. Mamantov frequently stresses the extreme thoughtfulness and delicacy with which Nicholas II treated his entourage, and indeed everyone with whom he came into contact (pp. 58, 131, 150, 231), adding that it was hard to govern in this way a country that remembered Peter I's club.

[15] Mamantov, *Sluzhbe*, 138; Bogdanovich, *Tri posdelnikh*, 447–8. The letters of Count Paul Benckendorff, the last *Oberhofmarschal*, to his brother, the Ambassador in London, are an excellent source on the imperial couple's attitudes and behaviour. Benckendorff first mentions Rasputin in a letter dated 16/29 August 1915. He stresses the fatal ignorance of the Empress, which was combined with a dislike of any political figure who was popular and with a total unwillingness to change preconceived ideas no matter what arguments or evidence were marshalled against them (see, e.g., a letter dated 26 Aug/8 Sept 1915). On 15/28 Nov 1915 Benckendorff described Alexandra as having 'a will of iron linked to not much brain and no knowledge'. Even before the war he was writing (e.g. 29 May/11 June 1914) about the Empress's character and the trouble she was causing her husband: Brooke MSS.

[16] Oldenburg, *Last Tsar*, III: 155. Nicholas II's conversations with the photographer S.M. Prokudin-Gorsky are of interest. See *Photographs for the Tsar*, ed. R.H. Allshouse (London, 1980), xvi–xx. Renewed efforts were made after 1905 to bring the Emperor into contact with the peasantry. On these efforts and their results Sir Arthur Nicolson, reporting in 1910, stated that 'the delight of the peasants at seeing their emperor was unbounded, and...they were much impressed by the simple, unaffected manner in which he spoke to them, and by the knowledge which he possessed of

their circumstances': Annual Report for 1909, in Bourne and Watt, *British Documents*, Part I, Series A: *Russia, 1859–1914*, V: 369. Documents 115 and 151 in ibid., vol. VI, have further comments on this theme. An intelligent and knowledgeable observer of Russian affairs such as Hugh O'Beirne could believe even in 1913 that 'there is no doubt that in this strong attachment of the masses of the Russian peasants to the person of the Emperor lies the great strength of the Russian autocracy. The Emperor does not often come into direct contact with the peasants, but when he does so the effect created appears to reduce political grievances and discontent to insignificance' (ibid., VI: 324). If O'Beirne could believe this, perhaps it is understandable that Nicholas did so too.

[17] See, e.g., the comment by Prince A. Obolensky that the Grand Duke Serge wholly failed to understand that the days of the nobility were numbered, and that the intelligentsia and particularly 'the rich, educated, numerous and very cultured merchant class required to be treated equally, not as an inferior estate': 'Moi vospominaniya', *Vozrozhdenie*, no. 40 (1955), p. 89.

[18] I was fortunate enough to be invited by Professor K. Möckl to attend a conference held at Büdingen in 1986 on German courts in the nineteenth and early twentieth centuries. The papers of this conference have yet to be published, but an earlier article by Professor Möckl, entitled 'Hof und Hofgesellschaft in Bayern' (see ch. 2, n. 11), is an excellent survey of this subject in one of Germany's most important states. On Prussia see Hull, *Entourage*, ch. 6.

[19] Shavel'sky, *Vospominaniya*, esp. II: 338–40, discusses the entourage. So too does A.A. Mosolov, *Court*, 14–16, 127.

[20] Ibid. (Mosolov), 28.

[21] Mamantov, *Sluzhbe*, 144–5, 151–3. Mosolov, *Pri dvore*, 11–12, states that Nicholas II never had a private secretary for fear of falling under his sway.

[22] The history of this episode is covered by documents in TsGIA, Fond 1409, Opis 4, Delo 14817. The memoranda of Count I.I. Vorontsov-

Dashkov. V.I. Neporozhnev, K.K. Rennenkampf and E.V. Frisch to Alexander III (pp. 1–39) outline the failings of the bureaucracy and the need to re-establish a civil-service inspectorate. The resultant decrees are on pp. 83–7, the protests of Witte and N.V. Murav'yov on pp. 61–75 and 153–6, and the minutes of the debate in and resolutions of the Committee of Ministers on 20 June 1895 on pp. 162–6. Given the size, quality, politicization and geographical dispersion of the bureaucracy, not to mention the lack of effective legal control over its activities, one could well argue that some kind of arbitrary punitive power in the hands of the civil service's ministerial chiefs was a necessity.

[23] Röhl, 'Germany', 273, e.g.: 'In the Civil Cabinet the Kaiser possessed a secretariat with a filing system almost as extensive as the Reich Chancellery's'.

[24] Naumov, *Iz Utselevshikh*, II: 533–4.

[25] Ibid., 532–3. Gurko, *Features*, 19, argues that a key reason for the domestic problems faced by Nicholas II's regime was the monarch's insistence on maintaining the principle of autocracy while being wholly incapable of himself embodying it in practice.

[26] The German chancellor was, however, unable to co-ordinate civilian and military aspects of policy. H.H. Herwig, the historian of the German navy, writes that 'a centralized, responsible Ministry of Marine could never be created so long as the monarch maintained the fiction of his personal "supreme command"': *Luxury Fleet: The Imperial German Navy 1888–1918* (London, 1980), 22.

[27] Kuropatkin, *Dnevnik*, 53, records an interesting conversation between himself and V.K. Plehve on monarchs' in-built distrust of their ministers and the ways in which they sought to control them.

[28] Röhl, 'Germany', esp. 198–202, 231–7.

[29] For Weber's views see his *The Theory of Social and Economic Organizations*, ed. Talcott Parsons (New York,

1947). Albrow, *Bureaucracy*, and D. Beetham, *Bureaucracy* (Milton Keynes, 1987), are useful short surveys of the field, though Downs, *Inside Bureaucracy*, was more useful for my purposes. J. La Palombara's 'Overview' (see ch. 3, n. 104) is a valuable early study of the relevance of Weberian notions to developing societies' administrations, and F.W. Riggs, *Administration in Developing Countries* (Boston, 1964), also awakened me to a number of comparisons and contrasts with Russian imperial bureaucracy. Studies of bureaucracy in specific empires and nation-states were also often of interest.

[30] See the General Index for precise references to the individuals mentioned here, whose characteristics have all been discussed earlier in the text.

[31] On Krivoshein see esp. Gurko, *Features*, 192–4; *Grazhdanin*, nos. 39–40 (1 June 1908), p. 12; K.A. Krivoshein, *Krivoshein*.

[32] Pareto's writings are certainly of relevance to a study of Russia's late-imperial élite, particularly perhaps if one looks at the court, upper bureaucracy, gentry and professional élite together, rather than just concentrating, as I have done, on a small and narrowly defined group of leaders. I consulted V. Pareto: *The Rise and Fall of the Elites; An Application of Theoretical Sociology*, introd. H.L. Zetterberg (Bedminster, N.J., 1968) and *Sociological Writings*, sel. and introd S.E. Finer (London, 1966). G. Parry, *Political Elites* (London, 1969) and K. Prewitt and A. Stone, *The Ruling Elites* (New York, 1973), were useful general guides to this field.

[33] An interesting detail is provided by V.P. Semyonov, who wrote that in his area of Ryazan the mentality of the peasantry changed sharply in an anti-gentry direction with the coming of the railway and the end of the relative isolation of local rural life. See Dostoevsky, ed., *P.P. Semyonov-Tyan-Shansky*, 149–51.

[34] Gentry agriculture in the immediate pre-revolutionary era has attracted relatively little attention from historians. The two most recent major works, both

Soviet, are A.N. Anfimov, *Krupnoe pomeshchichee khozyaystvo evropeyskoy Rossii* (Moscow, 1969), and I.D. Koval'chenko *et al., Sotsial'no-ekonomicheskiy stroy pomeshchichego khozyaystva Evropeyskoy Rossii v epokhu kapitalizma* (Moscow, 1982).

[35] A useful recent survey of Russian economic development is contained in P. Gatrell, *The Tsarist Economy, 1850–1917* (London, 1986). On labour, welfare legislation and modernization, the scholar's essential starting-point is the exceptionally thorough work by Olga Crisp: see 'Labour and Industrialization in Russia', *Cambridge Economic History of Modern Europe*, vol. VII, pt. 2 (Cambridge, 1978), 308–415.

[36] This was a major theme in *Vekhi*. P.B. Struve, for instance, wrote that the masses took into the revolution the same destructive and anarchical instincts, the same lack of constructive potential, that had graced the Razin and Pugachov revolts. See, e.g., pp. 166–70 of his 'Intelligentsia i revolyutsiya' in *Vekhi*, 2nd edn. (Moscow, 1909).

[37] This was an important factor in the political thinking of both Herzen and Bakunin, the gentry fathers of Russian socialism and anarchism respectively. In a sense who could be more of an anarchist than the feudal landowner who regarded himself as being the near-equal of his sovereign, resented all constraints on his will and independence, and traditionally exercised unfettered authority over the local population. The more Russian noblemen came to adopt Western notions of aristocracy, the more galling monarchical-bureaucratic absolutism became.

[38] Manfred Hagen provides an excellent sense of this in his recent study of the development of civil society in the constitutional era: *Die Entfaltung politischer Öffentlichkeit in Russland 1906–1914* (Wiesbaden, 1982).

[39] The links between domestic and foreign policy and the nature of the international environment in which imperial Russia existed are of crucial significance in interpreting the fate of the Old Regime. The best work on this subject is by Dietrich Geyer, initially published as *Der russische Imperialismus* (Göttingen, 1977), and now available in English as *Russian Imperialism: The Interaction of Domestic and Foreign Policy, 1860–1914* (Leamington Spa, 1987). My own *Russia and the Origins of the First World War* attempts to tackle this theme for the early twentieth century.

[40] See, e.g., Saburov's comment in the Tsarskoe Selo conference of April 1906: *Byloe*, no. 4 (Oct 1917), p. 225: 'One must punish only by law, however strict that law may be'.

[41] *SOGS*, Session 4 (4 Nov 1908, 15 Apr 1909), cols. 801–10, 1611–16; Session 6 (28 Mar 1911), col. 1653.

[42] The most recent major effort to fit the history of late imperial Russia into a comparative development context is by T. Shanin: *Russia as a Developing Society*, Vol. I: *The 'Roots of Otherness'* (London, 1985). In my opinion the idea of Russia as a developing society has had its uses in awakening Western scholars to obstacles to Anglo–American style political evolution in imperial Russia. On the other hand, leaving aside doubts as to some of Shanin's premises (e.g. the lasting homogeneity of the Third World), to equate the Russia of 1914 with the India, Africa or Asia of the post-1945 era raises many problems. By comparison with the leading powers of its day, imperial Russia was clearly far less backward than was the case with the newly emergent states of Asia and Africa after the Second World War. Could one not, after all, equate Russia just as readily with other states on the 'European periphery' (e.g., Spain, Italy), or imagine it occupying (as it indeed does today) a position somewhere between the 'First' and 'Third' Worlds? In my view C. Black, ed., *The Modernization of Japan and Russia: A Comparative Study* (London, 1975), remains an excellent introduction to this topic.

[43] N. Maklakov described himself in these terms when under interrogation by the Provisional Government: see 'Dopros N.A. Maklakova', *Padenie* 3 (1 May 1917), p. 89.

SELECT BIBLIOGRAPHY

This list includes principal sources, published and unpublished, cited in the text or of particular use to me; secondary sources cited in full in the chapter notes at p. 309 are not recapitulated here.

D.C.B.L.

I ARCHIVES

(i) Tsentral'nyy Gosudarstvennyy Istoricheskiy Arkhiv (TsGIA), Leningrad

Fond 1200	Delyanov and Peretz's Special Commissions reviewing entry into the Civil Service and the Civil Service Regulations
Fond 1409	His Imperial Majesty's Own Personal Chancellery. (First Section)
Fond 1162	State Chancellery
Fond 1615	M.G. Akimov
Fond 892	I.P. Balashov
Fond 899	Count Aleksei Bobrinsky
Fond 961	P.P. Kobylinsky
Fond 1642	A.N. Kulomzin
Fond 727	Baron E. Yu. Nolde
Fond 1650	Princes Alexander and Aleksei Obolensky
Fond 1010	Princess A.A. Obolensky-Neledinsky-Meletsky
Fond 1035	Prince N.V. Repnin
Fond 1044	A.A. and P.A. Saburov
Fond 1672	A.N. Schwartz
Fond 1675	I.G. Shcheglovitov
Fond 1088	Count S.D. Sheremetev
Fond 1112	A.N. Trubnikov
Fond 914	Prince M.S. Volkonsky

(ii) Tsentral'nyy Gosudarstvenyy Arkhiv Oktyabr'skoy Revolyutsii (TsGAOR), Moscow

Fond 730	Count N.P. Ignat'ev
Fond 564	A.F. Koni
Fond 568	Count V.N. Lambsdorff
Fond 1463	A.N. Mosolov
Fond 586	V.K. Plehve
Fond 1074	A.A. Saburov

Fond 1729   Prince P.D. Svyatopolk-Mirsky
Fond 542   V.V. Wahl

(iii) Otdel Rukopisey Biblioteki imeni Lenina (RO), Moscow

Fond 70   V.I. Guerrier (Ger'e)
Fond 126   A.A. Kireev
Fond 178   A.N. Kulomzin
Fond 514   A.N. Mosolov
Fond 215   M.M. Osorgin
Fond 358   N.A. Rubakin
Fond 338   A.N. Schwartz

(iv) Columbia University, Bakhmetev Archive (CUBA), New York

Unpublished memoirs and private papers of
P.A. Bark
N.N. Fliege
V.N. Kokovtsov
M.M. Kovalevsky
D.N. Lyubimov

(v) Harvard University, Law Library, Cambridge, Mass.
Materialy Kakhanovskoy Kommissii

(vi) Private sources

Prince B.A. Vasil'chikov, 'Vospominaniya'
Count P.K. Benckendorff, letters 1904–6; 1914–16 (Brooke MSS)

II PUBLISHED DOCUMENTS

Adamov, E.A., *Konstantinopol' i prolivy* (Moscow, 1925)
Anon., 'Pismo', *Russkaya Starina* 100 (1899), pp. 543–6
Frowein, E., ed., *Petergofskoe soveshchanie o proekte Gosudarstvennoy Dumy* (Berlin 1905)
Gosudarstvennyy Sovet. Pechatnye materialy, includes: *Smeta raskhodov Gosudarstvennogo Soveta na 1909 god* (SPB, 1908)
Lieven, D., ed., *Russia, 1859–1914* (1983), in K. Bourne and D.C. Watt, gen. eds., *British Documents on Foreign Affairs: Reports and Papers from the Foreign Office Confidential Print*, Part I, Series A
Ministerstvo Inostrannykh Del. Kommissiya po reorganizatsii zagranichnoy sluzhby, *Svod otchotov zagranichnykh ustanovleniy ministerstva na voprosnik kasatel'no reorganizatsii zagranichnoy sluzhby* (SPB, n.d.)
Padenie tsarskogo rezhima, Stenograficheskie otchoty doprosov i pokazaniy, 7 vols. (Leningrad, 1925)
'Revolyutsionnoe i studencheskoe dvizhenie 1869 v otsenke Tret'ego Otdeleniya', *Katorga i ssylka* 10 (1924), pp. 106–21
Riha, T., *Readings in Russian Civilization* (Chicago, 1964)
Schwanebach, P.Kh., 'Zapiski sanovnika', *Golos Minuvshego*, nos. 1–3 (Jan–Mar 1918), pp. 115–36
Soveshchaniya starshikh predsedateley i prokurorov sudebnykh palat po nekotorym voprosam

sudebnoy praktiki v svyazi s peresmotrom zakonopolozheniy po sudebnoy chasti (SPB, 1895)

Stenograficheskiy otchot Gosudarstvennogo Soveta (*SOGS*), Sessions 1–12 (SPB, 1906–17)

Trudy Iogo (-IXogo) s'ezda upol'nomochennykh dvoryanskikh obshchestv, 32 (−39) gubernii (SPB, 1906–13)

'Tsarsko-Sel'skie soveshchaniya 1905–6 gg', *Byloe*, nos. 3–6 (1917)

Vernadsky, G., *A Source Book for Russian History from Early Times to 1917* (London, 1972)

III WORKS OF REFERENCE

Adres kalendar' Rossiyskoy Imperii (SPB, 1829, 1840, 1860, 1881, 1894–1914)

Almanach de Gotha (Gotha, 1900, 1939)

Almanach de Saint Petersbourg, Cour, Monde et Ville, ed. M.O. Wolff *et al.* (SPB, 1910, 1911, 1912, 1913–14)

Almanakh sovremennykh russkikh gosudarstvennykh deyateley (*ASRGD*), pub. H. Goldberg (SPB, 1897)

Annuaire de la Noblesse de Russie (SPB, 1892, 1900)

Biograficheskiy slovar' professorov i prepodavateley Imperatorskogo S. Peterburgskogo Universiteta, 1869–1894 (SPB, 1896)

Bobrinsky, Count Alexander, *Dvoryanskie rody vnesennye v obshchiy gerbovnik vserossiyskoy imperii* (SPB, 1890)

Brockhaus and Efron. *Entsiklopedicheskiy slovar'*, 43 vols. (SPB, 1890–1906)

Deutschbaltisches Biographisches Lexicon 1710–1960 (DBL) (Vienna, 1970)

Dolgorukov, Prince P.V., *Rossiyskaya rodoslavnaya kniga*, 4 pts. (SPB, 1854–7)

Dvoryanskiy adres Kalendar' na 1897 god, pub. N.V. Shaposhnikov (SPB, 1896)

Dvoryanskiy adres Kalendar' na 1898 god, pub. N.V. Shaposhnikov (SPB, 1898)

Genealogisches Handbuch der Baltischen Ritterschaften (*GHdbR*):
   (i)   *Estland*, ed. O. von Stackelberg (Gorlitz, 1930–6)
   (ii) *Livland*, ed. A. von Transehe-Roseneck (Gorlitz, 1929–43)
   (iii) *Kurland*, ed. O. von Stavenhagen and W. von der Osten-Sacken (Gorlitz, 1930–44)
   (iv) *Oesel*, ed. N. von Essen (Dorpat, 1935–9; Hamburg, 1968)

Genealogisches Handbuch des Adels, Adelige Haüser B, Band VI (Limburg, 1964)

Gmeline, P. de., *Dictionnaire de la noblesse russe* (Paris, 1978)

Granat, A. and I., *Entsiklopedicheskiy slovar'*, vol. 23 (SPB, 1914)

Ikonnikov, N., *La Noblesse de Russie*, 2nd edn., vols. A1–Z2 (Paris, 1958–66)

Levinson, M.L., *Gosudarstvennyy Sovet* (SPB, 1907, 1915)
                   Pravitel'stvuyushchiy Senat (SPB, 1912)

Lobanov-Rostovsky, Prince A.B., *Rossiyskaya rodoslovnaya kniga*, 2nd edn., 2 vols. (SPB, 1895)

Lyons, M., *The Russian Imperial Army* (Stanford, Calif., 1968)

Modzalevsky, V.L., *Malorossiyskiy rodoslovnik*, 5 vols. (Kiev, 1908–14)

Pamyatnaya knizhka Imperatorskogo Aleksandrovskogo Litseya (SPB, 1851–7, 1880, 1886, 1898–9)

Pamyatnaya knizhka Imperatorskogo Uchilishcha Pravovedeniya na uchebnyy god 1914–15 (Petrograd, 1914)

Pamyatnaya knizhka litseistov (SPB, 1907)

Panchulidzev, S., *Sbornik biografiy kavalergardov, 1826–1908* (SPB, 1908)

Pol'noe sobranie zakonov (PSZ), lst and 2nd ser. (SPB)

Russkiy biograficheskiy slovar', 20 vols. (SPB, 1900–13)

Spisok chinam vedomstva Ministerstva Yustitsii (SPB, 1894, 1913)

Spisok general-adyutantam, general-mayoram svity Ego Velichestva i fligel-adyutantam po starshinstvu (SPB, 1913)

Spisok generalam po starshinstvu (SPB, 1907)

Spisok grazhdanskim chinam chetvyortogo klassa (SPB, 1881, 1895, 1908, 1914)

Spisok grazhdanskim chinam pervykh tryokh klassov (SPB, 1895)

Spisok lichnogo sostava Ministerstva Finansov (SPB, 1914)

Spisok litsam sluzhashchim po vedomstvu Ministerstva Vnutrennykh Del (SPB, 1894, 1914)

Spisok lits sluzhashchikh po vedomstvu glavnogo upravleniya Zemleustroystva i Zemledeliya (SPB, 1909)

Spikok lits sluzhashchikh po vedomstvu Ministerstva Narodnogo Prosveshcheniya (SPB, 1914)

Spisok vyshikh chinov tsentral'nykh ustanovlenii Ministerstva Vnutrennykh Del (SPB, 1912)

Svod zakonov Rossiyskoy Imperii (SZ) (SPB, 1842); vol. III (1896)

Tatishchev, S.S., *Rod Tatishchevykh* (SPB, 1900)

Vsya Rossiya. Russkaya kniga promyshlennosti, torgovli, sel'skogo khozyaystva i adminis-trsatsii. Adres-kalendar' Rossiyskoy imperii, pub. A.S. Suvorin (SPB, 1897, 1900)

Williamson, D.G., *The Counts Bobrinskoy – a Genealogy* (Middlesex, 1962)

IV OTHER PUBLISHED PRIMARY SOURCES

Abrikossow, D.I., *Revelations of a Russian Diplomat* (Seattle, Wash., 1964)

Alexandra, Empress, *The Letters of the Tsaritsa to the Tsar, 1914–1916*, introd. Sir B. Pares (London, 1923)

Anon., 'Shkola Gvardeyskikh Podpraporshchikov i Yunkerov v vospominaniyakh odnogo iz eya vospitannikov', *Russkaya Starina* 41 (1884)

Arsen'ev, K.K., 'Vospominaniya K.K. Arsen'eva ob Uchilishche Pravovedeniya 1849–55 gg', *Russkaya Starina* 50 (1886)

Bark, P.L., 'Vospominaniya P.L. Barka', *Vozrozhdenie*, nos. 43, 48, 157–70, 172–84 (1955–67)

Basily, N. de, *Memoirs: Diplomat of Imperial Russia: 1903–1917* (Stanford, Calif., 1973)

Bekhteev, S.S., *Khozyaystvennye itogi istekshago 45-letiya; mery k khozyaystvennomu podyomu* (SPB, 1902)

Bing, E.J., ed., *The Letters of the Tsar Nicholas and the Empress Marie* (London, 1937)

Bock, M. von, *Reminiscences of my Father* (New York, 1970)

Bogdanovich, A.V., *Tri poslednikh samoderzhavtsa* (Moscow, 1924)

Botkin, P.S., *Kartinki diplomaticheskoy zhizni* (Paris, 1930)

Cherevansky, V.P., *Dve volny. Istoricheskaya Khronika*, 2 vols. (SPB, 1898)
      Mir Islama i ego probuzhdenie, 2 vols. (SPB, 1901)
      Pod boevym ognyom. Istoricheskaya Khronika (SPB, 1898)
      Tvorchestvo russkoy sily (SPB, 1911)

Davydov, A.A., *Vospominaniya* (Paris, 1982)

Dellinghausen, E. Freiherr von, *Im Dienst der Heimat* (Stuttgart, 1930)

Denikin, A.I., *The Career of a Tsarist Officer* (Minneapolis, Minn., 1975)

Firsov, N., 'Novichki', *Russkaya Starina* 116 (1903)

Giers, N. K., *The Education of a Russian Statesman*, ed. C. and J. Jelavich (1962)

Golitsyn, Prince D.P., *V Peterburge* (SPB, 1892)
        Na bezlyud'e (SPB, 1910)

Gurko, V.I., *Features and Figures of the Past* (Stanford, Calif., 1939)

Ignatiev, A.A., *A Subaltern in Old Russia* (London, 1944)

Imperatorskiy Aleksandrovskiy Litsey, XL kurs (SPB, 1909)

Izvol'sky, A.P., *The Memoirs of Alexander Iswolsky*, tr. C.L. Seeger (London, n.d.)

Kalmykov, A.D., *Memoirs of a Russian Diplomat* (New Haven, Conn., 1971)

Kleinmichel, Countess, *Memoirs of a Shipwrecked World* (London, 1923)

Knyazhnin, P. (pseud. P. Popov), *Shest' let v Imperatorskom Aleksandrovskom Litsee* (SPB, 1911)

Kokovtsov, V.N., *Out of My Past* (Stanford, Calif., 1935)

Koni, A.F., *Na zhiznennom puti*, 5 vols. (Berlin, n.d.)
        'Pis'mo A.F. Koni', introd. V. Butchik, *Vozrozhdenie*, no. 24 (Nov–Dec 1952), pp. 161–6

Kropotkin, P.A., *Zapiski revolyutsionera* (London, 1902)

Kryzhanovsky, S.E., *Vospominaniya* (Berlin, n.d.)

Kulomzin, A.N., *Arkhiv sel'tsa Kornilova* (SPB, 1913)
        'Dmitri Nikolaevich Zamyatin', *Zhurnal Ministerstva Yustitsii*, no. 9 (Nov 1914), pp. 234–333
        Doma s deshyovimi kvartirami dlya rabochikh (SPB, 1912)
        Dostupnost' nachal'noy shkoly v Rossii (SPB, 1904)
        Opytnyy podshchot sovremennogo sostoyaniya nashego narodnogo obrazovaniya (SPB, 1912)
        Vsepoddaneyshiy otchot stats-sekretarya Kulomzina po poezdke v Sibir dlya oznakomleniya s polozheniem pereselencheskogo dela (SPB, 1896)

Kurlov, P.G., *Konets tsarizma* (Moscow-Petrograd, 1923)

Kuropatkin, A.N., *Dnevnik A.N. Kuropatkina* (Nizhniy Novgorod, 1924)

Lambsdorff, Count V.N., *Dnevnik V.N. Lamzdorfa*, 2 vols. (Moscow, 1926, 1934)
        'Dnevnik V.N. Lamzdorfa', *Krasnyy Arkhiv* 46 (1931)

Lieven, Prince A.A., *Dukh i ditsiplina nashego flota* (SPB, 1914)

Lopukhin, A.A., *Iz itogov sluzhebnogo opyta. Nastoyashchee i budushchee russkoy politsii* (Moscow, 1907)

Lykoshin, A.I., 'Pamyati A.A. Knirima (k istorii sostavleniya proekta grazhdanskogo ulozheniya)', *Zhurnal Ministerstva Yustitsii*, no. 10 (Dec 1905), pp. 1–29

Mamantov, V.I., *Na gosudarevoy sluzhbe* (Tallin, 1926)

Martens, F.F., *Sovremennoe mezhdunarodnoe pravo tsivilizovannykh narodov* (SPB, 1895)

Martynov, A.P., *Moya sluzhba v otdel'nom korpuse zhandarmov* (Stanford, Calif., 1972)

Masters, J., *Bugles and a Tiger* (London, 1973)

Meshchersky, Prince V.P., *Moi Vospominaniya*, 2 vols. (SPB, 1897)

Meyendorff, Baron A., ed., *Correspondence diplomatique de M. de Staal* (Paris, 1929)

Mosolov, A.A., *At the Court of the Last Tsar* (London, 1935)
        Pri dvore imperatora (Riga, n.d.)

Mosolov, A.N., 'Vil'nenskie ocherki', *Russkaya Starina* 41 (1884)

Naumov, A.N., *Iz utselevshikh vospominaniy*, 2 vols. (New York, 1955)

Nicholas II, *Dnevnik Imperatora Nikolaya II*, ed. S.P. Melgunov (Berlin, 1923)
    The Letters of the Tsar to the Tsaritsa, 1914–1917, ed. C.E. Vulliamy
    (New York, 1929)
Nikol'sky, B., 'Dnevnik Borisa Nikol'skogo (1905–7)', *Krasnyy Arkhiv* 63 (1934)
Obolensky, Prince A., 'Moi vospominaniya', *Vozrozhdenie*, no. 40 (Nov 1955),
    pp. 75–98
Obolensky, Prince D.A., *Moi vospominaniya o velikoy knyagine Elene Petrovne* (SPB,
    1909)
Pares, B., *My Russian Memoirs* (London, 1931)
Petrov, P.V., *Voennyy sobesednik* (SPB, 1910)
Pobedonostsev, K.P., *Dlya nemnogikh – otryvki iz shkol'nogo dnevnika* (SPB, 1885)
Polivanov, A.A., *Iz dnevnikov i vospominaniy po dolzhnosti voennogo ministra i ego*
    pomoshchnika (Moscow, 1924)
Polovtsov, A.A., *Dnevnik Gosudarstvennogo Sekretarya A.A. Polovtsova*, ed. P.A.
    Zayonchkovsky, 2 vols. (Moscow, 1966)
    'Iz dnevnika A.A. Polovtsova', *Krasnyy Arkhiv* 3 and 4 (1923), 46
    (1931)
Rosen, Baron R.R., *Forty Years of Diplomacy* (London, 1922)
Ryabushinsky, V.P., ed., *Velikaya Rossiya*, 2 vols. (SPB, 1910–11)
Sazonov, S.D., *Fateful Years, 1909–16* (London, 1928)
Schebeko, N.N., *Souvenirs* (Paris, 1936)
Semyonov-Tyan-Shansky, P.P., *Detstvo i yunost'*, vol. I of *Memuary* (Petrograd,
    1917)
    Memuary, Epokha osvobozhdeniya krestyan v Rossii
    (Petrograd, 1915)
Shavel'sky, G., *Vospominaniya poslednego protopresvitera russkoy armii i flota*, 2 vols.
    (New York, 1954)
Sheremetev, Count S.D., *Moskovskie vospominaniya* (Moscow, 1903)
Shipov, D.N., *Vospominaniya i dumy o perezhitom* (Moscow, 1918)
Simpson, J.Y., ed., *The Saburov Memoirs* (Cambridge, 1929)
Sorokin, V.I., 'Vospominaniya starogo studenta', *Russkaya Starina* 60, (1888)
Stasov, V.V., 'Uchilishche Pravovedeniya sorok let tomu nazad, 1836–42', *Russkaya*
    Starina 30, 31 (1881)
Struve, P.B., ed., *Vekhi. Sbornik stat'ey o russkoy intelligentsii* (Moscow, 1909)
Sukhomlimov, V., *Vospominaniya* (Berlin, 1924)
Svyatopolk-Mirsky, Princess E.A., 'Dnevnik kn. Ekateriny Alekseevny Svyatopolk-
    Mirsky za 1904–1905 gg', *Istoricheskie Zapiski* 77 (1965), pp. 236–93
Tagantsev, N.S., *Perezhitoe* (Petrograd, 1919)
Tcharykow [Charykov], N.V., *Glimpses of High Politics* (London, 1931)
Terner, F.G., *Gosudarstvo i zemlevladenie*, 2 vols. (SPB, 1896, 1901)
    O rabochem klasse i merakh k obespecheniyu ego blagosostoyaniya (SPB,
    1860)
    Vospominaniya zhizni, 2 vols. (SPB, 1910, 1911)
XXXI kurs Imperatorskogo Aleksandrovskogo Litseya cherez 25 let posle vypuska, 1871–
    1896 (SPB, 1896)
Tyutchev, I.A., 'V Uchilishche Pravovedeniya v 1847–52 gg', *Russkaya Starina* 48
    (1885)
Ustryalov, F.N., 'Vospominaniya o S-Peterburgskom Universitete v 1852–6 gg',
    Istoricheskiy Vestnik 16, 17 (1884)
Valuev, P.A., *Dnevnik Valueva*, 2 vols. (Moscow, 1961)

Vasil'chikov [Wassiltchikow], Princess L., *Verschwundenes Russland*, ed. T. Metter nich (Vienna, 1980)

Volkonsky, Prince S., *My Reminiscences*, 2 vols. (London, 1924)

Vorres, I., *The Last Grand Duchess* (London, 1964)

Vyrubov, A., *Memories of the Russian Court* (London, 1923)

Witte, S. Yu., *Samoderzhavie i zemstvo* (Stuttgart, 1903)
    Vospominaniya, 3 vols. (Moscow, 1960)

Zherebtsov, V.O., *Vospominaniya o Saratovskoy Pervoy Muzhskoy Gymnazii i SPB'om Universitete* (Saratov, 1912)

APPENDIX A

A NOTE ON SOURCES

The importance of a detailed and wide-ranging statistical analysis of the late imperial ruling élite is greatly increased by the fact that no adequate study of this sort exists to date. The three rather short works which have been published are both limited in scope and, most important, often thoroughly misleading because of the unreliability of the sources on which they are based.[1]

The most important single source used by me were the service records (*formulyarnie spiski*) contained in the Central State Historical Archive (TsGIA) in Leningrad. In the course of a year's study in the USSR I was able to use all but a handful of these records.[2] The *formulyarnie spiski* contain information about the social estate (*soslovie*) into which a man was born, his religion, his education, and his ownership of immovable property. In the latter case the records distinguish, at least in principle, between a man's property and property owned by his wife. They also state whether this property was inherited or bought. The *formulyarnie spiski* tell one whether a man was married, how many children he had, and what was the religion of his wife and offspring. In addition, the records go into great detail about an official's career, including his pay, his court rank and the orders and decorations he received. No other source comes close to providing such broad and detailed information. Indeed, without access to the service records it would have been wellnigh impossible to write my Chapter 2, at least in its present form.

Nevertheless, use of the service records has its problems. A minor difficulty was that in a few cases the records give not the estate in which a man was born but rather the job held by his father.[3] Far more important was the misleading information provided in the service records about landownership. In many service records one finds under the heading of property ownership the words, 'none possessed' (*ne imeet*) or simply 'no' (*net*). In other cases, however, this section was simply left blank or, rarely, filled in by a clerk with the words 'no information'. In all these cases the published *spiski*, which I will be discussing, said nothing about landownership, thus giving the impression that all the officials concerned were landless, which was by no means true.

Discovering just how many men did not report their ownership of land is very difficult. It is certainly not true that all those who left this section of their records blank were landowners, even when one finds the words 'no information' in the *formulyarnyy spisok*. On the other hand, quite a number of men were 'concealed' landowners, while others either reported only a small part of their property or simply specified that they owned land without saying how much. It is impossible at this distance to be confident that one has tracked down all these 'concealed' landowners, and indeed probable that one has not done so. Nevertheless, at least 16 men, 7.4 per cent of the total number, either reported only a small part of the land they owned or, in 13 cases, simply left that section in their service record blank. Between them 14 members of this group owned 136,547 *desyatiny*, just over 10 per cent of the known landownership of the appointed members of the State Council.[4] In addition, two men, both members of the aristocratic élite of the Russian nobility, did not record their ownership of estates which I know they possessed, but whose size I cannot discover.[5] As already mentioned, some other men confirmed their ownership of land without saying how much they possessed and, in most cases, I have simply had to enter them in my statistical tables (see Chapter 2) as owners of estates of unknown size. On occasion, however, I have been able to discover the dimensions of these men's estates. One man who falls into this category is P.P. Durnovo who, together with his wife, owned 123,600 *desyatiny*, in other words 9.16 per cent of the total land known to have been possessed by the members of the State Council.[6] In the face of statistics such as these the dangers of taking at face value the information on landowning provided by service records or published *spiski* become apparent.

The published *spiski* come from the same source as the service records but provide much less information. As regards civilian members of the State Council, the most useful *spiski* are those covering civil officials of the first three ranks (*chiny*).[7] On the rare occasions when a member of the Council belonged to the fourth rank, one can consult another volume, also issued annually by the Civil Service Inspectorate in the Emperor's Own Personal Chancellery.[8] These volumes provide information about a man's ownership of property which is, in the great majority of cases, the same as that cited in the service records.[9] In addition, the *spiski* tell one about an official's pay, as well as a few details about his past and present career and the posts he holds. As regards the military members of the State Council, the *spiski generalam* say nothing about ownership of property but do provide information on generals' religion and education as well as relatively full details about their careers.[10] The same information about the Council's admirals is available from the naval *spiski*.[11] For my purposes the *spiski* were useful on occasion to stop a gap in the service records; much more important, however, was the information with which they provided me about the whole of senior civilian and military officialdom, enabling me to see whether those at the apex of this élite, namely the members of the State Council, were typical of a broader group of the state's top servants.[12]

Five other published works are devoted specifically to providing biographical information about senior officials and generals under Nicholas II. They are the three volumes edited by M.L. Levinson on the members of the State Council and Senate, a section of volume 23 of the Granat Encyclopaedia, published in 1914, and the *Almanakh sovremennykh russkikh gosudarstvennykh deyateley*, published in 1897.[13] All these books concentrate on details of the men's careers, their information on the subject in general being accurate and full, though inevitably less complete than that contained in the service records. Their great value is, however, as sources on individuals' non-official activities, particularly their work as authors, playwrights and composers. In addition, a few high officials were of unusual interest to the editors of these volumes; as a result, aspects either of their lives, or of the histories of their families are described in detail.

Both Levinson and the *Almanakh* provide a little information on the social origins of some of the members of the State Council. Sometimes they describe men as nobles, on other occasions noting that they came from the hereditary nobility, in the latter case usually adding the name of the province on whose rolls the man was entered. Sometimes, however, these sources say nothing about a man's origins. Where Levinson or the *Almanakh* describe a man as a noble or as coming from the hereditary nobility, the service records confirm that the individual in question was indeed born into the hereditary noble estate. But the silence of these two published sources about a man's social origins by no means ensures that he was born a commoner. Not only the service records but also in many cases other published sources make this clear. Nor should any distinction be made between men described as nobles and others calling themselves hereditary noblemen from a specific province. Knowledge of the families in question makes it evident that no difference existed between the two groups. Moreover, Article 1104 of the 'Law on the Nobility' simply stated that commoners acquiring nobility could choose to be entered on the rolls of the nobility in any province, regardless of whether they owned immovable property or not.[14] The fathers and grandfathers of many members of the State Council availed themselves of this right.

Thus, to take one of many examples, A.V. Krivoshein is described in his service record as coming from the hereditary nobility of Simbirsk.[15] This is far from meaning that either he or his ancestors were landowners, or belonged to an old Simbirsk gentry family. On the contrary, Krivoshein's father had risen from the ranks into the officer corps and his grandfather was a peasant.[16] On the other hand, the *Almanakh* is silent about the social origins of, to take but two examples, K.K. Rennenkampf and N.I. Shebeko. The former, the son of a lieutenant-general, came from a Baltic landowning family ennobled in 1728.[17] The latter, the son of a court chamberlain (*tseremoniemeister*) and grandson of a lieutenant-general, was one of the biggest landowners in the State Council.[18] Statistics such as Mosse's, based on the idea that Krivoshein and his peers were 'old gentry', while the likes of Rennenkampf and Shebeko were commoners, are bound to produce very misleading conclusions.[19]

The service records and published works already cited provide a great deal of information about the members of the State Council. In two areas, however, which are important for Chapter 2, serious gaps remain in our knowledge. The first of these areas, landowning, has already been discussed. The second could be described as 'genealogical information', by which I mean not merely relationships of blood within the ruling élite, important as these were, but also a knowledge of families' antiquity, and of the positions occupied by fathers, grandfathers and other relatives in the state's service. Full information on these two areas was impossible to come by, and even the partial knowledge I acquired meant covering an immense amount of literature, of which I will mention here only the key works.

As regards landowning, the most important source, apart from the service records and *spiski*, are the two editions of *Vsya Rossiya*, published in 1897 and 1900 respectively.[20] Many important Russian landowners are not mentioned in this work, but the lists of estate owners contained in the two editions do allow one to fill some of the gaps in the service records. In addition, *Vsya Rossiya* provides useful information about how members of the Council exploited their estates, listing, for instance, the factories, mills, quarries, distilleries and other sources of income they had established on their land. As regards the Council's largest landowners, two Soviet works, one by A.M. Anfimov, the other by L.P. Minarik, are of considerable use; the list of great landowners provided by Anfimov is particularly valuable as a means of checking information given in the service records.[21] In addition, the work of N.A. Proskuryakova not only discusses important background material on Russian noble landowning but provides specific information, such as the average price of land in each province, which is an essential basis for some of my statistics.[22]

'Genealogical' information is even harder to come by than facts about landowning, for here one starts from scratch, since neither the service records nor the published sources already cited provide much information of value in this area. Above all what one lacks for the Russian nobility are systematic and comprehensive works on the British model of *Burke's Peerage and Landed Gentry*.

The closest one comes to system and comprehensiveness in Russian genealogy are the works of Prince P.V. Dolgorukov, Count Alexander Alekseevich Bobrinsky and Patrick de Gmeline.[23] Bobrinsky's book, however, does no more than list the more distinguished Russian noble families, including most of the older ones, according to the date at which they were ennobled. For the sixteenth and seventeenth centuries 'ennoblement' is often taken as the date at which someone was granted an estate. Dolgorukov also provides a list, in his case of noble families which can trace their origins to before 1600. With his volumes, as with those of Bobrinsky, one major problem is that they give one little means of determining whether a member of the State Council belonged to the old family whose surname was the same as his own. Dolgorukov does, it is true, provide detailed and useful genealogies of the Empire's titled and most distinguished untitled families. Unfortunately, however, it is precisely these families for which it is possible to derive information from other sources. Gmeline's work, unlike Dolgorukov's, is not a genealogy and does not therefore provide systematic information about blood relationships and ancestors' posts. Nor is even this work fully comprehensive, since some important noble families, such as the Strukovs and Krivskys, are not included. Nevertheless, Gmeline's book, providing brief histories of the major noble families and mentioning their most distinguished members, was of real service to me.

By far the most important source on Russian noble genealogy is the collection of 34 volumes produced by Nikolai Ikonnikov.[24] Ikonnikov's work is much more than a simple genealogy. He often gives short biographical notices on members of the noble families whose genealogy he is tracing, and his coverage of the official positions and estate-owning of fathers and ancestors of members of the State Council was of particular value to me.

Yet the lack of system with which Ikonnikov seems to have approached his task remains a major problem for scholars. Where a noble family is covered by Ikonnikov the scholar is assured of valuable information, but there is no guarantee that a family will necessarily find a place within his volumes.

As a result, although much of my knowledge about blood relationships within the élite, together with information about Russian[25] families' antiquity and history, comes from Ikonnikov, Dolgorukov and Gmeline, a great deal also had to be squeezed from a large number of other sources. Of these only one, the *Almanach de Saint Petersbourg, Cour, Monde et Ville*, published from 1910 to 1914, was sufficiently important in itself to warrant a mention here.[26] The *Almanach*, not a genealogical work but rather a social register of Petersburg high society immediately before the First World War, does occasionally provide useful snippets of information about families' histories.[27] Above all, however, the *Almanach* tells one about the town and rural residences of members of the State Council, their links by blood and marriage with other members of high society, and their membership of clubs. None of this information – certainly not that on club membership – is without value; indeed if one is attempting to define who belonged to the aristocratic élite of the Russian nobility, membership or otherwise of the Imperial Yacht Club is probably as good a dividing line as any other.

NOTES

[1] In order of publication these works are: N.A. Rubakin, *Arkhiv gosudarstvennoy mudrosti, ili zlachnoe mesto idezhe gosudarstvennye raki zimuyut* (SPB, 1906); a section of the work by P.A. Zayonchkovsky, *Pravitel'stvennyy apparat samoderzhavnoy Rossii* (Moscow, 1978); W.E. Mosse, in particular his two articles, 'Aspects of Tsarist Bureaucracy: Recruitment to the Imperial State Council 1855–1914', *SEER* 57, no. 2 (Apr 1979), pp. 240–54, and 'Russian Bureaucracy at the End of the Ancien Regime: The Imperial State Council 1897–1915', *SR* 39, no. 4 (Dec 1980), pp. 616–32. Rubakin's piece is propaganda rather than scholarship, but he is right to stress that the *spiski* underestimate the extent to which members of the ruling élite owned land. Zayonchkovsky's work is valuable but, like Rubakin's, is based on the *spiski*, which provide information which is neither comprehensive nor always accurate. Mosse's articles are also based largely on the *spiski*. In addition, however, he uses the *Almanakh sovremennykh russkikh gosudarstvennykh deyateley* (*ASRGD*), published by H. Goldberg in St. Petersburg in 1897, and the two editions of

Gosudarstvennyy Sovet, edited by M.L. Levinson, as his basic sources on social origins of members of the Council. Use of the *Almanakh* and Levinson for this purpose is bound to lead, and in Mosse's case does lead, to very incorrect statistics, and therefore inevitably to some false and misleading conclusions. I also have strong doubts about other ways in which Mosse divides the members of the Council into distinct categories for statistical and analytical purposes. To take but two examples: using the inheritance of titles as the only measure of membership of an 'aristocratic' group is a fundamental error: so too is any stress on the holding of the title of senator unless one realizes (a) that almost half of the Council's senators never actually sat in the Senate but merely held the honorary title of Senator; (b) even those who had worked as senators did not necessarily have any judicial or procuratorial experience. This was only essential if one sat in the third or fourth departments of the Senate, in other words in the civil or criminal cassation departments. My differences with Mosse on these and a number of other points are clear in the text. Nevertheless it is important to note both the value of part of his work and the fact that his errors are owed basically to the inadequacy and unreliability of the sources he has been forced to use.

[2] In most cases the records lacking were of ministers, whose prominence allowed me to draw abundant information with some confidence from alternative sources.

[3] An interesting example of this is V.K. Plehve, one of whose service records gives his father's estate and another his job: see TsGAOR, Fond 586, Opis 1, Ed. Khr. 2, pp. 1 and 14. On Plehve's background see E.H. Judge, *Plehve: Repression and Reform in Imperial Russia, 1902–1904* (Syracuse, N.Y., 1983), 12–13. On the very rare occasions when jobs rather than estate were cited I was usually able to check on a man's *soslovie* from other sources.

[4] The 14 men are Prince A.S. Dolgoruky, Prince N.S. Dolgoruky, D.A. Filosofov, Count A.P. Ignat'ev, A.P. Izvol'sky, V.V. Kalachov, P.A. Kharitonov, Prince V.S. Obolensky-Neledinsky-Meletsky, A.P. Salomon, S.D. Sazonov, S.A. Sheremetev, A.S. Stishinsky, N.N. Sukhotin, and Prince L.D. Vyazemsky. This is a distinctly aristocratic list.

[5] The two are Prince A.B. Lobanov-Rostovsky and Baron A.A. Budberg. Ikonnikov states that Lobanov-Rostovsky owned land in the Ostrogozh district of Voronezh province in 1897 and he is certainly listed among the noble landowners of this district in the genealogical rolls. See N. Ikonnikov, *La Noblesse de Russie*, 2nd edn., 34 vols. (Paris, 1957–66), here vol. I: 436; also *Dvoryanskiy Adres-Kalendar' na 1897 god* (SPB, 1896), 147. Witte says Budberg was a large landowner in Courland. See S.Yu. Witte, *Vospominaniya*, 3 vols. (Moscow, 1960), here III: 660. Budberg certainly owned until his death the estate of Widdrisch in Livonia, which had been in his family's possession since 1726. See *Genealogisches Handbuch des baltischen Ritterschaften* (*GHdbR*), Teil *Livland* (Gorlitz, n.d.), II: 657.

[6] P.P. Durnovo's service record in TsGIA, Fond 1162, Opis 6, Ed. Khr. 191, p. 77. See A.M. Anfimov, *Krupnoe pomeshchishchee khozyaystvo evropeyskoy Rossii* (Moscow, 1969), 382–7, for information on Durnovo's estate.

[7] *Spisok grazhdanskim chinam pervykh tryokh klassov* (SPB); I consulted the editions for 1881, 1894, 1908 and 1914.

[8] *Spisok grazhdanskim chinam chetvyortogo klassa* (SPB); I consulted the editions for 1881, 1895, 1908 and 1914.

[9] Not quite always: P.M. von Kaufmann, for instance, is said in his service record to have inherited 4,132 *ds.* with his brother, but there is no mention of this in the published *spiski*. His service record is in TsGIA, Fond 1162, Opis 6, Ed. Khr. 228. The published *spiski* before 1914 are often more accurate as regards land than service records completed during the period of abolition of the State Council in 1917–18.

[10] *Spisok generalam po starshinstvu* (SPB); I used the editions for 1897, 1908 and 1914. The *Spisok general-adyutantam, general-maioram svity Yego Velichestva i fligel-adyutantam po starshinstvu* (SPB, 1913) contains additional information.

[11] *Spisok lichnogo sostava sudov flota, stroevykh i administrativnykh uchrezhdeniy morskogo vedomstva* (SPB, 1913).

[12] See my 'The Russian Civil Service under Nicholas II: Some Variations on the Bureaucratic Theme', *JfGO* 29 (1981), no. 3, pp. 366–403.

[13] M.L. Levinson: *Gosudarstvennyy Sovet* (SPB, 1907; Petrograd, 1915) and *Pravitel'stvuyushchiy Senat* (SPB, 1912); A. and I. Granat, *Entsiklopedicheskiy slovar'*, vol. 23 (SPB, 1914); *ASRGD*.

[14] See *Dvoryanskiy Adres Kalendar'*, 'Zakonopolozhenie o dvoryanstve', Art. 1104, p. 81.

[15] TsGIA, Fond 1162, Opis 1, Ed. Khr. 263.

[16] K.A. Krivoshein, *A.V. Krivoshein, 1857–1921, ego znachenie v istorii Rossii nachala XX veka* (Paris, 1973), 1–2, 8–9, 12–13.

[17] *GHdbR*, Teil *Livland*, II: 776–85; also *Deutschbaltisches Biographisches Lexicon* (*DBL*) (Vienna, 1970), 620. *ASRGD*, 99.

[18] *ASRGD*, 158. Ikonnikov, *Noblesse*,

vol. B: 577–9.

[19] See n. 1. Mosse's mistake is easily made. Before gaining access to the Soviet archives I based my estimates of social origins in part on *ASRGD* and Levinson, inevitably getting a rude shock when I read the service records. There was never any conflict as regards men's social origins between the service records and the genealogical works cited in Chapter 2.

[20] *Vsya Rossiya. Russkaya kniga promyshlennosti, torgovli, sel'skogo khozyaystva i administratsii. Adres-kalendar' Rossiyskoy Imperii* (SPB, 1897, 1900).

[21] The list is on pp. 382–7 of Anfimov, *Krupnoe pomeshchishchee khozyaystvo*. L.P. Minarik, *Ekonomicheskaya kharakteristika krupneyshikh zemel'nykh sobstvennikov Rossii kontsa xix – nachala XXv* (Moscow, 1971).

[22] N.A. Proskuryakova, 'Razmeshchenie i struktura dvoryanskogo zemlevladeniya evropeyskoy Rossii v kontse xix – nachale xx veka', *Istoriya CCCP* I (1973), pp. 55–75.

[23] Prince P.V. Dolgorukov, *Rodoslovnaya kniga*, 4 vols. (SPB, 1854–7); Count A.A. Bobrinsky, *Dvoryanskie rody vnesennie v obshhiy gerbovnik vserossiyskoy imperii*, 2 vols. (SPB, 1890); P. de Gmeline, *Dictionnaire de la noblesse russe* (Paris, 1978).

[24] Ikonnikov, *Noblesse*; see n. 5.

[25] The only other sizeable group of old families, the Balts, provided few problems. Dolgorukov covered the best-known families and the volumes of *GHdbR* the rest. *DBL* was also useful.

[26] *Almanach de Saint Petersbourg, Cour, Monde et Ville* (SPB, 1910, 1911, 1912, 1913–14).

[27] E.g., the *Almanach* in its 1910 edition suddenly informs one (p. 26) that S.S. Bekhteev was living on an estate which had belonged to his family for 400 years.

APPENDIX B

MEN APPOINTED TO THE STATE COUNCIL
1894–1914

Akimov, Mikhail Grigorevich, b. 1847.

Alekseev, Evgeni Ivanovich, Admiral, b. 1843.

Altvater, Mikhail Grigorevich, General, b. 1840.

Anichkov, Nicholas Miliyevich, b. 1844.

Arsen'ev, Aleksei Aleksandrovich, b. 1849.

Arsen'ev, Dmitri Sergeevich, Admiral, b. 1852.

Avellan, Theodore Karlovich, Admiral, b. 1839.

Balashov, Nicholas Petrovich, b. 1841.

Beckmann, Vladimir Aleksandrovich, General, b. 1848.

Bekhteev, Serge Sergeevich, b. 1844.

Bezak (Besack), Nicholas Aleksandrovich, General, b. 1836.

Birilyov, Aleksei Alekseevich, Admiral, b. 1844.

Bobrikov, Nicholas Ivanovich, General, b. 1839.

Bobrinsky, Aleksei Aleksandrovich, Count, b. 1852.

Bobrinsky, Alexander Alekseevich, Count, b. 1823.

Bogolepov, Nicholas Pavlovich, b. 1846.

Bryanchaninov, Alexander Semyonovich, b. 1846.

Budberg, Alexander Andreevich, Baron, .b. 1851.

Bulygin, Alexander Grigorevich, b. 1851.

Butovsky, Peter Mikhailovich, b. 1852.

Cherevansky, Vladimir Pavlovich, b. 1836.

Dietrich (Deitrikh), Vladimir Fyodorovich, b. 1850.

Dikov, Ivan Mikhailovich, Admiral, b. 1835.

Dmitriev, Mikhail Dmitrievich, b. 1846.

Dolgoruky, Alexander Sergeevich, Prince, b. 1841.

Dolgoruky, Nicholas Sergeevich, Prince, General, b. 1840.

Dragomirov, Mikhail Ivanovich, General, b. 1830.

Dubasov, Fyodor Vassil'evich, Admiral, b. 1845.

Dukhovskoy, Serge Mikhailovich, General, b. 1838.

Durnovo, Peter Nikolaevich, b. 1845.

Durnovo, Peter Pavlovich, General, b. 1835.

Ekesparre, Oscar Reingoldovich, b. 1839.

Filosofov, Dmitri Aleksandrovich, b. 1861.

Frederycksz, Vladimir Borisovich, Baron (created Count 1913), General, b. 1838.

Freeze (Freze, or perhaps Fraser), Alexander Aleksandrovich, General, b. 1840.

Fuchs, Edward Yakovlevich, b. 1834.

Galkin-Vrasskoy, Mikhail Nikolaevich, b. 1834.

Ganetsky, Nicholas Stepanovich, General, b. 1815.

Gerhard (Gerard), Nicholas Nikolaevich, b. 1838.

Glazov, Vladimir Gavrilovich, General, b. 1848.

Golitsyn, Dmitri Petrovich, Prince, b. 1860.

Golubev, Ivan Yakovlevich, b. 1841.

Goncharov, Serge Sergeevich, b. 1842.

Goremykin, Alexander Dmitrievich, General, b. 1832.
Goremykin, Ivan Logginovich, b. 1839.
Grigorovich, Ivan Konstantinovich, Admiral, b. 1853.
Grippenberg, Oscar Kazimirovich, General, b. 1838.
Grodekov, Nicholas Ivanovich, General, b. 1843.
Gudim-Levkovich, Paul Konstantinovich, Lieutenant-General, b. 1842.
Guerrier (Ger'e), Vladimir Ivanovich, b. 1837.
Härbel (Gerbel), Serge Nikolaevich, b. 1858.
Heiden, Loggin Logginovich, Count, Admiral, b. 1806.
Hoyningen-Huene, Emil Fridrikovich, Baron, b. 1841.
Ignat'ev, Aleksei Pavlovich, Count, General, b. 1842.
Ivanitsky, Boris Evgenievich, b. 1857.
Ivanov, Appolon Viktorovich, b. 1843.
Ivashchenkov, Anatol Pavlovich, b. 1842.
Izvol'sky, Alexander Petrovich, b. 1856.
Izvol'sky, Peter Petrovich, b. 1863.
Kalachov, Victor Vassil' evich, b. 1835.
Kaufmann, Peter Mikhailovich, b. 1857.
Kharitonov, Peter Alekseevich, b. 1852.
Khilkov, Mikhail Ivanovich, Prince, b. 1834.
Khvostov, Alexander Alekseevich, b. 1857.
Khvostov, Nicholas Alekseevich, b. 1844.
Knirim, Alexander Aleksandrovich, b. 1837.
Kobeko, Dmitri Fomich, b. 1837.
Kobylinsky, Peter Petrovich, b. 1847.
Kokovtsov, Vladimir Nikolaevich (created Count 1914), b. 1853.
Koni, Anatol Fyodorovich, b. 1844.
Korff, Anatol Fyodorovich, Baron, b. 1842.
Kostanda, Apostol Spiridonovich, General, b. 1817.
Kosych, Andrei Ivanovich, General, b. 1833.
Kraemer, Oscar Karlovich, Admiral, b. 1829.
Krivoshein, Alexander Vassil'evich, b. 1861.
Krivsky, Paul Aleksandrovich, b. 1826.

Krshivitsky, Konstantin Faddeevich, General, b. 1840.
Kulomzin, Anatol Nikolaevich, b. 1838.
Kurakin, Anatol Aleksandrovich, Prince, b. 1845.
Kuropatkin, Aleksei Nikolaevich, General, b. 1848.
Kutaysov, Paul Ippolitovich, Count, General, b. 1837.
Lambsdorff, Vladimir Nikolaevich, Count, b. 1841.
Lazarev, Peter Mikhailovich, b. 1851.
Lieven, Andrei Aleksandrovich, Prince, b. 1839.
Linder, Konstantin Karlovich, b. 1836.
Lobanov-Rostovsky, Aleksei Borisovich, Prince, b. 1824.
Lobko, Paul Lvovich, General, b. 1838,.
Lukyanov, Serge Mikhailovich, b. 1855.
Lykoshin, Alexander Ivanovich, b. 1861.
Lyubovitsky, Julian Viktorovich, General, b. 1836.
Makarov, Alexander Aleksandrovich, b. 1857.
Makhotin, Nicholas Antonovich, General, b. 1830.
Mamantov, Vassili Il'ich, b. 1863.
Manukhin, Serge Sergeevich, b. 1856.
Markov, Paul Aleksandrovich, b. 1841.
Markov, Serge Vladimirovich, b. 1828.
Maslov, Nicholas Nikolaevich, General, b. 1846.
Medem, Otto Ludvigovich, Count, b. 1847.
Meller-Zakomel'sky, Alexander Nikolaevich, Baron, General, b. 1844.
Mohrenheim, Arthur Pavlovich, Baron, b. 1824.
Mordvinov, Semyon Aleksandrovich, b. 1825.
Mosolov, Alexander Nikolaevich, b. 1844.
Murav'yov, Mikhail Nikolaevich, Count, b. 1845.
Myasoedov, Nicholas Aleksandrovich, b. 1850.
Myasoedov-Ivanov, Victor Andreevich, b. 1841.
Nemeshaev, Klavdi Semyonovich, b. 1849.
Nikol'sky, Alexander Petrovich, b. 1851.
Nolde, Emmanuel Yul'evich, Baron, b. 1853.
Novitsky, Joseph Iosifovich, b. 1848.

Obolensky, Aleksei Dmitrievich, Prince, b. 1855.

Obolensky, Alexander Dmitrievich, Prince, b. 1847.

Obolensky-Neledinsky-Meletsky, Valerian Sergeevich, Prince, b. 1848.

Olive, Serge Vasil'evich, General, b. 1844.

Palitsyn, Fyodor Fyodorovich, General, b. 1851.

Panteleev, Aleksei Il'ich, General, b. 1838.

Pavlov, Platon Petrovich, General, b. 1834.

Petrov, Nicholas Ivanovich, General, b. 1841.

Petrov, Nicholas Pavlovich, General, b. 1836.

Pikhno, Dmitri Ivanovich, b. 1853.

Platonov, Stepan Fyodorovich, b. 1844.

Plehve, Vyacheslav Konstantinovich, b. 1846.

Pleske, Edward Dmitrievich, b. 1852.

Pokrovksy, Nicholas Nikolaevich, b. 1865.

Polivanov, Aleksei Andreevich, General, b. 1855.

Poltoratsky, Peter Alekseevich, b. 1842.

Puzyrevsky, Alexander Kazimirovich, General, b. 1845.

Rennenkampf, Konstantin Karlovich, b. 1826.

Repnin [Repnin-Volkonsky], Nicholas Vasil'evich, Prince, b. 1834.

Roediger (Rediger), Alexander Fyodorovich, General, b. 1853.

Rogovich, Aleksei Petrovich, b. 1861.

Röhrberg (Rerberg), Peter Fyodorovich, General, b. 1835.

Romanov, Peter Mikhailovich, b. 1851.

Rosen, Roman Romanovich, Baron, b. 1849.

Rozing, Iliodor Ivanovich, b. 1830.

Rukhlov, Serge Vassil'evich, b. 1853.

Sabler, Vladimir Karlovich, b. 1845.

Saburov, Andrei Aleksandrovich, b. 1837.

Saburov, Peter Aleksandrovich, b. 1835.

Sakharov, Vladimir Viktorovich, General, b. 1853.

Salomon, Alexander Petrovich, b. 1853.

Salov, Vassili Vassil'evich, b. 1839.

Samarin, Alexander Dmitrievich, b. 1872.

Sänger (Zenger), Grigori Eduardovich, b. 1853.

Sazonov, Serge Dmitrievich, b. 1861.

Schaffhausen-Schönberg och Schaufuss, Nicholas Konstantinovich, Lieutenant-General, b. 1846.

Schlippe, Vladimir Karlovich, b. 1834.

Schmemann, Nicholas Eduardovich, b. 1850.

Schreiber, Nicholas Nikolaevich, b. 1838.

Schwanebach, Peter Khristianovich, b. 1846.

Schwartz, Alexander Nikolaevich, b. 1848.

Selifontov, Nicholas Nikolaevich, b. 1836.

Selivanov, Andrei Nikolaevich, General, b. 1847.

Semyonov (-Tyan-Shansky), Peter Petrovich, b. 1827.

Sergeevich, Vassili Ivanovich, b. 1832.

Sergeevsky, Nicholas Dmitrievich, b. 1849.

Shamshin, Ivan Ivanovich, b. 1835.

Shatilov, Nicholas Pavlovich, General, b. 1849.

Shcheglovitov, Ivan Grigorovich, b. 1861.

Shcherbachev, Alexander Nikolaevich, b. 1845.

Shebeko, Nicholas Ignat'evich, General, b. 1834.

Sheremetev, Serge Alekseevich, General, b. 1836.

Sheremetev, Serge Dmitrievich, Count, b. 1844.

Shevich, Dmitri Egorovich, b. 1839.

Shevich, Ivan Egorovich, b. 1841.

Shidlovsky, Nicholas Vladimirovich, b. 1843.

Shipov, Ivan Pavlovich, b. 1848.

Shipov, Nicholas Nikolaevich, General, b. 1848.

Shirinsky-Shikhmatov, Aleksei Aleksandrovich, Prince, b. 1862.

Shishkin, Nicholas Pavlovich, b. 1830.

Shuvalov, Paul Andreevich, Count, General, b. 1830.

Sipyagin, Dmitri Sergeevich, b. 1853.

Sofiano, Leonid Petrovich, General, b. 1820.

Staal, George Georgievich (created Baron 1901), b. 1824.

Steven, Alexander Khristianovich, b. 1844.

Stishinsky, Alexander Semyonovich, b. 1857.

Stolypin, Peter Arkad'evich, b. 1862.

Strukov, Anani Petrovich, b. 1851.

Stürmer, Boris Vladimirovich, b. 1848.

Styurler, Alexander Nikolaevich, General, b. 1825.

Sukhomlinov, Vladimir Aleksandrovich, General, b. 1848.

Sukhotin, Nicholas Nikolaevich, General, b. 1847.

Svin'in, Alexander Dmitrievich, General, b. 1831.

Svyatopolk-Mirsky, Nicholas Ivanovich, Prince, General, b. 1833.

Svyatopolk-Mirsky, Peter Dmitrievich, Prince, Lieutenant-General, b. 1857.

Tagantsev, Nicholas Stepanovich, b. 1843.

Taneev, Alexander Sergeevich, b. 1850.

Tatishchev, Ivan Dmitrievich, Count, General, b. 1830.

Taube, Maxim Antonovich, Baron, General, b. 1826.

Terner, Fyodor Gustavovich, b. 1833.

Timashev, Serge Ivanovich, b. 1858.

Toll, Serge Aleksandrovich, Count, b. 1848.

Trepov, Fyodor Fyodorovich, General, b. 1854.

Trepov, Vladimir Fyodorovich, b. 1860.

Trubnikov, Alexander Nikolaevich, b. 1854.

Turau, Evgeni Fyodorovich, b. 1847.

Tyrtov, Paul Petrovich, Admiral, b. 1836.

Tyutchev, Ivan Fyodorovich, b. 1846.

Unterberger, Paul Fyodorovich, General, b. 1842.

Uxkull von Güldenbandt, Alexander Aleksandrovich, Baron, b. 1840.

Uxkull von Güldenbandt, Julius Aleksandrovich, Baron, b. 1852.

Vasil'chikov, Boris Aleksandrovich, Prince, b. 1863.

Velho, Ivan Osipovich, Baron, b. 1830.

Verkhovsky, Vladimir Vladimirovich, b. 1849.

Vlangali, Alexander Georgievich, b. 1823.

Voevodsky, Nicholas Arkad'evich, b. 1856.

Voevodsky, Stepan Arkad'evich, Admiral, b. 1859.

Volkonsky, Mikhail Sergeevich, Prince, b. 1832.

Vyazemsky, Leonid Dmitrievich, Prince, Lieutenant-General, b. 1848.

Wahl, Victor Vassil'evich, General, b. 1840.

Weber, Serge Fyodorovich, b. 1857.

Yanovsky, Kirill Petrovich, b. 1828.

Zinov'ev, Alexander Dmitrievich, b. 1854.

Zinov'ev, Ivan Alekseevich, b. 1835.

Zinov'ev, Nicholas Alekseevich, b. 1839.

Zverev, Nicholas Ivanovich, b. 1850.

APPENDIX C

RUSSIAN STATE INSTITUTIONS

The Emperor	Appointed all members of the State Council, ministers and senators, and could dismiss all officials but judges at will. He was not bound to accept State Council recommendations and could pardon anyone convicted of an offence and order any prosecution to be dropped.
State Council	Advised monarch on legislation and the annual state budget.
Special commissions	Set up to study and report on specific problems or projects. Submitted recommendations (often not unanimous) for the monarch's adjudication and decision.
Committee of Ministers	Settled disputes between ministries and co-ordinated administration. Serious disputes were arbitrated by the Emperor.
State Chancellery	Serviced the State Council: e.g., reported on draft bills, took minutes, etc. Headed by the so-called Imperial Secretary [*Gosudarstvennyy Sekretar'*].
Chancellery of the Committee of Ministers	Serviced the Committee and together with officials of the State Chancellery also serviced the special commissions.
The various ministries	Ministers reported directly to the Emperor in private audiences.
Senate	Its First Department was the supreme administrative court; its Second Department handled appeals from peasant courts; the Third and Fourth Departments handled criminal and civil cassation; the Fifth Department was the so-called Heraldry – it handled *inter alia* ennoblements.
Provincial governors	Officially the governor was the Emperor's viceroy in the province, but in practice the subordinate of the Minister of Internal Affairs. Exercised a limited degree of supervision over the provincial officials of other ministries and the zemstvos.
Vice-governors	The governors' deputies.

THE STRUCTURE OF RUSSIAN GOVERNMENT BEFORE 1905

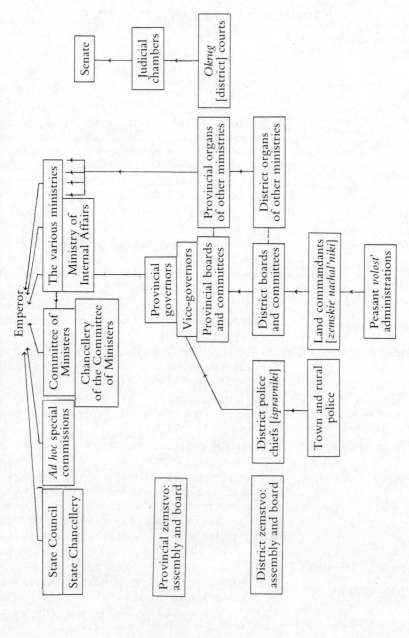

Provincial boards and committees	Covered various aspects of provincial affairs (e.g., peasant board; recruitment board; zemstvo board, etc.). Chaired by the governor and containing representatives of other ministries, the zemstvo, and the noble marshal.
District boards and committees	The same as the above but at district [*uezd*] level. In the *uezd* there was no equivalent to the governor and many boards and committees were chaired by the district marshal of nobility, who was elected by the local noble assembly, though the state had to confirm the election.
District police chiefs [ispravniki]	Subordinate to the governor; the chief was an official of the Ministry of Internal Affairs.
Land commandants [zemskie nachal'niki]	Officials of the Ministry of Internal Affairs, many of whom were local landed nobles. They supervised peasant *volost'* administrations and courts, possessing administrative and judicial powers.
Peasant volost' *administrations*	The *volost'* comprised a group of villages. Its administration and court had competence only over the peasants.
Town and rural police	These were the ordinary police – *gorodovie* in the towns, *uryadniki* etc. in the countryside. The political police (i.e. Gendarmerie and Okhrana) had a wholly separate organization, only partially under the governor's supervision.
Provincial organs of other ministries	E.g., state fiscal chambers (Ministry of Finance); procurators (Ministry of Justice), etc. All these officials were responsible to their respective ministries in Petersburg.
District organs of other ministries	Distinctly thinner and less impressive than their equivalents at provincial level. At both levels subordination to local boards and committees was slight.
Judicial chambers	Handled appeals in civil cases from *okrug* courts and were courts of first instance in certain cases (e.g., as regards officials' crimes).
Okrug [district] *courts*	The lowest tier of the judicial system. The judicial *okrug* was a much larger area than the administrative *uezd*.
Zemstvo	The district zemstvo assembly was elected by the local population, voting in social curiae (i.e., nobles, other property owners, peasants). It appointed an executive board and elected representatives to the provincial assembly. The zemstvo handled matters such as health, education and rural communications. Governors had some power to veto zemstvo deci-

sions and appointments, but zemstvos could appeal to the Senate (which often supported them) in many cases.

Certain institutions are not shown on the diagram at p. 392: The *Emperor's Own Personal Chancellery* was an extremely powerful institution until the early 1880s. In 1880 its Third Section, the brain of the Russian security police, was transferred to the Ministry of Internal Affairs, and two years later the Second (codification) Section was shifted to the State Chancellery. The old Fourth Section, which ran charities and schools, became independent in 1880, being known thenceforth as the department of the Empress Marie's Institutions. All that was left was the old First Section, whose many duties included preparing imperial rescripts and correspondence and, from 1894, running the civil service inspectorate.

The *Petitions Chancellery* was another imperial rather than governmental institution. It handled petitions to the monarch from individuals seeking help or redress.

The *Holy Synod* was a committee of senior clergy presided over by a lay official (the Chief Procurator), which ran the Orthodox Church's affairs.

N.B. Most of these institutions continued to exist post-1905, but certain changes occurred in the structure of Russian government: The *State Council* became the upper house of the legislature, a new institution, the elected *Duma*, becoming the lower house. The *Committee of Ministers* was abolished and the *Council of Ministers* created. The *Council* was intended to be powerful enough to impose co-ordinated policies on the various ministries.

General Index

(SC = State Council)

Akimov, M.G. (1847–1914), jurist,
  president SC, 60, 164, 183, 184
Aleksei Mikhailovich (1629–76), Tsar, 11,
  12, 281
Alexander I (1777–1825), Emperor, 281
Alexander II (1818–81), Emperor, 166, 242,
  250, 347 (n 56)
Alexander III (1845–94), Emperor, 57, 137,
  145, 156, 166, 179, 250
Alexander Lycée,·52–6, 91, 108–16, 117,
  118–19, 126, 133, 324 (n 89), 334 (n 73),
  335 (nn 80, 83), 336 (n 95)
Alexandra Fyodorovna (1872–1918),
  Empress, 141, 146, 204, 281, 284, 314 (n
  64), 364 (n 15)
Anichkov, N.M. (1844–1916), member SC,
  18, 80
Apraksin family, 11
aristocracy (Russian), 1–11, 12, 14, 16,
  19–20, 21–3, 26, 49, 57, 58, 81, 82, 134,
  155–9, 168, 199, 312 (n 29), 313 (n 31),
  315 (n 76)
armed forces (Russian), xi, 64–7, 173–7,
  208–9, 215, 218–19, 225, 273, 328 (n
  128), 356 (n 35)
Arsen'ev, A.A. (1849–1914), member SC,
  68, 163, 314 (n 61)
Arsen'ev family, 18–19, 314 (n 61)
Artillery Academy, 65
Artillery School, 94

Balashov, I.P. (b. 1842), courtier, 168
Balashov, N.P. (b. 1841), member SC,
  19–20, 58, 60, 168
Balashov family, 19–20
Balts, 32–4, 46–7, 49, 55, 82, 138, 170–3,
  319 (nn 22, 31, 34)
Bark, P.L. (1869–1937), Min. of Finance,
  77, 78, 145, 152, 188, 192–3, 196
Baryatinsky, A.I., Prince (1814–79), Field
  Marshal, 141
Bekhteev, S.S. (1844–1911), member SC,
  19, 68, 163, 314 (n 63)
Bekhteev family, 19
Benckendorff, Paul, Count, courtier, 139,

146–7, 157–8, 195, 364 (n 15)
Bezak, N.A. (1836–97), General, member
  SC, 51
Bezak family, 51–2
Bezobrazov, V.P., 115, 135
Birilyov, A.A. (1844–1915), Admiral,
  member SC, 175
Bobrikov, N.I. (1839–1904), General
  member SC, 62
Bobrikov family, 62, 327 (n 119)
Bobrinsky, Aleksei Aleksandrovich, Count
  (1852–1927), member SC, 58, 60, 68,
  81, 152, 156, 158, 159, 345 (nn 22, 25)
Bobrinsky, Alexander Alekseevich, Count
  (1823–1903), member SC, 44, 231, 377
Bobrinsky family, 45–6, 321 (n 52), 342
  (n 124)
Bogolepov, N.P. (1847–1901), Min. of
  Education, 80
Bryanchaninov, A.S. (1843–1910), member
  SC, 18, 187
Budberg, A.A., Baron (1853–1914), head
  Petitions Chancellery, 49, 203, 379 (n 5)
Bulygin, A.G. (1851–1919), Min. of Internal
  Affairs, 164, 165, 214
Bulygin family, 44
Bunge, N. Chr. (1823–95), chairman Comm.
  of Ministers, 78, 79, 145, 192, 243
bureaucracy (Russian), bureaucratic politics,
  see civil service
businessmen (Russian), 15, 16, 20, 28, 285
Butovsky, P.N. (1842–1912), jurist,
  member SC, 182
Buturlin family, 9

cadet corps, see education (Russian): military
Catherine II (1729–96), Empress, 21
Chaadaev family, 11
Chancellery of the Comm. of Ministers, 71,
  75, 77, 78, 83, 131, 186, 190–2, 240–1,
  242–4, 329 (n 155)
Cherevansky, V.P. (b. 1836), member SC,
  77, 200–1, 321 (n 44)
Chevaliers Gardes regiment, 52, 53, 56, 187,
  325 (n 90)

397

childhood, 85–91

chin (rank) system, 125–9, 339 (nn 53, 58), 358 (n 30)

civil service: (English) 30–3, 70, 119, 197; (French) 125, 132–3; (Prussian) 24, 30–1, 70, 72, 119, 124–5, 145, 152, 197, 280, 289, 341 (n 100)

civil service (Russian):
  10–12 (pre-Petrine); 22 (18th cent.); 23–5, 316 (n 81) (19th cent.); 289–96, 363 (n 10), 365 (n 22) (under Nicholas II);
  appointments and promotions, 124–33, 338 (n 32), 339 (n 53); bureaucratic politics, 138–47, 212, 288–9; clientelism, 129, 134–6; corruption, 211–12; gerontocracy, 146–7, 342 (n 132); minorities in, 31–6, 167–73;
  pay and pensions, 36–7, 136; professional training, 119, 123–4, 338 (n 20); provincial service, 68, 123, 337 (n 17); recruitment, 28–31, 121–3, 317 (n 7), 337 (nn 4, 7, 11); regulations, 121, 125–6, 336 (n 1), 340–1 (n 88)

clergy (Russian), 29–30, 318 (n 8)

clientelism, *see* civil service (Russian)

Corps des Pages, 52–6, 95, 98–100, 199

Crimean War, effects of, 86, 88

Danilevsky, N. Ya. (1822–85), Panslav writer, 115

Decembrists, 23, 156

Dellinghausen, E., Baron, Estland marshal, 171

Delyanov, I.D., Count (1818–97), Min. of Education, 103, 123

Demidov family, 20, 63

Dietrich, V.F. (b. 1850), jurist, member SC, 183

Dmitriev, M.D. (1846–1917), Asst. Min. of Finance, 61, 196, 302, 326 (n 108)

Dolgoruky, A.S., Prince (1841–1912), courtier, member SC, 5, 7, 49, 58, 161, 168

Dolgoruky, N.S., Prince (1840–1913), General, ambassador, member SC, 5, 49, 58, 80, 161, 168, 321 (n 52)

Dolgoruky, Olga Petrovna, Princess, 7

Dolgoruky [Dolgorukov] family, 1, 4, 315 (n 68)

Duma (Russian parliament), 31, 152, 218–19, 228–9, 254–5, 266–7, 270, 271, 288, 306, 351 (n 142), 362 (n 63)

Durnovo, I.N. (1834–1903), Min. of Internal Affairs 1889–95, chairman Comm. of Ministers 1895–1903, 123, 166, 243–4

Durnovo, P.N. (1844–1915), Min. of Internal Affairs 1905–6, 72, 83, 117, 136, 149, 152, 185, 190, 205, 207–30, 254, 293, 298, 299–301, 302, 303, 305, 308, 348 (n 75), 356 (n 35)

Durnovo, P.P. (b. 1835), member SC, 19–20, 60, 207

Durnovo family, 19–20, 207

education (European): classical, 102–3; military, 94

education (Russian): gymnasium, 98, 102–3; military, 91–102, 110, 117, 119–20; primary, 223–4, 246–8, 252; privileged school, 108–16, 334 (n 75); university, 103–8, 111, 334 (n 75)

Ekesparre, Oscar (1839–1925), member SC, 68, 171, 348 (n 83)

Elizabeth (1709–61), Empress, 21

Emancipation (of serfs), 89, 199, 205, 236–8, 259, 265, 361 (n 38)

Emperor's Own Personal Chancellery, 76, 129, 147, 286–7

Engineering Academy, 65, 96

family (Russian noble), 85–91

Finns, in Russian service, 34; *see also under individual names*

First Cadet Corps, 97; First Moscow Cadet Corps, 97

Frederycksz, V.B., Count (1838–1927), Min. of the Court, 51, 57, 161, 170, 286

Frederycksz family, 324 (n 84)

Fuchs, E. Ya. (1834–1909), jurist, member SC, 183

Ganetsky, N.S. (1815–1904), General, member SC, 60

Gendarmerie, 67, 175, 215

General Staff Academy, 62, 65, 93, 348 (n 92)

Gerasimov, A.V., Gendarme General, 214

Gerbel, *see* Härbel

Germans, in Russian service, 31–4, 169–73, 319 (n 22); *see also* Balts, *and under individual names*

Giers, N.K. (1820–95), Min. of Foreign Affairs, 122, 160, 167, 293, 345–6 (n 28)

Golitsyn, D.P., Prince (1860–1928), novelist, head Empress Marie's Institutions, 4, 48, 49, 141, 150

Golitsyn, G.S., Prince (1838–1907), General, Governor-General Caucasus, 96

Golitsyn, N.D., Prince (1850–1926), chairman Co. of Ministers 1916–17, 147

Golitsyn, V.M., Prince, Governor Moscow, 212

Golitsyn family, 2, 4–5, 7, 11, 48

Golubev, I. Ya. (1841–1918), jurist, member SC, 183

Goncharov, S.S. (b. 1842), jurist, member SC, 61, 164, 183

Goncharov family, 62

Gorchakov, A.M., Prince (1798–1883), Chancello R, 115, 197, 335 (n 80)

Goremykin, A.D. (1832–1904), General,
  member SC, 61, 206
Goremykin, I.L. (1839–1917), chairman Co.
  of Ministers 1906–7, 1914–16, 61, 72,
  81, 147, 150, 164, 184, 185, 271, 343
  (n 142)
governors, x, 70–1, 130, 186–8, 328 (n 144)
Grot, Ya. K. (1812–93), academician, 109,
  115, 118
Gudim-Levkovich, P.K. (1842–1907),
  General, member SC, 61
Gurko, V.I. (1862–1927), Asst. Min. of
  Internal Affairs 1906–7, 75, 160, 176,
  178, 191, 215, 268, 269
gymnasium, *see* education (Russian)

Härbel family, 61, 319 (n 24)
Heiden, L.L., Count (1806–1901), Admiral,
  member SC, 84
Heiden family, 44
Holy Synod, 79
Horse Guards regiment, 52, 53, 56, 170

Ignat'ev, A.P., Count (1842–1906), General,
  member SC, 16, 18, 174, 303, 327
  (n 121)
Ignat'ev, P.N., Count (1797–1879),
  General, chairman Comm. of Ministers,
  15–16, 94, 241
Ignat'ev family, 15–16
Isakov, N.V. (1821–91), General, member
  SC, 97–8
Ivan IV, Tsar (1547–84), 10, 281
Izvol'sky, A.P. (1856–1919), Min. of
  Foreign Affairs, 57, 81, 118, 197, 198,
  354, (n 190), 382 (n 4)
Izvol'sky, P.P. (1863–1916), Chief
  Procurator Holy Synod, 80, 81

Jews: anti-Semitism, 150, 179, 184, 193, 196,
  265, 275, 343 (n 139), 350 (n 133); state
  service, 35

Kapnist, D.A., Count (1837–1904),
  diplomat, 160, 345–6 (n 28)
Kaufmann, P.M. (1857–1926), Min. of
  Education, 118, 135, 293, 379 (n 9)
Kaufmann family, 44, 164, 324 (n 88)
Kharitonov, P.A. (1852–1916), State
  Controller, 51, 77, 164, 191–2, 354
  (n 199)
Kharitonov family, 52
Khilkov, M.I., Prince (1834–1909), Min. of
  Communications, 6, 8, 49, 79, 199–200,
  206, 303
Khilkov family, 1, 4
Khvostov, A.A. (1857–1922), Min. of
  Justice, 81
Khvostov, N.A. (1844–1913), jurist,
  member SC, 81

Khvostov family, 9, 14, 81
Kireev, A.A. (1833–1910), General,
  courtier, slavophil, 151, 153, 176, 188,
  198, 344 (n 155)
Knirim, A.A. (1837–1904), jurist, member
  SC, 55, 145, 180–2, 183
Kobeko, D.F. (1837–1918), historian,
  member SC, 118, 293, 301, 355 (n 17)
Kobeko family, 327 (n 115)
Kobylinsky, P.P. (b. 1847), jurist, member
  SC, 182
Kokovtsov, V.N. (1853–1943), chairman
  Co. of Ministers, 18, 72, 78, 79, 83,
  88–9, 91, 113, 118, 121, 125, 165, 190,
  194, 206, 321 (n 45), 334 (n 73), 337
  (n 17), 345 (n 11), 354 (n 199)
Koni, A.F. (1844–1927), jurist, member SC,
  61, 144, 178, 183, 184, 301, 303
Koni family, 61
Konstantin Surveyors' Institute, 63
Korhunov, N.M. (1853–1904), Professor,
  76, 107, 109, 115–16, 190
Kosych, A.I. (b. 1833), General, member
  SC, 67, 176
Krivoshein, A.V. (1858–1923), Min. of
  Agriculture, 62, 72, 83, 293–4, 343
  (n 144), 351 (n 142), 379
Krivoshein family, 62
Krivsky, P.A. (1826–1905), member SC,
  68, 163–4, 322 (n 69)
Kropotkin, P.A., Prince (1842–1921),
  anarchist, 100
Kryzhanovsky, S.E. (1861–1935), Imperial
  Secretary, 83, 131–2, 147, 185, 268
Kulomzin, A.N. (1838–1924), president SC,
  18, 75, 81, 83, 106, 117–18, 137, 143,
  164, 165, 166, 169, 190, 191, 220,
  231–55, 293, 301, 302, 303, 305, 306,
  321 (n 48), 357 (n 21), 358 (n 29)
Kulomzin family, 231–3
Kurakin, A.A., Prince (1845–1936),
  member SC, 4, 5, 49, 312 (n 24), 329
  (n 167)
Kurakin family, 2, 4, 11, 21
Kuropatkin, A.N. (1848–1925), General,
  Min. of War, 150
Kusov family, 15
Kutaysov, P.I., Count (1837–1918),
  General, member SC, 49
Kutaysov family, 21, 315 (n 70)
Kutuzov family, 9

Lambsdorff, V.N., Count (1845–1907),
  Min. of Foreign Affairs, 80, 95, 139,
  148, 160, 166–7, 171, 190, 198, 293,
  345–6 (n 28), 347 (nn 56, 64), 353 (n 179)
landownership (American), 8
landownership (Russian), 5, 8, 39–43, 45–6,
  82, 91, 238–9, 268
languages, 88, 90, 91, 100, 101, 115, 168, 233,

INDEX OF AUTHORS CITED

Principal secondary sources are indexed here under the first full citation in the Notes; for primary sources including works of reference see the Select Bibliography, p. 367